The Sydney Morning Herald
BEST OF SYDNEY

Published by SMH Books, a publishing division of
John Fairfax Publications Pty Ltd
ACN 003 357 720
First published 1998

Copyright © 1998 in text and compilation John Fairfax Publications Pty Ltd.
Copyright © 1998 in the introduction Leo Schofield.
Copyright © 1998 in photographs The Photographers

Typeset by DOCUPRO, Sydney
Printed by McPhersons Printing Group, Victoria

Design: Colin Rowan
Cover design: Michael McGuirk
Cover photograph: Palani Mohan
Maps: Anna Baker
Graphics: Remi Bianchi

National Library of Australia
Cataloguing-in-Publication Data

The Best of Sydney: an A-Z guide
ISBN 1 86290 123 6.
1. Sydney (N.S.W.) - Guidebooks. I. Muller, Ross, 1960-
919.4410465

All rights reserved. No part of this publication may be reproduced, stored in a retrieval system, or transmitted in any form, or by any means, electronic, mechanical, photocopying, recording or otherwise without the prior written permission of the publisher.

Every effort has been made to ensure that the information in this book is accurate and up to date at the time of publication.

CONTENTS

Photograph by Jennifer Soo

Photograph by Nick Moll

33 A TO Z LISTINGS

319 LOCALITY GUIDE

341 CALENDAR OF EVENTS

351 VISITORS' GUIDE

6 FOREWORD
by Ross Muller

8 THE METROPOLIS AS RESORT
by Leo Schofield

24 THE FIVE-RING CIRCUS IS COMING TO TOWN
by Matthew Moore

Photograph by David Marius

FOREWORD

For the resident and visitor alike, Sydney is one of the world's most desirable cities. It's the destination voted in the travel magazines as the one everyone would most like to visit, and seems to always pop up on top of those quality-of-life surveys of the world's great cities. The magic is not hard to explain. The good life is very good here indeed, with all the fine restaurants, designer shopping and vibrant cultural life expected of the modern metropolis. But the benevolent climate and close proximity to harbour, beaches and national parks mean the best of Sydney is mostly free and more often than not spent in the great outdoors. The 2000 Olympics are adding a superb collection of sporting facilities and venues, a complete (and sometimes controversial) overhaul of the city's infrastructure and public transport systems, and investment and revitalisation to long blighted urban environments.

The *Best of Sydney* is a book for anyone who wants to make the most of this city. It's more than just another guidebook, although visitors will find all they need to know about the Opera House, Bondi Beach, the harbour cruises, the museums and the galleries. It recognises that a city is different things to different people – that as well as seeing the sights, a visitor may also want to check out a local blues band, dangle a line for a flathead, play a hand of bridge, lick the tastiest ice-cream, buy a fabulous rug or even get a tattoo as a permanent souvenir.

The *Best of Sydney* is a user's guide to the city – an A to Z of the passions, the interests and the needs of its citizens – a handy companion volume to the phone book and the street directory for the Sydneysider for whom only the best will do. Whether you want to learn how to paint, look at the stars, hire an outfit for a fancy dress party, take up rockclimbing or redo the bathroom, it's all here in more than 280 cross-referenced categories. Sydney is a multicultural city, transformed by successive waves of immigration, so we've also included chapters on the best our Italian, Greek, Chinese, Vietnamese, Lebanese and Spanish and Latin American communties have to offer.

As well as being culturally diverse, Sydney is spread over a huge area, so we've included a separate index with listings in 10 areas for the best arts and entertainment venues, sport and leisure facilities, shops and services, restaurants and food outlets.

While the *Best of Sydney* doesn't replace word-of-mouth recommendations from friends, family and neighbours, it's the next best thing. With contributions from more than 80 specialist news, sports, arts and lifestyle reporters and writers for *The Sydney Morning Herald* and its online partner, CitySearch (www.sydney.citysearch.com.au), it's the collective knowledge of the people who know Sydney best. It's our job after all.

Ross Muller
Editor, Best of Sydney

Acknowledgements
Special thanks for their patience and assistance in getting a huge and unwieldy project off the ground go to Sara Conde (research) and Ann Atkinson (publishing consultant). Thanks also to Chris Dobney (CitySearch), Sarah Hodgkinson and Lisa Hunter (Fairfax Publishing), Anthony Dennis, Michael Howard, Bernadette Hudson, Tracey O'Brien, Donna Maiolo and Sue Bugler (*The Sydney Morning Herald*).

Photograph by Virginia Star

Bronte Baths. *Photograph by David Marius*

THE METROPOLIS AS RESORT

BY LEO SCHOFIELD

Sydney.

God, I love this town. I have done so ever since, at the age of five, I first breezed in by train from the bush for a holiday at the beach and inhaled the sacred smells of Sydney. Coal. Gas. Pork sausages. Sea air. Fairy floss. Waffles. Frying fish and chips. Commonplace urban smells but unencountered in the far west of New South Wales where the sausages were invariably beef and cooked on wood-fired stoves and the sea and its seductive attendant aromas were 625 miles and 22 hours away.

Sydney CBD, 1945. *Photograph by C. Gilbert*

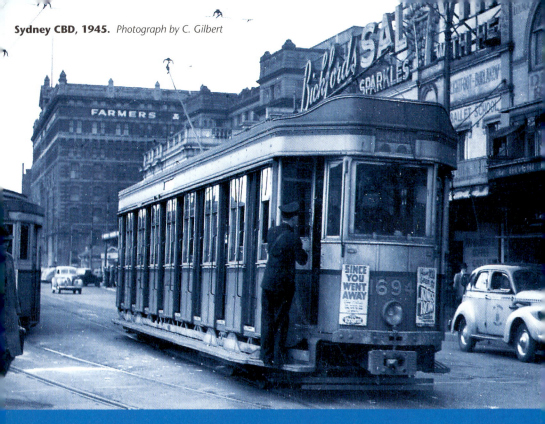

"Juddering from Central Railway to Bondi or Coogee on the tram was a magical excursion."

It was to be another six years before I moved here for good and, in the intervening half century, I have never wanted to live anywhere else. Well, hardly ever.

Sydney really was the Big Smoke. Still is, but bigger and brasher. Back then, the tallest thing in town was, or appeared to be, the AWA tower. Now it seems a pipsqueak thing, difficult even to see except from the terrace at Star City, a miniature and irrelevant mock Eiffel Tower, but in 1940 it reminded us of the logo for RKO pictures, symbolised metropolitan life and promised the remote high-tech future that is now upon us.

But what made Sydney seem so extraordinary then, as now and probably forever, is that primary source of this city's appeal to the citizen and the visitor – the seeming omnipresence of water of some sort.

Thirty years ago I travelled on a train through Italy. Just south of Genoa the line suddenly veered to run parallel to the Mediterranean. A small boy spotted the water, possibly for the first time, and ran to the window of the carriage crying out in wonder: "Il mare, il mare." I have a similar sensation here in Sydney each time I glimpse the ocean or some tranquil bay, for it is, as it was for him, unexpected. Other cities nestle on the edge of lakes or on rivers. Only Sydney is so intimately and inextricably and triumphantly locked in an embrace with the sea.

For a kid whose life had been circumscribed by the grid of the dozen or so streets that made up Brewarrina, the town where I lived the first 11 years of my life, juddering from Central Railway to Bondi or Coogee on the tram was a magical excursion. As the toast-rack swung round a corner, there it would be – the ocean, a quivering slice of intense blue water against a sky of a different but no less intense blue.

We would take a ferry to Manly – the Bellubera, the South Steyne, the Barrenjoey, the Narrabeen, the Curl Curl – pausing to be let through the boom net stretched across the Harbour in a puny effort to restrict the entry of Japanese submarines, dropping a penny or threepence in the collection box of the trio of musicians who patrolled the decks playing jaunty waltzes and polkas to distract us from thoughts of impending invasion or of the rolling swell as we passed across the Heads. Behind us was Sydney, rising like Atlantis from the haze and spray and dancing light.

Walking through the sandstone and granite city in our short pants, anxiously clasping the hand of fierce and powdery aunts, we would suddenly catch a glimpse, a flash of water and be reminded, if the buildings hadn't already done so, that we were in, as we used to call it, "town".

These experiences remain essentially unchanged. From a car one may still have the same heart-stopping experience as I had from a tram half a century ago. Travelling east along Bondi Road one sees first a wedge of the Pacific dead ahead. Then, as one throws a left into Campbell Parade there it is, a vast meniscus of white sand, a curvy froth of breaking waves, a slab of sea and a ceiling of purest blue. Intrusive masonry has only partially diminished the effect, the disappearance of the row of Norfolk Island pines that once delineated road from beach has made it more dramatic.

Ditto with the trip across the Harbour. Atlantis is now expanded to Megalopolis, more flamboyant and tricked out with towers and spires and curtain walls of glass, but the feeling is the same as I recall it from 1944, an eerie sense of being in two different places simultaneously.

Heading out to Watson's Bay on our very own grand corniche, there is that famous "reveal" as one heads steeply uphill past Rose Bay Convent ("The Catholics always get the best possies," people used to day) and makes an "eyes left" to see the City spread out below, wondrous at any time, but stupendous at dawn and sunset.

The truth is that Sydney is two cities, not discrete and mappable entities such as Buda and Pest, but conflated. Like paintings on mica, or animation cells, they can be read separately but when overlaid one on the other, they merge to assume a new and unexpected vibrancy.

The first Sydney is your standard-issue metropolis. It has all the physical components of a late 20th-century city – offices, banks, boutiques, hotels, department stores, places to buy books and places to sip coffee, theatres and cinemas. It has skyscrapers in which considerable amounts of money are managed or made and whose marble entrance halls are testament to that fact. It has that mandatory symbol of progress, or of what was once assumed to indicate progress, a tower with a revolving restaurant and observation deck on top, though what is to be observed from this lofty point is something more than an anonymous late 20th-century conurbation sprawling forth on all sides.

Martin Place, 1937. *Photograph by K. Rainsford.*

Governor Phillip Tower. *Photograph by Save*

What can be understood clearly from above is the form of Sydney, a kind of giant jigsaw. The dark assembled and patterned sections are the built city, the blank areas the ocean that edges it to the east and the waterways and bays that penetrate and course through it.

This is the second Sydney, an aqua-paradise, a place for swimming and sunning and lolling and picnicking and playing and boating and fishing and admiring. It has 240 kilometres of foreshore. It is a place of rest and refreshment. It is, in fact, a resort. And these two elements – metropolis and resort – have coalesced, telescoped, melded into this extraordinary, unique and sometimes schizophrenic place we call Sydney.

> *We got into Port Jackson early in the afternoon, and had the satisfaction of finding the finest harbour in the world.*

Captain Arthur Phillip, penning a despatch to his patron, Lord Sydney, in May of 1788, knew the world's best harbour when he saw it, even if, like Henry James, he had not made an extensive survey of maritime ports before delivering his unequivocal judgement.

There can be no underestimating the importance to Sydney of its harbour. Those who lack the means to live on it or look upon it can access it with ease and at little or no cost. "Our 'arbour" is Sydney's greatest asset and its greatest attraction. It provides us with our most acute sense of continuity with the past and with hope for the future. Whatever happens to the built city, the Harbour will stay pretty much the way it is. It is Sydney's salvation.

However, like Sydney, the Harbour is also two places between which exists an uneasy truce. There are the pristine headlands looking pretty much as they might have from Governor Phillip's pinnace, a curious mix of sandstone outcrop and scrubby, glaucous vegetation. This vestigial landscape now exists with a sometimes inappropriate built environment that makes further contribution to Sydney's schizophrenia.

North Bondi. *Photograph by Quentin Jones*

Are we to subside under profitable concrete? Or keep all of the remaining foreshore as it is so our children know what it once looked like?

We accept that, as well as being a source of leisure, this is also a working port, with all the usual appurtenances of container wharves and silos, lighters and tenders. Indeed, part of the appeal of the Harbour is the animation that commercial maritime traffic adds to it. Without tugs and fireboats and the increasingly numerous water taxis and cruise boats it would be as bland as a Swiss lake.

The Harbour, if not marking either its precise geographic or population centre, is Sydney's symbolic heart.

It is to the Harbour that Sydneysiders flock on great ceremonial occasions – in 1954 to greet the Queen on her first visit; in 1988 to inaugurate the Bicentennial festivities; annually to celebrate Australia Day; to watch the start of the Sydney to Hobart yacht race on Boxing Day; or to mark the annual transition from the old to the New Year. Gathering on the foreshores in hundreds of thousands to enjoy spectacle, we acknowledge, even if we live in far-flung French's Forest or Villawood, that the epicentre of Sydney is right here. On or about the Harbour. Just below the Bridge.

It is to the Harbour, too, that we turn when we want to show off the city to our guests. At interval during a performance at the Opera House we propel them out on to the terrace or towards the northern foyer where they can observe the coming and goings of liners and container vessels and ferries, admire the Bridge, wonder how they took so long to get round to visiting and how they can possible bear to leave.

We take them to restaurants that overlook the water, posh ones like Bilson's or The Pier or Catalina or the more modest eateries at The Rocks. We take them out on boats and stuff them with oysters and prawns and insist that they tell us, honestly and truly, what they think of Sydney because, in a sense, we are all insecure about the

"The second Sydney (is) an aqua-paradise ... a place of rest and refreshment ... a resort."

appeal of this city and, like good dogs that have fetched sticks, we pant for approval. Venturing forth on the water, with or without visitors, to gloat or to celebrate, remains, even after umpteen such excursions, a singular experience.

It happens in other Australian cities: "We have some visitors in town and we're taking them on a cruise." However, it has to be said that admiring Perth from the Swan, or Melbourne from a boat pootling up the Yarra, or contemplating Brisbane while floating on its olive-coloured eponymous river, are experiences akin to having telephone sex. The total, heady, full-on physical experience is to be had only in Sydney.

Nor does it have to be done from a boat. To cyclists and pedestrians, too, the Harbour offers a changing and endlessly beautiful prospect. Walk or ride across the Harbour Bridge in mid to late autumn and observe the beauty of the sun as it sets in a frenzy of pink and apricot. Wander down to the bottom of Erskine Street or through Millers Point or up on to Observatory Hill and do likewise. The best bike ride in Sydney is a compound experience, across the Bridge, weave down through Neutral Bay, around Mosman Bay and past Taronga Zoo to Bradley's Head. Here, as Jan Morris noted, is the quintessential Sydney view. After drinking it in, load the bike on a ferry to Watson's Bay if you're feeling energetic, or Rose Bay for a more leisurely ride, and head back into central Sydney. In just one morning one can sense the City's stupendous beauty and energy.

In some famous water cities, mostly man-made, the aqueous Venice or St. Petersburg or Stockholm perhaps, the water plays second fiddle to the architecture. In Sydney it's the principal performer. What Nature gave us, man has had a hard time improving and has so far proved unequal to the task.

> *In the morning I shall rise*
> *Red-raw and aching*
> *From memories of bronzed thighs*
> *And stupid sunbaking*
>
> **Ronald McCuaig, 1938**

The Harbour is only the half of it. There is the ocean, too. Running from Palm Beach to Cronulla are some of the most sensational surfing beaches in the world. There are other gorgeous ones further to the north and south, less regularly frequented, but Palmie, Collaroy, Dee Why, Harbord, Tamarama, Bondi, Maroubra are all within relatively easy striking distance of the City. It's not as if we have just one skirting a bay – a mono-beach as in Melbourne or Chicago. We have 'em in spades and beach culture has contributed as much to Sydney attitude as our climate. Business Sydney and resort Sydney cohabit comfortably. I can't see someone in shorts and thongs strolling along Collins Street or North Michigan Avenue. But it's a routine sight in Sydney.

Difficult to understand now but the early settlers, with one or two notable exceptions, turned their backs on the Pacific and its breathtaking beaches, preferring the tranquil millpond-ish Harbour. Perhaps, having crossed the ocean in one of the longest and roughest voyages then known, they wanted no more of turbulence and built their houses on the less troubled shores of Port Jackson. Thus it took some time for Sydney to get accustomed to the recreational possibilities of the surf. Our first surf lifesaving club was established in 1907 at Bondi, although both the fact and the place are disputed and Bronte claims primacy. But the Harbour beaches remained more popular than the wilder ocean ones.

There was a reluctance to slip into bathing costumes. I have a picture of my grandmother on Manly Beach. It was taken in February of 1913. She is wearing a high-necked black dress with long sleeves and voluminous skirt. A vast hat is her only item of apparel that we would today consider sensible. Her family is clustered about her in the shade of a tree. The kids' bare feet alone hint of the proximity of the cool inviting surf, stockings and shoes having been removed to facilitate paddling. For them, getting their gear off was a pleasure in store.

A pronounced Puritanism prevailed in the last

Botany Bay. *Photograph by Tim Clayton*

"Venturing forth on the water ... to gloat or celebrate ...remains a singular experience."

century and the first decades of this one. While the healthy effects of sea bathing were generally acknowledged, there was disapprobation of the concomitant pleasure and initiation to sexual congress that it implied. So for yonks, Sydneysiders went to the beach dressed as they might be for church. It was only after World War I that things eased up. But slowly. Even after World War II, men's and women's bathing costumes were manufactured with modesty flaps in front so as not to seem too provocatively crotchy. In the early '50s, one Aub Laidlaw, Australia's most famous beach inspector, patrolled Bondi Beach in blinding white shorts, navy singlet and panama with Waverley Municipal Council's coat of arms emblazoned on its hatband. Aub carried a foot-long ruler with which to measure bikini bottoms at their narrowest point on the hip. If they were narrower than three inches, the offending wearer was marched off the beach. Males as well as females were thus treated.

How would Aub and his municipal masters and minders of morals react if they could see a Sydney beach today, with half the women topless, the fitter, vainer men wearing not much more than a posing pouch?

In 1937 Max Dupain made his famous photographic image of *The Bather.* Had the Opera House not been built, this may have been the preferred image of this city. When Dupain clicked the shutter on the head and shoulders of an anonymous surfer, Sydney was developing an understanding of how important a part of its culture the beaches were. No point spending the week in a suit and tie if you had to wear the same clobber on the weekend. The beach became and has remained the antithesis of the office and an antidote to nine-to-five stress.

New arrivals were somewhat quicker to understand the luxury of having beaches to hand. Back home they travelled in large numbers to the beach for a brief summer holiday. During a Sydney summer, they are at the beach every weekend, families of Turks and Brazilians and Greeks and Russians, establishing early-morning occupancy of the famous picnic shelters at Bronte and frolicking until nightfall, often with accompanying live music from drum and bouzouki, as bemused Eurasia sit on a concrete pavement sipping their caffe lattes.

Certain tribes may flock to certain beaches – the inhabitants of Southern Sydney to Cronulla, the beautiful people to Tamarama, the backpackers to Bondi – but the common denominator is egalitarianism. In daily life, trappings and kit can signify power and position but, in a pair of Speedos or a bikini or, if you're under four, nothing, all are equal. The democracy of the surf prevails.

> Run of rocky shelves at sunrise, with their base
>   on ocean's bed;
> Homes of Coogee, homes of Bondi, and the
>   lighthouse on South Head;
> For in loneliness and hardship – and with just
>   a touch of pride –
> Has my heart been taught to whisper, 'You
>   belong to Sydney-Side.'
>   **Henry Lawson**

Henry Lawson slumbers atop one of those rocky shelves, in Waverley Cemetery, perhaps the most romantically located burial ground in the country. Set between Bronte and Clovelly with, beyond, the Coogee mentioned in his 1898 poem, it's the southernmost point of a famous recreational route that thousands of Sydneysiders take each day, some ambling, some scarlet and jogging, some so fit that they seem to bounce off the path, raising barely enough breath to extinguish a candle.

If the best vantage of the Harbour and City is from Bradley's Head, then the Bondi to Bronte cliff walk is the best way to get a sense of coastal topography and the union of city with sea.

Strike out from the southern end of Bondi Beach and follow your nose to the promontory beyond the rockpool at Bronte just short of the cemetery

"In daily life, trappings and kit can signify powe

where Lawson lies at rest. Or vice versa. Predictably, the view of coast and surf is spectacular, the impression of urban sprawl less so. But it's important to feel, yet again, how the beauty of nature can triumph over man's often ugly handprint.

One can imagine earlier walkers padding along this track, following the scalloped shoreline, then up to a rocky headland before another descent to another inwardly curving beach with sand almost as white as the caps of the waves, taking the sound of the surf below and the clarity of sky and water and the ongoing unravelling spectacle for granted, because it was always like this and all theirs. To us it is still a wonder, to a visitor more so, that such wildness, such beauty can exist as part of a modern city of around 4 million people.

> Sydney is a Rorschach test, and your
> interpretation of it reveals yourself.
>   **Ruth Park, 1973**

South Cronulla. Photograph by Craig Golding

"...nd position but, in a pair of Speedos or a bikini ... all are equal. The democracy of the surf prevails."

Barbarically glorious. That's how Blanche d'Alpuget described Sydney. She was right on both counts.

Beach and Harbour may be two of the twin attributes that set Sydney in unique distinction from other capitals, but this is after all a proper city and would probably exist without either. It's a pretty remarkable town, the most populous on this continent, sprawling in every direction except east, cosmopolitan in every sense, agog with activity of all sorts. In recent years it has, unchallenged, assumed the role of de facto capital of Australia.

Those who founded this city could never have imagined it thus. Their polite Georgian buildings dotted the foreshore and took advantage of topography and views but they were unable to actually create it or to impose on Sydney the kind of rational town plan that General Oglethorpe devised for Savannah, Georgia, 50 years before

Australia was claimed for Britain. Nature has always had the upper hand in Sydney and nature abhors a straight line. Our streets turn and twist like water finding the least resistant course, and our buildings have had to take into account dodgy foundations. The early colonists built where they could, first in wood, then in soft apricot brick, sometimes stuccoed, and later in Sydney's glorious sandstone that seems as ineffably right as does Bath stone in Bath.

By 1831, the town had grown from a small settlement into an early contender for a Tidy Town Award. Fortun Eydoux, a naval medical officer who visited here, described it as "a lovely town that could rival our prettiest in France".

Not even the City's most passionate advocates, in whose ranks I count myself, could make that claim today with a straight face but enough remains of our past to remind us that in the past century it was a more elegant place.

Waverley Cemetery. *Photograph by Joe Castro*

For the observant or the curious, the City's history is there to read in stone and sandstock brick – in St James Church and Hyde Park Barracks, remnants of Macquarie's Sydney, on our proudest street named, appropriately, after him; in the self-important public buildings that arose in the latter half of the 19th century, buildings that would be an ornament to any colonial capital; in the classical monuments to cultural pursuit, the Art Gallery and the State Library and, a century later, in the Opera House, the last great romantic building on earth.

In the Italianate Town Hall you can sense both affluence and optimism. The handsome Centennial Hall is the finest room of its kind in the country and the public staircases, paying decorative homage in iron and wood and stained glass and metal to wool, water, wattle and waratah, bespeak touching optimism, boundless faith in the city's and the country's future.

Much of historic Sydney has gone. Too much. All of the great private houses, such as the classical villa Greenway designed for Robert Campbell in Bligh Street and Burdekin House in Macquarie Street, are vanished, although more modest examples remain, particularly in Millers Point. The Strand Arcade is the sole survivor of a dozen such similar pedestrian connections between main streets. All our great Victorian theatres have been levelled along with good ones from this century. To have known Sydney in the 1950s is to be an unrepentant nostalgist, for the replacements have rarely matched original occupants of any site.

Enough still remains from our first century to provide a genuine feel of the past, particularly in the area on either side of the southern approaches to the Harbour Bridge, where Lower Fort Street and The Rocks area have the scale and charm and good manners that have been obliterated elsewhere; where an idle Sunday stroll in the afternoon sun can be a singular event.

A stroll from top to bottom of Bridge St is equally enlightening, the old Treasury (now a hotel), the 1878 Colonial Secretary's Office by James Barnet, the Education Department, the Lands Building of 1877, also by Barnet, with its decanter-shaped tower and the Burns Philp building, all cheek by jowl, a symphony in sandstone and collectively a compendium of 19th-century architectural styles.

Of course, Sydney has its horrors. What big city doesn't? There are things we all wish hadn't happened, like the Hilton Hotel and the monorail and the Cahill Expressway and, as if we had learned nothing from these design and planning disasters, the "Toaster" apartments at East Circular Quay. But whereas such excrescences might have marred a less naturally blessed city irretrievably, they merely scarred this one. It would take a lot to destroy Sydney's natural beauty, for there is always the redemptive topography and the ubiquitous ocean and bay. Chicago and Buenos Aires and Melbourne all have handsome architecture, handsomer than ours, but they sit on unpromising bodies of water. With Sydney, the reverse is true. Most of our buildings are fair to middling but we have the Harbour. And while the form of the City may change, that aqueous element remains and influences the way we live, see and enjoy the place.

The focus of early Sydney was a prime piece of waterfront land, the vast swathe of it between Darling Harbour and Woolloomooloo that formed the first settlement. The Governor, Captain Arthur Phillip, declared this land to be inalienable. He was, as the late Professor Max Kelly noted, probably hearing the distant drum of our economic history, trying to stem the tide of speculation as settlers scrambled to acquire and trade real estate. So important has real estate been to Sydney from the earliest days of European settlement, that it is jokingly observed that L.J. Hooker must have been Captain Cook's cabin boy.

Sydney's attraction to property speculation flourishes undiminished, as does the City's energy and raffishness. And its worship of money. Everybody is Sydney is chasing a dollar. Many of the families of Victoria who made their fortunes in the 1890s still have them, having largely been shrewd Scots as opposed to feckless Irish. Sydney fortunes are comparatively new, made as Sydney became and burgeoned as the business capital, not only of the country but also of the region.

It is also, despite claims to the contrary from the south, the cultural capital of the country. In the last 30 years Sydney has developed from a smug little town into an uncertain big one and out of that uncertainty has come a need to appear civilised, a need to construct monuments to sophistication. "World class" has become a favourite catchcry of our State and Federal politicians and sometimes, to their surprise and ours, the results of their initiatives turn out to be just that. Homebush Bay is a case in point. There has been general surprise at the discovery that facilities for the Olympics might be ready in time, let alone early, and that the predicted traffic chaos when public transport was trialled in April 1998, simply didn't happen.

For as well as a reputation for getting things wrong, Sydney also has something of a knack for rising to the occasion and getting it spot on. Or as, in the case of the Opera House, half-right which, I suppose, is better than total failure.

We are doing it as inexpensively as we can.
Joern Utzon

Not inexpensively enough for the rednecks of the Country Party as it then was. When the conservative coalition parties are in power in New South Wales, the Public Works portfolio goes by tradition to the most senior member of the National Party. In 1966, this was the dour Sir (then just plain Mr) Davis Hughes MLA, who decided that enough money had been spent on the Sydney Opera House and it was time to step in. Hughes made it impossible for Utzon to continue and, in getting rid of him, screwed up the inside of the building for all time, providing us with an acoustically impossible concert hall, a

"Sydney's glorious sandstone ... seems as ineffably right as does Bathstone in Bath"

Photograph by Belinda Pratten

Centennial Park. *Photograph by Steve Christo*

"The public flocks here on weekends for ... cycling and roller-blading ... but weekday mornings are for the pros"

woefully inadequate opera theatre and a desperate little drama theatre where the spectator feels as though proceedings are being watched through the slot in a post box.

We know now that no matter how much had been spent on the Sydney Opera House, it would have been worth it. Fortunately for us the outside form was irreversible and at least in that glittering cluster of shells we acquired a symbol that is not only universally known as a symbol of this city but of Australia, too.

We did not know it then but the Opera House architect and its political begetter, Labor Premier Joe Cahill, had bestowed on us a sense, probably undeserved then, of being a significant global player. What other city has a temple dedicated to the performing arts as its symbol? A clock, a steel tower, a sky needle and even a monorail are icons of London and Paris and Seattle and Wuppertal respectively, but Sydney has an opera house. Not any opera house but *the* Opera House.

Of all the additions to the foreshores, this is the one of which we can be proudest. Bradfield's great bridge links the two most populous parts of the city with, poised diagonally beneath, two kinds of egalitarian fun palaces, the Opera House and Luna Park. I do not buy the pejorative word "elitist". The Opera House is no such thing. Luna Park is just for fun and so is Utzon's pleasure dome. All manner of spectacles have graced its forecourt, from circus to the magnificent Els Comediants from Barcelona to the ancient smoking ceremony that inaugurated the 1997 Festival of the Dreaming, filling the air with the smell of eucalypt and the sound of didjeridoo and almost certainly conjuring up the ghost of Bennelong on whose eponymous point this wondrous structure has arisen.

There are not too many modern buildings that have lent grace and distinction and excitement to our City in the past few decades but this is one of them. It is appropriate that Sydney's most famous building should be a pleasure dome for, if there is one thing that Sydneysiders understand, it's how to have a good time. We do that frightfully well. And we're getting better at it.

Sydney's restaurants are now among the finest in the world (there's that old "world-class" idea again) and represent extraordinary value. The choice for the the diner is dizzying. And many of the old inane "regulations" have vanished. Thanks to the powerful axis of breweries and hotels, restaurant licences were restricted, one couldn't have a drink without having a meal, because the only place to have a drink, uncongenial though it might be, was the pub, wasn't it?

Those outmoded rules are gone or going. You can now actually sit on a milk crate on the tarmac outside a broom cupboard-sized caf and munch on a sticky bun without being worried by an inspector attempting to enforce some clause of the Pure Food Act of 1919.

Having embraced the macchiata, we then discovered another pleasure of urbanism, the *passeggiata*. In even the smallest towns in Italy people promenade in the evenings and on weekends. It's taken us some time to latch on to this civilised custom but now we have and strolling is in.

No shortage of places to stroll. Thanks to the foresight of our city fathers, we have the Royal Botanic Gardens, gloriously maintained these days, the Domain and the ground of Government House. We have waterfront parks studding the shore from Watsons Bay to Parramatta.

I can think of 20 places to lunch and fully experience Sydney, among them the Botanic Gardens caf, the MCA caf, the caf at the Museum of Sydney, the one at Palace Gate of the Gardens, the courtyard for Hyde Park Barracks, the Hyde Park caf, Pavilion on the Park in the Domain, either of two cafes at the Opera House, front and back. All are within a block or three of the CBD, all offer space and light and a seat in the sun.

Slightly further out one can use the Centennial Park caf in another green lung of the city. There have been attempts to make other parks that will be as inviting and as prodigiously visited as Centennial – Sydney Park at St Peter's and the Bicentennial Park at Homebush – but neither has become the magnet that Centennial is. Like lemmings, the public flocks here on weekends for picnics, duck feeding, and cycling and roller-blading, mostly inexpert. But weekday mornings are for the pros, the cyclists who roll by like a spilled packet of Smarties, the skilled roller-bladers who are the bitumen-bound equivalent of Brian Boytano or Michelle Kwan.

Centennial Park is open to all of Sydney, but some like to stay put, happy in their own chosen, self-contained precinct.

Newtown, with its cinemas, cafes, bookshops, all with a whiff of radicalism and a defiant air of anti-gentrification, is for the Newtownians. Woollahra is where a loaf of sourdough can cost a dollar more than at its place of origin 15 minutes away in Balmain or Haberfield. But the locals, happy with their swagger pub bistros like the Centennial and the Bistro Moncur, and jones the grocer, don't like to venture further than New South Head Road. Leichhardt, a suburb that has escaped the fate of its Melbourne counterpart, Carlton, simply by never becoming really modish, still has some of the best food emporia in Sydney, and is similarly self-contained. As are Mosman and Cabramatta.

These satellite communities revolve, like constellations, some brighter than others, around the dazzling central planet, planet Sydney.

When I returned to live here after the ritual stint in London that one felt, in the early '60s, obliged to undertake, I felt I had made a terrible mistake. One page of the *Herald* on cultural diversions seemed like starvation rations after London, where the nightly dilemma was choosing nightly between attractions at the Covent Garden and Festival Hall and Sadlers Wells and the National Theatre and the Aldwych. That was before one got to commercial entertainment. But gradually things here changed and now, while the choice is

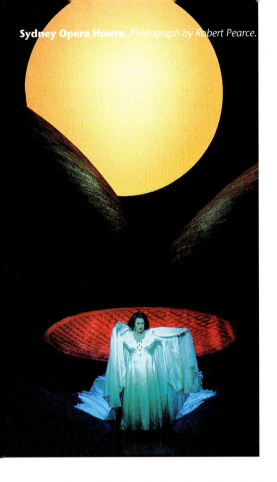

Sydney Opera House. *Photograph by Robert Pearce.*

not quite as dizzying as in London or New York and the quality may be somewhat variable, Sydney's cultural life is on a par with that offered in Paris or Berlin.

To a plenitude of opera, symphony, theatre, chamber music are added a dizzying array of popular entertainment. No one person could see everything. Sydney is a cinema city where going to the pictures has achieved the status of a ritual.

One need never be bored here. In fact, time is the enemy of the culturally voracious. To routine fare must be added the annual events, the Sydney Film Festival to which devotees dedicate an inordinate length of time, sometimes seeing four screenings a day. Its live theatres were allowed to vanish but Sydney had the sense to keep a couple of amazing atmospheric cinemas, one of which, the gloriously dizzy State, serves as the site for the film festival, which occupies half of June.

Twenty-two years old in 1999, the Sydney Festival takes care of January. And the arts festival and calendar of social events that precede the mighty Mardi Gras parade neatly take care of February. To these one may add the Spring Music Festival and a myriad of smaller events that effectively keep the City hopping on a 12-month cycle.

Culture is an elastic word. Sydney's culture can also be taken to include the City to Surf and the Sydney to the 'Gong ride in November. And it certainly includes sport. I am not the person to do more than observe that, although Sydney has developed film fever, gone coffee crazy and craves culture as an addict yearns for a fix, it remains as loyal as ever to sport of all kinds. Even new kinds. The prospect of Sydney crowding Swans' matches as they do Rugby once seemed as unlikely as the collapse of the Berlin Wall.

> *Sydney is a lower middle-class civilization suddenly got rich – the rich people have no public spirit and no cultivation and spend their time and money on racing.*
>
> **Beatrice Webb**

There is a grain of truth in the eminent Fabian's tart observation, delivered in 1898 in a letter to her sister, Catherine, in London. The popularity of racing may have waned, but Sydney remains sports-obsessed.

And the sense of pride in the city that is the spring to public beneficence is, as Webb correctly noted a century ago, not highly developed. Perhaps because so many of its citizens, those involuntarily settled here, later migrants coming not gladly but to escape oppression, even those like myself who came here because their parents thought we might have a shot at a better education and life than the bush offered, arrived here with little or nothing and have had to work so hard to achieve and are loath to throw money about on fripperies like philanthropy. Settled along different lines, Melbourne has many rich who see it as their duty to contribute to the public weal. But Sydneysiders, pleasure loving, with so much free on their doorsteps, demand more and give less.

That is not to say that Sydney has no heart, no soul. It can, at times, be the most open-hearted city imaginable, responding magnificently to the distress of others. But there is a difference between charity and philanthropy. One deals with the present, the other is an exercise in vision, a gift to the present but one that ensures a future.

Our cultural institutions bounce along, trying to avoid crisis rather than plan for growth. It would be nice for our gallery to have had a Fenton and his bequest. Perhaps it's too easy in Sydney just to sit in the sun and feel no need for improving anything but one's tan.

> You can form no idea of the beauty of this climate; our winters are delicious; the finest October day you can recall to mind is only a faint resemblance to the weather here.
>
> **Georgiana Lowe**, who, with her husband Robert Lowe, built Bronte House, in a letter to England, 1845.

To me at age five, Sydney's climate was part of its appeal. In the bush it was hot as hell, airless, dusty. But in Sydney, or at least the part of it I knew then, there always seemed, as now, to be a breeze coming from somewhere. In flat cities the air, particularly in hot weather, seems to sit material and motionless, trapped between buildings, lacking any force that might move the stale out and allow fresh in. But Sydney, being both a coastal and an undulating city, invites movement.

Its climate is part of Sydney's appeal. You can have terrible weather here – long humid days, sticky nights – but for most of the year one can move about without either freezing or deliquescing. It's a benign place. The odd willy-willy might rush through, providing an impromptu pruning for trees and flattening unprotected garden beds. It can occasionally become humid and the mould gathers on shoes and belts. But there are no wild extremes – no tornadoes or cyclones, no snow, no dark days in winter, no delineated seasons. If you want to see autumn leaves, what the Americans call Fall foliage, you can make a day trip in the appropriate season to Bowral or to the Blue Mountains. Sydney residents need no overcoats, no parkas, no second wardrobe.

A good climate is part of a city's appeal but people can endure terrible weather if there are other attractions. And in Sydney there are many, many, many, from the simplest to the most sophisticated. Which is why, despite minor irritations and exasperation, I don't want to be away from the place for long. Or in the words of Anthony Trollope:

> Sydney is one of those places which, when a man leaves it knowing he will never return, he cannot leave without a pang and a tear. Such is its loveliness.

Leo Schofield is a *Sydney Morning Herald* columnist, Director of the Sydney Festival until 2001 and Artistic Director of the Olympic Arts Festival, Harbour of Life.

"(Sydney) remains as loyal as ever to sports of all kinds. Even new kinds."

THE FIVE-RING CIRCUS IS COMING TO TOWN

BY MATTHEW MOORE

Photograph by Craig Golding

Sydney will never be the same. Of course, no city survives the Olympic blitz unaltered, but for Sydney the impact will be bigger than most. It's not just the Games themselves, it's the timing of them, the 2000 tag. As the first Games of the new millennium, they are in their own exclusive category. They will be first big international event of the next 1,000 years, looked to as a sign of how the world might do things differently. As far as most of the world sees it, they will take place in a far corner of the world in a land that's fresh and young and full of possibilities. Put that down as one big force for change.

Australia's cultural cringe mentality is another force that will transform the city. There's a widespread view that, at least on a project this size, Sydney, indeed Australia, will struggle to live up to the world's expectations. "How will Sydney ever cope with the Olympics when we can't even fix Parramatta Road?" is a common enough remark and it has organisers determined to do whatever's needed now to make sure the Games are something to be proud of.

Added to these reasons are the fact the Games are being paid for by the public, by taxpayers, unlike the last summer Olympics in Atlanta that were organised and funded privately. No Government, certainly no Australian Government, could survive serious international and local criticism that would come with any serious

Photograph by Peter Morris

"You won't need ... maps to find the Olympic Stadium ... at 110,000 seats it's the biggest in Olympic history."

problems, like venues not being completed or seriously inadequate transport plans. Governments have had little choice but to adopt a whatever-it-takes-and-whatever-it-costs strategy and make sure preparations are satisfactory. Put these three factors together and you get some understanding of the pressures to ensure that, at the closing ceremony, the IOC president, Juan Antonio Samaranch, will pronounce Sydney's Games "the best ever".

Proof of what pressure can do is everywhere. Roads are a good example. In the endless battle between residents and road-builder, the Olympics have tipped the balance and the engineers are in command. Construction signs beside the Eastern Distributor tollroad say the $600 million freeway linking northern suburbs to the airport will be finished in August 2000, a mere month before the Olympics. Just eight months after the Environmental Impact Statement for the tollway was released, fencing was up and the protestors were as good as beaten, surely a record for such a contentious project.

To the south of the city, the Olympics brought to a head a decade of debate and the Government resolved to build the M5 East freeway at a cost that was never finally decided. It is not an Olympic road, not needed for the Games, but it had a 2000 deadline until criticism from the local communities and skyrocketing costs saw a halt called. Along with a proposed railway to Bondi Beach, it remains one of the few big infrastructure projects not tied to an Olympics deadline.

Smaller freeways, like the City West Link, as well as a host of roundabouts and other road improvements, are being built to minimise delays that could frustrate the 200,000 visitors and hundreds of thousands of locals during the Games. Sydney has hardly had a new railway for years and now it's getting two (with a third to Bondi Beach still under consideration). By the time of the Games, visitors flying into Sydney will be able to take a train on the $750 million New Southern Railway straight to the City. Already they can take a 20-minute ride to Homebush Bay's Olympic Park. This purpose-built rail loop stops at the lofty Olympic Park station designed by Rodney Uren and Ken Maher of Hassell, right in the heart of the Homebush Bay complex of sports venues.

For anyone looking for a quick taste of Sydney's Olympics, this train trip is the way to get it. The ride through much of Sydney's inner west might be bleak and industrial but Homebush Bay, or Olympic Park as the venue complex is called, has its own big flavour. And it's called sport. Facilities built here shortly before and after Sydney's successful bid will host 15 of 28 sports, as well as the opening and closing ceremonies. Wherever you turn there is a mass of buildings, all new, almost all of them built for the Games.

The Visitors Centre, though, is from an earlier era. It's open every day and provides the best place to get an overview of the whole Olympics project. With photographs and models of all the venue sites, it gives you a feel for other venues, such as the velodrome and softball centre being built in other Sydney suburbs. You won't need one of the Visitors Centre maps to find the Olympic Stadium. Walk out of the airy platform, tilt your head back and it's hard to miss – at 110,000 seats it's the biggest in Olympic history. Ask at the Visitors Centre about getting inside.

Within a 2.5 kilometre radius you'll also find the Olympic village, where all 10,200 athletes and 5,000 team officials will stay for the Games. But with building and fit-out of the village continuing through the early part of 2000, getting a close look may be difficult. Much easier to see is the $380 million Showground complex, purpose-built for the Easter Show but designed to accommodate a host of Olympic sports. The huge dome and exhibition halls will be fitted out with some of the 340,000 temporary seats needed for the Games and will then host those sports Australians don't seem to win. Sports such as badminton, handball, table tennis and tae kwon do will be played here, while the animal pavilions will house a press centre where much of the media will work.

Bus tours run each day from the Visitors Centre. Check with the Olympic Co-Ordination Authority's Homebush Bay office on 9735 4800 for bus times and other details about the site.

The Sydney International Aquatic Centre, labelled by Juan Samaranch as the best in the world, is also worth a look. Thanks to its enormously popular leisure pool, where 85 per cent of swimmers go, the complex has become the second most popular sporting venue in the country after the Melbourne Cricket Ground. Temporary seats are being installed to increase capacity for the Games. For swimming nuts, it's possible to take tours of the centre that take you down into the bowels. Ring 9752 3666 for details.

You can drive to the Homebush site, too, and tour the venues at your leisure. With a car you can cruise through Bicentennial Park and take in other sites you may not get to on a tour. You should probably take a picnic, because Olympic

Olympic Park Station. *Photograph by Peter Morris*

Park is light on for food, although that is improving as more and more venues are completed.

However, the most spectacular way to arrive, is by ferry, the way Samaranch and the other senior members of the Olympic family are likely to travel during the Games. Standing out the front of the high-speed ferries that take you up the Parramatta River to Homebush Bay is one of the joys Sydney can offer, especially in spring when the Games will be held. This part of the Harbour is a mix of old and new, with enough industry remaining to remind you of how Sydney Harbour has been a working port, and enough new real estate development to illustrate how the Olympics are forcing change.

The shipping is just as mixed, with pleasure boats darting between the tankers and colliers and trawlers. The lovely new wharf at Homebush Bay suffers from one problem – it is several kilometres from the Homebush site. If you take one of the ferry and bus tours organised by State Transit (ph 13 1500), a bus will be there to meet and drop you at the wharf for the ferry back to the Quay.

Of course, the real reason to visit Homebush is to see sport, preferably Olympics-standard sport. If you're not going to be around for the Games themselves but like the idea of watching Olympic sport, then test events through 1999 and up until the Olympics could be the answer. Tests in every sport are planned to ensure organisers have a chance to sort out problems with equipment and planning in advance of the real thing. Test events will also give you a chance to visit Olympic venues at a fraction of the cost and the crowds of the Olympics. (Check this book's calender of events directory for test event dates.)

Australian sportsmen and women will use these events to prepare for the Games. With the Federal Government pumping an extra $135 million into preparing our athletes, Australia is expected to win 60 medals, a third of them gold, which would be an all-time record performance.

According to Australia's Olympic Committee president, John Coates, host nations judge the success of the Games according to how many medals they win. And the plan he's put together should see Australia finish fifth in the overall medal tally, and quite possibly higher.

With Australia's great performances at the January 1998 Perth world swimming championships, swimmers are likely to do well, as are athletes in other strong sports such as cycling, rowing, sailing, shooting, equestrian, triathlon and perhaps track and field.

Revellers celebrating victory are certain to congregate round Sydney Harbour, particularly The Rocks area. Hickson Road, the big wide strip that follows the Harbour under the Bridge and west past the Walsh Bay wharves, is likely to be full of temporary stores and stalls housed in acres of marquees where people can wander and eat and drink. The State Government has decided to remodel the wharves in time for the Games, to open them up to the light and the Harbour. Alfred Street, which connects all the wharves, is to be turned into a plaza with traffic all but removed. During the Games it is certain to be a popular meeting area with many visitors staying in hotels in the area or coming across the Harbour by ferry.

The Harbour itself is also undergoing changes thanks to the Games. A tunnel costing more than $300 million is being built underneath to take sewage to the ocean outfalls and reduce the overflows that pollute it whenever heavy rain falls.

Pin trading is always a big part of every Games and traders are sure to set up their tables throughout The Rocks once the Games begin. Already there's a pin-trading shop called The Pinworkx and an adjoining Olympic Pin museum at 8 Playfair Street.

Further up town, in the Pitt Street Mall, one of the Olympic Stores has hundreds of different items for Olympic souvenir hunters, where spending $500 will be easy. There are Olympic

State Sport Centre, Homebush. *Photograph by Tim Clayton*

"Test events will also give you a chance to visit Olympic venues at a fraction of the cost and crowds of the Olympics."

Homebush Aquatic Centre. *Photograph by Steve Christo*

"Australia is expected to win 60 medals ... swimmers are likely to do well, as are athletes in other

moleskin pants and tweed jackets, business shirts and bathrobes, cups, caps and even backpacks, all with SOCOG logos. If it's all too overwhelming, you can go downstairs and sit in the Olympic cafe, watch an Olympic video in the presence of paralympic wheelchairs and other sports gear. Check the phone book listings under Olympic Stores for locations of other outlets in the suburbs.

While most of the Olympic work is at Homebush, Sydney City Council is involved in a $200 million program to tart up the town in the lead-up to the Games. A large chunk of this is being spent on the "Look of the City" program. The French-based J.C. Decaux company, in partnership with an Australian firm, Manboom, won a $100 million tender for new street furniture that will change the look of streets in five Sydney local government areas. New benches, bus shelters, newsstands and public toilets, all paid for by the advertising they will carry, will appear in the City and surrounding areas, as well as at Darling Harbour, another site for Olympic sports competitons.

George Street has been the city's most neglected major street but that is changing with about $45 million being spent to give it a chance of coping with Olympic crowds. Footpaths are being paved with granite from Central Station to the Quay and are being substantially widened to give them a hope of carrying the numbers who use them on a normal day. New lights will be installed in George Street first and then throughout the rest of the city to prepare it for the Games. The Council has also decided to install closed circuit cameras at 35 locations in a move

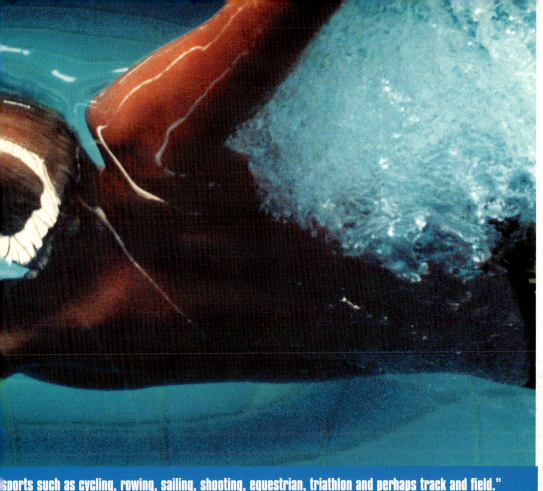

sports such as cycling, rowing, sailing, shooting, equestrian, triathlon and perhaps track and field."

it says will make the city safer for the Games. Hyde and Wynyard parks have been remodelled and a public art program has been approved.

The Council has calculated that $5.8 billion worth of development in the City is under way or has been approved. Much of this money is going into hotel developments. More than 4,000 new rooms are being built across Sydney, many in the City, not only to cope with the Games but in readiness for a tourism and convention boost that is expected to continue in the years after.

Not all projects are vast. Cook Park on William and College streets will be completed in time for the Games, so that locals and tourists can enjoy a swim in the heated pool after a day watching swimmers at Homebush Bay.

Getting a room in Sydney will be harder than getting a swim, unless you book a package through approved agents. SOCOG has signed up most of the accommodation. But if you can find a room it should be reasonably priced as the hotel owners have reached an agreement with Olympic organisers to hold prices during the Games.

Tickets for the Games are to go on sale in late 1999. A national ballot has been agreed to so that everyone can have an equal chance of getting those tickets to prime events which are not reserved by organisers and sponsors. While many events are likely to sell out, tickets should be easy to get for a host of the less popular events, such as rowing, handball, volleyball, badminton, baseball, softball and others. With more than 8 million tickets on sale, everyone will have a chance of seeing events. Sydney's venues are also very big, and the local population is relatively small, which means that it should be possible to get tickets for most events at the stadium. Scalpers normally sell tickets to most events during the Games and, if you really want to see an event, this can be a way to do it. Besides, tickets from scalpers are often a lot less than face price, especially five minutes before the start gun

But don't forget that some of the most spectacular events will be free. The marathon runs through Centennial Park and out and back along Anzac Parade, providing a chance to see runners twice. Road cycling will be on a spectacular course that runs on a loop also through Centennial Park and down to Bronte Beach before the climb up the long hill over the headland, providing a wonderful spot to watch events that can last more than four hours.

Rich or poor, on day one there will be only one place to be. Get to the Opera House early ready for the start of the first ever Olympic triathlon, where a spectacular harbour swim and a frantic cycle leg will end with a foot race through the City. With Australia's world dominance of both the men's and women's event, Australian gold medals seem as good as won.

Matthew Moore is the Sydney Morning Herald's Olympics Editor.

THE STYLE OF SYDNEY

Done Art and Design
123 George Street, The Rocks
Shop G46, Queen Victoria Building
Sydney International Airport

The Ken Done Gallery
Original paintings and drawings, limited edition silkscreens and posters

1 Hickson Road, The Rocks
Tel 02 9247 2740 Open 7 days

BEST OF SYDNEY
THE A-Z LISTINGS

INDEX OF THE LISTINGS

Aboriginal Sydney .... p 41
Abseiling, see Adventure & extreme sports
Accessories, see Women's shoes and accessories, Men's shoes and accessories
Accommodation .... p 43
Accountants .... p 44
Activism .... p 45
Acupuncture, see Alternative medicine
Adventure & extreme sports .... p 46
Aerobics .... p 47
Aircraft, see Flying
Air-conditioning .... p 48
Alarms, see Security systems
Alternative medicine .... p 48
Amusement parks, see Children's entertainment
Antennas .... p 49
Antiques .... p 49
Appliances .... p 51
Archery .... p 52
Architects .... p 53
Architecture & Urban Design .... p 54
Aromatherapy, see Alternative medicine, Beauty products, Beauty salons
Art conservation & framing .... p 56
Art galleries .... p 57
Art schools & supplies .... p 58
Asian restaurants .... p 59
Astrologers, see New Age
Astronomy .... p 60
Athletics .... p 61
Auctions .... p 62
Australian Rules .... p 63
Australian cooking, see Modern Australian restaurants
Baby supplies .... p 65
Backpacking .... p 66
Badminton .... p 67
Bags, see Luggage
Bakeries & patisseries .... p 68
Ballet, see Dance
Banks & financial institutions .... p 69
Barbecues .... p 70
Bars .... p 71
Baseball .... p 73

Basketball .... p 73
Bathrooms .... p 75
Beaches .... p 75
Beauty products .... p 77
Beauty salons .... p 78
Bed & breakfast, see Accommodation
Bed and bath linen, see Homewares
Beer .... p 79
Bicycles, see Cycling
Billiards, see Pool
Birdwatching, see Wildlife
Blinds & shutters .... p 80
Blues music .... p 80
Boat trips, see Ferries
Boating, see Fishing, Powerboating, Sailing, Water skiing
Body piercing, see Tattoos & piercing
Bodybuilding .... p 81
Books .... p 82
Bottle shops, see Liquor stores, Wine
Boules, see Bowling
Bowling .... p 84
Boxing .... p 85
Bread, see Bakeries & patisseries
Breakfast & brunch .... p 85
Bricks, see Building materials, Tiles & pavers
Bridal, see Weddings
Bridge .... p 86
Briefcases, see Luggage
Building contractors .... p 87
Building equipment .... p 88
Building materials .... p 88
Bush food .... p 90
Bushwalking .... p 90
Business lunches .... p 91
Business Services, see Translators, Couriers, Office furniture, Printing
Buskers .... p 92
Butchers, see Meat, Poultry & game
Cabaret .... p 92
Cabinetmakers, see Carpenters & cabinetmakers
Cafes .... p 93
Cakes, see Bakeries & patisseries
Cameras, see Photography
Camping & caravans .... p 94

Index of the Listings

Canoeing & kayaking .... p 96
Canyoning, see Adventure & extreme sports
Car hire .... p 97
Car parts & services, see Motor vehicle parts, accessories & services
Car racing, see Motorsport
Caravans, see Camping & caravans
Card games, see Bridge
Carpenters & cabinetmakers .... p 97
Carpets & floor covering .... p 98
Casinos, see Gambling
Catering .... p 99
Cats, see Pets
Caving, see Adventure & extreme sports
Cemeteries, see Dead Sydney
Charities .... p 99
Cheese .... p 100
Children's entertainment .... p 101
Childrenswear .... p 102
Chinese medicine, see Alternative medicine
Chinese restaurants .... p 104
Chinese Sydney .... p 105
Chocolates & confectionery .... p 107
Cigarettes, see Cigars & tobacconists
Cigars & tobacconists .... p 108
Cinema, see Film
Clairvoyants, see New Age
Classical music .... p 109
Cleaning .... p 111
Coaching (academic), see Tutors & coaching
Coffee & tea .... p 111
Collectables .... p 112
Comedy .... p 113
Compact discs, see Blues music, Classical music, Country music, Folk music, Jazz, Opera, Rock & pop music, World music
Compact disc players, see Stereo & home theatre equipment
Computers .... p 114
Concrete, see Building materials
Confectionery, see Chocolates & confectionery
Cooking classes .... p 116
Cocktails, see Bars
Cookware & kitchenware .... p 117
Cooling systems, see Air-conditioning
Costumes .... p 118
Country music .... p 119
Couriers .... p 119
Cricket .... p 120
Curriculums vitae, see Resumes

Curtains, see Soft Furnishing & fabrics, Interior designers
Cycling .... p 121
Dance .... p 122
Dating & introduction services ... p 124
Day trips, see Drives
Dead Sydney .... p 124
Decorators, see Interior designers & decorators
Delicatessens .... p 126
Demolition .... p 127
Dentists .... p 127
Department stores .... p 128
Design, see Furniture, Interior designers
Dieting, see Weight loss
Disabled Sydney .... p 129
Discount fashion .... p 131
Diving .... p 132
Dogs, see Pets
Domestic services, see Cleaning
Drama, see Theatre
Drawing classes, see Art schools & supplies
Drives .... p 132
Driving Schools .... p 134
Drycleaners & laundries .... p 134
Duty-free shopping .... p 135
Education, see Schools, Tutors & coaching
Electrical goods, see Appliances, Stereo & home theatre equipment, Television & videos
Electricians .... p 136
Environmental activism, see Activism
Equestrian, see Horseriding
European restaurants .... p 136
Evening classes, see Art schools, Languages, Cooking classes, Photography
Event management .... p 137
Extreme sports, see Adventure & extreme sports
Fabrics, see Soft furnishings
Factory outlets, see Discount fashion
Fairs, see Markets & fairs
Fashion, see Baby supplies, Childrenswear, Discount fashion, International designer fashion, Men's shoes & accessories, Menswear, Streetwear, Swimwear & surfwear, Vintage & recycled fashion, Women's shoes & accessories, Womenswear
Fastfood & takeaway .... p 138
Fences & gates .... p 140
Fencing .... p 140
Ferries .... p 140
Film .... p 141

Index of the Listings

Financial institutions, see Banks & financial institutions
Financial planning, see Investment managers & advisers, Accountants, Stockbrokers
Fine dining .... p 143
Fireplaces, see Heating & fireplaces
Fireworks .... p 144
Fishing .... p 145
Fish & seafood .... p 146
Fitness clubs .... p 146
Flora & fauna, see Wildlife, Zoos
Floor covering, see Carpets & floor covering, Rugs
Floors .... p 147
Florists .... p 148
Flying & gliding .... p 149
Football, see Australian Rules, Rugby league, Rugby union, Soccer
Folk music .... p 150
Food, see Bakeries & patisseries, Barbecues, Bush food, Cheese, Chocolates & confectionery, Coffee & tea, Cooking classes, Delicatessens, Fish & seafood, Fruit & vegetables, Gourmet food, Health food, Ice-cream, Meat, Poultry & game, Sandwiches
Formal wear, see Weddings
Fortune tellers, see New Age
Fountains .... p 150
Framing, see Art conservation & framing
French restaurants .... p 151
Fruit & vegetables .... p 152
Fun fairs, see Children's entertainment
Fun runs, see Running
Function venues .... p 153
Furniture .... p 153
Furniture restoration .... p 156
Galleries, see Art galleries
Gambling .... p 156
Game meats, see Poultry & game
Garage sales, see Junk
Gardens .... p 157
Garden supplies, see Nurseries & garden supplies
Gates, see Fences & gates
Gay & Lesbian Sydney .... p 159
Gelato, see Ice-cream
Glass, see Building Materials
Glasses & optical supplies .... p 160
Gliding, see Flying
Go-karts .... p 161
Golf .... p 162

Gourmet food .... p 163
Greek Sydney .... p 164
Greengrocers, see Fruit & vegetables
Greyhound racing .... p 165
Guided tours .... p 166
Gymnastics .... p 167
Gyms, see Aerobics, Bodybuilding, Fitness clubs, Gymnastics, Martial arts, Weightlifting
Hairdressers .... p 168
Hair replacement & wigs .... p 169
Handbags, see Women's shoes & accessories
Handball .... p 169
Handypersons, see Tradespeople
Hang-gliding, see Adventure & extreme sports
Hardware .... p 170
Hats .... p 171
Health & fitness, see Alternative medicine, Bodybuilding, Dentists, Fitness clubs, Health & medical matters, Massage, Personal trainers, Quitting, Yoga
Health & medical matters .... p 171
Health food .... p 173
Heating & fireplaces .... p 173
Herbal medicine, see Alternative medicine
Heritage Sydney .... p 174
Historic buildings, see Architecture, Heritage Sydney
Hobbies, see Toys & hobbies
Hockey .... p 175
Home appliances, see Appliances
Home help, see Cleaning
Homewares .... p 176
Horseracing .... p 177
Horseriding .... p 179
Hostels, see Backpacking
Hotels, see Accommodation, Backpacking
Ice skating, see Skating
Ice-cream .... p 180
In-line skating, see Skating
Indian restaurants .... p 181
Indigenous art, see Aboriginal Sydney, Art galleries
Indoor cricket, see Cricket
Insulation .... p 182
Interior designers & decorators .... p 182
International designer fashion .... p 184
Internet services, see Computers

Index of the Listings

Introduction services, see Dating & introduction services
Investment managers & advisers ....p 185
Italian restaurants .... p 186
Italian Sydney .... p 188
Japanese food .... p 189
Jazz .... p 191
Jetskiing, see Powerboating
Jewellery .... p 192
Jogging, see Running
Joy flights, see Flying
Judo, see Martial arts
Junk .... p 193
Karaoke .... p 194
Karate, see Martial arts
Kayaking, see Canoeing
Kitchen appliances, see Appliances, Cookware & kitchenware
Kitchens .... p 195
Kitchenware, see Cookware & kitchenware
Kites .... p 196
Korean restaurants, see Asian restaurants
Landscape designers & architects .... p 197
Languages .... p 197
Laotian restaurants, see Asian restaurants
Late-night food .... p 198
Latin American Sydney, see Spanish & Latin American Sydney
Laundries, see Drycleaners & laundries
Lawn bowls, see Bowling
Lebanese Sydney .... p 199
Lifesaving .... p 201
Lighting .... p 201
Lingerie .... p 202
Liquor stores .... p 203
Locksmiths .... p 204
Luggage .... p 204
Make-up, see Beauty products
Malaysian restaurants, see Asian restaurants
Manchester, see Homewares
Manicures, see Beauty salons
Marathons, see Running
Marinas, see Sailing, Powerboating
Markets & fairs .... p 205
Martial arts .... p 206
Massage .... p 207
Meat .... p 207
Medical matters, see Alternative medicine, Dentists, Health & medical matters
Meditation, see New age, Alternative medicine

Men's shoes & accessories .... p 208
Menswear .... p 209
Milliners, see Hats
Modern Australian restaurants .... p 211
Money, see Accountants, Banks, Investment managers, Stockbrokers
Motoring, see Car hire, Drives
Motorsport .... p 212
Motor vehicle parts, accessories & services .... p 213
Motorcycle racing, see Motorsport
Movies, see Films
Moving, see Removalists, Storage
Museums .... p 214
Music, see Blues music, Classical music, Country music, Folk music, Jazz, Musicians, Opera, Rock & pop music, World music
Musical instruments .... p 216
Musical tuition .... p 217
Musicians .... p 218
National parks .... p 219
Native animals, see Wildlife
Natural therapies, see Alternative medicine, Massage, New age
Naturopathy, see Alternative medicine, Beauty salons
Netball .... p 219
New age .... p 220
Newsagents .... p 221
Nightclubs .... p 221
Nurseries & garden supplies .... p 222
Observatories, see Astronomy
Office furniture .... p 224
Opera .... p 225
Op shops, see Vintage & recycled fashion
Optical supplies, see Glasses & optical supplies
Organic food, see Health food
Outdoor dining .... p 226
Outdoor furniture .... p 226
Paint .... p 228
Painters .... p 228
Painting classes, see Art schools & supplies
Paper hangers, see Painters
Paragliding, see Adventure & extreme sports
Parasailing, see Adventure & extreme sports
Parks, see Gardens, National parks
Party supplies .... p 229
Pastry, see Bakeries & patisseries
Patisseries, see Bakeries & patisseries
Pavers, see Tiles & pavers

Index of the Listings

Perfume, see Beauty products
Personal trainers .... p 250
Pest control .... p 231
Pets .... p 231
Photocopying, see Printing
Photography .... p 234
Picnics, see Barbecues, Beaches, National parks
Pies, see Bakeries, Fast food
Ping pong, see Table tennis
Pizza .... p 235
Plants, see Nurseries
Plumbers .... p 236
Pool .... p 236
Poultry & game .... p 237
Powerboating .... p 238
Pre-theatre dining .... p 239
Printing .... p 240
Public speaking .... p 241
Pubs .... p 241
Quitting .... p 242
Racing, see Go-karts, Gambling, Greyhound racing, Horseracing, Motorsport
Rafting, see Adventure & extreme sports
Record albums, see Blues music, Classical music, Country music, Folk music, Jazz, Opera, Rock & pop music, World music
Recycled fashion, see Vintage & recycled fashion
Relaxation, see Alternative medicine, Beauty salons, Massage, Tai chi, Yoga
Removalists .... p 242
Renovation, see Air-conditioning, Architects, Bathrooms, Blinds & shutters, Building contractors, Building equipment, Building materials, Carpenters, Carpets, Demolition, Electricians, Fences & gates, Floors, Hardware, Heating & fireplaces, Insulation, Interior designers, Kitchens, Landscape designers, Lighting, Nurseries, Paint, Painters, Pest control, Plumbers, Removalists, Restoration, Security systems, Skylights, Storage, Tiles & pavers, Tradespeople, Wallpaper
Restaurants, see Asian restaurants, Breakfast & brunch, Business lunches, Cafes, Chinese restaurants, Fine dining, European restaurants, French restaurants, Greek Sydney, Indian restaurants, Italian restaurants, Japanese food, Late-night food, Lebanese Sydney, Modern Australian restaurants, Outdoor dining, Pizza, Pre-theatre dining, Seafood restaurants, Spanish & Latin American Sydney, Steak, Thai restaurants, Vegetarian restaurants, Vietnamese Sydney, Yum cha
Rental cars, see Car hire
Restoration .... p 243
Resumes .... p 244
Rock & pop music .... p 245
Rock climbing, see Adventure & extreme sports
Roller skating, see Skating
Rowing .... p 246
Rugby league .... p 247
Rugby union .... p 248
Rugs .... p 249
Running .... p 250
Sailboarding .... p 251
Sailing .... p 252
Sales .... p 253
Sandwiches .... p 254
Scenic flights, see Flying & gliding
Schools .... p 255
Sculpture & public art .... p 256
Seafood restaurants .... p 257
Seafood, see Fish
Second-hand goods, see Junk
Security systems & alarms
Shoes, see Men's shoes, Women's shoes
Shoe repairs .... p 258
Shooting .... p 259
Shopping centres & strips .... p 259
Shutters, see Blinds & shutters
Skating .... p 261
Skiing & snowboarding .... p 262
Skydiving, see Adventure & extreme sports
Skylights .... p 262
Small goods, see Delicatessens
Snowboarding, see Skiing & snowboarding
Soccer .... p 263
Softball .... p 264
Soft furnishings & fabrics .... p 265
Software, see Computers
Spanish & Latin American Sydney .... p 266
Sporting goods .... p 268
Sports & outdoors, see Adventure & Extreme Sports, Aerobics, Archery, Athletics, Australian Rules, Badminton, Baseball, Basketball, Sailing, Water skiing, Bodybuilding, Bowling, Boxing, Canoeing, Cricket, Cycling, Diving, Golf, Greyhound

Index of the Listings

racing, Gymnastics, Handball, Hockey, Horseracing, Lifesaving, Martial arts, Motorsport, Netball, Rowing, Rugby league, Rugby union, Running, Shooting, Skating, Squash, Synchronised swimming, Table tennis, Tennis, Volleyball, Water polo, Weightlifting, Sailboarding, Wrestling
Sprinting, see Athletics, Running
Squash .... p 268
Sri Lankan restaurants, see Asian restaurants
Stargazing, see Astronomy
Stationery, see Newsagents
Steak .... p 269
Stereo & home theatre equipment ..... p 270
Stockbrokers .... p 271
Storage .... p 271
Street entertainment, see Buskers
Streetwear .... p 272
Sunglasses .... p 273
Supermarkets .... p 273
Surfing .... p 274
Swimming .... p 275
Swimming pools & spas .... p 277
Swimwear & surfwear .... p 277
Synchronised swimming .... p 278
Table tennis .... p 279
Tableware .... p 279
Taekwondo, see Martial arts
Tai chi .... p 280
Takeaway food, see Fastfood & takeaway
Tapes (audio), see Blues music, Classical music, Country music, Jazz, Rock & pop music, World music
Tattoos & piercing .... p 281
Tea, see Coffee & tea
Telescopes, see Astronomy
Televisions & videos .... p 281
Television, video & stereo repairs ..... p 282
Tennis .... p 283
Tenpin bowling, see Bowling
Thai restaurants .... p 284
Theatre .... p 285
Tiles & pavers .... p 287
Timber, see Building materials, Hardware
Tobacconists, see Cigars & tobacconists
Tools, see Hardware
Tours, see Aboriginal Sydney, Guided tours, Travel agencies & tour operators
Touch football, see Rugby league

Toys & hobbies .... p 287
Track sports, see Athletics, Running
Tradespeople .... p 288
Trains .... p 289
Translators .... p 290
Travel agencies & tour operators ..... p 290
Triathlon .... p 291
Trotting, see Horseracing
Tuition, see Art schools, Computers, Cooking classes, Driving schools, Languages, Photography
Tutors & coaching .... p 292
Upholstery .... p 293
Urban design, see Architecture & urban design
Vegetables, see Fruit & vegetables
Vegetarian restaurants .... p 294
Video stores .... p 295
Videos, see Television & videos
Vietnamese Sydney .... p 295
Vintage & recycled fashion .... p 297
Vitamins, see Alternative medicine, Health food
Volleyball .... p 298
Volunteering .... p 299
Walking tours, see Aboriginal Sydney, Bushwalking, Guided tours
Wallpaper .... p 299
Watches, see Jewellery, Men's accessories, Women's accessories
Water polo .... p 300
Waterskiing .... p 301
Weddings .... p 302
Weekends away .... p 303
Weightlifting .... p 305
Weight loss .... p 306
Whitegoods, see Appliances
Wigs, see Hair replacement & wigs
Wildlife .... p 306
Windsurfing, see Sailboarding
Wine .... p 307
Women's shoes & accessories .... p 308
Womenswear .... p 310
Woodworking .... p 313
World music .... p 314
Wrestling .... p 314
Yachting, see Sailing
Yoga .... p 315
Youth hostels, see Backpacking
Yum cha .... p 316
Zoos .... p 317

Aboriginal Sydney

Sydney's concrete, tar and grass lie over a landscape embedded with signs of at least 20,000 years of Aboriginal occupation. Some are still visible; the metropolis is a great outdoor gallery containing at least 1,000 known rock artworks. Simple and haunting, most are engraved, some painted. They depict lovers, fish, birds, roos, spiritual beings.

However, Aboriginal Sydney is not just a thing of the past. Although the First Fleet's arrival wrought devastation on the traditional owners, many descendants have survived. As well, indigenous people from all over Australia have been drawn to the city. They have created young, vibrant communities where great veins of anger and humour run side by side, spitting out artworks and music and politics which both confront and endear.

Thoughtful cultural teachers conduct tours for those who want to learn. Try contact. In these days of reconciliation, it's not that hard.

The Basin Track at Pittwater

Rock art is spread right across Sydney, from Bondi to the Blue Mountains. Consult Peter Stanbury and John Clegg's *A Field Guide to Aboriginal Rock Engravings* (Oxford University Press, $34.95). They say this site is 'five-star' viewing.
- Take the ferry from Palm Beach to the Basin.

Dharawal Education Centre

Rodney Mason, a descendant of the Botany Bay people, takes day tours from Bondi (dodge the balls across the golf course to see the clifftop engraved whales) to the Royal National Park to teach about rock carvings, bush tucker and culture lived then and now.
- 15 Murrong Place, La Perouse, ph 9661 1226.

Sydney Aboriginal Discoveries

See the Koori past along the city foreshores, from the great gathering place of Warraru (Circular Quay) to the fishing grounds of Kutti Kutti (Watson's Bay) on an indigenous-run harbour tour. Aboriginal chef Dallas Dodd offers glam bush tucker such as pipi consomme with native yams and damper. For a 24-hour cultural 'immersion', he and wife Margret Campbell also run overnight camps near Sutherland. There's campfire story-telling and traditional explanations of the night sky.
- PO Box Q507, QVB Post Office 1230, ph 9568 3226.

La Perouse Community Development Corporation

Need that liver cleansed? On the community's 'bush tucker' trail at Yarra Bay, an Aboriginal guide can explain the best berry to do the trick, or which native grass to choose to tie together your ti-tree gunyah. On weekends, Laddie Timbery, a descendant of the original 'La Pa' people demonstrates boomerang-throwing and sells arts and crafts at The Loop.
- Elaroo Ave, La Perouse, ph 9311 2999.

Yiribana, Art Gallery of NSW

Not a squeak from Lin Onus's cross-hatched bats nor the Hills Hoist they hang from in this wonderful space wherein permanently resides all manner of indigenous art. Furthermore, noontime visitors can do a croc or roo dance, get painted up or just drink in the enthusiasm and cleverness of Sean Choolburra, who chats informatively, does body art and dances (Tuesday to Saturday.)
- Art Gallery Rd, The Domain, ph 9225 1744.

Ngaramang Bayumi, The Powerhouse Museum

Tap into the fierce energy of Torres Strait Islander dancing, explore the power of the didj and wonder a little at how all that indigenous contemporary dance has exploded in our city at this exhibit, on until February 1999.
- 500 Harris St, Ultimo, ph 9217 0100.

The Edge of the Trees: Museum of Sydney

It's a shock for late-night revellers to find themselves outside the museum amid this sculptural work of 29 poles which literally talk in the Sydney Aboriginal languages. Artists Fiona Foley and Janet Lawrence haunt us with our past, as do flashes of indigenous life inside the museum.
■ **Cnr Bridge and Phillip Sts, ph 9251 5988.**

Indigenous Australians: Australia's First People, Australian Museum

Once attacked for clinging to Aboriginal bones, Ozmoz is now more sensitive and contemporary. This sweep across history includes re-creations of the 1972 Tent Embassy and a stolen child's painted documentation of the history of separated families. Live artists also perform regularly.
■ **6 College St, City, ph 9320 6000.**

Bangarra Dance Theatre

It's ochres rather than tutus for this world-dazzling company which has married traditional and contemporary dance values to say something about land, spirit and people. Sydney will see a special performance of a new work in November 1998. But catch them whenever they're home.
■ **The Wharf, Pier 4/5, Hickson Rd, Walsh Bay, ph 9251 5333.**

National Aboriginal and Islander Skills Development Association (NAISDA)

From this college has sprung the new generations of indigenous dancers like Kim Walker, but its end-of-year concert is little-known. In 1998 it's from November 27 to December 5 at the Performance Space, 199 Cleveland St, Redfern.
■ **3 Cumberland St, The Rocks, ph 9252 0199.**

Riberries Taste Australia

Not Aboriginal-run, but this restaurant seeks a path to reconciliation through the stomach, with pavlova made with wattleseed gathered by Central Australian Aboriginal women and Yolla, an ocean-going bird collected by Tasmanian Aborigines.
■ **411 Bourke St, Darlinghurst, ph 9361 4929.**

Edna's Table

The flavour is indigenous here, too, if not the ownership. French style is blended with native ingredients. Decor: outback meets city.
■ **Level 8/19 Martin Place, City, ph 9231 1400.**

Gavala

Aboriginal-run and staffed, this is where you can get your didj, T-shirt or modest dot painting. Regular dance performances, too.
■ **Shop 321, Festival Marketplace, Darling Harbour, ph 9212 7232.**

Blackbooks

Stop the search for that elusive title on indigenous issues. They'll locate it for you.
■ **11 Mansfield St, Glebe, ph 9660 2396.**

Boomalli Aboriginal Artists' Co-operative

Hip young inner-city urban indigenous artists have created a gallery where they hold regular exhibitions of often less-than-traditional works to broaden dot-dazzled minds about Aboriginal art.
■ **27 Abercrombie St, Chippendale, ph 9698 2047.**

Those with a yen to buy art from more remote regions should head for **Hogarth Galleries** (7 Walker Lane, Paddington, ph 9360 6839) and **Coo-ee Aboriginal Emporium and Aboriginal Art Gallery** (98 Oxford St, Paddington, ph 9332 1544).

Tranby Aboriginal Co-operative College

Has cross-cultural and 'black' history education by Aboriginal teachers. They also take overnight tours to Jervis Bay for bonding with the

land and the Jerrinja people, as well as odysseys through remote regions. Folk are also welcome to join Friends of Tranby to support the college's work – and socialise.
■ 13 Mansfield St, Glebe, ph 9660 3444.

Debra Jopson

Accommodation

see also backpackers, camping & caravans
It's not that hard for a hotel to be great, and a great hotel doesn't have to be expensive. Apart from obvious details such as bathrooms with two sinks, phones with ISD, tea-making equipment, a fridge, a TV with access to CNN, and free movies, a great hotel must, in my view, have these less tangible assets:
■ a role in the life of its city, whether through a restaurant that's loved by locals, or a ballroom where the power meetings take place, or a bar where the grooviest people pick each other up;
■ a sense of history, preferably scandalous, and a design that makes locals proud to look at it, even if they never step inside.

Sadly, few Sydney hotels meet all these requirements, but here are a few which get more than half way there – from the poshest to the most basic, but still special. The following selection starts at the posh end, moves on to some that are intriguing, or small and lively, and concludes with a few in the cheap and comfy category.

The Park Hyatt

Press a button to open your curtains for a view of the Opera House or to summon your butler for room service or a choice of videos. This is Sydney's most luxurious accommodation, wrapped around West Circular Quay and favoured by Diana Ross and Rod Stewart. Depending on demand, you might catch a double room with a view for $420 (plus the usual 5 per cent bed tax imposed by the NSW Government).
■ 7 Hickson Rd, The Rocks, ph 9241 1234.

The Regent

The pioneer of the grand-lobbied '80s hotels, it has smaller rooms than its '90s successors but its assets include a lively bar on George Street and the adventurous Kables restaurant. A double room with water view will cost at least $365.
■ 199 George St, City, ph 9238 0000.

The Observatory

Small but grand, with a star-ceilinged indoor swimming pool and an interesting Italian restaurant called Galileo. The Observatory emphasises calm discretion, at $350 or more for a double room with view.
■ 89 Kent St, The Rocks, ph 9256 2222.

The Ritz Carlton, City

Comfortable in a clubby kind of way, it has the honour of being housed in Sydney's former venereal disease clinic. If you sit in the opulent bar, you're on the spot where thousands of miserable souls over the decades awaited their test results. Basic doubles start around $300.
■ 93 Macquarie St, City, ph 9252 4600.

The Ritz Carlton, Double Bay

Historically, the home away from home of Diana Spencer, Bob Hawke, Madonna, and Michael Hutchence (who didn't survive his stay in room 514), the RC of DB would prefer to be quiet, discreet, Mediterranean in style and away from the city rush, instead of the buzzing publicity hive it became in the mid '90s. Double rooms start at $350.
■ 33 Cross St, Double Bay, ph 9362 4455.

Sebel of Sydney

Once the favourite of visiting rock stars, and the scene of much orgiastic adventuring in the

Accommodation

'60s and '70s, the Sebel now has a sexy downstairs bar and a somewhat seedy air, which is why communing with musical history will cost a mere $190 a night.
- 23 Elizabeth Bay Rd, Elizabeth Bay, ph 9358 3244.

The Russell
In the small and lively category. Right under the Harbour Bridge, and a victim of street noise when Sydney is partying (but then, why aren't you?), The Russell offers 19th century cosiness and a calming roof garden, starting at $170 a double.
- 143a George St, The Rocks, ph 9241 3543.

Ravesi's
Nothing could be more Sydney than waking to a view of Bondi Beach, and then crossing the road for a surf before tucking into a lavish breakfast in a buzzy restaurant. Ravesi's offers those options with style, and its cane furniture reinforces the beachside casualness. Without a view, you could pay $99 a double, and with one, $190.
- Cnr Campbell Pde and Hall St, Bondi Beach, ph 9365 4422.

The Stafford
Not so much a hotel as an eccentric collection of 64 renovated studios, apartments and terrace houses, all with their own kitchens as well as room service for the less energetic, starting from $200 a double.
- 75 Harrington St, The Rocks, ph 9251 6711.

Simpsons of Potts Point
A restored 1892 mansion, originally built for a NSW politician (and closely resembling the current Woollahra home of the former Prime Minister Paul Keating), Simpsons offers 14 elegant rooms, all with bathrooms, air conditioning, and windows that open, a minute's walk from two of Sydney's most interesting restaurants – Moran's and Cicada. Rooms for two start at $175.
- 8 Challis Ave, Potts Point, ph 9356 2199.

L'otel
Here's where under-40s who want to be groovy choose to stay. The noisy bar offers sightings of models, artists and actors on the way up. Basic rooms near the traffic go for $85 a night, while antique-decorated, bigger rooms can reach $160.
- 114 Darlinghurst Rd, Darlinghurst, ph 9360 6868.

Aaron's
Clean and cheap and close to Chinatown – what more could you want in a city hotel? Basic doubles with bathroom cost $112 a night, and rooms with their own tiny courtyards cost $132.
- 37 Ultimo Road, Haymarket, ph 9281 5555.

Bed And Breakfast Sydneyside
For those who prefer casual domesticity to formal efficiency, Alison Duncan has a list of 50 Sydney families, in such suburbs as Glebe, Rose Bay, Mosman, Manly and Bondi, who are keen to offer a bedroom and a seat at their breakfast table. She'll chat to the traveller and match the house with the personality (and the breakfast preference), at a cost around $60 for a single room and $90 a double.
- PO Box 555, Turramurra, NSW 2074, ph 9449 4430.

David Dale

Accountants

Even accountants have been known to tell boring accountant jokes. It's just that theirs aren't funny. However, Australia's labyrinthine tax laws have made this a booming business for budding number crunchers. And, not to be caught napping, Sydney's accountants have branched out into everything from investment advice to business consulting.

Good advice can be found in the smallest of suburban shops and bad advice in the most prestigious firms. But the big firms have the advantage of having more resources and a larger network to refer to.

The best accountants are generally to be found by word of mouth and, with this in mind, the *Sydney Morning Herald*'s Money section asked its readers to nominate their favourite accountants in April 1998. Nominations for almost 100 different accountants across the state – both big and small – bodes well for the quality of the profession. Most are members of one of the two main industry bodies, the Institute of Chartered Accountants or the Australian Society of CPAs, although other accountants were nominated and included in our final listing. Three firms scored particularly well.

Page Harrison

A three-partner chartered accounting practice at Milsons Point with a skew towards the entertainment industry, it received the highest number of nominations.
- Ph 9922 7144.

Gordon Hrnjak Rae

A member of the Count network of financial planners and accountants in Mona Vale (although the *Herald* was somewhat disappointed nominations for this firm came as form letters).
- Ph 9979 4300.

Morris Zammit

This Penrith firm is also a member of the Count network. Principal Craig Morris says a drawcard is special fixed-fee service packages, as well as the full range of financial and tax consulting.
- Ph (02) 4731 3333.

Annette Sampson

Further Information
- Australian Society of CPAs, ph 9375 6200: www.caponline.com.au
- Institute of Chartered Accountants in Australia, ph 9290 1344

Activism

see also volunteering, charities

It's not so much activist any more, as person with a conscience. No matter what your gripes are with the world, there will more than likely a group established to help voice your opinions. It's an age of recycling, being green, and standing up for basic human rights, so it's no surprise that these are the more popular groups.

People Living With HIV/AIDS

PLWH/A lobbies for policy changes on issues ranging from discrimination and housing to treatment access and funding.
- Suite 5, 1/94 Oxford St, Darlinghurst, ph 9361 6011 or 1800 245 677.

Planet Ark Environmental Foundation

An action-based, solutions-orientated environmental group with a strong focus on conservation.
- 160 Devonshire St, Surry Hills, ph 9319 5288.

Amnesty International

This grassroots, worldwide organisation works through individual action to prevent violations of human rights by governments.
- Level 3, 55 Mountain St, Ultimo, ph 9211 3566.

The Wilderness Society

Works for the conservation and preservation of wildlife and their natural habitats.
- Level 1, 263 Broadway, Glebe, ph 9552 2355.

Nicola Shenton

Adventure & extreme sports

see also flying & gliding, sporting goods

There's nothing quite like a good dose of adrenalin surging through your veins. No longer just for extremists, adventure sports have exploded in popularity. Sydney itself has a sense of adventure, so it makes sense that the city can cater to just about any death-defying feat you dare to tackle. Like most things here, risking your life comes with a view. Take your pick – the view from the plane as you leap out, the view of the CBD as you parasail above the harbour, or the view from the cliff face you're climbing in the Blue Mountains.

Adrenalin Club

The one-stop shop for all extremists, this club was put together by a couple of guys who found the standard corporate activities a little dull. The self-dubbed 'thrill sports club' runs a regular schedule of activities, including abseiling, caving, white-water rafting, bungee jumping, diving with sharks, aerial combat and rock climbing. One year's membership is $65.
■ Ph 9959 3934.

Sydney Skydivers

Imagine being hurled from a height of 4,000 metres into a terrifying free fall for 50 seconds. Nothing can prepare you for the rush of jumping out of a plane. If a beginner tandem dive sounds too tame, you may want to sign up for a training course and practise formations or night skydiving. The instructors here spend more time in the air than on the ground, teaching and doing stunts for television and film productions. Jumps start from $250.
■ Bankstown Airport, 677 Tower Rd, Bankstown, ph 9791 9155.

Sydney Harbour Parasailing

The easiest adventure sport of them all, parasailing simply needs the ability to sit when landing. Wave to the ferry passengers as you're dragged across the harbour, and enjoy one of the best views of Sydney.
■ Manly Wharf, ph 9977 6781.

Sydney Paragliding Centre

Like skydiving, being a beginner means tandem flights with an instructor. There are also one-day introductory courses involving groundwork and in-flight instruction. If after that you find yourself humming *Come Fly With Me* night and day, it may be time to get a licence so you can take a glide when the mood strikes. You must be 16 or older.
■ Stanwell Park, ph 4294 9065.

Ultimate Skirmish

Plot, plan and scheme against your boss/spouse/mate until a final confrontation when you unleash a rain of (paint ball) ammunition. The perfect revenge? If you can take a day of battering, and have a healthy vendetta against someone, this is the place to come. Choose from 10 playing fields and five package deals, including great incentives for group organisers. Players must be 18 years or older. Packages start at $55 a person.
■ ph 9790 1401 or 4776 1700.

High 'n Wild

The Blue Mountains have more than just aesthetic appeal. The area is an adventure sports haven. These guides take advantage of the area's cliffs and valleys with their beginners to advanced abseiling, rock climbing and canyoning courses (get ready for those water jumps; canyoning combines abseiling, bush walking and swimming). Two-day packages are also available.
■ 3/5 Katoomba St, Katoomba, ph 4782 6224.

The Adventure Shop

Extreme sports can be addictive, and once you've had your first taste you'll also realise they can be expensive. If your one-off abseiling adventure turns into a serious hobby, you can

save money by buying your own equipment. These guys stock everything from compasses and backpacks, to protective clothing and shoes. And they won't laugh at beginners who put their harnesses on backwards.
- 69 Liverpool St, City, ph 9261 1959.
  250 Military Rd, Neutral Bay,
  ph 9953 9340.

Rebecca Wallwork

Further information
- NSW Hang Gliding and Paragliding Association, ph 9327 4025
- Australian Parachute Federation, ph 02 6281 6830

Aerobics

see also fitness clubs, gymnastics, personal trainers

The sport of aerobics is diversifying, and the latest statistics say it's the largest sport in Australia. Aerobics is not just fat-burning steps choreographed to the latest top-40 sounds, it's part of a complete fitness regime. You can step, slide, pump or dance your way to fitness in one of the 200 centres in greater Sydney. Here are some of the best.

Bodyline Fitness Centre
Each week there are about 135 classes of aeroboxing, pump, step, and body sculpture. This is the first gym in Sydney to introduce the latest fad, spinning, where participants simulate the bumps and turns of road-bike riding.
- 100 Walker St, North Sydney,
  ph 9956 5533.

Healthland International
Many of the instructors at Healthland also appear on the television program *Aerobics Oz Style* (see further information below). There are 77 classes a week catering for beginners through to advanced. Classes include body power, circuit, step and yoga. The earliest class is 6.30am with the last one starting at 8.15pm.
- 110 Spring St, Bondi Junction,
  ph 9389 3999.

City Gym
Using the services of former world champion Marcus Irwin (as does Healthland), this centre caters for the CBD professional, offering the complete aerobics package. Classes are held before and after work, and during lunch hour.
- 107 Crown St, East Sydney, ph 9360 6247.

HotBodz
Forty thousand square metres of floor space hosts about 50 aerobic sessions each week. Whether you're a beginner or an experienced campaigner, dance, pump, step and slide classes are available to you.
- Level 2, 169 Port Hacking Rd, Miranda, ph 9544 7622.

Bloch for Dancers
The shop the aerobic instructors go to for all their tights. This chain supplies all the clothing required from the warming up to the cooling down.
- Strand Arcade, City, head office ph 9669 3777. Also at Chatswood, Liverpool, Miranda and Parramatta.

Fitness NSW
The controlling body of aerobics in NSW. All instructors are registered and accredited by this body. If you have any questions, this is the place to ask.
- Suite 3, 139 Alexander St, Crows Nest, ph 9460 6200.

Steve Samuelson

Further information
- Aerobics Oz Style, 6.30am, Channel 10, Monday to Friday, or buy a fat-burning video from its website: www.zero1zero.com.au/aos/ index.asp

Air-conditioning

Remember when having an air conditioner installed meant opening the window and pushing one in? Well, you can still buy room air-conditioners of this kind, but the most popular domestic units on the market nowadays are quiet, efficient, remote-controlled 'high-wall, split systems'. Best value and most appropriate to Sydney's humid summers are the popular Japanese-made brands, such as Mitsubishi, Panasonic, Fujitsu and Daikin. They're all good quality, reliable, and have large dealership networks. It's worth paying the extra for a 'reverse-cycle' unit, which will give you cost-effective winter heating as well. Have a reputable dealer come out and quote, or take in accurate room measurements – a unit that's too large can be as problematic as one that's too small.

Email

An established Australian company whose popular household brand, Kelvinator, is sold in retail stores. But its comprehensive Emailair range, from room air-conditioners to large commercial units, is marketed exclusively through dealerships. Email says it has the most sophisticated air-conditioning laboratory in the southern hemisphere. It mostly manufactures in Australia and for Australian conditions. For local dealerships, contact
- 46-48 Derby St, Silverwater, ph 9202 0444.

Carrier APAC

Established in 1905, this multinational company has been in it from the start. Its Australian factory specialises in both domestic and commercial ducted air-conditioning systems. While increasingly popular in new homes, they can be added to existing houses.
- 120 Terry St, Rozelle, ph 9818 9700.

Daikin Australia

A Japanese multinational air-conditioning specialist. Daikin says it produces the only 'true' multi-split system, allowing several interior units to feed off one external compressor. Owners of apartments, for example, can then air-condition several rooms without cluttering up the balcony with multiple machines.
- 77-83 Alfred Rd, Chipping Norton, ph 9755 3322.

Chris Dobney

Alternative medicine

see also health food, massage, quitting, new age, tai chi, yoga

Forms of alternative therapy range from acupuncture to iridology and aromatherapy. Eastern societies have practised such therapies in one form or another for centuries, while in Western culture it is only in the past 20 years that alternative therapies have not been frowned upon. It's important to remember there are literally hundreds of forms of alternative medicine, some credible and some dodgier than second-hand car salesmen. When deciding which therapies suit your needs, word-of-mouth recommendations are always good, as is checking that the practice has some form of accreditation. Lastly, some consultations are expensive, so it's not advisable to buy into 10 sessions before at least trying it out once.

Liu Lily

One of the few genuine, traditional Chinese herbal medicine practices left in Sydney. Here, herbalists determine your 'chi' energy by monitoring your pulse and checking your tongue. They then gauge the condition of your liver and kidneys to establish what vitamins are deficient in your body. A potion is brewed on the spot, using rare herbs and roots.
- 473 Crown St, Surry Hills, ph 9310 1685.

Herbal Solutions Annandale

Herbal Solutions is serviced by natural therapies accredited by the Australian Traditional Medical Society. It offers a wide range of natural therapy applications, including treatments for children. Clientele is offered prescriptions of herbal medicine and homeopathics. Iridology and remedial massage are recommended, along with other treatments.
- 45 Booth St, Annandale, ph 9660 6696.

UTS Chinese Medical School

Specialises in acupuncture, a Chinese healing practice dating back to 200 BC. Recognised by the National Institute of Health in the United States, acupuncture tries to relieve muscular, skeletal and sports injuries, stress and other emotional problems. The Chinese Medical School is both a teaching and healing centre, offering a 3½-year health science in acupuncture degree.
- 645 Harris St, Ultimo, ph 9514 2500 or 9212 5137.

Nature Care College

For those wanting to learn various forms of alternative medicine, the college offers programs ranging from 12-week courses to four-year diplomas in everything from astrology and aromatherapy to feng shui. The college has operated for 24 years and its courses are accredited by the Australian Traditional Medicine Society.
- 79 Lithgow St, St Leonards, ph 9438 3333.

Hellerwork at Zen

Hellerwork is best summarised as postural realignment. A good analogy is if a tent sags, you straighten up the ropes. Hellerwork also relies on the principal of gravity, and was developed about 30 years ago by a NASA engineer, Joseph Heller. Hellerwork concentrates on all areas of the body, from working inside the mouth for buck teeth to relieving prostate problems and scoliosis by moulding the body back into its intended shape. It is one of the more expensive therapies.
- 116-118 Darlinghurst Rd, Darlinghurst, ph 9361 4200.

Grant Gillies

Further information
- Australian Alternative Health Directory: www.aahd.com.au/index.htm

Antennas

It is rare, if not impossible, to find a house without a TV in it. And everyone knows, you can't watch TV without an antenna. So if you want to stay tuned, here's where to go.

Mr Antenna

Open 7am – 9pm, seven days a week, it offers everything from installation of basic antennas to Satellite and other complex installations.
- 40 Bowden St, Harris Park, ph 13 11 49.

Antenna Shack

For those who want to DIY, it has an enormous range of indoor and outdoor antennas, along with all the necessary accessories.
- 936 Anzac Pde, Maroubra Junction, ph 9349 2011.

Nicola Shenton

Antiques

see also collectables, auctions

Where to find the genuine antique article accompanied by the eye, the knowledge, the service. If it's mostly Queen Street, Woollahra, well that's the truth of it. And

Antiques

Discover Sydney's most exciting range of antique treasures. On three levels, all under one roof, 50 dealers display stunning gifts, superb souvenirs, precious investments as well as the most beautiful keepsakes you can imagine. Make a rewarding visit soon!

WOOLLAHRA ANTIQUES CENTRE
Opposite Centennial Park
160 Oxford St, Woollahra, N.S.W. 2025
Telephone: 9327 8840 Fax: 9327 7270

there's no need to take your copy of *What Polyurethane is That?*.

Antiques Avignon
Elizabeth Lindblom and John Taylor specialise in 18th- and earlier 19th- century French with a smattering of Swedish furniture, mirrors, barometers. Shop here for a light touch with watergilt, patinated woods, the imperfections of the real thing. Seductive prettiness enhanced by oriental works of art.
■ 120 Hargrave St, Paddington, ph 9362 1482.

W. F. Bradshaw
Queen Street's doyen dealer, layered with knowledge; clock and keyboard instrument expertise.
■ 96 Queen St, Woollahra, ph 9363 4453.

Hamish Clark
Energetic dealer in the solidly useful and atmospheric, with a very English architectural sense of style, more upmarket country than urban. Strengths: mirrors, gothic, *treen*, and the curious decorative object that might surprise you.
■ 94 Queen St, Woollahra, ph 9362 8628.

Martyn Cook
Supplies the imperially-minded end of town, with his expertise centred on English and European furniture. Works of art of the 18th- and early 19th-centuries Empire and Greek Revival are favourites. Gimlet-eyed, sophisticated and fun, Cook is rumoured to have actually read all the books.
■ 104 Queen St, Woollahra, ph 9328 1801.

The Country Trader
Geoffrey Clark's the right man for the rites of *paysage*. You may pay over the odds but achieve great French provincial with stone, ceramic, tapestry, curly wire, heavy glass and fruitwoods mixed with repro bergeres.
■ 122 Oxford St, Paddington, ph 9331 7809.

Lynette Cunnington Oriental Art
Dealer with an increasingly fine stock of Chinese and Japanese decorative arts – ceramics, glass, costume, paintings and furniture.
■ 80 Queen St, Woollahra, ph 9326 2227.

Grafton Galleries
Peter Cook and now his son Hartley mix Georgian and later furniture with a plethora of collectable objects. Good on antique silver and drinking glass.
■ 389 New South Head Rd, Double Bay, ph 9327 3567.

Howell & Howell Antiques
For ambience, for service, for desirable and extraordinary pieces – armoires, tables, fruity objects, proper bergeres, painted finishes – sourced by Georgina Howell in France. Specialises in the 17th to 19th centuries, and

best new repro by designer maker Frank Howell. No need for confusion.
- 84 Queen St, Woollahra, ph 9328 1212.

Alan Landis
Landis is Wedgwood man, the English ceramics expert.
- S2/155 Castlereagh St, City, ph 9267 7068.

Janet Niven
The authentic cosy end of Georgian English taste: china, needlework, paisley, silhouettes, miniatures, mourning rings – the small decorative pleasures.
- Shop 1, 118 Queen St, Woollahra, ph 9363 2211.

Anne Schofield
Australia's empress of antique jewellery and costume. Beautiful, intriguing, indeed bloody impressive stock.
- 36 Queen St, Woollahra, ph 9363 1326.

Raymond & Victoria Tregaskis Oriental Decorative Arts
Highly respected long-time dealers, mostly in fine Chinese antiques.
- 120 Hargrave St, Paddington, ph 9362 1582.

Jolyon Warwick James
Private silver dealer with knowledge of European and Australian in particular.
- Ph 041 042 155.

Sydney Antique Centre
This is Sydney's largest antique centre with 50 odd dealers. Gloomy but modernising, with a central cafe. Go for the off chance – antique toys, decorative smalls, jewellery, the occasional improbable object. And an interesting arts and antiquarian bookshop (Colin Randall).
- 531 South Dowling St, Surry Hills, ph 9361 3244.

Woollahra Antique Centre
Taken a newish lease of life. For decorative oriental, the best Majolica gleaming green, 20th century modern (great Italian glass) at Narcisse, and the All Arts bookshop for key reference.
- 160 Oxford St, Woollahra, ph 9327 8840.

Antonia Williams

Appliances

Thirty years ago, no home was complete without some nice linoleum, a floor polisher and a Mix Master. These days, it's a swish Smeg oven with laser hotplates, a bread maker and a stainless steel, six-slice toaster. What next? The appliances of the moment are always waiting to be superseded so it's good to get some expert advice.

Retravision
The biggest retailer of electrical appliances (not the retailer of the biggest electrical appliances as the ad would have it) has 58 outlets in greater Sydney. The stores sell every electrical product you can think of, from whitegoods to kitchen appliances.
- Ph 9745 1133.

Grace Bros City Store
Since its refurbishment Grace Bros city store has offered a huge range of appliances. In its electrical department there are currently more than 200 different products to choose from, and its strength is it will price-match any of its competitors. Grace Bros regularly offers special deals. These include six months interest-free terms to approved customers. It also has twice yearly sales that offer substantial discounts.
- Pitt St, City, ph 9238 9111.

Appliances

Rentlo
Most people associate Rentlo with television and stereo rentals, but it also has an extensive range of whitegoods for rent. It is one of the cheapest and friendliest rental companies in Sydney, and offers free delivery in the Sydney metropolitan area for goods that are being hired on a long-term basis. Rentlo provides free servicing and replacement of faulty goods.
- Ph 132 311 or 9475 2255.

Alpha Appliances Repair Company
Offers repairs for whitegoods and electricals. All labour comes with a warranty, the length of which is dependent on the product. Alpha also sells spare parts for those who feel confident enough to 'do-it-yourself'. Alpha has service people who do house calls, and also has a repair warehouse inside the shop if you want to save some money by taking the goods to them.
- 286 West St, Cammeray, ph 9929 8922.

Godfreys Vacuum Cleaning Specialists
This Australian company has been operating since 1930, and remains the only business that specialises in both domestic and commercial vacuum cleaners. Godfreys sells and repairs almost every brand of vacuum cleaner including its house brand. With 18 stores in Sydney, the Godfreys business is still run by the family of the same name.
- Ph 9748 7411 or 1800 047 718.

R. W. Winning
This family business has been around for 92 years selling a full range of world-class kitchen appliances, sinks, tapware and laundry products to Sydney homw renovators. After sales service is a top priority.
- 117 Phillip St, Waterloo, ph 9698 8099.

Designer Homeware
Superior kitchen and laundry products with a full range of leading brand names including Miele, Gaggenau, Scholtes, Ilve, Blanco, Jenn-Air, AEG, Bosch, Franke, Hansa, Maytag, Smeg, St George and Oliveri.
- 72 Gibbes St, Chatswood, ph 9417 8422.

Sydney Appliance Centre
This appliance showroom stocks all imported and major local lines of cooking and laundry equipment.
- 150 Parramatta Rd, Croydon, ph 9744 7966.

Sampford and Staff
A rare opportunity to try out exclusive designer range of Gaggenau and Jenn-Air appliances, Cannon gas cookers, Hansgrohe tapware and accessories. Trained staff are on hand to advise. Great because there is no retail pressure.
- 162 Crown St, East Sydney, ph 9331 8888.

Grant Gillies

Archery

Ever wondered exactly how William Tell split the apple with his arrow? Find out at your local archery club – there are 13 in Sydney. Archery, an Olympic sport, is experiencing a surge in popularity with 2000 approaching. The best part about the sport is that everyone, young and old, able and disabled, can participate. Secondhand equipment is almost always available to buy through clubs. If you're a beginner, you can also rent gear – but bear in mind that for safety reasons, you can't just rent a bow and have a go. Clubs will ensure you first complete a beginner's course, which are usually held on weekends and comprise three-hour lessons held over three to four weeks. All equipment is provided by the nationally accredited coach and you're taught the skills of shooting, tournament etiquette and archery safety. Courses cost about $50.

Major events in late 1998 include the NSW Outdoor Target Championships from October 31 to November 1 and the City of Sydney tournament on December 6.

Haslam's Creek
Near the athletes' village is the archery site for the Games, but it won't be limited only to elite use. Archery officials are planning some 'come and try' days, starting from October 1998, to help give locals an idea about the sport.
■ Homebush Bay.

Benson Archery
New bows range from around $300 to $2,000, while arrows cost $2 up to a pricey $40 each.
■ 164 Parramatta Rd, Granville, ph 9682 3080.

Abbey Archery
The second of Sydney's specialist archery suppliers. Prices as above.
■ 312a High St, Chatswood, ph 9417 0255.

Liverpool City Archers
This is the home club of giant Olympic archer Jackson Fear, along with national training squad members such as Michael Fisher and Jim Larven. Spectators are always welcome.
■ Helles Ave, Moorebank, ph 9644 3375.

Further information
■ Archery Society of NSW, ph 9569 1794

Heather Quinlan

Architects

see also interior designers
The tough thing about finding a decent architect is not that you have to sift real talent from mediocrity (there's plenty of both around) but that you need to find the right one for you – someone who can sensitively translate your needs and aspirations into a new home or renovation. The best place to start is **Archicentre**, advisory service of the Royal Australian Institute of Architects (3 Manning Street, Potts Point, ph 9356 3122). Archicentre can sketch a credible shortlist of architects best suited to your budget and taste. That way you'll be better equipped to put your wallet, relationship and nervous system through one of urban life's great proving grounds: the design and building process.

Glenn Murcutt
If you want a home that will, in characteristic Murcutt style, 'touch the earth lightly' you'll have to join a years-long queue. Despite internationally celebrity status (at least in architecture and design circles), Murcutt continues to work alone, refining his vision for houses predominantly of timber and steel.
■ 176a Raglan St, Mosman, ph 9969 7797.

Harry Seidler & Associates
The office of Australia's most famous architect has turned out an imposing number of celebrated commercial buildings and homes over the years. Commission a house by Seidler and you'll be assured of something well-planned, enduring and immaculately detailed.
■ Level 5, 2 Glen St, Milsons Point, ph 9922 1388.

Alexander Tzannes Associates
Tzannes' firm is one of Australia's most consistently celebrated designers of houses. In 1997 his company took out Australia's most prestigious national award for housing, the Robin Boyd, for the renovation of a 1950s harbourside home.
■ 63 Myrtle St, Chippendale, ph 9319 3744.

Architects

Grose Bradley

A thriving architecture practice headed by James Grose and partner Nicola Bradley famous for its crisp and innovative (lots of steel) designs. Grose Bradley regularly wins state and national architecture awards.
- 105 Reservoir St, Surry Hills, ph 9212 7074.

Allen Jack + Cottier

Managing director Peter Stronach is the company's star turn with his recent best works completed in league with interior architecture practice Tim Allison Architects.
- 59 Buckingham St, Surry Hills, ph 9699 9611.

Richard Le Plastrier

Like Murcutt (who is a friend and admirer), Le Plastrier is a purist, sole practitioner and considered something of a guru in the local architecture scene. He shuns awards and publicity and attracts clients by word of mouth (his phone number is unlisted).

Alex Popov Architects

Alex Popov is known for gracious, clean-lined homes at the upper end of the market.
- 2 Glen St, Milsons Point, ph 9955 5604.

Stutchbury & Pape

Noted of late for his Olympic archery centre design, Peter Stutchbury – like Murcutt, Grose and Le Plastrier – designs houses, often in lightweight materials, that capture a sense of place.
- Unit 4, 364 Barrenjoey Rd, Newport, ph 9979 5030.

Ken Latona

Best known for the eco-tourist lodges on the Freycinet Peninsula in Tasmania, Ken Latona was also the joint winner of 1996's Robin Boyd Award for Housing for the renovation on his own Sydney home.
- P.O. Box 234, Woollahra, ph 015 825 183.

Engelen Moore

Architect Ian Moore and interior designer Tina Engelen are unabashed advocates of the paired-back approach – no embellishments here. The firm achieved international notoriety for its design of a Redfern home which appeared in numerous overseas glossies (including *wallpaper* magazine).
- 64 Sophia St, Surry Hills, ph 9281 0372.

Guy Allenby

Further information
- Royal Australian Institute of Architects, ph 9356 2955
  www.raia.xom.au

Architecture & urban design

see also heritage Sydney, sculpture and public art, fountains

While Sydney is one of the world's most exhilarating cities, it also has some of the worst buildings in captivity. There are reasons for this, the most obvious being a culture nurtured from day one on the milk of property speculation. For all that, however, and not only because of the wonderful accidents of topography, Sydney boasts some of the world's most enchanting places and even the occasional gem. In Paddington, Woollahra, East Sydney and Glebe, for example, the interaction of Sydney's crazed network of streets, serried lacework terraces, luscious vegetation and the idiosyncrasies of the earth's crust makes for wonderful streetscapes. Paddo has the added attraction of being strewn with seminal houses, including Glenn Murcutt's house for Stuart Littlemore, two Ken Woolleys, a Leplastrier and several by Alex Tzannes. Neutral Bay, while less intense, has a wonderful internalised bay form and the gleam of well-oiled civilisation.

Architecture & urban design

Marathon Steps, Darling Point
Darling Point is a heady mix of '20s apartments, original mansions and modern residential towers that snuggle urbanely among the plane trees and paperbarks. As the aptly named Marathon Steps cascade – nay, gush – down to the even-more-seriously-moneyed Double Bay, they offer some of the happiest glimpses of dense but civilised urban living to be seen in Sydney.
■ End of Marathon Ave, Darling Point.

Governor Phillip & Governor Macquarie Towers
These 1993 towers, despite a rather curious history of government-developer collaboration, are among the few in Sydney that dignify their inhabitants as well as glorifying their designers. Joined at the navel by a fabulous glazed atrium, the Guvs P & M are consciously detailed so that the tower reads separately from the base. The architects, Denton Corker Marshall, won the RAIA's top gong for these towers and distinguished themselves further by insisting on receiving the medal jointly.
■ 1 Farrer Place, City.

The Bathers Pavilion
This curious, white, distinctly unscholarly pastiche of a Moorish palace (or similar) – now undergoing the Alex Popov treatment – has got to be one of the best places in Sydney for a lunch or a coffee. Restaurateur Victoria Alexander's genius for *objects*, *trouvés* and otherwise, is unparalleled.
■ 4 The Esplanade, Balmoral.

Christ Church, St Laurence
Edmund Blacket's most wonderful street church, in the drabbest CBD spot imaginable. With its hand-carved poppyhead pews and convincingly ancient ambience, it's enough to bring the heathen to prayer – almost. Another of Blacket's best moments, **St Stephen's Newtown** (189 Church St), has its own set of poppyhead pews and offers one of the most glorious churchyards in town. Walled, shaded and replete with the notable dead.
■ 507 Pitt St, City.

Rose Seidler House
Uninhabitable but a wonderful time piece. Harry Seidler tells the story of his mother's transplantation from the modish brown interior of pre-war apartment life in Vienna to the blasted heath of Turramurra in the late '40s. Alone in acres of market garden, the house and virtually everything in it sat on slender stilts, ensuring the modernist 'flow' of space. The glintingly modern cake trolley, especially designed for mother by son, is particularly poignant.
■ 71 Clissold Ave, Wahroonga.

Art Gallery of NSW
Andrew Anderson's first addition to the art gallery, with the cafe transparently overhanging the entrance like some modern minstrels' gallery, is probably Sydney's best example of elegant brutalism. The second addition wasn't up to scratch and, by all accounts, the third will take the cafe somewhere else. Pity.
■ Art Gallery Rd, Domain.

QVB & Strand Arcade
The Queen Victoria Building is more popular, the Strand more elegant. The Strand, too, sticks more closely to the European arcade model, running between streets so that only top- and end-lighting are possible, giving a very tight spatial dignity. The QVB, by contrast, with its fat 'n' fruity exterior and newly deepened (entirely ersatz) interior, has had more incarnations than Liz Taylor – as fruit market, library, municipal offices and now born-to-shop emporium. Every inch a lady who lunches.
■ Both in George St, City.

Wentworth Memorial Church, Vaucluse
Designed by Don Gazzard (assisted by Richard Leplastrier), this is an outcrop of a chapel on an outcrop of rock. Ancient Greek, Japanese

and brutalist traditions are detectable here, but most memorable is the light.
- Fitzwilliam Rd, Vaucluse.

Philip Cox Cat Pavilion, Homebush
Even if you hated Evelyn Waugh, you'll like this. A building designed for showing cats; dotty brief, serendipitous result. The witch-hatted cat pavilion at the new showgrounds is exquisite in every detail, absolutely self-possessed and coolly aloof in a barking menagerie of architecture great and small.
- 1 Showground Rd, Homebush Bay.

Hyde Park Barracks
The sheer, unassuming dignity and proportion of Greenway's original – and the intellectual minimalism of the rehab job – bespeak an exemplary collaboration between inventive designers, Tonkin Zulaikha Harford, and enlightened clients, Peters Emmett and Watts from the Historic Houses Trust. A splendid museum.
- Queens Sq, Macquarie St, City.

Hyde Park Avenue
The avenue of great figs forms a splendid gothic aisle between two of Sydney's best monuments – Bruce Dellit's Hyde Park Memorial and Francois Sicard's 1927 Archibald Fountain. Perch on the Memorial at dusk and watch the scavenging ibises and the homeward crowds, or take a paddle in the Archibald.
- Hyde Park, City.

The Rocks
The Rocks Authority, despite an inauspicious start and a few false moves early on, has managed a truly world-class conservation job. The trick is to limit the degree of Disney while retaining a real sense of time past. Much harder than it sounds. The result is picturesque without being plastic, genuinely old but also in parts stylishly new (D4's Rockpool, Tonkin Zulaikha's retail centre). The convict-hewn Argyle Cut is still the area's most magnificent single gesture.

Berowra Waters Inn
The fabled restaurant perched beside the great khaki Hawkesbury. In 1982 Gay Bilson commissioned Glenn Murcutt to design a self-cooling shed: the fully-louvred glass wall slices water, cliff and sky into a single, dazzling entity. Another memorable instance of Murcutt's trademark linear plan.
- Berowra Waters Rd, Berowra Waters.

Elizabeth Farrelly

Art conservation & framing

Let the experts frame and advise on measures to conserve, preserve or restore life to your masterpiece.

International Conservation Services
Will conserve or preserve rather than renovate and rarely reject seriously deteriorated works. Services include normal domestic paintings, furniture, metal, sculptures, textiles and photographs. It does on-site painted surfaces in historical buildings or removes layers to the original finish and preserves walls.
- 53 Victoria Ave, Chatswood, ph 9417 3311.

Paul Pribia Art Restoration
Restores works from oils to watercolours, charcoals, paper and canvas. It gilds frames, researches signatures of artists and can go on-site to work on large-scale pieces.
- 95 Windsor Rd, Dulwich Hill, ph 9569 0608.

State Library of NSW
The Library's Conservation Access gives advice and treatment for individuals and groups. It has specialist paper conservators for such items as torn documents and restoration of original photographs. As consultant on private collec-

tions, it advises on how to look after collections and has a 24-hour help line for disasters.
- Macquarie St, City, ph 9273 1676.

Metropolitan Framing
Specialises in conservation framing and a restorer is employed for canvas and paper works.
- 88 Penshurst St, Willoughby, ph 9958 8904.

Michael Commerford Gallery
Clients for customised framing include artists, designers and galleries. Services include gilding, painted finishes, recycled timbers and deep-profile perspex boxes – though it is not averse to framing a certificate.
- 16 McLachlan Ave, Rushcutters Bay, ph 9331 3338.

David Stein Fine Art Conservation
Primarily conservators, they can date and authenticate older paintings, track forgeries, restore paintings, works on paper, sculpture and frames, and stretch and frame Aboriginal art on canvas.
- Burton St, East Sydney, ph 9360 2201.

Zola McGoldrick
Offers new Asthetix custom-made framing, specialising in hand finishes, colour matching and gilding. Received multi recommendations in the *Sydney Morning Herald* Domain section's Tradespeople of the Year Award.
- 64 Denison St, Camperdown, ph 9517 2175 or 0419 989 798.

Trisha Treanor

Art galleries

see also photography, museums
Sydney's vast array of galleries seems to grow exponentially year on year. If you've a taste for the eyeball-teasing pleasures of images, it's not hard to find somewhere that hits the spot. The important thing to stress is that, no matter how posh the gallery looks, or how claustrophobic the space, you're always welcome to come in and look. Only the occasional show in one or two of the public galleries is likely to have an entry fee; the rest are free. Commercial galleries tend to slow down over summer, with their owners overseas (if they're lucky), sniffing out trends or overlooked artists.

Art Gallery of NSW
Excellent venue in The Domain with changing exhibitions, from drawing and photography through to Aboriginal, Asian and contemporary art, plus several big international shows a year. The permanent collections all repay multiple visits, and there are always extra activities – including guided tours, talks by experts, dance and music performances, workshops and children's activities.
- Art Gallery Rd, Domain, ph 9225 1744: www.artgallery.nsw.gov.au

Museum of Contemporary Art
The accent is firmly on 'contemporary' in this young and gorgeously located museum, in the thick of it at Circular Quay. Exhibitions are slow to change (up to four months), which can be disappointing if you're not a fan. But the atmosphere is tres chic, tres 'knowing', and, er, the staff are young and spunky.
- 140 George St, Circular Quay, ph 9252 4033: www.mca.com.au

Annandale Galleries
Puts on an inspired selection of shows – everything from modern British masters or Raoul Dufy to some of Australia's best contemporary artists, including Richard Goodwin, Guy Warren and Janet Laurence, plus excellent selections of Aboriginal bark painting. Good large space and conducive atmosphere.
- 110 Trafalgar St, Annandale, ph 9552 1699.

Art galleries

Gitte Weise Gallery
Newish space on Oxford St, run by an experienced hand. The work is self-consciously contemporary, but with an accent on poetics rather than concepts. Gitte Weise also has a space adjacent to her gallery which she puts up for submissions from artists not aligned with her. Exciting things are regularly discovered here.
- Level 2, 94 Oxford St, Darlinghurst, ph 9360 2659.

Ray Hughes Gallery
A jet-blast of sanity in the giddy world of Sydney art. Hughes is a fan of the vernacular, and the art reflects it. No-one on the scene has such a distinctive style or presence. His interest in tribal and voodoo art complements his Australian artists, including Tom Risley, Bill Robinson and Joe Furlonger.
- 270 Devonshire St, Surry Hills, ph 9698 3200.

Roslyn Oxley9
Snugly positioned in a Paddington cul-de-sac, Roslyn Oxley9 has been staging some of the funkiest and most talked-about shows for more than a decade. Regular exhibitions by Bill Henson, Robert Mapplethorpe, Fiona Hall and Lindy Lee.
- Soudan Lane, Paddington, ph 9331 1919.

Sebastian Smee

Further information
- See Sydney Morning Herald Metro (Fridays) and CitySearch listings
- Art Almanac ($2 at bookshops, galleries and newsagents)

Art schools & supplies

see also art galleries, photography

Express yourself! Whether you're an artist obsessed with light and dark, or struggling with perspective, mediocrity or the retrospective, classes inspire and fire your imagination.

Julian Ashton Art School
Established in 1890, the school teaches in the classical manner. Classes are mainly life drawing and painting and also etching, watercolours and sculpture. Daily day and evening classes and a sketch club run to a 10-week term with intensive school holiday courses.
- 117 George St, City, ph 9241 1641.

National Art School
Practising artists teach a 15-week program of evening or Saturday sessions in drawing, sculpture, painting, photography, ceramics, printmaking and photography. These short courses are of the same calibre as full-time day award classes and aimed at students of all ages, from beginners to advanced, and all backgrounds.
- Forbes St, Darlinghurst, ph 9339 8623.

Royal Art Society
A 10-week term of up to four classes a week in portrait and life drawing, watercolour, oil painting, pastel and outdoor landscape. Classes are two or three hours long. If you want more, there are art studios for use by members and a supervised sketch club.
- 25 Walker St, North Sydney, ph 9955 5752.

Balmain Art School
Flexibility means you can enrol at any time during the year or term for drawing and painting, and can attend day, night or weekend classes or in combination. Individual tutoring of small groups mixes 3 Unit HSC and mature-age students, beginner, intermediate and advanced levels. Summer schools, art tours and workshops complete the picture.
- 7a Campbell St, Balmain, ph 9960 2885.

Campus Art Store
Set up as a service to students, who get 10 per cent discount, and also open to the public, there is a low mark-up on product and the

staff has specialised knowledge on the broad range of materials.
- Cnr Napier St and Greens Rd, Paddington, ph 9331 7474.

Art on King: Discounted Art & Craft Supplies

Competitive discounts, savings schemes and bargains, a variety of materials and journals for serious artists. Also catering for children's and experimental craft art.
- 199 King St, Newtown, ph 9516 2342; 34 Hercules St, Ashfield, ph 9799 5793.

Discount Art and Drafting Materials

Operating for 20 years, it gives friendly personal service, discounts to students and specialises in framing.
- 184 Elizabeth St, City, ph 9281 5378; 279 Forest Rd, Hurstville, ph 9570 4138.

Eckersley's

Operating for about 30 years, its workers are artists who advise on an extensive product range and demonstrate techniques in mixed media. Its discount policy has loyalty programs and there is a kid's corner in each store.
- 21 Atchison St, St Leonards, ph 9439 4944. Also in the City, ph 9299 4151; North Sydney, ph 9957 5678; Parramatta, ph 9893 9191.

Trisha Treanor

Asian restaurants

see also Japanese, Indian, Chinese, Vietnamese, Thai restaurants

The less well-known Asian cuisines also offer a minefield of textures and flavours that are well worth exploring. Bring an open mind as well as an open mouth, and be prepared to be amazed occasionally.

Blue Elephant

The best place in Sydney to start exploring the subtleties of Sri Lankan food. Owner/chef Leonie Best and her friendly staff are always ready to steer the novice through the aromatic curries, the cashew-rich Jo Jo's chicken, stringhoppers (noodle like pancakes), and wattalapan jaggery custard.
- 36-38 Willoughby Rd, Crows Nest, ph 9439 3468.

Central Court Restaurant

A far cry from the more humble Korean eating houses around town, this newly refurbished restaurant comes with a karaoke room, electronic service buttons, and even a sushi bar. A line-up of specialist chefs serve up everything from bulgogi (barbecued beef) to naeng myon cold noodles.
- 382 Pacific Highway, Crows Nest, ph 9966 8855.

Kaysone's Kitchen

If you're expecting little luxuries like tablecloths, napkins, and um, walls, you might be disappointed. But if you want great, authentic Laotian food, then you won't mind sitting on plastic chairs in the middle of a shopping arcade. Do try the bible salad, teo chew rice noodles and fiery tom yum goong.
- Shop 13, Cabramatta Mall, 47 Park Rd, Cabramatta, ph 9755 0907.

Sam Won Garden

In an area overflowing with Korean restaurants and food shops, Sam Won!Garden stands out as one of the best. Seafood is a specialty but more popular Korean dishes such as chicken with ginseng, bulgogi and cold noodles are also available. The kim chi is amazing.
- 62 Beamish St, Campsie, ph 9718 6066.

Asian restaurants

Temasek
Such is the reputation of this Malaysian restaurant that hotheads from the far-flung Eastern Suburbs and North Shore head to Parramatta for their chilli fix. The beef rendang, prawn mee soup and laksa are all great, while milder souls can opt for the Hainan chicken rice and go easy on the chilli dip.
- Roxy Arcade, 71 George St, Parramatta, ph 9633 9926.

To's Malaysian Gourmet
There's nothing plush about this basic North Sydney eat here or take away, with its steaming bain maries. Yet the constant crowds must mean something. They do – they mean that this is where you'll find the best laksa lemak (curried noodle soup) in Sydney, plus wonderful Malaysian hawker food like hokkien mee noodles and char kuey teow.
- Shop 3, 181 Miller St, North Sydney, ph 9955 2088.

Ratu Sari
With its vinyl grey tablecloths, this is hardly the place for a big night out, or romantic tete-a-tete. It is, however, the ideal place to discover that there is more to Indonesian food than nasi goreng. Try North Sumatran beef rendang, the Menado style hot chicken and mini piata meat filled pastries.
- 476 Anzac Pde, Kingsford, ph 9663 4072.

Wockpool
Neil Perry has a knack of taking most forms of Asian cooking and making them irrevocably his own. At this glamorous Darling Harbour restaurant, he and chef Kylie Kwong take from China, Malaysia, Vietnam and Thailand to produce modern Asian cooking at its most glamorous and fluent.
- IMAX Panasonic Theatre, Darling Harbour, ph 9211 9888; 155 Victoria St, Potts Point, Ph 9356 2911.

Terry Durack

Astronomy

For purists, nothing beats the outback sky, far from dazzling city lights. But Sydney boasts enough starry fun – day and night – to appease even the fussiest viewing vultures.

Sydney Observatory
Australia's oldest existing observatory, now part of the Powerhouse Museum, has looked skyward for nearly 140 years. Recently the venerable observatory has been tarted up and opened a spanking new exhibition. Tickle the brain by day. Watch the cosmos by night.
- Observatory Hill, Watson Rd, The Rocks, ph 9217 0485.

Koolang Observatory
A one-hour drive from Sydney brings starrier skies and top solar viewing at this charming spot near Gosford.
- George Downs Drive, Bucketty, ph 02 4998 8216.

Science Centre and Planetarium
A mini-version of the big one in Canberra, just down the road near Wollongong. Let the kids loose on hands-on exhibits.
- Cowper St, Fairy Meadow, ph 02 4221 5591.

Orion Astronomy and Science Club
Join up, bring your telescope, hear talks, tour the campus observatory and even catch the star lab planetarium show, all courtesy of the University of NSW.
- Ph 9385 5752.

Space Shopping
Indulge in telescope envy at Sydney's best optical shops, including **Astro Optical Supplies** (9b Clarke St, Crows Nest, ph 9436 4360), **York Optical Company** (92 Wentworth Ave, City, ph 9211 1606) and **The Binocular and Tele-**

scope Shop (55 York St, City, ph 9262 1344). Come back to Earth with a browse at **The Sky and Space Shop**, 80 Ebley St, Bondi Junction, ph 9369 3344). Not content with publishing Australia's leading astronomy magazine, *Sky and Space*, Jonathan Nally and Lyle Rumble purvey all things spacey, from model spacecraft to sci-fi videos.

Leigh Dayton

Further information
■ 1998 Sydney Sky Guide (from Powerhouse Museum and Sydney Observatory, $12.95)

Athletics

see also running, sporting goods
You don't need legs like Carl Lewis. All you need is a pair of joggers to join the 5,200 registered athletes and 38,000 kids across NSW striving to go higher, faster and stronger. With the Games in 2000, Sydney is becoming a focal point for athletics with everyone from the US Olympic track-and-field team to kids inspired by Sydney's top sprinter, Melinda Gainsford-Taylor, hunting for the best local clubs. U-15s can attend free trial days during the September-to-March season at many of the 66 Little Athletics centres in the Sydney metropolitan area. And there are plenty of events for budding track stars, serious sweataholics and those who just want to have fun and enjoy the drinking afterwards.

Bankstown Sports
The athletics branch of this well-resourced club is putting in a new synthetic track during 1998 to add to its existing grass track. Active in recruiting, strong winter program, good athlete incentive program and coaching staff. Star performer is hammer thrower Debbie Sosimenkor.
■ Ph Peter Moore, 9604 6000 or 9609 4124.

Homebush Bay
An innovative club established in 1997, based at the Olympic warm-up track. Pro-recruiting, especially in schools. Olympic hockey gold-medallist-turned-sprinter Nova Peris-Kneebone is the club's biggest star.
■ Ph/fax 9552 2470.

UTS Northern Suburbs
Strong links with the University of Technology Sydney. 1990 Commonwealth 400m champion Darren Clark is a coach.
■ Ph 9983 1413.

Campbelltown Collegians
Links with local Little Athletics centres. Upgrade of the Orana Park facility is providing a new synthetic track in 1998. Elite program funded by the NSW Department of Sport and Recreation.
■ Ph 4626 6411.

Saucony Sutherland
One of the biggest Sydney clubs. Good incentive program, especially for country-based athletes. Strong winter program.
■ Ph 9528 6284 or 9524 4623.

Athletics East
High adult base and supporting coaching structure.
■ Ph 9388 1148.

Asics West
Own track with good coaching and sponsorship support. Upcoming sprinter Matt Shrivington is a member.
■ Ph 9622 9859.

Reebok Narrabeen
Has access to a new synthetic track. Good sponsorship support and coaching. Olympic triple jumper Andrew Murphy is a member.
■ Ph 9451 2075.

Athletics

Hills District
Well-maintained grass track and good links with local Little Athletics centres.
- Ph 9624 3419.

NSW and Sydney universities
Run by the athletes with strong social element. Good track facilities as well as access to gyms and pools. Scholarships available.
- University of NSW, ph 9327 3934; University of Sydney, ph 9428 5324.

Nepean and Blacktown City
Strong links with Little Athletics centres. Access to elite program at Western Sydney Regional Academy of Sport.
- Blacktown, ph 9626 1086; Nepean, ph 9623 6608.

Louise Evans

Further information
- Athletics NSW, ph 9552 1244: www.ausport.gov.au/aths/answhome.html
- Little Athletics, ph 9633 4511: www.laansw.com.au/
- Veterans, ph 9516 2139.

Auctions

see also antiques, building materials, collectables

Auctions are no longer an exclusive activity – we all trade up and down, buy, sell, fossick and dream.

The big international auction houses with few local sales but high market visibility and significant global reach operate small smart Sydney branch offices – Christie's, Sotheby's and Phillip's are all in Woollahra. Melbourne is head office and main saleroom for both Sotheby's and Christie's. Sell if you have something of sufficient quality, rarity or overseas interest. Sydney gets pruned sale previews (art, decorative and tribal arts) but more sales are promised. Learn to ask questions and visit to rifle through the catalogues.

Local Sydney auction rooms are many and varied. You might wait for a Langton's wine sale, a Brooks Goodman vintage car and automobilia sale, or an interesting Perpetual Trustees estate come ashore in **Tim Goodman's** Double Bay Rooms, or Herman Miller office furniture popping up at **Deans Auctions**. Keep your eye peeled for house contents sales by Sue Dobbyns of **Pickles**, lone operators **Alison Germaine McSweeney** or **Jonathan Alford**. And have the stamina to winnow the weekly **Raffan & Keleher** Leichhardt offering. But there's at least one very good reason for visiting all of those listed below after the international houses.

Remember, too, that these are service industries, with valuations (free if verbal, not if written for insurance or probate) and search facilities within their own sales network.

Sotheby's
Runs a corporately smooth ring around the upper floor of Queen's Court. Rooms to preview most of most Melbourne (spring and autumn) sales. November tribal art sale in Sydney. Charming desk assistance. Education program.
- Queen's Court, Cnr Queen and Moncur Sts, Woollahra, ph 9362 1000.

Christie's
Corner shop painted an esoteric grey. As above for charm, and helpfulness. Some selective previews of sales, shown out of office. In 1998, it offered Sydney's first major sale in five years (painting, decorative arts, jewellery, wine, Australiana, books and manuscripts). On site, decorative arts expert Ronan Sulich and paintings team Annette Larkin and David Cook. Education program.
- 180 Jersey Rd, Woollahra, ph 9326 1422.

Phillip's

Gleaming showroom/office where items for future sale shimmy at the Queen Street browser. Sydney-centred with spring and autumn 20th-century design and art sales currently held in Roslyn Oxley 9 Gallery. At least one mixed antique and decorative arts sale mid-year, possibly one garden-related decorative arts sale, and a November sale of antique and modern silver and jewellery. Melbourne sports related sale. Warm atmosphere with American MD Andrew Shapiro, and delightful consultant Alison Alford. Valuations and searches.
- 162 Queen St, Woollahra, ph 9326 1588.

Lawsons

Large, friendly, family-run, 19th-century firm. A popular fixture is the Friday big general sale at Annandale. Monthly – antique, decorative arts, silver, books, maps and prints. Occasional – toys and dolls, tribal art and textiles including antique rugs. Last Wednesday of the month – valuation mornings. Education program.
- 212 Cumberland St, The Rocks.
- 1a Bridge St, Annandale, ph 9241 3411.

Wemyss

New kids on the block, focusing on very large (vintage cars, motorbikes, planes, specialist area of petrol head MD Anthony Davies) and small collectables with specialist sales in 35 areas including tin toys, bears, luggage, art, marine, kitchenalia, the politically incorrect accessory. Features include new technology, in house cafe, occasional art exhibitions and first editions of Australian small collectables. Occasionally visit the more affluent suburbs north and south, and country towns with sales of small collectables.
- 10 Wentworth Ave, City, ph 9283 4900.

Gavan Hardy

Well-defined categories to suit the keen but not very cashed up collector. They sort everything. Regular weekly Monday general fossicker sale plus regular collector specials: mid 20th-century design, sports memorabilia, art, jewellery, radio, militaria, old tools and occasional erotica.
- 76 Mitchell Rd, Alexandria, ph 9310 7200.

Dalia Stanley

One woman band with mid-city rooms: monthly mixed furniture and decorative arts sales, good on collectable 20th-century smalls, modern glass and ceramics, with occasional antique gold amidst the solidly bourgeois. Specialist sales include art and Stanley's strong suit, the grown-up nursery – dolls, toys, bears, models.
- 9–15 Alberta St, City, ph 9283 3838.

John Williams

Convivial, shrewd, with a Queen Street background, a line to interesting, quality stuff (estates dead and alive). Most months has a mixed antique and decorative arts sale in Camperdown. Valuations.
- 57 Church St, Camperdown, ph 9326 2986.

Antonia Williams

Australian Rules

see also sporting goods

The game they go mad for in Melbourne came to Sydney in the late 1800s, but only truly arrived here in 1982 with the metamorphosis of South Melbourne into the Sydney Swans. So assured does the Swans future seem, after making their first Grand Final in 1996 and pulling average crowds of 33,000, that the talk has shifted to when, and not if, a second Sydney-based team should be included in the AFL (Australian Football League). The success of the Swannies has had a great impact on the popularity

Australian Rules

of the game in Sydney, which is very much amateur. The greater metropolitan area experienced an increase in junior playing numbers of 40 per cent in 1997. Senior football, which after 95 years of organised competition is still small (1400 registered seniors in seven clubs), looks set to expand accordingly.

Tony 'Plugger' Lockett

Raw, brilliant and occasionally brutal full-forward whose hairline has achieved celebrity status on its own. One of the league's hard men, Plugger is always vital to the Swans' fortunes. Other star Swans include captain Paul Kelly, who remains an inspirational figure with his blistering speed; veteran centre half-back Paul Roos; and newly-acquired midfielder Wayne Schwass. You can get autographs, if not in-depth conversations, at the training sessions, which generally begin at 2 or 4pm at the Sydney Cricket Ground five days a week.

Sydney Cricket Ground

The SCG is home turf for the Swans. Finding a park outside the ground is not a problem, but be prepared to endure bottlenecks that can crush even the euphoria of a win over the reigning premiers. Buses may be a better option, running direct to the ground every five minutes from Elizabeth St, outside Central Station. Dedicated bus lanes are in service for home games, which mean the journey is rarely more than 15 minutes. Shuttle buses also run from the Easts League Club, where parking is available.

- Moore Park Rd (opp. Oatley Rd), Paddington.

Redback Pass

This top-of-the-line season ticket will set you back $810. For your money you get reserved seating for two, a car pass, an autographed player photo, a sweater, entry to the official sponsors' luncheon, an invitation to the pre-season gala dinner and a post-training barbecue with the players and, last but not least, you get to play the footy tipping competition. For those on a budget, no-frills season tickets start at $109, while the cheapest match passes are a bargain $17.50.

- ph Ticketek 9266 4800, or Sydney Swans Football Club, ph 9339 9123.

Easts Leagues Club

Where diehard fans can rub shoulders with dead-tired players at after-match celebrations (or share commiserations).

- 97 Spring St, Bondi Junction, ph 9389 1011.

Sydney Swans Cheer Squad

That crazed, raucous battalion in red and white in Bay 22 is not there by coincidence – they are organised!

- Contact Catherine Marney, ph 9676 1612.

Sydney Swans Football Club

The Swans' head office has a merchandise shop, selling guernseys, scarves, caps, flags, posters and even replicas of the Swans' mascot, Cygnatius. Rebel Sports, Grace Brothers and K-Mart outlets also stock a limited range.

- Driver Ave, Paddington, ph 9339 9123.

NSW AFL

Administers senior football in NSW, which has been played since 1903. At present, the seven other clubs in town are: the Balmain Tigers (reigning Sydney Football League premiers), East Sydney Bulldogs (founding members of the Sydney Football League), Baulkham Hills Falcons, Pennant Hills Demons, North Shore Bears, St George Dragons and Western Suburbs Magpies.

- Contact Peter Hiscock, Operations Manager, ph 9552 6055.

Further information

- Swans website: www.sydneyswans.com.au
- Swans News, a newsletter, published

five times a season, featuring player profiles and club news, all for a mere $2.
- Gossip from the rest of the AFL can be gleaned from Inside Football Weekly for $3.50.

Peter Vincent

Baby supplies

see also childrenswear, toys & hobbies

For such small people, babies acquire an enormous amount of possessions even before they are born. To avoid overdoing it, parents-to-be should shop with their head, not with their heart. When baby arrives you'll want to show the little darling off as well as escape your four walls. Good places for a breath of fresh air, some exercise and baby watching are Bondi Beach, Centennial Park and the Manly-to-Shelly Beach walk. In the CBD, the Queen Victoria Building wins best and cleanest for its baby change room tucked away on the lower ground floor. In the suburbs, try Westfield shopping centres for the parents with prams, car spots and security-operated change rooms.

Baby's Stuff

Expecting? Parents who cannot find what they need here are not trying. Everything from change tables to cots, car seats and baby hammocks are on display. You can touch everything, ask staff anything and no-one will hassle you into buying.
- 305–309 Parramatta Rd, Leichhardt, ph 9518 1989; 189 Woodville Road, Villawood, ph 9725 7100.

David Jones

Emerge from the lift on the fifth floor of the Elizabeth Street store to find toys on the left, clothing and baby equipment on the right. Staff here are generous with their time and knowledge. There's something about going into town to shop that sets this apart from the suburban DJs.
- Elizabeth St, City, ph 9266 5544, customer inquiries 133 357.

The Baby's Ark

Co-ordinate the nursery from the sheets to the lampshades with fabrics specially imported from Laura Ashley and Designer's Guild. Mail orders are a specialty and a new catalogue, 'The New Baby Guide', costing $4.95, is available from newsagents.
- 81–85 Frenchman's Rd, North Randwick, ph 9326 5036.

Clothing Clearance Warehouse

Babies grow so quickly they are into the next size singlet or bodysuit before you say 'boo'. Stock up here on Bonds singlets and bodysuits and save up to half the cost. This is a factory outlet so styles will vary but there is always sleepwear, socks, rompers and tracksuits. For those inclined to advertise the 2000 Olympics on their youngster's clothing, there are plenty of factory seconds here.
- 47 Unwins Bridge Rd, Sydenham, ph 9519 5299.

Elandra's Baby Kingdom

Your baby will be treated like royalty. The range is enormous, with 60 types of cot and 100 prams on display and every possible baby accessory for sale. Even things like head rests that fit on to car seat straps.
- 234 Hume Highway, Bankstown, ph 9793 9322.

Baby Things

Take the guesswork out of buying and fitting a car seat by driving up and having your purchase installed. Even in the narrow aisles staff will take the time and trouble to demonstrate how to unfold a portable cot.

Baby supplies

You'll thank them when you take it on holidays.
- 145a Anzac Parade, Kensington, ph 9663 2320.

Adrienne & the Misses Bonney
An Eastern Suburbs institution in a revamped store. Grandmas who first came here as babes in arms are now returning to kit out the third generation. Everything for the ultra-pampered infant - from exquisite heirloom Christening robes to traditional smocked gowns.
- 20–26 Cross St, Double Bay, ph 9363 1723.

Margot Date

Backpacking

For most backpackers, Sydney is the first and usually last port of call in Australia. And what a gateway it presents: cosmopolitan, colourful, charismatic and, if you look in the right spots, cool on the cash. Each year about 250,000 backpackers eat, sleep, work, drink, sightsee and party their way through the city, staying, on average, for 3.2 days. Interestingly, while backpackers represent only six per cent of international visitors, they account for more than 14 per cent of money spent. And in Sydney, most of that money is splashed in Kings Cross, the City, Bondi Beach, Glebe, Coogee, Darlinghurst and Manly – the main hubs of backpacker activity.

YHA Travel Centre
For hostel bookings, travel information, YHA membership, travel books and accessories. With notice board.
- 422 Kent St, City, ph 9261 1111.

YHA
Budget accommodation with hostels in city centre and Glebe. The 530-bed city hostel has a rooftop swimming pool and sauna, self-catering kitchen or restaurant, bar in basement and YHA travel office (see above). Prices from $18 for dormitory, to $31 per person for double with en suite.
- Sydney Central YHA, 11 Rawson Place, City, ph 9281 9111; Glebe Point YHA, 262 Glebe Point Rd, Glebe, ph 9692 8418: www.yha.org.au

Nomads Backpackers
Hostel franchise with accommodation in city centre, Darlinghurst, Newtown, Glebe, Bondi Beach and Clovelly. Room prices from $15 for dormitory or $20 per person for twin or double room. All hostels with free linen, lockers, pick-up and tea/coffee.
- Bookings, freecall 1800 819 883.

VIP Backpacker Resorts of Australia
Budget accommodation franchise with 19 hostels across Sydney (including Kings Cross, Coogee and Manly) with discounted nightly rates for members. Contact head office in Brisbane or any of the hostels for membership and information.
- Ph 07 3268 5733.

International Travellers Advisory Service
ITAS offers a mail holding and forwarding service, with tax, insurance, banking, computer access and e-mail facilities. With fully furnished share houses and flats available.
- Level 6, 38 York St, City, ph 9262 5011.

Travellers' Contact Point
Travel agency specialising in bus passes and car hire, with mail holding and forwarding service, e-mail and internet facilities, and employment and accommodation notice boards.
- 7th Floor, Dymocks Building, 428 George St, City, ph 9221 8744.

Student Uni Travel
Travel agency specialising in domestic and international backpacking. With free e-mail service.
- Level 8, 92 Pitt St, City, ph 9232 8444.

Backpackers World
Travel agency with e-mail, internet, mail forwarding and tax file services, as well as a jobs board and accommodation assistance.
- 212 Victoria St, Kings Cross,
  ph 9380 2700 or 1800 67 67 63.

Greyhound Pioneer Australia
National coach carrier, with YHA or VIP backpacker discounts. Sydney terminal as below.
- Terminal 4, 7 Eddy Ave, Central Station, ph 132 030.

Oz Experience
National transport network providing off-the-beaten-track trips using bus passes valid for either 6 or 12 months. Free guidebooks.
- 3 Orwell St, Kings Cross,
  ph 9368 1766.

World Wide Workers
Private employment agency that finds work for travellers. Must have a work visa.
- 54 Rose St, Chippendale, ph 9699 8019.

Recruitment Solutions
Employment agency specialising in temporary work in accounting, business support, IT and sales and marketing.
- Level 12, 275 George St, City,
  ph 9377 9666.

Kyle Management Resources
Employment agency specialising in temporary work for travellers in accounting, administration and IT fields.
- Level 4, 507 Kent St, City,
  ph 9264 5777.

Travellers Auto Barn
Sell and rent cheap cars for travellers with buyback guarantee. Mostly early model Fords, Holdens, station wagons, panel vans.
- 177 Williams St, Kings Cross,
  ph 9360 1500.

Boomerang Car Mart
Sell fully-serviced campervans, station wagons and panel vans ($1500 to $3000) with a guaranteed buyback price. Supply camping gear.
- 30 Ewan St, Mascot, ph 9700 8595.

Pegasus Rental Cars
Rent cars, campervans, station wagons and panel vans and camping equipment. From $25 a day, with drop offs in most capital cities.
- 188 McElhone St, Kings Cross,
  ph 9368 1598.

Backpacker Campervans
Campervan rentals with drop-off locations in Melbourne, Sydney, Darwin, Cairns and Alice Springs. Prices from $60 per day.
- 342 King St, Mascot, ph 9693 2079.

Dugald Jellie

Badminton

see also sporting goods
Did you know that badminton – not swimming or athletics – is the most watched Olympic sport worldwide? This fast-paced, wrist-flicking sport is particularly popular in Asia and is taking off in Australia too.

Major events in late 1998 include the Sydney Badminton Association Senior Open on 17 October at the Dural Recreation Centre, 25a Kenthurst Rd, Round Corner (Dural). For events in 1999, phone the Sydney Badminton Association (see below).

Ross Pavilion
The badminton competition at the 2000 Olympics will be held here in the new Showground complex. The sport will host an international test event prior to the Games, which will be open to spectators.
- Sydney Showground, Homebush.

Badminton

University of NSW
One of Sydney's biggest badminton venues, with six courts, and the strongest university club. Competition is held in the UNSW gymnasium on Saturday afternoons and players are advised to just turn up and organise a game there.
- Anzac Pde, Kensington.

Five Dock Leisure Centre
To feel the thwack of the shuttlecock on racquet strings, head here on a Saturday to hire a court (other sports are held on the courts on week days and Sundays).
- Cnr Queens Rd and William St, Five Dock, ph 9744 2622.

Seaforth Badminton Club
Many of Sydney's 30 badminton clubs have limited membership numbers, but Seaforth welcomes new players.
- Seaforth Community Centre, Baringa Ave, Seaforth, ph 9451 6978.

Sydney Badminton Association
There are no specialty badminton shops in Sydney, but the association sells a range of racquets, shuttlecocks, nets and other gear, as well as providing information on the sport in Sydney.
- Ph 9451 6978:
  www.ozemail.com.au/-sydba

Heather Quinlan

Bakeries & patisseries

The fluffy focaccia is now but a crumb of its former self, and we're into real bread: real sour dough, real French baguettes, real Italian rosetta rolls, and real pain au chocolat. The same goes for cakes: goodbye Neenish tart and airhead cream puff, and hello choux pastry and fresh berry tarts. What you go for is up to you – it's your dough, after all.

Infinity Sour Dough Bakery
Chef Phillip Searle and bread-head Brent Hersee of the famous Blackheath Bakery now bake in Darlinghurst. The hand-crafted round sour dough loaf, made from certified organic stoneground flour, is like a bottomless loaf that will last you all week, and taste better for it. The pain au chocolat is a bittersweet breakfast experience, and the snails are life-sustaining.
- 225 Victoria St, Darlinghurst (next to Fire Station), ph 9380 4320.

La Banette
If you're heading for the northern beaches, don't take bread. Instead, pick it up fresh daily from Gilles Inkel's little gem, sweetly tucked away in Avalon like the *chocolat* in your *pain*. Not only great bread, but divine petits four, and football-worthy sausage rolls. You'll never bake a tart again once you've tried their mixed berry version.
- 28 Avalon Pde, Avalon, ph 9918 2948 (closed every February).

Victoire
Myriam Cordelier's sour dough baguette is the ultimate Sydney lunch. All you need is a ripe tomato or a slice of ham, and you're in (French) heaven. The shop is a slim haven of pretty lemon tarts, fresh cheeses, hazelnut swirls and wonderful, freshly baked breads that are worth crossing town for.
- 285a Darling St, Balmain, ph 9818 5529.

Haberfield Bakery
For those who love their bread with an Italian accent, Haberfield Bakery has crusty rolls that turn up on restaurant tables throughout the city. Buy some fresh pasta when you pick up your bread, and make lots of sauce so you can use the bread to mop up.
- 153 Ramsay Rd, Haberfield, ph 9797 7715.

Helios Demeter Bakery

Sure, you can buy Helios Demeter Bakery's health-giving bread at good food stores all over town, but why not bake it yourself? There's a big 'bake-in' on the first Saturday morning of every month, when you can mix, knead, shape and bake your own magical loaf of bread ($15 adults, $9 under 17 years, $45 families).

■ 65 Derwent St, Glebe, ph 9660 2555.

Paris Patisserie Francaise

Bondi residents swear by the Paris cake shop for traditional French patisserie and delicious almond croissants.

■ 91 Bondi Rd, Bondi, ph 9387 2496.

La Gerbe d'Or

Paddington dwellers line up on Saturdays for freshly made nougat and pastries from the affectionately nick-named Golden Gerbil, and Paddington dinner parties invariably start with their baguette and end with their glazed fruit tarts. Most sensual experience – biting into the St Tropez, two layers of light-as-air brioche between silky smooth crème patisserie.

■ 255 Glenmore Rd, Paddington,
  ph 9331 1070.

Fink's Fabulous Food

Northside, the new cake heaven is at Fink's Fabulous Food. Try Rosemary Fink's candied orange, chocolate and date, Greek coconut syrup or frangipane.

■ 69 Bay Rd, Waverton, ph 9957 5753.

Jill Dupleix

Banks & financial institutions

'Neither a borrower nor a lender be' isn't bad advice in Sydney – if you could only get away with it. The deregulation of financial markets and the smorgasbord of non-bank institutions which have entered the market means borrowers and other bank customers are offered a mind-boggling array of products, options, and bells and whistles. Unfortunately, it is all too easy to be swamped in the detail.

Bank accounts

If you can get by without a cheque account, give it some serious thought. In NSW debits tax (also known as BAD) applies to every withdrawal from accounts with a cheque facility. This will cost you 70 cents on a $100 withdrawal and operates on a scaled level. It doesn't sound like much, but it has been shown to be one of the biggest drains on everyday bank accounts.

For a basic transaction account, with minimum fees, try looking outside the banks to a building society or credit union. Endeavour Credit Union (ph 1800 224 008) is the state's largest. Metway Bank (ph 131 642) consistently pays one of the highest interest rates on savings accounts.

Savings

Banking is full of little ironies. One of the big ones is that the more money you have, and presumably the less you need to save, the better the deal you can get. One of the better developments of recent years has been the growth of bonus saver accounts. Most of the major banks now have them. You get a paltry rate of interest on your money (recently 0.25 per cent) but, if you add to the balance each month, you receive a bonus – generally 3 per cent – on your interest rate.

If you have at least $1,000 you should also consider a cash management account or cash management trust. The former are bank accounts which pay a higher rate of interest (although you'll need more money to get the top rate) while the latter are investment products which pay you market interest rates minus a management fee of around 1 per cent. Macquarie Investment Management in Sydney (ph 9237 3737) has Australia's largest cash management trust – more than $4 billion.

Term deposits will also pay higher rates if you are prepared to tie your money up for awhile. To check out the latest rates, the interest rate monitor, Cannex, has a MoneyLine service (1900 170 071) formed in conjunction with the Australian Consumers Association.

Credit cards

Many Australians pay their credit cards off in full each month which makes a card offering up to 55 days interest-free credit their best option. These come with an annual fee of $20-25 while cards offering no interest-free period generally have no fee. One of the more competitive cards on the market is the American Express Blue Card (ph 9271 1111) which was launched in 1997 and has no fees if you spend more than $1,500 a year. Reward-based cards are popular and fall into three groups: those offering flight-based rewards; those offering shopping vouchers; and those offering rebates on car purchases. Techno smart? Banksmart at www.banksmart has the latest details on all the reward offers.

Home loans

Super Home Loans (ph 1800 065 999), a joint venture between the ACTU (Australian Council of Trade Unions) and National Mutual, has consistently provided one of the lower-cost basic home loans on the market – especially for members of superannuation funds which provide finance for the loans.

For a mid-range loan, insist on a product with a redraw facility and full loan portability. This allows you to make extra payments and access the money later on if you need it for other purposes, rather than having to set up a new loan. Some of the non-bank lenders have these loans at near rock-bottom rates.

At the upper end of the scale, there has been growth in 'salary mortgages' and home equity loans which allow you to have your salary deposited direct into your loan account so that you can draw down the funds as needed.

Annette Sampson

Barbecues

see also outdoor dining, meat

Sydney has taken barbecuing to new heights since the first banger greased its way across a grillplate. Purists will head for the bush to throw a few chops on a disk plough, but urban dwellers will want to invest in the latest turbo-powered gas machine to fire up in the privacy of their own backyards. Sydney is well endowed with parks and beaches, many with barbecue facilities.

Best spots

Bronte and Tamarama are the best beachside barbecues. Inland try Centennial Park – while you are cultivating the perfect coal, the rest of the gang can stretch out. Harbourside, Nielsen Park is the most picturesque, especially at the end of the day. Catch the sunrays and silhouettes of sailing boats on one of the world's most beautiful harbours, swim and then rest in the shade of an ancient Moreton Bay fig tree. Northside, try Balmoral Beach.

Barbeques Galore

One-stop shopping for barbecue equipment, including the very latest models from Weber with the increasingly popular hoods for baking fish, bread and larger pieces of meat. Deluxe tools in stainless steel and rosewood, the Wiltshire brand with heat-resistant plastic handles and the new shiny chrome Turbot range by

Avanti. For a bargain, always check out the seconds warehouse first.
- 125 Parramatta Rd, Camperdown, ph 9388 1841; other locations, ph 131 254.

David Jones
A good range of barbecues, including the new Italian Barbe Cook, which looks terribly chic but only takes a handful of coals. DJs' Market St store also supplies certified organic Waramali Beef.
- Ph 13 3357.

Essential Ingredient
Go here for double-clipped wire grills for fish and meat and the expensive giant-sized German stainless steel Hofffritz brand of utensils. Also available is the non-stick barbecue wok and a dazzling array of the best knives. This is also the one-stop shop for BBQ condiments – Peter Watson's barbecue rubs and marinades, Paul Prudhomme's Cajun seasonings and amazing mustards and chutneys.
- 6 Australia St, Camperdown, ph 9550 5477.

AC Butchery
Legendary Roman butcher Carlo Colaiacomo makes arguably the best Italian-style sausages in town, cased in natural skins with the freshest ground meats and spices. Try chicken and rocket, duck and pistachio or pork and chili.
- 174 Marion St, Leichhardt, ph 9569 8687.

Other good suppliers include the following, who both sell high-quality grain-fed Federation sausages and sirloins: **B & J Lizard**, 186-188 Harris St, Pyrmont, ph 9660 3388; **La Mensa**, 257 Oxford St, Paddington, ph 9332 2963.

Nicole Lehmann

Bars

see also pubs, beer, wine, nightclubs, gay & lesbian Sydney

NSW has annoying licensing laws, which make it expensive to open a bar that doesn't serve food. As a result, many of the best spots in town for a cocktail are attached to great restaurants, where as long as you have 'the intention to eat' you are welcome to come in for a cold one. Others are found in international hotels and in social clubs, where you have to pay a nominal membership fee. A new breed is the groovy converted pub, which has kept the full pub licence, but slung out the poker machines.

Winebanc
Hurrah! A full bar licence – no need to eat, no poker machines. *Wallpaper* magazine would approve of the Dr No decor. We're keen on the best French champers by the glass and cool cocktails until midnight in the CBD. The drinks aren't cheap, but neither are this crowd's shoes.
- 53 Martin Place (enter from Elizabeth St), City, ph 9233 5399.

MG Garage
Just a restaurant licence, sadly, but worth coming half an hour early to have your pre-dinner at this designer bar. Make sure to drink a lot so you have to use the loos – they'll blow your mind (and probably your nose if you press the right button).
- 490 Crown St, Surry Hills, ph 9383 9383.

Horizons Bar, ANA Hotel
Better than Centrepoint views, with martinis. If you want more you'll have to take drugs.
- 46th Floor, 176 Cumberland St, The Rocks, ph 9250 6000.

Bars

The Krug Room
Not so much a bar as a life-changing experience. Krug champagne (from $29.50 a glass), Dietmar Sawyere's degustation menu of entree-sized dishes and that view, from 42 floors up (you climb a flight of stairs after entering at level 41).
- Forty One, Chifley Tower, 2 Chifley Sq, City, ph 9221 2500.

Bayswater Brasserie
Where the thirsty 30s glamour crowd meets on Friday nights, for a jug of margarita and a big flirt. Of course, they all intend to dine, although many of the female patrons look like they haven't had a square meal for weeks (in the nicest possible way).
- 32 Bayswater Rd, Kings Cross, ph 9357 2177.

Centennial
Are we in New York? It's hard to believe this deeply chic interior was formerly known as a pub. The bar throbs with a glamour crowd waiting for a restaurant table (no bookings) and perving through the open plan layout at who's already there (everyone, darling!).
- 88 Oxford St, Woollahra, ph 9362 3838.

East Village
Funkiness for grown-ups in the coolest of Sydney's many groovified pubs. You can eat upstairs, but the great thing is you don't have to.
- 234 Palmer St, Darlinghurst, ph 9331 5457.

Slip Inn
This place has it all. On the ground floor, it's a designer pub (glazed concrete-a-go-go) with pool. Downstairs there's a courtyard for summer evenings, a restaurant and two other bars. In the basement, a nightclub.
- 111 Sussex St, City, ph 9299 2199.

Penthouse Bar, Gazebo Hotel
For your post-modern moments, ironic chic '70s decor (the floor numbers in the lift will get you in the mood) with great views. Make mine a Cinzano.
- 17th floor, 2 Elizabeth Bay Rd, Kings Cross, ph 9358 1999.

Sebel Townhouse
This tiny round room, which closes when the last patron falls over, is a legend. Even when it's not full of the famous who stay at the hotel, it's the perfect place for a bourbon and Coke. After four of them, you're famous.
- 23 Elizabeth Bay Rd, Elizabeth Bay, ph 9358 3244.

Grand Pacific Blue Room
A restaurant, a bar and now, it says officially on its licence, a nightclub. But the high ceilings in this old building give it anything but a dingy club atmosphere, which is a good thing as you come here to be seen as you swill.
- Cnr Oxford and South Dowling Sts, Paddington, ph 9331 7108.

Bennelong
The ultimate Sydney experience. You're inside the Opera House, the bar snacks are from one of the best kitchens in town and the chair you're sitting on is a 20th-century design classic.
- Sydney Opera House, Bennelong Pt, City, ph 9250 7548.

Bondi Icebergs and Bondi Diggers
Bondi is full of awful 'trendy' bars, but nowhere beats these two for local colour. Don't expect fancy trimmings, but a cheap cold beer never came with better views. These are clubs, so you will have to take up social membership to get in (Icebergs $5, Diggers $2). In any other city, they would cost $5,000 a year to join.
- Bondi Icebergs Club, 1 Notts Ave, Bondi, ph 9130 3120.
  Bondi Diggers, 232 Campbell Pde, Bondi Beach, ph 9365 6747.

Anti Bar

Specially designed for the grazing punter who wants to toy with a plate of top chef Steve Manfredi's antipasto while sipping a chilled glass of Vernaccia di San Gimignano (or whatever). Ciao bella.
- bel mondo, Level 3, Argyle Department Store, 12-24 Argyle St, The Rocks, ph 9241 3700.

Maggie Alderson

Baseball

see also sporting goods

Although baseball has been an Olympic medal sport since Barcelona in 1992, the Sydney Games will be the first time that professional players will be allowed to compete, not only lifting the worldwide prominence of the sport, but significantly enhancing Australia's chances of winning a medal. With the inclusion of professionals at the Games, Australian players such as David Nilsson and Graeme Lloyd – who compete in US major league – could be eligible to participate. In 2000 baseball will be played at the RAS Showground facility at Homebush Bay.

Sydney Storm

Sydney's team competing for the FAI Cup in the Australian Baseball League.
- Loftus St, Concord, ph 9437 5546.

School baseball

Through programs such as Teeball and 'Pitch, Hit and Run', baseball has become one of the biggest school participant sports in the city.
- For details, contact the Australian Baseball Federation at Level 2, 48 Atchison St, St Leonards, ph 9437 4466.

Club baseball

There are numerous baseball clubs in Sydney catering for both junior and senior players.
- NSW Junior Baseball League Inc, ph 9639 3859; NSW Baseball League, ph 9552 4635.

Baseball Dugout

Specialist retailer of baseball and softball equipment.
- 39b Church St, Lidcombe, ph 9649 1347. Also at Thornleigh and Miranda.

Mike Cowley

Basketball

see also sporting goods

Think basketball, and instantly you think America, not Sydney. Sure, the US is considered the home of hoops, but it is hard to ignore the stature of Australian basketball, particularly when you consider that four of the ten national teams which Basketball Australia puts on the court are ranked with the world's elite. Our junior men's team and wheelchair men's team are both ranked number one, while at a senior level Australia's women and men were ranked three and four in the world respectively after their efforts at the 1996 Atlanta Olympics Games.

Basketball will be played at two venues during the Olympics – preliminaries at The Dome and finals at the MUA (Multi Use Arena) which will be completed in late '99.

Professional basketball in Australia underwent a major change in 1998, with the National Basketball League's traditional winter competition making way for a new summer competition. The opening game is on October 9 & 10, with the competition climaxing with the Championship decider in April '99.

Basketball

State Sports Centre

The administrative home of basketball in NSW and the venue for elite and international games. This is where you will see the Boomers and the Opals (Olympic men's and women's teams), as well as the crowd-pleasing national wheelchair team.

- Australia Avenue, Homebush Bay, ph 9763 0111.

Basketball NSW

Unlike many sports, basketball can be an individual game. All you need is the ball, then find yourself a hoop, and start shooting. Of course, if you want to be a little more serious, there are 15 basketball associations across Sydney, where you will be able to find an organised competition.

- Ph 9746 2969.

Sydney Kings

For the past 11 seasons this team has represented Sydney in the National Basketball League, but for the 1998-99 NBL season, they will have a cross-town rival in the West Sydney Razorbacks. For ticket details and a game schedule, contact the Kings.

- 48 O'Riordan St, Alexandria, ph 9319 7777.

Sydney Flames

Based at Alexandria with the Kings, this team is a title contender in the Women's National Basketball League season after season. Basketball is becoming extremely popular among women – to join a team contact Basketball NSW.

- Ph 9319 7777.

Shane Heal

The feisty 185 cm (that's practically a dwarf in basketball terms) point guard for the Sydney Kings and The Boomers is simply one of the most outstanding players Australia has produced. In 1997, he played with the Minnesota Timber-wolves in the NBA in the US.

Jodie Smith

While they spend their weekends on the court, the Sydney Kings players spend a majority of their time during the week visiting schools and conducting coaching clinics. For details contact Jodie, Development Co-ordinator at the Kings.

- Ph 9319 7777.

EG Whitlam Centre

This is the venue for home games and the base for the West Sydney Razorbacks.

- Memorial Ave, Liverpool, ph 9600 9333.
  West Sydney Razorbacks, ph 98240045.

Troy Sachs

A Sydney legend who scored 42 points for Australia in Paralympics basketball final at Atlanta. He plays for the Liverpool-based Slix, one of three Sydney teams in the National Wheelchair Basketball League. For details of matches and local competition, phone Basketball Australia (see below).

Rebel Sports

Just look around and you see basketball attire. Whether its caps or T-shirts or team singlets, basketball wear is everywhere. Most sports stores carry basketball equipment and paraphernalia, but Rebel has the widest range of both local and NBA gear.

- Mid City Centre, City, ph 9221 8633. Also at many suburban locations including Bankstown, ph 9707 3344; Bondi Junction, ph 9389 3822; Chatswood, ph 9419 2333; Parramatta, ph 9891 1611.

Michael Cowley

Further information

- Basketball Australia, ph 9369 5522: www.basketball.net.au

Bathrooms

see also plumbers

Bathware need not be merely functional – it can look good too, especially when luminaries like Philippe Starck turn their hands to their design. Whether your bathroom is contemporary or traditional, why confine yourself to a boring box when you can now get designer bathroom basics hot from Milan all over Sydney?

The Bath House

One of Sydney's best-known bathroom suppliers. Well established with a wide range of quality fittings from high-tech stainless steel to classically styled Czech & Speake chrome. The source for extremely practical whirlpool baths, spas, loos, showers, taps and accessories.
- 153 Sailors Bay Rd, Northbridge, ph 9967 4000.

Taps Design

The Prada of bathroom fittings by European designers, plus hard-to-find ranges. Impressive range of Agape timber wash basin units, porcelain lab-style sinks and coordinating accessories in clever combinations. As well as Philippe Starck pieces, there are the Spanish range of Cosmic accessories; Linea Beta wash basin units and mirrors in stainless steel (loved by architects); and Catalano white porcelain vanities updated with steel. Also own-brand stone bowls in three must-have shapes.
- 115 Flinders St, Darlinghurst, ph 9332 4800.

Candana

Classical and contemporary range of supremely practical bathroom products plus coordinated accessories.
- 120 Edgecliff Rd, Woollahra, ph 9389 8631.

Sampford and Staff

A rare opportunity to try out exclusive designer range of Hansgrohe shower heads and tapware.
- 162 Crown St, East Sydney, ph 9331 8888.

Melissa Walker Smith

Beaches

see also surfing, volleyball, swimwear & surfwear, windsurfing, lifesaving

With so many other leisure options in the city, and the modern bogeys of skin cancer and prematurely aged skin, Sydney beaches will never again see the teeming crowds of the mid century. However, the beach is now more than just a good spot to bask in the sun and the golden glow of nostalgia. Bondi Pavilion opens its doors to sandy summer hordes with concerts, festivals, a gallery and theatre, and a cafe downstairs that sells delicious gelato. The Rotunda at Balmoral Beach holds a summer season of music and theatre. And don't forget the climatically challenged (read colder) seasons. Due to the vagaries of ocean currents the water can be warmer in June than it is in December.

Bondi Beach

Australia's most famous beach, where cafe society gentrification is overtaking the seedy past. Join the **Bondi Life Saving Club** and really be a part of the Bondi scene. Call Peter Quartly, the club secretary to sign up for the 6-8 week training. Don't fancy wearing those little caps? Then don a wetsuit and head down to the south end for a surf. The **NSW Surf Riders Association** (ph 9518 9410) has professional teachers who'll have you riding waves with the best of them. Hire surfboards and boogie boards ($20–$40 for three hours) from the **Bondi Surf Company** (ph 9365 0870).

Tamarama Beach and Mackenzies Bay

If the tide is right, a strip of sand appears turning rocky Mackenzies into a tiny beach, enjoyed (illegally) by Sydney's dogs and their owners. Neighbouring Tamarama, a haven for the young gay scene and serious surfers, is a beach to bronze on – there are more models per square inch than any other beach in Sydney. Come armed with a g-string and a couple of months of gym classes under your well-toned belt.

Bronte Beach

The best beach for barbecues: you'll be surrounded by the mouthwatering smells of family feasts. Bronte has weathered the gentrification that has engulfed other Eastern Suburbs beaches, keeping an ethnic, family feel. You're as likely to come across a spicy Italian sausage on the barbecue as an Aussie pork banger. For people-watching, choose any of the Bronte Rd cafes.

Clovelly Beach

Next along the southern beaches is quiet little Clovelly with its long smoothly-cemented edges. This is a great spot for divers. **Pro Dive** (27 Alfreda St, Coogee, ph 9665 6333) offers a four-day diving course for $345.

Gordon's Bay

Best spot for dogs. Humans will also enjoy this beautiful bay secreted between Coogee and Clovelly.

Coogee Beach

Best spot for ocean pools. Wylies Baths won the Greenway Award for architectural re-use in 1995; about 200 metres south of Wylies is the Women's Only pool (pay a 20-cent donation for a peaceful swim).

Nielsen Park

A beach with shade. Bliss! After a swim at this netted harbour beach, retire under the cool Moreton Bay figs for a picnic. Check out the extraordinarily huge change rooms. Seems the local council was expecting hordes. Best spot for a night swim.

Camp Cove

Captain Arthur Phillip, the colony's first governor, landed in Sydney and set up camp here. Now locals park their boats in this bay and hang out gossiping and sipping chardonnay. A beach to be seen on. It's a tiny stretch of sand, so arrive early to stake a comfortable claim.

Lady Jane

A bathing-suit free zone, this minuscule beach is a short stroll along the cliffs from Camp Cove. Very popular with the gay community.

Manly

Laid-back and just a little tacky. Check out Oceanworld (West Esplanade, ph 9949 2644), where you can dive with sharks and swim with seals.

Balmoral Beach

A northside harbour beach. The southern end is great for windsurfing. Hire a windsurfer and get a lesson from **Balmoral Sailboard School** (ph 9960 5344).

Palm Beach

This is where the serious money goes to the beach. It's also the spot where the Australian soap *Home and Away* is filmed. Palmie, the northernmost of Sydney's surf beaches, is worth a look-in just to have a sticky at the mansions that overlook the water. Try the hike up to the Barrenjoey lighthouse through Governor Phillip Park; there are good picnic spots and the view of Pittwater is spectacular.

Bilgola Beach

The perfect antidote to Palm Beach is just a 10-minute drive south. Bilgola is never crowded and the steep headlands, heavy bush and creamy yellow sand make it feel like a secret hideaway.

Glenbrook Creek
Sick of all that salt? Try a fresh-water mountain beach. This creek runs through a gorge creating two perfect sandy swimming holes – Blue Pool and Jelly Bean Pool. Open to the public seven days a week. For details, call
- Glenbrook Visitors Centre, ph 02 4739 6266.

Cerentha Harris

Beauty products

see also **beauty salons, hairdressers**

Aveda Environmental Lifestyle Store
Pure, organic plant essences form the basis of all their skin, hair care and fragrance products. Petrochemicals and animal by-products do not feature and all staff are well trained to give advice.
- Shop 16, Lower Ground Walk, George St, Queen Victoria Building, ph 9264 8925.

Crabtree and Evelyn
This English classic works just as well in NSW, with the matching ranges of soap, talc, body lotion, etc., beautifully packaged and always the perfect gift. A nice range of accessories extends to the nighties and shortbread, as well as the more expected soap dishes.
- Shop 2, Level 7, MLC Centre, Martin Place, City, ph 9235 3826.
  Also at QVB, ph 9267 5140; Chifley Plaza, ph 9223 5397; Chatswood, ph 9415 4518.

David Jones
Best one-stop for all the big names in beauty, in the most elegant cosmetics and fragrance hall in Australia. A good bet for gift-with-purchase offers too.
- Elizabeth St, City, ph 9266 5544, plus suburban stores.

Julia's Perfumery
A specialist store with a highly committed owner. Julia Keogh is passionate about the products she imports (Annick Goutal fragrances, for instance) and is always on hand to advise. With hard-to-find perfumes like Calandre, Bal a Versailles and Fendi in stock, Julia will make it her mission to find your favourite scent when it has been discontinued elsewhere. Also a good range of interesting specialist cosmetics.
- Shop 8, Town Hall Connection, Park St, City, ph 9264 1619.

Jurlique
Made from herbs grown organically in South Australia, this super-pure line of cosmetics is achieving world recognition.
- Shop 1, Ground Level, Strand Arcade, ph 9231 0626; Chatswood, ph 9415 1738.

Napoleon
Formerly The Look by Napoleon, this is a make-up mecca started by a make-up artist. The colours are intense and the Luminizer sticks are a cult product. Make-up lessons also offered.
- 74 Oxford St, Paddington, ph 9331 1702.

Lush
Sydney branch of the famous British stores, where everything is so fresh you have to keep it in the fridge and the naturally perfumed soaps are sold by weight, carved off like cheese. All products are based on edible ingredients: chocolate and mint in the After 8:30 Massage Bar, fresh strawberries in the Possett Body Scrub, and fruit and vegies, such as bananas, lemons and oranges.
- Shop 14, QVB Walk, Queen Victoria Building, City, ph 9238 5746. Also at Warringah Mall.

Beauty products

Paradise Perfumery
Perfumeries as they have them in Europe, featuring top of the range skincare and cosmetics (Clarins, Lancome, Shiseido, Guerlain, Stendhal), plus those hard to find fragrances by Balmain, Donna Karan, Worth and Annick Goutal.
- Westpac Plaza, 273 George St, City, ph 9247 4481; branches in Mosman, Neutral Bay and Double Bay.

Red Earth
Australia's take on The Body Shop with cruelty-free, natural and innovative products at accessible prices.
- Shop 22-24 Lower Level, Queen Victoria Building, City, ph 9264 4019; plus many suburban stores, ph 1800 800 988 for details.

Showface
Where the professional make up artists buy their gear. Fascinating imported ranges, including brushes by Kryolan which are seriously worth investing in.
- 10 Argyle Place, Millers Point, ph 9247 4736.

Maggie Alderson

Beauty salons

see also beauty products, hairdressers

Sydney is a city particularly well-endowed with excellent beauty salons. You can phone **Clarins** (9315 9385), **Ella Bache** (9438 3911) or **Dermalogica** (1800 659 118) for their recommended venues. The following lists places which specialise, or offer something more.

Aveda Day Spa
A well of calm infused with the gorgeous natural aromas of Aveda products. You can go for the whole day (aaaaah . . .) or just for one treatment. Everything from waxing and eyebrow tinting, to massage and body treatments.
- 17 Oxford St, Paddington, ph 9380 5550.

Beauty on Crown
Small but beautifully-formed salon, offering all the usual services, plus special New Agey Heritage Healers treatments.
- Shop 2, 355 Crown St, Surry Hills, ph 9361 4363.

Ciao Bella
Good-humoured salon which features exotic 'French' waxing (think lap dancers . . .). Plus they play better music than the average salon, with the B52s more likely than Pan Pipes of Peru.
- Suite 2, Level 1, 32a Oxford St, Darlinghurst, ph 9361 0612.

Sylvia Deitch Beauty Therapy
Sydney's skincare specialist soothes many a famous furrowed brow. Book well in advance.
- 1st Floor, 37 Bay St, Double Bay, ph 9327 2102.

Efbee Hair, Body & Beauty
Attached to an excellent hair salon, the beauty area features a spa and hydrotherapy bath and personally blended, Aveda products.
- Shop 23, Level 1, Victoria Ave, Chatswood Chase, ph 9410 1033

The Ali Hamylton Makeover Shop
The nails queen of Sydney. There are women who would rather walk naked through Double Bay than give up their regular manicure appointment here. Everything else to make you beautiful is on offer too. Hamylton's own range of make-up is on sale and make-up lessons can be booked.
- 13 Transvaal Ave, Double Bay, ph 9328 1340.

Spa Chakra Potts Point

Four floors of glamour with air beds (specially imported from the US for ultimate comfort during facial treatments), hydrotherapy tubs, hair, make-up, facials, the lot. David Wehner, one of Australia's top aromatherapists, is head technician. And did I mention the valet parking?
- 170 Victoria St, Potts Point, ph 9368 0888.

Smyth and Fitzgerald

This buzzing beauty and hair salon is like a second home to its regulars and friendly to all. The manicures and pedicures are legendary, although you will have to book well in advance to get underneath the orange stick of part owner Christina Fitzgerald.
- Shop 18, The Ritz Carlton Promenade, 33 Cross St, Double Bay, ph 9326 1385.

Trumps

An oasis for the inner-city girl – or boy – fitting in that crucial waxing between board meetings. They do a special 'express facial' for just that purpose as well.
- Level 10, 300 George St, City, ph 9233 4888.

Venustus

The charming staff at this small sweet-smelling salon go out of their way to create a nurturing environment. As well as the usual roster of treatments, they sell their own range of products.
- 381 Oxford St, Paddington, ph 9361 4014.

Zen and the Art of Body Maintenance

A beautifully designed, high-class natural therapies centre (naturopathy, acupuncture, etc.) which also offers skincare treatments using Dermalogica's 100% organic products. Beauty for the body and soul.
- 116-118 Darlinghurst Rd, Darlinghurst, ph 9361 4200.

Maggie Alderson

Beer

see also bars, pubs

In a Sydney summer, all a beer needs to make it great is a cold fridge or an Esky. But if you're looking for something really special, try the following.

Lord Nelson Brewery Hotel

Sydney's original brew-pub has been producing English-style ales for more than a decade. Recommended: Three Sheets, Victory Bitter, Old Admiral (a strong ale) and Nelson's Blood (a seasonal stout). This fine old sandstone pub has dartboard, glassed-in mini brewery and excellent brasserie.
- 19 Kent St, The Rocks, ph 9251 4044.

George IV Inn

This delightful country pub on Sydney's outskirts is the unlikely producer of two excellent German style beers, Scharer's Lager and Burragorang Bock. It has budget accommodation and is easily reached by train. Both brews are also available at the Australian Hotel (100 Cumberland St, The Rocks) and Scharer's Lager is served at Bennelong restaurant in the Opera House.
- 180 Argyle St, Picton, ph 4677 1415.

Eastern Suburbs Brewmaker

A mecca for serious home-brew enthusiasts with an impressive selection of hops, specialty grains, yeast cultures, brewing literature, draft-beer-dispensing equipment and mashing paraphernalia.
- 149 Clovelly Rd, Randwick, ph 9399 8241.

Beer Importers & Distributors

If you're trying to track down obscure Belgian ales or exotic European lagers, these guys carry a range of 50-plus imported and domestic brews.
- 116 Queen St, Alexandria, ph 9698 2319.

Willie Simpson

Blinds & shutters

Blinds and shutters diffuse Sydney's strong light, control privacy and also give a hint of the view. And unlike curtains, you can always track down a blind or shutter that will be right for an awkward space, period sash window or modern interior.

Just Blinds
Do your own thing with this extensive range of made-to-measure plantation shutters. Privacy without total blackout and they look good anywhere.
- 25 Beaumont Rd, Mt Kuring-gai, ph 9457 9066.

IKEA
For a quick fix, you can filter your light with an off-the-peg roller blind or some timber venetians at cut-price. Check out the Brak cotton Roman blinds in white or sand.
- Stores at Gordon, Moore Park, Blacktown; inquiries, ph 9313 6400.

Silent Gliss
The big favourite with architects is the Sheer Weave quality roller shield, which provides sun, heat and glare control with a patented mechanism for slow, easy operation.
- 47-61 Pyrmont Bridge Rd, Camperdown, ph 9519 3899.

Sydney Plantation Shutters
Give your windows a fresh new view with these great plantation shutters which make for great light effects with a choice of 46mm, 70mm, 90mm or 115mm blades. You can choose from the standard range of colours or the company can custom paint, stain or lime to order.
- Unit 11, 888 Bourke St, Waterloo, ph 9319 1111.

Verosol
A simple, modern blind that really works, with more than 500 colours and textures to choose from.
- 2 Garema Circuit, Kingsgrove, ph 9750 3444.

Melissa Walker Smith

Blues music

see also jazz, folk music, country music, rock & pop music
When the sun is shining on the stunning expanse of the harbour, it's hard to sing the blues in Sydney. Nonetheless, a small number of blues bands play regularly around the city and deservedly have a passionate fan base. Major overseas blues acts also tour regularly with the bigger stars, such as BB King, attracting large and diverse audiences to the major venues.

The Basement
The city's premier blues venue. It can become very crowded, so book a table, have a meal, and enjoy the concert in comfort.
- 29 Reiby Place, City, ph 9251 2797.

Other venues include the **Harbourside Brasserie** (ph 9252 3000) and the **Sydney Blues Club**, Empire Hotel (ph 9557 1701).

Rose of Australia
Want to play blues? On the fourth Sunday of each month there's a jam session. All welcome. The quality of performance varies from the sublime to the offensive.
- 1 Swan St, Erskineville, ph 9565 1441.

The Backsliders
A talented three-piece (guitar, percussion and harmonica) specialising in acoustic Delta blues.

A distinctive Aussie variant of the blues with great panache and enthusiasm.

The Mighty Reapers
Excellent R&B band with soul inflections. Born out of the remnants of The Dynamic Hypnotics, on a good night they can sizzle, with lead singer Robert Susz setting the place ablaze.

The Foreday Riders
Grand old men of Sydney blues driven by the talents of Jeff and Ron King. Their 30th anniversary concert in 1997 attracted the cream of the city's blues players and crowds to The Basement.

Folkways Music
A music store with an extensive range of blues releases – local and international – including local rarities.
- 282 Oxford St, Paddington, ph 9361 3980.

HMV Shop
Excellent specialist blues section. Both Gordon Mignot and Dave Robson are a great source of knowledge and advice on good gigs around town.
- Mid City Centre, Pitt St Mall, City, ph 9221 2311.

Jacksons Rare Guitars
Want to play the blues on a rare dobro or National Steel guitar? Jacksons is recognised as one of the best vintage guitar shops in the world.
- 37 Parramatta Rd, Annandale, ph 9550 2985.

Bruce Elder

Further information
- Check Sydney Morning Herald Metro and CitySearch for listings.

Bodybuilding

see also fitness clubs, weightlifting

Critics argue it's not a sport but a parade for over-developed walking stimulant depositories. Those same critics will shrivel at the injustice to learn that bodybuilding is expected to be a demonstration sport at Sydney 2000, endorsed by a guest appearance from The Terminator himself, Arnold Schwarzenegger. Controversial, yes, but great for the sport in Sydney, which despite its popularity, hasn't hosted a major international competition since 1989. The anonymous view of what is always a touchy subject is that diuretic, synthetic growth hormone and steroid use is rife in Sydney. The official assertion is that the sport is clean and that early nights and eating your greens and will make you grow up big and strong – as big as a hot-air Zeppelin, in fact. In Sydney, as it is worldwide, the sport is highly fragmented with four major associations, each contesting its own cham- pionships. If you want to take up body building, a one-off visit to one of the more than 150 gyms city-wide should cost you about $10 and a year's membership no more than $600.

City Gym Health & Fitness Centre
Sydney's only 24-hour gym is the place to spot visiting international body building stars.
- 107 Crown St, East Sydney, ph 9360 6247.

Ultimate Gym
Run by the first Australian to win a professional title overseas, John Terilli.
- Level 2, Newtown Plaza, 328-338 King St, Newtown, ph 9557 2219.

Bayswater Fitness
A gym featuring a large, open training area with modern equipment. A stone's throw from Kings Cross station.
- 33 Bayswater Rd, Kings Cross, ph 9356 2555.

Bodyline Fitness Centre
The pick of North Shore gyms.
- 100 Walker St, North Sydney, ph 9956 5533.

Fernwood Female Fitness
Sydney's women's-only gym.
- Westfield Shopping Town, Marsden St (cnr Aird St), Parramatta, ph 9806 0202.

NSW Bodybuilding Supplies
Stocks the full gamut of essentials including dietary supplements, books, videos and equipment.
- 380 Cleveland St, Surry Hills, ph 9698 2422.

Stay-Fit Equipment
Excellent range of muscle-maximising material. Also repairs equipment.
- 397 Lyons Rd, Five Dock, ph 9713 2533.

Peter Vincent

Further information
- National Physique and Fitness Committee of Australia, PO Box 1, Blakehurst, ph 9583 2471
- National Amateur Body Builders Association, 45 Brougham St, Geelong, Victoria, ph (03) 5223 1776
- Australian Natural Body Building Federation, PO Box 31, Illawong, ph 9541 0038
- Australian Natural Body Builders Association, ph 9630 0338

Books

For a city whose image is outdoorsy hedonism, Sydney has built up a vivid literary life. OK, sometimes we like to combine it with food, drink and chatter at literary lunches, festivals and bookshop cafes. But we're serious about reading. Without spending a cent you can enjoy the vast collections of the **State Library of NSW** and its historic Mitchell wing (Macquarie St, City, ph 9273 1414), where there are public events and constantly changing exhibitions of books and artwork, even if you don't want to borrow or burrow into the vast collections. Over the past 20 or 30 years, independent bookshops have settled into most parts of the city and suburbs, offering collections as good as anywhere else in the world and now the superstores are arriving. The best shops have passionate owners, knowledgeable staff, speedy ordering and a sense of community that draws people in for a reading, a cappuccino, a chat or a solitary browse.

Major literary events in Sydney include the *Sydney Morning Herald*/Dymocks Literary Luncheons, celebrating its 10th anniversary year in 1998, with Australian and international writers. Bookings coupons can be found in the *Herald*'s Spectrum section on Saturdays or phone 9449 4366. The Sydney Writers' Festival is held annually in mid year. In 1999 it will take place on May 18-23 at Wharf 4/5, Walsh Bay and the Sydney Town Hall. For information phone 9265 9959 or 9265 9131.

Abbey's Bookshop
The clutter of 30 years gives Abbey's an unruly look but the shop has its own logic. Probably Australia's biggest and most authoritative crime collection; Greek and Latin classics; science and maths for lay readers; history, fiction and audiobooks. Upstairs the Language Book Centre has dictionaries in more than 100 languages; books, cassettes and CD-Roms for learning English and many other languages.
- 131 York St, City, ph 9264 3111.

Ariel Booksellers
Open until midnight seven days, this is just the place if you get a book craving after the

cinema or dinner on the Oxford St strip. An airy space, strong on cinema, cooking, design, architecture and current fiction.
- 42 Oxford St, Paddington, ph 9332 4581.

Berkelouw Books
More a village than a bookshop, this business has been run by the Berkelouw family since 1812, with headquarters in Berrima and a Los Angeles office that guarantees good US imports. New books on the ground floor, antiquarian and rare upstairs, quality second-hand up again, plus a cafe, all open until midnight, seven days.
- 19 Oxford St, Paddington, ph 9360 3200.

Bloomin' Books
Ex-teacher-librarian Kate Colley keeps a wide stock for children and teenagers 0 to 18, and a small adult section for parents and ambitious young adults. Restful blue-and-cream decor, beanbags and storytelling sessions make the shop a pleasant place to linger.
- Shop 1, 153 Denman Ave, Caringbah, ph 9540 3788.

Constant Reader Bookshop
This crowded Aladdin's cave specialises in animation, film, graphic design, architecture and computers as well as 'vicarious travel' and 'gratuitous sex and violence by the truckload', according to the owner, Peter Kirby.
- 27 Willoughby Rd, Crows Nest, ph 9438 1763.

Dymocks
Of the chains, this venerable 119-year-old company stands out, with 22 franchised branches in the metropolitan area. Its main city store carries more than 250,000 titles over three well-organised floors, including a specialised business, education and computer department, and a large audiobook section.
- 424 George St, City, ph 9235 0155.

Welcome to BOOKOCCINO

Good reading, good listening, good coffee, good times...

BOOKOCCINO

37a OLD BARRENJOEY ROAD, AVALON BEACH. TEL (02) 9973 1244

MONDAY TO SATURDAY 9.30AM - 7PM
SUNDAYS & HOLIDAYS 11AM - 5PM

'WE'RE MORE THAN JUST A BOOK STORE'

Galaxy Bookshop
Australia's oldest science fiction bookshop, with sections devoted to *Star Wars*, *Star Trek*, *Dr Who* and other media from *Aliens* to *The X-Files*. Also comprehensive collections of fantasy and horror. Plus T-shirts, signed photographs and other merchandise.
- 222 Clarence St, City, ph 9267 7222.

Gleebooks
Seems they have everything among the 35,000 titles squeezed into two shopfront floors and, if they don't, they get it in fast. Catering at first to local academics, the shop is particularly impressive in literature, fine arts, history, philosophy, politics and social theory. A second shop at No 191 sells children's and second-hand books. One of Sydney's most active programs of literary events.
- 49 Glebe Point Rd, Glebe, ph 9660 2333.

Lesley McKay's
Soothed by classical music, shoppers walk though a seductive array of glossy books on

art, interiors, food and wine to serious collections of new fiction, biography, history and full backlists of classics from Dickens to Waugh. Poet Robert Gray is the poetry buyer. A separate children's shop connects with the Double Bay branch and literary breakfasts are held at a nearby restaurant.

■ 346 New South Head Rd, Double Bay, ph 9327 1354; Queen's Court, Queen St, Woollahra, ph 9328 2733.

Louella Kerr Lorraine Reed Old Fine & Rare Books

A sumptuous shop whose owners love fine printings from private presses, artists' books, travel and classics. Plus a wide range of first editions (the oldest book in stock recently was a 16th-century Italian edition of Aristotle published in Venice).

■ 30 Glenmore Rd, Paddington, ph 9361 4664.

Nicholas Pounder Bookseller

Upstairs from Lesley McKay's, enter a subdued room with baize-lined shelves and Victorian lamps. The bespectacled Pounder presides over a second-hand and rare collection focused on 20th-century literature but is willing to hunt for almost anything. A catalogue every eight weeks listing 400 books in stock is worth reading if only for its humorous and/or belligerent comments.

■ 346 New South Head Rd, Double Bay, ph 9328 7410.

Susan Wyndham

Bowling

see also sporting goods

Indoors or outdoors, competitive or social, day or night, fast and furious or beer-in-the-hand relaxed – that's how diverse your bowling opportunities are in Sydney. Bowling – which encompasses the lawn, tenpin and boules varieties – can be enjoyed by people of all ages, making it a fabulous recreational activity for families. At the other end of the scale, lawn and tenpin bowls are also played internationally.

There are at least 18 tenpin bowling centres in the greater metropolitan area, where you can play a casual game, organise a birthday party, attend a 'Rock and Bowl' event (fog machines, glow-in-the-dark pins and balls, plus music) or sign up for league competition.

Rated Australia's second highest participation sport, behind netball, lawn bowls is played at more than 200 clubs in Sydney alone. The Hills, along with Merrylands and Engadine, are three of the most popular. Many clubs stage open days for people to try the game and all newcomers are made welcome. Coaching is always available and is mandatory before you can play in organised matches.

Boules is a French game, also known as petanque, in which players toss four steel boules at a wooden jack, or cochonnet. It's a convivial game, perfect for backyard barbecues or anywhere there's a square of gravel.

Major forthcoming events in bowling include the NSW State championships (lawn) at St Johns Park Bowling Club on September 27 to October 5, 1998; the Manhattan Super Classic (tenpin) at Manhattan Superbowl, Mascot, on April 24-26, 1999; and the final of the AGC Pennants (lawn) in June 1999.

Manhattan Super Bowl

This Mascot bowling centre is the most popular tenpin venue in Sydney, with more than 5,000 patrons a week.

■ 549 Gardeners Road, Mascot, ph 9317 2577.

Munsons Manor

This pro shop is highly regarded for its wide range of bowling equipment, accessories and clothing. The manager, Cheryl Munson, is the

honorary coach of the Australian women's tenpin bowling team, and is happy to offer advice to improve your bowling technique.
■ AMF Enfield Bowl, ph 9642 4547.

Boules To You
One of two local suppliers of boules.
■ 30 Fairy Bower Road, Manly, ph 9976 2034.

Australian Petanque Federation
Can help get you started and put you in touch with the four Sydney clubs (Austral, Glenfield, Rockdale and Canterbury).
■ Ph 9580 2342.

Heather Quilan

Further information
■ Royal NSW Bowling Association, ph 9283 4555:
www.rnswba.org.au
■ NSW Women's Bowling Association, ph 9267-7155
■ Australian Tenpin Bowling Congress, ph 99052733:
www.atbcmpx.com.au

Boxing

Boxing once enjoyed enormous popularity in Sydney, peaking in the 1950s and 1960s with weekly cards held before enormous crowds at the now demolished Rushcutters Bay Stadium. By that stage, the Stadium had long entrenched itself in Australian folklore, with Jack Johnson beating Tommy Burns for the world heavyweight championship at the Stadium in 1908. Sydney has continued to develop outstanding boxers, with champions such as Lionel Rose, Jimmy Carruthers and Jeff Fenech winning world titles out of Sydney. Television and the emergence of other sports have seen boxing crowds decline, with Sydney now holding only 10 per cent of the number of cards it held in its heyday. However, the healthy benefits of boxing, such as cardiovascular training, trimming fat and muscle toning, have seen boxing develop into a white-collar exercise phenomenon. Olympic competition will take place at the Convention Centre, Darling Harbour.

Newtown Police Citizens Youth Club
The home of famous Australian trainer Johnny Lewis, who has guided three men to professional world titles as well as countless national amateur and professional world titles. Classes are cheap and cater for everyone from the beginning boxer to the elite champion.
■ Angel St, Newtown, ph 9557 3480.

Nat Craig's City Boxercise
Retains the old-world charm of the authentic boxing gym, although specialises in non-contact boxing classes aimed specifically for cardiovascular workouts that tone the muscles and trim the fat. Classes are popular with women and corporate types.
■ Riley St, East Sydney, ph 0414 439 854.

Mick Simmons Sports Store
Carries everything for the serious boxer from gloves and clothing to hand-wraps and punching bags.
■ George St, City, ph 9264 2744.

Paul Kent

Further information
■ NSW Amateur Boxing Association, ph 9326 2891

Breakfast & brunch

see also cafes
Most doctors will tell you that breakfast is the most important meal of the day. This is especially true in Sydney, where it is effort-

Breakfast & brunch

lessly tamed into a meaningful act of early sun-drenched socialising. Here, it's not what you eat for breakfast that matters, but where you eat it.

bills

Pull up a seat at the giant communal table, order a sunrise (orange juice and yoghurt – warning: it's healthy) and maybe a plate of unbelievable wobbly, excruciatingly creamy scrambled eggs. Then rifle through the mags for the very latest air mailed copy of *GQ* or *wallpaper*, and try to do as little as possible for at least an hour.
■ 433 Liverpool St, Darlinghurst,
 ph 9360 9631.

Fuel

Next door to the mega-successful fine dining MG Garage restaurant is its little sister Fuel which, when it's not being a performance sports car showroom, or a with-the-lot produce store, is one of Sydney's hottest and most happening cafes. On weekends, feast on a breakfast of champagne sausages and oysters, or a mighty mixed grill. Just don't drool over the brand new Aston Martins.
■ 448 Crown St, Surry Hills,
 ph 9383 9388.

Sean's Panaroma

Sean's weekend breakfast is renowned in a suburb where weekend breakfast is an art form. The fresh juices are among Sydney's finest, the sheep's milk yogurt and palm treacle is miraculous, and if you're into eggs, you're in for a treat.
■ 270 Campbell Pde, Bondi,
 ph 9365 4924.

Tonic

What was once an anonymous hotel breakfast room is now a happening: white-clad space full of hip black-clad people. While lunch and dinner are always buzzy, breakfast has its own clutch of fans who fuel up on homemade toasted muesli, prawn and chive omelette and toasted bagel and lox.
■ Shop 2, 16-32 Oxford St, City,
 ph 9380 5077.

Sejuiced

Even film directors and movie stars do breakfast occasionally, especially at this beachy keen Bronte cafe. Eggs are great, and the porridge could start a fan club, but Sejuiced's fame is based on its vast range of fruit and vegetable juices. If it stands still long enough, they'll make a juice from it.
■ 487 Bronte Rd, Bronte, ph 9389 9538.

Terry Durack

Bridge

The world's most popular card game (apart from seducing money from ATM machines) is alive and well in Sydney. Locking horns with other enthusiasts close by is no problem, thanks to a bevy of affiliated clubs around the metropolitan area.

The Australian Spring National Championships are held each November in Sydney.

Double Bay Bridge Centre

Rubber bridge and duplicate. Comfortable, good table service. All-time great Tim Seres is a regular. Watch him make the cards dance.
■ 35 Bay St, Double Bay, ph 9326 2072.

Lindfield Bridge Club

Sydney's oldest and biggest suburban club, well organised and spacious.
■ Adjacent to Lindfield railway station,
 ph 9416 2500.

Pennant Hills

Night events Tuesday/Thursday at the Community Centre, daytime Wednesday at

Cherrybrook, all directed by the maestro Ross Folkard.
- Ph 9477 1454.

Trumps Bridge Centre
Friendly tournaments, lessons and supervision.
- 66 Spit Rd, Mosman, ph 9969 5959.

Ron Klinger
Essentially a bridge potato with little in common with the MASH character except his surname, this Klinger writes books, teaches the fundamentals and organises annual playing holidays to places like Norfolk Island and Tangalooma.
- Ph 9958 5589.

Postfree Bridge Books
Owned by star player Paul Lavings, and stocks a wide range of new and old books to suit all tastes. Has a store at the NSW Bridge Association, 162 Goulburn St, City, or phone order.
- Ph 9388 8861.

The Bridge Shop
The place to go to buy anything connected with the game – cards, scorers, tables, dealing machines, bidding boxes and books as well.
- 614 Willoughby Rd, Willoughby, ph 9967 0644.

Dick Cummings

Further information
- NSW Bridge Association, ph 9264 8111.
- Australian Bridge (ph 9967 0644 to subscribe to this magazine)

Building contractors

see also **bricklayers, carpenters, building equipment, building materials**

Finding a good builder is a tricky business. Open the Yellow Pages to the building contractor section and the list goes on for pages. But the best builders don't need to advertise and you will generally discover them by word of mouth. For the past several years, readers of the Sydney Morning Herald's weekly home section, Domain, have been recommending tradespeople for the Quote Unquote column. So either use the list below, which comprises the top seven builders from the Domain's 1998 Tradespeople of the Year Awards (each received at least 5 independent votes), call the Master Builders Association on 9281 3511 or ask at any of the big suppliers. Always seek a minimum of three quotes, and remember that the lowest is not always the best.

Mark Boudib
Specialises in architecturally designed buildings and furniture, and small extensions. Trade licence 18223C.
- Ph 0417 284 919 or 9797 6073.

Allan Bridekirk
Works mainly on the North Shore and northern beaches doing alterations and additions. Trade licence 9512.
- Ph 9451 9405.

Chris Francis, William and Francis Building Services
Works on older-style renovations and detailing for them, making them as authentic as possible. Trade licence 59599C.
- Ph 0418 410 669.

Colin Hobson
Does all renovations and additions. Trade licence 7096.
- Ph 9498 1150 and 0418 463 079.

David Jones, DB&HE Building Services
Provides full design and quality service for difficult and specialised building projects. Trade licence 39900.
- Ph 9802 8364 or 0418 211 051.

Building contractors

John Pearce
Builds architectural style houses generally on the Central Coast, not a project home builder. Trade licence 18518.
- Ph 02 4334 7500 or 0415 367 352.

Bill White
Works in the Inner West doing carpentry, gyprocking, painting and extensions. Trade licence 39533.
- Ph 9560 0747 or 0418 285 728.

Penny Harrison

Building equipment

see also building materials, hardware

Got a little job to do in the house or garden, but can't remember where you left the bobcat or the cement mixer? Why not hire one? Or better still, buy a new one. The following have been recommended by some of Sydney's top tradespeople.

Kennards Hire
Open seven days a week, Kennards has a huge range of equipment for hire, everything from air compressors to witches hats, catering to tradespeople, businesses and home handypersons. Chainsaws, ladders, vans, hedge trimmers, air hammers, nail guns, bobcats – you name it, they've got it at 20 branches in the metropolitan area.
- Ph 9747 6788.

Wreckair Hire
Catering to everyone from major building contractors to tradespeople to handypersons, Wreckair can supply you with power tools, generators, scissor lifts and boom lifts, and just about anything you might need – if they don't have it, they will find it for you.
- Unit 6, 1-15 Wentworth Rd North, Homebush, ph 9746 3855. Also Mascot, Pyrmont and Wetherill Park.

Tool Tech Australia
Sell a full range of power tools, including chainsaws, compressors, generators and hand tools, plus spare parts and accessories. Tool Tech also offers a repair service and saw sharpening.
- 483 Forest Rd, Bexley, ph 9597 6855.

Parra Power Tools
Offers competitive prices on a large range of power tools, including specialised tools and machinery, and carries all the biggest brand names.
- 280 Parramatta Rd, Granville, ph 9637 9055. Also at Castle Hill.

Gasweld Discount Tool Centre
Provides power tools and machinery to industry, tradespeople and home users, offering a greater range and more specialised tools than most hardware stores. This is a good place to come if you're looking for heavy-duty angle grinders, brick-cutters, bandsaws, air compressors, nail guns, milling machines, welding equipment, as well as more everyday tools and hardware.
- 170 Sunnyholt Rd, Blacktown, ph 9671 3888.
  Also Granville, ph 9637 8188; Leichhardt, ph 9569 5544; Penrith, ph 4721 5838; Taren Point, ph 9524 0708.

Benjamin Long

Further information
- Sydney Building Information Centre, ph 9319 3000

Building materials

see also hardware, building equipment
There are a few choices to be had when it comes to hunting down building materials.

Building materials

You can head to one of the larger hardware stores, stocking everything from bricks and mortar to timber and nails, and just about everything else you need. Or you might head to a specialist supplier that deals only in, say, bricks or roofing. Alternatively, there are a number of recycled building material suppliers offering a cheaper, and more environmentally sound, source of everything from timber, tiles and bricks to windows, fireplaces and antique fittings. And don't forget to keep an eye on the auctions listed in Saturday's Sydney Morning Herald.

Sydney Building Information Centre
A good place to start if you're contemplating building or renovating. It offers a specialist bookshop, lectures and courses for owner-builders, and nine floors displaying a range of products for every aspect of home building – from floorboards to roof tiles and everything in between.
- 525 Elizabeth St, Surry Hills, ph 9319 3000.

Hudson Timber & Hardware
Not just timber, but tools, cement, doors, insulation, frames and trusses, fencing and decking, particleboard and plywood, flooring, angle bars, bricks, and all your regular hardware.
- 84 Smithfield Rd, Bonnyrigg, ph 9610 3144.
  Also at Brookvale, Castle Hill, Eastwood, Kirrawee, Leumeah and Penrith.

The Brick Pit
More bricks than you can poke a trowel at, including new and recycled bricks.
- Cnr Lane Cove and Fontenoy Rds, North Ryde, ph 9888 7888.

Annandale Timber
Specialises in mouldings, architraves and skirting boards, carrying a large range of traditional and contemporary styles. It also stocks an extensive range of exotic timber.
- 11-13 Frank St, Wetherill Park, ph 9604 1555.

Terrace House Factory Building Materials
Everything for the home renovator including second-hand windows, doors, timber, bathroom fittings, claw-foot baths, fireplaces, staircases, mouldings, cast-iron lace panels and plenty more besides.
- 304-308 Harris St, Ultimo, ph 9660 6768.

Second Hand Building Centre
With a hectare of recycled timber beams, floorboards, skirting boards, bench tops, staircases, doors, windows, corrugated iron, tiles and more, this is one of Sydney's largest demolition yards. On-site sawing and milling is available as are made-to-order French doors.
- 432b West Botany St, Rockdale, ph 9567 1322.

Gray Eisdell Timms Auctioneers & Valuers
Holds auctions of building equipment every second Tuesday. Generally this includes a good range of timber materials – floorboards, decking, lattice, treated pine, fencing posts – as well as paving, roofing, paints, windows and doors, kitchen fittings and tools. Prices are significantly cheaper than buying retail, though you may need to buy in bulk.
- 60 O'Connell St, Smithfield, ph 9609 2699.

Law's Auctions
Has timber auctions every Wednesday and usually stocks a great variety of timbers and timber products. It also auctions every Wednesday a number of other building materials – tiles, roofing, windows and doors. Check the Saturday *Sydney Morning Herald* for details.
- 21 Frank St, Wetherill Park, ph 9604 0588.

Benjamin Long

Bush food

see also Aboriginal Sydney

Progress is slow, and not particularly steady, but when bush foods hit the supermarket aisles, you know their time has come. Next we'll have native pepper on the table next to the ground bush tomato, ready to season our crocodile, emu and wallaby. Here's where to go hunter-gathering.

Blackwattle Deli

A very small range – paperbark, wattleseed, lemon myrtle and a few others – sits in the middle of this something-for-everyone deli, but it's a good start.
- Sydney Fish Market, cnr Pyrmont Bridge Rd and Bank St, Pyrmont, ph 9552 3591.

The Essential Ingredient

Not only is there a fascinating range of Australian bush foods at the E.I., there is plenty of information on hand for those lost in the bush, as well as relevant cook books, paperbark, jams, chutneys and native meat products.
- 6 Australia St, Camperdown, ph 9550 5477.

Bush Tucker Supply

Australia's biggest indigenous ingredient supplier is wholesale only, but you can access all its products as well as helpful information on its web site: www.bushtucker.com.au
- Ph 9817 1060.

Also available from **Five Star Gourmet** (13 Willoughby Rd, Crow's Nest, ph 9438 5666).

Paris International Cooking School

This lively cooking school holds Australian Bush Food Workshops in 12 languages, which is very handy for tourists, and those who want to know how to order munthari berries and quandong in Japanese or French.
- MCA Ticketing, ph 9873 3575.

Jill Dupleix

Further information
- Tukka: Real Australian Food by Jean-Paul Bruneteau (Harper Collins, $39.95)
- Wild Lime, Cooking from the bush food garden by Juleigh Robins (Allen & Unwin, $24.95)

Bushwalking

see also national parks, camping, guided tours

When Sydneysiders want to step out in the bush, they don't have to venture far from the city centre. Bush tracks within Sydney Harbour National Park – including the 10-kilometre scenic walkway from the Spit Bridge to Manly – give spectacular city views as well as a taste of the bush. Slightly further away from the city, but still within the metropolitan area are hundreds of kilometres of walking tracks catering for walkers of all ages and all levels of fitness. Most are especially attractive in spring, when wildflowers add bright splashes of colour to the landscape. Slightly further afield, try the Blue Mountains and Morton National Park, which offer walks ranging from easy to challenging.

Royal National Park

The 26-kilometre coast walk from Bundeena to Otford takes in headlands, beaches, swamps, heaths, woodlands and rainforest. Allow two days or tackle it in sections. There are also shorter options.
- Visitors Centre, Farnell Ave, Audley, ph 9542 0648.

Ku-ring-gai Chase National Park
Follow one of the many West Head walking tracks through the bush to the beach, or take the Sphinx-Warrimoo Track and view Aboriginal middens along Cowan Creek.
- Kalkari Visitors Centre, Ku-ring-gai Chase Rd, ph 9457 9853.

Bushwalking Clubs
No-one to walk with? Join a bushwalking club and make new friends as you discover the bush. The **NSW Confederation of Bushwalking Clubs** (ph 9548 1228) keeps a list of clubs and publishes *The Bushwalker*. The **Wilderness Society** (ph 9552 2355) also organises weekend walks.

Paddy Pallin
For short walks around Sydney, all you need are comfortable shoes and clothing, a hat, sunscreen and refreshments. For longer walks, this shop (and nearby adventure outfitters in Kent St's 'Adventure Alley') have excellent ranges of clothing and equipment and helpful, enthusiastic staff.
- 507 Kent St, City, ph 9264 2685.

Jenny Stanton

Further information
- NSW National Parks and Wildlife Service, ph 9585 6333: www.npws.nsw.gov.au
- Sydney Bushwalks by Neil Paton (Kangaroo Press, $12.95)

Business lunches

see also Steak
Who said the business lunch was dead? Certainly not the well-fed, well-heeled and well-informed types who prefer to wheel and deal over the lunch table rather than the boardroom table. Of course the business lunch isn't dead. The figures don't lie.

Banc
Even though it's no longer a bank, 53 Martin Place still plays an important role in keeping Sydney's big business rolling along. With its marble columns, bottomless wine cellar and confident stylish food from chef Liam Tomlin, the business lunch is not only alive, it's never looked better.
- 53 Martin Place, City, ph 9233 5300.

Bistro Pave
Business restaurants are supposed to be more about who's eating, rather than what they're eating. Fortunately nobody's told Colin Holt, who continues to turn out some of the most dramatic, meticulous and satisfying French food in town. Funny how business talk comes so much easier after a good duck confit or boudin noir.
- 181 Miller St, North Sydney, ph 9956 8583.

San Francisco Grill
What year is this anyway? No, you're not dreaming – the padded booths, roast beef trolley and crepes flamed at your tables are all very, very real. Throw in a great red wine and a little cheese for good measure, and you're more than ready for the world of increased overheads and tax concessions.
- Hilton International, 259 Pitt St, City, ph 9266 2000.

Ristorante Mario
You won't find the best Italian food in Sydney at this popular, socially acceptable lunchtime meeting place. But you will find some the best-known, most influential, famous and infamous movers and shakers in town. Prepare for much air kissing.
- 38 Yurong St, East Sydney, ph 9331 4945.

Terry Durack

Buskers

Sydney is kind to buskers. Hot summer days, balmy evenings and mild winters mean you can always catch singing, juggling, guitar strumming, didgeridoo blowing try-hards all over town. And the vexed question of payment? Truly pathetic talent should not be encouraged – avoid eye contact and keep your hands in your pockets. Reward good buskers with at least a $2 coin. Coins are the way to go – they can't blow away and make the right sort of satisfying chink when thrown into the hat.

If you'd like to study music so you too can busk away an evening, call the Conservatorium of Music on 9351 2222 for class schedules. Also a good spot to catch a free concert on Wednesdays and Fridays during the school term.

Kings Cross

The entrance to Kings Cross station is a favourite spot for buskers. You'll catch didgeridoo players vying for attention and often on a Saturday night there's a Christian group with guitars, singing and preaching to a bemused crowd of sinners. There's also a busking competition at the Kings Cross Carnival in the first weekend of November.

Martin Place

Every lunchtime there's a free concert at the Martin Place amphitheatre. Join office workers juggling sandwiches on their knees as they take in a little jazz or some African drumming. Always worth checking out, the quality here is high.

Circular Quay

Under a trial ban by the City of Sydney, buskers are no longer allowed to perform between Wharf Two and Wharf Seven, so you'll have to wander to the western edge of the Quay to catch fire-eaters, didgeridoo players, stilt-walkers, jugglers, mime artists and the occasional saxophone player.

The Rocks

Every weekend, there are scores of musicians busking at The Rocks markets. The top end of George St is closed to traffic and there are more than 150 stalls set up with musicians playing throughout.

The tunnel between Central Station and Broadway

The best place to avoid. Attracted by the tunnel's excellent acoustics, it seems this spot pulls in the city's most tragic musicians. And you're trapped. Walk briskly, hum loudly and turn your Walkman up.

Cerentha Harris

Cabaret

see also nightclubs

Cabaret, that form of theatre designed to be enjoyed with a glass of something refreshing in hand, is in a difficult patch in Sydney at the moment. Chanteuses, talented groups and an audience abound—the problem is finding somewhere intimate to put them all. This is partly due to the closure in 1997 of Sydney's cabaret institution, the Tilbury Hotel. Founded and run by Michael Freundt and Geoffrey Williams in beautiful downtown Woolloomooloo, the Tilbury invented not just its own style of cabaret (sassy, smutty and silly) but also generated a loyal audience – who these days spend their time haunting old CD shops, waiting for this particular performance void to be filled. Rumours continue to float around town about one of the Tilbury Boys doing cabaret again in the embrace of an international hotel. It may have happened by the time you read this. At the time of writing,

Sydney has only three permanent cabaret nights, and only one purpose-built cabaret venue. However, most of Sydney's arts festivals have a cabaret component. Try the Sydney Festival in January, the Sydney Gay and Lesbian Mardi Gras Festival in February – especially its late-night cavalcade of extremities cLUB bENT – and the Olympics Arts festivals.

Sorlies
Attached to the Glen St Theatre, the acts range across the usual cabaret fare, with a lot of artists using Sorlies as a place to try out their new Adelaide/Edinburgh Festival show. The food's OK but the atmosphere – a reddish 1970s box – leaves much to be desired.
■ Cnr Glen St and Blackbutts Rd, Frenchs Forest, ph 9975 1455.

The Stables On Sundays
A special Sunday-night-only gig in the venerable Stables theatre. The space (and the crowd) seem to favour the more serious 'singer and song' style. Certainly some of Australia's best vocalists pop up here from time to time.
■ Nimrod St, Kings Cross, ph 9361 3817.

Showroom
The newest and most upmarket of the venues is at the Star City pokie palace. It's a 900-seat semicircle of cabaret glam, with acts ranging from the OS famed (Tom Jones, Tony Bennett) to the peculiarly local (Carlotta and Les Girls). Prices, ranging from the reasonable to the astronomic, depend on the show.
■ Star City, 80 Pyrmont St, Pyrmont, ph 9700 9000.

Marrickville RSL
At the lower end of the spectrum, many of the beer barns in Sydney's clubland have live entertainment. This is the most famed, boasting the world's richest popular singing prize ($75,000 for coming first) and live entertainment seven nights a week. Expect Elvis impersonators, accordion masters and well-groomed girls sucking on Celine Dion. But at least it's free, and the drinks are cheap.
■ 359 Illawarra Rd, Marrickville, ph 9559 1555.

Stephen Dunne

Cafes

Coffee has been with us in Sydney for 200 years but a powerful espresso and a crunchy rosetta stuffed with artichokes was a tall order until 1957, when Luigi Coluzzi opened his first coffee bar on William St. The idea took time to catch on. Through the '60s and '70s, the local cafe was a milk bar with an ill-used espresso machine at best. Then, in the '80s, cafes multiplied like bank loans and today we drink thick, aromatic espresso like residents of any other cosmopolitan city (Melbourne, for instance).

The search for a great cafe is not the challenge it was in 1957 – nor is it entirely dictated by the quality of the coffee. Feel comfortable perched on a milk crate on Victoria St? Prefer a faux Philipe Stark fitout or a cane armchair and a view across sparkling blue water to the Heads? Want to team your coffee with pumpkin risotto or ricotta hotcakes? Sydney has the lot. Sydney also has a handful of baristas who make a near perfect cup of coffee.

A&P Sulfaro
Sydney's best custard horns are stacked in shop-length cabinets with rare Italian pastries. At Christmas, boxes of panettone are piled nearly to the ceiling. Homemade gelato comes in dozens of flavours and pretty semifreddi. At a couple of stools in the far corner of the shop, chic Italian couples sip good, strong Vittoria coffee.
■ 119 Ramsay St, Haberfield, ph 9797 0001.

Cafes

Bar Coluzzi
The Coluzzi family's original Victoria St institution still serves up some of Sydney's best coffee (Robert Timms special blend) to night shift nurses heading home at sunrise, barristers on bicycles and Darlinghurst intelligentsia. Good focaccia and Turkish bread with cured-on-the-premises Italian fillings and eccentric boxing memorabilia on the four small walls.
- 322 Victoria St, Darlinghurst, ph 9380 5420.

Bar Italia
Local kids line up the at the gelato bar for legendary homemade flavours. Leichhardt home renovators stagger in at about eight for life sustaining bowls of pasta. Old Italian guys shoot the breeze over laminex tables and short, aromatic Vittoria coffees. A Sydney institution.
- 169 Norton St, Leichhardt, ph 9560 9981.

bills
bills 1 is all sunshine, white walls, big bowls of fruit, farmhouse kitchen; bills 2 goes the post-mod metallic route but delivers the same great breakfasts (golden ricotta hotcakes served with honeycomb butter, stupendous, fluffy scrambled eggs). Best of all, bills 2 opens for dinner with chic, light meals like soy glazed salmon sitting high on a bed of coriander noodles and crunchy pepper crusted tuna salad. Phenomenal mashed potato. Great Grinders coffee.
- bills 1, 433 Liverpool St, Darlinghurst, ph 9360 9631; bills 2, 355 Crown St, Surry Hills, ph 9360 4762.

Caffe Italia
Big Italian families waiting for Nonna's Alitalia flight rub shoulders with yuppies en route to Heathrow or JFK. They're here (as opposed to the burger barn with the runway view) for good Grinders coffee, housemade Italian snacks like pizzetta, frittata or arancini, crusty panini and Italian cakes.
- Shop 23, International Terminal, Sydney Airport, Mascot, ph 9669 6434.

Direction of Cure
Locals and daytrippers stop by Philippa White's cosy, sunsplashed cafe for homeopathic remedies or medicinal teas and indulge in cups of strong Lavazza coffee, raspberry and almond tarts, sticky chocolate and walnut fudge and plates of oat cakes served with crumbly, smelly slices of Mersey cheese.
- 23a Burnie St, Clovelly, ph 9665 5244.

Moran's Cafe
White paint, dark wood furniture, eccentric takes on Mount Fuji on the walls, terrific attitude-free service (regulars' drinks arrive as if by magic with their menus) plus the cafe shares its kitchen with Moran's much lauded restaurant next door. The coffee is a rich, aromatic Segafredo and locals have been known to eat three meals a day here.
- 61-63 Macleay St (enter via Challis Ave), Potts Point, ph 9356 2223.

Samantha Trenoweth

Camping & caravans

see also national parks
Big cities are not usually synonymous with camping and caravan parks, but Sydney has a couple of spots that are as popular with locals trying to get away from it all as they are with visitors. Several caravan parks provide grassy tent sites, hot showers and other amenities for campers looking for a budget base from which to explore the city. Sydney is also a good place to buy or hire camping equipment for an around-Australia trip. And for those

who want to get away from it all, and take it all with them at the same time? Consider the caravan. All you need is a car with a strong engine (preferably a V8) and you've got the best of both worlds – the freedom of camping and the comfort (well, almost) of a hotel.

The Basin

Camp on the shores of Pittwater in Ku-ring-gai Chase National Park and fish, swim or relax in one of Sydney's most idyllic spots. Access is by ferry from Palm Beach or on foot along a 4 km track, so travel light. Booking essential.
- Ph 9972 7378.

Bonnie Vale

Accessible by car and popular with families, this site overlooks a safe swimming beach and is perfect for exploring the Royal National Park. Bushwalkers can also camp, by permit, elsewhere in the park and in neighbouring Heathcote. Bookings essential.
- Off Bundeena Drive, ph 9542 0648.

East's Lane Cove River Van Village

Finding a caravan park in Sydney is not an easy task, but this one, in a scenic and leafy location, is just 10 minutes from the Harbour Bridge. You can park your own van for a minimal fee, or stay in one of the units and cabins.
- Plassey Rd, North Ryde,
  ph 9805 0500.

Also try **Lakeside** (ph 9913 7845) at Narrabeen and to the south **Silver Beach** (ph 9668 8215) at Kurnell.

NSW Caravan, Camping and 4WD Supershow

Held every year in April at Rosehill Racecourse, this is the place to check out the latest and greatest in caravan and campervan equipment.
- Rosehill Racecourse, Rosehill,
  ph 9633 9377.

Fulchers Caravans

In the business for 25 years, Fulchers has a large range of new and used caravans, campers and pop-tops for sale, including brand names such as Statesman, Windsor and Camp-O-Matic.
- 395-397 Great Western Highway,
  Wentworthville, ph 9688 2999.

Frontline Camper Conversions

Specialises in campervan conversions and can turn your van or four-wheel-drive into a mobile home. Frontline also sells and rents new and used campervans and motorhomes.
- 128 Parramatta Rd, Croydon,
  ph 9715 1166.

Caravan Accessories

A caravan supermarket with more than 8,000 items in stock. Everything you need for your caravan including spare parts, generators, LP gas equipment, portable toilets, air conditioners, awnings, stoves, fridges and more.
- Cnr Rocky Point Rd and Shaw St,
  Kogarah, ph 9587 4599.

Boots Great Outdoors

Has a great range of goods for car-based camping.
- 82 Parramatta Rd, Lidcombe,
  ph 9647 1488; 19 Stoddart Rd,
  Prospect, ph 9636 9266.

Also **Kangaroo Tent City** at Camperdown (ph 9519 1011) and **Barbeques Galore** branches (ph 13 1254 for details). For lightweight equipment for bushwalking, try **Paddy Pallin** (ph 9264 2685).

Benjamin Long and Jenny Stanton

Further information
- NSW National Parks and Wildlife Service, ph 9585 6333
- Caravan and Camping Association of NSW, ph 9637 0599
- NRMA Sydney Central and Greater

Western Sydney Holiday Guide ($10, free to NRMA members), ph 132 132

Canoeing & kayaking

see also rowing, adventure & extreme sports

Does a gentle paddle down a shady river sound like a relaxing weekend pastime? Is the adrenaline rush of zooming down a slalom course more your style? Or perhaps some sightseeing from a sea kayak appeals? Sydney's waterways are an integral part of the city's outdoor lifestyle, so consider taking a fresh view of them from inside a canoe. Best of all, you don't have to be an Olympic gold medallist to enjoy the simple pleasures of paddling. It's easy to hire equipment for a fun afternoon with the family and there is no shortage of lakes, estuaries and rivers to try. Canoeing encompasses a range of craft from canoes (one blade on paddle), kayaks (two blades), dragon boats, outrigger canoes, surf skis and sit-on-tops, and all can be mastered by the recreational paddler. Just be sure to pick a calm day, unless wave jumping and water dunking are part of your plans.

Narrabeen Lake

You won't be lonely canoeing here. NSW's elite kayakers, such as Olympian Shelley Oates, are based at the NSW Academy of Sport facility on Wakehurst Parkway and train here daily. Not only is this area scenic, but you might pick up some tips. For sales, hire and tuition, try **Pro Kayaks**, located at Narrabeen Lake (ph 9970 7020).

Natural Wanders

One of the most popular forms of recreational canoeing in Sydney is sea kayaking. Although traditionally fitted out for ocean paddling, the long, relatively stable sea kayak is perfect for taking in the scenery on open-water estuaries, such as Port Hacking, Sydney Harbour, the Hawkesbury river and Pittwater. This company offers sea kayak tours on Sydney Harbour.
■ Ph 9555 9788.

NSW Canoe Association

Improve your paddling with expert instruction from instructors. Two-day basic skills training courses are available and cost $185. There is a 10 per cent discount for groups of six or more people.
■ Ph 9660 4597.

Canoe polo

For something completely different, try this game – something like water polo played by five-person teams in canoes, usually in indoor swimming pools. Call the NSW Canoe Association (see above) for clubs and other details.

Sydney International Regatta Centre

The Olympic home of canoeing, both sprint and slalom. The sprint course is already completed and in regular use; the 300m rock and concrete-lined slalom course is due for completion late in 1998. While hard-nosed white-water canoeing enthusiasts head north to the Nymboida River, near Coffs Harbour, for rapids, the artificial slalom course here – complete with movable obstacles and variable water flow rates – will be open to recreational paddlers, as well as elite athletes.
■ Castlereagh Rd, Penrith, ph 02 4730 6790.

Southern Sea Adventures

After exploring Sydney's waterways, holidayers can head out of town and enjoy sea kayaking at places such as Cairns, Hinchinbrook Island and Yasawa Islands in Fiji on trips organised by this company.
■ Ph 02 6653 4815.

Heather Quinlan

Car hire

see also drives

Things get tricky with car rental. When renting, make sure that you check all of the rules and regulations pertaining to the company you choose. For example, payment for insurance and excess kilometres is common, yet not always the case. Always check for special deals. The big international companies – Avis, Budget, Hertz, Thrifty, etc. – are all in Sydney. Following are a few of the best that offer something a little different.

Discount Car and Truck Hire

With sites in the City and Bondi Junction, Discount Car and Truck Hire could be ideal for holiday-makers. It offers five different types of new cars – mainly from the Toyota range – at decent rates. It's less if you hire for more than five days. Insurance included and the first 100 kilometres are free.
- 204 Oxford St, Bondi Junction, ph 9389 7377.

Kings Cross Rent-A-Car

One of the cheapest deals in Sydney, offering a range from small hatches to large station wagons, plus mini-buses seating up to 11 people.
- 169 William St, Kings Cross, ph 9361 0699.

European Hire Cars

Acclaimed as Sydney's most professional and widely used chauffeur service, European Hire Cars has a fleet of 20 cars. Mercedes-Benz cars are available for general hire or weddings, where trimmings of ribbons, red carpet and champagne are included. Rolls Royces are used for weddings only, as is the red Ferrari convertible.
- 6-8 Waterloo St, Rozelle, ph 9555 7677.

All Districts Limousines

They offer personal chauffeurs for any amount of time, for any car you choose – yours, perhaps!
- 70-72 Park Rd, Homebush, ph 9746 8999.

The Chookmobile 'Limo' Act

A comedy act on wheels that will go through a whole load of wacky routines on the way from A to B.
- Ph 9906 2350.

Andrew Khedoori

Carpenters & cabinetmakers

see also building contractors, furniture

Fine timberwork and joinery are the details that lift a run-of-the-mill renovation into a work of art. The following carpenters and cabinetmakers received numerous nominations for the Sydney Morning Herald's 1998 Tradespeople of the Year awards, run by the weekly home section Domain. Satisfied clients emphasised their meticulous attention to detail, creative design skills and superior craftsmanship. An example of beautifully crafted furniture is worth a thousand words of recommendation but the Master Builders Association also suggests checking a tradesperson's licence with the Department of Fair Trading, getting at least three quotes and seeking references from previous clients. You can call the MBA for a recommended carpenter on 9281 3511.

Derek Chan Dekka Designs

Specialises in quality and budget kitchens, individually designed furniture and picture framing. Trade licence R91269.
- Ph 9529 7359 or 0414 585 753.

Carpenters & cabinetmakers

Mark Fitzroy
Specialises in kitchens and internal household cabinetry, including custom-made furniture. Trade licence 69601C.
- Ph 9905 4468 or 0418 968 618.

Amos Groth APG Designs
Makers of hand-crafted, fitted furniture, individually designed in contemporary and period styles. Includes bookcases, television and stereo cabinets, libraries, wall panelling, etc. Trade licence 45617C.
- Ph 9907 1256 or 0419 408 988.

Stuart and Cameron Reid
The Reid Brothers design and make fine traditional and contemporary furniture to order, including fully fitted timber panelling and cabinets.
- Ph 02 4883 6788 or 019 980 880.

David Smith
Anything, Anywhere, Anytime Builder and Carpenter . . . the name of the business says it all. Trade licence 11653C.
- Ph 0412 094 054.

Jorma Tahka
Restoration work on old buildings, repairing damaged timber, joinery, kitchens, installing new work in authentic style. Trade licence 04051.
- Ph 014 612 526 or 9958 6461.

Wayne Thorpe
Specialises more in cabinet-making than carpentry. Kitchens and custom-built furniture, antique restoration. Trade Licence 21798C.
- Ph 02 4576 1516 or 015 212 269.

Steve Forbes
Specialises in residential and second-storey extensions. Does a lot of work for owner builders. Trade licence 45207C.
- Ph 9498 7442 or 0419 803 430.

Penny Harrison

Carpets & floor covering

see also rugs
Our homes might be simpler than ever before, but the floor is still one of the areas where we can make an impact. Sydney's love affair with sisal and coir goes on, but there are alternatives. From wool carpet to vinyl that simulates timber, you can find it all here. Colours, textures and patterns depend on trends, your house and personal preference.

Amtico Studio
Amtico vinyl looks like timber parquetry. It's the Mercedes Benz of vinyl floor coverings and it doesn't come cheap but it's low maintenance, easy to install and highly durable.
- 86-88 Dickson Ave, Artarmon, ph 9901 4199.

Commercial and Domestic Flooring
Don't expect frills, just a dazzling array of vinyl and linoleum floorcoverings at affordable prices.
- 56 Macpherson St, Waverley, ph 9389 6059.

Hamilton Beach
This family business has been around for 55 years quietly selling some of the most luxurious wool carpets in Sydney. Can custom-dye carpet any colour from a small swatch.
- 9 Transvaal Ave, Double Bay, ph 9363 1361.

Natural Floorcovering Centre
Best range of coir, sisal and jute floorcoverings in Sydney with everything from Chinese latex-backed sisal to black weft flatwoven seagrass and Belgian sisal in biscuit hues.
- 5 Salisbury Rd, Stanmore, ph 9569 6999.

Premier Carpets
Premier has been in business since 1966 selling a full range of carpet, sisal and coir. The

Premier Weave in stone, celadon and piper (sand) is a perennial favourite. Owner John Osborne will happily custom-make to order.
- 525 Botany Rd, Waterloo, ph 9310 4455.

Melissa Walker Smith

Catering

see also party supplies, event management

Sydney knows how to party. And Sydney caterers know how to help them, whether it's a table for two in a special location, or a masked ball for 500. These days, catering is not just about food, but about hospitality, freshness, generosity, surprises and service.

Rockpool Catering
The first time you tuck in to Rockpool Catering food is a revelation. 'Aaah, so you can feed 200 people as well as you can one,' you cry, with your mouth full. The catering division of Neil Perry's Rockpool restaurant is all about fresh, simple, food, clever ideas and smart service.
- 107 George St, The Rocks, ph 9252 1888.

Juste Nous Catering
The award-winning Norma Willis has never dropped the ball – or the canape – in her 21 years of catering. Now she's in demand from Tokyo to New York, but can still do a fab party for 10 in Pott's Point without blinking.
- 64 Cameron St, Edgecliff, ph 9211 5819.

Belinda Franks' Catering
Belinda Franks makes a point of avoiding the cliché and gives you simple, stylish cooking based on excellent produce and fresh ideas. The hallmark of a good caterer is flexibility, and she can turn her hand from a small romantic to a large corporate whizzbang, with ease.
- Shop 8, 19-23 O'Brien St, Bondi, ph 9365 1299.

Culinary Edge
Their food has starred at the wedding of Baz Luhrmann and Catherine Martin, launched *Oscar and Lucinda*, and kept Diana Ross (Miss Ross, if you please) fuelled between shows. Richard Brown and Charles Wilkins love robust flavours and stylish cocktail food, and have the industry experience to put it together seamlessly.
- 13 Ramsay Rd, Five Dock, ph 9713 2322.

The Truffle Group
'From two to too many' is the motto for Tom Rutherford's Truffle Group. There is no chance of a boring function, as they will always come up with a little twist on tradition or a cute idea to add freshness to flavour.
- 19-21 Larkin St, Camperdown, ph 9557 8822.

The Mode Group
A high-profile catering group headed by Paul Clarke and Peter McCoskey of Taylor Square's hip Canteen restaurant and bar, with lots of energy and ideas and some of the best venues in town: the Art Gallery of NSW and the Sydney Town Hall among them.
- 129 Cathedral St, Woolloomooloo, ph 9326 9933.

Darren Taylor Catering
Will provide a full-scale, no-fuss, serious picnic for 24 people or more.
- Ph 9332 4415

Jill Dupleix

Charities

see also volunteering, activism

As the scale of human suffering in the world rises dramatically, and the welfare state retreats, the work of aid organisations and charities has never been more crucial. Sydney

Charities

has a number of extremely well-run charities which consume very little in administration and provide tremendous support to people in need, both here and abroad.

The Exodus Foundation
At a free restaurant at the Ashfield Uniting Church, the Reverend Bill Crews has provided more than 500,000 meals to those in need over the past six years. Three tonnes of food packages are distributed to families each week, as well as relief funds for rent and medical bills.
- 180 Liverpool Rd, Ashfield, ph 9799 2811.

Community Aid Abroad
This charity's strength is that it gives not 'patch-up' but self-help aid. It sends about $12 million a year overseas to hundreds of projects designed to help villagers break out of the crippling cycle of poverty and dependency. CAA shops and mail order sell handcrafts and foods produced in developing countries. The major focus of its work is in South and South-East Asia and Africa.
- Level 2, 16-22 Wentworth Ave, Surry Hills, ph 9264 1399.

APHEDA
The Australian People for Health, Education and Development Abroad has the direct support of more than 90 unions. Its strong links with labour organisations mean funds go directly to specific community projects. The aim is to engender professional and professional skills and knowledge in communities abroad, particularly the Middle East.
- Trades Hall Building, 4 Goulburn St, Haymarket, ph 9264 9343.

The Smith Family
The focus here is shifting from crisis services to education. Under the revamped Learning for Life scholarships, children will be eligible from primary to tertiary education and receive financial assistance.
- 16 Larkin St, Camperdown, ph 9550 4422.

United Way
Conducts fundraising programs for the benefit of a wide group of health and welfare agencies, and provides volunteers for many of their services – most of the work is performed by volunteers and with minimal administration costs. Of the funds you contribute, 90 per cent is distributed to beneficiary agencies.
- GPO Box 4083, City, ph 9299 5507.

Sydney City Mission
The biggest private trainer of unemployed people in Australia. Job placement has been one of the Mission's many success stories. It also offers telephone counselling, crisis services and accommodation, particularly for women.
- 4-10 Campbell St, City, ph 9219 2000.

Ali Gripper

Cheese

see also delicatessens
Overseas visitors are pleasantly surprised when they realise Sydney has a cheese culture as well as a surf culture, with tremendous blues, sheep's milk and goat's milk cheeses, washed rinds and fresh styles as well. Sydney also leads Australia in cheese trolleys, a recent but long overdue innovation. Enjoy cheese displayed in full splendour from **Banc** (53 Martin Place, City, ph 9233 5300) and **Pavilion on the Park** (1 Art Gallery Rd, The Domain, ph 9232 1322). And watch out for the Sydney Morning Herald's annual cheese show at the Regent Hotel. Held each October, it offers the chance to meet Australia's leading quality cheesemakers and taste their latest creations (inquiries: ph 9238 0000). Sydney's best cheese shops include the following.

Simon Johnson Purveyor of Quality Foods

Sydney's leading cheese emporium, with the best from here and overseas in walk-in, temperature-controlled conditions. Don't leave without Kervella goat's cheese or the Heidi gruyere, two of Australia's benchmark cheeses.
■ 181 Harris St, Pyrmont, ph 9552 2522.

Victoire

A good, neat range, with accompanying delicacies such as Maggie Beer's quince pate, perfect with a snowy goat's cheese. This is also one of Sydney's leading bakeries, so buy a sour dough baguette for your slice of nice, runny brie.
■ 285 Darling St, Balmain, ph 9818 5529.

jones the grocer

There are regular cheese tastings from an impressive range, including the latest fresh sheep's milkcurds and blues. Try anything from Meredith Dairy in Victoria.
■ 68 Moncur St, Woollahra,
   ph 9362 1222.

The Cheese Shop

Known for its friendly, personal service, this outlet offers the best range of cheeses on the North Shore. Sample one of their cheddars or blue cheeses.
■ 797 Military Rd, Mosman,
   ph 9969 4469.

Nicole Lehmann

Children's entertainment

Don't believe all the doomsayers. Kids are incredibly easy to keep entertained. Only dogs are easier. With them, you either take off to the nearest park and throw sticks around, you do cat-meowing imitations, or you wave your hand back and forth really quickly across their line of vision. That keeps them busy for hours. Kids are slightly more sophisticated. Thankfully, Sydney is that perfect mix of sensory overload and natural wonder. You can stick the kids in any number of indoor venues, museums or theatrical events, and you can take advantage of the great outdoors.

Many city parents these days bemoan the fact that, 'when I was your age, living in the country, we'd disappear after breakfast and mum wouldn't see us until dinner time'. Parenting is a little more hands-on in this day and age. Therefore, it's important to pick entertainment that isn't going to make the parent bilious. Naturally, every once in a while you're going to have to put up with a concert by visiting celebrity purple dinosaurs. A motion-sickness tablet, taken two hours before the performance, should cure queasy adult stomachs for this one.

So, you're in Sydney, Australia's largest slab of cement and humanity. What do you do?

Ride horses, naturally. **Centennial Park**, that huge hunk of green at the city centre, is much more than just a venue for hideously fit people wearing lurid skintight pants to roller-blade in. You can check out the ponds, the ducks and the horrible eels from the safety of horseback. The Centennial Park Horse Hire and Riding School can be contacted on 9361 4513.

Or, if you're a little more adventurous, you can head to **Maroubra**, where trail rides follow the gorgeous coastline. Be warned, though. The riding school is very close to a rifle range. If you're prepared, it's terrific fun to watch the riders take cover when the guns start popping. The horses are used to the noise and make no move at all. It's just the dorks on top who suddenly think they're in a John Wayne film. A one-hour trail ride at Maroubra costs $25.

All ages and sizes are catered for, although kids should really be over five. If they've never ridden or lack confidence, their ponies will be taken on a lead.

Children's entertainment

Gumption, too, is needed at the city's major theme park, **Australia's Wonderland**. Here, rides have been designed to frighten adults just as much as the small fry. The Demon, with its terrifying loop – going both forwards and backwards – even goes to the trouble of taking photographs of you in mid-scream. These, and all negatives, should be bought and immediately destroyed. Likewise, the newest attraction – the Space Probe 7, in which you essentially free-fall from 23 stories at 120kmh – has mercifully long queues, so you can tell your kids it's the delay that's stopping you having a go, rather than your cowardice. The small children's section of Australia's Wonderland is highly recommended, though, as is the giant water slide. A tip, here: don't give the slide a go while wearing Speedos. By the time you've hit the pool at the bottom, most of your swimwear will have gone painfully north.

Australias Wonderland is at Wallgrove Rd, Eastern Creek, ph 9830 9100. Adults $31.95; 4-12 years $21.95.

The animals at **Taronga Zoo** get to hang out on some of Sydneys best real estate. They've got sweeping views across the Harbour to the city, have the perfect spot to watch any fireworks spectacular, and enjoy plenty of open spaces. Visitors to their domain can enjoy the spot just as well, and there's no better bonding than having your kid say 'geez, daddy, that ape looks just like you'. The seal show – balancing balls on noses, eating fish, you know the pattern – is a favourite among children. Night openings of the zoo, which occur sometimes, are stunning. Taronga Zoo is at Bradley Head Road, Mosman, ph 9969 2777. Adults $15, concession $9, children $7.50.

Sydney's film strip will throw up the regular attractions for children, particularly in school holiday time. It's also close to **Chinatown**, where restaurants are loud, lively and very child-friendly. These are the places where a parent who walks in with kids doesn't bring the conversation and music to a complete stop, with diners looking down their noses as if you've ridden in on a stolen yak.

But for a more compelling film experience, check out the **IMAX theatre** in Darling Harbour. Its giant screen is the home for fantastic visuals (again, watch out for motion sickness), especially if a 3D presentation is happening. They're fabbo.

From here, you are in striking distance of most activities in **Darling Harbour** – a centre that is developing a lively soul after a scratchy beginning. You can take your kids to the giant games arcade that is Sega World and watch your wallet lose weight quicker than a bulimic actress. Then, if your purse is still looking a bit chubby, you can farm the kids out and visit the Star City casino.

Good luck.

Tony Squires

Childrenswear

see also streetwear, baby supplies

Teensy overalls, bold stars and stripes, hardy cottons and bright colour, all tied together with the cute-as-a-button tag: Sydney's childrenswear stores have all price ranges covered from mini versions of the international designer labels Mum wears, to longlasting Australian-made goodies.

Bonza Brats

This is almost your department store for kidswear. For babies up to size 14 is a large selection of local labels including Gumboots, Fred Bare, Scooter, Marquise, Freidelle, Uh-Oh, and French labels Confetti, Absorba and Petit Bateau. A large range of accessories, novelties and toys, as well as a separate shoe store at Mosman should just about have it covered.

■ 715 Military Rd, Mosman,
   ph 9968 1390. Also at Northbridge,
   ph 9958 4702; Gordon, ph 9418 2046;
   Dural, ph 9651 4343.

Childrenswear

Homegrown
Double Bay's designing mums recently came back to the job after a small rest from retail to continue with their signature black and white range, sweet gerbera hair twists and floral Alice bands that have attracted the likes of Paula Yates, Fergie, Jerry Hall, Nicole Kidman and Jack Nicholson in the past. Labels include Homegrown, Hot Tuna, and shoes by Doc Martens, Converse, and Keds.
- Shop 29, The Ritz Carlton Promenade, Cross St, Double Bay, ph 9328 7699.

Esprit Kids
Sporty weekend and casual wear plus shoes and accessories for boys and girls. The three ranges cater for Baby (6 to 24 months), Mini (sizes 3 to 6) and Big Kids (in sizes 8 to 14).
- Shop 222, Westfield Shoppingtown, 1 Anderson St, Chatswood, ph 9413 3426; Shop 141, Eastgardens Westfield Shoppingtown, 152 Bunnerong Rd, Pagewood, ph 9314 0787.

The House of Maxwell Mouse
Irresistible import clothes with impeccable attention to detail. Look out for cute co-ordinating accessories, like headbands to match dresses, and hats to match skirts and pants. French label's Catimini, Jean Bourget, Kenzo, Chipie, Les Robes, Dutch label Oilily, and Italian label Moschino covering ages newborn to 14 years, for boys and girls.
- 111 Queen St, Woollahra, ph 9328 6613.

Bow Blue
Wander through these adjoining stores with babywear in shop 3 at the front, to childrenswear, from ages 2 to 12 for boys and girls at the back which house French import labels like Kenzo, Elle, Naf Naf, and Confetti, and local labels Hiawatha and Mini Haha, Mambo and Freidelle. The store caters to a variety of price ranges. Look also for handmade dolls, bunny rugs, fairy dresses and made-to-order dolls houses.
- Shops 3 and 4, 74 Castlereagh St, City, ph 9231 5155.

Osh Kosh B'gosh
This American-based label, franchised in Australia 10 years ago, is known for its hardy, longlasting garments, and cute toddler overalls called Bongo's. Catering from 3 months up to size 12, the range also includes sun hats, swimwear with UVF 50, underwear, socks, and headbands, as well as a childrens shoes at the Mosman and QVB stores.
- Shop 22, Ground Floor, Queen Victoria Building, ph 9267 6187. Also at Mosman, ph 9968 2249; Warringah Mall, ph 9939 1640; Miranda, ph 9524 1431; Parramatta, ph 9893 7528; Bondi Junction, ph 9389 8970; Chatswood Chase, ph 9415 4833.

Gumboots
For 15 years this Australian made and designed label has been dressing boys and girls in hard-wearing, easy-care garments in signature bold colours, and their well-known star prints. The titles of the ranges that are divided into age are nearly as cute as the clothes; Gu-Gum (for new born to 9 months), GumGum (6 months to 2 years for girls and boys) and Gumboots (sizes 2 to 14), with labels GBG for girls and Woody for the boys.
- 740A Military Rd, Mosman, ph 9960 7420.

Fragile Maternity Wear and Kids
Colourful import kidswear, including Dries Van Noten, Paul Smith, Diesel, Bill Tornade, top quality cotton and wool knits from Belgian label Da-da, and look out for a startling new W&LT kids line for winter 1999. The store also has its own label maternity wear, for those who want to stay fashiony not frumpy, Baby Workshop cosmetics tailored especially for kids, and Baby Touch, Bees Knee's and New Born Necessities linen.
- 76a Paddington St, Paddington, ph 9362 0085. You can select stock at Mosman Fragile, ph 9969 0333.

Felicity Ward

Chinese restaurants

see also Chinese Sydney, yum cha

From Beijing in the north to Guangdong in the south, China offers an exciting variety of cuisines that go way beyond sweet and sour pork and lemon chicken. From Pymble in the north to Blakehurst in the south, Sydney offers exactly the same thing.

Chequers

Hidden away in shop-till-you-drop Chatswood, this smoothly run restaurant is pure Hong Kong with its fish tanks, glamorous marble and daily yum cha. Many of the really special specials are written only in Chinese, but show enough interest, and your waiter will happily translate.

■ Level 2, Mandarin Centre, 65 Albert Ave, Chatswood, ph 9904 8388.

Golden Century

One of the world's great Cantonese seafood restaurants is smack dab in the middle of Sydney's Chinatown. Don't expect frills. Do expect fabulously fresh fish. For a special treat try the king crab cooked three ways and, after 10pm, relax with a suppertime bowl of rice congee.

■ 393-399 Sussex St, Haymarket, ph 9212 3901

Golden Kingdom

When motels boast that they offer 'all mod cons', they don't usually include a top-rate Northern Chinese restaurant. But that's just what this Kensington motel offers. Try the wonderful hand-pulled noodles, the silky Shanghai won ton soup and the spicy picnic chicken.

■ 147 Anzac Pde, Kensington, ph 9662 1616.

Imperial Peking Blakehurst

If you're looking for the best Peking duck in Sydney, make the pilgrimage south to Blakehurst. In spite of its modern exterior, the feeling inside the restaurant is authentic and eye-catching, as is the food, from drunken chicken to hand-pulled noodles.

■ 979 King Georges Rd, Blakehurst, ph 9546 6122.

Kam Fook

Sydney's biggest Chinese restaurant, this 800-seater turns on the city's best yum cha by day and superbly crafted Cantonese banquets by night. The two giant shark's fins at the door give you a fair idea of the restaurant's specialty but everything is good from roast duck to claypots.

■ Level 3, Market City, 9-13 Hay St, Haymarket, ph 9211 8988.

Marigold Citymark

A marble-clad, two-storey monument to great Chinese eating. By day it is as busy as a crowded railway station, while at night the feel is more mellow and measured. Don't miss the Cantonese roast duck or the dried scallop and braised melon claypot.

■ Levels 4 & 5, 683-689 George St, Haymarket, ph 9281 3388.

Peking Inn

Somehow, it seems only fitting that a northern Sydney suburb should be home to some of the finest Northern Chinese food. Specialties include the highly flavoured and often fiery delights of Shanghai, Hunan, Peking and Sichuan. Try the mixed cold platter and the crispy Sichuan duck.

■ 390 Pacific Highway, Lindfield, ph 9416 3509.

Sea Treasure

This is not your average suburban Chinese restaurant by any means, as will become obvious when you try the whole fish, crab or prawns, straight from the tanks. Manager Ying

Tam is a warm and welcoming host. Leap upon anything he suggests.
- 46 Willoughby Rd, Crows Nest, ph 9906 6388.

Terry Durack

Chinese Sydney

see also Chinese restaurants, yum cha

Legend has it the first Chinese to arrive in Sydney were two cooks on the First Fleet in 1788. However, city records show the first registered Chinaman, Mak Sai Ying, didn't get here until 1818. Whichever version you believe, there is no denying the Chinese – Australia's oldest non-European migrant group – have made an indelible mark on Sydney: from the corridors of power in Macquarie Street, to the corridors of the city's most popular restaurants, Chinese Australians have emerged as some of Sydney's most engaging personalities, politicians and prominent restaurateurs. They include NSW Ombudsman Irene Moss, the Deputy Lord Mayor of Sydney, Mr Henry Tsang, late heart surgeon Dr Victor Chang, Liberal parliamentarian Helen Sham-Ho, restaurateur Robert Ho, and Chinatown personality King Fong.

Many Chinese came to Australia in the 1850s in search of gold and a better life. Few found gold, but many founded goldmines in the form of small businesses – most clustering around the Haymarket which in 1975 was declared the city's official Chinatown. It is Australia's biggest and oldest Chinatown, and is ranked the ninth most popular tourism destination for Asian visitors. It is home to more than 40 sit-down restaurants which serve more than 9,000 diners daily. Buzzing seven days and nights a week, it boasts four daily Chinese language newspapers, Mandarin and Cantonese cinemas, gaming houses, and even its own telephone book. You can find anything in the many Chinese greengrocer and emporium shops, from woks to bok choy, chopsticks to pressed duck.

But the face of Chinese Sydney is not just Chinatown. You will find members of Sydney's 150,000-strong Chinese community from the western suburbs of Canterbury and Fairfield to the north-west around Cherrybrook and Chatswood.

Helen's Cake Shop

It is worth coming here on Chinese New Year's Eve just to watch the spectacle of families frantically dashing to buy the Chinese New Year pudding – nin go. This is a traditional Chinese bakery selling Hong Kong-style buns and fresh cream cakes. Watch for moon cakes in September for the Moon festival and the ubiquitous darng tart (the custard tarts which make every yum cha experience complete).
- Cnr Sussex and Little Hay sts, City, ph 9281 1818.

Thai Kee Supermarket

More like Woolworths than your average Chinese grocery. Opened in 1997, this nine-lane supermarket is a favourite with the more well-heeled residents of Chinatown's residential towers. Recommended by Sydney Morning Herald Food editor Jill Dupleix.
- Shop 138, Level 1, Market City, Haymarket, ph 9212 4466.

Chinese Grocery Shop

You can find anything related to Chinese cuisine here from woks to bok choy, and chopsticks to chop suey. Despite the growth of similar smaller stores in the suburbs, this store, operating for more than 10 years, is still a favourite, particularly among Sydney's Chinese student population.
- 215 Thomas St, Ultimo, ph 9211 4860.

China Ginseng and Herbs Co

It is not just Asians who see the benefits of Chinese medicine. Acupuncture and herbalists are now being used to cure many ailments. The herbalist will take your pulse, look into your eyes, take a peek at your tongue and be able to tell you what's wrong with your internal organs. For those seeking relief from stress, arthritis or rheumatism, the needles used in acupuncture can help. Mr Kevin Lu, Chinatown's most prominent herbalist, has been curing locals for years.
- 75 Ultimo Rd, City, ph 9212 4397. Also phone Acupuncture Association of NSW, 5 Albion Street, Harris Park, ph 9633 9187.

Solomoda

The latest fashion from Italy at almost half the normal price. An example – an Armani women's woollen suit sells here for around $400. Versace and Gucci also at discount prices. Rest assured – it is the real thing.
- Shop R203, Market City, 9-13 Hay St, Haymarket, ph 9211 6420.

DB 2

Don't be fooled by the fact there is no name out the front of this shop, only a sign saying 50 per cent off. A typical Hong Kong style clothing company with the latest imports from France including Morgan, Zimmermann and Kookai.
- Ground Floor, Market City, 9-13 Hay St, Haymarket. ph 9211 2481.

John Wong

The deeply superstitious Chinese consult Chinatown's resident soothsayer and geomancist for all big events from Chinese New Year to elections.
- Shop G09, Dixon Centre, 413 Sussex St, Haymarket, ph 9281 0862.

The Art Gallery of NSW

Houses a permanent collection of Chinese art in its Asian arts and antiques wing.
- Art Gallery Rd, The Domain, ph 9225 1878.

The Powerhouse Museum

Has regular Chinese exhibits, the most recent on Chinese fashion through the ages.
- 500 Harris St, Ultimo, ph 9217 0111.

Chinatown Cinema

Catch the latest kung-fu film in either Mandarin or Cantonese.
- 27 Goulburn St, City, ph 9211 4546.

Po Hong

The most popular Chinese bookstore located in the heart of Chinatown. Not only can you buy books, but also Sydney's four Chinese daily newspapers.
- 419 Sussex St, Haymarket, ph 9211 5973.

Chinese Gardens

Opened in January 1988 as a gift from the Chinese Government to celebrate the Australian Bicentenary, these traditional gardens in the Darling Harbour complex are a tranquil island in the sea of madness that is Chinatown. Complete with its own teahouse, the gardens are open every day of the year. Entry: adults $3, concessions and children $1.50.
- Ph 9281 6863.

Go Yui Temple

The Chinese market gardeners began worshipping around Alexandria in their own makeshift temple from 1876. The Go Yui temple in Alexandria, which cost 'several hundred pounds of Chinese gold to construct', is the most ornamental of inner city temples. There are 75 Buddhist temples in the Sydney basin. The largest is the 700-member temple at Bonnyrigg in Sydney's west, which celebrates 53 special days in the Buddhist calendar.
- Visits to the Go Yui temple are made by arrangement with the Australian-Chinese Buddhist Society, 654 Cabramatta Rd, Bonnyrigg, ph 9823 3622.

Australian Chinese Community Association of NSW

Provides a comprehensive range of services for Chinese people from tai chi classes to translation. The president is Mr Benjamin Chow.
- 2 May St, Surry Hills, ph 9281 1377.

Chinese Youth League

Organises various activities for young people including lion dancing and dragon boat racing.
- 10 Dixon St, Haymarket, ph 9267 3166.

Jin Wu Koon – Kung Fu and Kick Boxing Academy

Kung-fu classes for self-defence and kick-boxing for the crazy. Lessons in both offered every other day. Chan Cheuk Fai is the chief instructor.
- 31 Dixon St, Haymarket, ph 9211 5395.

The Chinese Herald

This is the largest circulation daily Chinese newspaper with 30,000 copies sold daily (ph 9281 2966). There are three others – *Australian Chinese Daily* (ph 9261 3033), *Sing Tao* (ph 9264 2273) and *Independence Daily* (ph 9211 4611).

Chinese Christian Church

One of the fastest growing Christian churches in Sydney with an average weekly attendance of 800. Church services in Mandarin and Cantonese are held.
- Alfred St, Milsons Point, ph 9955 2800. (Rev Charles Cheung)

Chinese New Year

This annual event always starts with a bang on the streets of Chinatown on the first full moon after January 21. Fireworks, crackers, lion dancing and people wishing Kong He Fat Choy (Wishing you prosperity) fill the streets of Chinatown. Relatives gather for a huge New Year's Eve meal and give Chinese children and single people red packets usually containing money.
- Contact the Chairman of the Chinese New Year Steering Committee, Mr King Fong, ph 9452 3761.

Moon Festival

On the 15th day of the eighth lunar month – usually September – Chinese families traditionally gather for an evening of dining, moon giving and munching of moon cakes.

Dragon boat races

A colourful boat race at Darling Harbour, held every year in the week before Easter, with the winning team gaining the honour of representing Australia at the international titles in Hong Kong.

Tomb Sweeping Ceremony

Every Easter families gather for ceremonial sweeping of the tombs of dead relatives. The biggest gathering is at the Chinese section at Rookwood Cemetery.

Bonnie Tsui and Helen Pitt

Further information
- Red Tape, Gold Scissors, The story of Sydney's Chinese by Shirley Fitzgerald (State Library of NSW Press, $34.95)

Chocolates & confectionery

Somewhere just below world peace, fine hand-made chocolate is high on the list of things the world desperately needs. While Europe makes some exquisite examples, local wins because the fresher they are, the better they are, especially with cream fillings.

Chocolates & confectionery

Adora Handmade Chocolates
Dinner parties will never die early with a little platter of Adora lime truffles on the table. These fresh, hand-made chocolates promise no artificial ingredients or essences. Just fresh King Island cream, real liqueurs, real vanilla beans, real espresso coffee, and lots and lots of fine Belgian chocolate.
- 10 Homer St, Earlwood,
  ph 9559 5948.

Vanderwee Chocolates
Hendrik and Hilde Vanderwee-Rosseel have made Sydney a sweeter place to live, by air-freighting hand-made, carefully selected chocolates from the small makers of Bruges in Belgium. Vanderwee also stock a wide range of the famous Neuhaus chocolates, renowned for their packaging.
- Shop 4R4, The Glasshouse, 146 Pitt St (Mall), City, ph 9221 4020.

Belle Fleur Fine Chocolates
Belle Fleur hand-make a wide variety of melt-in-the-mouth yumminess. The chocolate mushrooms are enough to make you give up the non-chocolate variety.
- 658 Darling St, Rozelle, ph 9810 2690.

Sweet William Chocolates
The first test of a great chocolate shop is the smell. If you walk in and take a deep breath and remain transfixed, unable to move, then you're in the right place. It happens every time here. (But it's much more fun to buy.)
- 4 William St, Paddington,
  ph 9331 5468.

Bon Bon Chocolates
If Double Bay is a magnificent chocolate, then Bon Bon is the rich, creamy centre. The best of the European designer brands including the heavenly Godiva, flown in fresh monthly.
- Harris Arcade, 12 Cross St, Double Bay, ph 9327 4046.

Otello Chocolate & Patisserie
Because Otello Neutral Bay has a 12-seat coffee bar, you can scoff all your chockies with a caffe latte before you leave the store but don't). From the famous $50 boxes, to the old-fashioned chocolate ginger, Otello chox are quality on the outside (Belgian couverture) and the inside.
- 181 Military Rd, Neutral Bay,
  ph 9953 2344.
  17 Kendall St, West Pymble,
  ph 9498 8089.

Also try **jones the grocer**, 68 Moncur St, Woollahra, ph 9362 1222; **David Jones**, Westfield Plaza, Bondi Junction,
ph 9619 1111; **David Jones, Market St, City, ph 9266 5544**.

Jill Dupleix

Cigars & tobacconists

see also quitting
It's expensive, it's bad for you, it makes your clothes smell and your breath stale, but it's also as seriously trendy here as it is around the world. And, hey, if you have to smoke, a nine-inch Churchill is far classier than a pack of fags. While the worldwide upsurge in cigar smoking has created a few supply problems, especially for the favoured Cuban cigars, Sydney is well served by a number of cigar bars and tobacconists. These stock a range of Cuban cigars, including the brands with the best reputations, as well as brands from the Dominican Republic, Jamaica and Honduras, some of which are gaining reputations comparable with the Cubans.

Pierpont's Lounge Bar
Located within the Hotel Inter-Continental, Pierpont's is decorated like a 19th-century gentlemen's club, complete with chesterfield lounges, velvet drapes and paintings of horses and hunt scenes. It has a large walk-in humidor

and one of Sydney's best selections of cigars, including all the better-known brands as well as some more obscure ones. The bar has a wide selection of top-shelf cognacs, ports and single-malt whiskies.

■ Hotel Inter-Continental, 117 Macquarie St, City, ph 9252 0280.

Club CBD
On the third floor of Hotel CBD, a busy city pub that also houses the CBD Restaurant, a nightclub and a pool room, Club CBD is a posh bar with a relaxed ambience. It is decked out in explorer club style with Persian carpets, rattan chairs, zebra- and leopard-print cushions, Chinese lacquer cabinets and tropical plants. The smallish humidor stocks a choice of Cuban and Dominican cigars, with the cigar menu changing regularly.

■ 75 York St, City, ph 9299 8292.

Kingsley's Steakhouse and Cigar Lounge
Housed in an impressive sandstone building with exposed ironbark beams, Kingsley's offers diners prime steaks and top quality Australian wines. Downstairs, the cigar lounge is comfortably set up with couches and armchairs, a bar and a good-sized humidor with a stock of Cuban, Dominican and Jamaican cigars. Kingsley's hosts occasional cigar dinners.

■ 29a King St, City, ph 9262 4155.

The Dugout Bar
Underneath the Burdekin Hotel at the top of Oxford St, the Dugout is a classy watering hole that specialises in old-school cocktails – Martinis, Manhattans, Tom Collins and the like. It has a large humidor with a good selection of Cuban, Dominican and other cigars, including most of the popular brands, and hosts cigar 'smoke-outs' on Tuesday nights. The staff is knowledgable about cigars and cigar smoking and happy to advise customers.

■ Burdekin Hotel, 2 Oxford St, Darlinghurst, ph 9331 3066.

Sol Levy Tobacconist
Founded in 1890, Sol Levy is one of Sydney's oldest and best known tobacconists. In 1892 Sol Levy was awarded First Prize by the Agricultural Society of NSW for cigar making. They no longer make their own cigars, but they do stock as extensive a range of cigars as you'll find in Sydney, including Cubans, Dominicans, Jamaicans, Brazilians and Filipinos, alongside less fashionable brands from Europe and America. They also stock a good range of cigar accessories: cutters, scissors, leather cases and humidors.

■ 713 George St, City, ph 9211 5677.

Havana Tobacconist
You're at the Casino and you want to celebrate a win, or maybe you just want to 'look the money', then head to Havana Tobacconists, located within the Star City complex near the front entrance. They specialise in Cuban cigars, but also have a range of Dominican, Jamaican, Filipino and Dutch cigars. Havana also sells humidors, cutters, pouches and other cigar paraphernalia.

■ Shop RA, Star City, 80 Pyrmont St, Pyrmont, ph 9571 9881.

Nick's Tobacconist
Established in 1957 in the same location, Nick's specialises in Cuban cigars, but also has the full range of cigarettes, and pipe and rolling tobacco. It also stocks smokers' requisites – lighters, pipes, pouches and the rest – and men's accessories, including such unusual items as Indian trinket boxes and Victorian ox knives as well as the usual hip flasks and shaving gear.

■ 57 Darlinghurst Rd, Kings Cross, ph 9358 5771.

Benjamin Long

Classical music

see also opera
A piano came to Sydney with the First Fleet in 1788, but it was 1826 before the first public concert was presented by the Australian Amateur Concert Society in the Freemasons Tavern on George St with sing-

Classical music

ing and a flute obbligato. Sydney has been making up for lost time ever since, and today the city is rich in 'classical' music-making – a description that embraces music of the past and present. Audiences are like football crowds when it comes to old and new music: passionately divided. Subscribers to the Sydney Symphony Orchestra, Australian Chamber Orchestra and Australia Ensemble treasure the classic works, though they make time for an occasional world premiere. But you don't often see them among enthusiasts of late 20th century music at concerts by the **Seymour Group** (ph 9310 3716) with its new technology collaborations, by the virtuosic interpreters of the **Sydney Alpha Ensemble** (ph 9953 1108) or by the percussion ensemble **Synergy** (9518 0641), celebrating its 25th anniversary in 1999.

The range of Sydney's concerts and venues is exhilarating – from free lunchtime concerts in term time by **Sydney Conservatorium of Music** students (Tuesdays at St Andrews Cathedral, Fridays at Australian Technology Park, Cornwallis St, Redfern, ph 9351 1263) to the big and small choral events of the **Sydney Philharmonia Choirs** (ph 9251 2024) at the Sydney Opera House and St Jamess Church, King St. The **Sydney Festival** each January features an extensive classical and contemporary music program.

Sydney Symphony Orchestra

The largest in the southern hemisphere with 106 permanent players and more than 60 years experience. More than 20,000 subscribers pay $22 to $40 a concert, proving the popularity of its standard orchestral repertoire with occasional input from leading Australian composers such as Peter Sculthorpe, Ross Edwards and Carl Vine. The SSO's performing home is the Sydney Opera House Concert Hall, where it gives more than 100 concerts a year.
■ SSO box office, ph 9334 4600;
www.symphony.org.au

Australian Chamber Orchestra

Under the dynamic direction of Richard Tognetti, the ACO gives fresh life to old music so vibrantly and persuasively that in 1998 it had to add to its concert dates in Sydney and Melbourne to cope with its growing audience.
■ Ph 9357 4111; Sydney Opera House box office, ph 9250 7777.

Sydney Spring

An annual international festival of new music, a feast of contemporary work, founded and directed by pianist Roger Woodward. Often controversial, never dull, the program is diverse. In 1998 it will be held from August 29 to September 26, with composers-in-residence Franco Donatoni and David Lumsdaine, and featuring 14 world premieres including the 500-chorister *Dreams of the Earth* by Anne Boyd. At the Eugene Goossens Hall and Sydney Opera House.
■ Ph 9660 0140.

Australia Ensemble

Purveyor of fine music from the past three centuries, the Ensemble has an annual series of sustained high quality at the University of NSW, Sir John Clancy Auditorium, High St, Kensington.
■ Ph 9385 4872.

Musica Viva

The hub of intimate music-making, Musica Viva was established in Sydney in 1945 and is now the largest entrepreneur of chamber music in the world. It presents an international chamber music series at the Sydney Opera House and Seymour Theatre Centre.
■ Ph 9698 1711: www.mva.org.au

Australian Music Centre

Has all you need to know on the subject: recordings, scores, books and other publications for consultation and loan to members. Membership of AMC from $45 ($25 for students) and, for library only, $20 individual and $10 concession.
■ Argyle Centre, 18 Argyle St, The Rocks, ph 9247 4677;
www.amcoz.com.au/amc

HMV Music Store

Gets the vote ahead of Michael's Music Room for doing so well by Australian composers in addition to having a huge range of international CDs.
- Pitt St Mall, City, ph 9221 2311.

Jill Sykes

Further information

- Sydney Morning Herald: Metro section each Friday for performance listings; The Guide (Monday) for radio listings.
- Symphony Friends: joining fee $45 to discover more about the Sydney Symphony Orchestra, its music and musicians (ph 9334 4624).

Cleaning

How many people think they've found a good cleaner, only to find six months down the track that the mantelpiece has a film of dust and the table has lost its shine. So how does one find a truly great cleaner? Usually by word of mouth, but here's another handy hint: look in the classifieds in your suburban newspaper, you're bound to find a good one.

Billy Brown Domestic and Office Cleaning

The all-rounder of the cleaning game. Whether it's a house or a small business, Billy Brown offers the full range of cleaning services, including carpet and upholstery cleaning. There are 37 franchises throughout Sydney.
- Ph 9975 7717.

Happy Homes and Gardens

After three years in the business, this firm was so busy it had to mulch its gardening service. Servicing the Eastern Suburbs, Inner West and the lower North Shore. Its 65 clients can't be wrong.
- Ph 0417 251 039.

Kleenco

A company that provides the full gamut of services in the commercial and industrial cleaning spectrum. You name the business, this company has the skills and equipment to do the job, and they will deal with emergencies when they arise.
- Ph 9534 1111.

Sydney's Best Carpet & Upholstery Cleaning

With its high-tech continuous flow cleaners and special edging tools, this firm ensures every square centimetre of your carpet gets a thorough clean. As its name implies, it boasts that it's the best in town.
- Ph 9622 5822.

Steve Samuelson

Coffee & tea

see also cafes

Forget LA – coffee in Sydney has reached cult proportions and only the best beans will do. Camps are divided between the locally roasted blends such as Grinders, and those high-calibre companies such as Illy and Sega Fredo who roast overseas. But most agree the best beans hail from the Italian suppliers. Sydney is also tea-town and, while the end is not in sight yet for the tea bag, a number of suppliers now specialise in exotic loose leaf and herbal mixes.

L'Espresso Stop

Buy beautiful Illy coffee as beans, ground or in sachets, with specially designed cups to match.
- MLC Centre, Pitt St, City, ph 9231 3151.

The Blue Monkey

At this fairly new shop in the heart of Double Bay they roast their own coffee daily, and also have a range of house blend teas to choose from. Stop in for a cup and try before you buy.
- 9 Bay St, Double Bay, ph 9362 1373.

Cafe Hernandez

This Sydney cafe is an institution, for the quality of its home-roasted coffee and its rather Bohemian atmosphere, complete with oil paintings done by the owner. Open 24 hours for coffee nuts in need of a fix.
- 60 Kings Cross Rd, Potts Point, ph 9331 2343.

Penelope Sach

For the ultimate herbal experience. You have not lived until you have enjoyed her famous petal tea, used by local socialites and hard-drinking chefs as the penultimate hangover cure.
- 2 Moncur St, Woollahra, ph 9362 3339.

Simon Johnson Purveyor of Quality Foods

Refined, serious tea-drinkers stock up on the exquisite Mariage Freres range including the best available Darjeeling, Grand Yunnan and vanilla teas, while coffee lovers choose from the Giamaica Caffée or Grinders. Herbal tea fans like the new Husk brand or Penelope Sach.
- 181 Harris St, Pyrmont, ph 9552 2522.

David Jones

Offers a full traditional range of teas, including Twinings, and also some tea available in bulk.
- Lower ground floor, Market St, City, ph 9266 5544.

jones the grocer

For one-stop, comprehensive coffee and tea shopping, spanning the trendiest to the most traditional in a fun, social atmosphere.
- 68 Moncur St, Woollahra, ph 9362 1222.

Nicole Lehmann

Collectables

see also antiques, auctions

A collectable is a Steiff bear, is a Segusi vase, is a tribal rug, is a Depression clothes peg – and is impossible to pin down. All sorts and kinds are here reduced to a handful of currently fruitful, mostly collector friendly sources.

Dennis Eccles

For antique clocks, if it's not Bill Bradshaw (see Antiques listing), it's this quiet expert and restorer.
- 9 Regent St, Paddington. 9331 2280.

Paul Kenny

Original French mirrors and armoires revamped, plus elegant copies of English 18th and 19th-century originals that are hard to tell from the triple-the-price originals. Will reproduce anything from a snapshot. Interspersed among his repro furniture is beautifully worn wood and stone, doors and fireplaces.
- 19–21 Byrnes St, Botany, ph 9316 7856.

Andrew Simpson

Simpson is the prime dealer in authentic untampered with early Australian colonial cedar and curious artefact. Also writes the books that rise in price almost as rapidly as the subject matter. With Kevin Fahey, has published *Australian 19th Century Furniture*.
- 40 Queen St, Woollahra, ph 9363 3424.

Hordern House

In their nobly proportioned Potts Point terrace, Ann McCormick and Derek O'Donnell deal in the cream of travel and exploration – manuscripts, books, prints, paintings.
- 77 Victoria St, Potts Point, ph 9356 4411.

Josef Lebovic

Bereted and busy dealer in works on paper, broad spectrum, with specialist learning to local early photography, all printed matter.
- 34 Paddington St, Paddington, ph 9332 1840.

Tim McCormick Rare Books

Goes beyond books and deals, as does Hordern House, in fine travel, exploration, history, manuscripts, pictures, curiosities.
- 92 Queen St, Woollahra, ph 9363 5383.

John Sommerlad

For Industrial memorabilia – authentic, large-scale salvage, objects and practical, sometimes reworked, furniture.
- Dock One, 80 O'Connell St, Newtown, ph 9557 4359.

Nicholas Pounder Bookseller

For 20th-century first editions. Above Lesley McKay's bookshop.
- 346 New South Head Rd, Double Bay, ph 9328 7410.

Bottom of the Harbour Nautical Antiques

For marine and maritime collectables.
- 104 George St, City, ph 9247 8107.

Art of Food and Wine

John Cunnington is the man for the well-dressed antique kitchen. From the back of his wife's oriental emporium, he has just what the wine buff or Oscar-winning stylist dreams of: old corkscrews, drinking glass, taste de vin, faience, menus, kitchen art, much sourced in France.
- 80 Queen St, Woollahra, ph 9363 2817.

Hugh Webb is another good source of gourmet collectables (ph 9331 5335).

Caspian Gallery

Bill Evans has refocused and sells fewer rugs, more tribal art, specialising in Aboriginal and Melanesian.
- 469 Oxford St, Woollahra, ph 9331 4260.

Nomadic Rug Traders

Ross Langlands deals in African and Melanesian objects to spice up his extensive antique and tribal rug trade. Holds regular educational exhibitions.
- 125 Harris St, Ultimo, ph 9660 3753.

I. & B. Perryman

Attractive old and antique carpets with the most friendly uncalculated service in a tough business.
- 100 Queen St, Woollahra, ph 9327 3910.

Chee Soon & Fitzgerald

Worth regular visits for Casey and Brian's passionate interest, Marikmekko textiles, Murano glass, modernist ceramics and other good smalls.
- 387 Crown St, Surry Hills, ph 9360 1031.

Copeland & de Soos

Best eye in the modernist business, with lashings of sculptural style: arts and crafts oak to exotic French vases of the 50s and 60s, Italian lamps, tribal objects, art deco jewellery.
- 66 Queen St, Woollahra, ph 9363 5288.

Tyrone Dearing

Interior designer, dealer in art deco modernism, now creating good repro to supplement the increasingly rare real thing.
- 88 Queen St, Woollahra, ph 9363 3225.

Ken Neale

Maverick, wonderfully well-informed dealer in the mid-century moderns. More of his buried treasure may be visible in the new shop. Don't expect bargains, but do expect the goods.
- 283 Liverpool St, Darlinghurst, ph 9361 4869.

Antonia Williams

Comedy

see also cabaret

You don't have to check out the Monorail to get a laugh in Sydney. There aren't many

Comedy

venues but they bristle with the high and lowbrow, mean and gentle, fast and deadpan. Sydney's comedians range from hardcore stand-up merchants such as Anthony Mir and Peter Egner to situational storytellers such as James O'Loghlin. Other names of note are Peter Berner, Alan Glover, Sarah Kendall, Mark Mywords and David Callan.

The Comedy Hotel

It used to be the Harold Park Hotel, a gambling man's watering hole outside the Harold Park trotting track, then a venue for small, dark-hued bands. Now it's renamed itself after its raison d'etre. On Monday nights it's an open mic Comics in the Park where both novices and seasoned comics can test their wits in this relaxed and (sometimes) encouraging atmosphere. Wednesday night is improv night with The Gong Show; and the rest of the week there are stage comedies and live comics. Unfortunately in 1998 there was news that the hotel might close down by the end of the year.
- 115 Wigram Rd, Glebe, ph 9552 2999.

Double Bay Comedy Club

This is dinner and show territory on Friday and Saturday nights. Live comics and a meal or just the show later in the evening. This is not the rough and tumble world of bucks' nights.
- 16-18 Cross St, Double Bay, ph 9327 6560.

The Comedy Store

The home of the old-style raw and in-your-face comedy scene. There are stand-ups early and late and food is available. A popular spot for groups, particularly those on their 'last night of freedom'.
- Cnr Crystal St and Parramatta Rd, Petersham, ph 9564 3900.

The Old Manly Boatshed

A rare northside comedy venue opens up on Mondays for comedy and dinner. Bookings are recommended for dinner.
- 40 The Corso, Manly, ph 9977 4443.

Unicorn Hotel

Another Monday night favourite, this time in the centre of Sydney's pink strip. Out of town acts are regularly featured here.
- 106 Oxford St (cnr Hopewell St), Paddington, ph 9360 3554.

Jokers

Star City's own contribution to the Sydney comedy scene. It is a big supporter of local comedians, old style and new, as well as featuring many overseas comedians. And apparently you can gamble.
- Star City Casino, 80 Pyrmont Rd, Pyrmont, ph 9777 9000.

Bernard Zuel

Computers

It's not just the Sydney nightlife that's wired. From Bondi to Blacktown and beyond, an increasing number of people are discovering what the nerds have tried to keep a secret and failed – that computers can be not only good for your business but great for your lifestyle. Add an Internet connection, take it all away into the great outdoors with a notebook computer and Bill's your rich uncle.

Gateway 2000

Founded by a fourth-generation Iowa cattle rancher (the reason why their corporate colours are the black and white markings of a Friesian cow), Gateway is one of the world's leading direct-to-you computer retailers. They offer an excellent range of desktop and notebook PCs at sensible prices: less expensive than many name brands but a cut above the cheaper corner store machines. Boffins can also have their PC built to order by adding more

memory, a bigger hard drive or monitor, and so on.
- 225 Clarence St, City, ph 1800 500 332.

Harvey Norman Computer Superstores

Your best bet for seeing all the hardware, software and who-knows-what-else-ware under one very long roof. Harvey Norman's monuments to the megabyte scope from educational games for kids to productivity programs for businesses. Watch for seasonal price reductions as companies roll away their current models to make way for the new cyber-stars.
- Cnr South Dowling St and Dacey Ave, Moore Park, ph 9313 6500.
  Other superstores include Auburn and Caringbah.

Dick Smith Electronics

Dick no longer owns this chain but his bespectacled face beams down on enthusiasts looking for the most popular names in hardware and software. There's great after-sales service including free delivery and setup of your PC and a free telephone help line with the most obliging and knowledgable tinkerers this side of the elves' workshop. Shoppers can now roll their own specification for the house brand DSX desktop computers.
- Bankstown Powerhouse, Christies Homemaker Centre, 173 Canterbury Rd, Bankstown, ph 9793 9677. Also at 30 other locations in NSW.

Laptop Land

Whoever said you can't take it with you? Laptop Land is one of Australia's only specialists in portable computing. Notebooks remain most prevalent amongst business people, especially that breed of roaming tyros called 'road warriors', but are also finding their way into schools, universities and even living rooms. Laptop Land sells major brands such as Compaq, Digital, Toshiba, NEC and IBM plus software and accessories for the mostly mobile user.
- 60 Miller St, North Sydney, ph 9957 4090.

Luggage Land

It's an oddity that you can spend from $2,000 to $10,000 on a portable computer and be given a shoulder bag most kindly described as 'functional', if you get one at all. That's when George St landmark Luggage Land should be on your map. Walk past the backpacks on the left and valiantly (but probably unsuccessfully) try to avert your eyes from the highly desirable Zero Halliburton cases on the right. Head straight to the rear wall for Sydney's widest selection of notebook computer carry bags and, even better, real-world advice. Their range extends from student-proof backpacks (good for concealing expensive hardware) to expanding bags suitable for overnight business trips. It is, dare we say, a best case scenario.
- 397 George St, City, ph 9299 6699.
  Also at Chatswood and Miranda.

Hunt Leather

This leather paradise is worth visiting just to enjoy the aroma. But hiding among the classy luggage and leathergoods are the highly regarded Tumi notebook briefcases. Their 'SafeCase' protects your notebook with a patented shock absorbing system (sans airbag, but that will surely come). Inside are pockets and pouches galore. The hardest choice is between the soft calfskin or purportedly 'bulletproof ballistic nylon'.
- MLC Centre, Martin Place, City, ph 9233 8702. Also Greenwood Plaza, North Sydney.

Telstra Big Pond

Not Australia's cheapest Internet service provider – the generic name for any mob which gets you online – but the largest and best for beginners to intermediate users. Internet access is usually charged at a per-hour rate. While you'll see tariffs as low as $1 per hour at some smaller suburban providers, Big Pond has a pleasing combination of speed (fast pipelines into the US heart of the Internet), support (extended hours and weekends, from anywhere in NSW for the cost of a local call) and price (including a monthly $44 all-you-can-surf

Computers

deal). Both personal and business customers are catered for. Unlike most ISPs, there's no joining fee, and you also receive 8 free hours with which to get your feet wet in the cybersurf. You can then wave goodbye without paying a penny or sign up for one of several well-constructed monthly plans, all of which include a free personal Web page.
- 157 Walker St, North Sydney, ph 9934 9200.

The Well-Connected Cafe

If you don't have a computer and need access to the World Wide Web but fast, this is one of several 'cyber cafes' where you can surf for a price, mouse in one hand and machiatto in the other. The going rate is $6 per half hour, with free assistance from the staff to get you up and running. But first, check if your local library has free Internet terminals. Also ask around at the office – it's almost guaranteed there will be some form of Web access in the building, even if it's nominally for work purposes only.
- 35 Glebe Point Rd, Glebe, ph 9566 2655.

Dymocks

Despite the attempts of software companies to make their programs easy to use, the market for computer books continues to boom. Maybe that's because most programs come with a thin pamphlet that's a very poor excuse for a manual. Join the lunchtime crowds on the mezzanine floor at Dymocks City store. They're all trying to get ahead in the computing game with a book that actually teaches them how to get the most from their software – such a radical concept! And newcomers, don't let the title of those 'Dummies' books fools you. They're an enjoyable and affordable first step.
- 428 George St, City, ph 9235 0155.

Books Buy & Sell

This has long been a favourite late-night haunt. Open until 9.30pm for 364 days a year, Books Buy & Sell is the only place you can immerse yourself in a den of second-hand computer books (along with every other subject dreamt of by Dewey) while listening to ABC FM or debating almost any subject with store owner Peter White. The selection of computer texts covers recent and older software and often includes decidedly meaty tomes.
- Downstairs at 711 George St, Haymarket, ph 9212 2478.

WEA

Books are fine for some people; others learn best by seeing, doing and discussing in a group environment. The WEA's Computer Training division offers a variety of courses, beginning with computing basics through to taking charge of popular applications such as Microsoft Excel, CorelDRAW and PageMaker. More recent additions to the roster cover the World Wide Web. You can opt for intensive two-day sessions held over a weekend or attend evening classes one night each week. Also don't forget to see what's available at your local community and TAFE college.
- 72 Bathurst St, City, ph 9264 2781.

David Flynn

Cooking classes

see also bakeries & patisseries, bush food

If you learn just one good thing from a cooking class, you're ahead. If you learn great wads of things and have a great time in the process, you're way, way ahead. Sydney's home cooks have a great array of local classes, visiting chef demonstrations, and regular cooking programs to choose from.

Simon Johnson Quality Foods

This food-filled emporium is a Pandora's box of temptations, including a lively, ongoing program of seminars entitled Talk, Eat, Drink. Renowned cookbook authors, famous chefs,

and specialist suppliers all talk, while you eat and drink.
- 181 Harris St, Pyrmont, ph 9552 2522.

Sydney Seafood School
As the name suggests, this is the place to learn about everything from seafood paella to a luscious laksa, and from sushi to sugarcane prawns. The classes range from simple demonstrations to hands-on four-hour intensive workshops with famous chefs (it's OK, you still get to eat). Early morning market tours are a great way to dip your toes in.
- First Floor, Sydney Fish Market Building, Blackwattle Bay, Pyrmont, ph 9552 2180.

Accoutrement
Sue Jenkins and her crew run a tight ship of hand-picked chef demonstrations aimed at the competent home cook, right in the middle of her you-need-it-we've-got-it-in-three-sizes cookware store. Check out the new extension devoted to fine foods, olive oils, rices and chocolates, and you may never leave.
- 611 Military Rd, Mosman, ph 9969 1031.

Johanna Minogue Cuisine
Holiday cooking classes for food-friendly teenagers mingle with sybaritic cooking sojourns to southern Italy at Johanna Minogue Cuisine.
- Ph 9331 5176.

Elise Pascoe Cooking
A charming teacher, an emphasis on matching food and wine, and a well-balanced program of entertaining-oriented classes.
- 1/44 Darling Point Rd, Darling Point, ph 9363 0406.

Much Ado About Cooking
Vicki Harrington celebrates the local – in her Chefs of Balmain cooking program – and the far, far away (in 1998 Chianti, Ireland, and Spain).
- 5 Donnelly St, Balmain, ph 9810 5172.

Jill Dupleix

Cookware & kitchenware

see also tableware
Good kitchenware shops have all the big names and, more importantly, they have all those funny little things that you have just decided you can't live without, such as good twine, trussing needles and $500 Dualit toasters. Avoid those shops with too many decorative, shiny things, and go with the pro.

Accoutrement
The hearth of Sydney's food world, Accoutrement deals only with the best, and the staff have good reasons for every acquisition. Great for bakers, moussers and hard-core chocolatiers, as well as gracious hostesses who want pretty plates.
- 611 Military Rd, Mosman, ph 9969 1031; Shop 9, 808 Pacific Highway, Gordon, ph 9418 2992.

Bay Tree
Inside this cosy cottage is a warehouse worth of beautiful kitchen things. It takes a while to see the wood for the trees, but you'll always find a great masher, copper couscoussiere, or appealing little coconut spoon for your sugar.
- 40 Holdsworth St, Woollahra, ph 9328 1101.

Kitchen Kapers
The great home cooks of the North Shore flock to this corner store for everything from apple corers to giant electric slicers. The emphasis on professional kitchen tools, plates and glasses makes shopping for a domestic kitchen even more fun.
- 160 Willoughby Rd, Crows Nest, ph 9906 4655.

Peter's of Kensington
The mighty Peter's is a giant foodie fantasyland, filled to bursting with Spring pots and pans, Wursthof knives, Good Grips tools, Alessi

gorgeous things, Dualit toasters, and Scan Pan semi-nonstick fry pans, all at reasonable prices. Keep an eye out for sales and specials.
- 57 Anzac Pde, Kensington, ph 9662 1099.

Basic Essentials

A very gleamy, shiny shop that shows off our passion for stainless steel and designer goodies. It's perfect wedding-present-land, but it's not all glamour. This stuff actually works once you put it in the kitchen.
- Shop 11, 20 Bay St, Double Bay, ph 9328 1227.

Jill Dupleix

Costumes

If all the world's a stage, there must be a lot of customers for costume shops. Whether the event is a fancy dress party, the Mardi Gras parade or a local amateur dramatic society production, at some time we all feel the need to be someone else for a night.

The Costume Shop

Ostensibly the largest collection in Sydney, with more than 15,000 period costumes and fancy dress outfits now centralised in one location. Costumes can be made to order, and items from the ever-expanding collection can be rented by the day or year. Accessories and theatrical make-up are also available.
- 7/61 Marlborough St, Surry Hills, ph 9318 2511.

The Costume Design Centre

Probably the classiest costumier in Sydney, making to order from large-scale productions to individual Mardi Gras costumes. It also has an entire floor devoted to rental costumes.
- 288 Abercrombie St, Redfern, ph 9698 7440.

ABC TV Marketing

Perhaps this isn't the first place you'd think to look, but all those period costumes have to go somewhere. Why not to your next fancy dress party?
- 221 Pacific Highway, Gore Hill, ph 9950 4284.

Amazing Costume Hire Company

Although it doesn't have a dazzling array, there are some buried treasures if you're prepared to search for them.
- 112 Oxford St, Paddington, ph 9361 3878.

The Little Shop for Horrors

You can't leave the kids out when it comes to costumes. From school plays to that irritating *Star Trek* theme birthday party, you'll find it here. They'll even make it to hire to you if they don't have it in stock.
- Level 1, 302 Pacific Highway, Crows Nest, ph 9437 5339.

Powerhouse Museum

No, the curators will not let you borrow items from their long-running costume exhibitions, *Stepping Out* and *Lace for Fashion*! But many more such extravaganzas are planned for the coming year. There is art, armour and armoury in *Nights from Imperial Austria*, which runs until October 11, 1998, music dance and costume of Australian Aborigines and Torres Strait Islanders in *Ngaramang Bayumi* until February 1999, and *Korean Wrapping Cloth* until April 1999.
- 500 Harris St, Ultimo, ph 9217 0111.

Chris Dobney

Country music

see also **blues music, folk music, rock & pop music, jazz**

The real bootscootin' home of Sydney country music is the 'wild west', the city's outer western suburbs. The likes of Campbelltown and St Marys may be a long way from rolling paddocks and bushland, but this is where some of Australia's best country music acts – Lee Kernaghan, Shanley Del, Slim Dusty, John Williamson, The Bushwackers – perform regularly. It's also where they go to promote their new albums. Occasionally, mainstream American country acts play major city venues.

Campbelltown Catholic Club
The best venue for authentic Australian country music, although nearly an hour's drive from the city centre. All the major local acts include it when touring.
- 2022 Camden Rd, Campbelltown, ph 02 4625 0000.

Also check out **Rooty Hill RSL** (ph 9625 5500), **Canterbury-Hurlstone Park RSL** (ph 9558 0422), **Evan Theatre, Penrith** (ph 02 4720 5555) and **Tropicana Hotel, Wilberforce** (ph 4575 1603).

Yesterday & Today Records
Far and away the best shop in Sydney for country music obscurities, imports from the US and hard-to-get collectors' items. Beware of Steve Reid, the strongly opinionated owner, if your choice tends towards the mainstream.
- 255 Church St, Parramatta, ph 9633 3585.

St Marys Sound Centre
Recognised as the leading mainstream country music shop in Sydney. Lee Kernaghan once spent six hours here signing more than 500 copies of his latest release. Also provides information on concerts and venues in the western suburbs.
- 116a Queen St, St Marys, ph 9623 4262.

Linedance Association of Australia
The city's source of all bootscootin' knowledge. As most enthusiasts prefer to find their own level and their own club, they will tell you where to join the nearest bunch of bootscooters.
- PO Box 363, Seven Hills 2760, ph 9624 3129.

Australian Linedance
Gay and lesbian enthusiasts of the arcane art have a regular night at a mystery location. The gay bootscooter squad are a wonder to behold and make everyone else seem like two-left-feet amateurs. Their float is one of the highlights of the city's Gay & Lesbian Mardi Gras parade.
- Ph 9557 2763.

Bruce Elder

Further information
- See Sydney Morning Herald Metro and CitySearch for listings.
- The Country Music Association, ph 6766 1577: www.immedia.com.au/amid

Couriers

In a world without Harry Houdini and Dale Buggins, we have to rely on couriers to be our daredevils. Laying their bodies and vehicles on the line, all for your benefit. Well, not quite – but when it has to be person-to-person (and who can resist the personable touch of a sweaty, dreadlocked bike rider?) the courier can be a relatively cheap way to get the goods delivered.

Snap Courier Services
For a simple Sydney metropolitan pick-up and delivery, Snap Courier Services charge a low, flat fee.
- Ph 9748 0755.

Crisis Couriers

Crisis Couriers are especially popular with businesses within the city and North Sydney (where it's based), as it specialises in using pushbike couriers in those areas. A small, flat fee is charged for this service, and you if need to go further, a distance fee is applied. It will upgrade to a motorbike or car where applicable.
- Ph 9964 0000.

Ansett

Of course, they can ship by air, do the bigger jobs, and it is Australia's largest airfreight network. Ansett offer an airport-to-airport, or door-to-door service, and can guarantee overnight service. The airline is especially good for sending market produce.
- Ph 9352 1900.

Andrew Khedoori

Cricket

see also sporting goods

Organised cricket has been played in Sydney since 1826, and despite the game's 19th-century slowness and the obscurity of its many laws, it remains Australia's biggest spectator and participation sport, a summer institution. Competitive cricket is a complicated affair, requiring at least 22 players, a large field with a proper 21-metre cricket pitch – real or artificial turf, concrete or matting – and expensive equipment. Organised cricket of this kind is played in five tiers in Sydney, from international down to the city and suburban, schools and shires competitions. But cricket is a democratic game, and all a social game requires is a batter, a bowler, a bat and a ball, and some improvised playing area, be it a backyard, a garage, the local nets, a park or a strip of beach. Most sports stores sell cricket gear. Bat prices range from $50 to $300, balls and stumps from $40 a set. Cricket equipment can be hired from universities. Contact the UNSW Sport Store (ph 9385 4885), the University of Sydney Sports Union (ph 9351 2039) or Macquarie University Sports Association (ph 9850 7635).

Sydney Cricket Ground

As the name suggests, this is Sydney's cricket mecca. It has hosted cricket matches since 1854. Renovations during the 1980s scaled its capacity down to 42,000 seats – and increased its comfort – and the famous Hill disappeared beneath concrete and tiered seating. At this time the SCG slipped somewhat as Australia's best, or second-best (rivalling the Melbourne Cricket Ground) cricket venue. It is regenerating in the late '90s, however. The SCG hosts one Test match a year, traditionally in the first week of January, and about four day-night limited-overs internationals in December and January. The SCG also hosts the NSW team in domestic competition, the Sheffield Shield (four-day matches) and the interstate one-day competition through the summer.
- Sydney Cricket Ground Trust, ph 9360 6601; match information, ph 0055 63132.

Match coverage

Tune into the ABC's 2BL (702 on the AM band); Channel 9 has the television rights to one-day and Test cricket played in Australia.

North Sydney Oval

This picturesque old ground north of the Harbour Bridge is hosting an increasing number of Sheffield Shield and State one-day matches. It is the regular grade cricket venue for the North Sydney club.
- Ph 9936 8100.

Club cricket

Sydney has 20 clubs in the main grade competition, each fielding four to six teams. First grade is intensive with many semi-professional players, including national representatives

when available. The lower grades are also competitive and very serious. Grade cricket matches are usually two-day affairs at suburban grounds as widespread as Penrith, Campbelltown, Sutherland, Manly and Hornsby. Below that level, Sydney has three thriving competitions: the Sydney Shires (suburban teams), City and Suburban (schools old-boys, corporate associations etc) and the NSW Churches Union.
■ NSW Cricket Association, ph 9339 0999.

Women's cricket
The NSW Women's Cricket Association has eight clubs playing a four-grade competition (not all clubs field four grades) and an under-18 competition. The popularity of women's cricket is rising fast across Australia, though club-level participation has fluctuated over the years.
■ NSW Women's Cricket Association, ph 9339 0999.

Indoor cricket
Attracting men and women, indoor cricket is a specialised game played in a netted area the size of a basketball court on artificial turf. There are eight players a team, and everyone gets an equal amount of batting and bowling. Games last 60-90 minutes. Indoor cricket centres are mostly in western Sydney – Five Dock, Gladesville, Bankstown, Thornleigh, Windsor, St Marys – and also in Sutherland.
■ Indoor Cricket Federation of NSW, ph 9566 2492.

Kanga cricket
Played with plastic bats and balls, as opposed to the standard willow and leather, Kanga cricket pits players in pairs against other pairs, grouped in teams of 10.
■ NSW Cricket Association, ph 9339 0999.

Malcolm Knox

Cycling

see also triathlon
You know the saying: it's like riding a bike, you never forget how. And with 2000 providing a rush of adrenaline, there is no time like now to hop into the saddle and get the legs pumping. As in any major city, cycling can be dangerous on Sydney's main roads, but there is an ever-increasing number of cycle paths to smooth the way of the enthusiast. Paths from as far west as Penrith, through Windsor, Dural and Riverstone all the way to Botany Bay and the North Shore are now available to cyclists. Sydney's Olympic velodrome for 2000 is under construction at Bankstown, with the current velodrome at Tempe being used for all major NSW events. Olympic mountain bike events will be held at a special track at Fairfield City Farm. The track has traditionally been a winner for Australia and cycling is one of Australia's major medal hopes for 2000.

Centennial Park
One of the more picturesque cycling venues. The park will be used as part of the road race at Sydney in 2000, its open plan allowing riders to reach impressive speeds. There are few cars, but you may have to share the dedicated cycle lanes with horses, in-line skaters and recreational runners.

Roads and Traffic Authority
For free maps and a complete list of Sydney's cycling tracks, contact the RTA. Some of the best include: an uninterrupted run from Tempe to Homebush along the Cooks River; the Botany Bay waterfront at Brighton; Glebe to Parramatta along the Parramatta River.
■ Ph 1800 060 607.

Waratah Veteran Cyclists Club
This club, formerly Homebush Veteran Cyclists Club, caters for over-35s interested in racing or

Cycling

simply enjoying a ride. Average age is 50, although some members are in their 80s. Races begin at 8am each Sunday from the northern end of Bennelong Rd, Homebush Bay, spanning 60 to 80 minutes over a distance of 40km to 70km.
- Ph 9449 8501.

Western Sydney Mountain Bike Club

For the radical, mountain-bike riding might be more the go. This club organises social rides and races at the foot of the Blue Mountains. The club caters for all ages, from juniors through to experienced riders.
- Ph (02) 4751 1928.

Chatswood Cycles

Part of Australia's largest cycling chain. Buyers can walk in off the street and find a wide variety of bikes. Expert knowledge from hobby rides to racing.
- 160 Victoria Ave, Chatswood, ph 9411 5772.

Bates Bikes

Provides bikes, parts, repairs and advice for serious road racers, mountain bikers and even the family of four which wants a child carrier for junior on the back.
- 124 Forest Rd, Hurstville, ph 9585 1230.

Clarence St Cyclery

The largest cycle store in the city. Three floors of every thing for the cycling enthusiast, from workshops to specialised clothes to custom-made facilities.
- 104 Clarence St, City, ph 9299 4962.

Centennial Park Cycles

For those who are looking for a few glorious hours in the saddle, there are all types of bikes that can be hired for a lap or six around inner-city Centennial Park. Mountain bikes, road bikes, tandem bikes, baby carriers, pedal cars, you name it. Prices start from $6 an hour with the fourth hour free.
- 50 Clovelly Rd, Randwick, ph 9398 5027.

Paul Kent

Further information
- NSW Cycling Federation, ph 9796 1344
- Discovering NSW and Canberra's Bike and Walking Paths (Sabey and Associates, $16.95)
- www.cyclery.com.au

Dance

Sydney loves dance of all kinds. From its early years, the city welcomed diverse examples of the art form. Excerpts from Giselle were seen in Sydney within 15 years of its 1841 Paris premiere – fast travelling for those times. The same year, 1855, Lola Montez scandalised and delighted audiences with her spider dance. In the late 1990s, styles range from classical to acrobatic, from the cool depths of Swan Lake at the Sydney Opera House to the hot beat of Dein Perry's industrial tap at the Casino.

Homegrown dance and dancers top the bill these days, with occasional visiting companies adding to the variety. Though the **Australian Ballet**, the national company, is based in Melbourne, it spends more time performing in Sydney where it has regular March–April and November–December seasons at the Sydney Opera House (ph 9250 7777). What was Sydney's newest and most exhilarating contemporary group, Gideon Obarzanek's **Chunky Move**, is also making its home in Melbourne on a generous government grant.

Small groups and independent artists spark up the scene. For cool thrills in the postmodernist mode, try Russell Dumas' **Dance Exchange** (ph 9357 3576). Traditional insights into other cultures are offered by Diana Reyes' **Flamenco** (ph 9557 1825) and the Indian classical styles of Anandavalli's **Lingalayam Dance Company** (ph 9764 4530). **Bodies**, the umbrella title of a diverse dance selection, offers the best sampling of new work by independent artists.

Notable upcoming events in the world of dance include the Parsons Dance Company at the Sydney Opera House Drama Theatre in November–December 1998 and the premiere of Hydra, Gideon Obarzanek's Chunky Moves new work, at the Sydney Festival in January 1999 (ph 9265 0444).

Sydney Dance Company

The city's flagship contemporary dance company has been producing an eclectic range of theatrical dance works for more than 30 years, the last two decades under the direction of national treasure Graeme Murphy. The SDC's next program of its own work will be in the Opera Theatre, Sydney Opera House, in May 1999.
- ph 9221 4811:
  www.sydneydance.com.au

Bangarra Dance Theatre

At the forefront of a new wave of truly Australian dance, mingling the essence of Aboriginal and Torres Strait Islander dance traditions with universal contemporary styles. Artistic director Stephen Page came to world attention with *Ochres*, which he choreographed with Bernadette Walong, followed in 1997 by *Fish*.
- Bangarra Studio Theatre, Pier 4, The Wharf, Hickson Rd, Walsh Bay, ph 9251 5333.

For an interestingly different take in the same dance area, look out for performances by the **Aboriginal Islander Dance Theatre** (ph 9252 0199).

One Extra Company

Concentrates on new Australian work, curating seasons by leading young choreographers. Based at the Seymour Theatre Centre.
- Ph 9364 9468:
  www.ozemail.com.au/oneextra

Ausdance

A professional association for dance. Membership is open to anyone from professionals to enthusiasts, starting at a concessional rate of $25. Ausdance NSW offers promotion of activities and resources, advocacy and lobbying, career advisory service, education and training. Resources include a book and video library with video viewing, access to computers and database, workshops, courses, discounts on classes, performances, books and a variety of services.
- Pier 4, The Wharf, Hickson Rd, Walsh Bay, ph 9241 4022:
  http://sunsite.anu.edu.au/ausdance

Australian Dance Week

This festival will be held from April 25 to May 2, 1999, with a packed program of dance activities and performances to celebrate the art form. Further details from Ausdance (see above).

Performance Space

The venue most likely to have interesting experiments in dance and theatre, as well as more polished performances by established but adventurous creative groups.
- 199 Cleveland St, Redfern, ph 9319 5091.

Performing Arts Bookshop

This is consistently the best for the latest dance books off the shelf.
- 280 Pitt St, City, ph 9267 2257.

Astam Books

A wide-ranging dance list for its core business of mail order, but also invites people to check its current stock.
- 57-61 John St, Leichhardt, ph 9566 4400.

Jill Sykes

Dance

Further information
- Sydney Dance Company Friends: informative and social activities, joining fees from $40, ph 9221 4811
- Friends of the Australian Ballet: informative and social activities, joining fees $25 for the public, $20 for subscribers and concessions, $10 for under-18s, ph 9264 6436
- Dance Australia, bimonthly magazine with features, reviews and information on dance (Yaffa, ph 9281 2333)

Dating & introduction services

Desperate and dateless? There is someone out there just for you, it's just a matter of trying the right places. If the agencies are just too much of an admission of defeat, why not try the clubs and classes route. Pick a hobby and find someone who shares your passion. Check the Yellow Pages clubs listings for everything from rabbit fanciers to language schools.

Yvonne Allen and Associates
Psychologist Yvonne Allen is a mainstay of the scene, having been around since 1976. She charges around $975 for the basic four month program and caters to people of all ages.
- Ph 9241 3066.

Carolyne Hardwick and Associates
Carolyne Hardwick has been in the business for 17 years and prides herself on running a very personal service that mostly caters to professionals. $1,500 for 12-month membership, with a minimum of 10 introductions with no upper limit.
- Ph 9440 0477.

Six for Supper
Trudy Colless, the woman behind this outfit, gathers three men and three women and sends them off to a restaurant. A good way to meet people in a low-pressure situation if you dread that initial meeting.
- Ph 9417 5890.

The Singles Sailing Society
A very popular club with regular twilight cruises.
- Ph 9337 1946.

Online
Put down that phone, chat lines are passe. Head to the computer and log on. RSVP and Catch are the two of the biggest internet dating agencies. But the best place to meet a like-minded soul is at a newsgroup. Pick a topic – music is very popular – and get in there and trade email addresses so you can talk in private.
- www.rsvp.com.au
  www.catch.com.au

Further information
- Sydney Morning Herald: Single Scene column for regular singles parties, balls and events
- Sydney Star Observer: for gays and lesbians, the best place to start for singles listings (free at inner city venues or ph 9380 5577)

Dead Sydney

How do you get to see the rich and famous in Sydney? Your best bet is to visit a cemetery, where you can reflect on how well or badly the former colossi of the city are being remembered. And if you bring a picnic, you can be assured of a peaceful and picturesque day out. These are our nominations for the most fun you can have with dead people . . .

Dead Sydney

Waverley Cemetery

Sydney's most spectacular graveyard, on a cliff overlooking a raging sea. Established in 1877, it now has a population of 250,000, including the republican author Henry Lawson; the poet Dorothea Mackellar (who wrote 'I Love a Sunburnt Country'); the cricketer Victor Trumper; Dante The Great, a magician shot by his orchestra leader; and the aeronautical pioneer Lawrence Hargrave. There's also an elaborate memorial to the convicts transported from Ireland after the rebellion of 1798. Our favourite gravestone is carved in the shape of a man about to make a dive. It honours Charles Peart, High Diving Champion of the World, 'accidentally killed while diving from a great height into a tank of water' (in 1896 near Redfern station).
■ St Thomas St, Waverley.

South Head Cemetery

Here's another place for gorgeous views, and useful proximity to the lighthouse and other sites of Watson's Bay, with the chance to see the tombs of Jack Moses, author of 'The Dog Sits on the Tucker Box' and various members of the Fairfax family, who once owned the *Sydney Morning Herald*.
■ Old South Head Rd, Vaucluse.

St John's Cemetery

This is Australia's oldest cemetery, in the grounds of the now vanished St John's Church. An unnamed nine-year-old child was the first recorded burial, in January 1790, and the earliest identified grave belongs to Henry Dodd, butler to Governor Arthur Phillip, who died in 1791. There's a variety of convicts (such as Sarah Tunks, transported for stealing seven yards of silk for handkerchiefs) and early settlers, including D'Arcy Wentworth (a doctor on the First Fleet and father of the political crusader William Charles Wentworth), Baron Augustus Theodore Henry Alt, first surveyor-general of NSW, and Samuel Marsden (known as 'the flogging parson', who joined John Macarthur in founding Australia's wool industry).
■ O'Connell St, Parramatta.

Eastern Suburbs Memorial Park and Crematorium

Small but elegant, this graveyard near Botany Bay was founded in the 1880s, mainly to accommodate convict and free settler graves moved from the ancient Devonshire St cemetery near Central Railway. Its art deco crematorium benefited from a handsome refurbishment in the early 1990s.
■ Military Rd, Matraville.

Gore Hill Cemetery

Known as 'a headstone history book', this graveyard had its first burial in 1877, and its last in 1977. It contains Louisa King, Sydney's first female pharmacist, and John Sulman, an important architect of the late 19th century whose name is now remembered in the annual Sulman Prize for genre painting.
■ 211 Pacific Highway, St Leonards.

Rookwood Cemetery

Founded in 1867, and sprawling over 315 hectares, it contains many Sydney politicians (such as controversial NSW Premier Jack Lang), tycoons (merchant Anthony Hordern), and entertainers (comedian Roy Rene, aka Mo McCackie). The cemetery is divided into sections according to religion and nationality. The epitaphs offer hours of puzzlement, such as: 'William Moon, who was so suddenly cut down in the vigor of life, while engaged in that pleasure to which he was so devotedly attached. Leaving a wife and 7 children to mourn their loss. 29th March. 1871. Aged 38 years.' Tours are held on the first and third Sundays of the month.
■ East St, Lidcombe, ph 9746 2177.

David Dale

Delicatessens

see also gourmet food

Delis are where we go after we grow out of sweetshops. The word comes from the German Delikatesse, meaning 'delicacy'. We define it here as having high-quality groceries, smallgoods, cheeses, and luxury foods, while still leaving you with some things to cook yourself.

Five Star Gourmet

The deli section of this specialist food store is an island of free flavour. Pick up Italian mascarpone, naturally coloured frankfurts, Alligator Brand ravioli, English stilton, bush foods, emu eggs, Jonathan's of Melbourne hams, and even tubs of fish stock.

■ 13-19 Willoughby Rd, Crows Nest, ph 9438 5666.

Arena's L'antipasto Deli

This is Little Italy on the North Shore, a bustling long spaghetti strip of a deli, lined with great food platters of antipasto, fresh pork salsiccie, real parmigiano, freshly-made grissini, good wood-fired breads, Italian pasta and homemade pasta sauces.

■ 908 Military Rd, Mosman, ph 9969 9905.

Cyril's Delicatessen

Go to Cyril's before we lose it. Cyril Vincent runs a sweet-smelling, gorgeous little shop stocked with eastern European specialties, and small goods, fine chocolates and baking needs. Not only do they have the right cream cheese for your cheesecake, they'll tell you how they make it at home.

■ 183 Hay St, Haymarket, ph 9211 0994.

Delicacies on King

There is food at your feet, in front of you, behind you and hanging over your head. Olives, hams, cheeses and the world's canned and jarred delicacies lie in wait, all at low King St Newtown prices.

■ 257 King St, Newtown, ph 9557 4048.

Martinez Bros

You know those mornings you wake up and just crave something South American? No? Well go here anyway, for the home-made empanadas, the mate (South American tea), chorizo sausages, and lively atmosphere.

■ 47 Spencer St, Fairfield, ph 9724 5509.

jones the grocer

It's our own little Dean & De Luca gourmet food store, so dress up to go, and take your Prada wallet to stock up on hand-made chocolates, Jonathon's famous meats and smallgoods, Asian bowls and chopsticks, Queensland Falwasser wafers, Portuguese custard tarts, char-grilled vegetables, and mesmerising local and imported cheeses. Plus cook books, teas, ice-creams, whatever.

■ 68 Moncur St, Woollahra, ph 9362 1222.

Torres Cellars & Delicatessen

Spanish lovers love the Torres Deli, with its Portuguese bread rolls, Serrano-style jamon, hanging strings of chorizo and morcilla sausages, and cans of anchovy-stuffed olives. You can even buy a Spanish rioja to have with your anchovy-stuffed olives.

■ 75 Liverpool St, City, ph 9264 6862.

Bonaventura

A milk bar with an Italian accent, this tiny old-fashioned little shop tucked away in Paddington is filled with extra virgin olive oils, jelly snakes, prosciutto and olives and milk and bread. We wish all local milk bars were like this. Grazie, Lidia, Angelo e Gianni.

■ 2 Hopetoun St, Paddington, ph 9332 3395.

Simon Johnson Quality Foods

Eating in Sydney wouldn't be the same if this fine food providore vanished. We need it, for its wonderful temperature-controlled cheese

room, its atmospheric warehouse room of pasta, extra virgin olive oil, sea salt, French pralines and tea leaves, unpasteurised Iranian caviar, fresh truffles, and even fresh local breads and smallgoods. And for its espresso coffee while we shop.
■ 181 Harris St, Pyrmont, ph 9552 2522.

Jill Dupleix

Demolitions

You can't stop progress and obstacles in its path must be removed. These home-wreckers are the ones to call when your redundant building needs removing.

Ronnies Demolition
Whether it's commercial or residential, this company will wreak a path of destruction once given the green light. They're licensed to remove hazardous materials and they re-sell building materials, kitchen and bathroom fittings.
■ 66 Riverside Rd, Chipping Norton, ph 9755 1399.

Delta
Commercial and industrial demolition is their domain. Removal of hazardous materials, such as asbestos, and synthetic mineral fibres presents no problems to these demolishers.
■ 7-11 Little Buckingham St, Surry Hills, ph 9310 4327.

Bassett Demolition
Specialising in housing demolitions, this company's motto 'All we leave is a memory' sums up their approach to the job.
■ 12a Parramatta Rd, Lidcombe, ph 9748 7899.

Steve Samuelson

Dentists

Sydney's best dentists do not congregate in one place. They can be found throughout the suburbs as well as in the heart of the city, and the recommendation of friends is probably the surest way to track down the one with the chair-side manner that suits you best.

Dentists can charge whatever fees they like, so cost will be an important consideration for many people when choosing a dentist. Don't be afraid to ask for an estimate of the total charge if the dentist recommends extensive work, or to inquire about alternative, less expensive options. Get a second opinion and quote if the price still seems too high.

The fees charged do not necessarily reflect standards of practice, and consumers should also feel free to quiz practitioners about their infection-control procedures. The vast majority of dentists can be expected to comply with regulations about wearing gloves and masks, and autoclaving equipment between patients to prevent the spread of viruses such as hepatitis C.

Another important indicator of quality is the emphasis placed on preventative dentistry, and on efforts to preserve all of your existing teeth. A good dentist will also be happy to explain what needs to be done, and why.

The NSW branch of the **Australian Dental Association** (ph 9906 1660) will provide a list of their members in a particular location. While membership does not guarantee high standards, member dentists are bound by the association's code of ethics and formal complaints procedures. As well, member dentists may be more likely to keep up to date by undertaking the continuing education programs provided by, or promoted by, the association.

On issues of safety, the association backs the international consensus that amalgam is

Dentists

a safe and very effective material for fillings, although a composite resin may be preferred on aesthetic grounds, for example, for front teeth. Patients should be provided with lead aprons for protection during X-rays.

In an emergency, dentists who practise after hours can be found in the Yellow Pages, or you can ring the Dental Association's after hours number (9369 7050) for a list of available dentists.

Only people who hold health care cards, health benefits cards or pensioner concession cards can obtain free treatment at public clinics including at the **United Dental Hospital** in Surry Hills (9293 3200) and **Westmead Hospital** (9845 6766).

Most health funds have packages which include dental cover. The economics benefits of insurance can only be weighed up by each individual family according to their circumstances, but as a general rule you should read the small print on any restrictions, such as waiting periods for entitlements, or the number of times you can access a service and still be covered.

Melissa Sweet

Department stores

Go to any major city in the world and the best place for one-stop shopping is always the big department stores. We hate to say it, but Melbourne is actually has better variety with the new Georges and an outpost of the Japanese Daimaru chain. However, Sydney boasts the flagships of the two mega department stores – David Jones and Grace Bros – plus a number of speciality department stores. Here in shoppers' heaven you can find virtually anything you crave from a needle and thread to designer fashion to a bunch of grapes to an icemaking refrigerator.

The Argyle Department Store

More a cluster of boutiques than strictly a department store, the Argyle Department Store is located in an historic building that was the site of the first shop in Australia. It houses fashion stores like Brian Rochford, Dinosaur Designs, Surf Dive 'N' Ski, Duo, Helen Kaminski, Claudia's Collection, Pierre Cardin, Timberland, Johnny Dexter and Table Eight. All topped off with one of Sydney's top restaurants, bel mondo.

■ 12-24 Argyle St, The Rocks,
ph 9251 4800.

David Jones

Billed for many years as 'the most beautiful department store in the world', David Jones Elizabeth St store is a women's shopping nirvana. It starts at the glamorous marbled cosmetics and perfumery ground floor, goes through floors of women's fashion from funky young style to designer labels and on to the hushed elegance of the top international designer floor on seven. Also check out the kids' floor busting with clothes and toys and the manchester floor for bed, table and bath. Over the road in Market St is the men's store boasting a great Food Hall in the basement, men's clothing and shoes in the middle and topped by furniture and electrical goods. Its 'we will match prices' policy has kept a loyal following from straying elsewhere.

■ Elizabeth and Market Sts,
ph 9266 5544. Suburban stores include the smart store at Chatswood in Chatswood Chase, ph 9844 4111; and at Brookvale, Bankstown, Bondi Junction, Castle Hill, Miranda, Pagewood and Parramatta.

Grace Bros

Part of the megapowerful Coles Myer group, the Grace Bros stores provide a popular alternative to David Jones. Its ambitious renovation of the city store, surrounded by the new Sydney Central Plaza, opens in October 1998. It promises to provide six floors of 'innovative

Australian and overseas brands that will be displayed in a way which will be unique for Australian department store retailing'.

- 436 George St, City, ph 9238 9111. Also at Bondi Junction, ph 9387 0222; Warringah Mall, ph 9938 9111; Chatswood, ph 9412 01111; and Blacktown, Burwood, Carlingford, Hornsby, Hurstville, North Ryde, Parramatta, Liverpool, Roselands, Miranda, Mt Druitt. Inquiries: ph 1800 626 611.

Gowings

This classic men's department store, established in 1868, is famous for its cluttered retro windows. It's full of Aussie basics and beyond – RM Williams, Drizabone, Bonds underwear, and Akubra hats and all sorts of camping gear and gadgetry. Upstairs is Gowing's barber shop – $5 for short back and sides but don't go on pension day. Now also near Wynyard Station is their new upmarket store in George St with its fun boy toy department for grown-up lads, cafe and even hardware (one of the few places you can find it in the city).

- Cnr Market and George Sts, City, ph 9264 6321. Also at Wynyard, ph 9262 1281, and Darlinghurst, ph 9331 5544.

Jane de Teliga

Disabled Sydney

The streets of Sydney are narrow, winding and convoluted and can pose considerable difficulties for people with disabilities. Buildings or shopping centres which have more than one frontage can also easily confuse when you enter at ground level at one end and have to use a lift or escalator to enter from another street entrance.

It is impossible to provide, in a short article, a complete guide to the best services for the disabled to Sydney. *Accessing Sydney – a handbook for people with disabilities and who have trouble getting around* is extremely comprehensive, with detailed listings of facilities at hundreds of hotels, restaurants, shops, entertainment and transport. The book is available from the Australian Quadriplegic Association (AQA) (ph 9661 8855). With the help of the APA and advice from the Disability Access Service of the State Library of New South Wales, here are a selection of some of the services and facilities for the disabled in Sydney.

Transport

Train stations are increasingly building ramped or lift access into their upgrading programs to help the disabled. Some of the best-designed stations are: Circular Quay, Kogarah, Hurstville, Sutherland, Parramatta, Strathfield, Westmead and Wollstonecraft.

Most of the ferries services are good, particularly the Rivercat service which glides under the bridge, stopping at ports down the wide Parramatta, and the Jetcat to Manly.

The 888 bus service to Circular Quay and Star City and the 478 to Rockdale, Ramsgate and Miranda are able to transport wheelchair users, and the State Transport Authority is attempting to improve bus design with features such as handrails and slip-resistant floor surfaces.

Parking is available for 'authorised disabled people' within the city of Sydney at a number of places including: two spaces outside the Art Gallery of NSW, three spaces near the State Rail Authority Booking Office at Central Railway Colonnade, two spaces outside the Conservatorium, and two on the West Side of Martin Place in Macquarie Street.

Accommodation

There is quite a wide variety of accommodation available in Sydney generally offering good facilities for the disabled across a broad price spectrum.

The Sydney Central Youth Hostel has seven fully accessed rooms and the YWCA has one access unit with a bathroom. Many of the good quality hotels offer good access and facilities with ramps or no steps. These include: the Renaissance, Sydney Marriott, Parkroyal, Regent, Wentworth International, Furama Hotel, Southern Cross, Nikko, Observatory, Park Hyatt, ANA and Sheraton. Notoriously poor is the Sydney Hilton, which has wheelchair access to seminars only through its kitchens.

Restaurants

Most of the restaurants at the top hotels have good access. The Forecourt Restaurant at the Sydney Opera House has a level entrance with access to a toilet, as does City Extra and Rossini's at Circular Quay and the Sydney Cove Oyster Bar.

The Australian Quadriplegic Association recommends highly the Sydney Rowing Club at Abbotsford, which has toilets, parking, and access to Abbotsford wharf. Signatures at Brighton Le Sands goes to extra effort with two small lifts giving access to its restaurant. The Malaya in George St is recommended, as is Lipinis in Cronulla and the Cleveland in Double Bay – all well-known for their easy access.

Communications

Telephone Typewriters or TTYs which allow communication between two deaf people or one deaf person and a hearing person are becoming increasingly prevalent in offices. Using a typewriter keyboard the two people can type messages to each other over the telephone line. TTY pay phones have also become available at the following locations: the Pay Phone Centre at 100 Pitt Street, City; the Ansett Domestic Terminal, opposite the ticket counter; the International Airport, downstairs at the opposite end of arrivals; Westfield Shopping Centre, Parramatta.

The Australian Communications Exchange also offers a TTY relay service where an operator connects the call between a hearing and deaf person and a tremendous range of services for the hearing impaired (ph 132 544).

Cinemas

The Verona in Oxford St is noted for its lifts. Greater Union George St Cinema Complex is accessible as are the nearby Hoyts Village and complexes.

Sporting facilities

Hurstville Aquatic Centre and Homebush Aquatic Centre are outstanding, according to the AQA.

Collaroy Beach is noted for its beautiful rockpool, ramp and submersible wheelchair. Shelley Beach has a boat ramp which is sheltered and makes wheelchair access easy.

Centennial Park has certain facilities which are excellent, as does part of the Royal National Park.

Other entertainment

The Art Gallery of NSW has good access as does the Botanic Gardens. Darling Harbour is also a location with good facilities.

Specialised services

The Royal Blind Society of NSW (ph 9334 3333) is a non-profit organisation which helps with sensory development, braille, vocational skills, activities of daily living, counselling service and recreation resource service. They also have a free library service with large print books, talking book machine and tapes and a tactile mapping service.

Accessible Arts Inc. (ph 9555 1022) is a community based organisation which acts as advocacy service promoting integration of disabled people within all arts/cultural activities, venues, facilities and resources.

The NSW Council for Intellectual Disability (ph 9211 1611 or fax 9211 2606) is a computer-based information service to help people with intellectual disabilities, their families and carers and to keep in touch with services available to them throughout NSW – data includes accommodation, employment, leisure activities, respite care and activity therapy centres.

The Deaf Education Network (ph 9764 4600) provides programs for deaf people such as Reading and Writing, Office Administration and Sign Language interpreters, as well as job placement.

The State Library of NSW (ph 9230 1540) has a special needs service – large print materials, talking books, captioned videos, tape and text kits, scanners, computer software.

Sydney Community College (ph 9555 7411), which runs more than 5,000 courses from belly dancing to bread making, has an Access Project, run by Frank Storey, which offers volunteers to help with transport, sign language and peer support. It also offers fee reduction in cases of hardship.

The Intellectual Disabilities Rights Service (ph 9318 0144) provides help with accommodation, services, advocacy and self-advocacy.

The Australian Quadriplegic Association (ph 9661 8855), as well as providing the book Accessing Sydney, as above, has a range of services including information, training and employment, accommodation, counselling and support.

Discount fashion

see also sales

Sydney has a growing discount fashion market with Birkenhead Point Shopping Centre, the new Market City in Chinatown and a concentration of factory outlets across Redfern and Surry Hills. Here a shopper with a keen eye can find great pieces at bargain prices among mainstream labels' discontinued stock and samples.

Brian Rochford

Competitively priced swimwear can be found at this factory outlet, filled with bikinis and one-pieces in an array of brilliant fluorescents, prints and classic colours.
■ Market City, ph 9212 7381.

Country Road Wearhouse Store

Billowing with shirts, jackets, shift dresses, pants, skirt and accessories, the Country Road Wearhouse store is well worth a look for quality clothing at discount prices.
■ Birkenhead Point, ph 9819 6222.

Esprit

A wide variety of stock with basic pieces plentiful and at very reasonable prices. Cotton t-shirts priced from $4.95.
■ Market City, ph 9211 6511; Birkenhead Point, ph 9719 8364.

Jigsaw

Heavily discounted samples, faulty garments, previous seasons ranges, as well as current stock at regular retail prices. Worth a look for pretty floral print dresses, tailored skirts, pants, dresses and individual knitwear pieces.
■ Birkenhead Point, ph 9719 9324.

Mambo

Renowned for its funky surfwear range, Mambo's outlet store is filled with board shorts, signature tees and swimwear. A great place to find savings of around 30 per cent, and one-off pieces in among discontinued stock and samples.
■ Birkenhead Point, ph 9719 9327.

Marcs

At factory outlet stores in Redfern, Market City and Birkenhead Point, popular label Marcs has men's and womenswear reduced by 30-75 per cent. Filled with brightly coloured tees and

shirts, Italian label Diesel jeans, and men's casual and business shirts.
- 152 Redfern St, Redfern, ph 9319 7561. Also at Market City and Birkenhead Point.

Oroton Factory Outlet
Beautifully made wallets, handbags and accessories at 25-75 per cent less than retail. Also carries discounted Polo Ralph Lauren men's chino pants, business and casual shirts.
- 418a Elizabeth St, Surry Hills, ph 9281 9520; 52-54 Balgowlah Rd, Balgowlah ph 9951 0500.

Georgina Lucas

Diving has been described as one of the most graceful – and one of the most difficult – sports. Whether it be off the one-metre springboard, the three-metre springboard, or the 10-metre platform, spectators consistently watch in awe as competitors take part in diving events.

In the lead-up to the Olympics in 2000, the Sydney International Aquatic Centre will play host to numerous national, and international diving events, including the Southern Cross International in January 1999. Australian will be sending one of its strongest teams in history to the Commonwealth Games in Kuala Lumpur in September 1998, with the summer diving season in Australia beginning after they return, in late October. For information on events, contact the NSW Diving Association (see below).

Sydney International Aquatic Centre
While several aquatic centres around the city have diving pools, the main diving venue is the pool which will be used in the Sydney 2000 Olympic Games. If you go on a guided tour of the centre one morning or afternoon, chances are that you will see the NSW Institute of Sports elite squad training in the diving pool.
- Sydney Olympic Park, Homebush, ph 9752 3666.

NSW Diving Association
The place to go for all information relating to diving events in Sydney. It also offers learn-to-dive classes.
- ph 9589-0370. For information on classes, contact the director of coaching, Eric Brooker, on 4933 3061, or Alan Cheetham on 9808 3834 or (0414) 260 360.

NSW Diving Association Troupe
For a corporate event with a difference why not hire this troupe for a spectacular exhibition of diving at the Sydney International Aquatic Centre.
- Contact coach Madelaine Barnett on 9799 2193 or (015) 247 115.

Michael Cowley

Further information
- Australian Diving Association, ph (07) 3823 1444

Drives

see also national parks, car hire
Sydney and its hinterland offer spectacular roads and scenery, most within an hour or so of the CBD. Even if time is short, every visitor to Sydney should travel the Bays to Bondi loop.

Bays to Bondi
Don't try this in the rush hours. Take New South Head Rd through Double Bay and Rose

Bay. Follow it all the way to Watson's Bay for sensational views and a real slice of Sydney life. Plenty of restaurants and coffee shops. Return via Old South Head Rd with a turn off to Military Rd for the run over Dover Heights and down to Bondi Beach. Head back to the city via Bondi Rd.

Heading south

A solid four- to five-hour round trip. Head for Royal National Park, 20 minutes due south of Sydney Airport. You'll find it by taking the Princes Highway then a left turn (Route 68) to Audley. For a concentrated dose of bushland, big coastal views and good picnic spots, the park is impossible to beat. Stop at peaceful Wattamolla for a swim.

Pile back in the car for the drive to Kiama, home to the famed blowhole – try to catch it on a high tide. A little further south is the very twee Berry – home of coffee shops and overpriced antique stores. Then loop inland through Kangaroo Valley up and over two rainforested mountain passes to Fitzroy Falls and on to Bowral for a late lunch or early dinner at one of the restaurants on Bong Bong St. (The Catch has great fish). Pick up the Hume Highway for the trip back to Sydney.

Northern exposure

Everyone thinks their route to Palm Beach is quicker, less trafficked and has fewer stop lights. The only real concern is to get onto Pittwater Rd before Collaroy so you can stop at the best pie shop in the area, the Uppercrust, for a morning snack. Drive on to Mona Vale (south end) to eat your pie. This is where all the locals hand out and they swear it's the best spot for a swim. If you fancy a surf along the way the best place is definitely North Narrabeen. Veer off Barrenjoey Rd (Pittwater turns into Barrenjoey at Mona Vale) onto Beach Rd for a sweep through Whale Beach and the most picturesque entry over Little Head to Palm Beach. Hang out on the beach, work up an appetite and head for a delicious late lunch at the best restaurant in the area, the Beach Rd. Head back to Sydney truly satiated and probably a little sunburnt.

On the other hand, it can be a crowded drive up the peninsular to Palm Beach. A more relaxed option: head up the Pacific Highway to Hornsby, then leave the freeway for a meandering run along the Old Pacific Highway. A challenging road, much favoured by Sunday morning motorcyclists, it opens out to reveal the mighty Hawkesbury river at the fishing village of Brooklyn (worth a detour for coffee or lunch). Continue up the old road to Gosford or make a bee-line back to Sydney on the adjacent freeway. Or both. Pick up the freeway close to Gosford.

Country Life

A day trip: north-west of the city are Wisemans Ferry and St Alban's. Great views of the Hawkesbury, towering sandstone escarpments, a chugging car ferry and if you're feeling adventurous a run through St Alban's common on an unsealed but good-quality road to the famous convict pub. On weekends it really hops (jazz bands, string quartets), but during the week it's tranquil. Reach it via the Old Northern Rd (through Castle Hill, Dural) which wends its way through orchard and farm country before diving down to Wisemans Ferry, a river town with a long history. Buy a map and you'll see it's possible to link up the return journey via the Gosford freeway (or a run over the Old Pacific Hwy, as above).

The Blue Mountains

The key here is to get into the country as quickly as possible. Head north to Hornsby on the Pacific Highway, cutting west at Galstn. Wind your way west from Galston through the countryside to Richmond where you'll join up with Bells Line of Road and begin the ascent into the Blue Mountains. Just past Bilpin is the beautiful Mt Tomah Botanic Garden and Restaurant, a perfect place for lunch (try the baked Bilpin apples for dessert). Continue west to Bell and loop down to Mt Victoria where you pick up the Great Western Highway for the trip back through the mountains to Sydney. Stop at artist Norman Lindsay's bohemian grove at Springwood for an afternoon stroll in the breathtaking gardens dotted with some of the artist's sculptures.

Phil Scott and Cerentha Harris

Further information
- 200 Kilometres Around Sydney (Gregory's, $19.95). Available from good book stores or try Map World, 388 Pacific Highway, Lindfield, Lane Cove, ph 9428 3566.

Driving schools

As if teens don't get enough learning in the classroom, they are subjected to mastering a four-wheeled potential death trap with mum or dad tut-tutting away in their ear each weekend. So, it's not surprising that schoolies make up about half of all driving school pupils. There are no hard and fast rules about how to learn quickly, though there are on how to pass the Roads and Traffic Authority's theory test which must be sat in order to gain L plates. Driving an automatic, as unfashionable as it is with retro-favouring youth, is simpler and therefore easier to reach a competent standard.

When choosing a driving school, bigger does not necessarily mean better. Look for the more established schools and ones with Australian Driver Training Association affiliated instructors. Getting on with the instructor is vital – so choose carefully. Most learners take at least 10 lessons (at an average $35-40 a pop) to reach a passable standard. If cost is an issue, try learning in the second half of the year, when most driving schools reduce their fees to meet a drop-off in clientele. Students tend to try and pass before the business-end of the school year. Above all, remember: if you don't succeed at first, try, try again – almost 50 per cent of all first-timers fail.

ABC
Australia-wide school claiming a 95 per cent pass rate. Does overseas licence conversions and offers student discounts.
- Head office: 28 Princes Highway, Kogarah, ph 9587 1899.

Norman Driving School
North Shore company with excellent rates. Sympathetic to nervous drivers.
- 9/12-14 Landers Rd, Lane Cove, ph 9418 6544.

Eastern Suburbs Driving School
One of Sydney's most established and least expensive schools.
- 8 Govett St, Randwick, ph 9314 6919.

Royce Driver Training School
Specialises in tuition for truck, bus, semi-trailers and forklift licences. Runs heavy vehicle assessor courses for the Roads and Traffic Authority.
- PO Box 119, Five Dock, ph 9648 7233.

Stay Upright School
Specialises in motorcycle tuition.
- Annangrove Rd, Annangrove, ph 9679 1578.

Jim Murcotts Advanced Driving Centre
Worried about young Jimmy's temperament behind the wheel? This post-licence driver training school also offers corporate discounts.
- PO Box 30, Jannali, ph 9589 1970.

Fleet Taxi Training Centre
Has been helping put cabbies on the road since 1974. Assists with the mandatory 35-hour training program and exam.
- 357 Glenmore Rd, Paddington, ph 9360 6139.

Peter Vincent

Further information
- Roads and Traffic Authority (RTA),

ph 9218 6641 (motorcycle training);
ph 9218 6221 (heavy vehicle permits)
- Driver Rehabilitation Centre,
Cumberland Health & Research Centre, University of Sydney, East Lidcombe, ph 9351 9282

Drycleaners & laundries

Laundrettes are becoming popular these days, with many people having less and less time to worry about such trivial things as washing. They're also becoming something of an icon, stemming from popular music videos and a love for the '50s. Here are a few of the gems found around Sydney.

Blue and White Dry Cleaning
Now this is well and truly a service. A drive-through drycleaners that's reasonably priced, friendly and super-speedy.
- Cnr Falcon and West Sts, North Sydney, ph 9955 6044.

Hang Out Bondi Laundry
Washing your knickers has never been so much fun. A thoroughly modern laundrette and drycleaners with a trés cool coffee bar. It's quite a popular place to meet people, so make sure you're wearing clean boxers.
- 97 Glenayr Ave, Bondi Beach, ph 9300 9733.

TLC Dry Cleaning
A franchise found across the city. They're reliable and efficient, and conveniently placed near metropolitan train stations.
- Martin Place, Town Hall, Wynyard, North Sydney stations; locations around the city. Head office, ph 9363 1711.

Nicola Shenton

Duty-free shopping

You have your plane ticket and now you're ready to shop. Is buying duty-free in Sydney worth it? Perfume, cosmetics, jewellery, alcohol, tobacco and electrical goods are the areas you can buy duty-free and it's possible to get some very good deals. You aren't paying customs duty or sales tax, some of which can hike the price 70 per cent. Always make sure you check the equivalent retail prices before buying. The individual duty-free allowance per adult is $400, plus 1.125 litres of alcohol, 250 cigarettes and any amount of fragrance. A recent study by Sydney Airport Retail Marketing shows that duty-free prices in Sydney are comparable with and sometimes lower than other countries. Singapore was the only country where every item tested came up substantially cheaper than in Sydney.

Downtown Duty Free
There are 15 stores all over Sydney and DDF also own City Duty Free and the Allders stores. The chain's buying power allows big ranges at competitive prices. They are strongest in cosmetics and fragrances, but you can also find good deals on alcohol and electronics. The staff are well trained and there's no pressure to buy. Don't be afraid to bargain, especially if you are buying a number of items. DDF offers a pre-order phone service (ph 9319 5599) with pick-up at the airport before departure or after arrival. Far more economical than buying at DDF's airport store, where prices can be 10 per cent more than at other branches.
- 105 Pitt Street, City, ph 9233 3166.
Also at many other locations.

Camera House
All prices clearly marked retail and duty-free. This is the best place to buy digital videotape (retail and duty-free) for your digital camera.
- 201 Clarence St, City, ph 9299 4404; 364A Kent St, City, ph 9299 6745. Also at Parramatta and many other locations.

Duty-free shopping

Paxton's Camera and Video
Retail and duty-free. You'll find everything from a beaten-up, second-hand Pentax to the newest, slick little Leica. A good spot for comparison shopping. Plus you can get money off your duty-free purchase if you trade in your old camera.
- 258 George St, City, ph 9299 2999.

Angus & Coote
The best spot for jewellery, especially watches. They have a shop at the airport and in the city selling tax-free items to travellers. Jewellery doesn't attract duty, but it does get taxed. Tag Hueur men's 2000 series watch sells for around $1495 tax-free and for about $1995 retail.
- 19 Pitt St, City, ph 9247 7611.

Cerentha Harris

Electricians

While many people are left in the dark when it comes to electricians, a good, reliable one is not that difficult to find. Instead of randomly scanning the Yellow Pages by candlelight you should have the name of a trusty electrician or two on hand in case of emergency. The five electricians listed below received top votes in the 1998 Tradespeople of the Year Awards, run by the Sydney Morning Herald's weekly home section Domain, and are renowned for their dedication to clients, flexibility and professionalism. You can also seek advice on electricians from the Electrical Contractors Association on 9744 1099 or the Master Builders Association on 9281 3511.

Keith Blakemore
Work varies between industrial, commercial and domestic and includes installation of intercom and security systems. Trade licence EC23363.
- Ph 0418 228 070.

Eaton Electrics
Specialises in luxury homes and prestigious developments. No problems, only solutions. Trade licence 37174.
- Ph 9909 8822.

Peter Gooden, Coogee Bay Electrical Pty Ltd
Domestic, commercial and property maintenance. Trade licence 40895C.
- Ph 0411 192 919.

Jim Graham
Domestic and commercial installations and repairs in the St George area and Sutherland shire. Trade licence 27503C.
- Ph 0418 140 726 or 9525 6679.

Leo Robertson
Domestic and commercial work on the North Shore. Trade licence EC6255.
- Ph 9427 1881.

Penny Harrison

European restaurants

see also French restaurants, Italian restaurants, Italian Sydney, Greek Sydney, Spanish Sydney

A grab-bag category this, covering what we once called 'Continental food' – anything from a golden crumbed schnitzel to a creamy beef stroganoff or a smoky, chunky sausage. For a nation brought up on lamb chops and canned beetroot, it had all the makings of a long-time love affair.

Double Bay Steakhouse

Yes, the steaks are very good and generous, but you're really here to enjoy some of Sydney's most authentic Hungarian food. Chef Imre Halasz has cooked at the famous Gundel restaurant in Budapest and it shows in his goulash, his schnitzels and his creamed cabbage.
- 15 Knox St, Double Bay, ph 9327 1115.

Una's

That old Darlinghurst staple, Una's, is selling more schnitzels, goulash and strudel than ever under its new owners and recent refurbishment: amazing, considering how many things they're doing wrong. The servings are far too big, the prices are way too small, and at around $10 a main course they even have the nerve to be nice, and to ask if you enjoyed it.
- 340 Victoria St, Darlinghurst, ph 9360 6885.

Northern Lights

The food is a mixture of the cuisines of Sweden, Denmark, Finland and Norway, though every one of those nationalities claim it as their own. But wherever you come from you'll enjoy the Danish frikadeller, the salmon gravlax, the herring with blackbread, and the Swedish pancakes.
- 188 Pacific Highway, Hornsby, ph 9482 7364.

Terry Durack

Event management

see also **party supplies, catering**

Next time you feel like inviting 500 of your closest friends round for cocktails, but are too busy to commission the florists, field the RSVP phone calls and put all those sausages on sticks, these are the people to call. Most of them will organise the full range of events (an ultra-luxe dinner for eight, a 50th birthday, a mega budget corporate bash for 2,000 . . .), looking after everything from invitation design to clearing up, although a couple specialise in giant-scale events. Whatever it is, their special skill is to make any party ultra-stylish, unique and unforgettable. And fun for the hosts.

The ARC Factory

They're equally at home doing the Princess Diana dinner, the launch of *Harpers Bazaar Mode* and *Cleo* magazine's Eligible Bachelors party – so not really the choice for a coffee morning . . .
- Ph 9332 4744.

Cavanagh Consulting

The groovy side of town. Mark Cavanagh's PR clients include Ray Ban sunglasses and Absolut vodka.
- Ph 9331 1322.

Cinch

Very stylish visual concepts for the entire party spectrum.
- Ph 9380 9335.

Colvin Communications

The Triple A list party organisers – the legendary Cointreau Ball is their gig.
- Ph 9380 6822.

David Grant Special Events

Nothing is too big, or too ambitious. David Grant does the biggest corporate parties in town with wild ideas and unique concepts. If there are woodchoppers, flying trapezes and eight different kinds of music, David did it.
- Ph 9241 4790.

James Gordon Workshops

The most beautiful events, from the party for the premiere of *Romeo and Juliet* to high society weddings.
- Ph 9929 6952.

Event management

Hospitality Hire
Very grown up. Gorgeous weddings a speciality and the perfect choice for the smart corporate set. They will do the complete event, or hire out the details that make it look good – tablecloths, chair covers, candelabra, fake flowers etc.
- Ph 9699 8600.

Mary Cummins Special Events
Corporate events specially designed and managed by the owner of Hospitality Hire (see above).
- Ph 9817 0734.

Maggie Alderson

Fast food & takeaway

Forget greasy fish and chips, overheated pies, MSG-laden chop suey, and soggy pizzas. Fast food does not have to be junk food – it can be just as serious as slow food, so long as it's made with fresh, topnotch ingredients, and it's made by someone who really cares. There are rules in the world of the perfect pie, best burger, flaky fish and flavoursome falafel. It must be quick – that means 10 minutes max. Here's where to get it in Sydney.

Patchett's Pies
Best spot for the classic, all glazed and golden and crammed with chunky beef. There's a perky little English pork pie and a rich, peppery steak and kidney in its repertoire, too.
- 2 Ewan St, Mascot, ph 9667 3799. Also sold in shops, restaurants and cafes around Sydney.

King Wally's Pies
Nothing new-age about these pies. The pastry is super flaky and golden brown and the plain steak pie oozes with a juicy dark beef gravy.
- 209b Coogee Bay Rd, Coogee, ph 9665 5588.

Burgerman
All the burgers are stacked with fresh ingredients between halves of crunchy white or wholemeal and sesame buns. The juicy, ground beef burgers (with cheese, onion, pickle, bacon-style combos) draw the crowds but the vegetarian number (crispy rocket and yam chips, goat's fetta, garlic mayo, just-cooked beetroot, grilled capsicum, iceberg and tomato slices) is a winner, too.
- 249 Bondi Rd, Bondi, ph 9130 4888; 116 Surrey St, Darlinghurst, ph 9361 0268.

Paul's Famous Hamburgers
A great, traditional burger with snappy crisp salad on a fresh-like-it's-just-baked bun. An institution. Take it away with a pineapple crush.
- 12 Princes Highway, Sylvania, ph 9522 5632.

Bronte Chippa
Hugely popular with locals and daytrippers braving the crazy Bronte surf. A fillet of whiting, a serve of chips and a view of waves crashing from the grassy park makes a perfect conclusion to a jog along the Bondi-to-Bronte track.
- 491 Bronte Rd, Bronte, ph 9387 7956.

Seafood at the Beach
The shop is as fresh as a daisy, chips are greaseless and crisp and the fish taste as though they have just jumped out of the ocean across the road.
- 12a The Strand, Dee Why, ph 9971 9666.

Blue Bells
This old-style fish shop offers fast, friendly service and super juicy fillets of fish in a good crunchy batter.
- 218 Lyons Rd, Five Dock, ph 9713 8954.

El-Manara
This shop prepares everything on the spot, from great kebabs and kofta (lamb mince) to a breakfast special called fatteh (crispy flat bread topped with tahini, yogurt, pine nuts and chick peas).
- 143 Haldon St, Lakemba, ph 9740 6762.

Victoria Yeeros
These kebabs, like the falafels, are an Inner West staple – all freshly prepared ingredients, crunchy tabouli, rich hommos and baba ghanoush.
- 301 Victoria Rd, Marrickville, ph 9560 1478.

Fu Manchu
Takeaway Chinese goes funky in a modern Mao sort of way at this tiny shoebox of a restaurant. The san choy bao is reliable, the duck wraps are highly recommended, and the roast pork and dumpling soup is life supportive. Best of all, the food comes in those cool cardboard containers you see in *Seinfeld*. And, yes, they deliver.
- 249 Victoria St, Darlinghurst, ph 9360 9424.

Samantha Trenoweth

Fences & gates

'Don't fence me in' runs the old song. Yet our need for security and desire to define boundaries have never been greater. Gates and fences can be purely utilitarian, or they can be designed to enhance the look of your property. Quality does not necessarily cost more, but it can take a little longer to find.

Australian Wrought Iron
As its old-fashioned name suggests, this is a well-established company with a reputation for quality. Of course, it works in steel these days, producing everything from structural work to architect-designed gates and doors.
- 29 College St, Gladesville, ph 9817 1311.

Designer Iron Craft
Twenty-five years in the business, Designer Ironcraft manufactures gates, security doors, window grilles and fences with the same quality materials, care and attention that they use when making their wrought iron furniture. Available in a variety of finishes.
- 4 Booralee St, Botany, ph 9666 3398.

Edwards Engineering
A small company producing extremely good work, often on fast-turnaround times. From steel security gates to swimming pool fencing, Edwards will make and install to your specifications.
- 23 Ada Ave, Brookvale, ph 9938 5320.

Steel Fitter Security
Frank Fanaian may not be the biggest in the business, but he'll work with you to achieve your desired end, however unusual your request. As an added bonus, he'll also fit electric security locks to your choice of gate.
- Unit 24, 1 Adept Lane, Bankstown, ph 9707 3322.

Fence Magic (Southside) Pty Ltd
Face it, steel fences are cheaper, last longer and provide better privacy than those old paling jobs. And they don't deplete our rapidly diminishing forest resource. Fence Magic is known in the trade for competitive prices and good turnaround times. Installation can be arranged.
- 116 Caldarra Ave, Engadine, ph 9548 2700.

BBC Hardwarehouse Stores
When it comes to that fancy colonial picket fence, or if you're determined it's good old-

fashioned palings for you, builders we spoke to still reckon BBC has the best range in town.
- Located in many suburbs. Head office: Cnr Cambridge and Chester Sts, Epping, ph **9876 0888**.

Chris Dobney

Hordern Pavilion at the old Sydney Showgrounds has been chosen as the venue for the 2000 Olympic fencing competition.
- Church St, Lidcombe, ph **9646 5666**.

Heather Quinlan

Fencing

En garde! Make like a Musketeer and experience the thrill of one-on-one combat – minus the threat of injury, of course – with a foray into fencing. One of the traditional Olympic events, fencing is an athletic, skilful and very challenging sport. And for spectators, it's nothing less than spectacular to watch, with its eye-catching lunges and duels. Australia does not have a strong background in Olympic fencing competitions, but with the 2000 Games approaching, Sydney is doing its best to hone the local talent.

NSW Amateur Fencing Association Inc

There are three fencing weapons: foil, sabre and epee. For obvious reasons, you can't just pick one up and start lunging away. First you need to approach a qualified coach, through one of Sydney's five private fencing clubs, to give you some basic tuition. There are also four clubs based at the University of Sydney, University of NSW, UTS and Macquarie University.
- ph **9918 2456**.

Equipment

Clubs will also provide the protective gear and equipment, but if you want to purchase your own, call **Jeff Gray** (ph **9773 4515**) or **Terry Bowen** (ph **9642 7193**).

Anne Clarke Netball Centre

This is the venue for elite championship fencing events, though after much debate the

Ferries

What could be more peaceful than a ferry trip across the harbour on a summer's evening with the city twinkling around you. But don't limit yourself to the Harbour. There's a profusion of waterways to explore by ferry.

Cronulla National Park Ferry Cruises

Best southern ferry tour. For $8, tour the bays and inlets of the Hacking River with the Royal National Park bordering the whole southern shoreline. Check out Aboriginal sites, historic settlements and have a sticky at some of Sydney's most magnificent waterfront properties. Morning tea provided.
- Tonkin Street Wharf, just below Cronulla Station, ph **9523 2990**.

Sydney Ferries

Still the cheapest way to enjoy the Harbour. Choose the ferry to Manly for the best view of the big three – Opera House, Harbour Bridge and the East Circular Quay extravaganza. The 30-minute ride costs $3.80. For the very best view of the Harbour Bridge, catch the Hunters Hill or Balmain ferry. Both ferries glide right under the giant span of the bridge.
- Sydney Ferry Infoline, **131 500**.

Hawkesbury River Ferries

The last riverboat postman in Australia travels up and down the Hawkesbury carrying mail, milk and groceries. You can join the skipper for the 3½ hour ride up the river. Tickets are

$25 for adults, $20 for pensioners and $10 for children.
- ph 02 9985 7566 for bookings and information.

Australia Day Ferry Race

Watch these lumbering queens of the Harbour dash off from Fort Denison, careen around Shark Island and swoop to the finishing line at the Harbour Bridge, all vying to win the coveted Lord Mayor's Trophy. In 1997 the speedy catamaran ferries were included in this 18-year-old race, giving it a whole new spin. Starts at 11am. Best viewing points are Mrs Macquarie's Chair, Bradleys Head and under either end of the Harbour Bridge.

River Cat

A one-way ticket to Parramatta will set you back $4.80, but the hour-long trip along some of the most beautiful waterfront property in Sydney is well worth it. Make sure you get one of the seats outside, they go fast. The River Cat glides along the Parramatta River, and if you are going to Homebush, hop off the ferry at the Meadowbank wharf. The Olympic site is just across the river.
- Ph Infoline 131 500 for schedule information.

Cerentha Harris

Film

see also video stores

It was an Australian who invented the ('Take thirty-two!') clapperboard, an Australian who made the first feature-length film (Soldiers of the Cross), an Australian who recorded the first 'talkie'. Still today this country is a strong force in film-making, and Sydney its focus. At last count 37 Aussie directors were in Hollywood action, but increasingly they're 'working from home'. On one day at Lindfield's post-production complex, you could find Phil (Patriot Games) Noyce, Bruce (Driving Miss Daisy) Beresford and Gillian (Oscar and Lucinda) Armstrong all at work. Baz Luhrmann has a Sydney-centred deal with US studio, Fox – the company that's banking on more Bazzes to fill their new film-making studios in Paddington. Fox will feature its own multiplex from 1999, but meanwhile the big screens are clustered in the CBD – George St is blockbuster bonanza, with Greater Union, Hoyts and Village. Check out Hoyts new state-of-the-art cineplex at Broadway.

Chauvel Cinema

With the most innovative programming in Sydney, this cinema in Paddington Town Hall has a great bar, great balcony and classics showing at Monday night cinemateque.
- Cnr Oxford St and Oatley Rd, Paddington, ph 9361 5398.

Academy Twin

Also keeps a caffeinated crowd of arthouse stalwarts happy.
- 3a Oxford St, Paddington, ph 9361 4453.

The Verona

Here, the slick, chardonnay-sipping crowd comes for what the trade calls 'cross-over product' – part arthouse, part-Hollywood. Great bookshops nearby, too.
- 17 Oxford St, Paddington, ph 9360 6099.

Palace Leichhardt

Like the Verona but in the heart of Little Italy. New for the caffeinated cool crowd.
- 99 Norton St, Leichhardt, ph 9550 0122.

Cremorne Orpheum

The main theatre in this restored art-deco cinema features a live organist on a hydraulic

platform, so your matinees come with music – just like the good old days.
- 380 Military Rd, Cremorne, ph 9908 4344.

Roseville
This family-run cinema still draws a door prize! Wait for it here, rather than rush to the multiplex down the road.
- 112 Pacific Highway, Roseville, ph 9416 8555.

Walker Cinema
Small but special, this hole in the wall of advertising firms shows smart art fare.
- 121 Walker St, North Sydney, ph 9959 4222.

Dendy Cinemas
Three cinemas all showing passionately picked films from Australia and around the world.
- 19 Martin Place, ph 9233 8166; 624 George St, ph 9264 1577; 261 King St, Newtown, ph 9550 5699.

IMAX Theatre
Shows specially made mega pictures on a mega-mega-screen. Go for the full vertigo of a flying adventure, or see whiz-bang special effects splashed on screen, or jungle animals, Antarctic explorers . . . family fun, but not cheap.
- Southern Promenade, Darling Harbour, ph 9281 3300.

Randwick Ritz
This art-deco treasure would have been knocked down but for a late-discovered Heritage order. Now it's restored and offering blockbuster fare for less money – $7.50 leaves you room for popcorn.
- 43 St Pauls St, Randwick, ph 9399 9840.

Valhalla
The champion of independents, this big old cinema lets true art-house pictures find their audience – always an eclectic mix, from foreign to animation to documentary to plain entertaining.
- 166 Glebe Point Rd, Glebe, ph 9660 8050.

Sydney Film Festival
This is the premiere fest event on the cineaste's calendar. Held every June, it shows a mix of first-look local pictures, hard-to-see foreign films, and intelligently curated retrospectives, plus forums, a great club and always a good cocktail crowd. In summer, the international short film fest is Flickerfest, under the stars at iconic Bondi Beach.
- www.oze-mail.com.au/~sff/

Tropicana Film Festival
A monster street party every February where, incidentally, they show short films. 'TropFest' screens all around Victoria St, Darlinghurst, and in 1999 will also be at either The Domain or Centennial Park. Next, it's in cafes all over Australia.
- www.infolearn.com.au/tropfest/

Great Inflatable Film Festival
Dive-in drive-in – the latest Australian 'first'. Held each December with the audience floating on pool-ponies, li-los and rafts while the movies drown out the waves of Coogee.

Cinestore
Chock-a-block with movie books, scripts (even before the movie is out!), manuals, memorabilia and all things fun for a movie buff.
- 37 Liverpool St, City, ph 9283 3049.

Lauren Martin

Further information
- See Sydney Morning Herald Metro and CitySearch for listings
- Australian Film Television and Radio School (AFTRS), Epping Rd, North Ryde, ph 9805 6444: www.aftrs.edu.au/

Fine dining

There was a time when fine dining meant heavy drapes, inch-thick carpet, black-tied waiters and a stuffy, all-enveloping air of pretension. These days it means dining finely in restaurants that know well that having a good time is what it's all about.

bel mondo
The Manfredi family is something of a legend in this town, having honed its reputation in a hard-to-find restaurant in the back streets of Ultimo. Now that it's moved to this glamorous location in The Rocks, with theatrical open kitchen and stupendous, innovative Italian food, the legend is growing by the minute.
- Level 3, The Argyle Department Store, 12-24 Argyle St, The Rocks, ph 9241 3700.

Bennelong
Michael Moore, former executive chef of Terrence Conran's groundbreaking Bluebird restaurant in London, returns to Sydney to take over the premier restaurant of the even more groundbreaking Sydney Opera House. Rarely has the finest Australian produce had such a glamorous stage on which to perform.
- Sydney Opera House, Bennelong Point, ph 9250 7548.

Bilson's
Normally, having a view that encompassed the Sydney Harbour Bridge, Circular Quay and the Opera House would be enough to guarantee a good night out. But to make absolutely certain, Bilson's throws in the fine, assured French-based cooking of former Joel Robuchon chef, Guillaume Brahimi.
- Overseas Passenger Terminal, Circular Quay, ph 9251 5600.

Cicada
Few chefs push themselves as hard or as far as Peter Doyle. As a result, his food manages to be stimulating, finely honed and impeccably balanced without being overworked or over-fussy. Even his special vegetarian menu is so beautifully put together it makes you forget you were ever a carnivore.
- 29 Challis Ave, Potts Point, ph 9358 1255.

Claudes
It's such a small, plain little room, you wonder how it manages to squeeze in a reputation as large as the one that Tim Pak Poy has earned for himself. It's BYO, so bring a bottle fine enough to do justice to Pak Poy's delightful smoked salmon broth with cod roe crostini and salt-baked cockerel.
- 10 Oxford St, Woollahra, ph 9331 2325.

Claudines
You know the whole concept of fine dining has changed considerably when you find yourself going to suburban shopping centre for a big night out. Yet Claudines is a warm woody, appealing space made even more appealing by the measured, classy cooking of Meyjitte Boughenot who has worked with French greats including Alain Pic and Georges Blanc.
- Chatswood Chase, Victoria Ave, Chatswood, ph 9411 1688.

Forty One
What was once earmarked as Alan Bond's private penthouse now has a much more public life as one of Sydney's most deluxe big-time restaurants. The views are positively breathtaking, as is Dietmar Sawyere's exquisitely honed food including his renowned crown roast of hare. Yes . . . hare.
- Level 41, Chifley Tower, 2 Chifley Square, City, ph 9221 2500.

MG Garage Restaurant
It's not every day you get to eat rock lobster cabbage rolls, and guinea fowl baked in clay in a car showroom. Yes, we admit it's a weird combination, but thanks to Janni Kyritsis's inspired touch in the kitchen and one of the

Fine dining

best service teams in town, it works. Don't be surprised if every major car dealer in Sydney starts advertising for a chef.
- 490 Crown St, Surry Hills, ph 9383 9383.

Rockpool
Now a seasoned performer on the Sydney restaurant scene, Neil Perry's Rockpool has never lost its sparkle or its glamour. The place still feels like a perpetual movie premiere, the crowd is still scattered with household names and the food, including slow-cooked abalone with black fungus and roast jewfish with braised vegetables, still startles.
- 107 George St, The Rocks, ph 9252 1888.

Tetsuya's
Don't even think about calling this fusion food. Guided by a Japanese heart and underscored by masterful French technique, Tetsuya Wakuda's food defies any attempt to pigeonhole or classify. Split second timing and inspired innovation has produced classics such as his slow-cooked ocean trout confit, sea urchin and truffle custard, and blue cheese bavarois.
- 729 Darling St, Rozelle, ph 9555 1017.

Terry Durack

Fireworks

It seems Sydneysiders love a bit of flash and will use any excuse to see their harbour lit up. It's illegal for the general public to buy fireworks in Sydney without a permit so it's probably best to leave it to the professionals (they're licensed and insured).

New Year's Eve
The night of nights for fireworks. Last year, more than a million people packed the Harbour foreshores to watch 70 pyrotechnists set off five tonnes of explosives. Wherever you want to be, arrive early; the foreshores get crowded quickly. On land, the best viewing spot is the front of the Opera House. But why not hire a boat to bag an unbeatable spot on the water?

Darling Harbour
If you miss New Year's Eve, Australia Day is your second chance for larger-than-life fireworks. Darling Harbour also lights up with at least five smaller-scale events a month. The best spot to watch is from the new steps at the south end of Cockle Bay. Call the Darling Harbour Authority for a schedule.
- ph 9286 0100.

Syd Howard Fireworks International
Perhaps best known for their New Year's Eve Harbour shows, Syd Howard split from the other Sydney firework giant, **The Original Howard and Sons Pyrotechnics** in a rather contentious family feud. Both are excellent technicians and if you've a major event and money to burn these two are the pick of the bunch.
- Syd Howard Fireworks, ph 9652 2244; The Original Howard and Sons Pyrotechnics, ph 9627 1694.

The Stockade
The DIY alternative. Tony Garland will help you apply for a permit to let off your own fireworks and supply you with a 6-page how-to pamphlet along with your fireworks. Or Garland will design a show for you to fit any budget.
- 9/53 Myoora Rd, Terry Hills, ph 9486 3221.

Cerentha Harris

Further information
- Sydney City Council, ph 9265 9333

Fish & seafood

see also cooking classes, seafood restaurants

Do not pass Go, but go directly to Pyrmont, where the Sydney Fish Market is awash with snapping-fresh fish and seafood. Make sure you visit Claudio's, Musameci's, de Costi's, and Christie's. Outside Pyrmont, there are still plenty more fish shops in the sea. So to speak.

Costi's at David Jones

While there are always a lot of perfectly fresh fillets awaiting your pleasure at Costi's, it's good to see a display of whole fish as well, in case we forget what they look like. Bound to have what you want, or get it in for you.
- David Jones, Westfield Plaza, Bondi Junction, ph 9369 6290 or Market St, City, ph 9266 5544.

Haymarket Seafoods

This is the closest you'll get to a market atmosphere without going to the wholesale markets: stacked boxes of snapping-fresh small fish, squid, prawns, and you name it. Because it serves so much of Chinatown, there is a particularly large array of you-name-it.
- Level 1, 35A Market City, Hay St, Haymarket, ph 9211 7858.

Mohr Food

Not a fish shop, but a smoker of salmon, trout, and purveyor of all sorts of delicious delicacies. John Wilson's Lacroix-pink salmon is dinner party de rigueur, and you can pick it up fresh from the smokehouse.
- 4 Luff St, Botany, ph 9316 6126.

Jill Dupleix

Fishing

see also powerboating

To catch a fish is a bonus, to land dinner truly marvellous, and nowhere is city fishing as productive – or as therapeutic. Anglers of all sizes, creeds and cultures find their own piece of Sydney and hook into a lifestyle. And amid the daydreaming there are fish to catch. Big bream from scenic Blues Point, sweet leatherjackets from the rickety wharves at Pyrmont, dusky flathead from Lane Cove river, sand whiting from famous Bondi, and even the mighty marlin miles out to sea. There are also trout in the mountain streams, an hour's drive west, or luderick for those game enough to partake in rock fishing – Australia's most dangerous sport. By contrast, Sydney's estuaries are safe, serene and fishy havens, where you can leave your worries behind, cast a line and catch the true charm of Sydney – and a seafood dinner.

Rocks

The rocks around south Whale Beach pool are safe in all but a big north-east swell. Fish for bream, tailor, salmon, luderick, maybe a snapper at first light.

Beaches

Every beach has its day, but Narrabeen appears to have more than most. Cast a beachworm for whiting and bream, or soak a whole fresh squid bait for a big jewfish. A 32 kg jewfish was caught here on the December full moon in 1997.

Estuaries

Balls Head for bream and small jewfish on bloodworms, the pylons at Clifton Gardens wharf for leatherjackets on peeled prawn, Rose Bay wharf for fun with the kids, and the park beneath Roseville Bridge for bream and flathead. If you have a boat, Sow and Pigs Reef

Fishing

at the entrance to Port Jackson yields bream, trevally, tailor, luderick and kingfish.

Fishabout Tours
Craig McGill, the only qualified fishing guide on the harbour, has a knack for finding fish when others flounder. A day out includes boat, bait and tackle, tea and biscuits, tuition and tips.
- Ph 9418 4704.

Fishfinder Charters
Tony Davis heads to sea for snapper, morwong and kingfish big enough to feed a football team. Pick-up from all harbour wharves.
- Ph 9818 1718.
  Or jump aboard Avalon IV at Palm Beach with a wise old salt called Jimmy Dempsey, ph 9918 3914.

Mountain River Riders
Fly by chopper from Parramatta helipad into the Cox's River in the Blue Mountains. Fly-fish for spawn-run rainbow trout averaging 2 kg each from April each year. Truly a wonderful experience.
- ph 02 6336 1890.

The Sheriff
Chase striped black and blue marlin, yellowfin tuna and mahi mahi from spring to autumn with father-and-son team Leon or Brett Thomas.
- Ex Pittwater: ph 018 64 8189.

From Sydney Harbour, head out on a glorious 50-foot Precision yacht called *Yackatoon*.
- Ph 018 253 625.

Balmoral Boat Shed
Hire a 3.5m tinnie with outboard motor and cast adrift from Balmoral, haunt of the succulent summer flathead and winter john dory. No licence required.
- 2 The Esplanade, Balmoral Beach, ph 9969 6006.

Narrabeen Bait
Live bait is the ticket for catching fish in Sydney. Buy a tangle of bloodworms, some fresh Hawkesbury prawns, live nippers or bottle squid from Narrabeen Bait.
- 1469 Pittwater Rd, Narrabeen, ph 9970 6204.

On the south side, Macs Bait is open from 4 am.
- 428 Princes Highway, Blakehurst, ph 9546 1341.

Compleat Angler
Row upon row of rods, reels, lures and the latest lines to tempt anglers who say they have it all.
- Level 3, 428 George St, City, ph 9241 2080.
  Northside: **Bohm Bait and Tackle**. 1246 Pittwater Rd, Narrabeen, ph 9913 7878. Southside: **Bluefin Sports** 186 Railway Pde, Kogarah, ph 9553 8730.

David Lockwood

Further information
- Video: Fishing Sydney Harbour by Craig McGill ($24.95 from tackle shops)
- Gregory's Australian Fishing Guide ($22.95)

Fitness clubs

see also aerobics, personal trainers, martial arts, bodybuilding

So you've made a resolution is to go to the gym. Or at least buy a membership. Before you sign up, pay a few casual visits to ensure it isn't about to go broke and that it has what you're looking for. Are you after one with a sprung aerobics floor or a heavy-metal weights room that exudes the smell of sweat? Choose your gym according to what it specialises in. Shiny new equipment is all well and good, but it doesn't help if there's no-one there to show you how to use it.

City Gym
The daddy of the Sydney gym scene, City Gym has been in business for more than 20 years under the astute guidance of proprietor Bill Moore. The shopfront window, with a view to the bodies working out, says this is a 'working gym'. It's open 24 hours a day and Moore says the equipment may not be the newest in town, but the angles are always correct.
- 107 Crown St, East Sydney, ph 9360 6247.

Pumphouse
Unlike many North Shore gyms, this one does not have an aerobics floor the size of a footy field. It does, however, have one of the most complete weight-training areas on the north side. Offers separate weight, cardio and aerobics rooms, and a friendly family atmosphere with child care.
- Level 1, 199-207 Military Rd, Neutral Bay, ph 9953 4099.

Ultimate Fitness
The mood at Ultimate Fitness reflects Newtown's casual atmosphere. Baggy shorts and T-shirts are more the go than form-fitting Lycra, and Ultimate has a separate 'easy start' area. Owner John Terilli is a former Mr Universe, whose unusual philosophy for successful body-building is eating more and working out less.
- Newtown Plaza Shopping Centre, King St, Newtown, ph 9557 2219.

Temple of the Body & Soul
This lavish new women-only venue boasts a rock-climbing wall and virtual-reality gym equipment, as well as beauty therapy, spas and body scrubs to pamper you after all that adventuring. The Temple's holistic approach reflects the philosophy of the founders, Edwin Phillips and Barry Wain, who set up Camp Eden in Queensland.
- 100 New South Head Rd, Edgecliff, ph 9362 9988.

Christopher Dobney

Floors

see also carpet & floor covering, tiles & pavers
Rolling back flea-infested carpet to reveal the honeyed patina of aged baltic pine is the dream of every '90s home renovator. If you plan to polish your own floors, expect dust in every pore and hope that you discover floorboards, not chipboard, under that nasty '70s shag pile. This is where to go for all eventualities.

Decorator Flooring & Interiors
A vast array of all flooring types, including timber, parquetry, vinyl, carpets and rugs.
- Central Park, A2/4 Central Ave, Thornleigh, ph 9484 9967.

Planet Floorcoverings
Planet specialises in parquetry, both the Swedish-made veneer variety and the traditional Australian hardwood styles. You'll learn something just standing in the queue.
- 3-5 Hogan Ave, Sydenham, ph 9516 2577.

Sydney Flooring Pty Ltd
One of the oldest and largest suppliers of Australian hardwood tongue-and-groove floorboards in Sydney. Chances are your tradesman will buy from them. Or they will supply and lay for you, even over existing floors.
- 21-23 Governor Macquarie Drive, Chipping Norton, ph 9755 1899.

Balmain Floorsanding

Brian van Koeverden's business is a one-man-and-machine operation. He'll fix, sand and polish at reasonable rates, and recommend if replacement is the best option.
- PO Box 448, Carlingford, ph 9890 9243.

Kennards Hire

Probably the largest in the business, they have branches in most suburbs hiring all types of floor sanding, stripping, edging and polishing equipment. Staff are generally helpful and knowledgeable.
- 21 locations, ph 9318 2777.

Christopher Dobney

Florists

It's a very sorry bunch of flowers you can get for less than $10 these days, which makes the Flemington Markets such a bargain. For Sydney's leading floral exponents, stylemakers and others in the know, it is the place to go at 6am on Mondays, Wednesdays and Fridays for bulk blooms. However, if you don't have the time or the talent, don't worry because help is at hand. Here's a bunch of floral designers who make fabulous flowers look easy.

Susan Avery Floral Decorator

Longtime florist to Sydney society, Avery is a floral decorator in the grand manner. Her fairy-tale arrangements have a visual sensibility uniquely hers. She can design anything from a single posy to a complete environment.
- 59 Jersey Road, Woollahra, ph 9363 1168.

Alison Coates

The grande dame of Sydney florists no longer runs a shop, preferring to focus on private parties, functions and installations. Her signature is lush exuberance in exotic shapes and eye-catching colours. If you want to pick up tips (enough to last you a lifetime), book now for her popular bi-monthly two-day workshops at the Vaucluse House Tea Rooms.
- Ph 9360 2007.

Andrew Birley

His training began as an artist, yet his work encompasses everything from corporate event design to food-clad floral arrangements, from flowers for Bill Clinton to art-directing mega weddings. Despite the diversity of his projects and the objects he creates, there is an unchanging core to Birley's distinctive work.
- Ph 9699 4100.

Tracey Deep Floral Sculptures

Deep can put a stripped frangipani branch in a pot and make lotus flowers and a piece of string or a handful of cocoa pods look like art. A favourite with film directors and celebrities, her sensational and exotic creations are renowned for their shape, colour and texture.
- 223 Sutherland St, Paddington, ph 9328 7321.

Grandiflora

Saskia Havekes and Eva Seltner have developed a strong, individual style, finessing a new minimalism for flowers. Acclaimed for their simple but original style, the duo have gained a huge following. Their look is not about statements, it's about flowers. Pure and simple.
- Shop 1, 12 Macleay St, Potts Point, ph 9357 7902.

Juliet Justice Floral Design

This shop is full to bursting with eye-catching and exuberant flowers in vibrant colours and elegant shapes. Repeat clients include Armani and Emporio Armani whose boutiques Juliet fills regularly with beautiful white oriental lilies and camellia foliage.
- 402 Darling Street, Balmain, ph 9810 9089.

Roses Only

The name says it all. Tucked away in Chifley Plaza, this clever florist is the place to go for some of the best roses around — colours and varieties are endless. Will source any rose on the planet.
- Shop 12a, Chifley Plaza, 2 Chifley Square, City, ph 9232 4499.

Litsa Flowers

Noth Shorites in the know head for here for beautiful bunches of fresh-cut flowers.
- 149 Blues Point Rd, McMahons Point, ph 9922 6749.

Melissa Walker Smith

Flying & gliding

see also adventure & extreme sports

On November 12, 1894, a bushy-bearded inventor called Lawrence Hargrave helped start something big when he strapped four box kites to his back and rose five metres into the air at Stanwell Park, south of Sydney. Since then, Sydney has been a good base for amateur aviators. You need at least 55 hours of training and about $8,000 to gain a private pilot licence. If you want fun, try a smaller school, take it one lesson at a time and enjoy the flying as well as the learning. No interest in ever touching a joystick but still want to leave the earth behind? Try a joyflight. Just choose your craft and take off.

Sydney Harbour Sea Planes

The breathtaking flight in a six-seater from Rose Bay along the coast to Palm Beach is recommended. Rose Bay to Palm Beach return flight including three course a la carte lunch, $180 per person. Return flight only $120 per person.
- Lyne Park, Rose Bay, ph 9388 1978.

Sydney Heli-Scenic

Fly by chopper over the Opera House, the Harbour Bridge, Luna Park and any other Sydney landmark that tickles your fancy. Four-, six- and seven-seater helicopters are available and 25- to 30-minute flights start at $95.
- Ph 9317 3402.

Red Baron

Indulge your Biggles fantasies in a Pitts Special two-seat biplane. Survey Sydney from behind leather helmet and goggles from the open cockpit.
- Ph 9791 0643.

Fearless Flyers

Flights hold no joy for you? This group has a 90 per cent success rate in curing the deepest fears within eight weeks. Held at Mascot, a psychologist teaches relaxation techniques and during the lessons you fly a simulator to Hong Kong. The course ends with a graduation Qantas domestic flight. $550, includes flight.
- Ph 9522 8455.

Navair International Flying College

One of the bigger schools, with 40 aircraft including Cessna and Piper types. Cessna 152 dual training from $120 an hour.
- Bankstown Airport, ph 9791 0100.

Australian Flying Training School

Fleet includes 28 aircraft. Cessna 152s from $125 dual and T-bird trainers at $130.
- Bankstown Airport, ph 9791 9042.

Sydney Aerobatic School

Aerobatics is guaranteed to lift your adrenaline level if flying straight gets boring. Run by former RAAF fighter combat instructor Noel Kruse, who has trained many national champions.
- Bankstown Airport, ph 9791 0044.

Curtis Aviation

The Steve Curtis fleet includes three aerobatic Citabria planes. Camden is less busy than Bankstown and offers a pleasant rural feel – $145 dual.
- Camden Airport. ph 4655 6789.

Southern Cross Gliding Club

For silent flight and the thrill of soaring thermals, try this Camden-based club. Trial flight $100.
- Camden Airport. ph 4655 8882.

Sydney Ultralight Flying Club

Based at The Oaks, near Camden. Ultralights are a simpler and cheaper way of going flying.
- Ph 018 217 841.

John Sharpe, Cerentha Harris

Further information
- Learning to Fly, Australian Flying or Australian Aviation (from newsagents, or ph 9281 2333).

Folk music

see also country music, rock & pop music, blues music

Sydney has pubs belting out Irish music, active suburban folk clubs and a number of venues where overseas acts such as Steeleye Span, Fairport Convention and Rory McLeod perform when touring the country. Australia's premier folk performers live outside of Sydney, but keep an eye out for Judy Small, Eric (And the Band Played Waltzing Matilda) Bogle and Enda Kenny.

The Loaded Dog

A traditional folk venue which holds concerts on a semi-regular basis.
- Annandale Neighbourhood Centre, Johnston St, Annandale, ph 0411 821 286.

Also specialist venues such as **The Basement** (ph 9251 2797), **Harbourside Brasserie** (ph 9252 3000) and **The Three Weeds** (ph 9810 2244).

Sunday Folk

Sunday mornings at 9am on 2SER-FM (107.3-FM), international and local folk music and news of the folk scene is broadcast.

Further information
- See Sydney Morning Herald Metro and CitySearch for listings.
- Cornstalk Gazette (a newsletter available from Folkways, ph 9361 3980)

Bruce Elder

Fountains

Transfixed by the waters of its great sprawling harbour, Sydney has had little truck with such small-scale civic fripperies as fountains, apart from the landmark Archibald Fountain in Hyde Park. The long-buried Tank Stream and Busbys Bore, which made the convict settlement possible, are marked only by Stephen Walker's fountain on the corner of George and Alfred streets (its 'Children's Fountain' deemed a great playing place by kids) and John Byrom's uninspiring Busby's Bore in Hyde Park North. In the 1960s and early '70s, city fathers made valiant efforts to introduce fountains to the city, and succeeded in producing the El Alamein fountain at Kings Cross, two in Martin Place and one in Chifley Square – the last now removed because of its tendency to spray passing pedestrians.

Archibald Fountain

The gift of Jules Francois Archibald to commemorate the World War I alliance between Australia and France, cast in bronze to the design of Francois Sicard. Apollo, Diana, Pan

and Theseus, with attendant tortoises, provide a focal point of the park, and a meeting place for Sydneysiders. Right on axis to another great Art Deco monument, Bruce Dellit's Anzac Memorial.
■ Hyde Park North.

El Alamein Fountain
The gorgeous puffball designed by Robert Woodward which, since its installation in 1961, has been copied around the world.
■ Fitzroy Gardens, Kings Cross.

Tinkers Well Fountain
Made from the base of one of Pyrmont Bridge's light columns, Lucy Bleach's 1996 fountain is named for an old spring which once rose near the site. A sheer curtain of water slides gently over the incised stone; surrounding seats are recycled sandstone coping, and the fountain is nestled among metre-high foxtail grasses. Scattered blocks of sandstone nearby are engraved with plants grown or eaten in the area over the past 200 years.
■ In the park above the Fig St cutting, Ultimo.

Geraldine O'Brien

Further information
■ Open Museum Map Guide (Sydney City Council, ph 9265 9775)

French restaurants

While Australians have stopped thinking of French cuisine as something akin to a religion and French chefs as all-powerful gods, we haven't totally lost our taste for the odd slice of lush pate, or a perfectly roasted duck, or a light-as-air souffle.

Bilson's
While chef Guillaume Brahimi has been cooking in Australia for some years now, both his voice and his cooking have retained a distinctive and very charming French accent. A former disciple of the great Joel Robuchon, his knockout basil-infused tuna, silky scallop ravioli, and rare beef tenderloin with merlot sauce would still drag in the crowds, even without one of the best harbour views in Sydney.
■ Overseas Passenger Terminal, Circular Quay, ph 9251 5600.

Bistro Moncur
Damien Pignolet first made a name for himself as a practising perfectionist and devout Francophile at the mighty Claudes. Later, when he moved around the corner and down market to open an honest French bistro at the Woollahra Hotel, you could practically hear the locals cheering. The twice-cooked gruyere souffle and prime sirloin Cafe de Paris are must-haves.
■ Woollahra Hotel, 116 Queen St, Woollahra, ph 9363 2782.

Bistro Pave
Thanks to the efforts of chef Colin Holt, what once was a nice, honest, business lunch restaurant has blossomed into a temple of French cooking. Colin Holt transforms bistro classics into minor works of art without sacrificing form or flavour. From the boudin noir to the duck confit and stunning stuffed tripe, this is food that could make France the flavour of the month all over again.
■ 181 Miller St, North Sydney, ph 9956 8583.

Claudes
For more than 21 years, Claudes has remained a staunch bastion of fine French cooking. While current chef Tim Pak Poy is not afraid to innovate, and is quick to pounce on the very finest of Australian produce, his effortless command of French technique always manages to shine through on every plate.
■ 10 Oxford St, Woollahra, ph 9331 2325.

Merrony's
It is rare for French bistro flavours to be treated with such finesse and such respect. It is rarer

still for them to come with views of Sydney Harbour and the bridge. This is one of Sydney's most consistent restaurants, with food that never disappoints. Try the pan-fried pig's trotter terrine, rack of veal with shallots and leeks, and the sumptuous chocolate tart.
- The Quay Apartments, 2 Albert St, Circular Quay, ph 9247 9323.

Terry Durack

Fruit & vegetables

There used to be one type of lettuce (iceberg), one tomato (pale red and tasteless), and two potatoes (washed and unwashed). Now, our great greengrocers immediately announce the season, with smaller quantities of lots of things: fresh, strong herbs, baby cresses, oxheart tomatoes, and labelled potatoes. It almost makes cooking fun again.

Sydney Markets
One of the joys of the keen home cook is to head to the real markets, the wholesale ones, early in the morning. But we mean early. Get out to Flemington by 6am, because it's all over by 9am, when you can feast on a big breakfast in one of the atmospheric Italian cafes on site. Saturday morning farmer's markets are great fun, with heaps of cheap and seasonally adjusted fruit and veg. Take the kids – it's good for them to know where their food comes from. $7 car entry fee.
- Parramatta Rd, Flemington, ph 9325 6200.

Joe and Sam Antico's Northbridge Fruitworld
Fresh horseradish, fourteen types of chilli, exotic mushrooms, Asian vegetables, fragrant fruits, wonderful salad greens, and always, always, a few things you've never heard of or seen before. It's a great shop, run by a very fruity family.
- Shop 24, 83 Sailors Bay Rd, Northbridge, ph 9958 4725.

Arena's Quality Fruit and Vegetables
A Mosman fashion boutique that just happens to deal in fruit instead of fabric. If you want it, they've got it, from rambutans to rhubarb.
- 906 Military Rd, Mosman, ph 9969 6114.

B&J Lizard
The opening hours are late here (opens midday) so that the crew can clear out all the wholesale orders to some of the best restaurant and hotels in town. Then in come the foodies to pick up the perfect peach, pear, pumpkin, potato, pea, parsnip, passionfruit, papaya, and pineapple.
- 186-188 Harris St, Pyrmont, ph 9660 3388.

Parisi's of Rose Bay
It's huge, but the quality is there, right down to the smallest baby rocket leaf. Tool around and load up with fresh fruit juices, ice creams and salads as well as the original fruit and veg they were made from.
- 15 Dover Rd, Rose Bay, ph 9371 0870.

Emile's
Emile's is so cute to visit, it's a wonder they have so many people who take advantage of their shop-by-fax service. Under the hanging garlics and behind the big, bright flowers is a very caring fruit and veg shop that is an asset to the whole area.
- 321 Darling St, Balmain, ph 9810 2759.

Top Fruit
It takes a while to get the hang of this place, but it's worth it. Apparently what you do is wander in, point a diamond-encrusted finger at a few things, and wander out again with dinner. Special bonus: fresh nuts, and some terrific homemade Lebanese breads and

pastries. Ask for the ingredients of that delicious Lebanese fattoush salad of tangy greens, and you'll get a grin from one of the Sawan family.
- 53 Bay St, Double Bay, ph 9328 7420.

Waterside Fruit Connection
This isn't particularly designery or gourmetish – but it's open when you need it (10am Sunday, for instance, with eight coming for lunch), is no fuss, no mess, and is immensely reliable in quality and price.
- Shop 9, Sydney Fish Market, Pyrmont, ph 9552 2104.

Top Score Fruit Market
The Scala family have been in fruit-and-veg for 50 years, and now brothers Ray and Charles run this bustling mini-market with an eye for quality and price.
- Shop 211, Westfield Chatswood, Spring St, Chatswood, ph 9419 5998.

Jill Dupleix

Function venues

see also party supplies, event management
Throwing a successful party, whether it is a wedding, birthday or bar mitzvah should be the work of a cool-headed organiser. If your friends are frisky, don't have the party at home. Where then? Following are star venues guaranteed to please the boss and her husband or even fussy Aunt Babs.

Museum of Contemporary Art
The elegant atrium features polished marble and huge, bronze-framed doors and windows – a dramatic Gotham City backdrop with a postcard harbour view. Rockpool caters.
- East Circular Quay, ph 9252 4033.

Curzon Hall
This neo-Gothic mansion was built as a private home, then became a seminary. Today you can hire the castle-like space for groups of 10 to 300 people.
- Cnr Balaclava and Agincourt Rds, Marsfield, ph 9887 1877.

Athol Hall Function Centre
This weatherboard building's past incarnations include Catholic Youth Club dance hall, and before that a brothel. Set in bushland with sweeping lawns down to the harbour and a distant city skyline.
- Ashton Park, Bradleys Head Rd, Mosman, ph 9968 4441.

Sydney Opera House
Best venue in Sydney for a party and possibly one of the best backdrops in the world. For a 'do' with a difference, hire the Bennelong or Harbour restaurant, a panoramic front foyer, or even the opera stage.
- Bennelong Point, ph 9250 7578.

Locomotive Workshops
At the Australian Technology Park, Redfern, these sheds need a little more work, but the old workshops have plenty of character and space and few noise restrictions.
- Cornwallis St, Redfern, ph 9209 4444.

Kate Ryan

Furniture

see also carpenters & cabinetmakers, homewares, antiques, collectables, outdoor furniture, woodworking
You don't have to travel far in Sydney to check out good design. As well as a fantastic range of import furniture by high profile international greats, there is a wealth of local talent in a design precinct in Sydney's

Furniture

inner-city. There's also affordable second-hand finds, repros that are good enough to pass for the real thing and bargain flatpack basics that will work in any place with any look.

Anibou

With work by Sydney's most talented and celebrated young furniture designer, Caroline Casey, this designer showroom also stocks the Jorge Pensi Toledo aluminium chair from Spain, own-brand cane sofas from the Philippines, the Mini chair by Antonio Citterio and the Leeuwin woven leather sofa. In 1998 it celebrates the centenary of Alvar Aalto with an exhibition of his design classics plus a special edition of glassware by Iittala.
- 726 Bourke St, Redfern, ph 9319 0655.

Chee Soon & Fitzgerald

This is a well-sourced collection of groovy one-offs from the '30s to the '80s with everything in between.
- 387 Crown St, Surry Hills, ph 9360 1031.

Country Road Homewear

Our premier lifestyle store supplies furniture and accessories for every aspect of our homes. It is simple and pure and to the point for interiors with modern leanings. The latest range of Furniture For Neat Living in blackbutt takes in Japanese economy with a whiff of Conran minimalism.
- Paddington Homewear, 332 Oxford St, City, ph 9360 2533; David Jones Homewear, Level 6, 9 Elizabeth St, City, ph 9266 5544.
  Inquiries: 039 267 1400.

Darryl Gordon

A traditional range of 12 classic couture designs at ready-to-wear prices. There's a deep sprung sofa, plus a variety of upholstered armchairs, bergere chairs and ottomans with solid refinement.
- 100 Cathedral St, Woolloomooloo, ph 9380 2600.

Dedece

In business for 20 years, this design hothouse is the epitome of structural rigour. Stockists of original Fritz Hansen series 7 chairs, Knoll, Cappellini, Marc Newson, Alberto Meda, Jasper Morisson plus streamlined pieces by Melbourne-based MAP.
- 263 Liverpool St, East Sydney, ph 9360 2722.

Echo Echo

It may say '90s cool but this fab range of big, modernist furniture plus that of Melbourne-based company Design Ecru is no intended fashion statement. Lots of bold shapes and timber veneers offering all the advantages of modernist design without the overkill. It's smart stuff.
- 211 Bourke St, Woolloomooloo, ph 9361 6699.

Form

Keith Glover and partner Trudi Scrymgour sell covetable one-off mid-century furniture from the funky to the sublime.
- 415 Bourke St, Darlinghurst, ph 9331 6227.

Funkis

Carina Enstrom sells a well-edited selection of mod Swedish designs that are simple, functional and affordable. You can buy Bruno Mathssons '30s classics as well as innovative designs from leading contemporary designers.
- 23c Curlewis St, Bondi, ph 9130 6445.

IKEA

A huge bustling department store where you're sure to find a bargain. Modern range of smart and practical tables, cupboards and chairs which flat pack. The Swedish chain's manufacturing muscle and good taste yields great deals.
- 19 Stoddart Road, Prospect, ph 9636 9222; South Dowling St, Moore Park, 9313 6400; 924 Pacific Highway, Gordon, 9498 3822.
  Inquiries: 9313 6400.

Furniture

Inne
This is the spot to see some of the best of Swedish design. Contemporary furniture from two of Sweden's most innovative companies, Swecode and Kallemo, with a fab range of furniture and designer basics by Magis.
- 47 Queen St, Woollahra, ph 9362 9900.

Ken Neale
Form and function meet in a groovy and amusing way here. For the past 14 years Neale has been collecting retro chic with everything from Pierre Paulin freeform chairs to '60s plastic.
- 283 Liverpool St, Darlinghurst, ph 9331 2187.

Loot
You can sniff out groovy bits and pieces from the '50s to the '70s here at bargain basement prices. It's full to bursting with must-haves.
- Shop 119, Level 2, Strand Arcade, City, ph 9223 5150.

Make
This swinging little newcomer has taken Sydney by storm. Stockists of stuff from the '60s to the '70s with original items by Robin Day, Douglas Snelling, Gordon Andrews, Grant Featherstone, Eeri Aarnio and Parker Knoll. Plus modern accessories by local designers.
- Shop 2, 17 Elizabeth Bay Road, Elizabeth Bay, ph 9326 9424.

Mobili
Long-time retailer of modern design classics: Corbusier, Costes, Jacobsen, Ripiego and more.
- 38 Queen St, Woollahra, ph 9328 6366.

Norman and Quaine
In business for more than two years now, this showroom has gained a cult following keen to buy into its raw, modernist aesthetic. From the distilled designs of Korban Flaubert in ply and steel to its own label, everything is designed and produced locally. Also work by Charles Wilson, ISM Objects, Astrid Huwald and Gordon Mather Industries.
- 74 Commonwealth St, Surry Hills, ph 9212 3542.

Pad
Good source of mid-century furniture with the Charles Eames style factor at a better price, plus modern pieces by Sydney-based designer Marc Veenendaal.
- 134 Darlinghurst Road, Darlinghurst, ph 9326 0321.

Planet Furniture
Ross Longmuir has made a vivid impact on Sydney's design scene with his beautiful furniture range made from our neglected native woods plus batch productions of other local talent.
- 374 Crown St, Surry Hills, ph 9360 8677.

Sedia
Among the best for upholstered furniture with a classic (but not boring) spin. Renowned for its famous hump-back and Chesterfield sofa designs.
- 84 Cathedral St, Woolloomooloo, ph 9356 3166.

Space
Excellent source of affordable contemporary Italian furniture with decidedly modern attitude. More than 20 of the leading Italian furniture and accessory manufacturers to choose from.
- 111 Flinders St, Darlinghurst, ph 9380 6000.

Spence & Lyda
Tucked away in Surry Hills, this store is bursting with buy-me vintage American steel renovated with a secret recipe to stop the rust. Easy care, low maintenance stainless steel pieces from the '30s to the '50s that are well designed.
- 51-57 Holt St, Surry Hills, ph 9212 6747.

Furniture

Stylecraft
Good source of affordable contemporary sofas by Sydney designers Schamburg + Alvisse plus local and imported cafe chairs and tables and office systems.
- 221-225 Liverpool St, East Sydney, ph 9331 8388.

Studio Wilkhahn
Huge range of design-led desks, chairs and filing systems with a multitude of add-ons suitable for the home office.
- Level 6, 227 Elizabeth St, City, ph 9264 6588.

West Eight
If the style pundits are to be believed, British design is the furniture of choice for the '90s. Check it out here: Mark Brasier-Jones, Tom Dixon, Procter Rihl, JAM, Terence Williams and more.
- Suite 4, 144 Cathedral St, Woolloomooloo, ph 9326 9877.

Melissa Walker Smith

Andrew Farquhar
One of only a handful of craftsmen who are working in the specialised field of fine furniture in this country. The backbone of his business is cabinetmaking, but more than 30 per cent of his work is restoration using ancient skills.
- 25 Loftus St, Bowral, ph 0248 62 2210.

Major & Tom
Arts graduate Georgina Tom and cabinetmaker Paul Vane (Major left some years ago) are renowned for restoring and rebuilding old furniture, sometimes from scraps.
- 23 Doody St, Alexandria, ph 9693 2404.

Restoration Scene
Ros Speirs restores antiques by hand and uses the traditional method of hand french polishing. Received multi recommendations in the *Sydney Morning Herald* Domain section's Tradespeople of the Year Awards.
- 7 Cambridge Rd, Artarmon, ph 9411 3983.

Melissa Walker Smith

Furniture restoration

see also antiques, interior designers & decorators, carpenters & cabinetmakers

Restoring a period piece of furniture is a tricky business. Ardent restorers will carefully repair the fabric of the piece and give it the appearance of being properly maintained with the patina of time. Respect is the golden rule among Sydney's restorers.

Brian Barrow
Among the best craftsmen in Sydney for restoration with an authentic spin. Loved by leading antique dealers and interior decorators.
- 105 Carrington Rd, Waverley, ph 9389 1950.

Gambling

To some, gambling is a fun flutter; to others, it's an uncontrollable addiction. Gambling, in moderation, can be an enjoyable experience. But remember, don't bet big unless you know what you're doing; odds are always stacked against the punter and successful gamblers are dispassionate and calculating. Forget feng shui and lucky numbers, just play the odds. If it's all gone beyond a bit of fun and you keep thinking your lucky streak is just around the corner, you may be addicted. Don't panic, there are several groups who can help. Call them before you are in too deep: Gamblers Anonymous, ph 9564 1574; Gambling Counselling and Support Service, ph 9858 1377; Gambler's Counselling Service, ph 9951 5566.

Star City
If it's not the best gambling haunt in Sydney, it's certainly the biggest. A total of 1,500 slot machines and 160 tables of blackjack, roulette, sic bo, two-up, baccarat and craps is spread across a gaming area of 145,000 square metres. Their motto of 'bet with your head, not over it' is one worth remembering.
- 80 Pyrmont St, Pyrmont, ph 9777 9000.

TAB
This organisation takes bets on horse racing, greyhounds, rugby league, soccer, motor racing and yachting, and with 560 locations throughout Sydney, there's bound to be one close to you. Don't forget, all betting is totalised – which means that the odds you get when you layout your money is not necessarily the odds you have at race time. Don't worry if you know nothing about sports, just try one of their mystery bets.
- Ph 9211 0188.
  Website: www.tabnsw.com.au

Lotteries NSW
If your newsagent is selling it, these people produce it. As a general rule, the higher the odds the greater the booty. Here are your chances of success with each product. In Lotto, a basic three-game systems entry has a one in 1.76 million chance of success and a $2 Lucky Lottery ticket has a one in 180,000 chance, although these odds can fluctuate with jackpots. Powerball is a whopping one in 27 million chance, although the prize pool is often more than $10 million. The Pools results are loosely related to the soccer scores, although you probably stand a better chance picking your numbers randomly. Your chances here are one in 2.76 million. The odds of winning the big one in the $5 Scratch Lottery is one in 500,000, but you do have a one in 3.3 chance of scoring a smaller prize.
- Ph 1300 363 444.

Thommo's
It's name is derived from the illegal two-up school of the 1930s, but their specialities are card and poker machines. Thommo's has 56 outlets (and counting) in pubs throughout Sydney, just waiting for you to hit the big time with a royal flush.
- Ph 1800 677 330.

Centrebet
Located in Alice Springs, this sporting agency provides online betting for all sports. Net surf in and open an account and you can bet on the English soccer, American baseball plus the Australian favourites: cricket, Aussie Rules and rugby league.
- Ph 08 8955 5800:
  www.centrebet.com.au

Two-up
Get into the spirit of Anzac Day (April 25) by playing the game of diggers. Clubs and pubs receive special dispensation to toss the coins on this iconic day.

Steve Samuelson

Gardens

see also nurseries & garden supplies
There are many beautiful gardens in Sydney and surrounding areas open to the public on various days through the year. All gardens in Australia's Open Garden Scheme are listed in its annual guidebook (ABC Books, $12.95, ph 9328 0173) and local garden openings are given publicity in newspapers and on radio. There are a couple of rules in garden visiting – no dogs, no high heels, no stealing plants or cuttings.

Waterfall Cottage
Jean Villani's exciting garden is part natural rainforest gully, part garden setting for a stone

Gardens

cottage. Bush paths lead to natural waterfall, rocks, pool and creek and it is a haven for native birds. Open for Australia's Open Garden Scheme and also for various charities through the year.
- 90 Cabbage Tree Rd, Bayview.

The Lilian Fraser Garden

A historical garden developed privately by Dr Lilian Fraser, the third woman in Australia to qualify as a biologist, now open to the public every day; unusual mature trees and shrubs underplanted with woodland plants. A botanical jewel.
- Cnr Bellamy and Laurence Sts, Pennant Hills.

Arborea

Formerly the garden of horticultural writer, broadcaster and nurseryperson, the late Valerie Swane, developed as a shade garden under a canopy of tall trees. Part of the Open Garden Scheme.
- 414 Pennant Hills Rd, Pennant Hills.

Eryldene

The garden of the late Professor E.G. Waterhouse, with house designed by William Hardy Wilson, garden by Professor Waterhouse and Hardy Wilson. Combines a series of beautifully planted garden rooms with elegant garden structures plus Australia's most significant collection of camellias. Open on designated weekends through camellia season.
- 17 McIntosh St, Gordon.

Betty Maloney's Garden

A bush garden classified by the National Trust and owned by Reg and Betty Maloney. A delightful combination of naturalness with order and a joy for all seasons, this garden was the inspiration for the *Bush Garden* books by Betty Maloney and her sister Jean Walker. Part of the Open Garden Scheme.
- 18 Hurdis Ave, Frenchs Forest.

Joseph Banks Native Plants Reserve

Botanist Banks collected plants to send back to England for study, and this reserve on the banks of the Georges River was the repository for all manner of exotic flora. Visit the temperate rainforest trees and the exquisite scented gardens.
- Manooka Place, Kareela.

E.G. Waterhouse National Camellia Garden

A gem in Caringbah, and busy with weddings during camellia season. Call Sutherland Council (ph 9710 0251) for the best time to see the different varieties of blooms.
- Corner of Kareena Rd and President Ave, Caringbah.

Moidart

The property of Mr David Burns, this is the best garden to see in the Southern Highlands. Special features include splendid mature, cool-climate trees, rhododendrons, sunken rose garden, stone walling, ha ha, bluebell walk, formal garden of white roses and annuals and herbaceous borders. Beautifully designed, planted and cared for, this large garden can be visited daily 9am to 4pm during its open period (last weekend September to last Sunday October; and Anzac Day weekend to following Sunday in autumn).
- Eridge Park Rd, Bowral, ph 4861 2600.

Nooroo

In the cool climate of Mount Wilson is one of Australia's most famous gardens, honoured on a postage stamp. Special features include the summer house built to celebrate the garden's centenary and collections of rhododendron, maple and wisteria collected and planted by two generations of the Valder family. Mature chestnuts and other cool-climate deciduous trees are underplanted with spring bulbs. Now owned by Drs Tony and Lorraine Barrett and open daily from April to May and again from mid September to mid November.
- Church Lane, Mount Wilson, ph 4756 2018.

Shirley Stackhouse

Gay & Lesbian Sydney

1998 was the 20th anniversary of the Sydney Gay and Lesbian Mardi Gras parade. The presence of the '78ers contingent was a vivid reminder of how things have changed. In that first parade the police arrested marchers, rather than marching themselves. The Sydney Morning Herald, which in 1998 ran a supplement on the Mardi Gras Festival, in 1978 published the names and addresses of those arrested.

Not all the changes have been for the better. AIDS has decimated a generation of gay men, but it has also forced a franker public discussion of sexuality and led to the forging of some strong and enduring community organisations. Many of the old venues are gone forever: Capriccio's with its legendary drag shows; The Rex with its Jean Genet mix of sailors and drag queens; and Costello's with its notorious retiring rooms. Others, like the community they serve, are constantly reinventing themselves to move with the times.

Sydney Gay and Lesbian Mardi Gras Ltd
By far the nation's largest gay and lesbian group, and the one you have to join if you hope to be invited to its (Mardi Gras and Sleaze Ball) parties. Membership is open to sympathetic and supportive heterosexuals, but be prepared to show your commitment. The 1998 Sleaze Ball is on October 3; the 1999 Sydney Gay & Lesbian Mardi Gras Festival will run from January 29 to February 27 when the Mardi Gras Parade and Party will take place.
- 21-23 Erskineville Rd, Erskineville, ph 9557 4332.

PRIDE (Sydney Gay & Lesbian Community Centre Ltd)
Provides a home for many community groups and activities, most notably the Fitness Exchange, a non-commercial gay and lesbian gym. It conducts a popular New Year's Eve party at the old Showgrounds, and fosters community art projects including the Funny Farm gay and lesbian stand-up comedy nights.
- 26 Hutchinson St, Surry Hills, ph 9331 1333.

Gay and Lesbian Counselling Service
First established as CAMP Inc in 1975, GLCS is Australia's oldest gay and lesbian community group. It continues to dish out tea and sympathy to people coming out and those experiencing relationship or family hassles. Operates a phone service (4pm to midnight), limited face-to-face counselling and a regular mixed coming-out group.
- Ph 9207 2800 or 1800 805 379 (within NSW).

AIDS Council of NSW
Developed in the early '80s as the gay male community's response to AIDS/HIV, ACON continues to provide information, education, advocacy and support specifically for this group. It has grown into a large, government-funded organisation with branches around NSW. ACON has sections targeting various groups, including men from ethnic backgrounds, youth, drug users and older gay men.
- 9 Commonwealth St, City, ph 9206 2000 or 1800 063 060.

Bobby Goldsmith Foundation
Bobby Goldsmith was the first Sydney gay man to contract HIV. During his illness his friends formed an informal support group. After his death they formalised it into a foundation which they gave his name. Today BGF is the largest AIDS charity in the State, with regular fundraisers, including the annual Shop Till You Drop held on the Saturday before Mardi Gras (February 20, 1999).
- 2/9 Commonwealth St, City, ph 9283 8666.

Luncheon Club AIDS Support Group
Ladles out free Monday lunches and entertainment to people living with and affected by HIV/AIDS at the Exchange Hotel, Oxford St.

The aim is to 'bring the nightlife to daylight hours'. The Luncheon Club Larder gives food and supplies to the needy, and its bright yellow van is regularly used to raise cash by catering for community events. For all that, the service is still run out of the living room of its founder, the indomitable Carole Ann King.
- Ph 9389 7477 or 0416 040074.

Albury Hotel
In many ways the Albury is the archetypal Sydney gay pub, complete with nightly drag shows behind the bar. It's strictly standing room only on most nights. The erstwhile piano bar has recently been converted into a snappy new cocktail bar. The Albury is famed for its muscle-bound barmen, generally dressed in no more than shorts and singlets. The crowd is youthful and the atmosphere buzzy.
- 6 Oxford St, Paddington, ph 9361 6555.

Midnight Shift
For more than a decade the Midnight Shift has been at the heart of the gay male clubbing scene. The fact that it now has a regular girls' night is a sign of the times, and probably something of a shock for those who remember when it was the bastion of boydom. Downstairs, the Shift Bar has been expanded to include Locker Room, a back bar equally suited to a round of pool and a round of drinks.
- 85 Oxford St, Darlinghurst, ph 9360 4463.

Stonewall
The advent of Stonewall – as its name suggests – created a revolution on the Sydney scene when it opened in 1997. Gone are the days of smoky, pokey gay bars. Built over three levels, this sumptuous venue has something for everyone: pub, club and cocktail lounge. It's also that rarity in Sydney: a venue people dress up to go out to.
- 175 Oxford St, Darlinghurst, ph 9360 1963.

Class Act at Sublime
Gay nights in otherwise straight venues have become almost a thing of the past. A valuable exception is Class Act, a regular Sunday night gig featuring popular gay house DJs Stephen Allkins and Ben Drayton. Take an RDO next Monday.
- 244 Pitt St, City, ph 9264 8428.

On the Other Side at X Site
Under the rule of Mistress Gigi, OTOS has had great success where others have failed miserably, offering a girls-only event, on an off-night of the week in someone else's venue. It worked a treat at the top level of Kinselas, packing them in for several years running. The new venue boasts even more: two levels, two dance floors, six DJs, pool, video, a chill-out area and a happy hour. What more could a girl ask for? Who knows, maybe you'll find her there.
- 171 Victoria St, Potts Point, ph 9358 6511.

Christopher Dobney

Further information
- Capital Q Weekly, Sydney Star Observer (weekly), and Lesbians on the Loose (monthly) are Sydney's regular gay and lesbian publications. All three are available free in venues and gay-friendly shops and cafes.

Glasses & optical supplies

see also sunglasses
Brand names abound, as do competitive services. To overcome the conflict between what looks cool and what is functional, your specs specialist should be able to advise on a frame that suits your face.

Budget Eyewear
At 16 one-stop-shop metropolitan locations, prices of frames to suit all budgets are said to be 15 per cent below those of leading competitors.
- Fifth floor, Dymocks Building, 428 George St, City, ph 9231 3910.

OPSM

Niche market stores – Next for boutique designer frames and Face It for a younger trendy choice – incorporate inhouse optometrists, as do traditional OPSM stores. All guarantee replacement within four weeks if dissatisfied, free replacement and repair within six months and life-time adjustments from any branch.
- Face It OPSM, 446a Oxford St, Paddington, ph 9331 4619.

Paris Miki Optical Vision Express

Its unique service is the Japanese Mikissimes computer graphics design system where a digital camera captures an image of your face and, by combining keywords of your style preferences, can design the appropriate spectacles. You can then view your new look on computer. This is a free service with no obligation, available at five stores.
- Shop 15-16, Level 1, Chifley Plaza, City, ph 9231 4699.

Merringtons

A family company operating in Sydney since 1899, this has 11 centres with in-house optometrists and one-stop services. Practitioner warranties include guaranteed frame and lens workmanship, and if you're not happy with the results of your eye test, you can come back within three months.
- Shop UC9, Macquarie Shopping Centre, North Ryde, ph 9870 7811.

Masterspecs

For single-vision lenses, the prescription price is included in the cost you see on the frame. Its two-for-one offer starts at $159 and you can choose the second pair. A video facility for those who can't see themselves in the mirror means you can view yourself onscreen in up to eight varieties of tints, shapes and lenses.
- 245 Oxford St, Bondi Junction, ph 9387 5531.

Trisha Treanor

Go-karts

see also motorsport

The great world champion drivers Ayrton Senna and Michael Schumacher jump-started their careers in go-karts. You may never be a world champion, but the thrills and speed that lured these men to racing can be experienced in Sydney. Check out these venues and see if your fastest time is a lap record.

FastLane Go-Karting

This track has an undulating, 500-metre-long course and all the features you'd expect from a Formula One circuit, plus a bank corner from NASCAR racing. This centre prides itself on providing the complete family day out with corporate functions and birthday parties catered for.
- 20 Swettenham Rd, Minto, ph 9820 4422.

Mini Grand Prix

Is the longest indoor track in Sydney. Have your time electronically recorded as you tackle a 330-metre track of chicanes, hair-pins and sweeping turns. Corporate and individual hiring packages are available.
- 24-26 Lillian Fowler Place, Marrickville, ph 9516 1302.

Eastern Creek International Karting Raceway

Here on any (fine) day, you can temporarily become a Jacques Villeneuve in a rent-a-kart, at a cost of $20 for 10 minutes. Its way cheaper than spending $250,000 on a touring car and then discovering you drive like great-grandma.
- Brabham Drive, Eastern Creek, ph 9672 7530.

Kingsgrove Megatrack

An indoor track with no electronic timing, but it's the only circuit with a tunnel and bridge

just like the Formula One Suzuka track in Japan.
- 1 Garema Circuit, Kingsgrove, ph 9750 2252.

CRG Racing Centre

If you're sick of hiring other peoples karts and want to buy your own, this is the place to visit. CRG proudly boasts its the largest go-kart retailer in Australia, selling the complete range of machines, accessories and clothing.
- 40 Ernest Ave, Chipping Norton, ph 9755 4321.

Steve Samuelson

Golf

see also sporting goods

With more than 100 courses, ranging from verdant parkland to windswept moors reminiscent of the game's origins in Scotland, Sydney's golfers are well served. Try playing the NSW Golf Club out at La Perouse, or nearby St Michael's when the prevailing wind blows, and you'll find a golfer dedicated to his or her game. A handicap is easy to come by if you're a member of a private club, but really no more difficult if you are a member of a social golf club that is registered with the NSW Golf League (call Rod Clark on 9264 8433). Cost of 18 holes ranges from $7 to about $80 on a public course, but dig deeper if you're playing prestigious courses such as **The Australian** (Bannerman Crescent, Rosebery, ph 9663 2273), **Royal Sydney** (Kent Rd, Rose Bay, ph 9371 4333), **The Lakes** (cnr King St and Vernon Ave, East Lakes, ph 9669 1311), and **Concord** (Majors Bay Rd, Concord, ph 9743 6111), which host the major tournaments. Private club membership fees range from $300 to $4,000 a year, and most have a waiting list – between five and ten years at some clubs.

For the price of a week's wages, you can get a game at one of the more exclusive clubs; others have green fees which are minimal.

Camden Lakeside

Carved out of the cow paddocks by five-times British Open champion Peter Thomson and his partners, this is Sydney's best public course. An hour from the CBD, it not only has touches of St Andrews, the home of golf, but also shades of Carnoustie, Royal Troon, Royal Birkdale and Royal St Georges, all of them on the British Open rota.
- 50 Raby Rd, Catherine Field, ph 9606 5277.

NSW Golf Course

Forget the Australian! Too expensive and too tough. (Jack Nicklaus redesigned it, with the help of Kerry Packer's chequebook, and, off the back tees, it is a nightmare even for the most seasoned of touring professionals.) Try instead this course on the cliffs of La Perouse where Captain Cook first took a look at our soon-to-be Olympic city. Greg Norman says, with a few design changes, it could be in the top 10 of world courses.
- Henry Head, off Anzac Pde, ph 9661 4455.

Best bargains

Watch the television coverage of the major events in world golf to catch the advertisements. For consistent discounts through the year, try **Sharpies Golf House** (220 Elizabeth St, City, ph 9212 2452), **Al's Golf Centre** (cnr Coronation Pde and Hume Highway, Enfield, ph 9744 3633), or one of the six **Geoff Scott** outlets spread across the metropolitan area (North Turramurra, Gordon Golf Club, Hudson Park Homebush, Canterbury Golf Club, Casula and Auburn Public Golf Course). All of them will have a ball which goes further, a driver which goes straighter and further, and whatever else the latest gimmick is.

Best golf teachers

Advice on this is always going to put many noses out of joint. So be it! Try **Ron Luxton** at The Australian (ph 9663 2273), **Greg Hohnen** at Killara GC (ph 9498 2700), **Kyle Francis**, formerly at Concord and now at North Turramurra (ph 9144 5110), **Harvey Graham** at Roseville (ph 9417 7222), and **Max Hawkins** at Massey Park (ph 9743 4113), who, if he doesn't teach you the right grip, will at least amuse you with his wry sense of humour. If in doubt, contact the NSW PGA on 9439 8111.

Peter Stone

Further information

- NSW Golf Association, ph 9264 8433: www.agu.org.au
- Golf in Sydney (Gadfly, $9.95, ph 9948 4049).

Gourmet food

see also delicatessens, bakeries & patisseries, cheese, coffee & tea, chocolates, ice-cream, wine

In these hectic times, we rely on outsourcing to do the things we would do if only we had the time. When it comes to getting a fast dinner on the table – for one, with a video, or for ten, with Champagne – you should be able to stand in the middle of a great gourmet food store and simply buy your way out. And you can.

Gusto

Always bubbling with espresso-sipping people pondering the array of dips, breads, take-home soups, curries, cold meats, cheeses, ice-creams, cakes and biscotti. There are shelves groaning with good things they could actually cook if they wanted to, but – surprise, surprise – nobody seems to want to.

- 16 Hall St, Bondi, ph 9130 4565; Cnr Broughton and Heeley Sts, Paddington, ph 9361 5640.

Sydney Cove Providore

By rights you should be wearing a crinoline in this tiny shop in the heart of the touristy Rocks, as you pop cakes, bottles, pasta and jams and other trachalments in your basket. Very cute, very helpful, and very necessary for the area.

- 39 Argyle St, The Rocks, ph 9247 8833.

David Jones Food Hall

Where do you start? With freshly opened oysters, or the specialty breads? With whole baked dinners and accompanying vegetable accessories, luscious smoked salmons, fine wines, irresistible cakes, the mountainous salads? It doesn't matter where you start, you'll end up with a great no-fuss dinner at this exemplary food hall.

- David Jones, Elizabeth St, City, ph 9266 5544; Westfield Plaza, Bondi Junction, ph 9369 6333.

Pasta Rosa

It's been there for years, and is in danger of being overlooked, but Pasta Rosa quietly gets on with feeding half of Woollahra with freshly prepared, simple, tucker like crumbed veal, good pasta, scrummy salads, and the brightest, greenest, freshest pesto in all of Sydney.

- 134 Queen St, Woollahra, ph 9328 6368.

Simmone Logue

It's gorgeous, it's bright, it's fresh, and it's even garnished with the odd fresh daisy just for fun. And best of all, it's delicious – from the glazed chicken drummies to the ornate pies, the motherly soups, the rice paper rolls, and the drop-dead bread-and-butter puddings.

- 470 Oxford St, Paddington, ph 9360 1314; 349 Darling St, Balmain, ph 9555 7426.

Jill Dupleix

Greek Sydney

Love or hate their mansions, pebbled concrete and marbled floors, not to mention their Ionic columns, the Greeks have made an immense contribution to Sydney since the first arrivals back in 1829. And not just to the building industry. Young and penniless, in some cases barefoot or with a baoulo (trunk) in tow, the new arrivals stepped off liners such as the Patris at Circular Quay displaying a thirst for work and financial independence.

Their efforts – in factories, oyster bars and later fish'n'chip shops – helped shape a vibrant, multicultural Sydney. And they can still be found in every suburb from Surry Hills to Marrickville and Canterbury.

Food and feasting play a major role in Greek Sydney. Good Greek food, cooked from the heart, is the essence of life. It is not surprising therefore that Sydney boasts more than 60 Greek restaurants, tavernas and cafes. So when in a Greek restaurant, do as the Greeks do. And that means eat, drink and be merry.

Eleni's

Terry Durack, *The Sydney Morning Herald* restaurant critic, says: 'Forget everything you ever knew about Greek food. Eleni Conistis, with a little help from son Peter, is about to change all that in this innovative Greek restaurant. Even the taramasalata gets the beauty treatment, made here from cod, salmon and flying fish roes.'
- 185a Bourke St, East Sydney,
  ph 9331 5306.

Perama Greek Restaurant

A buzzy and lively restaurant with ever so friendly staff. Oh, and delectable, fresh food. From the traditional favourites such as dolmades (rice, pork or beef wrapped in cabbage or vine leaves) to dishes the owners describe as 'modern Australian with a Greek twist' such as the mouth-watering seafood parcel (fresh seafood in filo pastry).
- 88 Audley St, Petersham,
  ph 9569 7534.

Steki Taverna

Small is probably the best word to sum up this taverna; another is fun. The atmosphere, especially on music nights, not to mention the excellent food and hospitable service, makes this taverna a true Greek night out. Friday, Saturday and Sunday are the nights to go, if you feel like a bit of live Zorba. Try the tender BBQ octopus or the succulent lamb, slow-baked for six hours then barbecued. Bookings advised.
- 2 O'Connell St, Newtown, ph 9516 2191.

Hellenic Club Restaurant

Simple and informal. Or, as the 1998 *Sydney Morning Herald*'s *Good Food Guide* describes it, hearty, reliable and comfortable. According to the guide, neither the menu nor the calm service has changed in 40 years. Hence the appeal, not to mention the views of Hyde Park from the large dining room.
- 5th Floor, 251 Elizabeth St, City,
  ph 9261 4910.

Athenaikon Continental Cake Shop

This is the first Greek cake shop in Sydney, having opened in 1955, and arguably the best, with cakes and pastries to die for. From the simple koulourakia (plain or sesame sweet biscuits) to the deliciously rich baklava (almond and filo pastry with heavenly thick syrup) and galaktoboureko (baked custard slice), there is something for everyone and for all occasions. The sweet bun known as tsoureki is a must during Easter – complete with dyed-red egg – and so is the Christmas bread.
- Baveas House, 409 Bourke St, Surry Hills, ph 9360 4878.

Picuba Food Wholesalers
This is the place to buy your kalamata olives, taramosalata (fish roe dip), fetta cheese and imported goods including olive oil.
- 105a Illawarra Rd, Marrickville, ph 9560 8441.

Greek Art and Book Shop
Need a komboloi (worry beads)? No problem, they're next to the backgammon sets, which are next to the Greek pottery sitting alongside the Byzantine and other religious icons. And for the widest selection of books, from the classics to cooking, and latest newspapers and magazines from Greece, there is no other place to shop. Popular with Greeks and Australians, it is even rumoured that items bought from the shop are passed off as gifts that have made the 24-hour flight from Greece in someone's suitcase.
- 251 Elizabeth St, City, ph 9264 7795.

Nicholson Museum
Founded in 1860, the museum has the largest and most important collection of Greek artefacts in Australia, including some magnificent painted vases from the Classical period. Open Monday to Friday from 10am to 4.30pm. Closed in January. Free admission.
- Main Quadrangle, University of Sydney, ph 9351 2812.

Odeon Music
This shop boasts the latest and largest range of Greek music in Australia, even promising to have CDs in stock within four days of their release in Greece – barring any strikes in the homeland. From modern music from artists including Keti Garbi to the old rembetika (urban blues). Yes, even closet Nana Mouskouri and Demis Roussos fans will be happy.
- 94 Bathurst St, City, ph 9267 6480.

Greek Festival of Sydney
This is a month-long festival held to promote Greek-Australian local artists and to uphold the Greek culture, language and tradition. It kicks off with a grand opening at the Opera House forecourt the first Sunday of every March complete with music and Greek dancing. This is followed by daily events including plays, art exhibitions, lectures, and international acts.

Nick Papadopoulos

Further information
- Greek Orthodox Community of NSW, ph 9740 6022
- Hellenic Council of NSW, ph 9267 2349

Greyhound racing

see also gambling

For sheer excitement, greyhound racing has a unique appeal. From the moment the greyhounds explode from the starting boxes in pursuit of the mechanical hare or 'bunny', these speed merchants put their bodies on the line. Blink once and the race is half over, blink again and the quest to find the winner of the next race begins.

Wentworth Park
Metropolitan greyhound racing is conducted here every Saturday and Monday evening by the National Coursing Association (NCA) and NSW Breeders' Owners and Trainers' Association (GBOTA). The track is easily accessible by public transport, with light rail and buses leaving the track on a regular basis. Both associations cater for parties and special functions, with restaurant and bar facilities available on both levels of the complex. Greyhound racing is generally regarded as a 'family sport' and kids are most welcome.
- Wentworth Park Rd, Glebe, ph 9660 4308.

Greyhound racing

AWA National Derby and Eukanuba Golden Easter Egg

These are the two premier races in NSW and both carry Group One status with a winners' purse of $100,000. The Derby is in late February while the Eukanuba is on Easter Saturday.

Don McMillan

During the 1997 racing year, this Llandilo based trainer averaged more than a win a week at the Glebe Circuit with 62 winners. His nearest rival was Carolyn Reinke, who trained 26 winners. Worthy Reward was the leading sire, with 67 winners, while Kedo's Polly, was the leading dam with 22 wins.

Greyhound Racing Authority

Can provide several free brochures on getting started in the sport, along with videos on the rules, feeding and training methods, leading trainers and greyhound adoption. Greyhounds have a gentle nature and retired racers make excellent family pets.
- Ph 9646 3933.

Tony Zuccarini

Further information
- NSW National Coursing Association, ph 9646 5711
- NSW Greyhound Breeders, Owners and Trainers' Association, ph 9649 7166
- The Greyhound Recorder (weekly newspaper), ph 9646 5855
- Sydney Morning Herald, sport section daily, The Form liftout on Friday
- De Fax Form Guides, ph 9649 7277

Guided tours

No need to wander aimlessly through the streets of Sydney, take advantage of someone else's knowledge and attach yourself to a guided tour.

The Rocks

For something different, follow Master Christopher through The Rocks on his two-hour History, Convicts and Murder Most Foul night tour. Book at Quayside.
- Ph 9555 2700.

Royal Botanic Gardens

Take a guided walk through the gardens and check out the site of the first European farm. The tours leave daily from the Visitor's Centre at 10.30am and are free and very informative.
- Ph 9231 8125.

NSW National Parks and Wildlife Service Guided Walks

Check out bats feeding in Gordon or take an early morning walk along West Head and help collect information for the NPWS Wildlife Atlas. 120 volunteers give guided tours through Sydney's parklands.
- Ph 9457 9853.

Quarantine Station Ghost Tour

Follow a night guide armed only with a torch through the empty buildings of quarantine, the first stop in Sydney for immigrants suspected of carrying disease. Opened in 1832, hundreds of people died here before it was closed in 1984. $17 will get you a three-hour ghost tour. Book through the National Parks and Wildlife Service.
- Ph 9977 6522.

Centennial Park Guided Tours

Track possums and flying foxes, learn about the park's great trees, immerse yourself in Centennial history or hire a guide to take your children on a night time traipse. Call the Centennial Parklands for bookings and times.
- Ph 9360 4215.

The Hunter Valley Wine Tasting Tour

The best bus tour must be short – no sitting for more than three hours – and there must

be treats at the end. This tour cover both bases. Organised by AAT Kings, you visit Petersons Champagne House, McGuigans Hunter Estate, Wyndham Estate and the Golden Grape Vineyard. Lunch at Wyndham Estate is included in the $92.00 fee. Best of all, there's no way you can get busted for drink driving.
- Ph 9252 2788.

Cerentha Harris

Further Information
- Sydney Visitor's Centre, 106 George Street, ph 9255 1788

Gymnastics

see also aerobics, sporting goods

Here's the good news – gymnastics isn't only a sport for impossibly flexible and athletically talented mites aged 18 and under. This is a sport which, in its modified forms, can be enjoyed by toddlers aged 18 months and up, through to active older people in their 80s. The NSW Gymnastic Association runs programs for every kind of participant, so even if a triple back somersault is beyond you, there are many other gymnastic activities to be enjoyed. Gymnastics is one of Australia's most watched sports during the Olympics and Sydney boasts several potential Games stars, including rhythmic gymnast Shaneez Johnston and artistic gymnast Ian Bartlett, both of whom train with the NSW Institute of Sport. The Multi-Use arena (MUA) is the brand new venue for artistic gymnastics and trampolining at the 2000 Olympics, in Kevin Coombs Ave, Homebush. Rhythmic gymnastics will be held in one of the pavilions attached to the Showground complex in Murray Rose Ave, Homebush. An Olympic test event will be held there in November 1999.

State Sports Centre
Currently Sydney's only fully equipped international-standard gymnastic training facility, the SSC hosts elite squads from the NSW Institute of Sport, plus other regular groups. With a viewing balcony and cafe nearby, it's the perfect place to watch Australia's up-and-coming Olympic gymnasts tumble, swing, handspring, vault and somersault their way through training. The Centre will be the venue for the World Championships (trampoline) on October 9-11, 1998, and the Australian Championships, artistic (men and women), in March 1999.
- Australia Ave, Homebush.

Gym for kids
Kindergym, a gymnastics program for under fives, is designed to help children develop their creativity, physical development and thought processes. Coaches organise the kids' activities, using gymnastic equipment, in a safe environment and encourage social interaction between the children. Other programs, such as Gym Skills (12 years and over) and Aussie Gym Fun (12 years and under) are run in schools as part of the government's Aussie Sports program.
- Contact the NSW Gymnastic Association, ph 9763 0177, for more details.

Epping YMCA
One of Sydney's largest gymnastic clubs, renowned for producing top level gymnasts. All clubs, of course, supply gymnastic equipment and will usually provide a club leotard for competition. When you're starting out, however, you can wear whatever you feel comfortable in.
- Ward St, Epping, ph 9869 8966.

NSW Gymnastic Association (NSWGA)
Can direct you to one of the 150 Sydney clubs and provide information on all of its programs, events and where to buy gear or equipment. Veterans groups are a rapidly growing area of gymnastics.
- Ph 9763 0177.

Heather Quinlan

Hairdressers

see also beauty salons

A city which swims almost as much as it walks, Sydney polarises into people who seem to have their hair blow-dried almost every day and those who rarely wash it anywhere except in the Bondi surf. For the rest of us, there are good salons right through the suburbs (asking a well-coiffed local is often the best way to find out which is best), but the big names tend to be concentrated in Darlinghurst, Paddington, the City and Double Bay, simply because this is where the fashion and modelling industries are based. These are destination salons that are worth travelling kilometres to. Double Bay, in particular, is the 'beauty suburb', with a profusion of hairdressers, beauty salons and nail boutiques; monied women drive from all over Sydney to have their does done there.

Blondes, Brunettes, Redheads

Owner Alyson Schoer was the Senior Colourist at Vidal Sassoon in New York for five years and has trained hair colourists all over the world. In 1997 she was ordered a 'World Master of the Craft' lifetime achievement award for her colouring work at the hairdressing equivalent of the Oscars. As well as colouring, the salon also does cutting and make-up.
- 132a Foveaux St, Surry Hills, ph 9331 7211.

Efbee Hair, Body and Beauty

One of Melbourne's best hairdressers comes to Sydney. Excellent for all treatments, with great service.
- Shop 23, Level 1, Chatswood Chase, Victoria Ave, Chatswood, ph 9410 1033.

Helmet

Literally cutting edge, but they don't force wild styles on you. Owned by one of Australia's top make-up artists, Glen O'Reilly, who will also do special make-ups by appointment.
- 49 Flinders St, Surry Hills, ph 9380 5103.

Joh Bailey Hairdressers

The Versace of hairdressing – for the bold and the beautiful. They specialise in dressed hair.
- Shop 30, Level 1, Chifley Square, City, ph 9223 7673; 7 Knox St, Double Bay, ph 9363 4111.

Andrea Connolly Hairdressing Double Bay

Ladies who lunch have their hair done here first.
- 2 Short St, Double Bay, ph 9326 1799.

Smyth and Fitzgerald

Not just a salon, but a way of life for some of Sydney's most glamorous women. Excellent hairdressing in a friendly environment and one of the best beauty salons too.
- Shop 18, The Ritz Carlton Promenade, 33 Cross St, Double Bay, ph 9326 1385.

Toni and Guy

The Sydney branch of a legendary London salon, this is the place to go for the newest look from the Swinging City.
- 35 Oxford St, Darlinghurst, ph 9267 6299; 194 Pitt St, City, ph 9267 6011.

TSB

A very trendy salon, with excellent cutters (especially owner Troy S. Brennan). A nice touch is that they serve wine and cheese as well as the usual coffee.
- 71–73 Campbell St, Surry Hills, ph 9211 7373.

Wink Hair

Award winning salon in the CBD, great for colour, cuts and those essential pre-party blow drys.
- 165 Castlereagh St, City, ph 9264 1648.

Antony Whitaker

Consistent award winners, providing directional looks.
- 10 Oxford St, Paddington, ph 9360 9411.

Maggie Alderson

Hair replacement & wigs

see also hairdressers

If you're getting a bit thin on top (like Greg Matthews), or just need a bit of an image revamp (a la Kylie Minogue and Tina Turner), there are dozens of avenues within the hair industry to help you get that desired look. As common baldness now effects up to 75 per cent of men at some stage of their lives, more are turning to hair-replacement therapies. That's not to say wigs aren't still a multi-billion dollar business – just ask Dolly Parton who has made extra millions by selling her trademark Dolly wigs.

Ahead In Wigs

After 15 years in the business, Sharon Geyer and the staff know their wigs. The shop retails and hires wigs and toupees made from both synthetic materials and human hair. They specialise in wigs for people with medical conditions and are contracted by many film and theatrical agencies. The motto here is 'anything is possible', and extra services such as wig cleaning and styling are available.
- 125 Oxford St, Darlinghurst, ph 9360 1230.

Hairline Institute

Specialises in natural hair replacement, using the latest microscopic technology to transplant your own living hair. The treatment also covers scar tissue, burns and blemishes that have resulted from previous scalp surgery.
- Suite 919, 185 Elizabeth St, City, ph 1800 243334.

Advanced Hair Studios

Begun in Australia, Advanced Hair is now one of the largest hair replacement companies in the world, with more than 60 stores worldwide. Hair consultants will identify the extent of your hair loss, then tailor a treatment program to maximise hair regrowth. Using laser therapy and scalp and follicle treatments, significant regrowth usually takes between four and twelve months.
- City, Parramatta and Chatswood locations, ph 9267 6084.

The Academy of Hair Transplantation

'Hair transplantation' is a general term that includes a number of surgical procedures. The three major procedures are: micro and macro mini grafts, where the hair roots are taken from the back and sides, then transferred into the bald or thinning areas; hair lifting which works in a similar way to a face-lift, where unwanted bald skin is removed or tightened; the so-called flaps procedure, when a strip of hair bearing scalp is rotated from the side of the head, then sutured in place at the hairline. All of the procedures involve minor skin surgery, and the academy offer a refund if your hair falls out after surgery.
- 14th floor, 187 Macquarie St, City, ph 9233 3103.

Grant Gillies

Handball

The Olympic sport of handball is just starting to gain recognition in Australia. A traditional favourite in Eastern Europe, handball has rules similar to soccer, but the ball is thrown with the hands. Each team has 12 players, with seven on court at any one time. The court is 40m long by 20m wide and has goals at either end. The Olympic handball event will be played in one of the halls attached to the main showground arena at the Homebush Games site.

Sydney University Sports Aquatic Centre

Far and away the best current venue for handball. The University's handball court – located within the Sports Centre – can be hired for $80 an hour, which works out cheaply when divided between two teams of 12 players. The centre also has many other facilities, such as a gym, swimming pool, squash and tennis courts.

■ Ph 9351 4978.

NSW Handball Association

The best starting point for any newcomer to the sport. The association handles all queries, provides information about the sport, Sydney clubs and can even import for you a pair of shoes specifically made for handball. Many players, however, use normal sports shoes or runners because the imported gear is very expensive. Handballs can also be bought through the Association.

■ Ph 9327 3785.

Clubs

Sydney University is the biggest of the four clubs, due to its strong student membership. All membership enquiry details for this club, or the Hills District, Harbourside and North Sydney clubs, can be directed to the NSW Handball Association, as above.

Heather Quinlan

Hardware

see also building materials, building equipment

For some, size is what counts when it comes to hardware stores. They like their hardware stores to be as big as aircraft hangars, with aisle after aisle of gadgets, widgets, power tools and absolutely everything the home handyperson could ever dream of. Others prefer something on a more human scale, where products are easy to find, and the service is friendly and helpful. While the megastores have changed the hardware business in recent years, with new outlets opening around Sydney, the smaller stores have held their own, matching or even bettering them for price, service and convenience. Sydney has plenty of both to choose from.

Carroll's Hardware

One of the few hardware stores near the CBD, Carroll's has been serving the public, and winning a loyal following since 1923. It recently moved into new premises, over the road from where it had been, but still offers the same friendly service and good value. In addition to the usual hardware goods, it also stocks a range of building materials – sand, cement, timber and such. It is independently owned, but a member of the John Danks Thrifty-Link chain, which enables it to offer competitive prices.

■ 161-165 William St, Kings Cross, ph 9331 5555.

Booth & Taylor Hardware

Another member of the Thrifty-Link chain, Booth & Taylor Hardware is in the unusual position of having a competitor next door – which means the prices here are some of the cheapest you'll find in Sydney. Serving the Annandale, Glebe, Camperdown and Leichhardt area, the store is tailored to the needs of the home renovator, specialising in, among other things, materials for attic conversions, such as attic ladders and windows. It also carries a large range of paints, competing with specialist paint stores in this market.

■ 8 Booth St, Annandale, ph 9552 2910.

Hardwarehouse, Mascot

As big as a football field and filled from floor to ceiling with row upon row of tools, building materials, gardening supplies and plenty more besides. You may get lost a few times, but you can be pretty sure it'll have what you're after. Where your average hardware store will stock in the vicinity of 10,000 products, a Hardwarehouse has more like 35,000.

■ Cnr Bourke St and Gardeners Rd,

Mascot, ph 9700 8599. Also at Ashfield, Bankstown, Blacktown, Bonyrigg, Campbelltown, Caringbah, Minchinbury, Rockdale and Thornleigh.

Home Hardware
There are 10 of these large-sized hardware stores (around 15,000–20,000 products) in the Sydney area (plus others all through NSW) supplying tradespeople and the serious do-it-yourself market as well as the common home handyperson.
- 1 Brennan Close, Asquith, ph 9477 3355. Also at Birrong, Brookvale, Dural, Five Dock, Gladesville, Gymea, Pendle Hill, Riverstone, West Hoxton.

Benjamin Long

Hats

Millinery is alive and well in Sydney, judging by the flourishing number of hatmakers. It's not the fear of skin cancer that drives sales, however, but rather the frenetic social schedule of racing, weddings and lunches that keeps the whole business afloat.

Jane Lambert
Sydney's milliner to the smart set around town. The light-filled store is packed with pretty accessories – silk flowers, beaded evening bags and wraps, as well as Jane Lambert's clothing range.
- Shop 1, 23-25 Bay St, Double Bay, ph 9327 8642.

Axel Mano
Quirkier millinery with a bohemian air – squashy straw chapeaux and raffia baskets.
- 46a Ocean St, Woollahra, ph 9362 3756.

Neil Grigg Millinery
Ladies who lunch and/or go to the races, corporate clients, wedding guests, mothers of the bride, and even the brides themselves pop into Grigg's shop just near Cooper Park.
- 123 Manning Rd, Double Bay, ph 9281 8613.

Moray Hats
Sydney's classic milliner has been making hats for Sydney society for 65 years. Also at the swanky Moray hat boutique at David Jones on Seven (Elizabeth St store), where you can make appointments with Moray's master milliner, David Waddell.
- Studio, 3rd floor, 306 Strand Arcade, 195 Pitt St, City, ph 9233 1591.

Strand Hatters
Classic old hat shop carrying traditional hats by the Australian icon Akubra as well as smart panamas and straws for both men and women. Hats are steamed to fit on the premises.
- Strand Arcade, 412 George St, City, ph 9231 6884.

Isabella Klompe
Glamour hats favoured by the racing fraternity with as much personality as the milliner herself.
- Shop 10, 20 Bay St, Double Bay, ph 9363 0822.

Jane de Teliga

Health & medical matters

It would be pointless to even try to name Sydney's best doctors and hospitals. Not only would such a list be misleading – you may hate my favourite doctor's bedside manner – but the reality is that it is impossible to compile any objective guide.

The sorry fact is that there is very little data to guide consumers when selecting

GPs, specialists or hospitals, and most people have to rely on word of mouth, which is not always reliable or based on any meaningful evidence. Doctors traditionally have not welcomed outside moves to evaluate their performance.

As well, there are many practical reasons why the collection of comparative data is extremely difficult. One hospital, for example, may have relatively high rates of patients with hospital-acquired infections. But this may simply reflect that it treats more cancer and HIV patients, whose suppressed immune systems make them more likely to contract such infections.

Nonetheless, many well-meaning people in the medical profession, health departments and consumer organisations are working hard to develop more objective systems of evaluating standards of care. Who knows: in future there may even be report-cards to help us evaluate performances in a variety of areas, as has already happened with hospitals in some places overseas.

In the meantime, following are a few suggestions for what to look for in your GP, specialist and hospital. The one bit of advice that applies to them all is this: don't be afraid to ask questions, the more the better.

GPs

Choose your GP carefully – they are the 'gatekeepers' to the health system and a good GP will increase your chances of finding a good specialist, should you need one. Perhaps the most important issue is whether a GP is someone with whom you can develop a trusting, comfortable relationship where you will feel free to speak your mind and be confident that your concerns are being heard. Some patients will want to be fully involved in their health care and others will prefer to have decisions made for them; the important thing is that the doctor is meeting your needs.

Surgeries with long waiting times, rushed consultations and unsympathetic receptionists are best avoided. So are messy, dirty ones. Be more confident in doctors who advertise their commitment to continuing education programs and to proper infection control procedures. GPs who engage in preventive healthcare, such as asking about other aspects of your life and not just the immediate reason for your visit, may bring long-term health benefits. Written advice and information about support groups can be helpful.

Specialists

It is more difficult to be actively involved in choosing a specialist. But not impossible. Ask the GP why they are referring you to this person: are they known to have a particular interest in your complaint and have they produced good outcomes for similar problems before? Ask about the specialist's discipline and what this means for you – a surgeon, for example, will take a different approach to managing back pain to other specialists. Does the specialist provide detailed written reports back to your GP? Many don't, although this is important for ensuring continuity of care. Ask about the specialist's qualification and experience in treating your complaint. Any doctor who discourages a second opinion and is reluctant or too busy to answer your questions is probably best avoided.

Don't be afraid to ask about fees. If you are privately insured and undergoing surgery, you may face bills from several areas – for tests, the surgeon, anaesthetist, intensive care doctors, etc., so find out as much as you can about the charges.

Hospitals

Many patients don't have much choice about their hospital, especially if in a rush or not privately insured or living in smaller centres. Pragmatic issues can be very important. Is parking easily available and at what cost? Are the visiting hours convenient? What charges can you expect? What is the hospital policy on discharge planning, complaints, and what are the arrangements in case of emergency – a particularly important issue in smaller hospitals which may not have 24-hour backup? Not all hospitals are accredited with national standards bodies, so it may pay to check. If you want to go to a specific hospital, check which specialists have admitting rights there.

Melissa Sweet

Health food

see also alternative medicine

Health food stores are no longer just repositories for vitamin supplements and body-building seaweed elixirs, but have also turned into great food shops that offer naturally leavened bread, organic avocados, yummy muffins, wild honey and a happy mix of fresh and preserved foods and Japanese ingredients. They are, in fact, what all good food stores should be.

Macro Wholefoods

With its great breads, nuts, fruit and vegies (there is always an interesting pumpkin!), and not-too-lentilly takeaway food, this is a health food shop that makes you hungry. Also good for wholegrains and seeds, yogurt, cook books and world-friendly detergents.
- 328 Oxford St, Bondi Junction, ph 9389 7611; 170 King St, Newtown, ph 9550 5422.

Annabel's Natural Food Store

Annabel's is like a country town's general store, with its mix of hormone-free beef, terrific breads, huge bins of seeds and grains, free-range eggs, natural skin care and takeaway felafel rolls.
- 18 Willoughby Rd, Crows Nest, ph 9906 6377.

Russell's Natural Food Markets

Russell's main store, a healthy walk from Sydney University, is a large, rambling place filled with everything from macrobiotic Japanese thingies for lunch to fresh fruit and vegies, grains, honeys and an imposing array of water filters.
- 55 Glebe Point Rd, Glebe, ph 9660 8144. Also at Chatswood, Dee Why, Neutral Bay, North Sydney, Rockdale and City.

The Health Emporium

A bright and airy half-cafe, half-shop arrangement that is serious about grains, seeds and pulses, and about stocking the good stuff (like all organic fruit and veg) for allergy sufferers. The takeaway food is so tempting it stops meat-eaters in their tracks.
- 263 Bondi Rd, Bondi, ph 9365 6008.

Jill Dupleix

Heating & fireplaces

Yes, it does get cold in Sydney. The most cost-effective (and environmentally sound) method is gas heating, though there's more romance and character in a working fireplace to keep the winter chills out. But where do you go when the chimney is blocked and the prior owners have 'modernised' your once-gracious hearth?

AGL Showcases

Gas heaters have never been so smart, slim and portable. For solid good looks, check out the Convector 516 TR in gunmetal.
- For your nearest outlet, ph 9922 0101.

Cheminee Philippe

The European manufacturer has been in business here for more than 14 years with a fully operational showroom featuring its heavy-duty

Heating & fireplaces

range of Radiantes cast iron fire boxes in a variety of sizes.
- 130 Pyrmont Bridge Rd, Camperdown, ph 9517 2740.

Jetmaster

The South African based manufacturer has been selling its hugely successful Jetmaster range to Sydneysiders for more than 20 years. The basic black box and metal flue system comes in around 10 different sizes which can be fitted easily into an existing or new fireplace. There's even a freestanding model. The most recent addition is the Heat and Glow series of gas heaters made in America.
- 10 Martin Ave, Arncliffe, ph 9597 7222; 167 Eastern Valley Way, Castlecrag, ph 9958 1777.

Architectural Heritage

Sydney-based Bowin's ultra-efficient unflued fires fit into natty little Victorian or Federation upright antique grates in cast iron. Make sure you ask for extra logs and cones.
- 62 Glebe Point Rd, Glebe, ph 9660 0100.

Chippendale Restorations

Replacement parts for your fireplace: grates, fire bricks and ash pans.
- 505 Balmain Rd, Lilyfield, ph 9810 6066.

Randwick Restoration Store

Specialises in the restoration of original fireplaces and the installation of new ones. The Store can also supply marble and timber fire surrounds.
- 31 St Pauls St, Randwick, ph 9399 9312.

Anglo Master Chimney Sweeps

Recommended by the National Trust.
- 86 Old South Head Rd, Bondi Junction, ph 9369 4889, mobile 018 963 131.

Sydney Chimney Sweep Company

As well cleaning your chimney and flue, the company can install and repair period fireplaces.
- 6 William St, Tempe, ph 9558 4879, mobile 018 296 351.

Peter Jordan & Melissa Walker Smith

Heritage Sydney

see also architecture, monuments

Around Macquarie St, the politicians have cared well for their surrounds, with Greenway's Hyde Park Barracks superbly reinterpreted as a museum, the old Rum Hospital buildings reworked as the Mint Museum and Parliament House, and icons such as Sydney Hospital and the government buildings of Bridge St undergoing refurbishment. Elsewhere, the picture is not so happy, so don't take your eyes off what remains.

Sydney Town Hall

It took Sydney some time to establish a civic headquarters. Early city council meetings took place, fittingly perhaps, in the back room of a pub. But when, in the 1860s, work began on a town hall, the project proceeded with gusto, producing what is now one of the most important, and lavish, Victorian interiors in Sydney. Up the marble steps from George St is the vestibule, restored in 1991 by Howard Tanner and Associates to a dazzling array of 35 original colours. The Centennial Hall beyond, though magnificent, is subdued in comparison.
- Cnr George and Parks Sts, City.

GPO, Martin Place

Now destined by Australia Post to be little more than a 'front' for a posh hotel and some Sydney-standard office blocks. But James Barnet's magnificent colonnade – one of the city's finest public spaces – will be restored and will stand as a fitting monument to our sad habit of bastardising our heritage.

Opera House

Despite criticisms – the interiors aren't up to scratch, it isn't a satisfactory place to stage opera, etc – Joern Utzon's fabulous dream at Bennelong Point is still the building of the century, architecture that sends a shiver down the spine at the sheer *rightness* of it there, and the sheer daring. Not so long ago, Utzon's daughter, Lin, brought a 1965 scale model of the building to Sydney at her father's behest, with 'my best wishes to the people of Australia'. 'What lives with him is that the building is a success and Australians love it,' she said. How could we not?

Susannah Place, The Rocks

Three brick terraces and a corner store (operating once again), built in 1844, probably for Edward Riley, and named for his niece, Susannah Sterne. Their continuous history of working-class family occupation up to the late part of this century has been carefully preserved in a joint Historic Houses Trust/Sydney Cove Authority project. Here are the backyard dunnies, the coppers, the wall finishes, furniture and layers of paint recording the lives and living conditions of the not-so-rich or famous.

Elizabeth Bay House

Worth its five-star rating, if only for the 'finest staircase in Australian colonial architecture'. Designed by John Verge for Alexander Macleay and his family, it was built between 1835 and 1839, and occupied by Macleays until 1911. Its 22-hectare garden, a 'botanist's paradise', has long since disappeared, but from the portico and the upstairs windows there are glimpses of what the Macleays once surveyed.
■ 7 Onslow Place, Elizabeth Bay, ph 9358 2344

Pier 4/5, Walsh Bay

One of the ranks of Sydney Harbour Trust wharves built from the early 1900s, reminders of how Sydney came to be and how it was sustained by maritime commerce for most of the first 200 years of its existence. The greatest and grandest of these at Woolloomooloo is being remade as a housing/hotel development; but Pier 5 at Walsh Bay, converted in 1984 by architect Viv Fraser for the Sydney Theatre Company, captures the spirit of Sydney. You don't have to be going to the theatre, or to the restaurant at the end – just walk along the massive, lanolin-polished timber floors, glimpsing green water all the way, to the theatre of glittering harbour, thundering Bridge and Luna Park on the opposite shore. Or walk past the Sydney Dance Company headquarters on the lower level and join the fishermen at pier's end. And hope that other redundant industrial sites will be treated with such care.

Geraldine O'Brien

Further information
■ NSW Historic Houses Trust, ph 9692 8366.

Hockey

see also sporting goods

Hockey has long been one of the most popular participant sports in Sydney, with many clubs in all parts of the city fielding hundreds of teams in men's, women's and junior's competitions. The Sydney Olympics will ensure the sport receives a greatly enhanced profile as a spectator sport, as well as leaving the lasting legacy of one of the world's best hockey stadiums. The current dominance of the Australian women's team, the Hockeyroos, is likely to create great interest in the hockey competition, while the Kookaburras, the Australian men's team, will also be a strong gold medal contender.

Olympic Hockey Centre

While Sydney hockey has long had its headquarters at the State Sports Centre at Homebush where the 1994 men's World Cup final was played, the Olympic competition will

be contested in the new 15,000 seat stadium, also at Homebush Bay. After the Olympics, temporary seating will be removed leaving a stadium that will seat up to 7,000 spectators. This will be the focus of the major inter-city competitions and also, it is expected, be the venue for major international tours and series.
- State Sports Centre, Sydney Olympic Park, Australia Ave, Homebush Bay, ph 9764 1911.

Hockey NSW

Men's and some women's competitions are organised by the central administrative body for hockey in Sydney. Most clubs field multiple teams in graded leagues.
- PO Box 522, Concord, ph 9764 1911.

NSW Arrows and NSW Warriors

The Arrows and the Warriors are the NSW teams in the women's and men's national league competitions. The teams play their home games at the State Sports Centre, Homebush. The seasons vary, depending on the commitments of the national teams. For information about the Arrows and Warriors contact Hockey NSW.

Just Hockey

Specialist retailer of hockey equipment.
- 110 Parramatta Rd, Homebush, ph 9746 0231.

Richard Hinds

Homewares

see also **tableware, cookware & kitchenware, furniture, soft furnishings**

The fashionable home decorator can find all the newest home-design trends in one concentrated shopping strip stretching from the Sydney CBD to the Eastern Suburbs. From the functional and affordable to a well-deserved indulgence, Sydney is brimming with great, modern homewares to complement or contrast with modern and classic interiors.

Bibelot

Showcase for up and coming designers with the nattiest objects from a portfolio of young local talent and high profile designer pieces from international luminaries. Authentic, plastic, fantastic, mass-produced domestic products plus hard-to-find ranges such as tactile office products in pale timber.
- 445 Oxford St, Paddington, ph 9360 6902.

Brook Street Trading

Heritage-hungry Sydneysiders will delight in Ros Palmer's glam showroom which is decorated in epic style and stuffed with English classics: Bennison fabrics, covetable Vaughan repro lighting and needlepoint in convincing shapes and forms, creamware plus an elaborate mix of sofas, chairs, mirrors, ottomans and tables.
- Shop 1, 50 Bayswater Rd, Kings Cross, ph 9380 6502.

Empire

Targeting the busy, design-savvy urban dweller, this new one-stop shopping emporium has an understated selection of furniture, bed linen, bathroom basics, rugs, glassware and kitchen kit.
- 18-20 Oxford St, Paddington, ph 9380 8877.

Home

Located near the hurly burly of Taylor Square, this is a modern, lively shop selling quirky placemats, cool ceramics, bold bathroom basics and loads more.
- 153 Oxford St, Darlinghurst, ph 9332 4840.

Castone

Kim Kunnerman has her own edgy spin on pretty. A good range of household kit: chenille

throw rugs, cushions, lampshades and bed linen plus made-to-measure armoires and beds with the patina you want.
- 31 Ocean St, Woollahra, ph 9363 5794.

Mondo
Simple and uncompromising, with a well-sourced collection of hot contemporary homewares in a limited palette of white, black and stone.
- 27 Bay St, Double Bay, ph 9362 4964.

Orson and Blake
An amazing array of beautiful homewares that are right in tune with our craving for things that are simple, useful and functional. Attractively laid out with cushions, ceramics, wickerware and other accessories in shades of white and brown, so that you feel inspired just stepping through the door.
- 55 Queen St, Woollahra, ph 9326 1155.

Papaya Studio
A recently opened shop with a modern soul. Robyn Connelly and Karen Lange share an earthy aesthetic with a clever slant on the global marketplace. They bring together a subtle mix of everyday household objects from around the world in wood, stone, metal, terracotta and natural fibres.
- 15b Transvaal Ave, Double Bay, ph 9362 1620.

Pigott's Store
A godsend for those in search of affordably priced decorative items that take their cue from English classics. The shop is brimming with a festival of cheery chintzes, lots of toile de jouys and snappy cotton checks. Also locally made furniture and a vast array of accessories: fabric-clad boxes, wall brackets, trays, lamps, wastepaper bins, lamps and prints.
- 53 Ocean St, Woollahra, ph 9362 8119.

R.G. Madden
That pillar of the hip Melbourne set now has two stores in Sydney selling everything for the self-respecting groover: Alessi, Dualit toasters, Hamilton Beach retro-look kitchen appliances, Lexon luggage, DDT vases and heaps more.
- Shop 207, Skygarden, 77 Castlereagh St, City, ph 9231 2257.

White & White
Freshen up with white linen and household accessories from this small shop which shows you different ways with white. There's stacks of crisp bed linen, useful bathroom bits and bobs plus cuddly throw rugs to lose yourself in.
- 785 Military Rd, Mosman, ph 9968 4559.

Melissa Walker Smith

Horseracing

see also gambling

If you want to find out exactly what makes Sydney society tick, walk onto a racecourse. Blue-collar battlers push and shove along with the big end of town as each strives to secure the best odds. Racing has always played a big part in the life of this city. Officers of the 73rd Regiment conducted the first formal race meeting in 1810. The venue: Hyde Park. From that initial meeting, racing has grown to become a multi-billion dollar business. In NSW, more than 50,000 people are employed directly or indirectly in the racing game.

However, racecourse crowds numbering 80,000 are long gone. The introduction of the NSWTAB, the off-course betting shop, in 1964 was responsible for a steady decline in on-track patronage. The majority of pubs and clubs also cater to the punting public's demands.

In the metropolitan area, race meetings are conducted every Wednesday, with exceptions for country cup meetings, and on

Saturdays. Public holidays are reserved for Royal Randwick while Sunday meetings are on the increase. Carnival days, in the autumn and spring, are major events. The latest fashions from the catwalks of Milan are paraded in front of the best trainers, jockeys and horses, making for a delightful day of punting and fun.

And it's worthwhile remembering the Government is richer to the tune of some $300 million each year due to the racing game. The money is used to build hospitals, roads and associated infrastructure which may help ease the pain if you've failed to back a winner.

Royal Randwick

The home of thoroughbred racing in Australia. The famous track has played host to some of racing's greatest duels, both human and equine. Easily the biggest of the four courses in the metropolitan area, Randwick is renowned for its rise in the home straight which provides a stern test for the thoroughbred as it reaches top speed.
- Alison Rd, Randwick, ph 9663 8400.

Rosehill Gardens

Home to the Golden Slipper, a race restricted to two-year-olds, who sizzle over a 1,200m course to secure a share in prize money of $2m which makes it the richest race for juveniles in the world. A train will take you straight there.
- James Ruse Drive, Rosehill, ph 9930 4000.

Warwick Farm

On Sydney's western outskirts, this course's tranquil surrounds make for great picnic days.
- Hume Highway, Warwick Farm, ph 9663 8400.

Canterbury Park

The racecourse has recently been completely rebuilt and realigned while all betting facilities are now housed indoors. All redevelopment was carried out with a view to the tight course becoming Sydney's home to night racing which is due to commence at the end of 1998.
- King St, Canterbury, ph 9930 4000.

Shane Dye

Flamboyant, highly controversial but the consummate professional. Jockey R.S. Dye does things differently – his own way. There is no doubt the former Kiwi is a big race rider. Premierships have been won. Major races are what it's about. And keeping him busy are the likes of Jim and Larry Cassidy.

John Hawkes

Backed by Australia's biggest owners, Jack and Bob Ingham, Hawkes commands stable operations in four states from his Warwick Farm base. Won his fourth Sydney trainers' premiership in 1998 and will be hard to beat in 99.

Gai Waterhouse

Without doubt Australian racing's first lady. Waterhouse is the daughter of legendary trainer T.J. Smith and has set about changing the relationship between owner and trainer. Open days are held most Sundays at her Randwick stables.
- 16 Bowral Ave, Randwick, ph 9662 1488.

Sydney Autumn Carnival

Kicks off in early March and culminates in late April. On the Saturday of the Easter long weekend in April the AJC Australian Derby is run at Randwick along with the time-honoured Doncaster Handicap. On the preceding Saturday the Golden Slipper is run at Rosehill. The nine races carry a total of $3.7 million in prize money making it the richest racing carnival in Australia.

Sydney Spring Carnival

Starts in September and runs through to the long weekend in October.

William Inglis & Son Australasian Yearling Sale

The biggest sale of its kind in the southern hemisphere and held each Easter. If you've a spare $100,000 or so, head to the famed Newmarket sale complex situated just near Randwick racecourse. Buy tomorrow's champion today.

Harold Park

The inner city track is home to harness racing, or 'the trots' as it is affectionately known. The circuit has been completely rebuilt at a cost of several million dollars. Apart from a brand new cambered track the facilities for patrons are first-class, with a fully-enclosed grandstand, restaurants and a poker machine lounge.
- Ross St, Glebe, ph 9660 3688.

Further information
- Sydney Morning Herald: sport section daily and The Form guide on Fridays.
- Australian Jockey Club, ph 9663 8400: www.ajc.org.au
- Sydney Turf Club: ph 9930 4000: www.stc.com.au
- NSW Thoroughbred Racing Board: ph 9694 6200

Craig Young

Horseriding

Horses have been at home in Sydney since the turn of the 19th century, when settlers shipped in European working breeds to share the labours on their new land. Today's massive thoroughbred industry is based in the Hunter Valley, but Greater Sydney remains the stronghold of the nation's horse-riding talent. Of the 74 names in Australia's latest equestrian squads, 47 are from NSW and most of them could drive to its capital inside an hour. The best are Maraylya's Stuart Tinney, our best home-based eventer, and Arcadia's Rachel Downs, who surprised the Europeans on the national dressage team's 1997 tour.

But you do not have to be a regular Roy Rogers to enjoy what Sydney has to offer horse lovers. One-time thrill-seekers (and those who just like to watch) can get involved, too. From Mt White to Camden and the Royal National Park, Sydney has hundreds of clubs, extensive training and stabling and breathtaking trail rides. Sydney and nearby areas also host many exciting events, which in late 1998 include the Hermes Show (showjumping) at Moore Park on October 25 (ph 9233 5844); the NSW Dressage Championships at Clarendon on November 6-8; and the Berrima Horse Trial (three-day event) on November 28-29.

Centennial Park

You cannot get more central than this favourite spot for all things horsey. Reopened in early 1998 after redevelopment. The revamped site is smaller, with fewer stables (270, down from 999), but is first-rate. Includes dressage arenas, vet care, schooling and a 4km walking track.
- Lang Rd, ph 9339 6699.

Kurnell Boarding Stables and Riding School

Agistment, tuition and, at Quibray Bay (southern side of Botany Bay), the only beach trail rides you'll go on without being chased off by a council officer.
- Captain Cook Drive, Kurnell, 9668 9817.

Sydney Horse Riding Safaris

Offers an hour ride up and down (and up and down) the Malabar Headland, all within sight of the Centrepoint Tower. Get on the second of the two daily treks to see the horses released into the bush at the ride's end.
- Ph 0419 289 155.

Equitrek

If too far is not far enough, this horseback holiday specialist can give you saddle sores in

Horseriding

four states. Closest trek is a three-day trot through the sprawling Yarramalong Valley.
- 5 King Rd, Ingleside, ph 9913 9408.

Kellyville Riding Club
Equestrian club for 8- to 80-year-old riders. It specialises in dressage, eventing and showjumping.
- Cnr Withers & Commercial roads, Rouse Hill, ph 9632 2203.

Northside Riding Club
Club catering for riders from every weird and wonderful equine discipline, including showing.
- St Ives Showground, Mona Vale Rd, St Ives, ph 9979 8203.

Glenworth Valley Horse Riding
Set in 2,500 acres, this popular establishment features barbecue areas and natural rock pools for swimming. It is open seven days a week from 10am till 5pm. Cost of rides vary. The longer you ride, the cheaper it becomes. You'll pay $40 for 2 hours, $50 for 3 hours and $65 for 6 hours.
- Cooks Rd, Peats Ridge (20 minutes from Hornsby, 1 hour from Sydney's CBD), ph (02) 4375 1222.

Charltons Horseland
This chain saddlery is a Sydney institution, and imports from Germany and the UK. Open late Thursdays.
- 989 Pacific Highway, Chatswood, ph 9419 5070.

Goodwood Saddlery
Horsey megastore in the CBD. Stocks all imaginable saddlery, and specialises in traditional countrywear.
- 237 Broadway, ph 9660 6788.

Mt White Stockfeeds
Run by the World Cup showjumper Krissy Harris. Home-delivers its freshly cut, dust-free feed across the metropolitan region.
- 136 Ashbrooks Rd, Mt White, ph (02) 4370 1133.

Sydney Mounted Police Stables
The oldest mounted force in the world – older even than the Canadian mounties. Stable tours Tuesdays and Thursdays.
- 7 Baptist St, Redfern, ph 9319 2154.

National Parks and Wildlife Service
If you are planning an unaccompanied trek and give a whinny about the future of Sydney trail riding, clear your path here first.
- ph 9585 6333.

Peter Vincent

Further information
- Australian Bushmen's Campdraft and Rodeo Association, ph (02) 6766 5863
- Equestrian Federation of Australia (NSW), ph 9571 8777
- Hack Council of NSW, ph 4358 2662
- NSW Dressage Council, ph 4777 4965
- NSW Horse Trials, ph 6547 9212
- NSW Polo Association, ph 9552 1260
- NSW Showjumping Council, ph 9629 5830

Ice-cream

Good ice-cream must be freshly made of quality ingredients, naturally coloured and flavoured, and stored at the right temperature. Just as importantly, it must be stored at exactly the right time and place that you crave it. Sadly, many of our beachside shopping strips are taken over by waffle-selling franchise chains, but it is well worth seeking out the more individual quality makers and putting them to the test lick by lick.

Nice Cream
Nicola Smith and Wolfgang Groh make Sydney's richest, creamiest ice-creams (including an angelic passionfruit and lime), and now sell direct from their Paddington factory. Their ice-

cream ingredients are so pricey we mortals would probably only buy them as special treats.
- 300 Glenmore Rd, Paddington, ph 9380 8011. Also available from some delicatessens and gourmet food outlets, including Glebe St Deli (Glebe), Avenue Rd Deli (Mosman), and Goldy's Deli (Mosman and Lindfield). ph 9386 9161 for details.

Serendipity Ice Cream

Black licorice, peach Melba, passionfruit and chilli, and Japanese green tea flavours keep Serendipity one of the most licked ice-creams in town. Eat in or take away by cone and tub from Passionflower.
- Shop G12, 730 George St, next to Capitol Theatre, City, ph 9281 8322.

Also available from some delicatessens and gourmet food outlets, including **Five Star Gourmet** (Crows Nest), **David Jones Food Hall** (City and Bondi Junction) and selected **Clancy's Supermarkets** (Darlinghurst and Paddington). ph 9557 8986 for details.

Glace

Flavours (fresh peach, watermelon, lemon verbena) that would melt the hardest heart, and a texture that is less cloying and creamy than most put Glace in the top handful – and on as many dinner party tables as possible.
- Available from delicatessens and gourmet food outlets, including **Jones the grocer** (Woollahra), **Mosman Cheese Shop** (Mosman), **Simmone Logue** (Balmain) and **Luigi Bros** (Double Bay). ph 9716 6451 for details.

Gabriel's on Swanson

One of the few places you can get a real quality ice-cream, such as Glace, by the cone, direct from a genuine ice-cream trolley. One of Sydney's newest food stores, Gabriel's is handily situated across from a park so you can lick and dribble your fresh lime ice-cream or mango sorbet in peace.
- 110 Swanson St (cnr Park St), Erskineville, ph 9565 4171.

Bravo Trattoria

One of the North Shore's most popular lick stops, the Bravo Trattoria will top your cone with mango, lemon, watermelon or guava gelati that is made only from fresh fruit, with not a bottled syrup in sight. Eat in or take-away.
- 6 Falcon St, Crows Nest, ph 9906 6629.

Bar Italia

A favourite Norton St stop for those indulging in *la passegiata*, the long, slow stroll that is so much a part of Italian daily life. And what motivation – fresh pistachio (that's from real nuts), and fresh mango are worth the walk, even from the city.
- 169 Norton St, Leichhardt, ph 9560 9981.

Jill Dupleix

Indian restaurants

Great! You love tandoori chicken and Kashmiri naan. Now you've got just 15 Indian provinces to go. It's time to discover the rich vindaloos of the west, the lush sambars of the south, the beautifully balanced lamb dishes of the north, and the glorious fish dishes of the east. Luckily, most of Sydney's Indian restaurants can take you around the whole subcontinent in a single meal.

Abhi's

They seem so genuinely pleased to see you at this neighbourly Indian eatery, you wonder if they haven't mistaken you for a regular. And once you've tried the fish hariali kebab,

chicken makhani and tandoori meats, chances are it won't be too long before you are a regular.
- 163 Concord Rd, North Strathfield, ph 9743 3061.

Flavour of India, Edgecliff
The menu is a round-India package tour with the usual selection of pakoras, tandoori meats, breads, and beef vindaloos, but there is a liberal sprinkling of more unusual offerings that lift it out of the cliché class. Service is genuinely helpful, and the wine list contains some interesting bottles.
- 128 New South Head Rd, Edgecliff, ph 9326 2659.

Malabar
Most of the what we call Indian food is actually north Indian. Malabar on the other hand specialises in the spicier, more fiery cuisines of the southern states with their beautifully balanced vegetable dishes, and magical rice and lentil pancakes known as dosai.
- 332 Pacific Highway, Crows Nest, ph 9906 7343.

Oh! Calcutta!
If you're expecting sitar music and Kama Sutra wall hangings, you may be disappointed. Basil Daniell's restaurant looks more like a mod Oz bistro than an Indian restaurant, although the smells coming from the kitchen are decidedly of the subcontinent variety. As well as classic north Indian dishes, the menu features contemporary touches such as stir-fried kangaroo.
- 251 Victoria St, Darlinghurst, ph 9360 3650.

Terry Durack

Insulation

Few people like the extremes of Sydney weather, be it a sultry January day or a cold August night (what was Neil Diamond going on about?). Central heating or reverse-cycle airconditioning might be going too far if sealing your roof and walls is all that's required to make your home more comfortable. Here are some leading operators.

Roof and Wall Home Insulation
Its cellulose fibre bats are fireproof, rodent resistant and recycled, which makes them the most environment-friendly insulators in town. Residential properties are their specialties, but will also do commercial premises.
- Gordon, ph 9418 2131; Hurstville, ph 9580 0733; Liverpool, ph 9893 7386; St Marys, ph 9623 0607.

NSW Insulations
Supplier and installer of the two major insulation products, ACI and Bradford. They can cocoon your home from the temperature and noise extremes of suburban living with their glasswool and rockwool bats.
- Ph 9894 9100.

Ifco Insulation and Air Supply
Suppliers and installers of Bradford bats, specialising in residential properties.
- Ph 9477 5455.

Steve Samuelson

Interior designers & decorators

see also architects
The days are over when a decorator simply appeared, clapped their hands and said, 'I see the whole thing in raspberry silk'. In the design-conscious '90s, most of us want to work with the interior designer or decorator from the start to create something that reflects our individual style and personality. Surveying the old Sydney hands and the new talent, you will discover world-class

Interior designers & decorators

designers and decorators on your doorstep. Many are trained; however some of the most supremely gifted are not – but all have taste, confidence, perfectionism and a professional attitude. An interior designer can change a space structurally; a decorator is generally a surface person. Unlike architects, interior designers and decorators are not legally required to be registered.

Tim Allison
As well as an architectural understanding of structure, interior architect Alison has a formidable ability with colour, shape and detail.
■ ph 9356 4204.

Pia Francesca Design
As one of Sydney's most successful designers, what makes Francesca notable is that she views furniture as real pieces rather than elitist one-off collector items. Minimalist logic with maximum comfort. Favours a sludgy palette.
■ ph 9331 7184.

George Freedman
Guru of Sydney interior design, Freedman is a designer with his roots in the '60s but his finger firmly on the pulse of the contemporary. Eternally modern, his work fuses a refined sophistication with classical elements from the past.
■ Ph 9360 2600.

Darryl Gordon
There is something fresh and young in a Gordon interior. The thirty-something decorator won the prestigious SIDA Young Designer of the Year award in 1995 and is renowned for combining the pleasures of simplicity and ornament.
■ Ph 9380 2600.

Burley Katon Halliday
Iain Halliday and David Katon's total commitment to simplicity and modernism has given them a special place in the rollcall of contemporary Australian designers. One of Sydney's most talented design duos, they marry modern furniture classics with their own custom-made pieces. Renowned for their meticulous attention to detail and their disciplined colour palette which goes from matt to gloss white.
■ Ph 9332 2233.

Margot Montgomery
She revels in faded glory: the patina of age, original paintwork, the grain of real timber and the texture of cotton and linen. She is renowned for her innate ability with colour.
■ Ph 9363 0043.

Cameron Kimber
Not shy of colour, comfort or decoration, the honed graciousness of his interiors marks him out as the one to watch. He trained under Leslie Walford and Thomas Hamel before branching out on his own in 1997.
■ Ph 9362 8766.

Thomas Hamel
King of Sydney society decorators, Hamel is the man of the moment. Virginian-born, London-schooled and New York-trained, his interiors are loved, not just because they are beautiful, but because they actually work. No matter what your look, he can make it work.
■ Ph 9363 3738.

Michael Love
The master of modern glamour, whose interiors are remarkable for their chic serenity, a combination of luxury and suave sophistication.
■ Ph 9327 8383.

Ros Palmer
Palmer is an accomplished decorator in the grand manner with a career spanning three decades. She is best known for her epic style.
■ Ph 9362 3062.

Interior designers & decorators

Scott Weston
One of Sydney's most inventive and dynamic designers: radical, bold, elemental and funny. He trained as an architect and is renowned for his rigour and bold palette which seems to be an alien concept to many contemporary designers.
■ Ph 9331 3317.

Melissa Walker Smith

Further information
■ Society of Interior Designers of Australia, ph 9633 4055
■ Design Institute of Australia, ph 9929 5188

International designer fashion

see also womenswear, menswear
Sydney is seen as the last frontier for all the big international labels bent on colonising the world, so in the last decade the big names have been coming thick and fast. Don't forget the big department stores for international designer labels – for example, the 7th floor of David Jones Elizabeth St store. The On Seven floor is a haven for labels like Donna Karan, Valentino, Yves Saint Laurent and Jil Sander, while Grace Bros city flagship store stocks many top international labels.

Celine
Parisian label for the well to do, with the highlight on smart handbags.
■ 65-71 Castlereagh St, City, ph 9223 4209.

Chanel
The ultimate label for the ladies who lunch. Nothing beats Karl Lagerfeld's Chanel, with its much prized double CC logo and the legendary quilted chain-handled handbag.
■ 70-70A Castlereagh St, City, ph 9233 4800.

DKNY
Donna Karan's taste of supercool New York for the young man and woman.
■ 19 Castlereagh St, City, ph 9232 1222.

Emporio Armani
One of the world's most popular labels, Italian master Giorgio Armani has taken the stuffing and stuffiness out of tailoring. Very popular among the his and hers corporate set who love to lunch in its terrific cafe.
■ 4 Martin Place, City, ph 9231 3655.

Gap
The cult American label for basics like the simple T-shirt, white shirts and the chino pant for both sexes.
■ 155 George St, The Rocks, ph 9258 7663; Terminal C, International Airport, ph 9313 5744.

Guess
Young and sexy American label with sportswear emphasis. Big on trendy accessories.
■ Queen Victoria Building, City, ph 9267 8554. Also at Parramatta, ph 9891 9062; Drummoyne, ph 9819 7754; Chatswood, ph 9415 4411.

Gianni Versace
The legend lives on, despite the death of this Italian designer. Glamorous clothing for men and women who want to be noticed. Plus homewears laden with gold and classical motifs.
■ 128 Castlereagh St, City, ph 9267 3232.

Giorgio Armani
Enter the stylish, calming world of Giorgio Armani, the Italian designer synonymous with good taste. For those men and women who value quiet refinement and have the wherewithal to buy the best.
■ 173 Elizabeth St, City, ph 9283 5562.

Gucci Boutique

One of the hottest labels on the fashion planet, the revitalised Gucci now boasts two stores in Sydney. The Gucci shoe and handbag are tops on the fashion hit list.
- MLC Centre, cnr King and Castlereagh Sts, City, ph 9232 7565; 136-140 George St, The Rocks, ph 9252 1663.

Hermes

The luxury French label, with a thoroughbred pedigree, whose expensive accessories like their famous Kelly handbag and printed silk scarves have long epitomised class and good breeding.
- 77 Castlereagh St, City, ph 9223 4007; The Regent, 199 George St, The Rocks, ph 9247 1396.

Kenzo

Paris-based but Japanese-born Kenzo is renown for his rich and vibrant florals.
- Shop 2.2, Chifley Plaza, 2 Chifley Square, City, ph 9223 9669.

Loewe

Spanish label with the emphasis on luxury leathergoods.
- 63 Castlereagh St, City, ph 9236 9625.

Louis Vuitton

The world's most coveted leathergoods whose famous monogrammed bags and luggage are sought after worldwide from Paris to Tokyo. Part of the huge French luxury goods company LVMH (Moet Hennessey Louis Vuitton).
- 63 Castlereagh St, City, ph 9236 9605.

Max & Co.

The young and hipper little sister label to Max Mara.
- Shop G13, Chatswood Chase, Victoria Ave, Chatswood, ph 9410 0211.

MaxMara

Elegant Italian style for the well-heeled woman, including the world's best cashmere coats.
- Shop 2.1, Chifley Plaza, 2 Chifley Square, City, ph 9223 2686; Cnr Bay St and Guilfoyle Ave, Double Bay, ph 9362 9155.

Polo Ralph Lauren

American designer Ralph Lauren's new classics for men and women who share his nostalgia for polo fields, upper crust sportswear and cowboy denim.
- Greenwood Plaza, North Sydney, ph 9956 6828; Queen Victoria Building, City, ph 9267 1630.

Prada

Newest arrival on the designer scene, Prada is the cult label for fashion aficionados. Prada's black nylon accessories and clothes have become a modern fashion classic.
- 44 Martin Place, City, ph 9231 3929.

Salvatore Ferragamo

Begun by the famous Italian shoemaker whose family dynasty continue making the women's (and men's) shoes, handbags, women's clothing, and printed silk scarves and ties that sell all over the world.
- MLC Centre, Castlereagh St, City, ph 9221 3036.

Jane de Teliga

Investment managers & advisers

see also accountants, stockbrokers

Investment advice is a fiercely competitive market in Sydney, where quality varies widely depending on the individual or people you are dealing with. Advisers should be licensed by the Australian Securities Com-

Investment managers & advisers

mission (ASC) so make it your first port of call or check out its Web site (see below) to check that your adviser is licensed and has not been banned from practising. The ASC also publishes a booklet, Don't kiss your money goodbye, on how to choose an adviser. This is recommended reading. Investment advice is available from a wide range of practitioners – big national groups, accountants, stockbrokers, sole operators and even lawyers.

Australia's investment management industry is dominated by a relatively small group of companies. Unit trusts are the predominant investment vehicle and these are pooled investments where each 'unit' entitles you to a share of the fund's earnings.

The following lists the three investment advisers who were ranked at the top by principal members of the Financial Planning Association in a survey conducted by Personal Investment magazine, followed by a selection of highly rated investment managers.

Godfrey Pembroke
Voted as 1997 adviser of the year by the *Personal Investment* survey, this major group has more than 10 offices throughout NSW and was formed by one of the industry founders, John Godfrey.
- Ph 9299 7500.

Bain Investor Services
A subsidiary of the Deutsche Morgan Grenfell group, this firm came second in the *Personal Investment* survey.
- Ph 9258 1862.

RetireInvest
Now fully-owned by Mercantile Mutual, this is another of Australia's major advisory groups and ranked third in the *Personal Investment* survey.
- Ph 9262 1111.

Bankers Trust
This manager has proven its merit over the long haul – although it does not have the stand-out performance it did in the late 1980s. It was still highly rated in a recent *Sydney Morning Herald* Money section survey of Australia's best investment funds.
- Ph 9259 3555.

First State Fund Managers
Owned by the Colonial group, this is a newer fund manager with highly regarded skills in selecting investments. Its funds were also highly rated in the *SMH* Money survey.
- Ph 9273 3000.

Perpetual Funds Management
An offshoot of the once-staid trustee company, Perpetual has several funds highly rated by researchers and advisers. Its Industrial Share Fund is one of the originals.
- Ph 1800 022 033.

MLC
MLC is unusual in the funds management industry in that it contracts most of the investment management of its funds to other companies. However, the advisers say it works well and has delivered consistent performance for many of the MLC funds.
- Ph 9957 8000.

Annette Sampson

Further information
- Australian Securities Commission, ph 1300 300 630: www.asc.gov.au
- Financial Planning Association, ph 9299 8300
- Investment and Financial Services Association, ph 9299 3022

Italian restaurants

see also Italian Sydney, pizza

While there is an alarming trend to put things in spaghetti that don't belong there

Italian restaurants

(like smoked chicken) and an increasing tendency to forget the basic tenets of good regional Italian cooking, all is not lost. Fortunately, Sydney is blessed with a special breed of restaurateurs who know that good Italian food goes way beyond spag bol and veal cooked six ways.

bel mondo

The kitchen stands on a raised theatrical stage. The views are snatched glimpses of The Rocks and the harbour. The wine list can bring tears to the eyes. The food, courtesy of Stefano Manfredi and his mother Franca is solid, worldly and inspired. And the whole thing feels like a modern opera in which you are a major player.

■ Level 3, The Argyle Department Store, The Rocks, ph 9241 2700.

Beppi's

You don't get to stick around 43 years unless you're doing something right. Actually Beppi and Norma Polese do an awful lot of things right, as their loyal and devoted clientele will happily attest. The food may not shock or startle, but it nearly always satisfies.

■ Cnr Yurong and Stanley Sts, East Sydney, ph 9360 4558.

Buon Ricordo

No, it's not a theatre restaurant, but it's show time every night with the show going on behind the plate glass window that looks into the kitchen, and on the dining room proper where Armando Percuoco meets and greets and generally holds court. From the glorious antipasto to the truffled egg pasta, everything is recommended.

■ 108 Boundary Street, Paddington, ph 9360 6729.

Elio

For an area that is so decidedly Italian, Leichhardt has amazingly few top-notch Italian eateries. Elio is one of the newest and one of the best, with a nice, easy, laid back feel and food that runs from an antipasto served on a freshly baked pizzetta to a towering pile of spatchcock pieces perched on crisped polenta.

■ 159 Norton St, Leichhardt, ph 9560 9129.

Lucio's

Lucio's seems to get better and more popular (if that's possible) every year. It's always a delight to dine here, as much for the striking art on the walls as for the equally striking food on the plates. Young chef Timothy Fisher takes on modern Italian cooking and shows wisdom and wiles that far exceed his years.

■ 47 Windsor St, Paddington, ph 9380 5996.

Mezzaluna

While Beppi's has a lovely, old-fashioned way of doing things, the Polese family's second restaurant is far more modern and forward looking, plus it has an absolutely stunning view of the city skyline from its outdoor terrace. Try the lobster and prawn-filled squid ink ravioli and the fresh eel on creamy polenta.

■ 123 Victoria St, Potts Point, ph 9357 1988.

The Mixing Pot

It might be almost 20 years old, but age certainly hasn't caught up to this perennially popular and perpetually packed Glebe Italian restaurant. Under the watchful eye of Peter Zuzza, service is genuinely helpful and nice to boot, while the food puts flavour first as with squid inky spaghetti alla Chioggiotta.

■ 178 St John's Rd, Glebe, ph 9660 7449.

Pazzo

Pazzo doesn't pretend to be anything but a nice, well-run neighbourhood Italian restaurant. As a bonus, both owners are blessed with Italian mothers who cook, and if you're lucky, the night's specials might well include their mighty lasagna or feather-light gnocchi.

■ 583 Crown St, Surry Hills, ph 9319 4387.

Italian restaurants

Ristorante Riva

It's small, it's cute, and it has a neighbourly feel that's almost old-fashioned. Yet, for its size, Ristorante Riva is an amazingly well-rounded restaurant thanks to the efforts of Eugenio Riva in the kitchen and of his wife Beverley Wood on the floor. The house-made pasta is special.

- 379 Liverpool St, Darlinghurst, ph 9380 5318.

Terry Durack

Italian Sydney

see also Italian restaurants, pizza

One of the great joys of life in Sydney has long been the diverse, lively and spirited presence of the many immigrant communities that settled here after World War II. The Italians, the first big wave of non Anglo Saxon arrivals and still the largest ethnic community, have had an unquestionably profound influence on modern Australian culture over the past 30 years, from the arts and commerce to the way we dress, furnish our homes, eat, drink and even shop. The national construction industry is dominated by Italo-Australian companies founded in the wake of the Snowy Mountains Hydro-electric scheme.

Sydney's Little Italy, in the suburb of Leichhardt, began as the Italian immigrant community's residential and commercial enclave in the late 1950s but the main street, Norton Street, has now transformed into a vibrant restaurant and caffé precinct. Italian supermarkets, fresh fruit and vegetable providores, video and bookshops are still the dominant force in the suburb's commercial heart in Marion Street. If you are looking for a truly extensive variety of Italian produce, from high-quality pastas (Barilla, Del Verde) to olive oils, cheeses, cured meats, chocolates and biscuits, Leichhardt remains the place to go. However, there are several very good delis outside Leichhardt (see below) that have attracted Italo-Sydneysiders from far and wide.

There are literally thousands of Italian restaurants in greater metropolitan Sydney, from home-style trattorie to the elegance of harbourside, al fresco ristoranti. Lovers of regional cuisines will find the south and the north heartily represented while gastronomes looking for Italian food with an Australian bent will also rejoice. Our favourites are included in the listing below.

Good Italian coffee, from an espresso corto to caffé latte, can now be found everywhere. However the very best is concentrated around the cafe district in Darlinghurst (around Riley St) and Norton St, Leichhardt. The very best coffee, consistently good, freshly ground and served in cups, not those blasted Duralex glasses, can be found at the cafes listed below.

The great Italian fashion designers can now be found easily throughout Sydney, from the boutiques of Double Bay, to the big city department stores like David Jones to their own CBD precinct in and around Castlereagh, Elizabeth and Market Streets where you will find Giorgio Armani and Gianni Versace boutiques. Specialist fashion and accessory boutiques stocking Moschino, Ferragamo, Prada and many others are also in the area, as is the jeweller Bulgari. The arcade in the Chifley Plaza is also worth perusing.

Today, with nearly one quarter of a million Italian-born Australian residents and many more in the second and third generations, the influence of Italy is visible everywhere and in every field of endeavour. Here is a selection of the best of Italian Sydney.

A.C. Continental Butchery

Entering this small shop is not dissimilar to visiting a gastronome's Aladdin's cave. Fridges full of freshly made pasta (the pumpkin ravioli are delectable), tiny quail's eggs, Parmigiano

Reggiano and gnocchi and a mind-boggling array of fresh and cured meats. Prosciutto, hand-made sausages (try the pork and fennel specialty) to milk-fed veal cuts and organic chicken. You can also find all sorts of game meats as well as good olive oils and tomato-based products.
- 174 Marion St, Leichhardt, ph 9569 8687.

Paesanella Cheese Manufacturers Pty Ltd

Established in a tiny Federation house nearly 30 years ago by the late Umberto Somma, this is now the label to look for if you want truly fresh, locally made Italian cheeses. However if you want to buy direct from the factory – and enjoy watching white-robed staff stirring huge vats of fresh ricotta or serving bulk orders of just made bocconcini – this is the place to go. And factory direct is cheaper too.
- 27 Gerald St, Marrickville, ph 9519 6181.

Bonaventura

A Sydney institution for Italo-Australians, Bonaventura has been in the same spot for at least two decades and stocks a huge variety of items from good pastas to fresh cheeses, biscuits, cured and smoked hams and more.
- 2 Hopetoun St, Paddington, ph 9332 3395.

Ralph's Delicatessen

Service here is usually bedlam but it would be unusual for this deli not to stock even the most obscure or specialist ingredients. A great variety of fresh breads and focaccia, great prosciutto, mortadella and salame, every type of cheese imaginable as well as Christmas and Easter fare such as Panettone.
- 337 Darling St, Balmain, ph 9810 2340.

The Arch

What is lacking in decor (boring to say the very least), is more than made up by the fantastic coffee and lively clientele – from the inner city grunge crowd to visiting CBD professionals – sharing the back room pool table.
- 81 Stanley St, Darlinghurst, ph 9361 5598.

Bar Italia

Big, noisy, often surly service but always great coffee and authentic gelato made in-house. Some say this is the best gelato in Sydney.
- 169 Norton St, Leichhardt, ph 9560 9981.

Corso de Fiori

If you want Italian ceramics, glassware (including Murano glass) and stylish indoor furnishings, visit one of the three Corso shops in Sydney. Owner Massimo Murgia stocks an incredible array of dinner ware designed and hand-painted in a variety of Italian regions, from Sicily in the south to Tuscany in the north. The biggest selection can be found in the Darlinghurst showroom.
- Shop 216/77 Castlereagh Street, City, ph 9223 7647. Also at Darlinghurst, ph 9360 5151; and North Willoughby, ph 9417 8126.

Libreria Italiana

For Italian magazines, newspapers, current affairs mags and fashion tomes.
- 430 Parramatta Rd, Petersham, ph 9569 4514.

Europress Distributors Pty Ltd

If you want to find Italian literature, this is the place to phone or visit.
- 3/123 McEvoy St, Alexandria, ph 9698 4922.

Paola Totaro

Japanese food

Twenty years ago, Sydney boasted a grand total of two Japanese restaurants. These

Japanese food

days, we have everything from sushi bars and noodle shops to tempura temples and full-on kaiseki restaurants. That Sydney can support such specialist endeavours in one single cuisine benefits everyone, as chefs hone and preserve their skills, and Sydney diners choose from a dazzling array of authentic dining experiences.

Azuma
That might be Crows Nest outside, but inside it is pure Tokyo. English is at a minimum, but the sheer quality of chef Kimitaka Azuma's cooking makes it worth making the effort to crash through the language barrier to order his succulent sashimi, wonderful tempura garfish and must-have chimni appetisers.
- 125 Falcon St, Crows Nest, ph 9955 3316.

Kamogawa
When it comes to the formal kaiseki banquet, few Sydney restaurants can match Kamogawa's finesse and attention to detail. Every flavour has been honed to its very essence, while presentation is breathtaking in its refined simplicity. It's worth taking a private room to make the most of this very special dining experience.
- Cnr Market and Sussex Sts, City, ph 9299 5533.

Isaribi
Noisy and cheerful like a good-natured party, Isaribi specialises in robatayaki, serving a variety of simply grilled food accompanied by copious quantities of merriment, beer and sake. Just about everything goes on the grill, from mini steaks to whole mackerel and octopus tentacles.
- 41 Elizabeth Bay Rd, Elizabeth Bay, ph 9358 2125.

Matsukase
Located in the first floor of Chifley Tower is a tempura bar where deep frying reaches greater heights than the tower itself. Chef Takaaki Nakoji's wondrous deep-fried whiting, eggplant, and super fresh prawns are so light, you expect them to float off your plate. At night, a larger, pricier kaiseki menu is featured.
- Level 1, Chifley Plaza, 2 Chifley Square, City, ph 9229 0191.

Sakana-ya
While seafood is a highlight of every Japanese restaurant, few take it as seriously as this specialist. Fish here is immaculately cooked, whether tempura grilled, or in the nimono style. The sunomono of pickled fish, sea urchin on rice, and moist grilled mackerel are all recommended.
- 336 Pacific Highway, Crows Nest, ph 9438 1468.

Shimbashi Soba
Yoshi Shibazaki is one of only 50 chefs recognised by the Japanese government as a master of soba (buckwheat) noodles. Every day, he makes fresh soba and thick white udon noodles by hand, serving them in soup, cold, or with a variety of flavourings. Welcome to noodle heaven.
- Cnr Young and Grosvenor Sts, Neutral Bay, ph 9908 3820.

Shiki
In the middle of the historic Rocks area, Shiki has all the style and feeling of a modern, sophisticated Tokyo nightspot. What makes Shiki different is its range of 'sakana' dishes, the Japanese answer to tapas, except that sake is the drink of choice, and not sherry.
- Cnr Argyle and Harrington Sts, The Rocks, ph 9252 2431.

Unkai
When people call this the height of Japanese dining in Sydney, they're not necessarily referring to the spectacular 36th floor location, or the breathtaking views of Sydney and the harbour. The food here can be equally breathtaking from the kaiseki banquets to the sushi in the adjacent sushi bar.
- Level 36, ANA Hotel, 176 Cumberland St, The Rocks, ph 9250 6123.

Yoshii

Having honed his craft at Futaba sushi in Tokyo, Ryuichi Yoshii is probably Sydney's most highly qualified and most skilled sushi chef, as a visit to the modern, curvy sushi counter will attest. In the restaurant proper, he offers riskier, more inventive creations such as snapper with meringue and quail with blue cheese miso sauce.

- Ground Floor, Mercure Apartments, 50 Murray St, Darling Harbour, ph 9211 6866.

Tokyo Mart

Your one-stop Japanese shopping stop. Pick up exquisite lacquered bowls for your soba noodles, finely cut beef for your sukiyaki, all those mirins, tamaris and sakes those pesky recipes call for, and enough rice to sink a ship.

- 27 Northbridge Plaza, Northbridge, ph 9958 6860.

Terry Durack & Jill Dupleix

Jazz

see also blues music, country music, folk music, rock & pop music

Sydney is Australia's jazz capital. Whether you are interested in the traditional styles, big band swing, contemporary or avant-garde forms, there are groups playing your type of music. The venues are as diverse as the sounds they emit. There are late-night clubs presenting overseas ensembles, high-quality Sydney groups playing in corner pubs on weekend afternoons, and open-air performances at popular city attractions such as Darling Harbour and the Martin Place amphitheatre.

Major annual jazz events in Sydney include the Newport Jazz Festival on the weekend before Easter (ph 9997 7787); the Darling Harbour Jazz Festival on the Queen's Birthday long weekend in June (ph 9286 0100); the Manly Jazz Festival on the Labour Day long weekend in October (ph 9977 1088); and the Sydney Harbour Jazz Festival in December (ph 1902 261 059).

The Basement

A Sydney icon and the city's best-known jazz club. It presents some of the best improvised music in town and is a great place to hear touring overseas acts. If you want dinner, book a table in front of the stage. Otherwise, stand at the bar.

- 29 Reiby Place, Circular Quay, ph 9251 2797.

Soup Plus

This long-running basement restaurant in the heart of the CBD presents trad, mainstream and occasional bop groups from Monday to Saturday.

- 383 George St, City, ph 9299 7728.

Wynyard Hotel

A relatively new home for lovers of traditional styles. Perennial favourites Eclipse Alley Five play every Saturday afternoon.

- Cnr Clarence and Erskine streets, City, ph 9299 1330.

Woollahra Hotel

This popular venue presents accomplished contemporary groups on Sunday evenings.

- Cnr Queen and Moncur Sts, Woollahra, ph 9363 2782.

Unity Hall Hotel

A Balmain institution where trad group the Roger Janes Band have played every Friday for more than 20 years.

- 292 Darling St, Balmain, ph 9810 1331.

ReZerection

A newish venue that features a cross-section of contemporary music, including jazz.

- Cnr Cleveland and Chalmers Sts, Surry Hills, ph 9690 0287.

Jazz

Bernie McGann
This alto saxophonist is arguably our most original jazz stylist. He is an emotionally direct player who can oscillate between anguish and exaltation, often in the same phrase. McGann has won three ARIA awards for best jazz album and was the recipient of the 1997 Don Banks Music Award for his sustained and distinguished contribution to Australian music. Other leading contemporary musicians and groups include pianists **Mike Nock** and **Cathy Harley**; **Clarion Fracture Zone**; **the catholics**; **Wanderlust**; former Jazz Messenger tenor saxophonist **Dale Barlow**; singer **Michele Morgan**; and large ensemble **Ten Part Invention**. **Australysis** is the pick of the experimental or avant-garde ensembles.

Bob Barnard
His dazzling trumpet-playing has won him an international reputation. Influenced by Louis Armstrong, Buck Clayton and Bobby Hackett, Barnard's triumph has been to reinvigorate the traditional repertoire, making well-known material sound exciting and fresh. Other leading classic and mainstream jazz artists include multi-instrumentalists **Tom Baker**, **Don Burrows** and **James Morrison**; guitarist **Ian Date**; singers **Marie Wilson** and **Janet Seidel**; and pianist **Kenny Powell**.

Birdland Records
Sydney's only jazz specialty shop. A treasure trove of new and old recordings.
- 3 Barrack St, City, ph 9299 8527.

Folkways Music
Long-established shop with comprehensive jazz and world music sections.
- 282 Oxford St, Paddington, ph 9361 3980.

Sounds Australian
Specialises in Australian releases.
- Shop 33, The Rocks Centre, 16-23 Playfair St, The Rocks, ph 9247 7290.

Peter Jordan

Further information
- See Sydney Morning Herald Metro and CitySearch for listings
- Jazz Action Society, ph/fax 9281 2230
- Sydney Improvised Music Association, ph 9938 2180
- Sydney Jazz Club, ph 9557 6550

Jewellery

From ritzy and grand to fun and funky, Sydney stores have jewels to suit all styles and pockets.

Anne Schofield
Exquisite antique jewellery for lovers of fine decorative arts.
- 36 Queen St, Woollahra, ph 9363 1326.

Bulgari
The Roman family jewellers known particularly for their elegant use of coloured stones.
- 91 Market St, City, ph 9267 8866.

Cartier
French jewellers, established more than 150 years ago, and one of the first luxury goods brands to come to Sydney.
- 43 Castlereagh St, City, ph 9235 1322.

House of Cerrone
Most recent winner of the DeBeers Diamond International Awards, Sydney's Nic Cerrone designs and imports glamorous pieces.
- 83 Castlereagh St, City, ph 9232 6186; 15-19 Catherine St, Leichhardt, ph 9569 8922.

Dinosaur Designs
Funky, colourful and clever resin jewellery and homewears by a Sydney artistic threesome that is always being refreshed with new ideas.
- 399 Oxford St, Paddington, ph 9361 3776. Also in the City, ph 92232953, and the Rocks, ph 9251 5500.

Fairfax & Roberts

A longstanding Sydney company with an elegant store on Martin Place, for classical fine jewellery.
- 44 Martin Place, City, ph 9232 8511; Westfield Shopping Centre, Miranda, ph 9524 1506.

Hardy Bros

One of the oldest established jewellery firms in Sydney (established 1853) with serious fine jewellery and silverware.
- 77 Castlereagh St, City, ph 9232 2422.

Jan Logan

Antique pieces and Jan Logan's modern jewellery pick up the trends, making them affordable, wearable and desirable.
- 36 Cross St, Double Bay, ph 9363 2529.

Paspaley Pearls

The Paspaley family are the biggest producers of Australian South Sea Pearls with a store full of these lustrous beauties including Collette Dinnigan's peerless collection.
- 142 King St, City, ph 9232 7633.

Makers Mark

A gallery-style store full of Australian artist designer jewellery and objects.
- Chifley Plaza, 2 Chifley Square, City, ph 9231 6800.

Percy Marks

Established in 1899, this family company is still going strong.
- 60-70 Castlereagh St, City, ph 9233 1355.

Perri Jewellers

Ritzy jewels and contemporary Faberge pieces.
- MLC Centre, Castlereagh St, City, ph 9231 1088.

Musson

Contemporary but classical jewellery by award-winning jeweller Robert Musson.
- Chatswood Chase, Victoria Ave, Chatswood, ph 9412 2780.

Rox Gems and Jewellery

A little gem of a store with designer jewels.
- Strand Arcade, Pitt St, City, ph 9232 7828.

Stefano

Stefano began as a suburban jeweller and is now headed for the big time even hiring Linda Evangelista for a big campaign.
- 80 Castlereagh St, City, ph 9231 1799; 120 Rawson Rd, Greenacre, ph 9790 6496.

The Watch Gallery

A cornucopia of swanky watch labels all under the one roof.
- 142 King St, City, ph 9221 2288.

Tarasin Jewellers

Jeweller John Tarasin, who has a passion for anthropology, creates unusual pieces that run from the sumptuous to the affordable in his studio/retail outlet.
- 39 Ridge St, North Sydney, ph 9922 4782.

Tiffany & Co

The New York jewellers that has become a legend. Who doesn't love those blue boxes swathed in ribbon?
- Chifley Plaza, 2 Chifley Square, City, ph 9235 1777.

Jane de Teliga

Junk

The lime green toilet seat lies haphazardly on the footpath during a council clean-up. To most it says 'junk', but for you it is the piece de resistance of your new '60s-look bathroom. It's amazing what people throw out these days – all you need to pick up a bargain is a keen eye. Contact your local council to find out when there's a clean-up in your area. The

Junk

North Shore is your best bet for quality junk (Mosman Council, ph 9978 4000; Lane Cove Council, ph 9911 3555; Hornsby Council, ph 9847 6666). Check out your local paper for details of garage sales, another great source for that perfect piece of junk. Try your luck in any area of Sydney.

Brookvale Bazaar
So you're out of vintage car parts, wind-up gramophones and brass nautical gear. Head straight down to the definitive junk shop of Sydney. Describing itself as a shop that sells 'anything and everything' Brookvale Bazaar will entice you with its vast array of useful (and useless) objects.
- 505 Pittwater Rd, Brookvale, ph 9905 0384.

Recycling Works
Set up to promote recycling and to help local disadvantaged people, Recycling Works sell pre-loved junk. Discover second-hand furniture, bric-a-brac and eclectic one-off pieces (such as old red telephone booths) at very cheap prices. Staff and students from Sydney University are given discounts. Open seven days.
- 45 Parramatta Rd, Annandale, ph 9517 2711.

Reverse Garbage
A non-profit co-operative that collects industrial discards for creative community use. Assisting in the reduction of waste is its primary aim. It stocks everything from leather, fabric, foam, rubber, plastic, timber, cardboard, perspex to individual furniture pieces.
- 142 Addison Rd, Marrickville, ph 9569 3132.

Barry's Garage Sale
For general household appliances, sportsgoods and obscure pieces of junk, make a trip to Barry's. You'll pick up a bargain.
- 83 Curlewis St, Bondi, ph 9365 5303.

Sara Conde

Karaoke

see also party supplies, pubs
There are two schools of thought regarding karaoke. One says the full cathartic effects of this form of ritual humiliation can only be achieved in a crowded public venue with a few sakes under the belt and your equally soused mates egging you on. The other insists it should only be done between consenting adults in the privacy of their own homes. If you must do it, there is no shortage of choices for either option.

Fivestar Karaoke
A division of Planet Entertainment, who can also supply you with sumo suits, velcro walls, surf machines and other party essentials, Fivestar Karaoke has karaoke machines for any occasion. They have 12 different systems for hire, including one for kids, and, if you like, will even host your evening.
- 18 Susan St, Annandale, ph 9519 0500.

Accent Entertainment
Provides top quality, professional karaoke equipment and operators for a range of corporate and private functions, as well as hosting karaoke nights at different hotels. Accent has a huge range of songs on its playlist, including recent hits, and can also provide songs in Chinese, Italian, Japanese and Spanish. The karaoke operators are all trained vocalists and act as comperes. Lighting and disco music are also provided.
- 3 Wellington Rd, Hurstville, ph 9570 7070.

Hotel Bondi
Karaoke nights are held every Wednesday night in the Cage Bar attracting a crowd of backpackers and Bondi locals. Cash prizes are awarded and the singing standard can be quite

high. Don't let this put you off – plenty of donkeys also get behind the mike.
- 178 Campbell Pde, Bondi Beach, ph 9130 3270.

Time & Tide Hotel
This Dee Why watering hole has been running karaoke nights on Wednesdays for the past five years, attracting an appreciative audience of mostly 20- and 30-year-olds. Cash prizes are awarded, although champagne, shirts and caps are more common giveaways. Standards range from the 'not bad' to the 'atrocious'.
- 30 Campbell Ave, Dee Why, ph 9971 2311.

Triple-8 Hotel
This city pub, between Scruffy Murphy's and the Mandarin Club, has a 24-hour licence. It holds late-night karaoke on Saturday and Sunday from around 10pm until 2 or 3am, attracting a mixed crowd of travellers and inner-city regulars.
- 2 Cunningham St (cnr Goulburn St), City, ph 9211 6888.

Benjamin Long

Kitchens

It started with the food and now we're working on the visuals, according to Geoff Solomons, chairperson of the HIA NKBA (Housing Industry Association National Kitchen and Bathroom Association). Just as Sydneysiders have grown to love a multicultural gamut of tastes and flavours on the plate, they now expect designers to offer a broad range of shapes, styles and moods for the kitchen. This selection should satisfy the most discerning palate.

Homebush Home Improvement Centre
If you haven't a clue where to begin, head for this venue opposite the Sydney Olympic Centre, formerly the HIA Building and Renovation SupaCenta. With more than 80 kitchens by different makers on display, the only problem can be too much choice.
- Cnr Homebush Bay Drive and Underwood Rd, Homebush, ph 9746 8744.

Gelosa
Slick custom kitchens for people who want the best. A big investment – but these kitchens will last the distance.
- 111 Flinders St, Darlinghurst, ph 9380 6100.

Freedom Kitchens
As affordable and style-conscious as its furniture, Freedom offers a selection of looks from contemporary and traditional country to the Asian-inspired Lombok. With the help of CAD (computer-aided design), 12 designs can be adapted with 15 different worktops to fit the client's dimensions. DIY installation or use Freedom recommended tradespeople.
- Moore Park SupaCenta, 2a Todman Ave, Kensington, ph 9697 0044. Also at Caringbah, ph 9542 7200, and Blacktown, ph 9896 4044.

De Gabrielle Kitchens
Owned and run by the De Gabrielle brothers for the past 18 years, this multi-award winning business has built its reputation on the custom-designed, custom-built kitchen. They offer a minimum 10-year guarantee on their handiwork, a lifetime on their top-of-the range designs in the Marque series.
- 2 Turbo Rd, Kings Park, ph 9831 4777. Also at Willoughby, ph 9958 5668 and Homebush, ph 9746 0006.

Capell of Chatswood
No problem is insurmountable for this boutique kitchen centre which specialises in very

Kitchens

personalised service for the top end of the market. MD Keith Capell counts his rewards in terms of satisfying customers who know what they want but sometimes offer little more than a picture from an overseas publication or even a single antique tile as a starting point.
- 169 Victoria Ave, Chatswood, ph 9411 4998.

Sydney Kitchen Centre

Acclaimed for their custom-made kitchens which are, above all, extremely workable, this company prides itself on using the best components such as Hafele drawer mechanisms and door hinges to achieve its mission.
- 96 Penshurst St, Willoughby, ph 9958 4546; 693 South Dowling St, Surry Hills, ph 9698 7937.

Nouvelle Designer Kitchens

Top-flight service for the busy professional (there's even a kids' play centre so parents can concentrate) incorporates the latest American CAD (Cabinet Vision) to produce 3-D colour images of the client's selection. An 'international selection centre' allows customers to confirm their choices with actual kitchen-sized mock-ups of doors, floors and benchtops.
- 372 Pennant Hills Rd, Pennant Hills, ph 9484 8299.

In Kitchens

If your style is European and money is no object, consider this German company which combines the best design with brands such as Miele, Gaggenau, Scholtes and Four Seasons.
- Homebush Home improvement Centre, ph 9764 4900.

By Dezign

A rarity in the kitchen industry, this company provides the total package from CAD technology to cabinetry, tiles, lights, benchtops, appliances (and their installation). They even have a range of decorator wares (vases and artworks) to inspire or complete your project.
- Homebush Home Improvement Centre, ph 9763 1077.

Kirsty McKenzie

Kites

The perfect combination of artistic flair and engineering innovation, kiting caters for everyone from starry-eyed children to do-it-yourself hobbyists. It also has an extreme version, power kiting (using kites to pull you along, for example on a skateboard), which is just taking off in Australia. All you need to fly a kite is windy land free of powerlines, but some councils do have restrictions, particularly on popular surf beaches. Don't give power kites to young children or they might fly over the horizon.

On the second Sunday in September the Festival of the Winds is held at Bondi. This annual event attracts kite-makers from all over Australia and overseas. There are great prizes on offer over a wide range of categories. Phone 9130 3325 for information.

Dobroyd Point, Balgowlah Heights

A combination of consistent winds, open spaces and spectacular views makes this the best kiting spot in the Sydney.

Christison Park, Vaucluse

Situated near Sydney's sensational South Head, this park has no shortage of wind, guaranteeing all kite enthusiasts a full day's flying.

Kite Site

Home of the largest kite in Australia, a 25-metre-long octopus called Romeo. Kite Site

caters for all devotees and they just love the kite buggies and power kites.
- 169 Dolphin St, Coogee, ph 9315 7894.

Steve Samuelson

Further information
- Australian Kite Society, ph 9449 1165

Landscape designers & architects

see also nurseries & garden supplies, gardens, gardeners & garden services

Some landscape architects or designers become very fashionable (like Paul Bangay in Melbourne) but you need to select your landscaper for more than fashion. Choose someone whose designs you and your garden site will be comfortable with.

Terragram
The name to conjure with is Vladimir (Tom) Sitta of Terragram. Vladimir is hot – a rising star whose big work in progress is the garden around the Australian National Museum, Canberra . His work in domestic gardens and courtyards is innovative, interesting and exciting.
- 105 Reservoir Rd, Surry Hills, ph 9211 6060.

Award Pools & Landscapes
If you want more of your backyard pool than being able to swim in it, Brad Baxter is tops for original and inspiring environments created round water.
- 4 Old Windsor Rd, Kellyville, ph 9629 3494.

Imperial Gardens
Specialises in the art of oriental gardens – the place to go for Chinese, Japanese and water gardens. They understand rocks, oriental style plants and ornaments.
- 18 Myoora Rd, Terrey Hills, ph 9450 2455.

Bay Street Nursery
For courtyards and all those tricky spaces in eastern suburbs gardens, see Scott Williams.
- 41 Bay St, Double Bay, ph 9327 3936.

Timothy Abrahams & Associates
A landscape architect who does terrific roof gardens.
- 68 New South Head Rd, Vaucluse, ph 9337 5551.

Coastal Care Horticultural Services
Geoff Burton is the one for those beachside gardens.
- 27 Park Ave, Avalon, ph 9973 1471.

Joanne Green Landscape Design
Now concentrates on mainly domestic work and has won numerous awards including two for Landscape of the Year.
- 10d Ponderosa Rd, Warriewood, ph 9979 5363.

Co-Ordinated Landscapes
This company has won more awards for commercial landscaping than any other. They must have got it right.
- Level 3, 33–35 Belmont Rd, Sutherland, ph 9914 7311.

Shirley Stackhouse

Languages

see also translators

It's cool to be bilingual these days. Studies range from four-week crash courses to four-year university honours. Recruitment agencies predict employment opportunities for bilingual people will be up to 70 per cent greater, especially leading up to the Olympic Games.

InSearch Language, University of Technology Sydney
Offers intensive and part-time courses for overseas students, visitors and residents. Class sizes range from eight to 18 persons, and it offers certificate and diploma courses in almost all Asian and European languages, and intensive between-term courses, interpreting courses and business language and culture programs.
- 10 Quay St, City, ph 9281 4544.

Australian Institute of Modern Languages
Established for more than 30 years and endorsed by a whole host of corporate clients, the institute covers most languages, and teaches design, presentations and typesetting. It also acts as Australia's largest translation centre, and its accreditations are approved worldwide.
- 109 Pitt St, City, ph 9369 3800.

National English Academy
For overseas students and visitors there are courses that range from two weeks to one year, covering all levels of English competency. There is a computer and audio centre so students can learn at their own pace. Suitable for those people who can't speak English at all or those who want to increase their fluency.
- Level 6, 1 Newland St, Bondi Junction, ph 9369 1110.

National Centre for English Language Teaching and Research (INCELTA)
This is the country's key centre for English language teaching and research. To undertake its Postgraduate Certificate in Teaching English to Speakers of Other Languages you must have an undergraduate degree in English or an equivalent qualification. The course is one year part-time or six months full-time, and provides a teaching qualification.
- Macquarie University, ph 9850 7111.

Sign Language at The Deaf Education Network
Provides courses in conjunction with community evening colleges. Most courses take eight weeks to complete, and are primarily for hearing people who are interested in learning how to communicate via sign language. The average cost of the course is $90.
- ph 9764 4600 (TTY 9764 4972).

Grant Gillies

Late-night food

see also pre-theatre dining
You've worked all day and played all night in that most typical of Sydney lifestyles, and now you're hungry, really hungry. And you're not going to let a little thing like the time come between you and something delicious, are you? Anyway, can you help it if you're suddenly starving at midnight?

Golden Century
From 10pm through to 3am, Chinese waiters, night owls and casino refugees wander in for noodles, hot pots and the famous rice porridge, known as congee or jook.
- 393-399 Sussex St, Haymarket, ph 9281 1598.

Cafe Hernandez
Hernandez is like a 24-hour safe house for the Spanish community, cabdrivers and party hoppers who have run out of hop. The empanadas, churros, focaccie and house-roasted coffee can make that empty gnawing feeling disappear in no time flat.
- 60 Kings Cross Rd, Potts Point, ph 9331 2343.

BBQ King
Five out of six chefs can't be wrong. When they're not cooking their own stuff, they're

relaxing at this highly unassuming Chinatown favourite. Why? Because the roast duck, soy chicken and barbecued pork are probably the best in town. But more importantly because it's open until 2am.

- 18-20 Goulburn St, Haymarket, ph 9267 2433.

The Fireplace

A quirky and cosy King's Cross late-opener based on the *izakaya* – the simple taverns of Japan where customers can snack and drink in a cheerful, easy going surroundings. The food can be best described as a Japanese take on tapas.

- 19 Bayswater Rd, Kings Cross, ph 9357 3300.

Merrony's

Sydney's classiest late-opener. From Monday to Saturday, the kitchen stays open until eleven-ish, dishing out some of the most beautifully crafted French bistro food in town.

- 2 Albert St, Circular Quay, ph 9247 9323.

Terry Durack

Lebanese Sydney

Behind the tabouli and falafel rolls, Sydney's Lebanese community is vibrant in style, diverse in its mix and rich in culture. Take the route to western Sydney suburbia and you'll find village traditions alive and well in the backyards, corner shops and main streets of Lakemba, Punchbowl and Bankstown. Sample the best the community has to offer in the main streets in and around these suburbs. From sweet palaces stocking an array of bargain, high-quality pastries to restaurants and nightclubs that are alive with the striking beats of Lebanese music, dance and spirit, Sydney offers a truly authentic taste of all things Lebanese. And if you can't make it west, try **Cedars Wing** in North Sydney (ph 9964 9766) for authentic food in comfortable surroundings. Sydney's Lebanese forgo the strip along Cleveland St, Surry Hills, where you're unlikely to come across Arabic speakers except for the staff.

Golden Nights

A reception centre which doubles as a restaurant/nightclub on Saturday night, the Golden Nights is one of the more popular and among the first to spring up in Sydney. Here you will experience the fast pace of an indulgent Lebanese nightlife: food, music, dance and more food. Bellydance the night away on the spacious dance floor and be prepared for the loud and striking rhythm of a band featuring the Arabic derbeckieh drum. Stay until after midnight when the lights are dimmed and the bellydancer takes centre stage. Best enjoyed with a group of friends after 9 pm. Many partygoers don't leave before dawn.

- 12 Restwell St, Bankstown, ph 9790 5555.

Star Light

This is Lebanon every Saturday night. When you taste the 20 different mezza (Lebanese appetisers), such as baba ganouge and vine leaves, you will be forgiven for thinking the mezza is the meal. In this comfortable setting the night features a bellydancer and four singers accompanied by a six-piece band.

- 299 Belmore Rd, Riverwood, ph 9153 0303.

Summerland

In the heartland of Sydney's Lebanese community, Summerland takes its place as one of a handful of restaurants offering authentic Lebanese cuisine all week long. Specialises in charcoal grilling. You won't forget the generous banquet in a hurry. It has a minimum meal of 17 dishes (including hommos, oregano salad, labni or yoghurt dip and a cheese called shanklish). Puff on a hookah pipe, drink arak or enjoy the live music on Saturday nights.

- 741 Punchbowl Rd, Punchbowl, ph 9708 5107.

Rimal

An intimate setting with a view to the water. Choose from up to 35 mezza dishes before dinner is even served. Try the samke harrah – a fillet or whole fish baked or pan-fried, coated in a sauce of tahini, lemon juice, coriander, pine nuts and chilli. Live music on Friday and Saturday nights.
- 2nd Floor, cnr Bay St and Grand Pde, Brighton-Le-Sands, ph 9567 6422 (free parking under the Novotel Hotel).

Lebanon: Imprisoned Splendour

This multi-award-winning documentary by Sydney film-maker Daizy Gedeon provides a historic and modern-day account of Lebanon narrated by Omar Sharif. Last year, it opened the Beirut Film Festival, had a special screening before the US Congress and qualified for nomination for the 1998 Academy Awards. Price $39.95.
- Ph 9744 5178 or 9744 6041.

Sorry My Love

Rich businessman wrongly accuses loving wife of cheating on him . . . This drama-action feature film, produced in Australia and set in Sydney's Arab community, features serving police officers, real police cars and scenes shot in Lakemba police station. Made for Arabic speakers and non-speakers alike – the dialogue is in English and Arabic and the film is subtitled in both languages. It screened to sell-out audiences at Hoyts in Bankstown in 1997 and has generated so much interest that it is sure to screen again.
- Stars Production, ph 0414 221 111.

The Arabic Bookshop

Established in the 1980s when Lebanon was engulfed in turmoil, this shop provided a creative pipeline between Lebanon and Australia. Today, it remains an important link, offering a range of political, educational and historical books, handy crafts, pictures of Lebanon, music and film that have been imported from Beirut.
- Cnr Haldon St and the Boulevard, Lakemba, ph 9758 2444.

Cedars of Lebanon Folkloric Group

A 20-minute-long performance of the Lebanese dabki (traditional dance) by a group of 25 men and women is a popular and regular feature at social functions. The group, who recently celebrated their 20th anniversary by completing a successful tour of festivals in Lebanon, average 75 performances a year. They have a long history of contributing to community events, dance to traditional music and can be commissioned for a fee. Group leader is Elie Akouri.
- Ph 9750 0134.

Lakemba Mosque Tour

Of the 20 mosques in Sydney, it is the sight of the bell-shaped tower and crescent moon spire of the main mosque in Wangee Rd, Lakemba, that instantly transports you to the Middle East. A guided tour can be organised through the Lebanese Moslems Association.
- Ph 9750 6833.

El Bahsa

This is my pick of the pastry palaces of Lakemba, Punchbowl and Bankstown. If your eyes miss it, don't worry, your nose won't. All shops are fragrant with rosewater and honey, offering fresh sweets filled with dates, nuts or clotted cream. Be warned. Selection is not easy when choosing from the more than 20 different sweets sitting in enormous circular trays. Eat in or take away. There's something for all taste buds on offer: sweet finger foods (birds' nests, ladies' fingers, king's crown and honey balls), fruit ice-cream and petits fours (biscuits dipped in crushed pistachio nuts or chocolate). The average price for a kilo of mixed baklava is only $12.
- 288 Chapel Rd South, Bankstown, ph 9796 4818.

Also good are **Abla Pastry** (ph 9637 8092), **Rabieh Sweets and Gelato** (ph 9708 4103) and **Al Afrah** (ph 9708 2774).

Venice Nuts

Don't be put off by the warehouse-look. Once inside, you'll find shelves of any sort of nut

you desire (macadamia, hazelnut, cashew, pistachio and almond), quality Lebanese coffee, dried oregano, cinnamon, cloves, Lebanese flower tea, herbs and spices, every kind of dried bean, hookah pipes and a range of delicacies imported from all over the Middle East.
- 81 Chapel St, Lakemba, ph 9759 1206.

Also good for Lebanese groceries is **Harkola** (180-186 South Pde, Auburn, ph 9649 4448).

Further information
- An Noujoum Productions: commissions singers from the Middle East for live concerts in Sydney all year round, ph 0414 900 000
- Arabic Community Business Directory: a free guide to Lebanese services and products, ph 9740 3444
- Australian Lebanese Association, ph 9564 3506

Nadia Jamal

Lifesaving

see also triathlon

Sydney is blessed. How many cities in the world can boast surf beaches just minutes from the CBD? Of course, with beaches come surf-lifesavers, that remarkable movement mixing athleticism and community service. Sydney has 36 lifesaving clubs, 21 north of the harbour and 15 to the south. In terms of members, Cronulla is the biggest, boasting about 600 members. No qualifications are needed to join a club, but to be a surf-lifesaver you do need the Bronze Medallion.

Bondi Beach Surf Lifesaving Club
Situated on one of the world's most famous beaches, this club proudly boasts that it's Australia's oldest (a claim hotly disputed by Bronte and Manly clubs). Formed in 1907, its surf patrolling, performance at championships and general up-keep of the beach make this the best club south of Sydney Harbour.
- ph 9300 9279.

Freshwater Surf Lifesaving Club
Tucked away between Curl Curl and Queenscliff, this club's performances at state and national championships belies its relative obscurity. Often overshadowed by the famous Manly clubs, Freshwater is a hidden gem and is arguably the best club on the northern beaches.
- ph 9905 3741.

South Maroubra Surf Lifesaving Club
This will be the venue for the 1999 State Lifesaving Championships.
- ph 9344 5491.

Uncle Toby's Super Series
Every summer, the best lifesavers in Australia run, swim, surf ski and paddle-board across a series of courses in search of the Ironman title.

Steve Samuelson

Further information
- Surf Life Saving NSW Incorporated, ph 9984 7188

Lighting

see also electricians
Different lights do different things but basically lighting is about mood, drama and feeling. The big lighting chain stores are scattered throughout Sydney's suburbs, but the best (as is the case with most quality design) is to be found in the inner-city design precinct.

Lighting

Brook Street Trading
A traditional mix of classic English lighting for the home.
- Shop 1, 50 Bayswater Rd, Kings Cross, ph 9380 6502.

DeDeCe
Always expect an emphasis on purity of form here. As well as dramatic and geometric floor and wall lights by Frank Lloyd Wright, there is a wide range of Kreon lighting systems including its ingeniously simple adjustable spot lighting using the latest lamp technology. Also the Faulkland pendant light designed in 1964 by Bruno Munari.
- 263 Liverpool St, East Sydney, ph 9360 2722.

ECC Lighting
Modernise your rooms with these hard-edged and highly desirable designer pieces that are superb diffusers of light. Stockists of Iguzzini, Artemide, Antonangeli, Cinni Nils, Les Actuels plus local designer Hotlux.
- 36 Gosbell St, Paddington, ph 9380 7922.

IKEA
Modern, chic and affordable selection that competes well with the more costly versions. Several stores.
- 924 Pacific Highway, Gordon, ph 9498 3822. Also at Prospect, ph 9636 9222, and Moore Park ph 9313 6400.

Lightwise
The biggest contemporary lighting showroom in town. Represents Flos, the multinational manufacturer of modern illuminations by the most creative designers in the world. Also Luceplan and Reggiani as well as ranges from Studio Italia.
- 99 Flinders St, Darlinghurst, ph 9380 6222.

Louis Poulsen Lightmakers
Danish manufacturing giant of eclectic mix of contemporary and classic designs by Arne Jacobsen, Alfred Homann, Jens Moller-Jensen and Poul Henningsen.
- 755-759 Botany Rd, Rosebery, ph 9667 0222.

Spence & Lyda
Great one-off anglepoise desk lamps that have been revamped.
- 51-57 Holt St, Surry Hills, ph 9212 6747.

Tangent Central
The most recent addition to this line of fun, contemporary Spanish lighting is the extensive Italian range of Nemo lights and the Constellation range of exterior wall lights in cast aluminium. Lots of sculptural shades.
- 20 Boronia St, Redfern, ph 9698 5088.

West Eight
Maverick lighting designer Tom Dixon's Jack Stack plus pieces by Jam, renowned for using recycled and ready-made materials in groovy lighting.
- Suite 4, 144 Cathedral St, Woolloomooloo, ph 9326 9877.

Melissa Walker Smith

Lingerie

Who wants to wear clothes in summer? With the distinction between outerwear and innerwear blurring, and sheer styles abounding, lingerie is more and more important as a fashion statement. Sydney's best stores run the gamut from luxury imports to local heroes, such as Collette Dinnigan.

White Ivy
Established more than 50 years ago, White Ivy has been serving generations of families with

silk nighties and robes, satin chemises, satin-trimmed showercaps and hand-quilted flat slippers. The store stocks imported labels, such as Gossard, Chantelle, the trendy Dolce & Gabbana's fine cotton underwear and sleepwear, as well as Cara Martin slippers.
- Shop 2, 365 New South Head Road, Double Bay, ph 9326 1830.

Adrienne and The Misses Bonney
For decades, this quaintly named shop has been specialising in dainty hand-embroidered cotton nighties and robes, as well as the Misses Bonney's exquisite christening robes and baby wear.
- 20–26 Cross Street, Double Bay, ph 9363 1723.

IM Designer Bodywear
Specialising in high-impact international luxury labels – the sizzling Italian name La Perla, the lacy Aubade from France and the hip young brand Marvel from Italy – IM Designer Bodywear has the kind of racy and expensive lingerie suitable for prancing around the boudoir.
- Shop 18, First Floor, Queen Victoria Building, City, ph 9261 2180; Shop 1, Wentworth Arcade, Phillip St, City, ph 9221 6328; also at Westfield Miranda, ph 9524 1307.

JayeM Underfashion
Old-fashioned service and professional fitting of a kind that's hard to find these days. Specialist corsetieres for first bras, maternity bras and mastectomy requirements.
- 1st floor, Strand Arcade, City, ph 9231 2796.

David Jones
Don't forget Sydney's premier department store for the biggest selection of lingerie labels – for women in the Elizabeth Street store and for men in the Market Street store.
- Ph 9266 5544.

Collette Dinnigan
Australia's international success story. Dinnigan's lingerie and lacy dresses are sold in the world's most prestigious department stores and boutiques, as well as right here in her original Paddington terrace-house store.
- 39 William St, Paddington, ph 9360 6691.

Jane de Teliga

Liquor stores

see also wine, beer
Home is where the heart is and, despite Sydney having every conceivable type of watering hole, we need to know where to get good grog for BYO dinners, barbecues, dinner parties and Tuesday's stir-fry. The listed liquor stores have free delivery and glass hire for parties.

Crown of the Hill
Discounts on mixed dozens, endless stock of wine and spirits, weekly deals and cheap prices – this chain has it all. All locations have handy parking, right outside.
- 682 Warringah Rd, Forestville, ph 9451 6413. Also Harbord, ph 9938 5122; Naremburn, ph 9439 3902; West Lindfield, ph 9416 8711.

Kemeny's Food and Liquor
Shop for discount liquor, solicit excellent advice and pick up the groceries while you're there – you could be forgiven for thinking it's Europe.
- 137-141 Bondi Rd, Bondi, ph 9389 6422.

Oddbins
Oddbins takes its name from the excess-of-production lines, which were not bottled by the maker. They buy bin-ends and label them,

Liquor stores

producing quality wines at discounted prices. Oddbins also stocks your favourite spirits.
- 140 Parramatta Rd, Camperdown, ph 9550 3177. Also Belrose, ph 9452 2099; Alexandria, ph 9310 4937; St Ives 9488 7466; City, ph 9299 5075.

Sixty Darling Street
Expert wine service, corners (behind boxes) to explore, legendary stocktake sales and merry wine tastings – this is serious wine territory. Oh, and they have spirits too.
- 60 Darling St, East Balmain, ph 9818 3077. Also Eastwood, ph 9874 1208.

Kate Ryan

Locksmiths

A locksmith can be your best friend, especially when it's 3am and you've lost your keys.

North Shore Locksmiths
This business specialises in both domestic and commercial locks, and security systems. They not only crack safes, they make them.
- 12 Frederick St, St Leonards, ph 9439 6300.

Independent Locksmiths
With 20 mobile workshops, Independent will be at your place or car quickly. Specialists in creating master keys.
- 79 Phillip St, Parramatta, ph 9633 5877; a.h. 0418 465 753.

B 'n' S Locksmiths
Sydney's only 24-hour locksmiths. Convenient whenever you've mislaid or had keys stolen.
- 1/888 Bourke St, Alexandria, ph 9310 1888.

Kate Ryan

Further information
- Master Locksmiths Association of Australia, the locksmiths' watchdog for your complaints or compliments, ph 1 800 810 698

Luggage

Australians seem to work not just to live but also to travel. Whether you're after briefcases for work or luggage for business trips and summer holidays, they're all available here.

Hunt Leather
Stockists of luggage, handbags and small leather goods. There are pieces by the chic French travel brand Longchamp, luggage from business-orientated brand American Tumi, natural leather bags from Il Bisonte of Florence, and MH Way's ultra-modern collection from Milan. English brands include Mulberry, Launer and Papworth, an old firm making traditional attaches and briefcases.
- MLC Centre, City, ph 9233 8702.

Oroton
An Australian brand of quality leather goods, designed here but mostly manufactured in Italy. Oroton specialises in small leathergoods and briefcases, including the Macquarie, designed to fit your laptop computer.
- Shop G02, Gallery Level, Centrepoint, City, ph 9232 2242. Also at Greenwood Plaza, North Sydney, ph 9956 5112; Queen Victoria Building, City, ph 9261 1984; Chifley Plaza, City, ph 9235 3351; Chatswood Chase, ph 9415 3567; Westfield Parramatta, ph 9687 0393; Sydney Airport, ph 9969 2656.

Luggageland
Main brands include Samsonite, Paklite (especially in the trendy new bright colours), Delsey,

Condotti and Zero Halliburton's aluminium cases.
- 397 George St, City, ph 9299 6699. Also at Chatswood, ph 9410 0288; Westfield Miranda, ph 9524 0966.

Strandbags

In their big new store on George Street, Strandbags stocks not just handbags but also a big selection of luggage, such as Samsonite, Carlton (from England), Paklite and Hedgrin, plus super smart cases from Zero Halliburton, and briefcases from Targus, Hide design, Cellini, Samsonite and Paklite.
- 413 George St, City, ph 9262 4737. Also in the Strand Arcade, ph 9233 2816, and many suburban locations.

Louis Vuitton

The LV monogram adorns the most sought-after luggage in the world. In Sydney, these status leather goods are housed in an elegant building on the corner of King and Castlereagh streets, in the heart of the luxury goods precinct. There are the famous trunks and new suit packs. Look also for the newer plain-coloured grained leather range, Taiga, in forest green and mahogany.
- 63 Castlereagh St, City, ph 9236 9624.

Jane de Teliga

Markets & fairs

Sydney's markets get crowded, revitalise the streets on weekends, and offer a diverse range of shopping choices. You can search through trash and treasure for rare finds, browse for bargains, discover the latest fashions, be entertained, and shop for fresh produce.

Bondi Beach Markets

If you like old junk, it's here. You'll also find refurbished antiques, imported furniture from Asia and works of Bondi artisans. Prices are fair and wares are hip and attractive. Fashion ranges from designer-graduate styles at affordable prices to savvy second-hand clothing. Held each Sunday.
- Bondi Beach Public School, Campbell Pde, Bondi Beach.

Glebe Markets

Bohemian and grunge-style stalls make for a lively market and provide good scavenging for students and the budget-conscious. Indian food, fresh juice, wind chimes, beeswax candles, and jewellery mix well with alternative, contemporary and second-hand clothing, CDs and books. Held each Saturday.
- Glebe Public School, Glebe Point Rd, Glebe.

Kings Cross Rotary Market

This Rotary-sponsored community market is designed to serve its neighbourhood – a mixture of long-term residents, artists and tourists. You can browse through old treasures, discover unusual collectables, have a tarot reading or a Chinese massage, pick up underwear, indigenous handicrafts and fashionable second-hand clothing. Held on Sundays.
- Fitzroy Gardens, Macleay St, Kings Cross.

Leichhardt Sunday Market

Latin-American and jazz bands provide the rhythm for cosmopolitan shopping at a leisurely pace. The market aims to please the 25- to 45-year-olds, with fashions from new designers, children's clothing, plants and flowers, and music stalls with new and used CDs. For foodies, there's organic and gourmet choices; homemakers can browse for knick-knacks, furniture, ceramics and handicrafts.
- Leichhardt Public School, cnr Norton and Marion Sts, Leichhardt.

Markets & fairs

North Sydney Market
A shopping expedition can be a family affair among the market's 190 stalls laden with books, antiques, jewellery, plants, clothing, fresh food, children's wear and toys. Kids can use the playground equipment and adults can whet their appetites with choices ranging from pancakes to barbecued sausages. Entertainment includes wandering performers, street theatre and bands. Second Saturday of every month.
- Cnr Miller and Ridge Sts, North Sydney.

Paddington Bazaar
About 250 artisans and designers of handicrafts, furniture, homewares and fashion display an eclectic mix, catering to modern, antique, funky and alternative tastes. Sydneysiders and tourists travel here en masse to shop, be seen and be entertained. Street theatre and bands perform each week, and there are fashion parades, jazz events and craft exhibitions year-round. Held each Saturday.
- Cnr Oxford and Newcombe Sts, Paddington.

The Rocks Market
A 150-metre-long canopy adds a modern touch to this historic locale and encourages a welcome breeze through the bustling marketplace. Stalls display homewares and decorative items, antiques and old wares, arts, crafts and curios from around the world. Street theatre and musical groups entertain and other attractions include art exhibitions, antiques fairs and craft shows. Saturdays and Sundays.
- George and Playfair Sts, The Rocks.

Trisha Treanor

Martial arts

see also tai chi, fitness clubs, personal trainers, sporting goods

Martial arts are not only an age-old tradition, but also a sport for all ages. The various disciplines include kung-fu, tae kwon do, karate, jeet kune do, judo and kick boxing. The more traditional forms, such as kung fu and judo, which are not based on brute strength, are popular with people more interested in fitness and self-defence. There will be two forms of martial arts at the Sydney Olympics: judo, which has no punching or kicking but revolves around throw and hold techniques, and tae kwon do, which will be introduced as a full medal sport. Australia will have full teams in both disciplines for the first time. Major judo events are held at the Michael Wenden Aquatic Centre at Liverpool.

International Wing Chun Academy
For practical self-defence as a weapon against brute force. The academy, specialising in kung fu, also deals with weight management, fitness, relaxation and concentration and stress relief.
- 335 Sussex St, City, ph 9264 9947.

Sydney City Karate
Teaches a style known as *kyokushinkai*, a tough but effective form of self-defence with an emphasis on discipline, perseverance and respect. Teaching is tailored to various age groups and skill levels. All ages welcome.
- Ultimo Community Centre, Ultimo, ph 9319 2644.

Metapower Martial Arts Supplies
Specialises in martial artists' needs – uniforms, punching bags, gloves, training equipment and clothes, such as T-shirts, sweatshirts and track pants.
- 42 Elizabeth Dr, Liverpool, ph 9600 8985.

Paul Kent

Further information
- Judo Federation of NSW, ph 9773 0166
- Australian Tae Kwon Do Association, ph 9979 7788
- Australian Karate Federation: www.pcug.org.au/~djm/akf/
- Women in Martial Arts Association: www.dot.net.au/~ssands/winma.htm

Massage

see also alternative medicine, new age

Hard day at the office? A recent study found that more than 60 per cent of people come home from work stressed. If your back's got more knots that a Scouts' jamboree, good sleep will not solve the problem. Varieties of massage available in Sydney include remedial, reflexology, Hawaiian, shiatsu and, the most popular, Swedish.

Aveda

For the ultimate pampering, the tranquil surrounds of Aveda should appeal to your senses. Relax in the spa, with some essential oils burning, before a body rub and massage. Aveda prides itself on being socially and environmentally responsible, and offers the best money can buy. It smells, looks, feels and sounds beautiful. The staff offer everything from advice on herbal medicines to full-scalp massages. It doesn't come cheap, but go on, you're worth it. Heaven on earth.
- 17 Oxford St, Paddington, ph 9380 5550.

Hotel Capital Relaxation Centre

Offers a wide range of services, including wet and dry saunas, foaming ginseng baths and the famous skin scrubs. Bear in mind 'no pain no gain', as a Korean masseur gives you a body slapping or sets off on a jog up and down your back.
- 111 Darlinghurst Rd, Kings Cross, ph 9368 0818.

NSW School of Therapeutic Massage

Established for 12 years, offers 10-week certificate courses (cost $280) in a variety of massage, including sports, remedial and Swedish. Courses run during the day, in the evenings or on weekends. If you complete five different strands, you are eligible for a diploma, which is recognised by the Association of Massage Therapy (AMT). The staff are extremely helpful, and for $20 you can have a massage and a tour of the school.
203 Pitt St, City, ph 9283 2588.

Grant Gillies

Further information
- Association of Massage Therapists Australia:
  www.amta.asn.au/
- Massage Australia:
  www.massageaus.com

Meat

see also poultry & game

Why buy your meat shrink-wrapped onto plastic trays, when there are dedicated professionals who age their beef and cut to order, who saw marrowbones for you, trim your lamb rack on the spot, or know just what ribs you need for your recipe? Good butchers know when to leave good meat alone, and when to do things to it. They can even tell you how to cook it.

Thai Kee Meats

The one-stop shop for all your Asian meat needs, as well as being a perfectly good source of meats for non-Asian dishes. But here, they know the difference between pork for a stir-fry, pork for a soup, and pork for those steamed pai gwat (spare ribs) you love at yum cha.
- Shop 138, Level 1, Market City, Haymarket, ph 9212 4466.

Penny's Quality Meats

A gem of a butcher, who puts personal service in front of enticing displays. If you can't see it, ask for it, and watch them bend over backwards to get it for you.
- Royal Arcade, 401 New South Head Rd, Double Bay, ph 9327 3826.

Meat

Cliff Penny's Butchery

Cliff Penny's great-great-grandfather started the business in King's Cross in 1880. The shops still do things the old-fashioned – as in good – way, with some of the most exciting, ever-changing and inspirational meat displays in town.

- 880 Military Rd, Mosman, ph 9969 3372; Shop 2, 18 Bungan Rd, Mona Vale, ph 9997 1581.

AC Butchery

If so many of Sydney's finest restaurants trust Carlo Colaiacomo's meats, then so can you. Shopping here is a joy, for anything from young Illabo lamb and sensational pork and fennel sausages to a very good prosciutto, free range eggs, and excellent poultry.

- 174 Marion St, Leichhardt, ph 9569 8687.

Iseli Swiss Butcher

If Heidi ever went to the butcher, this is the butcher she would go to, for the most delicate European sausages, fine pork and veal, sweet-smelling smallgoods, and very Heidi's-mum service.

- 8 Charlotte St, Ashfield, ph 9798 6406.

T.J. Wright's Gourmet Meats

About the size of a standing rib roast, this little shop is filled with great meats, eager foodies, and butchers who really know their craft, as well as their hams, kangaroo, veal and venison.

- 32 Clovelly Rd, Randwick, ph 9398 1038.

Jill Dupleix

Men's shoes & accessories

see also **menswear, international designer fashion**

Because men's dressing codes are so restricted, the accessories are often the way for men to display a little more individuality – with a clever cufflink, a whimsical yellow floral tie or a multicoloured striped business shirt. Menswear stores like Five Way Fusion and Robby Ingham have great accessories. Don't forget the great array of men's shoes and accessories for men in David Jones Market St store, or go to the cult International label names such as Gucci and Prada.

Aquila

Founded in 1959, this Australian company has been manufacturing shoes for 40 years, inspired by the latest in European style and design. They also import Italian-made shoes.

- 460 Oxford St, Paddington, ph 9360 4591. Also in the City at Sydney Central Plaza, ph 9232 3884; Skygardens, ph 9221 4806.

Baubridge & Kay

Baubridge & Kay's two Sydney stores are stocked to overflowing with businessmen's accoutrements – business shirts (Australian made from Italian and English cottons), ties, braces, cufflinks (including Links of London). They also have an Australia-wide mail order service.

- 1st floor, Queen Victoria Building, City, ph 9261 1539. Also at Skygardens, ph 9223 6729. Mail order: 1800 818 658.

Declic

Makers of their own business shirts and importers of quirky cufflinks from English label Duchamp. Melbourne-made Declic shirts are available in a range of styles for business (including French cuffed), casual and dress. Declic also stocks ties and accessories from international labels like Dolce & Gabbana, Moschino and Paul Smith.

- 450 Oxford St, Paddington, ph 9361 6662. Also at Queen Victoria Building, ph 9264 9936.

Jane de Teliga

Menswear

Australian men have gone way past the old stubbies and thongs stereotype these days, with every possible sartorial option now available in Sydney's stores – from funky streetstyle and designer yuppie threads to the classical besuited attire of the urban professional.

Bisonte
Men's and women's contemporary leather clothing that has the fine tailoring and soft leather of international leathergoods, designed by this Melbourne-based company (not to be confused with Italian leathergoods label Il Bisonte).
- 452 Oxford St, Paddington, ph 9331 3999.

Brave
Funky menswear label for the fashion-forward male, full of the latest trends designed by Wayne Cooper, a Londoner now based in Sydney. Wayne's two ranges are Brave, a less expensive label and his more up-market label, Wayne Cooper.
- 302 Oxford St, Paddington, ph 9332 2940.

Calibre
A Melbourne menswear label that is as cool and modern as its minimalist store in Paddington, with suiting for the hip urban male in wool lycra blends through to dark indigo denim jeans and jackets.
- 416 Oxford St, Paddington, ph 9380 5993.

Country Road
The Australian label that has changed the way Australian men dress, by taking classic country style and making it fashionable for the urban male at work and play. Head-to-toe dressing from suiting to tracksuits and all the accessories – ties, shoes and belts.
- 142-144 Pitt St, City, ph 9394 1818. Also at Mosman, ph 9960 4633; Chatswood, ph 9419 5570; and other city and suburban locations.

Emporio Armani
The label the affluent urbanite loves to wear. This store sells the more affordable line of Giorgio Armani's famous unstructured soft tailoring that has revolutionised men's suiting.
- 4 Martin Place, City, ph 9231 3655.

Five Way Fusion
An institution in Sydney, Five Way Fusion has been going for an amazing 26 years importing clothing from some of the world's leading designers. The current line-up includes Comme des Garcons, Issey Miyake, Dolce & Gabbana, Missoni Menswear and Thierry Mugler as well as Romeo Gigli and Bagutta shirts and Cesare Paciotti shoes.
- 205-207 Glenmore Rd, Paddington, ph 9331 2828. Also in the Queen Victoria Building.

Giorgio Armani
The ultimate for the well-heeled urban male who likes top-of-the-range contemporary Italian style. A Giorgio Armani suit is a must-have status symbol.
- 173 Elizabeth St, City, ph 9283 5562.

Cutler Bespoke
Classic bespoke tailor to Sydney's upper crust for more than a century. Handmade suits tailored entirely in Sydney, as well as made-to-measure suits from Italian samples and ready-made suits from Italy. Made-to-measure shirts with an dazzling array of fine cotton shirting from Italy, ready-made business shirts, and beautiful handmade silk ties from Italy and England and other accessories.
- 17 O'Connell St, City, ph 9232 7122.

John Pardoe
Established more than 25 years ago, Pardoe specialises in everything for the affluent businessman from local made-to-measure suiting through the much-coveted Italian suiting name Ermengildo Zegna, as well as Roman label Brioni and handmade Canali suiting from

Milan. He also carries Churches shoes, Zegna yachting gear, George Trumper toiletries.
- 23 O'Connell St, City, ph 9232 4255.

Ian McMaugh
Directional menswear by Sydney-based McMaugh, who keeps a low profile but has been plugging away at relaxed urban style for more than a decade, including funky knitwear and wide-legged pants.
- Strand Arcade, City, ph 9221 3357. Also at Darlinghurst, ph 9360 2911.

Marcs
Mark Kieghery's stores run the gamut from his own popular label of casual Australian separates ($39.95 basic T-shirt through to $495 for a tailored Marcs jacket) to the most directional, edgy, trans-generational urban wear from international designers like Helmet Lang, Yohji Yamamoto, Dries Van Noten, and Issey Miyake, along with Diesel jeans.
- Mid City Centre, Pitt St, City, ph 9221 5575. Also at Paddington, ph 9332 4255; Mosman, ph 9968 1298.

Morrissey
Peter Morrissey continues his urban cool for both men and women post the Morrissey-Edmiston split. Soon to open in Double Bay.
- 76 Oxford St, Darlinghurst, ph 9380 8787.

Plot
Since 1969, Plot Clothiers has been providing the latest trends in menswear translated into affordable prices and easy care microfibre. Plot has a huge following around Australia, with its inexpensive suits ranging from $300 to $450.
- Mid City Centre, 197 Pitt St, City, ph 9221 5120. Also at Paddington, Neutral Bay and a factory outlet in Waterloo, ph 9318 2499.

Polo Ralph Lauren
The diffusion range of this designer's hugely popular all-American sportswear crossbred with gentrified English style. Perfect for the affluent middle-class Australian male with classic navy blazers, business and casual shirts, golf wear, Polo tees, classic chinos and leathergoods.
- Queen Victoria Building, City, ph 9267 1630. Also at North Sydney, ph 9956 6828.

Robby Ingham
Four stores in an Oxford row house Robby Ingham's mix of imported labels for men and women. His men's specialities include his own directional suiting for the young urban professional, along with imported suiting from G. Gigli and Paul Smith. Other labels include Comme des Garcons men's shirt line, Stone Island from Italy, and Paul Smith jeans line.
- 422-428 Oxford St, Paddington, ph 9332 2124.

RM Williams
Australian classic bushman's clothing that looks great in the city – Drizabone coats and beautifully crafted, elastic-sided boots that supermodel Linda Evangelista stocked up on for boyfriend Kyle Maclachlan.
- Chifley Plaza, 2 Chifley Square, City, ph 9233 1949; 389 George St, City, ph 9262 2228. Also at Chatswood, ph 9411 4388.

Saba
The contemporary Melbourne label that's been going for 30 years and still looks hip. Known particularly for smart suits and knitwear for both men and women. Has just opened a flagship store in New York.
- 270 Oxford St, Paddington, ph 9331 2685; Skygardens, 77 Castlereagh St, City, ph 9231 2436.

South West Trader
Stocks English menswear by Tokyo-based by Nigel Curtiss. Very modern and directional from suiting to hi-tech sportswear. Also collectable silver jewellery from Mexican-based

William Spratling as well as native American jewellery.

- 36 Oxford Street, Paddington, ph 9332 2311.

Vince Maloney

Classic suiting by Ermengildo Zegna, favoured by Sydney's business, banking and legal fraternity. Also stocks V2 suiting and shirts, Paul & Shark leather jackets, casual cords and tracksuits plus Rossetti shoes.

- 177 Elizabeth St, City, ph 9264 8837.

Jane de Teliga

Modern Australian restaurants

To debate fully whether or not there is such a thing as Australian cuisine would probably take more pages than this book has. But Australia does have a special way of looking at food – of taking the sunshine of the Mediterranean and the wisdom of South-East Asia and presenting them both anew on a plate.

The Boathouse on Blackwattle Bay

Enjoy some of the finest bridge views in Sydney. No, not that bridge, but its little sister, the starkly dramatic Glebe Island bridge. You also get a good look at the Pyrmont fish markets which seems right and proper, considering the restaurant's emphasis on shellfish and crustaceans from the kitchen tanks.

- End of Ferry Rd, Glebe, ph 9518 9011

Number Seven

The next time you dine at the Park Hyatt's premier restaurant, prepare to be amazed, and not just by the staggering harbour and Opera House views. It might look like just another hotel fine dining room, but it is now home to some of the finest Asian-influenced, Mod Oz cooking in town, courtesy of former Rockpool head chef, Ross Lusted.

- Park Hyatt Sydney, 7 Hickson Rd, The Rocks, ph 9256 1630.

The International

Remember when a big night out meant booths, top-of-the-town views and really zoomy cocktails? No? It doesn't matter. The International is the hippest retro dining room in the town where Sydney's gorgeous young things sip martinis and guavaritas, listen to the coolest New York vibes, and tuck into chef Brian Duncan's refined, good-looking take on Mod Oz.

- 14th floor, 227 Victoria St, Kings Cross, ph 9360 5188.

Moran's

The full gamut of Mod Oz flavours can be experienced at this friendly, whiter than white restaurant. But it's Matthew Moran's way with Mediterranean flavours that really impresses. Try his striking ravioli of salt cod, char-grilled tuna with piperade and fig-stuffed quail with de puy lentils.

- 61-63 Macleay St, Potts Point, ph 9356 2223.

Paramount

White blonde Chris Manfield is the golden girl of Mod Oz cooking. Every visit to her strikingly modern Potts Point restaurant rewards with flavours that burn themselves into your memory, such as hot and sour coconut prawn soup, soy braised Barossa corn-fed chicken and brandied cherry and coconut trifle.

- 73 Macleay St, Potts Point, ph 9358 1652.

Ravesi's

Once, the ultimate Sydney summer's day used to be eating fish and chips on the beach at Bondi. Now it's eating Martin Teplitsky's char-grilled King George whiting and blue swimmer crab salad on the Ravesi's balcony overlooking the beach.

- Cnr Campbell Pde and Hall Sts, Bondi Beach, ph 9365 4422.

Modern Australian restaurants

Rockpool
Neil Perry might not have invented Modern Australian cooking but he sure did give it direction and substance. Every year he and chef Ross Lusted enliven it with even more nous and nuance, producing gems such as mudcrab, paw paw and sweet pork salad, and herb and spice-crusted tuna on braised eggplant.
- 107 George St, The Rocks, ph 9252 1888.

Sean's Panaroma
With its bomb-shelter feel and awkward, cast-off school-chair seating, this might not strike you as a particularly serious restaurant until you start eating. You can't get much more serious than Sean Moran's preserved duck salad with black figs and borlotti beans and white peach and raspberry trifle.
- 270 Campbell Pde, Bondi Beach, ph 9365 4924.

Terry Durack

Motorsport

see also go-karts

Motorsport is near the top of the list when it comes to charges we lay against Jeff Kennett for stealing Sydney's thunder. Melbourne has the Formula One World Championship opener and pinched back the Australian Motorcycle Grand Prix. Even our touring car national champions like Glen Seton and Mark Skaife have relocated to the Victorian capital. But motorsports have a proud history in Sydney, dating back to the days of 50,000-plus crowds at the speedway in the 1920s. Today, local petrolheads still have plenty to cheer and steer, from super-trucks to motocross, from drag racing to touring cars and the ever-popular speedway. If it has wheels and an engine, you can race it, or watch it being raced, in Sydney.

Oran Park Raceway
This raceway south-west of the city hosts such events as the Shell Australian touring car championship (grand final in August) and the supertruck, sports sedans and Formula Xtreme motorcycle series. It is the home of truck-racing in Sydney and host for the annual Transtasman Supertruck Challenge each June.
- Cnr Northern and Cobbitty Rds, Narellan, ph 4646 1004.

Parramatta City Raceway
Home of Sydney speedway, held every Saturday night from October to April. Sydney has four of the best Sprintcar drivers in the country – Garry Brazier, Skip Jackson, Brook Tatnell and Kerry Madsen – who between them have a brace of Australian titles.
- Wentworth St, Granville, ph 9637 0411.

Eastern Creek Raceway
Largely responsible for taking clandestine drag racing off Sydney's streets. The raceway hosts bimonthly Off-Street Meets (aka The Runs) where beginners are welcome to show up with a registered car and $30. Major events here include the Premier State Nationals (drag racing) on October 16-17, 1998.
- Horsley Rd, Eastern Creek, ph 9672 1000.

Bathurst
Sleepy NSW town two hours from Sydney which is overrun by up to 50,000 motorsport fanatics during two nation-stopping touring car races in October and November. The Bathurst 1000 Super Touring Car Championship (Oct long weekend) is the original hoonathon, pitting overseas drivers against Australia's best. Five weeks later the V8 Supercars take the town for the Bathurst Australian 1000 Classic in a battle

Motor vehicle parts, accessories & services

of home-grown talent which is just as fiercely contested.

Confederation of Australian Motor Sport

CAMS is the ruling body for Oz motor sports, with the exception of speedway and bikes. A good place to start for answers to your racing car queries.
- Unit 24, St Johns Ct, OConnell St, Parramatta, ph 9635 1366.

Motorcycling NSW

The folk to ring for anything to do with competitive motorcycling.
- 67 High St, Harris Park, ph 9635 9177.

Women In Motorsport Association

WIMSA was established to support women in motorsport.
- Jenni Thompson, ph 0417 255 619 or Cristine

Race and Rally

Retail outlet specialising in circuit racing equipment and safety gear.
- 37 Rosedale Ave, Greenacre, ph 9709 4655.

A Rally Experience

Rally school offering one-off forest runs at Amaroo Park, corporate team building and specialist rally training.
- Rydalmere, ph 1800 648 846.

Revolution Racegear

Retailer stocking its own brand race suits, boots and gloves.
- Unit 4, rear of 191 Parramatta Rd, Auburn, ph 9648 4044.

Insex Leathers

Mail order and retail outlet stocking custom-made leathers.
- Yagoona, ph 9743 7619.

Peter Vincent and Peter McKay

When having your car repaired, how can you be certain that (a) the price is fair, (b) the work is up to standard and (c) the work done was necessary in the first place? The answers are: you can't, you can't and (you guessed it) you can't. If you have a doubt of this kind (who hasn't!) you can only make reasonable inquiries. Start with the person who did the work – find out exactly what parts were required (these are usually surprisingly inexpensive), whether they were new or used, and how long the work took. Labour costs are the easiest to bump up, but if you ask how much your repairer charges by the hour, you should have an idea if your bill has been exaggerated. But prepare to be surprised by hourly labour rates – they vary wildly across the city, usually corresponding roughly to property rentals. Therefore, head gasket repairs will probably cost you more in the central city or North Sydney, than at Lidcombe or Strathfield. Prices in the Eastern Suburbs should be somewhere in between. But labour costs also vary according to what car you have – if you have a sick Jaguar, you'd best have your overdraft extended. If you talk to your garage and are still not happy, there are further options open to you. The first three in the following list are organisations that can help.

Motor Vehicle Repair Disputes Committee

A statutory government authority set up to intervene on customer/repairer disputes. Will examine and rule on the the standard and/or the fair cost of the work done. They hold the *Standard Times Manual*, which outlines reasonable labour times for most repairs.
- 239 Great North Rd, Five Dock, ph 9712 2200.

Motor vehicle parts, accessories & services

Department of Fair Trading
This State department rules on disputes over car warranties and the purchase of spare parts.
- 175 Castlereagh St, City, ph 9286 0006.

NRMA
They can put a potential purchase through its paces, give you a valuation or pick up the pieces if it all goes horribly wrong somewhere back of Bourke.
- Ph 9292 6777 (technical advice line) or 13 1111 (road service help line).

Autopro
Spare parts superstore for all makes and models with 19 outlets city-wide, open 7 days.
- Head office: Percy St, Auburn, ph 9704 4350 or 13 2776.

American Auto Parts
Specialises in parts and accessories for Valiant, Chevrolet, Ford and the great Aussie tank, Holden.
- 478 King Georges Rd, Beverly Hills, ph 9502 1030.

Unique Autosports
Parts and accessories for imported coupes and high-performance vehicles including Nissan, Lexus, Soarer, Supra and MR2.
- Unit E1/2a Victoria Ave, Castle Hill, ph 9634 8000.

Tempe 4x4 Spares
Wrecking specialist for new and used Japanese jeep and ute parts.
- 661 Princes Highway, Tempe, ph 9558 4931.

JS Craig Panelbeating
Well-established company boasting a five-year guarantee on its work.
- Head office: Artarmon, ph 9906 2577.

Roof Rack City
Sells and hires new and second-hand racks for surf boards, skis, bikes, windsurfers and anything else that can fit on your roof.
- Head Office: 42 Whiting St, Artarmon, ph 9901 3000.

Town and Country Vehicle Accessories
Excellent range of RTA-authorised child restraints.
- Cnr King Georges and Moorefield Rds, Roselands, ph 9758 2500.

Clifford Powell
Leatherwork specialist for prestige cars including BMW, Porsche and Mercedes-Benz.
- Cnr Crown and Burton Sts, East Sydney, ph 9360 6892.

VIP Car Care
Valet and detailing service.
- Cnr Brunker and Rookwood Rds, Yagoona, ph 9707 1744.

Peter Vincent

Museums

see also art galleries, photography
Sydney's museums offer something for everyone – from small specialised displays to the mega collections of the science and technology museums. They offer history and learning, information and entertainment, whiz-bangery and games – for young and old. Special exhibitions are mounted regularly to make a return visit worthwhile, while the museum bookshops offer a wide range of books, educational toys, gifts and unusual souvenirs.

Australian Museum
Science, natural history (dinosaurs!) and anthropology are the star attractions here. Dis-

plays are geared to learning and fun, so it's a perfect place to take the kids.
- 6 College St, City, ph 9320 6000: www.aust-mus.gov.au

Australian National Maritime Museum
There are exhibitions devoted to every imaginable aspect of the sea. And for kids – and their parents – the chance to explore a submarine, a battleship and several other ships makes this a most exciting museum visit.
- 2 Murray St, Darling Harbour, ph 9552 7777: www.anmm.gov.au

Hyde Park Barracks Museum
Designed by the convict architect Francis Greenway, one of Sydney's earliest buildings now houses displays about Australia's colonial history and convict life. Excellent bookshop and cafe.
- Queens Square, Macquarie St, City, ph 9223 8922.

Justice and Police Museum
Chilling relics from our criminal past – from bushrangers to the pyjama girl – in an historic building. The police charge room, the magistrate's court and several remand cells survive and give the visitor a taste of the other side of the law.
- Cnr Albert and Phillip Sts, Circular Quay, ph 9252 1144.

Macleay Museum
Out of the way, but worth the effort. This museum still possesses a 19th-century atmosphere. Lots of exhibits, including dinosaurs, a dodo and a Fijian cannibal fork. A great family visit.
- Gosper Lane, University of Sydney, ph 9351 2274.

Manly Art Gallery and Museum
A great visit after a day at the beach for the displays devoted to the history of Manly and its surf culture.
- West Esplanade Reserve, Manly, ph 9949 2435.

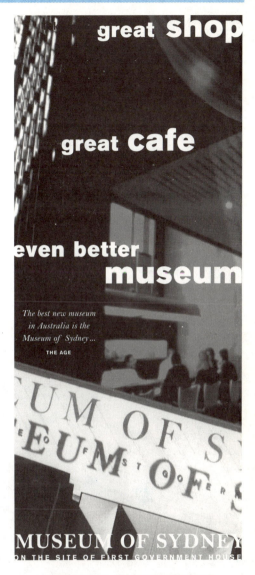

The best new museum in Australia is the Museum of Sydney...
THE AGE

SPECIAL EXHIBITIONS

8 AUGUST – 8 NOVEMBER 1998
WANDERLUST
Journeys through the Macleay Museum, University of Sydney

21 NOVEMBER – 21 FEBRUARY 1999
FLESH & BLOOD
Family Connections in Sydney 1788-1998

6 MARCH – 31 MAY 1999
TERRA NAPOLEON: TERRA AUSTRALIA
Captain Baudin's Voyage of Discovery to the Southern Lands 1800-1804

Museum of Sydney on the site of first Government House
Cnr Phillip and Bridge Streets, Sydney OPEN DAILY 10AM – 5PM
Ph 02 9251 5988 Fax 02 9251 5966
A PROPERTY OF THE HISTORIC HOUSES TRUST OF NEW SOUTH WALES

Museums

Museum of Sydney
One of Sydney's most exciting contemporary buildings on an historic site with innovative and participatory displays about the changing face of the city. Excellent shop and a very smart cafe.
- 37 Phillip St, City, ph 9251 5988: www.mos.nsw.gov.au

Nicholson Museum
The best display of antiquities in town. Neolithic artefacts, Greek pots and even a mummy make it a place to explore while learning about ancient history.
- Main Quadrangle, University of Sydney, ph 9351 2812.

Powerhouse Museum
A mega museum with lots of science and technology and whiz-bangery for kids (and grown-ups). Social history and decorative arts – fashion, ceramics and gold and silver – too.
- 500 Harris St, Ultimo, ph 9217 0111: www.phm.gov.au

Sydney Jewish Museum
Exhibitions concerned with Judaism and the history of the Jewish people, such as *Whoever Saves a Life Saves the World*, honouring those who saved Jewish lives during the Holocaust, and *From Bondage to Freedom, from Darkness to Light*, looking at the lives of 20 Holocaust survivors now living in Australia.
- 148 Darlinghurst Rd, Darlinghurst, ph 9360 7999.

John McPhee

Musical instruments

see also musical tuition

Whether you're after a snare drum or a Stradivarius, finding the right instrument shop is the best way to ensure your music-making gets off to a harmonious start.

The Bass Player
This shop, which has operated for 10 years, sells new and used electric bass guitars, and boasts a good range of vintage instruments. It also will sell your unwanted guitar on consignment. A guitar technician and a teacher both operate from the premises.
- 35 Parramatta Rd, Annandale, ph 9550 4048; freecall 1800 805 825.

Billy Hyde's Drumcraft
Billy Hyde's has been synonymous with drums for many years and claims to be the biggest retailer of its kind in the southern hemisphere. In addition to selling a large range of percussion instruments, it offers repair and hire services. Also tuition by leading musicians is available.
- 104 Commonwealth St, Surry Hills, ph 9211 1700.

Drum City
Drum City has been in business for 33 years and knows a thing or two about percussion. While it specialises in selling and hiring drums and accessories to professional players, it also stocks beginner kits and gives lessons.
- 14 City Rd, Chippendale, ph 9281 0255.

Ensemble Musical Instruments
Ensemble specialises in orchestral instruments – such as violins, woodwind and brass – and sells a range of accessories from reeds to music stands. Players of all levels are catered for: the Department of School Education and the Sydney Symphony Orchestra are customers. The shop distributes Selmer in Australia.
- 42 Sailors Bay Rd, Northbridge, ph 9958 3640.

Hutchings
This long-established firm has adjoining shops selling keyboards and pianos. Computer-based

recording specialists Hutchings Keyboards sells Yamaha, Korg and Kurzweil electronic instruments, digital samplers and other related equipment. The shop also hires keyboards, amplifiers, DAT recorders and mixers. The Hutchings family has been selling pianos for 43 years. They also have a rental stock of more than 500 instruments from beginner models to concert grands.
- 5-9 Edgecliff Rd, Bondi Junction, ph 9387 5011 (keyboards); 9387 1376 (pianos).

Jackson's Rare Guitars
The Ferraris and Porsches of the guitar world are lovingly bought and sold by Steve Jackson and his team (which includes AC/DC's original bass player, Mark Evans). The shop attracts customers from bands such as Metallica, Aerosmith and Midnight Oil looking for that old Martin acoustic, vintage Telecaster or rare Gibson. The shop, which offers a repair service, will buy your old instrument or sell on consignment. Also amplifiers are stocked.
- 37 Parramatta Rd, Annandale, ph 9550 2985.

Sound Devices
Specialises in providing hardware and software for hard-disc recording. This includes sequencers, MIDI keyboards and mixers. The majority of the shop's customers work in professional studios or are setting up home studios.
- 265 Sussex St, City, ph 9283 2077.

Steve Giordano
The former jazz saxophonist repairs and reconditions woodwind and brass instruments.
- 53 Church St, Camperdown, ph 9519 9424.

Theme and Variations Piano Services
Well regarded by professional players, the shop sells Yamaha, John Broadwood and other makes from beginner models to concert grands. The shop also deals in quality second-hand pianos and can rebuild old instruments.
- Suite 1/178 Pacific Hwy, Greenwich, ph 9439 5277.

Turramurra Music Centre
The shop has been operating for 21 years and sells instruments suitable for players at all levels, although the professional end of the market is Turramurra's speciality. Members of major bands are regular customers. In addition to the usual range of guitars, violins and clarinets, the shop stocks electric keyboards and recording studio equipment. A music school, the Northside Academy, is upstairs.
- 1267 Pacific Hwy, Turramurra, ph 9449 8487.

Peter Jordan

Musical tuition

The days of music teachers rapping their students' knuckles for playing a wrong note are largely over. Nonetheless, finding the right tutor is still an important part of ensuring that you or your child enjoys the learning experience. After all, music is supposed to be fun.

Sydney Conservatorium of Music
The Conservatorium's Access Centre offers non-tertiary semester, weekend and day courses for students of all ages and abilities. Most programs are offered across the year in three 10-week terms, giving students the chance at three entry points a year. Course fees begin at $150 a term, averaging less than $15 an hour. There are programs for primary and secondary students in jazz, classical, musical theatre and music technology, and general courses in basic music skills, song writing, composition, and jazz improvisation.
- Macquarie St, City, ph 9351 1206.

Australian Institute of Music
The AIM is an independent, non-profit, secondary and tertiary educational academy. While much of its focus is on award courses (at HSC, diploma and bachelor degree levels),

Musical tuition

it also offers general tuition on most instruments, including voice, and music technology to people of all ages and abilities. There is a young musicians' program that caters for children as young as 18 months through to students at an intermediate level. Entry is available all year.

- 17-51 Foveaux St, City, ph 9212 2333: www.aimusic.com.au

Australian International Conservatorium of Music

Located in Harris House, a heritage building set on an acre of land, the Conservatorium offers a wide range of individual and group classes in most instruments, as well as musicianship, theory and composition, to students at all levels of musical development. The school operates on a European model that emphasises performance. Students can choose to participate in the school's choir, ensemble groups and master classes. Early childhood music classes are also available.

- 31-33 Allen St, Harris Park,
  ph 9637 0777:
  www.eisa.net.au/~austcon

United Music Teachers of NSW Inc.

The group can recommend qualified music teachers for private tuition based on geographic location. While many of its members specialise in classical music, some teach contemporary forms.

- Vice-president Faye Lake, ph 9569 8009.

Peter Jordan

Musicians

While you may remember the great band playing at a function or party, you will certainly remember a lousy one, or one that just didn't suit – no matter how good they were. The right musical backing is crucial to a function's success. Ask for a sample of the act's work in advance; most should have something on cassette.

The Engine Room

Drummer John Pochee, pianist Roger Frampton and bassist Steve Elphick are some of Australia's best jazz musicians. They regularly perform at functions and have a great library of standards at their disposal as well as their own material.

- Ph 9311 7783.

Bernie McGann

Arguably Australia's finest saxophone player, he has his own trio that are also able mix it up with all styles of jazz.

- Ph 9569 8925.

Enormous Horns

As the name suggests, this band has a large brass section, and a risque sense of humour in its act. They have a huge repertoire of chart hits from the past few decades.

- Ph 9870 7180.

Australia Live!

A bush band could be ideal for a convention of overseas delegates, and this agency has many to choose from, including the award-winning Eureka! Traditional Australian songs and ballads are the order here. Dance callers and line dancers are also available. Yee-ha!

- Ph 9876 6667.

Sydney Wedding Strings

A business that changed its name from Soiree Musicale in 1997. Nigel Parry was a cellist and pianist with the Australian Opera for 12 years, and his son, Nicholas, accompanies him at many functions playing cello or violin. To suit desired styles and group sizes, it draws from a base of more than 20 classical musicians.

- Ph 9869 0753.

IMC

This agency books some of Australian rock music's finest talent. They are also responsible for the hugely successful Homebake music festivals.
■ Ph 9699 1611.

Andrew Khedoori

National parks

see also bushwalking, camping, barbecues

It is little wonder that Sydney is marketed as the city of national parks. There are more than a dozen designated national parks and one state forest within an hour's drive of the city centre. They protect aspects of the city's Aboriginal and European history, many of its native plants and animals and some of its most unspoilt beaches and bush. Whether you visit for a quiet picnic beside a creek, to try to spot an elusive bird or animal or indulge in a range of more strenuous activities, there is something for everyone to enjoy in every season. Entry fees ($7.50 a car or $60 for an annual pass) apply to some parks and dogs and other pets are not allowed.

Sydney Harbour National Park

The five islands and sections of harbour foreshore that make up this fragmented park are rich in history and natural beauty. Take guided tours of Fort Denison and Goat Island to discover their convict history, explore the underground tunnels and forts built at Middle Head and Georges Head to defend Sydney and visit the haunted quarantine station at Manly. There are excellent walking tracks at North Head, Bradleys Head, Watsons Bay and Vaucluse – and plenty of secluded beaches.
■ Ph 9337 5511.

Royal National Park

Gazetted in 1879, this is Australia's oldest and best-loved park. Its 15,014 hectares include Aboriginal art sites, swimming and surf beaches, cliffs, rivers, waterfalls and a wide variety of vegetation. Hire a boat on the Hacking River, cycle the length of Lady Carrington Drive or step out on one of the many walking tracks.
■ Ph 9542 0648.

Ku-ring-gai Chase National Park

Look for Aboriginal engravings and middens, walk through eucalypts to a deserted beach or hire a boat and admire the sandstone-dominated landscape as you explore Pittwater or the Hawkesbury River.
■ Ph 9457 1049.

Jenny Stanton

Further information
■ NSW National Parks and Wildlife Service, ph 9585 6333: www.npws.nsw.gov.au

Netball

When the lazy, hazy days of summer have disappeared and there's a pleasant chill in the morning air, that's when the estimated one million netballers around the country take to the courts. Netball is the most popular female team sport in the country and, with the growth in popularity of mixed-team games, is spreading its appeal. It is the one sport in which Australia is the undisputed world champion, having won the official World Championship seven times out of the nine the competition has been held. Netball is to be included for the first time at the Commonwealth Games in Kuala Lumpur in 1998 and Australia is hot favourite to take the gold medal.

Netball is fairly simple to learn, requires little specialised equipment and can be played on grass, asphalt or bitumen. There is a court in almost every Sydney suburb.

Netball NSW

The game has been adapted to cater for all ages with Fun Net for the 5-7 years age group; Netta for the 8 to 10s; and then netball proper for those over 11. Netball NSW can provide the details of the nearest association (there are 110 in the State) for anyone wishing to play.
- Ph 9552 6077.

Commonwealth Bank Trophy

The national competition runs from late March until early August. There are two Sydney-based teams – the Swifts and the Sandpipers – among the eight competing for the trophy. Games are usually held on a Friday night, occasionally Saturday, at the State Sports Centre, Homebush. Dates for all matches are available from Netball Australia, ph 9633 2533.

State League

The NSW competition runs from April to September with games played at the Anne Clark Centre, Church St, Lidcombe. Information from Netball NSW.

Jennie Curtin

Further information
- Netball NSW and Netball World: both magazines are published during the season and available from newsagents or by subscription from the NSW organisation or the national body. Both include player profiles, match reports, fitness and diet tips and playing strategies.

New age

see also alternative medicine, massage, yoga

In a society of mindless materialism, there are new sets of belief systems to heal our soul (or, at least, that pain in the lower back). Forget about the Old World, this is the New Age, man. It's an age of astrology, of reiki, of shamanic and spiritual healing, of getting in touch with your inner child. In essence, it is the age of balming your body, mind and spirit with palm readers, clairvoyants and tarot card readers.

It all comes together at the popular Mind, Body, Spirit Festival, held at Darling Harbour mid year.

Crystal Forest

Spiritual development classes, reflexology, spiritual healing, vibrational medicine, crystal and colour healing, aura diagnosis and drawing, tarot and clairvoyant readings, and astrology. With vegetarian cafe.
- 253 Forest Rd, Hurstville ph 9580 2925.

Destiny

Natural therapies clinic that offers massage, shiatsu, spiritual healers and counsellors, hypnotherapy, reflexology, colour therapy, clairvoyant readers, astrology.
- Shop 3, 143 Military Rd, Neutral Bay, ph 9953 9030.

Essential Energies

Nurture the inner being with tarot and clairvoyant readings, palmistry, astrology, reflexology, spiritual and vibrational healing, and chakra balancing.
- 207 King St, Newtown, ph 9557 7269; 16 Glebe Point Rd, Glebe, ph 9552 3538.

Higher Octave

Alternative and metaphysical bookstore with palm, tarot and clairvoyant readings.
- 852 Military Rd, Mosman, ph 9968 2034.

Highest Aspirations

Holistic healing with acupuncture, clairvoyants, counselling, hypnotherapy, inner-child work, massage, reiki, shamanic healing, tarot reading.
- Suite 3, 5/11 Hollywood Ave, Bondi Junction, ph 9387 8411.

Mysteries in Balmain

Work on your mind, body and spirit with tarot readings, palmistry, clairvoyants, spiritual channelling, radionics, crystal healing, energy massages and colour therapy in the float tanks.
- Level 1, 314 Darling St, Balmain, ph 9818 2274.

Siren Song

The sweet smell of soaps and aromatic candles, as well as tarot readings, palmistry, counselling, numerology, feng shui services and psychic readings and healings.
- Shop 2c, Jacques Ave, Bondi Beach, ph 9130 8505.

Dugald Jellie

Further information
- New Age Online Australia: www.newage.com.au/

Newsagents

Australia is the world's largest consumer of magazines per capita; an odd claim to fame but, at the very least, it proves we love a good newsagent. Here's a cross-section of large and small agents offering papers, stationery, glossy mags and helpful service.

Central Newsagency

Specialists in airfreight (current) copies of the grooviest magazines and journals globally including *wallpaper*, *Collezione* and *The Face*. Subscriptions can be delivered.
- 300 Elizabeth St, Surry Hills, ph 9211 5886.

World News Centre

Stocks a large number of foreign airfreight newspapers and magazines, with a nice view of the harbour as a bonus.
- 402 Harbourside Festival Marketplace, Darling Harbour, ph 9281 3707.

Humphreys Newsagency

Walk through the turnstiles before your feet get sandy and behold the sea of magazines, pristine stationery and paperbacks. Perfect beach distractions.
- 60 The Corso, Manly, ph 9977 1699.

The Papershoppe

A large agency with high turnover so plenty of neatly piled, popular magazines, and plenty of browsing space.
- S49 Stockland Mall, Baulkham Hills, ph 9639 4112.

Taylor Square Newsagency

The place you can get the *Herald* earliest is the newsstand outside the Oxford Hotel, which is part of this agency. Be first with the news at 12.30am.
- 165 Oxford St, Darlinghurst, ph 9331 2026.

Kate Ryan

Nightclubs

see also late-night food, bars, pubs

So what makes a good nightclub? It seems Sydneysiders think if the queues are a mile long, it must be a ripper. Clubbers are paying cover charges of up to $25, and venues are still filling with 2,000-strong capacity crowds. It appears, however, that promoters finally are pumping some of their substantial earnings back into the venues, as Sydney's club scene seems to be flourishing, with the inner city still considered the place to go.

Sublime

Established in late 1996 to fill the hard-house void, Sublime is Sydney's only club of its kind. Closely resembling some underground New York clubs, Sublime prides itself on retaining

Nightclubs

credible, deep house sounds. A little pretension, and a lot of fun for serious punters.
- 244 Pitt St, City, ph 9264 8428.

The Milk Bar

After a successful run in both Melbourne and the United States, the Milk Bar opened in Sydney in 1997. This novel club, true to its name, offers vodka-laced ice-blocks, cigars, lollies and various other kooky milk bar delights, including some of the finest cocktails in town. By midnight, the club's atmosphere is electric with some of Sydney's best DJs playing decadent disco, handbag house and all the big dance anthems. Provides a fresh alternative to mainstream clubbing.
- 2 Kellet St, Potts Point, ph 9331 0058.

DCM

Officially voted the best club in the southern hemisphere by *Harper's Bazaar* magazine, DCM is the place to go for discerning clubbers. It has been unrivalled as Sydney's most popular venue since 1991, with more than 1.5 million patrons visiting by the end of 1997. Disco bunnies, drag shows, weirdos and a queue outside as long as a Mardi Gras parade make this club the place to be seen – just ask Molly Meldrum, Janet Jackson or the Pet Shop Boys.
- 33 Oxford St, Darlinghurst,
  ph 9267 7036.

The Underground Cafe

If you're not in the mood for mirror balls, smoke machines and steroid-popping clubbers, the Underground provides a more relaxed atmosphere. The grungy venue is becoming increasingly popular, due to some fantastic house/garage music and a friendly informal crowd. The DJ line-up changes regularly, and the Underground often has special international guest DJs.
- 22 Bayswater Rd, Kings Cross, ph 9358 4676.

The Temple

If R&B is your thing, Friday night's Chocolate City at the Temple is your best bet, with two levels of the smoothest grooves. It's dark and dingy with great sofas and a comfortable chill-out space, making it one of the few quality R&B nights in Sydney.
- 34 Oxford St, Darlinghurst, ph 9331 1936.

Grant Gillies

Nurseries & garden supplies

Every year there are Nursery Industry Association Awards for the best nurseries in Australia and several Sydney nurseries have won 'Best' awards in recent years. Judging is based on standard of appearance, cleanliness and appeal of premises; health, variety and organisation of stock, extra facilities such as child-minding, tea-room etc., friendliness and skills of staff. Winning an award (or several) is a guarantee that the nursery is excellent – the best.

Rast Bros

A cosy, friendly nursery, long established and simple but very attractive (includes a historic palm grove) with colourful plant displays. Staff helpful and interested in plants and clients. Frequent Gardeners Card provides good discounts.
- 29 Kissing Point R, Turramurra,
  9144 2134.

Swane Bros

One of Australia's largest nurseries with both wholesale and retail areas. A long-running, family-owned business with family members very hands-on in the nursery, famous for roses grown at their Narromine nursery. Large new country-style building; good glasshouse for displays and exhibitions, pleasant tea-room; kids playground. Preferred Customer Card provides a discount system.
- 490 Galston Rd, Dural, ph 9851 1322.

Nurseries & garden supplies

North Manly Garden Centre
Enthusiastic owners, trained staff, helpful and willing to find wanted plants for customers. Customer service ranges through garden advice to gift-wrapping. Plenty of big features – an extensive gift shop, stunning bronze statuary, garden ponds with fish and aviaries full of pet birds which entertain the kids.
- 510–512 Pittwater Rd, North Manly, ph 9905 5202.

Tim's Garden Centres
Famous for funny signs which attract passing trade and lots of signage in the nursery giving helpful gardening tips. Mt Annan nursery, near the Mt Annan Botanic Gardens, is very large and has huge stock of plants including natives, especially grevilleas. Good coffee shop, sensational pots imported direct from Malaysia and Vietnam. Kid's Garden Club and Tim's Garden Club have regular meetings. Tim Pickles is one of Sydney's most energetic and innovative nursery people.
- 2 Queen St, Campbelltown, ph (02) 4626 7022; Cnr Mt Annan Drive and Narellan Rd, Mt Annan, ph (02) 4647 3788.

Longview Nursery
Beautifully laid out general nursery which also specialises in excellent cool climate plants such as hard-to-buy rare maples, conifers, rhododendrons and David Austin roses. Customer discount card.
- 29 Great Western Highway, Wentworth Falls, ph (02) 1223.

Camellia Grove
Prettiest, best cared for nursery and a pleasure to visit. Specialty is 'best in Sydney' camellias, azaleas and magnolias plus seasonal plants including rhododendrons (including vireyas), gardenia, hibiscus and cyclamen. Advice from trained staff. Pot range includes special camellia pots. Annual camellia and azalea catalogue.
- Cnr Mona Vale Rd and Killeaton St, St Ives, ph 9144 3402.

Michele Shennen's Garden Centres
Boutique nurseries with high-quality plants (new releases and standards a specialty), water features, pots and ornaments. Michele offers a garden design service. The Balmain nursery is geared specially to inner-city living. At Willoughby a coffee shop and a great kids garden club, Scotty's Junior Garden Club, are big features.
- 427 Darling St, Balmain, ph 9810 8892; 132 Penshurst Rd, Willoughby, ph 9958 6631.

Greenjade Exotic & Rare Nursery
The best nursery for rare and exotic plants including a range of interesting Asian plants, rare fruit trees, imported and tropical plants. The Lucketts at Greenjade will have the plant other nurseries haven't even heard of. Nursery includes bookshop.
- 2530 Silverdale Rd, Wallacia, ph (02) 4774 1112.

Rainbow Ridge Nursery
A specialist nursery, which is a fairly rare thing for the Sydney area. It is the best place to find iris and daylilies. Graeme Grosvenor and John Taylor not only import, collect and grow these plants, they are also involved in breeding new varieties with emphasis on the international award-winning Louisiana iris. They have a beautiful, full-colour catalogue; the best book on irises, *Iris the Flower of the Rainbow* by Graeme Grosvenor; take mail-orders; and are open to the public during the flowering season October, November and December.
- 8 Taylor's Rd, Dural, ph 9651 2857.

Parkers Nursery
This is Sydney's poshest (count the rollers, jags, mercs and volvos in the car park), a boutique nursery specialising in good quality plants including a great range of topiary, camellias and perennials. Customer service (trained staff to give horticultural advice and a landscaping service, Parker's Garden Solutions). There is a good range of tools and a really upmarket gift show-

Nurseries & garden supplies

room with interesting teak furniture and desirable decorative objects.
- 45 Tennyson Rd, Turramurra, ph 9487 3888.

Materials in the Raw
A complete one-stop for all garden materials including mulch, compost, pebbles, gravel, pots and a free trailer service to help you haul bulk materials home. There are five outlets conveniently positioned round the Sydney area so that there will be one not too far away from you.
- 619 Hume Highway, Casula, ph 9821 1132. Also at Gladesville, ph 9817 4377; Guildford, ph 9892 3000; Menai, ph 9543 2233; Penrith, ph 9627 5919.

Elders Stockmans
The place to go if you are into bulk buying – you might get a lifetime's supply in one hit. A wide range of fertilisers, sprays, good tools, gates, fencing, stockfeeds, pet and bird food – the whole farm bit.
- 282 Newline Rd, Dural, ph 9651 1222. Also at Camden, ph (02) 4655 9235; Riverstone, ph 9627 2602; Windsor South, ph (02) 4577 3705.

Shirley Stackhouse

Office furniture

Imagine if dialling for a complete office was as easy as ordering a pizza – now that would be nice. Well, it actually is possible these days. Every home office needs a photocopier, fax machine and filing cabinet, but comfortable, aesthetically pleasing furniture is hard to get. So with ergonomics the buzzword of the '90s office, you may find out that a good gas-lift chair is just a phone call away.

Studio Wilkhahn
At the top end of the market, Wilkhahn supplies high-quality German-designed chairs and Dutch-designed desk and filing systems. Its modular desks are adaptable, which is ideal for the oddly-shaped home office. As you would expect for the price, its furniture is pleasing to the eye.
- Level 6, 227 Elizabeth St, City, ph 9264 6588.

Grosvenor Antique Centre
This store sells furniture from the days when the mention of gas-lift chairs would have earned you an appointment with the executioner for witchcraft. If you prefer elegance to practicality in your home-office, try antique fittings. This store holds stock of 19th and early 20th century desks, bookcases, clocks and prints. And, you never know, you might even find an old-style telephone.
- 216 Pacific Highway, Lindfield, ph 9416 1779.

Resource Office Pty Ltd
Offering the full range of ergo chairs, from the executive style to the simple meeting-room chair. All chairs exceed the Australian occupational health and safety standards, and are reasonably priced.
- 37 Shepherd St, Chippendale, ph 9281 3303.

Affordable Office Furniture
This is the place to go for a range of ergonomical chairs such as the Therapod, the Synchro and even the Managerial (with gas-lift, action swivel and headrest). They will deliver in the metropolitan area.
- Warehouse 13, 7 Packard Ave, Castle Hill, ph 9899 4359.

Total Office Solutions
The place to go if you'd rather sit back, relax and let someone else plan your office. It has fitted out offices for American Express and the Australian Stock Exchange. But if it's an exclusive leg system you're after, you may want to check out its range of accessories.
- Level 1, 2-14 Mountain St, Ultimo, ph 9281 3638.

Officeworks
More for the home office. Its stock stationery and office equipment include fax machines, shredders and photocopiers. If you ever get a copy of their pamphlet, you may be lucky enough to get a bonus lipstick with your next Magic Tape order.
- Ph 131 533 (orders); 131 505 (inquiries).

Melanie Pattison & Steve Samuelson

Opera

see also classical music
Sydney is Australia's opera city, home of the national company Opera Australia, which gives more performances of classic and (just occasionally) contemporary works in Sydney than in any other State capital. Australia's first operatic performance took place in Sydney in 1796 – an English ballad opera by William Shield called The Poor Soldier. Sydney was also the home of diva Dame Joan Sutherland, who helped put the city on the map musically as her career blossomed overseas. Sydneysiders enjoy their opera in many forms. Crowds topping 100,000 go to Opera in the Park, a Sydney Festival summer tradition. The best tickets for Opera House performances cost upward of $100 but standing room only is a reasonable option. Traditionalists support the venerable Rockdale Municipal Opera Company (ph 9562 1832) while more adventurous souls tap into the exotic theatrical originality of Opera Project Inc (ph 9516 3762). Between these extremes, Music Theatre Sydney (ph 9310 3716) is making up Australian creative ground that was lost to Melbourne for a few years by concentrating on new operas written by Australians.

Sydney Opera House
The building that was Australia's coming of age in the arts – 17 turbulent years in the making from Joern Utzon's competition win to its opening in 1973 – finished up with a rather small and not entirely satisfactory opera theatre. But it will always be an icon and there are many advantages in a smaller theatre for singers and audiences, who benefit from its intimacy.
- Bennelong Point, ph 9250 7777: www.soh.nsw.gov.au

Opera Australia
Mainstay of operatic performance in Australia, the national opera company has summer and winter seasons at the Sydney Opera House, presenting about 16 operas in new and revived productions. Geographical isolation makes its high quality core ensemble of local singers both essential and a rarity, topped up by expatriate and overseas stars.
- Opera Centre, 480 Elizabeth St, Surry Hills, ph 9319 1088: www.opera.australia.org.au.

Opera-Opera
A Sydney-based monthly publication, *Opera-Opera* is tops for information on opera in Sydney and beyond. It also has 150 opera videos in stock, plus librettos and scores, many self-published. Subscriptions $44 a year.
- Ph 9247 2264.

Michael's Music Room
This shop's diverse selection of opera CDs just pips HMV's city store as the greatest temptation for collectors of opera on record.
- 19 Town Hall Arcade, City, ph 9267 1351.

Performing Arts Bookshop
Opera books from basic to esoteric.
- 280 Pitt St, City, ph 9267 2257.

Friends of Opera Australia
Joining fee from $50 for activities including lectures, dress rehearsals and introductions to new productions by the creative team and singers.
- Ph 9699 1099.

Jill Sykes

Further information

- See Sydney Morning Herald Metro and CitySearch for listings
- Radio: John Cargher's Singers of Renown, ABC Radio National 4pm Saturday or 6am Sunday. See press listings for programs on ABC Classic FM and 2MBS-FM
- Sydney Conservatorium Opera, for studies and student performances, ph 9351 1222

Outdoor dining

Let's face it, Sydney is best enjoyed outdoors rather than in, and that goes double for dining. Sydneysiders love eating on balconies, verandas, courtyards and streetside tables – anywhere the food comes laced with fresh air and garnished with sunshine. There is usually something nice to look at (water, if you're lucky), some shade when you need it, and a tree or something green nearby, even if it's just parsley.

Catalina Rose Bay

Sit on the beautiful sweep of balcony with the harbour lapping at your feet as you sip chardonnay, and watch the pelicans and seaplanes take off and land. Throw in some oysters, a little sushi or maybe some vitello tonnato, and pretend you never have to go home.

- 1 Sunderland Ave, Rose Bay, ph 9371 0555.

Watermark

The water's so close you could almost reach and touch it from your terrace table. This is one of Sydney's favourite sun traps, made even more enjoyable by chef Kenneth Leung's beautifully conceived, Asian-inspired dishes.

- 2a The Esplanade, Balmoral Beach, ph 9968 3433.

Pavilion on the Park

There's nothing like a walk in the park, unless of course you're eating in it. Slip into your moulded Philippe Starck chair, and take up a prime people-watching position on the balcony as you tuck into Anthony Musarra's beautifully crafted Mod Oz food.

- 1 Art Gallery Rd, The Domain, ph 9232 1322.

Mezzaluna

Sitting on the sunny back deck at Mezzaluna is like being handed Sydney on a plate. Everything about this meticulously run restaurant is so gloriously Italian that even good old St Mary's on the skyline looks positively Florentine.

- 123 Victoria St, Potts Point, ph 9357 1988.

Wockpool Darling Harbour

There are heaps of things to do and see at Darling Harbour, but they can all wait until after lunch. Book a table outside and watch the action close up as you enjoy the best Modern Asian food outside of Modern Asia. Don't miss the chilli salt squid or the Sichuan duck with Mandarin pancakes.

- Panasonic IMAX Theatre, Darling Harbour, ph 9211 9888.

Terry Durack

Outdoor furniture

Transforming your bit of Sydney turf into an outdoor room is easy. Simply turn a potential no-go space into an outdoor living room by adding some great furniture. Designs, colours and finishes depend on personal preference. But even so, there are a handful of products that shine out among the rest.

Outdoor furniture

Australian Squatters Chair Company

For more than 10 years this company has been manufacturing good-value Australian teak furniture from its Dee Why based factory. Everything is well made with mortice and tenon joints and comes with a 10-year guarantee. The range is endless with a variety of garden benches including the popular Lutyens design plus folding slatted chairs, squatters chairs, pool lounges, adirindak chairs, canvas directors chairs, swing seats, rocking chairs and recliners. And there is also a range of imported Indonesian folding tables and chairs which are more reasonably priced from $150.
- 5 Vista Street, Mosman, ph 9968 2291.

Barlow

This is the place to find good affordable metal Italian cafe chairs and tables. Great designs in aluminium, vinyl wicker, polypropylene and timber. Headache-free.
- 42 Alberto Street, Lilyfield, ph 9555 1333.

de de ce

Great editions of contemporary outdoor furniture with clean lines and simple materials from Jasper Morrison, Mark Newson, Alberto Meda, Eero Saarinen and modern designers. Pricey, but museum-worthy. Check out the Alias Outdoor range of furniture with dark grey powder-coated steel frames designed by Belotti including chairs and chaises with polyester net upholstery in black or white and tables and trolleys with glass inserts. Also stocks the covetable Alias Frane chaise, foot stool and easy chair with natural anodised aluminium tubing and PVC coated mesh upholstery in eight different colours. The Cappellini Lima easy chair and foot stool by Jasper Morrison comes with polypropylene slats in blue, green or white. You can also see (and order) Mark Newson's Orgone large dog-bone shaped plastic chaise or Felt fibreglass chair in six different colours. Most recent addition is the Knoll Bertoia range of tables and chairs which can be ordered with vinyl upholstery for outdoor use.
- 263 Liverpool Street, East Sydney, ph 9360 2722.

Cotswold Garden Furniture

This company pioneered teak garden furniture in Sydney more than 15 years ago. It stocks a full range of quality Burmese plantation teak furniture that you can expect to last. There is everything from chairs and tables to benches, recliners and pool beds. A recent addition to the Cotswold collection is a range of woven-fibre verandah furniture that is made in brown paper twisted around wire to resemble cane. It comes in natural or can be custom coloured to order, but you have to drag it indoors at night.
- 42 Hotham Parade, Artarmon, ph 9906 3686.

Freedom

The source of useful, modern outdoor furniture that is cheap and well-designed. Designs come in every shape and size imaginable from director and steamer chairs to bistro tables and chairs in powder-coated metal and French-style cafe folding tables and chairs. Also a variety of smart designs in colourful plastic, woven plastic and timber.
- 247 Condamine St, Balgowlah, ph 9948 0238. Also eight other locations, ph 9951 9000.

Kalinka

The source of good decorative French garden furniture. Stockists of a massive selection of around 100 different bistro chairs in timber and metal dating from the 19th century to the mid 20th century priced from $120 to $400. And always more than 20 different tables to choose from, priced from $400 to $1,200. Grand and florid English and French benches in cast iron priced from $1,500 to $4,000.
- 281c Old South Head Rd, Bondi, ph 9300 0406.

Melissa Walker Smith

Paint

Paint manufacturers call it offering a choice, we prefer to call it creating confusion. When faced with the vast array of products on offer, sorting the good from the bad becomes impossible. Most of us end up choosing by brand (a word-of-mouth recommendation always helps) and according to price.

Amazing Paint Discounts

There are more than 10 discount outlets in Sydney selling Dulux, Wattyl and Taubmans products to the public at rock bottom prices.
- 105 Oxford St, Bondi Junction, ph 9389 0736. Also at Camperdown; Maroubra Junction; Marrickville; North Ryde; Padstow; Randwick; St Marys; Seven Hills; Willoughby.

Dulux Trade Centres

Choosing a paint here is not easy. There is a full range of quality acrylic, enamel and plastic paints in thousands of different colours. Famous for its White Birch, Dairy Cream, Burmese Beige, Potters Clay and Beacon Hill.
- 324 Cleveland St, Surry Hills, ph 9319 6453; 613 Pacific Highway, Chatswood, ph 9412 2411. Also at many other locations. Inquiries: ph 132 525.

Dumaster Paint Discounts

Get your discount paint here. If you're uncertain of what's what in paint, don't worry because the Vecchio brothers will point you in the right direction. For more than 10 years they have been supplying the public with big brand paints at trade prices.
- 24 Burwood Rd, Enfield, ph 9747 6728.

3D Paint Stores

The buying muscle of this national co-op means great deals on quality paint at any of their independent Sydney outlets. The prices at each store varies, so its worth shopping around. Check out the Yellow Pages for your nearest outlet. Leading painters recommend these members of the 3D paint group:
- Hornsby Paint Warehouse, 89 Hunter St, Hornsby, ph 9477 7122; Merilux Paint'n'Paper, 577 Parramatta Rd, Leichhardt, ph 9569 3744.

Murobond Coatings

Smart Sydney renovators head straight here for its brilliant cement paint for exterior surfaces. More recently, the company has developed Murowash – a premium waster-based paint that can be used indoors or out on virtually any surface including metal and aluminium. A big favourite with architects who like it for its colour accuracy and simplicity.
- 27 Dickson Ave, Artarmon, ph 9906 7299.

Porter's Original Paints

Sydney's preferred painter Peter Lewis has inspired a whole generation to splash out on limewash. He revived the look of wishy washy walls in singing colours and has more recently developed Limecote an acrylic paint that achieves the same pleasing decay as trad aged finishes. And which can be successfully applied to plastic, timber and metal. Also great line of own-brand cement paints, plaster, acrylics, milk paint, distemper and special finish products. Also specialises in corrosive solutions for verdigris, rust and steel. Porter's also offers courses on how to paint.
- 895 Bourke St, Waterloo, ph 9698 5322. Also at Bondi Junction, ph 9389 2228, and Willoughby, ph 9958 0753.

Melissa Walker Smith

Painters

see also interior designers & decorators

The ideal painter must be a craftsperson, not a tradesperson, according to the Painters Association. This means he or she should be adept, not only with a paintbrush, but in the art of decorating, colour consultation and restoration. Sixty per cent of a painter's work is preparation but a good painter will also be familiar with paperhanging, marbling and stencilling. These are the top five painters from The Sydney Morning Herald Domain section's Tradespeople of the Year awards. You can also call the Painters Association on 9746 2477 or the Master Builders Association on 9281 3511. The Painters Association recommends asking for references from previous clients, checking trade licences with the Department of Fair Trading and never accepting the cheapest quote.

Roberto Adoncello
Wallpaper, restoring plaster working, ceiling work and decoration, house painting. Trade licence R65365.
■ ph 9744 1909 or 0417 228 283.

Lynne Campbell, Wall FX
Works in Sydney and interstate on painted finishes, design and decoration and colour consultations. Mostly interior work. Trade licence R96083.
■ ph 018 475 844 or 9436 0662.

William Franca
Works mainly on the North Shore in all aspects of painting and decorating. Residential work includes both interior and exterior and spray painting. Free quotes, 7 days. Trade licence R89648.
■ ph 9488 9448 or 0418 608 061.

John Le Carpentier
Painter and decorator, specialises in domestic work. Trade licence 52898C.
■ ph 9987 4406.

Lou Montuoro
Domestic and commercial painting, specialising in interior painting, decorating and paper hanging. Trade licence R53467.
■ ph 9417 2340.

Penny Harrison

Party supplies

see also **catering, event management, function venues, cakes & pastries, beer, wine, liquor stores**

What's your style? A Renaissance banquet with French champagne, snapping paparazzi and a six-figure budget? Or a barbie – pass the cold beer, please? The sight of a sturdy jumping castle and jugs of cordial is likely to send a herd of five-year-olds into raptures. A good party should have certain tangible elements: a comfortable or interesting venue, enough appropriate food, plenty to drink, 'up' music (Wiggles to Barry White) and possibly an attractive theme. Sometimes, these elements aren't enough to whip up a dull crowd, but when you're the host your job is to think positive. Some parties work with no planning. When impressions are important, consider professional assistance.

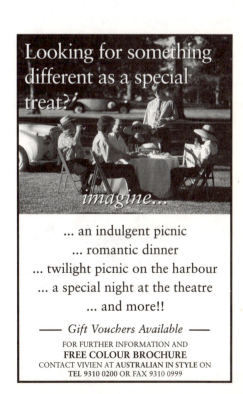

Looking for something different as a special treat?

imagine...

... an indulgent picnic
... romantic dinner
... twilight picnic on the harbour
... a special night at the theatre
... and more!!

—— *Gift Vouchers Available* ——

FOR FURTHER INFORMATION AND
FREE COLOUR BROCHURE
CONTACT VIVIEN AT **AUSTRALIAN IN STYLE** ON
TEL 9310 0200 OR FAX 9310 0999

Party supplies

Pages Hire Centre
Pages Hire has three locations across Sydney, catering to every aspect of your party. Page's motto is 'you can hire everything but the guests'.
- Kogarah, ph 9587 1755; Chatswood, ph 9417 3381; Lidcombe, ph 9646 4000.

Partytime Hire
These are the people to go to if you're a novice at hosting parties. They can do a free site inspection so the guesswork is taken out of installing your marquee, awning and dance floor. If you're still feeling a little nervous about your choices – or the guest list, for that matter – there's a 24-hour hotline.
- Unit 6/331 High St, Chatswood, ph 9417 7477.

Planet Entertainment
Specialises in providing interactive entertainment for parties and businesses. Erect your own inflatable rock-climbing wall, bungee jump or have guests hop into sumo suits for a friendly wrestle.
- 18 Susan St, Annandale, ph 9519 0500.

Reverse Garbage
Feeling creative? This recycling centre has everything from unused cigarette filters to used theatre sets. A great place for cheap party decoration ideas.
- 142 Addison Rd, Marrickville, ph 9569 3132.

Kate Ryan

Personal trainers

see also fitness clubs, martial arts
If it's good enough for Madonna, it's good enough for me. Work it, baby, work it. Sydney, if you hadn't noticed, is a city that worships the body beautiful. All tanned. All taut. All toned. Beef up those pecs and work off that butt. And if gym membership isn't enough, the next step is a PT: a personal trainer. Yep, even amateur exercise needs some one-on-one coaching for those tummy curls, sit-ups and star jumps. There are about 500 accredited personal trainers in Sydney, most of whom are associated with a gym.

Andrew Markham, The Personal Training Dept
A posse of personal trainers for rehabilitation, sports training, weight loss and general fitness.
- Contact the Bodyline Fitness Centres: North Sydney, ph 9956 5533; Castle Hill, ph 9899 4299; and Bankstown, ph 9708 5033.

Clinton Kerr
No pain, no gain – boxing, kick-boxing, boxercise and weight training in a gym where you smell the sweat.
- Eastern Suburbs Police and Community Youth Club, 1 Underwood St, Paddington, ph 9331 5921.

Janet Norton
More than 15 personal trainers to improve body shape, muscular strength, help with injury rehabilitation, offer nutritional advice and programs.
- Chatswood Fitness, 1a/372 Eastern Valley Way, Chatswood, ph 9417 4277.

Keiran Barry
University-qualified trainers who specialise in massage, fitness training, fat loss, sports-specific training, group sessions, nutritional advice and house visits.
- The Energy Lab, 232 Campbell Pde, Bondi, ph 9130 4921.

Peter Cosgrove
Personal training in a spacious air-conditioned gym with the latest high-tech electronic equipment.
- Club Physical, cnr Port Hacking Rd and Princes Hwy, Sylvania, ph 9522 4155.

Storm Hughes
A 24-hour gym providing personal trainers for full fitness assessment and tailored individual workouts.
- City Gym, 107 Crown St, East Sydney, ph 9360 6247.

Dugald Jellie

Pest control

Who to call when it's cockroach infestation season and there's an army of them camped in your kitchen? And how can you be sure the treatment will be effective, but not kill the dog or make the cat glow? A few things to remember: ask the pest controller to show you his/her licence (it is mandatory in NSW to have one). You should also find out how long the company has been in business; how much experience it has had with your problem; whether it has professional indemnity insurance.

Flick
A large pest-control company that operates throughout the Sydney region. It uses gels and baits, placed where they can't be seen or smelt, and are safe around children and pets.
- Ph 9418 7422 or 13 1440.

Systems Pest Management
It describes itself as an environmentally responsible pest-control company. Toxins are not used, but low-hazard chemicals are sometimes employed.
- Ph 9564 1614.

Australian Pest Controllers Association
The group recommends companies on the basis of the type of pests to be eradicated and the suburb you live in. It also will intervene on behalf of customers if there is a dispute. The organisation represents a small number of companies only, but its help may be better that picking a name from the phone book.
- Ph 9771 2533.

Chris Dobney

Pets

Sydneysiders now have some 500,000 dogs (about one dog for every six people), not to mention all the cats, birds, fish, rabbits, chickens, ferrets, guinea pigs, horses, mice and rats. So where do you find the most fabulous facilities for pets – anything from a naturopath to treat your cat's anxiety attacks to an award-winning groomer to make your dog look good enough to take to the Cointreau Ball?

Adelar Pet Motel Boarding Kennels
Set in landscaped country surroundings. Dogs sleep in brick kennels with their own grassy backyards; the cats are in a brick building set in a U-shape around an internal courtyard full of plants where they bask in their own three-level, cushion-strewn sleeping quarters. Dogs $12-$20 per day; cats $10 per day.
- 14 Hulls Rd, Leppington, ph 9606 5955.

Contented Cat Inn
Specialises in treating your cat like you do at home – or even better. Plenty of grooming, attention and affection. Cats are fed whatever they usually eat at home, $9 per day.
- 1403 Old Northern Rd, Glenorie, ph 9652 1162.

Hanrob Pet Care Centre
Huge complex which offers the convenience of a free pick-up and delivery service to 53 veterinary hospitals around Sydney. Dogs have runs with adjoining sleeping quarters, piped

music, automatic water drinkers. Daily brushing, play and exercise available (for a fee). Dogs from $14 per day; cats from $11. There's also in-house obedience lessons under head trainer Steve Austin.
- Lot 927 Princes Highway, Heathcote, ph 9520 6633.

Home Alone
Liz Scott provides a cheerfully impeccable and professional pet care service. She walks dogs or takes care of pets in your home (from $15 per visit or walk). She has been walking those dogs, rain or shine, for six years.
- Ph 9564 3938.

Monika's Mouse, Moggy & Mutt Minding
Monika has been pet pampering for six years. Smaller critters such as birds, mice and rabbits are looked after in her home. Larger animals are visited, fed and exercised (dogs walked individually). Rates from $15 per visit.
- 12 Hudson Close, Turramurra, ph 9488 7189.

Canine Good Citizen Courses
A Canine Good Citizen Course teaches small groups of dog owners how to make their dogs fit into their family and their lives. It's a friendly, fun, few weeks, which teach humans how to be the leader of the pack. For details, contact the NSW Animal Welfare League.
- Ph 9606 9333.

Animal Antics
The place for designer pet accessories, even collars where the bandana is part of the collar (won't that save a lot of time?) Toys, cat and dog baskets and, if you have $1,200 to lavish on your pet, snap up their gorgeous paw print rug.
- 333 South Dowling St, Darlinghurst, ph 9331 8144.

Four Legged Friends
One of the few places where you can buy pina colada flavoured shampoo for your dog. Yuppy puppy heaven, but also a large pet shop with an excellent range of accessories. Sells pets and an exotic array of pampered cats such as Himalayan, Persian and chinchillas.
- 107 Military Rd, Neutral Bay, ph 9953 1695.

Cremorne Pet Centre
Great for the latest thing from America, anything from funky collars and leads to the latest in jogging-with-dog accessories. Only mice and fish sold on premises.
- 104 Spofforth St, Cremorne, ph 9909 2174.

Campbelltown Pet and Aquarium Centre
With two shops, this is one of the largest retailers in the pet industry. Great for anything to do with fish, from ponds to marine and tropical fish. One of the few shops accredited by the NSW Canine Council and Pet Industry Joint Advisory Council to sell pedigree puppies from approved breeders.
- Shop 6 and 7, 266 Queen St, Campbelltown, ph 4625 1838.

NSW Animal Welfare League
Do your good deed by adopting an abandoned or stray animal, at their West Hoxton complex: puppies and dogs $110, kittens and cats $70. The excellent Manly-Warringah-Pittwater AWL has kittens for $100 and cats for $70. All animals desexed, microchipped, wormed, vaccinated and de-flea'd. The AWL has a full-time trainer who makes home visits to help the dog settle in or help you through a free 10-week behaviour modification training course.
- 45 Herley Ave, West Hoxton, ph 9606 9333; 160 Mona Vale Road, Ingleside, ph 9913 8731.

RSPCA
Another place to buy a stray or abandoned animal: $100 for dogs or puppies, $70 for cats and kittens. Open 9am to 3pm seven days a week (except public holidays).
- 201 Rookwood Rd, Yagoona, ph 9709 5433.

Canine Coiffure

Susan MacDonald efficiently runs this grooming service, right under the Warringah Animal Hospital. Animals are kept in cages but the room is airconditioned. Grooming starts from $23, pick-up and delivery $15. Open 7.30am to 6pm.
- 104 Spofforth St, Cremorne, ph 9909 2174.

Sydney Pet Grooming Centre

A 'pet salon' with its own taxi service – the taxis even have airconditioning and seat belts. Specialising in clipping cats' and rabbits' claws. No sedatives or cages. Prices $10 for clipping and grooming, Monday to Saturday.
- 333 Forest Rd, Bexley, ph 9597 7270.

Messy Mutts

Warm, friendly, open-plan business, where pets are not kept in cages but on their leads. They'll 'style' every dog, from mixed breeds to pure poodles. Open 9 to 5, Tuesday to Saturday, by appointment only.
- 56 Moore St, Leichhardt, ph 9564 5010.

Tytaff Grooming

Everything from basic bath and groom, to creative clipping, nails, even hair colouring. Prices star from $35, open Monday to Saturday, 9 to 'when we finish'.
- Shop 8, 201 High St, Willoughby, ph 9967 2740.

Centennial Park

Centennial Park has sections devoted to dogs where pets are allowed to run free, with drinking areas, bushwalks and plenty of open space. Afterwards, tether the mutt outside a cafe and have brunch or coffee where he can sit and gaze at you adoringly. Queens Park next door is also a friendly, off-leash exercise park.
- Grand Drive, Centennial Park, ph 9339 6699.

Botany Dog Beach

Not a very glorious stretch of beach but your dog will love it. It's a long sliver that runs from the airport to the ports. Dogs are welcome and the shallow water makes it ideal for paddling canines as well as swimmers.
- Sir Joseph Banks Park, Foreshore Rd, Botany, ph 9317 0555 (Botany Bay Council).

Tivoli Esplanade, Como

Sutherland has an excellent free-range, off-leash exercise area, down by the mangrove swamps. Fully fenced in, with rubbish bins for faeces (plastic bags provided) and big tubs of water dogs can drink from or dive into. Contact Sutherland Shire Council.
- Ph 9710 0333.

Rossmore Dog Pool

A clean, well-maintained saltwater pool in a rural setting behind the Rossmore Vet Surgery. Much favoured by greyhound trainers, but also excellent for exercising dogs with limb problems, recovering from surgery or just breeds who love to swim. $2.50 per swim.
- 651 Bringelly Rd, Rossmore, ph 9606 6984.

Sirius Cove

Adjacent to Sirius Park, Sirius Cove offers an increasingly rare chance in Sydney to exercise your dog on both the park and the beach. Open all day Monday to Friday, but on weekends or public holidays you can only walk until 9am and after 4pm. When the tide is out, the beach offers a massive stretch of sand, reaching back to the park where dogs are allowed to be exercised off lead.
- Down Illawarra St, Mosman, ph 9978 4000 (Mosman Council).

The Pet Health Food Shop

This shop, owned by Beeline Natural Solutions, specialises in dog and cat health food and customised diets. You can pick up a standard weekly food pack, containing raw chicken, lamb, liver, heart, ricotta cheese and herb/fruit/vegie pulp, plus chewing bones and healthy treats. Dogs and owners are welcome to drop in to the big warehouse to sample

food or use the canine play area. Open daily 9am to 7pm, Saturday 9am to 5pm and Sunday 10am to 4pm.
- 4 Annandale Street, Annandale, ph 9560 9666.

Pets Pantry

A light, bright, airy pet shop, plenty of room to move around to see the wide range of stock. Huge array of pet foods, such as Eukenuba, and it is easy to get helpful advice from the attentive staff.
- Gray St, Bondi Junction, ph 9387 1912.

Jane Freeman

Photography

see also art galleries, books, museums

Sydney has enchanted its photographers for more than 150 years. Investigate the works of Harold Cazneaux, Max Dupain, Olive Cotton or David Potts and discover images that have defined the city. Whatever your skills as a photographer, this most photogenic of cities will challenge them. The camera's love affair with Sydney is most passionate during the 'magic' hours just after dawn and just before nightfall, when lights radiate from a thousand skyscrapers and homes. There is a lively, growing community of professional photographers in Sydney, from traditional photojournalists to experimental artists. A network of galleries and curators supports this new wave of contemporary Australian photography, and there are opportunities for aspiring professional and amateurs to study and improve their craft.

Lorrie Graham

Few photographers have seeped more into the texture of modern Sydney than this typically durable Australian photojournalist with an abrasive, poetic sense of observation. She can capture nuns or punks on Bondi beach with equal sensitivity.

Roger Scott

The quiet achiever of the Australian 'Decisive Moment' school. Works passionately on self-assignments and is one of the few Australian photojournalists to be consistently amusing.

Robyn Stacey

A digitally based photographic artist and remarkable teacher.

Jon Lewis

His definitive coverage of Bondi Beach in the '80s remains unsurpassed. Lewis has also taught photography at Goulburn TAFE and the University of Technology Sydney for a number of years. Other artists enlivening the Sydney photographic scene are **Wendy McDougall**, **Bill Moseley**, **Emmanuel Angelicas**, **Marco Bok**, **Louise Lister**, **Gilbert Bel-Bachir** and **Peter Elliston**.

NSW State Library

Home to a superb collection of contemporary and historical photographs of Sydney, curated by Alan Davies. The work, wit and scholarship of freelance curator Anne Loxley has also been seen here. Houses the Image Library, which provides a photographic picture research service.
- Macquarie St, City, ph 9273 1482: www.slnsw.gov.au

Art Gallery Of NSW

An impressive exhibition program.
- Art Gallery Rd, City, ph 9225 1878: www.art-gallery.nsw.gov.au

STILLS Gallery

After six years in a tiny Paddington terrace, directors Cathy Freedman and Sandy Edwards have moved to an elegant, former film studio, where their commitment to contemporary Australian photography is on display.
- 36 Gosbell St, Paddington, ph 9331 7775.

Josef Lebovic Gallery
Consistently exhibits a rich variety of 19th- and 20th-century photography.
- 34 Paddington St, Paddington, ph 9332 1840.

Byron MAPP Gallery
Superb international exhibitions and a wide selection of Australian photographers. Also carries an excellent range of photographic books for sale, as do nearby book stores Ariel and Berkelouw.
- 178 Oxford St, Paddington, ph 9331 2926.

Photographer's Showcase
Lewis Morley, famous for documenting London in the '60s, often appears embarrassed at having to charge for work he would display for love alone at this unpretentious space.
- 76 Parramatta Rd, Stanmore, ph 9516 5191.

Point Light
Relatively new to Sydney, but has already gathered impressive credentials. From the standard of a recent students' exhibition, co-director Gordon Undy can be regarded as one of Sydney's premier photography teachers.
- 465 Glebe Point Rd, Glebe, ph 9552 3304.

Australian Centre for Photography
Explores 'the cutting edge of the photographic experience', and occasionally stumbles into the abyss of obscurantism. The ACP also has a fine teaching workshop, accepting private students.
- 257 Oxford St, Paddington, ph 9332 1455.

European Cameras
In a tiny showroom, Phil Stekhoven and Bruce Searle sell quality new and second-hand cameras.
- 178 Oxford St, Paddington, ph 9360 6383.

Fletchers Fotographic
A large, traditional camera store which, like Paxtons and G&V Imaging, has a strong commitment to the growing digital camera market.
- 317 Pitt St, City, ph 9267 6146; 253 Church St, Parramatta, ph 9891 5545.

L&P Photographics Supplies
Stocks a large range of digital cameras for amateurs and professionals. Richard Williamson and Andrew Sala, resident digital experts, welcomes inquiries.
- 96 Reserve Rd, Artarmon, 9906 2733.

Charing Cross Photo
Will process your film and then bind finished prints into an elegant booklet for a small added charge.
- 261 Bronte Rd Waverley, ph 9369 5783.

Windsor Lab
Provides a more comprehensive service (with larger prints) and caters for black-and-white and colour photography.
- 119a Alexander St, Crows Nest, ph 9438 1261.

Robert McFarlane

Pizza

see also Italian restaurants, Italian Sydney
Ah, pizza! Real pizza that is, with a deliciously crisp crust, all golden and still smokey from the wood-fired oven. And to think, once upon a time pizza was something you had to be drunk to eat.

The eDGE
The eDGE was one of the first restaurants to pioneer two dining traits that have now become de rigeur in Sydney: the wood-fired pizza and the no-bookings policy. Mind you, these pizzas are worth waiting around for,

Pizza

especially the legendary seafood pizza and the pumpkin pizza with feta and olives.
- 60 Riley St, East Sydney, ph 9360 1372.

La Disfida

Purists swear by Rino Lattanzio's pizzas. The dough is made with the addition of extra virgin olive oil while the pizzas themselves are cooked in an ornate wood-fired oven. If you had your heart set on a Hawaiian or a Ned Kelly, you might just be in the wrong place.
- 109 Ramsay Rd, Haberfield, ph 9798 8299.

Napoli in Bocca

If you like pizza bases thick and your toppings piled high then this not the place for you (neither, by the way, is Italy). Neapolitan Ben Riccio makes his pizzas in the Neapolitan manner, with thin, delicate bases and just enough smeared tomato, or olives, or mushrooms, or mozzarella to let you know they're there.
- 73 Dalhousie St, Haberfield, ph 9798 4096.

Uno Uno

Marino Maioli, who many will remember from his Lucio days, has brought his finely honed style to this simple, easy-going pizza and pasta spot. Pizzas are thin, classy numbers running from a classic margherita to a fresh grilled calamaretti with rocket and shaved parmesan.
- 152 Liverpool St, Paddington, ph 9361 0520.

Terry Durack

Plumbers

The winner of the 1998 Sydney Morning Herald Domain section's Tradesperson of the Year award, run by the weekly home section Domain, was plumber Rick Lucas. Plumbing crises have to be among the worst of all domestic emergencies, so having a good plumber on hand is absolutely vital.

Use this list of tradesmen, who all received numerous nominations in Domain's awards or contact the Master Plumbers Association on 9797 7055 or the Master Builders Association on 9281 3511.

Matt Etherington

Specialises in small and medium commercial developments and maintenance work. Trade licence L13697.
- Roseriver Pty Ltd, ph 9482 2722 or 0418 445 919.

Bruce Gammie

Works along the northern beaches on small domestic jobs and maintenance. Trade licence L2054.
- Ph 9971 4150 or 014 034 341.

Rick Lucas

Fulfils general plumbing and roofing needs for domestic maintenance and renovations. Trade licence L7249.
- Ph 018 294 788 or 9736 1374.

Anthony Ross

Works in the North Shore area in general plumbing jobs including drains, gas fittings, maintenance, roof repairs and leaks. Trade licence L12465.
- Ph 9415 2120 or 0418 287 155.

Nick Storey

Works in Balmain and Inner West area on renovation and maintenance work. Trade licence L6834.
- Ph 0412 473 084.

Penny Harrison

Pool

This popular game has slowly but surely taken over Sydney. From corner pubs to ritzy clubs, it's rare to find a venue without a pool table. The pubs are the main players, but their style has changed a lot in the past couple of years to accommodate the increased popularity of the game.

Beach Road Hotel
The Pavilion Bar boasts 28 pool tables, a well-stocked bar and live entertainment on the weekends.
- 71 Beach Rd, Bondi Beach, ph 9130 7247.

Sutherland's Hotel
Has 11 tables and an energetic atmosphere, with music being the key element.
- 2 Broadway, City, ph 9211 2321.

Green Park Hotel
Only three tables here, but the competition's fierce.
- 360 Victoria St, Darlinghurst, ph 9380 5311.

Billiards & Snooker Association of NSW
A good way to get in touch with other players and find out about competitions and 'friendly' games with professionals.
- 296 Pitt St, City, ph 9267 6894.

Elite Pool Table & Amusement Machines
Elite's specialty is to recloth and repair commercial and home tables. It also hires out tables, mostly to pubs and clubs, though they will do daily hire for parties.
- 31b Chester St, Petersham, ph 0418 293 448.

Action 8 Ball Tables
Action manufactures and retails world-standard tables. It also repairs tables and cues, on site if necessary. Short-term rental is available.
- 28 Lawson St, Balmain, ph 018 618 279.

Nicola Shenton

Poultry & game

Sydney isn't as well catered for in this field as it should be. The good stuff is there, but tends to be sent directly to restaurants rather than end up in retail. Perhaps we should all go back to having a chook in the backyard.

Game Birds
A very swish poultry specialist with corn-fed, free-range poussin and quail in the window instead of Gaultier and Escada. There are Double Bay residents who live on their spit-roasted chickens and baked spuds, and others – who actually cook – who rely on the high quality poultry and game, always fresh and always immaculately cleaned and ready to cook. A bit of inside trading: theirs is the best chicken stock in town.
- Shop 32, Cosmopolitan Centre, Double Bay, ph 02 9327 6126.

David Jones
You want free-range, corn-fed? You want two kilograms of chicken wings? You want chicken livers for a pate? You want a whole chook boned, and rolled for you? You want quail, squab, fresh eggs, you name it? Go to David Jones chicken specialist, and just point.
- Market St, City, ph 9266 5544; Westfield Plaza, Bondi Junction, ph 9619 1111.

DeliFarm
Half fresh chicken shop and half a good deli, DeliFarm offers free-range, corn-fed chooks, Thirlemere poultry, Kangaroo Island chickens, and good eggs, alongside AC Butchery's snags, Patchett's Pies and Blackheath Bakery bread.
- Shop 2, Eastpoint Food Fair, New South Head Rd, Edgecliff, ph 9328 7435.

Jill Dupleix

Powerboating

see also waterskiing, fishing

So long as you've got a boat with a motor, you can do Sydney in a day in style. Start with a tour of the best waterfront mansions in the eastern and northern suburbs, then stage your own harbour cruise. Pass all the big sights – Fort Denison, Kirribilli House, the Opera House and Harbour Bridge – into the new 38-berth marina in Darling Harbour, where shopping and eating beckon. Better still head for the Fish Markets in Blackwattle Bay. The marina is free, the prawns and oysters fresh, and there's a baker, bottle shop, deli and fruit and veg for the big lunch out. Continue winding upstream on the Parramatta River, past Sydney's oldest boatshed at Abbotsford Point, to the Olympic site in Homebush Bay. The best anchorages are downstream: Store, Castle Rock or Cobblers beaches, depending on wind direction. When you've done your swimming, weigh anchor and nip across to Doyles at Watsons Bay – one of more than 20 harbourside restaurants that you can get to by powerboat. Devour fish and chips for dinner before slinking off into the night to secluded Bantry Bay or Sugarloaf Bay in upper Middle Harbour, where a peaceful sleep on a public mooring is assured.

If you think Sydney is good by powerboat, wait till you've tried the Hawkesbury River. There you'll find better facilities, more public moorings, less boat traffic and wonderful, deep, calm and well-protected inlets flanked by scribbly gums, sandstone bluffs and lots of wild National Park shores. Cowan Creek is a powerboating mecca.

Store Beach

The best beach in the best harbour in the world. A superb anchorage but you'll need to get there early to find a spot. Super swimming, a clean beach, interesting foreshores with trees and shade for a picnic in summer. Look for the cave on the northern end behind the big boulder where mullet fishermen perch in autumn and wait for the fish to arrive.

Andrew Short Marine

An aluminium dinghy, better known as a tinnie, is where powerboating begins for many. Small enough to roof rack or tow behind the family car, big enough to tour the Harbour, Botany Bay, Port Hacking or the Hawkesbury. Add a 15hp outboard and away you go.

■ 96 Taren Point Rd, Taren Point, ph 9524 2699.

Hunts Marine

The home of family boating since 1943, run by a family of powerboaters and frequented by Sydney families looking for a trailer-boat to keep everyone happy. And there is such a creature – an Australian-made fibreglass Haines Signature or Whittley, or an aluminium Quintrex runabout.

■ 629 Princes Highway, Blakehurst, ph 9546 1324.

Chapman Marine

Sydney's high-performance centre where power is everything and going fast the measure of success. Buy the latest American-made Wellcraft and let the little boats eat your wake as you steam along Sydney Harbour for a lunch spot.

■ Shop 61, Birkenhead Point Marina, ph 9719 8188.

Riviera Sales Sydney

Pleasure is the principle behind the Australian-made Riviera range of 34- to 48-foot flybridge cruisers. Designed for the whole family, from the Harbour to the Hawkesbury and beyond. And when summer arrives, you can head offshore and tow a big lure for a marlin.

■ d'Albora Marina, New Beach Rd, Rushcutters Bay, ph 9363 0000.

Eastsail

Charter a Riviera 33-foot cruiser with twin Cummins turbo-charged 210 hp diesel motors for a fast day out doing 24 knots. You must hold a NSW boating licence and demonstrate some skills to drive it, or hire a skipper. A Riviera 39-foot and a 40-foot sportscruiser are also available for hire.
- d'Albora Marina, New Beach Rd, Rushcutters Bay, ph 9327 1166.

Halvorsen Boats

Reminisce aboard a wonderful wooden Halvorsen hire boat from Bobbin Head. Pack the friends and fishing gear and chug down timeless tree-lined Cowan Creek to an overnight public mooring in Smiths Creek.
- Ku-ring-gai Chase National Park, ph 9457 9011.

Clipper Cruiser Holidays

Powerboating is pleasantly slow aboard these 30- to 34-ft Clipper charter boats. Set sail from Akuna Bay, make Cottage Point a dinner stop, and take in Brooklyn in the morning for local oysters.
- d'Albora Marina, Akuna Bay, ph 9450 0000.

Best marinas

d'Albora Marina at Rushcutters Bay has a 5-Gold Star rating, meaning it's among the world's best. d'Albora Marina Akuna Bay is better again. It has a laundry, gym, general store, bottle shop, restaurant and casual berths.
- Akuna Bay, ph 9486 3000.

David Lockwood

Further information
- Waterways Authority, ph 13 1256
- NSW Boating Industry Association, ph 9438 2077
- NSW Water Ski Association, ph 9552 4311
- Australian Powerboat Association (NSW), ph 4573 6351
- Boating Weather Information, ph 11 541
- The Waterways of Sydney Harbour by Phillip Mathews ($24.95, from Boat Books, ph 9439 1133)

Pre-theatre dining

see also late-night food

Popcorn and a choc top just don't measure up to a nice glass of wine and a plate of delicious food. If there were more of the latter and less of the former, there'd be a lot more movie and theatre fans in Sydney.

BBQ King

When you feel like something no-frills and nourishing, hit the roast duck on noodles, or roast pork and rice. Don't feel you have to hurry either. The George St cinemas, the Capitol theatre and the Entertainment Centre are just around the corner. Open until 2am.
- 18-20 Goulburn St, City, ph 9267 2433.

Casa Asturiana

It opens at 5.30pm. So sit down with a glass of sherry or a white wine, and allow for three tapas dishes per person. With Sydney's cinemaland just a garlic clove's throw away, you could even make it four tapas dishes.
- 77 Liverpool St, City, ph 9264 1010.

Concourse

Being part of the Opera House complex, it's not exactly surprising that the Concourse has become adept at getting out a full Mod Oz meal with all the trimmings and still pack you off in time for the opening curtain. By the time the show's over, the staff will have enough breath back to serve you supper.
- Lower concourse, Sydney Opera House, Bennelong Point, ph 9250 7300.

Pre-theatre dining

la mensa
If you're heading for the Chauvel cinema or maybe the Verona or Academy down the road, this easygoing mod Med canteen is the perfect spot for a quick bite before the show. If the Federation sausages are on, grab 'em. Otherwise try the pastas, the roast Ilabo lamb or any of the light, breezy salads.
- 257 Oxford St, Paddington, ph 9332 2963.

Merrony's
A time and motion expert would have a ball here. Merrony's manages to get out a full meal, beautifully cooked and artfully served in not much more than the time it takes to eat it. With the kitchen open from 5.45pm to 11.30pm, it works just as well post-theatre as pre-theatre.
- 2 Albert St, Circular Quay, ph 9247 9323.

Terry Durack

Pink Panther
Pink Panther have 13 offices in Sydney and can take your files electronically from most common storage media or the Internet. It also has an electronic document distribution network.
- Ph 9660 2222.

Kinko's
The oddly named Kinko's is omnipresent in the United States, and have opened a 24-hour store in Sydney.
- Shop 1, 175 Liverpool St, City, ph 1800 244 432.

Centatime
These book printers can bind your academic thesis or first novel.
- 18 Primrose Ave, Rosebery, ph 9313 7811.

Andrew Khedoori

Printing

We all know about first impressions. If it doesn't look good, there can be an uphill battle. From student essays to business affairs, getting the right printing and photocopying is essential. We've come a long way from the humble photocopier, and services in Sydney reflect the change. There are several chains stretching to many sites in Sydney and opening later than usual business hours – no-one wants to travel too far to get their documents printed, and some people have needs after hours.

Snap Printing
Snap is the largest in Sydney with more than 40 locations. It efficiently caters for general needs, such as letterheads, menus and reports.
- Ph 9630 7744.

Public speaking

Sweaty palms, quavering voice, rubber knees, a deep urge to burst into tears. It's public speaking time. Defeat those nerves with a little help from the professionals. Depending on the nature of the event there are organisations to help you through the most trying speech. Or, better still, hire a professional and really enjoy yourself. Professional speakers start at around $300 to $500 for an average of 45 minutes while big names can cost up to $10,000.

Celebrity Speakers
Looking for a big name? You can't go past Margaret Throsby or Phillip Adams, just a few of the names on CS's books. They also offer personal training for everyone from a shy chairperson to a nervous father of the bride.
- Ph 9251 1333.

Fairfax Communicators

Specialises in the business market with financial luminaries from the Fairfax press including Max Walsh, Robert Gottliebsen, Ross Greenwood and Trevor Sykes and also offering lifestyle speakers.
- ph 1800 240 241.

Dale Carnegie Training

For 85 years has produced brave and eloquent public speakers. $1,995 for a 13-week course.
- ph 9816 1822.

The Speech and Drama Association

Has more than 200 qualified teachers on its books and will give you the details of those in your area. Perfect for polishing a speech or prepping for an audition.
- ph 9498 1537.

Toastmasters

Holds speech craft courses at more than 300 clubs in Sydney. Around $275–$300 for an 8-week course. Phone for details of a club in your area.
- ph 9790 2968.

The Domain

Practise your new skills here every Sunday when speakers from around town sound off about current affairs, aliens and local politics. BYO soap box.

Cerentha Harris

Pubs

see also bars, nightclubs, beer

In the social life of Sydney, the public house is king. Like the city itself, the archetypal Sydney saloon is relaxed, friendly, regularly raucous, sometimes saucy and frequently flashy. There are pubs to dine in, pubs to rock in and pubs to chill out in. There are pubs for blowing off steam on Friday nights and pubs for sipping beer on slow Sunday afternoons. Being in Sydney, some also come with views.

Lord Nelson Brewery Hotel

Opened in 1841, the Lord Nelson is one of Sydney's oldest and best pubs. It has nautical decor, appropriately, and its own microbrewery making beers with names such as Old Admiral, Three Sheets, Victory Bitter and Nelson's Blood. There's a brasserie upstairs, an informal bistro on the ground floor and accommodation available on the top floor.
- 19 Kent St, The Rocks, ph 9251 4044.

Watsons Bay Hotel

The pub is a fairly drab building, but nobody comes for the architecture – they're all out in the waterfront beer garden enjoying spectacular harbour views. Make sure you bring your sunglasses – that west-facing garden can get pretty glary in the afternoon.
- 1 Military Rd, Watsons Bay, ph 9337 4299.

Newport Arms Hotel

On the Pittwater side of Newport, overlooking Church Point, Scotland Island and the Ku-ring-gai Chase National Park, the Newport Arms has views to rival those of the Watsons Bay Hotel. The beer garden is a popular spot, especially on sunny weekends.
- Kalinya St, Newport, ph 9997 4900.

Annandale Hotel

The Annandale has presented quality original music ('everything except middle of the road') seven days a week for 11 years. It offers an intimacy that can't be matched by bigger venues, but it can turn into a sweatbox on busy nights. Highlights in recent years include You Am I (playing under a pseudonym) and Nick Cave's guest appearance with the Dirty Three.
- Cnr Nelson St and Parramatta Rd, Annandale, ph 9550 1078.

Riverview Hotel

A good neighbourhood pub that, some connoisseurs say, pulls Sydney's best draught Guinness. The downstairs bar is styled after an English country pub, while the upstairs restaurant serves modern Australian cuisine. A jazz group, the Robber's Dogs, plays every second

Sunday, alternating with the Irish band Spud. The one thing it doesn't have is a view of the river. Well, not unless you stand on the roof.
- 29 Birchgrove Rd, Balmain, ph 9810 1151.

Benjamin Long

Quitting

Cough, cough, cough, splutter, splutter, cough. Some things are just plain no good for you. We all know our vices – whether it be smoking, bad relationships, alcohol, drugs – but what are we doing to quit the habit? Yes, it's hard; yes, it means a change of lifestyle; and yes, we've promised ourselves umpteen times before that this would be our very last cigarette . . . ever. Well, there's no time like the present to make a real break. Listed below are a batch of organisations that can help us quit . . . forever.

Alcohol and Drug Information Service
ADIS has a 24-hour telephone information service providing counselling, information and referral on alcohol and other drug issues.
- Ph 9361 2111.

Alcoholics Anonymous
There are daily AA meetings across Sydney for people with alcohol problems, organised by those who have shared the experience.
- Ph 9261 0055 or 9799 1199.

Centre for Education and Information on Drugs and Alcohol
CEIDA provides education and information on alcohol, tobacco and illicit drugs (including tranquillisers).
- 24-hour recorded information service: ph 9818 0488 or 1800 816 210 (within NSW). Office hours: ph 9818 0444.

NSW Users & AIDS Association
NUAA provides information, advice and counselling about illicit drugs, AIDS, safe sex, hepatitis B and C.
- Ph 9369 3455 or 1800 644 413.

Quitline
A 24-hour telephone counselling service to help kick the smoking habit. Call the Quitline for tips and advice and for a free copy of the QuitKit.
- Ph 131 848.

Relationships Australia (NSW)
Provides personal and telephone counselling, mediation advice, relationship education programs and workplace programs.
- Ph 9418 8800 or 1800 801 578.

St Vincent's Hospital
For information about drug and alcohol programs, and counselling, ph 9339 1111. For quit-smoking programs, ph 9332 6540.

Dugald Jellie

Further information
- National Heart Foundation, ph 9219 2444
- Smokers' Clinic, Royal Prince Alfred Hospital, ph 9515 7614
- Web sites:
  www.heartfoundation.com.au
  www.quitnow.info.au

Removalists

see also storage

The most traumatising events of our adult life, so they say, are death of a loved one, followed by divorce and moving house. So it's not surprising we want to be extra sure that the removalist isn't going to smash our favourite china in the process.

Grace Removals

One of the biggest in the business, Grace will move you from Sydney to Melbourne overnight. It also has links with overseas companies, giving it worldwide coverage. The Grace Valet service involves packing up your goods and chattels, and unpacking them again at the other end – leaving you nothing to do but walk in the door.

■ Carter St, Lidcombe, ph 9704 2222.

China Bear

This company specialises in antique and art removals. It employs a unique method of wrapping furniture, using giant elastic bands to hold pads of protective felt around your precious pieces. This is generally done in situ, before the piece is moved, to minimise any likelihood of damage.

■ 10/1307 Botany Rd, Mascot, ph 9317 5322.

123 Removals and Storage Australia

Joseph Verner is the brawn and brains behind 123 Removals while his wife, Rosemary, coordinates Storage Australia's Gladesville depot. The friendly, hardworking Czech offers highly competitive rates for two men and a van (charging from door to door, not depot to depot). Storage can be arranged by the month, or for just a couple of days if needs be.

■ 401 Victoria Rd, Gladesville, ph 9816 5555.

Dyke Energy Removals

For five years this all-woman, all-gay removalist has given great service at economical rates. A business with a conscience, it offers discounts to people living with HIV/AIDS, community groups and women fleeing violent domestic situations. In case of emergency it has moved clients within greater Sydney the day they call.

■ Ph 0412 99 1648.

Christopher Dobney

We offer an unpacking and setting up house service that is tailored to your needs. The moving house team transforms a house full of boxes into an organised home in one day. All items placed into cupboards, clothes into wardrobes, beds made up, bathrooms and kitchens ready for use, books and ornaments on shelves, children's rooms set for study and play, cartons folded and ready for collection.

For more details and a quote call the moving house experts on:
Ph: 9380 5112
Fx: 9380 6889
Mob: 0412 232447

The Unpacking And Setting Up House Service

Restoration

Today's desirable address is one with an inner-city postcode. And with its return to favour has come a renewed appreciation of older houses and the period detail which gives them their character. Throughout Sydney's older suburbs skips are taking up vital car-parking spaces as people strip their restoration gems of the excrescences of the '50s and the '60s. If you've just entered the restoration game, be prepared to spend your weekends combing the demolition yards for missing authentic details.

Balmain Stripping Factory

Don't let the misnomer confuse you. The Balmain Stripping Factory is actually in nearby Leichhardt. It is one of the last places

Restoration

in Sydney where furniture, doors and mantelpieces can be stripped of unwanted layers of paint. And that's not all. The Factory also sells sound and particularly charming secondhand architectural fixtures and fittings, while the showroom upstairs is full of restored antique furniture.
■ 124 James St, Leichhardt, ph 9560 3083.

Architectural Heritage
This two-storey building on Glebe Point Rd is crammed with exceptional pieces at (often) exceptional prices, with most of the stock having an impressive and sometimes foreign provenance. Even if your budget doesn't stretch to the lengths required, any house restorer worth his or her heat-gun will gain enormous pleasure and inspiration just being in the presence of such treasures. A secondhand store of museum quality.
■ 62 Glebe Point Rd, Glebe, ph 9660 0100.

Chippendale Restorations
Two staff are not enough to cope with the queue of customers on a weekend who wait for assistance in choosing from the vast range of secondhand doors, light fittings and fireplaces, reproduction brass hardware, hearth tiles and letterboxes. This is a restoration emporium with an inhouse joinery where the patience required waiting for the attention of the harassed owner or his co-worker is ultimately worth it. Few leave empty handed.
■ 505 Balmain Rd, Lilyfield, ph 9810 6066.

Terrace House Factory Building Materials
Three adjoining terrace houses form the ramshackle premises for this secondhand supplier with a fondness for cast-iron – whether it be Victorian lace balustrade panels, veranda posts, pedestal basins or fireplace inserts.
■ 304 Harris St, Ultimo, ph 9660 6768.

The Restoration Centre
If the patina of age doesn't turn you on or you simply can't find what you want secondhand, then take a look at the reproduction items here – everything from brass taps to fireplace tools.
■ 267 Cleveland St, Surry Hills, ph 9698 5511.

Sydney Building Information Centre Centre
The bookshop here is the best place to find most titles ever published on restoring old houses, including the latest from Maisy and Ian Stapleton, *Australian House Styles*.
■ 525 Elizabeth St, Surry Hills, ph 9318 2977.

Jennifer Reed Burns

Further information
■ The Period Home Renovator Buyer's Guide, a good annual guide to suppliers of restoration products. Available from many newsagents. Enquiries: Publicity Press, ph (03) 9646 6788

Resumes

The modern resume has to be snappy and tailored to the prospective employer. Don't send reams of paper minutely detailing your education, employment and personal histories. Some of the best agencies in Sydney, which will help you highlight your best selling points and make your resume as relevant as possible, follow.

The Centre for Worklife Counselling
Director Paul Stevens is an expert in resumes and interview skills. Two sessions, costing $215 altogether, will produce a beautifully designed resume, perfectly pitched at the job you are applying for.
■ 5 Earl St, Mosman, ph 9968 1588.

Dominique du Maurier

With a background in advertising, marketing and graphic design and as the author of *The Chosen Resume*, du Maurier has become well known for helping people to highlight their skills and will work with you to create a tailor-made resume.
- Ph 9326 5006.

Career Edge

Under the umbrella of Morgan and Banks recruitment, it provides coaching and teaching to help you construct a resume which stands out from the rest. A one-on-one consultation – which involves a one-hour meeting, several fax follow-ups with feedback and suggestions and a final face-to-face follow-up -costs $150. It also runs resume-writing workshops every two weeks, including an hour's follow-up consultation for $200.
- Level 6, 220 George St, City,
  ph 9252 4822.

Ali Gripper

Further Information
- Careersonline web site:
  www.careersonline.com.au

Rock & pop music

see also nightclubs, pubs, blues music, country music, folk music, jazz

Sydney is the heart of Australia's rock and pop scene. The major record companies have head offices here, the national radio networks come out of Sydney and the city's live music scene is a barometer of the health of the industry.

It was in Sydney that Johnny O'Keefe nearly tore down the old Stadium with one of his barnstorming concerts, that the Pope, Billy Graham and Led Zeppelin all shared the one venue (Randwick Racecourse – though not at the same time). It was where Michael Jackson married Debbie Rowe and, in 1984, Elton John wed Renata Blauel. Music, madness, religion and marriage – who could ask for anything more?

Sydney also has spawned some of the biggest international names out of Australia. Midnight Oil and INXS both sprang from the northern beaches, while Air Supply first strummed in view of the harbour. The Hoodoo Gurus emerged out of the inner city, You Am I came out of the western suburbs and The Church quickly moved from Canberra to Sydney to establish themselves before their first album.

Jackie Orszaczky

The man for soul or funk in any one of half a dozen bands. Look for his name and be assured of a laugh, a boogie and great playing.

Doug Williams

Good-time soul shows just made for dancing and a party night.

Leonardo's Bride

One of the most successful bands in Sydney's booming acoustic scene, with soft voices and sweet melodies. Also keep an eye out for **The Whitlams** and **Cactus Child**.

Love Me

Droll but melodic country rock done with a touch of Velvet Underground. **Karma County** do it more traditionally and acoustically.

You Am I

One of the best bands in the country play guitar pop with plenty of classic English influences mixed with a real Sydney lyrical feel. **Knievel** do wonderful things with catchy melodies, too.

Skunkhour

Once heavy on the rapping funk, now mixing rock and funk in equal measures.

Rock & pop music

Robyne Dunn
Singer/songwriters such as Dunn and David Lane prove you can be esoteric/jazz influenced but still pop at heart (such as Dunn) or low-key and melodic (such as Lane) in a world of guitars and drum machines.

Sydney Entertainment Centre
The Ent Cent is the city's biggest, but not a venue for aesthetics. Here is where you will find the biggest-name touring acts and spectaculars.
- Harbour St, Haymarket, ph 9266 4800.

State Theatre
There is atmosphere in spades here. The venue is all seated and is the best place to hear the softest of folk singers, the most complex of arthouse musicians or the most vibrant of African acts with clarity.
- 49 Market St, City, ph 9373 6655.

The Metro
This is the city's main rock venue, where good sightlines, facilities and sound combine and up to 900 fans can all enjoy it.
- 624 George St, City, ph 9264 2666.

Other venues
Inner city, the best venues are the **Annandale Hotel** (17 Parramatta Rd, Annandale, ph 9550 1078) and the **Globe** (379 King St, Newtown, ph 9519 0220). The Eastern Suburbs' chief venue is **Selina's**, **Coogee Bay Hotel** (Coogee Bay Rd and Arden St, Coogee, ph 9665 0000). On the north side, **Dee Why Hotel** (cnr Pittwater Rd and Sturdee Pde, ph 9981 1166); **Narrabeen Sands** (1260 Pittwater Rd, Narrabeen, ph 9913 1166) and the **Mona Vale Hotel** (2 Park St, Mona Vale, ph 9999 4214) are the pick. Westwards, it's the **Collector Tavern** in Parramatta (100 George St, ph 9689 1122), while the southern suburbs' picks are the **Sutherland Trade Union Club** (cnr Kingsway and Manchester Rd, Gymea, ph 9540 1933) and the **Caringbah Inn** (343 Port Hacking Rd, Caringbah, ph 9526 1166).

Red Eye
The best alternative music store – for local rock and experimental music and those rare imports.
- Tank Stream Arcade, City, ph 9233 8177.

Anthem Records
The CBD home of funk, soul and R&B whose customers include many of the city's best DJs who know this is the place to score those rare pieces of vinyl as well as the latest CDs.
- 9 Albion Place, City, ph 9267 7931.

Utopia Records
Not just a heavy metal store. There are hard rock, classic rock rarities and some alternative music you won't find anywhere else.
- 636 George St, City, ph 9283 2423.

Time Warp Records
If you wish you had lived in the '50s, never really left the '60s, or just can't get enough of those '70s sounds, this is the store. Vinyl is still loved here but if it's been rereleased on CD it's bound to be here.
- 289 Clarence St, City, ph 9283 1555.

Bernard Zuel

Further information
- Check Sydney Morning Herald Metro and CitySearch for listings.

Rowing

see also canoeing
Like rugby union, this quintessential white-collar sport is on the verge of growing up and leaving home, to be embraced by a broader faithful. Gad, sir, even the ladies are getting involved! In NSW, particularly at school level, the participation rate is close to 50-50, a mix encouraged by the gold medal success of Kate Slatter and Megan

Still at the 1996 Atlanta Olympics. This is a new wrinkle on a sport which can trace its history in Australia back to the early 19th century, with records of a four-oared race from Bradley's Head to Sydney Cove.

Head of the River
Sydney's major private schools race each other in this annual sporting/social event in early April. The passion and level of public attention to the race prompted the schools' principals, in the early '70s, to ban all publicity, such was the extent of the stress and attention they felt their pupils had to endure.

International Regatta Centre
The site for the Head of the River and every other rowing event of significance since its opening in March 1996. Before a month-long plague of ribbon weed in the water in early 1997, the course was regarded as the best of its type in the world.
- Castlereagh Rd, Penrith, ph 4730 6790.

Riverview Gold Cup
Upper-crust Sydney's love affair with this sport is perhaps ideally viewed and experienced at this event, the social event of the rowing calendar. Staged by St Ignatius' College on a not entirely straight stretch of the Lane Cove River, the event is becoming more spectator-friendly, with barges moored along the course, and extra seating.

NSW Rowing Association
From St George in the south, Middle Harbour and Narrabeen Lake in the north, to the Nepean River, way out west, Sydney has no shortage of clubs or venues. NSW Rowing will point you in the right direction, although the nature of the sport, of course, means that will be backwards.
- ph 9552 1263.

Iron Cove
Sydney's most popular course – upwards of 50 boats will meander up and down from sunrise until 8.30–9am. Be warned: a single sculler was tipped from her craft by a shark not so long ago.

Middle Harbour
This is in the eye and heart of the beholder, but the Mosman rowers' course at along this stretch at first light is hard to beat.

Gerard Wright

Rugby league

see also sporting goods
More than any sport, Sydney identifies with rugby league. The game began in a now abandoned shop front in George St, where dissatisfied rugby union players decided to form a breakaway game where players could be paid for their toil. That was in 1908, and in the years that followed rugby league developed into the city's number one sport, spreading along the east coast until it went national in 1995. Yet almost immediately the game was under siege when News Ltd, owned by billionaire Rupert Murdoch, attempted to set up Super League, a rival competition to the Australian Rugby League, and poached many of the game's top players. After numerous court battles and ill-feeling, rugby league finally got back together in 1998 and the major series is now called the National Rugby League Competition. The Competition is played throughout the winter months, with the finals series starting in late August (weekend August 28-30, 1998) and the Grand Final in late September (September 27, 1998).

While not an Olympic sport, rugby league enjoys enormous participation levels from children as young as five to senior levels. In the '80s, regular touch football competitions – a rugby league spin-off – began surfacing around NSW. Competitions now take place regularly around the city.

Rugby league

Australian Rugby League

The ARL is responsible for running rugby league in NSW and Australia with the exception of the elite competition, which is a partnership with Super League. For anyone looking to play the game, or to simply watch a match, the ARL can handle all enquiries.
- NSW Leagues Club, 165 Phillip St, City, ph 9232 7566.

NSW Touch Association

There are more than 150 affiliated touch clubs in NSW, most coming from within the city area. All members are required to pay membership fees which help cover registration and insurance costs. The NSWTA also sells merchandise and referees' gear and is responsible for organising State tournaments across NSW.
- 2 Bayview Ave, Burwood, ph 9580 7333.

The Domain

Every lunchtime, summer and winter, the NSWTA organises lunchtime competitions for the hundreds of CBD workers looking for a fun sweat. The competitions run for 15 rounds. A variation of touch, called Oztag, is also played at the Domain.
- Contact the NSW Touch Association or Sporting Spectrum, PO Box 495, Crows Nest, ph 9959 4269.

Peter Wynn's Score

Probably the largest retailer of rugby league gear in Sydney. Sells everything from sponsored football jumpers to old-style foundation jumpers. Has a large variety of safety equipment, training gear, footballs and football boots. Also stocks touch football equipment. Even sells posters.
- 197 Church St, Parramatta, ph 9891 2655 or 9891 2677.

Paul Kent

Further information
- Australian Rugby League, ph 9232 7566
- Super League, ph 9285 1555

Rugby union

see also sporting goods

Sydney is the home of Australian rugby. Since 1829, rugby has been one of Sydney's most popular winter sports, with virtually every suburb having a team playing in either district or sub-district competition. As most clubs are desperate for players, owning a pair of football boots is enough to get a game, while for the spectator, a match is usually as close as the nearest municipal park.

Randwick Rugby Club

The home of the Ellas, this club is among the most successful in the world, winning countless premierships. A visit to their licensed premises will convince you of their power, as it is crammed full of trophies, and reminders that this is THE rugby club in Sydney. Ask for Randwick president, club coach, rugby legend, chief bottlewasher Jeffrey Sayle, who will delight you in everything Galloping Green.
- 104 Brook St, Coogee, ph 9665 4143.

Campo's

Most sporting greats never raise their head in public. But David Campese can be regularly sighted behind the counter of his sports and leisurewear shop. Will gladly sign anything you place in front of him – and even give you tips on how to become a rugby star.
- Shop 30, St Ives Shopping Village, Mona Vale Rd, St Ives, ph 9449 3974.

Coogee Oval

The Sydney club competition provides excellent football at a reasonable price for spectators. This is one of the most interesting venues, especially on the halfway line, where you will find the city's most abusive football supporters (Brook St, Coogee). Also try **Woollahra Oval** (O'Sullivan Rd, Bellevue Hill) where the beautiful people meet; **Chatswood Oval** (Albert Ave, Chatswood) where many beautiful relationships have started; and **Pittwater Rugby Park** (Welsh St, Narrabeen) which has the best after-match entertainment around.

Best footy pies
Go immediately to T.G. Millner Field, Eastwood's home ground, for the meatiest and freshest pie in Sydney, or Pittwater Rugby Park, which boasts an excellent steak, tomato and onion dogs-eye.
■ Vimiera Rd, Eastwood.

Greg Growden

Further information
■ NSW Rugby Union, ph 9747 2400.

Rugs

see also carpet & floor covering, floors
If hard floors are the practical, no-fuss, Sydney answer for good looks underfoot, rugs set the tone and can also be a clever way of adding good lines to a space. From shag pile flokatis to grandiose Aubusson styles, Sydney has it all. Colours, weaves and patterns depend on trends, your house and personal preference. The good news is that you should be able to find just about anything you want in Sydney at a price you can afford.

Amalgamated Textiles
Importers of flokati rugs woven from New Zealand wool. There are more than eight sizes in lusciously soft cream priced from $375 for a 2 x 3m medium size rug. Also a must-have brown swirl design with a definite whiff of the 1960s.
■ 35-39 Trafalgar St, Enmore, ph 9519 8160.

Anibou
Since the designer showroom launched the Finnish range of Woodnotes paper and twine rugs in 1997, the natural weaves with dramatic accents have quite simply taken Sydney by storm.
■ 726 Bourke St, Redfern, ph 9319 0655.

Designer Rugs
If you don't like what's around, you can always design your own rug to fit a particular room or decorating statement. Designer Rugs has been custom making rugs on site for more than 10 years using pure New Zealand wool. There are two inhouse designers to help you create anything from contemporary abstract images to highly decorative French designs. The service takes four to five weeks and is reasonably priced.
■ 509 Parramatta Rd, Leichhardt, ph 9550 9933.

Tibet Gallery
Rugs inspired by ancient Tibetan patterns with a contemporary edge. You can order any size or colour at less than $550 a square metre..
■ 22 Queen St, Woollahra, ph 9363 2588.

Nomadic Rug Traders
Ross Langlands sells an exquisite range of quality Persian, tribal and village rugs from the Middle East with refined good looks.
■ 125 Harris St, Pyrmont, ph 9660 3753.

Form
You can sniff out thick woolly original 1950s rugs with geometric designs from around $500 here.
■ 415 Bourke St, Darlinghurst, ph 9331 6227.

Ray Hughes Gallery
The gallery's wonderful range of striped abstract rugs designed by artist Peter Cooley will jazz up even the dullest floor. Plus an extraordinary collection of Afghanistan war

Rugs

rugs enlivened with tanks, rifles, helicopters and bombs.
- 270 Devonshire St, Surry Hills, ph 9698 3200.

Robyn Cosgrove Rugs
Stockists of a magical range of handmade rugs, wool dhurries, kilims, Turkish rugs, needlepoint and chainstitch rugs in a mesmerising range of colours and designs using vegetable dyes. Cosgrove's eye is impeccable: you won't go wrong here.
- 18 Transvaal Ave, Double Bay, ph 9362 3663.

Astro Design
Stockist of Christopher Farr designer rugs from Britain.
- 10 Cecil St, Paddington, ph 9360 0003.

Melissa Walker Smith

Running

see also athletics, sporting goods

One of the cheapest and easiest ways to get fit. With trails as gorgeous as those around Taronga Park Zoo, Balgowlah Heights and Bondi on your doorstep, you have no excuse. So, as the ads say, Just Do It. But a quick checklist first: sunblock, shades, shorts, shirt, shoes and hat. Winter is the most comfortable season to jog in Sydney, when the heat won't (as one avid harrier said) 'melt your brain'. Those serious enough to stick to a regular program over summer will find the early morning the most pleasant time to train.

Botanic Gardens and the Domain
Wide open spaces, right in the CBD. At lunchtime on Wednesdays, an informal Corporate Challenge is held in the Domain.

Centennial Park
If you jog inside the fence then add on the horse track, you'll get a gentle 10-kilometre crosscountry run, but beware horses and cyclists.

North Bondi to Coogee
For a spectacular (if blustery) 16-kilometre run, follow the headlands to Coogee and back through Clovelly, not forgetting to doff your cap in respect to the residents of Waverley Cemetery, which is on the way.

Sutherland National Park
A training run for all comers starts at the sheds on the old Lady Carrington dirt road in the Royal National Park on Sundays at 7.30am. Beautiful and shady in summer, you'll run past lyrebirds and maybe the occasional snake.
- Lady Carrington Drive, off Sir Bertram Stevens Drive, Audley.

Sydney Striders
A club organising regular 10 km training runs for all paces in Parramatta and on the North Shore.
- Ph 9959 4269.

Billy's Bushies
For the more adventurous souls, this club sets off at 6.30am on Saturday from Sutherland swimming pool for a morning of sometimes wild bush running.
- Ph 9525 5126.

Southside Runners
Serious runners have a golden rule when shoe shopping: go somewhere owned by another runner, as this establishment is.
- 29 East Pde, Sutherland, ph 9545 6010.

Kenso Discount Sports
Recommended by *Fun Runner* magazine for its knowledgeable staff.
- 210 Anzac Pde, Kensington, ph 9663 1714.

Kim Gillard
Local gun who covers his specialist 10 km in a terrifyingly fast sub-29 minutes. Young **James Barker** is another of Sydney's best speedsters and could be a name to remember come Sydney 2000. Our best woman is probably mother of two, **Liz Miller**, City to Surf winner.

Olympic marathon
The 42.195 km slog in 2000 is likely to be based on the Sydney Marathon (next scheduled for mid-1999), which starts in North Sydney, crosses the Harbour Bridge, wiggles past the Opera House and Mrs Macquarie's Chair, cuts across the city into Darling Harbour, then rolls up its sleeves for the suburban crawl out to Homebush.

Sun-Herald City to Surf
The toughest road race in Australia, held the second Sunday in August. This 14 km race draws the nations best (plus 40,000 others) to battle the near-mountainous Eastern Suburbs course. A good, if painful, time is about 50 minutes.

Sydney Morning Herald Half Marathon
You'll need to train for months to tackle this testing, 21.1 km, two-lap gutbuster late in May.

Peter Vincent

Sailboarding

see also beaches, sailing
This is sailing in its purest and fastest form, and, on the waves, the most spectacular. For many, it's just for fun. For a bank of Sydney professionals, it's a lifetime of serious and successful competition. The sailor beside you could be world windsurfer champion Sue Calvert or Adam Quinn or a four-week novice, each pursuing individual searches for the increased skill and exhilaration that make this sport so satisfying. They probably won't be on the Sydney Olympics course, which will be sailed on the Harbour out of Rushcutters Bay, but they will be on the more popular beaches north and south, away from the no-go harbour shipping channels. Beginners, remember this is a sport where boards and rigs must match conditions and skill. Don't attempt the surf beaches or big winds unless your gybing and water starting are good. Always check the boating weather forecast before going out (ph 11541). Conditions can change suddenly.

Palm Beach
The northernmost of Sydney's string of wave havens, with Newport just to the south. Out here on good day, you'll find the likes of longtime wave men Mark Paul and Rohan Cudmore. The shallow water west of the peninsula can be crowded as the north-easterlies strengthen offshore – shorter boards to the east please.

Narrabeen Lake
Excellent for beginners and intermediates, one of the few spots where you can hook onto a westerly and not worry about having to book a return ticket from New Zealand. Good also in northeasterlies.

Long Reef
One of the premier wave sites. Match aerials with Mark Pedersen, world champion and long-time competitor at windsurfing's highest levels.

Balmoral
A beautiful flatwater location, best in a north-easterly.

Rodd Point
Best in north-easterlies. Short runs and in the crowds you can share a gust with Barcelona bronze medallist Lars Kleppich.

Sailboarding

Botany Bay

The crowds of jellyfish have front-row seats at this arena that works around the compass, for everyone from first-day beginners to senior competitors such as Nathan Clift. There's good speed in the north-easterlies on the flat water south of the airport, a mess of jumping ramps when wind meets tide at the Georges River mouth and battlefields of space for mining westerly bullets off Silver Beach at Kurnell. Attack the southerlies from the beach north-east of Captain Cook Bridge.

Wanda

Home and heaven for southern suburbs wave sailors praying for summer's nor'easterlies.

Best shops and suppliers

Long Reef Sailboards and Surf (ph 9982 4829); Botany Bay Sail-boards (ph 9599 2814).

Instruction and hire

Balmoral Sailboard School (ph 9960 5344); Palm Beach Water Sports (ph 018 862 000); Narrabeen Water-sports (ph 9913 2636).

NSW Boardsailing Association

Can advise on your nearest club and on competition from beginner to Olympic level.
- Keith Single, president, ph 9268 7861 or 9528 6258.

Jim Darling

Sailing

From wet behinds and speed demon rides to cruising for views and champagne and chicken lunches, sailing offers something for everyone in Sydney. There is the independence that comes with going places and catching your own puff of wind. And sailing is a great leveller, of course. On the harbour, you might rub shoulders with Lachlan or Rupert Murdoch, Iain Murray or Syd Fischer, or your next-door neighbour. Come 2000, there will a spectacular display of Olympic sailing on the harbour, surely the world's best natural amphitheatre for this sport. While the traditional dinghy classes will be tested by fickle winds and big southerly busters, the 49er, a skiff making its Olympic debut in Sydney, will relish the going. The new two-man, high-performance dinghy has been designed by Sydney's Julian Bethwaite to put the sizzle back into Olympic sailing. Needless to say, it goes like the wind.

For most, however, the best part of sailing is the traditional wake at the end of the day. The camaraderie at the yacht club between like-minded salties sharing tales and drinks as the sun sets on another great weekend and the steaks sizzle behind. If you like the sound of that, sign up with a sailing school or try for a free berth by putting your name down on the crew-wanted list at your local club.

Eastsail

Forge friendships as you learn to sail a yacht on the harbour and hob-nob with the high-rollers at stylish Rushcutters Bay. This slick sailing school offers tuition from experts, yacht charters on French-designed Beneteau yachts, and a corporate racing program so you can con the whole office onto the water.
- d'Albora Marina, Rushcutters Bay, ph 9327 1166.

Hugh Treharne Sailing

Learn to sail across oceans with ex-America's Cup sailor and master seaman, Hugh Treharne. He is based in Pittwater, but often heads for Lord Howe Island or Queensland in his 15.5 metre yacht, with a pastry cook who bakes fresh loaves at sea.
- 10 Princes St, Newport, ph 9997 3036.

Ausail Sailing School

A summer camp aboard safe but exciting Catalina Capri 16.5 dinghies built for four budding sailors and a qualified instructor. Courses

develop communication skills, self-confidence and a useful working knowledge of sailing – something every kid in Sydney should have. Also charters Catalina yachts.
- 235 Spit Rd, The Spit, Mosman, ph 9960 5511.

The Sailing Scene
Get going on a Laser dinghy, throw a Hobie Cat behind and ease off the beach, or step up to a racy Elliott 7 trailer-yacht. A summer of sailing options for sale.
- Cnr Darley St and By The Sea Rd, Mona Vale, ph 9979 6546.

Sydney Yachting Centre
Go for a trusty, locally-made Northshore yacht or buy a preloved beauty for social and club racing in both twilight and weekend regattas.
- 81 Parriwi Rd, next to The Spit Bridge, Mosman, ph 9969 2144.

Vicsail Pittwater
Up the style factor in the new French-designed Beneteau 33.7, a yacht with panache and practicality. Sail as a couple and sleep the weekend away, or dash about the harbour buoys with a crew of keen club sailors for the day.
- Heron Cove Marina, Queens Pde, Newport, ph 9999 0944.

Bashford International
Designed by Iain Murray and Associates and winning yacht races all around the world, Sydney Yachts from Bashford International are Australia's biggest and best-selling yachting export. Buy a 36- to 60-footer and head for Hobart at high speed.
- Suite 8, Prince Alfred Yacht Club, Mitala St, Newport, ph 9979 8044.

David Lockwood

Further information
- Yachting Association of NSW, ph 9660 1266: www.yachtingnsw.org.au

- The Waterways of Sydney Harbour by Phillip Mathews ($24.95 from Boat Books, 31 Albany St, Crows Nest, ph 9439 1133)

Sales

see also shopping centres, discount fashion

Resourceful shoppers reserve their credit cards for notable dates on Sydney's sales calendar. Behind the scenes, competition among retailers for our patronage hots up. Traditionally, major department stores and shopping centres start the ball rolling post-Christmas and at the end of the financial year, with ads heralding the events. Other retailers follow suit, though there is a new trend to pre-empt this domino effect. Some stores now start price reductions in early December, as is the custom in cities overseas, to gain the edge over larger competitors. Prestige brand names, not wishing to be associated with the stigma of bargains, advertise one-off clearance sales under disguised identities. Others, well known for reduced prices all year round, cut their prices further twice a year, to compete for our dollars. Your shopping sense is enhanced, if you know where to go and when.

Birkenhead Point Shopping Centre
Factory outlets of fashion and homewares.
- Cary St, Drummoyne (off Victoria Rd).

Westfield Shoppingtowns
The Parramatta and Miranda sites have the widest choice. All shops have the usual clearance sales at the beginning of January, but watch out for one-day 'mega sales' in February.

Sales

Holy Sheet!
Competitively priced manchester, gifts and homewares are reduced by 20 per cent during post-Christmas sales at its six Sydney stores.
- ph 9565 1163.

Home
The annual 'recovery' sale of top-of-the-range homewares and objets d'art takes place the day after the Gay and Lesbian Mardi Gras parade.
- 153 Oxford St, Darlinghurst, ph 9332 4840.

Thurlstane
This manchester supplier to five-star hotels also sells everything from big fridges and small electrical appliances to fine and commercial china to the public at 30 per cent less than retail prices all year round.
- 62-68 Riley St, Darlinghurst, ph 9361 0661.

Peter's of Kensington
Well-priced brand names in dinner and tableware, cookware, crystal, small electrical appliances and gifts. Watch out for the January sale.
- 57 Anzac Pde, Kensington, ph 9662 1099.

Strand Arcade
Fashion designers cut their prices each fortnight at sale time by 25, 50, then 75 per cent. Summer lines go on sale straight after Christmas.
- George St to Pitt St Mall, City.

Riada
The summer sale offers 20 to 40 per cent reductions on ranges of European 'mainline' women's collections.
- 118 Queen St, Woollahra, ph 9363 0654;
  681a Military Rd, Mosman, ph 9969 4269.

Flash Trash
Prices for antique, reproduction and recycled furniture, decorator items and gilt mirrors are normally sold at 20-30 per cent less than retail prices and even less for cash payment.
- Cnr Missenden and Parramatta Rds, Camperdown, ph 9557 3793.

QCC Grande Cuisine
Trade prices of commercial kitchen equipment and utensils, crockery, cutlery, glassware and electrical appliances are reduced by at least 20 per cent after Easter.
- 53-59 William St, East Sydney, ph 9331 4124.

Trisha Treanor

Sandwiches

see also cafes
Sydney is one big culinary, cultural sandwich. Within minutes whole grain was superseded by the baguette, the foccacia and now the flatter, chewier Turkish pide reigns supreme. But that's just this week. Fillings can also get a little out of hand. Try sticking to two or three.

The Olive Italian Food Bar
In the heart of the CBD, it's three-deep everyday for beautifully pliant Turkish pide bread filled with gorgeous Italian fillings such as crisp, golden zucchini, great schnitzel, and superlative green bits.
- Shop 18, Strand Arcade, Pitt St, City, ph 9231 2962.

The Sidewalk Cafe Coffee Lounge
For old-fashioned toasted ham and cheese, asparagus, even prawn cocktail sandwiches; a real mothers-and-daughters hang.
- G22 Centrepoint, City, ph 9232 3486.

Parmalat
On Victoria Street's famous cafe strip in Darlinghurst for tuna with S&W mayo, or black olive, egg and whitlof, and great coffee to match.
- 320b Victoria St, Darlinghurst (no phone).

Loreto's Larder
You don't have to go to New York to get a good Reuben. They make their own bread, the fillings are mile-high and you can watch the

passing parade. Try the potato salad, leg ham and chives. Mmmm.
- Shop 4113 Oxford St, Darlinghurst, ph 9360 6810.

Nicole Lehmann

Schools

see also tutors

With more than 3,000 primary and secondary schools in NSW, finding the best one will depend on what you are looking for. If best means high academic results, then there is no doubt government selective schools and independent schools dominate the top rankings in the Higher School Certificate. But selective schools take in only the brightest students so serious questions would need to be asked if they were not producing excellent results. If best is based on sporting achievements, then a school like **St Joseph's College** at Hunters Hill, with 50 Wallaby players to its credit, may be more what you are looking for. In dance, drama and music, **Newtown School of the Performing Arts** specialises in these fields, while **Wenona** at North Sydney, **MLC Burwood** and **Pymble Ladies College** could claim an edge in the technology stakes by equipping each student with their own laptop. Or perhaps the best school is one that simply gets on with the job quietly and efficiently.

HSC results

Analysis of the 1997 HSC results found a great divide in school performance with high performing students concentrated in a small number of schools. Just 30 schools accounted for 44 per cent of the places on last year's merit list for HSC English and in maths about 5 per cent of all schools accounted for 38 per cent of students on the list. The list included students who scored over 90. **James Ruse Agricultural High School**, an academically selective school at Carlingford, had the highest percentage of students on the English merit list, followed by **SCEGGS Darlinghurst**. **North Sydney Girls**, also a selective school. **Wenona School**, **Sydney Girls** and **Pymble Ladies College** also finished with high numbers of students on the merit list. In maths, **James Ruse Agricultural High**, **Sydney Boys**, **North Sydney Boys** and **North Sydney Girls**, **Fort Street High** and **Sydney Technical High School** had the most students on the merit list.

While private school students as a group do tend to perform better academically, their success may have a lot to do with the ability of students coming into the school rather than the teaching at the school. A school such as **Canley Vale**, a disadvantaged school in Sydney's west, finished among the top 100 schools for maths, while **Homebush Boys** and **Ashfield Boys**, both government schools, finished among the top 50 schools.

Sports

Sporting competitions in NSW schools are played at levels from local knock-out competitions to state and national championships and are organised by several different associations. **St Joseph's College** is regarded as Australia's greatest rugby nursery, although **The King's School** won the premiership in 1997. In general terms, of the eight Greater Public Schools, **St Ignatius, Riverview**, at Hunters Hill is known for cricket and athletics, while **Sydney Church of England Grammar School** (Shore) at North Sydney and **Newington College** at Stanmore are known for their outstanding performances in rowing. More than 100 independent schools compete in 20 different sports under the banner of the Combined Independent Schools Sports Council.

Independent girls schools play in a separate competition involving 13 different sports. **Pymble Ladies College** is known for its strength in athletics, diving and swimming, while **Abbotsleigh**, **Ravenswood** and **St Catherine's Anglican School for Girls** do well at basketball. **Tara** is another school strong in diving while **Ravenswood** has a good reputation in the tennis competition. Rowing is traditionally dominated by **Loreto Normanhurst**.

Government school sport is run by the Combined High Schools Sports Association. There are five sports high schools in the government school system – **Endeavour Sports High**, at Caringbah, **Westfield Sports High**, at Fairfield West, **Berkeley Sports High**, near Wollongong, **Narrabeen Sports High** and **Hunter Sports High**.

Stephanie Raethel

Further information

- *The Sydney Morning Herald Guide to Schools.* (Available from book stores and newsagents, $19.95)

Sculpture & public art

see also art galleries, fountains, architecture, heritage Sydney

Maybe you could see the Sydney Opera House as the city's greatest sculpture – otherwise, the city is poorly served. For a town that generates so much wealth, there is precious little returned to the public domain. There are sculptures, of course – many ill-conceived or ill-sited or both. No wonder the Irish gave Sydney the statue of Queen Victoria that squats like an overblown toad outside 'her' building. And the copies of copies of 'antique' sculptures or images of national worthies that adorn the Botanic Gardens and other parks hardly inspire the late 20th-century imagination.

However, the City Council has allocated funds for a Sculpture Walk of major pieces around the city, to be in place by 2000.

THE EDGE of the TREES

Janet Laurence and Fiona Foley's 1994 piece, on the forecourt of the Museum of Sydney. Their columns of timber, 'I'-beam steel and sandstone incorporate the memory of the site from its botanical fragments and traces of the original Eora inhabitants – shells, bone, hair – through to the first layers of white settlement. Walking among the 'trees' triggers a whispering of voices, a forest of memory.
- 37 Phillip St, City.

Angles

Henry Moore's reclining figure outside the Art Gallery of NSW was bought from the artist by the gallery in 1981 (the plaster maquette donated by the artist is inside). Moore has said that, as a boy, he rubbed his mother's broad, rheumatic back and, according to gallery director Edmund Capon, the 'maternal image has the impressive power of an archetypal form of Earth Mother'. She also enjoys a great view.
- Art Gallery Rd, The Domain.

Ben Chifley

This modest hero has been given suitably heroic treatment in a recently unveiled tribute in the city square named for him. An example of the City Council's efforts to integrate design and art works with the sculptor, Simeon Nelson, working with the architects, Hassells, from the beginning of the project. Some say the eight-metre figure could be taller still but he's impressively placed in the grid of palms.
- Chifley Square, City.

Geraldine O'Brien

Further information

- Open Museum Map Guide, Sydney City Council, ph 9265 9775.

Seafood restaurants

Think about eating in Sydney and the mind's eye doesn't automatically conjure up visions of roast beef, cured hams and racks of lamb. Sydney is a glisteningly fresh rock oyster; a whole fish, steamed with a little soy and ginger; a marinated, char-grilled baby octopus; or a crab salad rich with glorious white flesh. Here's a quick guide to Sydney's best fishing spots.

Pier
Greg Doyle and Steve Hodges are Sydney's seafood royalty. Rarely is fish and shellfish handled with such class, or in such classy surroundings as at their bright, sunny, waterside restaurant.
- 594 New South Head Rd, Rose Bay, ph 9327 6561.

Boathouse on Blackwattle Bay
It's got it all: to-die-for water views looking over to the dramatic structure of the Glebe Island bridge; a smart modern feel that's a cross between a hip glasshouse and a funky factory; and crabs, lobsters, mussels and clams from the tanks in the kitchen.
- End of Ferry Rd, Glebe, ph 9518 9011.

Rozelle Fishbowl
Fish and chips were never like this. At this tiny, crowded, glorified fish shop, chef Brett Stephenson gives fish a touch of class that the locals go mad for. Special favourites are the beer battered fish with lemon myrtle mayonnaise, tandoori baked salmon and a great little bouillabaisse.
- 580 Darling St, Rozelle, ph 9555 7302.

Golden Century
No, it's not an aquarium, it's a gloriously noisy, buzzy, Cantonese seafood restaurant. Indulge in a little window shopping before you order, then discuss price with your waiter. If your inheritance has come through, order whole fresh abalone, Murray cod and king crab served three ways.
- 393-399 Sussex St, City, ph 9212 3901.

Sea Treasure
Don't even bother with the menu. Simply ask manager Ying Tam or one of his staff for what's freshest, brightest, and tastiest. Chances are they will respond with a whole steamed Morwong, crab with butter and garlic, or perhaps some prawns in the shell with chilli sauce. Do not mention the words sweet or sour. We're all over that.
- 46 Willoughby Rd, Crows Nest, ph 9906 6388.

MCA Fish Cafe
Get a seat on the outside balcony and watch the Circular Quay ferries scuttle by. Neil Perry (of Rockpool fame) runs a neat little cafe sourced by his own fish wholesaling arm. All fish are line caught, fresher than you'll find at most markets, and simply presented with a good dash of style.
- Museum of Contemporary Art, The Rocks, ph 9241 4253.

Harbour Restaurant
While not as glamorous as its big brother the Bennelong, the Harbour does have its advantages, including a nice close-up view of the world's most beautiful harbour, and good, fresh fish cooked with mod Med flavours. Try char-grilled marlin with spiced Puy lentils.
- Sydney Opera House, Bennelong Point, ph 9250 7191.

Azuma
That might be Falcon St, Crows Nest, outside, but inside it is pure Tolyo, as straitlaced expatriate businessmen mix with a younger, looser crowd. Kimitaka Azuma is a masterful, highly refined chef, turning out some of the best sashimi in town, must-have chimni appetisers, incredibly fresh tempura garfish and a perfectly tender medium-rare mini-steak.
- 32 Falcon St, Crows Nest, ph 9436 4066.

Terry Durack

Security systems & alarms

A car alarm that goes off every time a cat approaches. A PIN number you remember only after you've woken the neighbours. Is protecting your property endangering your life? It needn't be.

Secom Security
One of the world's best-known office security companies, they will also wire up your house – for a price. No more forgotten PIN codes, a magnetic key enables you to control who goes where and when. If you get it wrong, they'll call you. Security guards patrol nightly.
- 45 Murray St, Pyrmont, ph 9660 7111.

Specialised Security Systems
Tenants, install this wireless alarm system and take your protection with you when you move. Comes with optional sensors for fire and glass-breaking and a remote control that fits on your key ring. Can also monitor your car.
- 603 Victoria Rd, Ryde, ph 9809 1711.

QuikTrak Networks
With this new technology, when someone steals your car, a radio signal enables it to be traced. QuikTrak involves the police. When your car is in sight, another signal immobilises it, meaning the thieves are often caught red-handed.
- 345 Pacific Highway, Lindfield, ph 9415 6700.

Chris Dobney

Shoe repairs

Shoes reveal all. Those who know the value of putting their best foot forward also know that trained shoemakers who repair stand apart from the rest. They'll look after your well-worn favourites and if you're down at the heel, they'll labour to restore your stance.

Andrew McDonald
McDonald makes ready-to-wear and custom-made men's and women's footwear. He repairs his own shoes and he can do yours too. His specialties are hand stitching for upper-shoe repairs and sole reconstruction, and referrals from the high-end footwear brands.
- Jour & Nuit, 50 Erskine St, City, ph 9299 1419.

Chifley Shoe Worx
Louis repairs shoes, handbags and leather apparel for R M Williams, Celine, Ferragamo and Versace stores. He also cares for the humble individual.
- Shop 25, L1, Chifley Plaza, Hunter St, City, ph 9223 9670.

The Original Michel's Shoe Repairs
Michel grew up making shoes in Lebanon and he now operates a family-style business of seven stores. All of his staff are fully qualified shoemakers, some working for him for more than 30 years. Specialties include alterations, tints, covering, orthopaedic work and repairs for footwear stores.
- Brices Shoe Repairs, Shop 860, Imperial Arcade, City, ph 9233 2836; Coombs Shoe Service, Shop 21, Strand Arcade, City, ph 9231 1784.

Jaede's Orthopaedic Made-to-Measure Footwear
This third-generation family trade specialises in bespoke and surgical orthopaedic shoes, and repairs. John Darragh consults at nursing homes and hospitals and is referred by specialists and podiatrists. Walk in off the street for adjustments; he takes into account the shoes you wear and studies your walking pattern.
- 25 Everton Rd, Strathfield, ph 9744 7864.

Trisha Treanor

Shooting

The widely-publicised success of elite athletes such as Olympic gold medallist Michael Diamond has put shooting firmly back into the sporting spotlight. There are 17 Olympic events in four disciplines (pistol, rifle, shotgun and running target) but shooting, of course, isn't restricted to targets only. There are also numerous hunting disciplines, although, of course, they are all practised outside the metropolitan area. There are literally hundreds of different shooting clubs and organisations in and around Sydney – the difficult part is deciding which area of the sport you'd like to target.

Cecil Park
The venue for the 2000 Olympic Games shooting events. By the time the complex is completed in mid-1999, it will feature rifle, pistol and shotgun ranges, with over 60 shooting lanes. Seating for 10,000 spectators will be provided for the Olympic competition. The 1999 Oceania championships will be held here.
■ Off Elizabeth Drive, Cecil Park.

Horsley Park Gun Shop
Australia's largest firearms dealership, based in Sydney's west, carries shotguns, rifles, pistols, reloading equipment, scopes and accessories. Also buys and sells second-hand guns.
■ 1848 The Horsley Drive, Horsley Park, ph 9620 1235.

Smith's Sports Store
Sydney's oldest established firearms dealer, it specialises in guns, ammunition, antiques and re-loading equipment. Also buys second-hand guns.
■ 773 George St, City, ph 9211 0166.

NSW Gun Club
Boasts state-of-the-art facilities and is a regular venue for elite competitions. All newcomers to gun clubs receive introductory training courses; juniors must be 12 years or older. While Australia's gun laws require that only licensed persons use or possess firearms, new members of a club receive an exemption for up to three months before they must obtain a licence.
■ Booralie Rd, Terrey Hills, ph 9450 1775.

NSW Shooting Association
The peak body for shooting in NSW, the Association can provide information on any of the shooting disciplines and put you in touch with the relevant club or affiliated organisation. They will also organise tours for shooting and hunting parties.
■ ph 9552 6349.

Heather Quinlan

Shopping centres & strips

From the commercial and crowded to the small and exclusive, Sydney boasts some of the most eclectic and fascinating shopping arcades, malls and strips. Whether it's Paddington markets or Parramatta Westfield, what better way to cheer yourself up than to set out for a good old shopping spree?

Strand Arcade
One of the most striking architectural features in the CBD, the Strand opened its doors in 1891. Today it is home to many of Sydney's most exclusive boutique and specialty stores. The designer gallery on level one boasts the best creations of Australia's leading fashion designers, including Leona Edmiston and Ian McMaugh, through to the unusual outlets, such as Dinosaur Designs. Stroll through the Strand and discover 90 shops, and a wealth of history unlike any other Sydney mall. Also located in the Pitt St Mall are the Skygarden shopping centre, boasting a beautiful food

Shopping centres & strips

court and designer shops and galleries, and the newly renovated Sydney Central Plaza.

- 412-414 George St (through to Pitt St Mall), City, ph 9232 4199.

Westfield Shopping Centres

For those who want 'everything under the one roof', Westfield complexes are Sydney's biggest, and Miranda Westfield the biggest in the southern hemisphere. They offer free parking facilities and are home to all the major retail chains. The larger centres house almost 400 shops, including huge food courts and cinemas. All of Sydney's nine Westfield centres are 'parent friendly', and offer free stroller hire and parents' rooms with televisions.

- Head office, ph 9358 7000.

Parramatta Road

If you're after a new set of wheels, there are more new and used cars dealers along Parramatta Road than anywhere else in the country. Starting at Camperdown in the inner city, right through to Parramatta, this is where you are likely to find the best deal.

Double Bay

Probably Sydney's most exclusive (and expensive) shopping precinct. Fashion boutiques, such as Solo Baci and Belinda, sell imported labels and there are plenty of shops to treat the tastebuds, such as the exclusive Bon Bon chocolate store. For beauty treatments there's a spectrum of choice, from facials by Sylvia Deitch to the hair salon of 'stylist to the rich-and-famous' Joh Bailey. If you want to go all out, retreat to the Temple of Body and Soul.

Newtown

A mecca of shops selling used clothes, books, furniture and incense, scattered between the best cafes, makes King Street one of the most eclectic and colourful strips in Sydney. Noticeably absent are the retail chain stores, which allows the small stores to flourish.

Castlereagh Street

Sydney's own Rodeo Drive. If you want names, names, names, this is your strip for international fashion labels. DKNY, cK Calvin Klein, Louis Vuitton, Chanel, Gucci, Ferragamo, Celine, and Versace adorn Castlereagh Street, and just off the glamorous mile is Emporio Armani and Prada. Get out the gold Amex and off you go!

Moore Park SupaCenta

For all your homewares and electrical needs you can't go past the Supa Centa. Freedom Furniture and IKEA are the two big names, stocking everything from kit kitchens to sofas and general homewares. Also in the complex are Chandlers, Toys 'R Us, and the Harvey Norman Computer Centre for all your home office needs.

- 2a Todman Ave, Kensington, ph 9313 8340.

Oxford Street, Paddington

Home to what was once one of the country's most eclectic markets, Paddington is made up of beautiful shops, especially appealing to the 20-something shopper. From the flamboyant D-Po and skate/surf shops such as General Pants and Mambo, to the up-scale fashion designer shops Wilson Stuart and Robbie Ingham.

Chatswood Chase

Relaunched in 1997 after a $150-million face-lift, Chatswood Chase provides an elegant, yet comfortable, environment for shoppers. The Chase offers valet parking for just $2 and houses more than 100 retailers, including many retail flagships such as Diesel and Kookai, and an extensive food court complemented by a fine dining French restaurant. Parking facilities are available for 2,500, and the centre prides itself on its five-star customer service.

- 345 Victoria Ave, Chatswood, ph 9419 6255.

Queen Street, Woollahra

The leafy streets of the inner east's most prestigious zone are scattered with some of the best antique shops and art galleries in the city. From the exclusive Howell and Howell, who specialise in decorative art and furniture and one-off pieces from the 17th, 18th and 19th centuries, to Appley Hoare who stock 18th-century French furniture. Home shopping heaven when money is no object.

Military Road, Neutral Bay to Mosman

One of Sydney's more affluent strips, Military Rd has something for everyone, from one of Sydney's biggest supermarkets to recycled designer clothes shops, exclusive boutiques such as Marcs, a host of galleries and beauty shops.

Roselands

This shopping centre has always been the place to meet. Opened as Sydney's first shopping 'mall' in 1968, 30 years on several of the original shops are still trading, with a kitsch '60s feel. Not to be superseded, all the major chains also now trade here.
- Roselands Drive, Roselands, ph 9750 0533.

Surry Hills/Redfern

One of the city's oldest working-class precincts today abounds with factory outlets for many top labels, such as Country Road, Sportsgirl and Howard Showers. Many of the outlets sell slightly damaged stock, and there are also many fabric shops in the area, especially along Foveaux Street, just off Central Station.

Grant Gillies

Skating

Whether your skating interest is board, roller, ice or in-line, Sydney has the ramps, rinks, parks and shops to satisfy your needs.

Macquarie Ice Rink

Home of the Sydney Bears ice-hockey team, this place attracts crowds as large as 900 on weekends. Glide along to the latest music with each program catering for both the experienced and inexperienced skater. Host of the 1991 world short-track speed-skating championships, this is a world-class venue.
- Macquarie Shopping Centre, Waterloo Rd, North Ryde, ph 9888 1100.

Manly Blades

A shop with the latest in skateboards and in-line skating kit. Providing for beginners and experts, it offers free coaching by trained staff with any purchase. This store regularly holds demonstrations.
- North Steyne, Manly, ph 9976 3833.

Bondi Beach

A spot world famous for its surfing, but fast getting a reputation for in-line skating. One of Sydney's most popular recreational in-line skating places. Walkman-clad skaters weave their way around joggers and walkers enjoying the views. Not quite LA's Venice Beach, but the closest thing Sydney has.
- Campbell Pde, Bondi Beach.

Majestic Rollerink

Xanadu eat your heart out! At the Majestic Rollerink every Tuesday and Thursday night is Gay Skate. Stilettos are swapped for roller-skates when this venue plays host to Sydney's most glamorous drag queens on wheels. It may not be a Raquel Welch roller derby, but with plenty of music by Kylie Minogue and Diana Ross it certainly lets the good times roll.
- New Canterbury Rd, Petersham, ph 9569 3233.

Mona Vale skate ramp

Regarded by the experts as the best ramp in Australia. It's not an aesthetically pleasing structure, but its transition angles makes this the smoothest ramp in town.
- Kitchener Park, Mona Vale.

Skating

Manly Skate Park
Great for beginners. A well-designed ramp that provides the young skater with the scope to learn the craft in relative safety.
- Keirle Park, Manly.

Steve Samuelson

Skiing & snowboarding

OK, snowboarders and skiers, it's time to bury the hatchet, and realise that the ski slopes are there to be shared and enjoyed by all users. After all, many shops and ski resorts cater for both – here's just a few.

Alpine World
Anything this company doesn't know about ski travel isn't worth knowing. Boasting it's the largest ski travel agent in Australia, Alpine World's consultants are avid skiers who've skied the slopes they're sending you to. Individual and package tours are available for the Snowy Mountains, New Zealand, North America and Europe.
- 343 Pacific Highway, Crows Nest, ph 9955 3744; www.alpineworld.com.au

Mountain High Travel
A travel agency that specialises in ski tours. All the major destinations are catered for, plus a few lesser known Japanese and South American resorts. All staff are skiers and between them have skied all the world's great slopes.
- 304 Willoughby Rd, Naremburn, ph 9901 3111.

InSki
A store that offers the full gamut of skiing and snowboarding equipment. The top-shelf ski products, such as Rossignol, are available plus great deals can be secured on ex-demo equipment. All the gear is available for hire.
- 46 York St, City, ph 9233 3200.

Balmoral Snowboards
Specialists who claim they're Australia's biggest year-round snowboarding stores. They sell brands of proven quality, both new and second-hand, with hiring, maintenance and repairs facilities also available.
- 73a Spit Rd, Mosman, ph 9968 1044.

STM
Another of Sydney's stores that caters for both specialities. Expert skiers and snowboarders can help you find the equipment that suits you. It also provides hire packages ranging from budget to high performance.
- 125 Bronte Rd and 237 Oxford St, Bondi Junction, ph 9386 0430.

180 Degrees
Prepare yourself for your next downhill run by improving your cardiovascular fitness, strengthening your legs and lower back. Tailor-made courses at 180 degrees give you the stamina and the strength to survive your next skiing holiday.
- Shackle Ave, Concord, ph 0412 008 605: www.180degrees.com.au

Roof Rack City
For snow chains and ski racks – if you're driving to the Snowy Mountains you may need these. Hiring facility also available.
- Head office, 42 Whiting St, Artarmon, ph 9901 3000.

Steve Samuelson

Skylights

Shed some light on your situation. Install a skylight in the kitchen, bathroom, stairwell or that creepy attic storeroom.

Velux Skylights
Popular imported Swedish, precision-made timber and glass units. You're welcome to visit the showroom, but you'll need to buy from a dealer or your installer.
- Princes Highway, St Peters, ph 9550 3288.

Sky Solutions
Makes and supplies tubes, domes and traditional window-style skylights. It claims to have the best performing 'sky tube' in the world, using a patented 'silver lux' lining to give maximum efficiency to this small-area skylight. Will supply, or deliver and install.
- 77 Queens Rd (cnr William St), Fivedock, ph 9745 1522.

Glass Bricks and Skylights
The Sydney distributor for Australian manufacturer Woodroofe Industries, it supplies roof windows, sun-tubes and skylights to suit all types of roof, from flat to almost 90-degree angles. They come with a seven-year guarantee, are on display at the Sydney Building Centre in Elizabeth St, Surry Hills, and available in kit form from hardware stores.
- 19a Linley Way, Putney, ph 9807 7850.

Attic Access Company
As the name suggests, it specialises in building attic rooms, but installing skylights is a logical extension of this highly successful business.
- 163 Taren Point Rd, Taren Point, ph 9524 2334.

Chris Dobney

Soccer

see also sporting goods
On the streets on Munich, they call it fussball. In Brazil, it remains the jogo bonito (beautiful game). Played by an estimated 400 million people worldwide, soccer's simplicity is its greatest attraction. Across Sydney that popularity is evident every afternoon and every weekend. There are more than 100,000 registered players in the metropolitan area – more than the other football codes combined.

Come the 2000 Olympics, Australia's quaintly-named Olyroos team will be in the frame for a medal. The Olympic soccer tournament is for under-23 players only, but don't be fooled. Next to the World Cup, it offers the best quality of football you're likely to see. Games will be played in four cities apart from those in Sydney. And don't forget the Matildas, our national women's team. The girls, under the guidance of coach Greg Brown, range in age from 16 to 34, and with the benefit of a professional preparation are definitely a medal contender.

Soccer NSW
The state federation has a semi-professional arm, which controls the NSW Super League and the six divisions below, and a women's State league. For those not wanting to be paid for the privilege of playing, the NSW amateurs administer the multitude of district-based associations, who in turn control the local clubs. At all these levels, soccer remains a winter sport.
- Ph 9629 1800.

Ericsson Cup
The elite National League competition which, unlike State and amateur leagues, is played in a summer season from October to May. Clubs from every state play, including local flagships Sydney Olympic (home ground Belmore Oval), Sydney United (Parramatta Stadium), Marconi-Fairfield (Marconi Stadium) and Northern Spirit (North Sydney Oval).
- Ph 9380 6099.

Club Marconi
Fancy a foccacia and a frothy cappuccino? Recently refurbished and serving the rapidly expanding suburbs of Sydney's south-west,

Soccer

this sprawling social club boasts a distinct Italian heritage among its 30,000 members. But in a sign of the changing times, more than 35 different nationalities are now represented on the members' roll. Long-standing club president Tony Labbozzetta proudly proclaims that visitors are witnessing multiculturalism in its purest form. Recent expansions include a multi-storey car park, while plans to add a new grandstand to the adjacent soccer stadium have been completed. Home to perennial National League powerhouses Marconi-Fairfield, the Marconi Stadium is one of the best venues in the country.

■ Maroni Rd, Bosley Park, ph 9823 2222.

Northern Spirit

Get into the Spirit. Watch out for the National League's newest, trendiest, grooviest, and most ambitious franchise, Northern Spirit FC. Starting in summer '98, they will play out of North Sydney Oval on user-friendly Friday nights. The Spirit have assembled an all-star cast of internationals for their debut season, including former Socceroos Graham Arnold and Scott Ollerenshaw, and star English import Ian Crook, once of Tottenham Hotspur FC. With Kathryn Greiner as president, and ARIA boss Peter Rix on the board, expect the unexpected. Residents of the northern suburbs (22,000 registered players) have never had a professional club before and should respond in their thousands.

■ Ph 9460 2187.

Soccer City

The place to go now that soccer stripes are a fashion statement – the black and white stripes of Juventus, the red of Liverpool, the yellow and blue of Brazil. Major sportswear companies such as Nike, Reebok and Fila have recently entered the market as soccer jerseys have replaced basketball singlets as favoured teenage clobber. Most major sports stores carry them, but they are all here under one roof.

■ 538 Princes Highway, Rockdale, ph 9567 5189.

SBS

Affectionately known as 'Soccer Bloody Soccer' by the basket-weaving brigade, the ethnic broadcaster has traditionally shown most free-to-air soccer coverage – from the Slovenian league to the Libertadores Cup. The ABC brings a weekly highlights program from the English premier league, while pay television broadcasters Optus Vision and Fox Sports cover a cosmopolitan mixture of leagues from Holland to France to Germany to our own Ericsson Cup. Gooaaaallll!

Michael Cockerill

Further information
■ Soccer Australia, ph 9380 6099

Softball

see also sporting goods

This sport has been taking off like a fly ball to the outfield since its inclusion as an official medal sport at the 1996 Atlanta Olympics. Sydney produces some of Australia's best softballers, such as champion pitcher and Olympic bronze medallist Melanie Roche, and boasts some of the country's most impressive facilities. Although better known as a sport played by women, softball is actually unisex and an ideal activity for families. Slowpitch is the fun, social version of softball and features modified rules so everyone can have a go. Beginners, mixed teams and masters competitions are all catered for by softball, while other modified versions of the sport, such as Teeball and Modball, are aimed at junior players and people with disabilities.

Major competitions to be held in Sydney in 1999 include the U23 men's invitational in January at the sports fields, Meurants Lane, Glenwood; the Youth Girls Pacific

Soft furnishings & fabrics

International in April at the same venue; and the Women's International in October at the Olympic Softball Stadium, Eastern Creek.

The NSW Softball Association
Can provide details about specialised clinics and coaching courses for those wanting to learn how to play softball. The association will also put you in touch with your nearest local association or club.
- ph 9746 1611.

The Strike Zone
You'll strike it lucky at this well-known outlet, with softball gear including clothing, caps, shin guards, knee pads, shoes, gloves, bats, balls, bases and catcher's equipment.
- 34 Anderson Ave, Panania, ph 9774 4767.

Olympic Softball Stadium
Work on the new home of softball will be completed in July 1999. The public will be able to hire diamonds and other facilities at the site, which will host the 2000 Olympic softball competition.
- Aquilina Reserve, Eastern Rd, Eastern Creek.

Cumberland-Nepean
With more than 1,300 players, this club is renowned as one of the biggest – and friendliest – in Sydney. Any level of player, from E-grade up, is welcomed. Call NSW Softball Association for up-to-date contact details.

Heather Quinlan

Soft furnishings & fabrics

see also interior designer & decorators
Dealing with home furnishings in this age of the fast and fashionable needn't be hell. All you need is an expert with an eye for detail and lots of bright ideas.

Interiors Soft Furnishings
Suzannah Adin trained under soft furnishing guru Christine Jeffery for eight years before branching out on her own two years ago. Made-to-measure soft furnishings at reasonable prices. Will visit your home and come up with creative solutions.
- Unit 11, 29 Scrivener St, Warwick Farm, ph 9600 9730.

Fabric With Finish
Guru of wall upholstery, Gerard Van der Bossche is a trade secret among leading decorators. His shop offers a full interior design service and can custom-make soft furnishing to order.
- 131 Booth St, Annandale, ph 9552 4576.

No Chintz
Save time and trouble by heading straight here. Sells the best range of furnishing fabrics for less than $30 per metre in Sydney as well as offering a brilliant made-to-measure service. There's also a loan arrangement so you can borrow swatch books to take home and compare colours and patterns. No Chintz can visit your home and from $65 give curtain ideas and trim suggestions.
- 574 Crown St, Surry Hills, ph 9318 2080; 509 Willoughby Rd, Willoughby, ph 9958 0257.

Stitches Soft Furnishings
Christine Jeffery is the acknowledged queen of Australian curtain making and has gained a huge following among Sydney's elite for her couture curtains which are designed and detailed to fantastic effect. Her custom work room can hand stitch window treatments that are as elaborately constructed as a Christian Lacroix gown.
- Level 1, 895 Bourke St, Waterloo, ph 9698 4399.

Soft furnishings & fabrics

Tempo Interiors
When you get stumped Kathy Abbott can help you get it right. Bursting with clever solutions, she is loved by the Mosman mob.
- 515 Military Rd, Mosman, ph 9960 2844.

Decorating Recycled
Best known for their great range of curtains and blinds: cotton through to Colefax and Fowler and beautiful chintzes. They sell all manner of decorating stuff including lamps and small items of furniture. Eighty per cent comes from people's homes, the rest from photo shoots and decorators. Prices about a third of original price. Monday to Friday 10am–5pm, Saturday 10am–2pm.
- 735 New South Head Rd, Rose Bay, ph 9388 1841.

Arkitex
There are two 13 metre long arcades from which you can study more than 3,000 textile swatches which are delightfully colour free from such big-name fabric houses as Donghia, Larsen, Jim Thompson, Pollack & Assoc, as well as Arkitex's own line by hot New York based designer Lori Weistzner.
- 44-46 McLachlan Ave, Rushcutters Bay, ph 9331 4544.

Ascraft Fabrics
You won't go wrong here with its extensive range of affordable cottons, damasks, crewels, linens damasks and paisleys.
- 19a boundary St, Rushcutters Bay, ph 9360 2311.

Boyac Decorative Furnishings
If you want to go over the top, check out the beautiful range of fabrics here including Mulberry, Boussac, Manuel Canovas, Le Filandiere, Faeini Borghi, Garin and Watts of Westminster.
- 19c Boundary St, Rushcutters Bay, ph 9360 4515.

Cloth
The latest addition to this weighty handprinted range of textiles is rawcloth, a crushingly contemporary collection of five groovy geometric designs handprinted on hemp, jute, canvas and muslin.
- Studio 51, 61 Marlborough St, Surry Hills, ph 9310 5095.

Order Imports
Top-end range of couture quality fabrics from legendary houses such as Lelievre, Houlse, Manuel de Lorca, Gassinari et Chatel, Le Crin, Zuber, Trelle, Burger and Zerel de Belval.
- 11a Boundary St, Rushcutters Bay, ph 9360 3565.

St James Furnishings
Lots of decorative grandeur here with big names that include Rubelli, Brunschwig & Fils, Marvic, G.P. & J. Baker, Gaston y Daniela.
- 15-19 Boundary St, Rushcutters Bay, ph 9332 1900.

Wardlaw
Those dedicated to the art of understatement will delight in the range of elegant fabrics here. Lots of traditional favourites such as Osborne & Little, Nina Campbell, Pierre Frey, Designers Guild, Schumacher, Warner and Liberty.
- 100 Harris St, Pyrmont, ph 9660 6266.

Melissa Walker Smith

Spanish & Latin American Sydney

If only Luis Vaes de Torres hadn't taken a wrong turn back in 1606, Sydneysiders would be eating paella, drinking rich Rioja reds, dancing to Cuban music and enjoying late-night tapas washed down by a cold Corona. Hang on, that's more or less what we do, anyway. Still, most Australians don't realise just how close the country came to being colonised by those red-blooded Spaniards rather than their slightly more dour English cousins. No matter. Over the past 50 years or so, planeloads of Spaniards and later on, Latin Americans, have found their way to Terras Australis Incognita, especially to Sydney, the Australian city with the largest – and most lively – concentration of Spanish-speakers.

The Spanish Club
Founded in the early '60s, the Spanish Club remains the spiritual centre of Hispanic Sydney. Old-timers there still recall fondly the night visiting King Juan Carlos and Queen Sofia turned up unexpectedly to chat with the locals. Open till late most nights, the club has a restaurant upstairs, and an array of activities, from language lessons to flamenco.
- 88 Liverpool St, City, ph 9267 8440.

La Viña
After several very successful years on the edge of Sydney's Little Italy, La Viña moved to bigger premises in Surry Hills about five years ago – and hasn't looked back. Good spot for a drink, some food and plenty of Latin music, including salsa and merengue, on weekends.
- 504 Elizabeth St, Surry Hills, ph 9319 0423.

Rio's Brazilian Cabaret
A huge barn of a place, with long rows of tables made for large, boisterous parties. The food is traditional southern Brazilian (lots of barbecued beef and black bean stews), but really, you come here for the Latin bands and the Brazilian floorshow, which includes scantily-clad dancers and even, occasionally, an acrobat.
- 128 Pyrmont Bridge Rd, Camperdown, ph 9557 1371.

Capitan Torres Restaurant
This has never pretended to be anything more than a family-style eatery catering to both its traditional Spanish-speaking clientele, and to all those *canguros* out to have a good night. The paella is still among the best in Sydney, the wine list is comprehensive and prices reasonable.
- 73 Liverpool St, City, ph 9264 5574.

Don Quixote Restaurant
Remember those '70s restaurants with lots of heavy furniture and impossibly low lighting? Say hello to Don Quixote. In these days of simple decor and small portions, it sticks out like a sore thumb. But who else makes spit-roasted suckling pig like Don Quixote? No-one.
- 1 Albion Place, City, ph 9264 5903.

Casa Asturiana Restaurant
This is *Sydney Morning Herald* restaurant critic Terry Durack's pick of the Spanish restaurants in Sydney. He recommends a meal of tapas, the generously proportioned paella, or char-grilled pork ribs. The Garcia Villada family come from the Asturias region of Spain, hence the name and the cuisine.
- 77 Liverpool St, City, ph 9264 1010.

Miro Restaurant
Tapas heaven, with a dash of modern Spain. Sit at the long bar and pretend you are somewhere off the Plaza Mayor in Madrid – a glass of Rioja and a selection of tapas before hitting the town.
- 76 Liverpool St, City, ph 9267 3126.

Torres Cellars and Deli
The original Spanish deli. This is the place to buy the local version of jamon serrano (a close cousin of the Italian prosciutto), turrones de Navidad (traditional sweets eaten by Spaniards and Latinos at Christmas time), and chorizo (cured sausage with a touch of paprika). Plus Spanish and South American wines.
- 75 Liverpool St, City, ph 9264 6862.

Martinez Continental Deli
South Americans from all over Sydney travel to this mega-deli in Fairfield. You can get just about everything here, from good-quality Brazilian coffee to Argentinian condiments. And of course, plenty of mate, the traditional South American 'tea'.
- 47 Spencer St, Fairfield, ph 9724 5509.

La Torre Cake Shop

Three words to describe the cakes here: rich, rich, rich. This is the place to visit for dulce de leche, the South American version of milk caramel, which is found in every second pastry. Who needs to diet?
- 1/9 Nelson St, Fairfield, ph 9724 4565.

Music Front

You can buy Spanish and Latin American music at several other places in Sydney, including **Odeon** in Bathurst St, in the City, but Music Front probably has the most ambitious collection, especially when it comes to up-to-the-minute salsa.
- Ashfield Mall, Liverpool Rd, Ashfield, ph 9799 7795.

Luis M. Garcia

Sporting goods

see also sports listings

Sydney is sports mad. It has more general sports shops than you can poke a hockey stick at. Needing more tennis balls? A pump for your football or a bike riding helmet? Here are a just few stores that cater for everyone.

Mick Simmons

Once one of the biggest names in the sporting goods industry, this is the last relic of an empire. Boasting equipment for a vast range of sports, it caters best for the popular ones such as cricket, tennis, golf and the various football codes. It's one of the oldest names in the business and has an equipment expert for each sport. It proudly claims its old-fashioned service is the best in Sydney.
- 478 George St, City, ph 9264 2744.

Rebel Sport

A retail chain with nine branches clustered around the city. This is the supermarket of sports stores. Mostly located near major shopping centres, they are designed for convenience. As a general rule, the more popular the sport, the greater the range. Central city store:
- Shop 401, Gallery Level, Mid City Centre, City, ph 9221 8633.

Sportscene

In terms of outlets, this is the largest sporting retailer in Australia. In the Sydney region alone, there are 14 shops. The general rule for this chain is if the schools are playing it, Sportscene caters for it.
- Shop 202, Bankstown Shopping Square, Bankstown, ph 9790 5385; for other locations, ph 9896 2003.

Peter Wynn's Score

A sporting goods shop with a difference, supplying equipment across a range of sports, particularly the various football codes. It also sells a wide range of rugby league paraphernalia including boxer shorts, docks, cap, mugs, nightgowns and autographed jumpers and photos. Its slogan is 'If you can't score here, you'll never score.' That may explain the range of boxer shorts!
- 197 Church St, Parramatta, ph 9891 2655.

Steve Samuelson

Squash

see also sporting goods

At a participation level, few sports in Sydney have the numbers to beat squash. Everyone, it seems, has belted that black rubber ball around the local court at one stage or another. About 7,000 Sydneysiders play pennant squash in the spring and autumn, but many more are just social players.

Riverview Squash Centre

Sydney's biggest squash facility, with 12 courts.
- 497 Victoria Rd, Ryde, ph 9816 1855.

But there are plenty of others with eight or more courts – meaning you have a better than reasonable chance of being able to book one. Try **Forest Squash** (Belrose, ph 9452 2288), **Evergreen Tennis & Squash** (Dee Why, ph 9971 4233), **Thornleigh Squash** (Thornleigh, ph 9484 5255), **Castle Fitness** (Castle Hill, ph 9634 3111), **Seven Hills Squash** (Seven Hills, ph 9674 2699), **Jannali Squash** (Jannali, ph 9528 5233) or **Rockdale Squash** (Rockdale, ph 9597 6129). Most Leagues clubs also have squash facilities.

Michelle Martin

Opponents have been known to tremble in their sports socks when Michelle Martin walks onto a squash court. The 1997 British Open champion and former world No 1 lives in Fairlight when she isn't playing in tournaments around the globe and practises her wicked backhand at the Willoughby, Forest and Powerhouse Mosman squash centres. Martin is such a strong and feared player that when she's in Sydney she plays in the men's Premier League competition – no-one can beat her in the women's league!

Thornleigh Squash Centre

Has the largest number of teams playing in the pennant competition, with clean, tidy courts and a reputation for friendliness. Centre manager Geoff Roberts is rated one of Sydney's best squash coaches. Also boasts a well-stocked pro shop.
- 6 Duffy Ave, Thornleigh, ph 9484 5255.

Canterbury-Bankstown Leagues Club

Many elite-level events are held here because the venue is large and it has glass-backed courts. It hosts the Premier League and first grade pennant finals twice a year.
- 26 Bridge Rd, Belmore, ph 9759 8733.

Heather Quinlan

Further information

- NSW Squash Ltd, ph 9660 0311
- Off The Wall, quarterly magazine available through Squash Australia, ph 07 3367 3200

Steak

see also meat

This humble slab of protein is without doubt the great survivor of the food world. It has outlasted cholesterol and heart disease scares, carcinogenic slurs, and obesity murmurings. While it has suffered the ignominy of being exiled to the fashion desert for the best part of 20 years, make no mistake: the steak is back.

Armstrong's

Mark Armstrong ages his meat in a special coolroom fitted with ultraviolet light and programmed to a constant 2 degrees centigrade. He generally presents four different steaks, but his personal favourite is the butt fillet seared on each side, then roasted whole in the oven.
- 1-7 Napier St, North Sydney, ph 9955 2066.

Bistro Moncur

There are perfectly well-adjusted adults living in Woollahra who have no idea that Bistro Moncur does anything else other than its famous grilled prime sirloin Cafe de Paris served with a zippy, herby sauce, and legendary chips.
- 116 Queen St, Woollahra, ph 9363 2782.

Kable's

Chef Serge Dansereau is renowned for his ability to source topnotch Australian produce. Fortunately for steak lovers, his finds include Kobeef – Kobe style beef produced from locally reared Wagyu cattle. With its pronounced marbling and rich flavour, it's the nearest thing to going to Japan.
- The Regent Sydney, 199 George St, City, ph 9255 0226.

Steak

Kingsley's Australian Steakhouse
It's all very Australian with its exposed sandstone and pictures of Ned Kelly and Captain Cook, not to mention the Vegemite next to the salt and pepper. Yet the steak is very good indeed, taken from 'the best Hereford and Hereford Poll cattle' and aged for a minimum of 21 days.
■ 29a King St, City, ph 9262 4155.

Lennons
Scott McFadyen has three different steaks on offer, aged in his own coolrooms. They include a beautifully aged piece of rump, rested and sliced into thin pieces which are then layered over a mounded of wilted spinach and young onions. All crusty on the outside and melting inside, it's a steak lover's dream.
■ 105 Victoria Rd, Drummoyne, ph 9819 7511.

Rengaya
You may have do a bit of the work in this cook-at-the-table Japanese grill restaurant, but at least you'll be working with some of the best meat in town. The special sirloin is magnificently marbled and obligingly sliced into chopstick friendly pieces.
■ 73 Miller St, North Sydney, ph 9929 6169.

Terry Durack

Stereo & home theatre equipment

see also televisions & videos, television, video & stereo repairs

It's fitting that a city with the world's most spectacular Opera House should also be home to several of the world's finest hi-fi and home theatre stores. These days, a stereo or home theatre system is a major purchase. You should be able to sit down in a private room and relax with a cup of coffee in one hand and a remote control in the other, to audition a wide range of components in comfort, without the pressure of pushy salespeople.

Len Wallis Audio
Voted by *Hi-Fidelity Magazine* as one of the top five stores in the world, Len Wallis has been keeping hi-fi buffs happy for more than 20 years. And with seven architect-designed listening rooms, 23 experienced staff, free installation and a 14-day money-back guarantee, it's no wonder.
■ 64 Burns Bay Rd, Lane Cove, ph 9427 6755.

Audio Excellence
You won't have to search all three floors to find your genial host, Ceto Sandoval. Just choose the room with the loudest music! You'll find he's listening to Australia's most expensive hi-fi system. Opulent though the store is, it caters for all tastes, from those who demand the finest equipment in the world to those who'd prefer something a little more modest.
■ 137 Victoria Rd, Drummoyne, ph 9819 6499.

Audio Connection
Aladdin's Cave has nothing on Josef Reidiger's store. There are more brands and models, from more places in the world, amassed here than you'll find in any other store in Australia, as well as the country's largest assembly of bargain-priced second-hand hi-fi and video components.
■ 455 Parramatta Rd, Leichhardt, ph 9518 3000.

Khai Hi-Fi
Sydney's multicultural diversity is no more evident than here, in Minh and Cindy Ong's store, where you'll find karaoke on one wall, laser disc on another and everything in between. If it's available in Asia, it's here.
■ 1/98 John St, Cabramatta, ph 9726 8308.

Greg Borrowman

Stockbrokers

see also investment managers

Sydney's stockbrokers have learned to love the mums and dads who flocked into the sharemarket on the back of the big share floats of recent years. These days you can find a broker to suit any budget and meet a wide range of needs. Just remember, it's a buyer's market.

Australian Stock Exchange

This should be everyone's first port of call. It has a free referral service which will provide you with contact names of at least three brokers who will suit your needs – no pressure, no obligations. Don't miss the Stock Exchange's free seminars each week – jam-packed with useful information.
- 20 Bond St, City, ph 1300 300 279.

Macquarie Equities

Offers the crème of retail broking services through its Inner Circle club. It costs $100 a year to join, but that entitles you to benefits such as portfolio evaluation, itemised monthly statements, and lower brokerage fees as well as Macquarie's research. It has an online broking service at cheaper rates.
- Ph 9237 3434.

Dicksons

One of Australia's oldest specialist private-client broking firms offering full service stockbroking with discounts for Seniors Card holders.
- Ph 9229 4700.

Rivkin Croll Smith

Founded by Sydney's most flamboyant stockbroker, the bead-worrying Rene Rivkin, it was responsible for making discount broking a force in Australia and offers cheaper broking without research and other extras.
- Ph 9251 2277.

Sanford Securities

Claims to offer Australia's lowest brokerage rate at $28.95 for orders up to $50,000.
- Ph 1800 819 3888:
  www.sanford.com.au

Annette Sampson

Storage

see also removalists

Whether you're renovating, going overseas, or in between addresses, storage charges vary depending on your need for either limited or unfettered access. If you need reassurance, take a look at the space first. Most companies offer incentives and budget rates for combined packing, removal and storage.

Zebra Discounts

Competitively priced furniture removal and warehouse-type storage, if you don't want access. Good for long-term storage if you're going overseas.
- 1 Gladstone St, Newtown, ph 9557 2122.

Grace Removals

Established since 1911, removalists measure and pack. Payment is gauged by the cubic metre. Large wooden boxes are stacked to a height of four and placed in wooden storage modules.
- North Shore, ph 9979 6100; Eastern Suburbs, ph 9666 6177; Western Suburbs, ph 9704 2222.

Global Self Storage

Ten branches offer incentives such as two months' storage free, if you sign up for six months and pay in advance, and a 20 per cent discount on another company's quote for periods of one to five months.
- Ph 1800 677 784.

Storage Australia

You can drive into its storage warehouse or it can recommend removalists who can estimate

Storage

the storage size needed and know how to pack in the space.
- 28 Salisbury Rd, Hornsby, ph 9482 7404.
- 401 Victoria Rd, Gladesville, ph 9816 5555.

Trisha Treanor

Streetwear

Sydney's streetwear outlets are segregated into very specific niche markets, all of which are based on youth subculture and cult dressing. Whether you consider yourself skate, hip hop, mod, or vintage rocker there is a store to meet your needs.

Cobra Athleisure

A department store for the label-crazed teen. Tommy Hilfiger, Guess?, Levi Strauss, Nike, Adidas, Oakley, Champion, Vans and Puma, to name a few.
- Shop C75, Castlereagh St level, Centrepoint, 100 Market St, City, ph 9223 5511. Westfield Shoppingtown, Parramatta, ph 9687 8588.

Fila

Italian sportswear label Fila's concept store has a great range from the original black Fila high tops of early '90s Hip Hop craze, to the too-cool sweatshirts for boys and demi tops for the gals.
- Shop G52, Queen Victoria Building, George St, City, ph 9267 6638.

Dotti

Ranging from funky daywear to spandangly clubwear, the cheap and cheerful clothes at Dotti stores are always a hit with teenage girls and club-goers.
- Shop 227, Mid City Centre, Pitt St Mall, City, ph 9223 4028. Also at Paddington, ph 9332 1659; Bondi Junction, ph 9389 0526; Chatswood, ph 9415 3482; Parramatta, ph 9633 2342; Miranda, ph 9540 9022.

D-PO

For simple jeanswear with a wild, streak look to labels G-Star and Diesel, or thoroughly insane 'cyberwear' from Belgian label W.&L.T (Wild & Lethal Trash).
- 441 Oxford St, Paddington, ph 9361 4339.

General Pants

For an affordable, lightening-fast interpretation of current street trends, General Pants can dress most youth cultures from surfer to raver. Everything from Lee to Rip Curl for clothes, Oakleys to Blackflys sunglasses, and the latest Converse or Vans for your tootsies.
- 391 George St, City, ph 9299 3565; with stores from Blacktown to Brookvale to Bondi.

Rif Raf

Great shopping for anything lycra, especially tops.
- 414 Oxford St, Paddington, ph 9331 2292. Also at Darlinghurst, ph 9361 5545; Bondi, ph 9130 3201; Brookvale, ph 9938 6610; Parramatta, ph 9687 2034.

Run For Your Life, Nike

From the sports and fitness company that just cannot shake being fashionable comes a concept store with everything Nike you could ever want in the footwear and apparel departments.
- 44 Bronte Rd, Bondi Junction, ph 9389 0414.

Swellstore

Casual wear with just the right dose of cult background to make it cool. For men, hooded sweatshirts from Fred Perry, and mod shirts from Ben Sherman; PIGSINSPACE, Saba knitwear and Mossimo for the girls; and Clarks desert boots and Wallabies for both.
- 256 Oxford St, Paddington, ph 9331 5822.

Wheels & Doll Baby
Quirky accessories and retro glam-rock clothing from a selection of local and American labels.
■ 259 Crown St, Surry Hills, ph 9361 3286.

YPV
A nice mix of street attire for day that will take you out that night as well. Stock includes, for men, own label YPV; for women, PIGSINSPACE; and for both, Mooks and comfortable John Smedley knits.
■ 314 Crown St, Darlinghurst,
ph 9332 4090.

Felicity Ward

Sunglasses

see also swimwear & surfwear, hats, glasses & optical supplies
With the depleting ozone layer, sunglasses are not only a hot fashion item but a health must-have for all seasons.

Dioptics
For prescription sunglasses and snazzy imported brands, Dioptics' tiny store is brimming with labels such as French Beausoleil, LA Eyeworks, Japanese Bada and Australian Jonathan Sceats.
■ Shop 320, Mid City Centre, City,
ph 9221 0049.

George Skoufis Optometrist
Just at the start of the hip and happening Paddington precinct, Skoufis has a host of cool brands – Anne et Valentin, Alain Mikli, Donna Karan, Robert la Roche, LA Eyeworks, Arnette, DSO and Mossimo.
■ 38A Oxford St, Paddington,
ph 9360 7487.

K Optica
Full of interesting imported labels, such as Alain Mikli, Lafonte, Icon, Selima, X Japan, Matsuda, Jil Sander and Kirk Originals. And the shop itself is a design statement with its wavy wood and aluminium cabinets.
■ 432 Oxford St, Paddington, ph 9331 3400.

Sunglass Hut
This chain store is bursting with anything from the cheap and cheerful (Fiorelli, Polaroid and Cancer Council) to the funky (Stussy and Dirty Dog) and the designer labels (cK, Gucci and Armani).
■ Glasshouse, Pitt St Mall, ph 9223 8185.

Face It
This is OPSM's answer for the young and funky market, stocking hip brands Arnette, Oakley, Ray Ban, Bolle, Black Fly, Diesel, Adidas, Fossil, Dakota Smith, Red Ant and Dirty Dog, plus designer labels Gucci, Giorgio Armani and Cutler and Gross.
■ 446a Oxford St, Paddington,
ph 9331 4619; Macquarie Centre,
ph 9805 1511.

Shades
Devoted entirely to sunglasses, this Adelaide-based company stocks some of the hottest labels around – Stussy, Killer Loop and Arnette – and international designer labels Dolce & Gabbana, Giorgio Armani and Gucci.
■ Shop 309, Mid City Centre, City,
ph 9221 1949.

Jane de Teliga

Supermarkets

The supermarket has changed. It is now a greengrocer, hardware store, fashion boutique, bottle shop and specialty store. Most are bland and boring, but there are a few

Supermarkets

that make shopping more fun than going to the dentist.

Thai Kee Supermarket
Seek and ye shall find, at the Thai Kee. With whole aisles devoted to Korean, Thai, Japanese, Indian, and most of all, Chinese food products and serving utensils, you can feed yourself in every Asian language. Also fresh breads, ancient Chinese medicines, frozen goods and 'normal' supermarket stuff like loo paper.
- Shop 138, Level 1, Market City, Haymarket, ph 9212 4466.

Franklins Big Fresh, Marrickville
In a *Choice* magazine national survey in 1996, this branch of the Franklins chain was found to offer the cheapest available standard basket of groceries. For brand name products, the cheapest basket was to be found at the Franklins Big Fresh as Mt Druitt.
- Cnr Smidmore and Murray Sts, Marrickville, ph 9565 1029.

Woolworths Neutral Bay
If life were an episode of *Star Trek*, Neutral Bay Woollies would be a friendly but alien planet. It's huge. You can get lost between the asparagus and the barbecue beads, but at least you'll never starve. Now that the management have started promoting that thing about singles nights, it's only for losers.
- 43 Grosvenor St, Neutral Bay, ph 9908 3055.

Five Star Gourmet
It may look like a supermarket but it's really a gourmet food store in disguise, with a fantastic deli section, great imported goods, specialty cheeses and even those hard-to-find American favourites.
- 13–19 Willoughby Rd, Crows Nest, ph 9438 5666.

Tokyo Mart
Your one-stop Japanese shopping stop. Pick up exquisite lacquered bowls for your soba noodles, finely cut beef for your sukiyaki, all those mirins, tamaris and sakes those pesky recipes call for and enough rice to sink a ship.
- 27 Northbridge Plaza, Northbridge, ph 9958 6860.

Jill Dupleix

Surfing

see also beaches, lifesaving, swimwear & surfwear

James Cook, 18th-century English watersports hero, obviously was well briefed before he left London. Australia's first settlement had to be located on a prime stretch of surfing coastline. He favoured the southside, proposing the city centre be located at Botany Bay. But perhaps he'd sailed past Voodoo – at the northern end of Cronulla – in a nor'easter, witnessed those gaping left-hand barrels and decided that was good enough for him.

As we all know, Cook later journeyed to Hawaii where he (in surfing parlance) was 'badly eaten' after an altercation with some heavy locals. Some things never change. But it wasn't until 1957, and the introduction of the malibu boards, that Sydneysiders appreciated Cookie's foresight.

In the right conditions, every ocean beach in Sydney turns on, from the infamous Shark Island at Cronulla in Sydney's deep south to the left-hander down the side of Barrenjoey at the northern end of Palm Beach. And, yes, this includes Coogee.

It doesn't get very big very often, but Sydney's beaches regularly produce crisp, clean waves that have nurtured the talents of more world champions than any other area in the world. World titleholders Midget Farrelly, Nat Young, Tom Carroll, Damien Hardman and Barton Lynch all hail from Sydney's northern beaches.

Pipeline master Larry Blair cut his teeth at Maroubra, consistent world runner-up Cheyne Horan learnt his skills at Bondi and born-again shredder Mark Occhilupo grew up at Cronulla.

There are tens of thousands of avid surfers in Sydney. And since the birth of the modern malibu – a revamped version of the '60s longboard – there are almost as many surfers with no hair as those with long hair. Its popularity has made Sydney an ideal venue for including surfing as a demonstration sport during the 2000 Olympics.

Local clubs on every beach hold regular contests. But the big event on the competitive Sydney calendar is the Coke Classic, one of the richest contests in the world, traditionally held at North Narrabeen just after Easter.

Breaks

Shark Island, Cronulla Point and Voodoo in the south. Maroubra, Bronte and Bondi in the city. Fairy Bower, Dee Why Point, North Narrabeen, Newport Peak and Whale Beach wedge in the north.

Seasons

There are two distinct seasons. Prime time is winter, from May until September, when westerly winds create beautiful waves from swells generated by Antarctic storms. From then it is relatively quiet until the cyclone season – between February and May – when the Coral Sea sends mammoth swells down the NSW coast.

Shops

Every major beach has at least one surf shop. Cronulla has six. **Surf, Dive 'n Ski** (ph 9299 4920) has eight shops in major suburban shopping malls and three in the city, while **Surfection** (ph 9387 1600) has six, stretching from Bondi to Mona Vale. Few hire boards, as catering to tourists lacks cred, man. But almost all sell good quality, reasonably priced used boards. All carry mals, short boards and boogie boards.

Shapers

Ask 20 surfers and you'll get 20 answers, as the best surfboards are all hand crafted. Brookvale and Mona Vale on the north side and Caringbah in the south are the surf equivalents of auto alley. The big names are **Insight** (4/76 Darley St, Mona Vale, ph 9997 8266), **Aloha** (Unit 8, 111 Old Pittwater Rd, Brookvale, ph 9939 1831) and **Hot Buttered** (Unit 1, 3 Vuko Pl, Warriewood, ph 9970 8000). In the south, **Jackson Surfboards** (57 Captain Cook Drive, Caringbah, ph 9524 2700) caters for an older crew, while **Force 9** (43 Captain Cook Drive, Caringbah, ph 9526 1007) and **Vudu Liquid Equipment** (41 Captain Cook Drive, Caringbah, ph 9524 9022) are strong local names.

Australian Surfriders Association

There is a large number of professionally accredited surfing coaches on its books, spread along the entire stretch of Sydney coastline. Most coaches operate in conjunction with local surf shops and provide all equipment in surf schools held throughout the school holidays. Private lessons also can be arranged.
■ **Ph 9976 0657.**

Ian Verrender

Swimming

see also beaches, surfing, swimwear & surfwear, triathlon

Whether it's the sand and surf of a beach, the grass and concrete around a local pool or a sandstone rock ledge above a gum-shaded creek, when the weather warms Sydneysiders get wet. While there's nothing quite like throwing yourself in the cool surf on a summer's day, local swimming pools and centres have one big advantage – they are just that . . . local. North, south, east or west, a pool is never far away.

Swimming is part of the city's consciousness. It is the Olympic sport at which we expect to do best, with the state-of-the-art

Swimming

Sydney International Aquatic Centres open and hosting major events.

And, whether you're a babe in arms or an octogenarian wanting to improve your stroke, there's a swimming class somewhere for you in Sydney. As well, most metropolitan pools have specialised staff, ready to turn toe-dippers into swimmers.

Coogee Women's Pool

A women- and kids-only rockpool. Great for Muslim women (who can't swim with men) and just going topless, unhassled by blokes. Also at Coogee is **Wylies Baths**: sluiced by ocean tides, you can see the shells and seaweed as you do your laps.
- Beach St, Coogee.

Bondi Icebergs

Swim year-round with the Bondi Icebergs at the south end of the beach.
- Notts Ave, Bondi, ph 9130 3120.

Chinamans Beach

At the Spit, just round from Balmoral. Sheltered, quiet, clean sand, a great picnic spot, with a park backing onto the beach.

Parsley Bay

A secluded, netted spot for swimming, set off by an expanse of bright-green grass. Like being in the front yard of your own harbourside mansion.
- Parsley Rd, Vaucluse.

Warringah Aquatic Centre

Before Homebush this was the venue for most of the major events held in Sydney. Caters for all swimmers, from competitive to beginners.
- Aquatic Drive, French's Forest, ph 9451 8000.

North Sydney Olympic Pool

Just under the Harbour Bridge near Luna Park, a historic favourite. Full of strictly-business lap-pounders in the early morning, but empties out by 9am.
- Alfred St, North Sydney, ph 9955 2309.

Sutherland Leisure Centre

The south's premier swimming venue, with an indoor and outdoor pool, a children's pool with toys and games to keep youngsters amused, a gymnasium and learn-to-swim classes for babies through to senior citizens.
- Rawson Ave, Sutherland, ph 9545 2400.

Sydney International Aquatic Centre

Site for swimming events in 2000. Swimming classes for children and adults held throughout the week. Also competitive swimming, or just splash around.
- Sydney Olympic Park, Homebush Bay, ph 9752 3666.

Andrew (Boy) Charlton Pool

Like the Olympic gold medallist it was named after, the pool is part of Sydney's swimming history. Wedged between the Botanical Gardens and the Harbour, this pool is unheated and bracing.
- Mrs Macquaries Rd, The Domain, ph 9358 6686.

MacCallum Pool

Surrounded by timber decking, this North Shore pool has uninterrupted views back across the harbour to the Opera House and the Bridge.
- Milsons Rd, Cremorne Point ph 9936 8100 (North Sydney Council).

Matthew Dunn Swim School

An innovative learn-to-swim program run by swimming star Matthew Dunn. Home delivery swimming classes aimed at increasing confidence and safety in your backyard pool.
- ph 9487 8744.

Mike Cowley and Ali Gripper

Further information
- NSW Swimming Association, ph 9552 2966: www.nswswimming.com.au
- Swimming in Australia: www.netspace.net.au/~logan/

Swimming pools & spas

Choosing the right builder is the key to ensuring to that your vision of a backyard water-world is realised painlessly. The Master Builders Association can provide a list of builders in your local area (ph 9281 3511 or 1800 451 393).

Blue Haven Pools
One of Australia's largest pool builders, Blue Haven can construct pools of any size and style from above-ground models to the fully landscaped concrete variety.
- ph 13 2025.

Crystal Pools
'Quality without compromise' is the company's motto. The firm has been in the pool business since 1957, designing and building pools for private, commercial, school, hospital and municipal clients. Crystal, which has won numerous awards, recently built a pool for Admiralty House.
- ph 9875 4555.

Mirage Pools
Mirage caters to the middle to upper end of the market. Sophisticated in-floor cleaning systems are a speciality. The company recently built the penguin pool at Taronga Park Zoo.
- Moorebank, ph 9601 8677; Chatswood, ph 9954 5705.

PoolWerx Mobile Pool and Spa Care
Poolwerx styles itself as the complete pool and spa care company, says it does 'everything except build them'. With mobile franchises in 20 suburbs throughout Sydney, Poolwerx will maintain or repair your pool, and deliver pool equipment and chemicals. In addition, they promise a 'less than one hour response' to emergency situations.
- ph 1800 812 025.

Corfu Pools & Spas
Installs concrete pools and spas, and specialises in renovations. Corfu's Harry Trifonas received multi recommendations in the *Sydney Morning Herald*'s Tradespeople of the Years Awards.
- ph 9872 2894.

Peter Jordan

Swimwear & surfwear

see also sporting goods, surfing

If there's one thing Australians excel at above all others in fashion, it is swimwear and surfwear. Our surfwear labels are booming around the world and some of our swimwear labels are making inroads into international markets, too. Lucky us, we just have to nip down to our nearest beach to buy it.

Bikini Island
The quintessential swimwear shop that's been going since 1961, on Australia's most famous beach. Bursting with bikinis and one-pieces from a wide range of local labels such as Ozone Aware, Seafolly, Finch, Moontide (New Zealand) and their own '60s-style crochet bikinis in silver and gold lame.
- Shop A, 38 Campbell Pde, Bondi Beach, ph 9300 9446.

Cool for Cats
A popular Bondi shop packed with swim- and surfwear for women, men and children. Labels include Jets, Sunseeker, Paradise Express, Charlie Brown, Beach Patrol (US) and Elements.
- 74 Campbell Pde, Bondi Beach, ph 9365 4457.

Mambo
Australian cult surfwear label that has grown into one of the hottest street-style favourites

around the world with shops in London (Covent Garden and a new store opening in Carnaby St) and Brighton in the UK, Singapore, Denpasar, Kuta and Tokyo. With a quirky, irreverent sense of humour and great prints, Mambo is famous for its iconoclastic T-shirts – like the farting dog which has now reached classic status. Surfwear and streetwear for men, women and children all in one concept store.
- 17 Oxford St, Paddington, ph 9331 8034.

Hot Tuna
Aussie surfwear label like Mambo that grew to include men's, women's and children's gear plus all the accessories, covered with characteristic Hot Tuna prints. Everything from clothes, bags, jewellery, sunglasses, watches, caps, beach towels and even furniture.
- 180 Oxford St, Paddington, ph 9361 5049.

The Quiksilver Boardriders Club
Strictly surfwear label that is big on the Australian surf scene and now making inroads into the US market. Sold from Brazil to Indonesia.
- 88 The Corso, Manly, ph 9977 8444.

Surf Dive 'n Ski
The full surfie bit with stores from Brookvale to Parramatta. Everything from surfboards, swimsuits, sportswear, surf and skatewear for men, women and children. Big range of surfwear labels like Billabong, Quiksilver, Rip Curl, Aztec Rose, Mambo, Just Add Water, SMP, Volcom, Rusty and Kuta Lines. Surfboards, skateboards, sunglasses, clothes and shoes from all the funky surf labels.
- City store, 462-463 George St, City, ph 9267 3408.

Lorna Jane
Queensland style comes to Sydney with somewhat kitschy but ingeniously cut swimwear using unusual fabrics and retro-style prints like op-art patterns, marbled velvets and animal prints. Also a lot of active wear.
- 391 Oxford St, Paddington, ph 9360 5113.

Zimmermann
The hippest swimwear by young Australian designer that is being sold around the world. As far away from fluoro as you can get – dark and funky fashion colours and her own prints are her swimwear speciality.
- 24 Oxford St, Woollahra, ph 9360 5769.

Jane de Teliga

Synchronised swimming

The myths of synchronised swimming are that you need cast-iron lungs and a goal to compete at the Olympics before you can attempt this sport. In reality, you just need to be a competent swimmer and have a willingness to try something a bit different. Another myth is that this is a girls-only sport. Boys are very welcome to join a club and learn the sport's many skills. The 1999 championships will be held in February, at Auburn and Granville pools.

Sydney International Aquatic Centre
The Olympic event will be held here and Australia, ranked 12th in the world, will of course be competing. Along with Granville and Auburn pools, it is one of three Sydney venues with water deep enough to practise synchronised swimming properly.
- Sydney Olympic Park, Homebush Bay, ph 9752 3444.

NSW Synchronised Swimming
This is the association for the sport. They can put you in touch with the club closest to your area. Sydney's champion synchronised swim-

ming club is Ariel. There are six clubs in total, the others being Northern Beaches, Swans, Knox Pymble Aquatic, Holroyd and Auburn.
- Ph 9632 5449.

Danz Design
Specialises in colourful, sequined synchronised swimming costumes.
- 13 Penshurst Rd, Penshurst, ph 9580 1966.

Sylphides
Another costume maker recommended by NSW Synchronised Swimming.
- Ph 9874 1388.

Heather Quinlan

Table tennis

Countless ping pong stars of all shapes and sizes lurk behind Sydney garage doors, where championship matches are played out on family table tennis tables. It's a game loved by millions around the world and, happily, can be played at all levels. Many licensed clubs have table tennis tables, as do some YMCAs and Police & Citizens Youth Clubs. The main teams competitions are played in the Sutherland, Western Districts and Manly areas, but Table Tennis NSW Inc (ph 9660 0710) can help you find a club wherever you are. Bats at the ready . . .

Combined Sports Traders
For all your table tennis equipment.
- 959 Canterbury Rd, Lakemba, ph 9750 4211.

Greenacre YMCA
The most popular spot for table tennis, with 16 tables for hire on Thursday, Saturday and Sunday nights. Anyone can turn up and find a willing opponent here.
- 87 Waterloo Rd, Greenacre, ph 9740 3476.

NSW Veterans Table Tennis Association
Calling over 40s . . . whether you hanker to join a team, play competition table tennis or just line up a social game, the NSWVTTA can help. Beginners are welcome.
- ph 9796 7000.

Cumberland College
Elite events are played on an irregular basis (about once a month) and when Sydney's top table tennis players get together they frequently play in the sports hall of the University of Sydney's Cumberland Campus. Table Tennis NSW (see introduction) can supply further information.
- East St, Lidcombe, ph 9660 0710.

Heather Quinlan

Tableware

see also homewares, cookware & kitchenware
From plastic plates and tin cups on the back of a boat to an alfresco lunch with porcelain plates and bone-handled cutlery, Sydney serves up a spirited mismatch of tabletop textures that will add sure-fire chic to your table.

Pavillion Christofle
Get your couture crockery here. As well as the silver-plated splendours of Christofle, there is a full range of porcelain, linen, silver and crystal by Christian Lacroix. Each piece oozes with originality and fantasy.
- 11 Bay St, Double Bay, ph 9363 4166.

Dinosaur Designs

Seriously sexy designer tabletop accessories handmade in resin. Every form imaginable from organic pitchers to bowls and spoons in a colourful palette.
- 339 Oxford St, Paddington, ph 9361 3776. Also at the Strand Arcade, ph 9223 2953, and The Rocks, ph 9251 5500.

IKEA

Thoroughly modern bargain basics with everything from plain white plates to stainless steel cutlery and chic glassware.
- 19 Stoddard Rd, Prospect, ph 9636 9222. Also at Moore Park, ph 9313 6400 and Gordon, ph 9498 3822.

Ma Maison en Provence

Few looks can match the drama of faience earthenware. The colours are to die for: there's really no comparison. Check out the dreamy range of enamel-glazed terracotta plates and pitchers for everyday use.
- 158 Queen St, Woollahra, ph 9363 1500.

The Bay Tree

Stockists of William Yeoward glassware, Rambouillet crystal, Duralex tumblers, Pillivuyt, Apilco and Limoges porcelain, Maryse Boxer, Gien and Luneville ceramics plus must-have Belgium table linen.
- 40 Holdsworth St, Woollahra, ph 9328 1101.

The Butler's Pantry

Stockists of china, glass and silver plate dating from the 18th century to the present day with everything in between. Cam McEachern will happily scour Australia for a missing piece of china dating from any period. Also handles glass repairs.
- 36 Gurner St, Paddington, ph 9360 4736.

The Art of Wine and Food

An old favourite with magazine editors and food stylists looking for character glassware, corkscrews, faience earthenware and champagne buckets. Great mix of the decorative and the practical.
- 80 Queen St, Woollahra, ph 9363 2817.

Melissa Walker Smith

Tai chi

see also martial arts, alternative medicine

The ancient and serene Chinese exercise has grown steadily in popularity during the past two decades. Experienced teachers offer classes in most Sydney regions.

Australian Academy of Tai Chi

Senior master Gary Khor has taught in Australia for over 20 years. The group runs classes at venues throughout Sydney.
- 686 Parramatta Rd, Croydon, ph 9797 9355.

Tai Chi College of Australia

The highly-experienced Dr Tennyson Yiu runs classes in Manly and Kensington.
- 3 Wentworth St, Manly, ph 9977 7122.

Tai Chi Hung Ging Academy

Master Peter Yiu has 42 years' experience and teaches at venues in Chinatown and Chatswood.
- 176 Commonwealth St, Surry Hills, ph 9211 1353.

Tai Chi Qi Gong Centre & Yoga Centre

Classes in the Eastern and Inner Western suburbs.
- PO Box 89, Petersham, ph 9569 3249.

Kellen Chia

Grand master Kellen Chia teaches the traditional form of Tai Chi in classes throughout Sydney.
- Ph 9954 0806.

Peter Jordan

Tattoos & piercing

Every second bank teller in Sydney, it seems, has a red rose tattooed on their shoulder, and you can't blade along Bondi Beach without seeing a parade of pierced belly buttons. Tattooing and body piercing are a tribal body art that's hip along every fashionable Sydney strip.

Celtic Dragon Tattoo Art Studio

Non-smoking tattoo emporium where Kiwi Kim – as she's known in the trade – specialises in Celtic designs, Japanese motifs, tribal images and realistic portraits. The place for Newtown punks, bikers and businessmen.
- 41 Enmore Rd, Newtown, ph 9516 5120.

Harry's Tattoo World

Light and clean with a friendly atmosphere. On the edges of Taylor Square, a popular parlour for travellers after a permanent memento of Sydney. Mostly custom work.
- 22 Flinders St, Darlinghurst, ph 9331 5385.

The Illustrated Man

A famed Sydney tattoo parlour, owned by the award-winning troubadour of tattooing, Toney Cohen. The name is from the counter-culture 1968 film in which Rod Steiger's skin is covered with fantastic tattoos that foretell the future.
- 228a Elizabeth St, City, ph 9211 3761.

The Piercing Urge

The best-known place to get pierced and pricked in Sydney. They sell only surgical stainless steel and solid 18-carat gold jewellery, all bio-compatible with such body parts as eyebrows, tongues, lips and naughty bits.
- 322 Bourke St, Darlinghurst, ph 9360 3179.

Polymorph Body Piercing Studio

The widest range of piercing jewellery in Sydney, with a gallery upstairs for local and international artwork. Specialists in skin stretching.
- 82 Enmore Rd, Newtown, ph 9519 8923.

Dugald Jellie

Televisions & videos

see also stereo & home theatre, television, video & stereo repairs

It doesn't matter what you call it – the 'box', the 'telly', or the 'TV' – that flickering screen dominates our lives. Choosing a set from amongst the bewildering array of widescreen, flat-screen, projection and plasmatypes that are available can be tough. When you're buying, remember to compare sets side by side, under the same lighting conditions, and make certain that the colour, brightness and contrast controls are all at their factory pre-set positions.

Sound & Vision

Offers a wide range of European and Japanese-made TVs and VCRs, plus excellent advice, a ten-day home trial and double-length warranty.
- 67 Ebley St, Bondi Junction, ph 9387 5222.

DME

Good range of sets, specialising in European, but other makes sold.
- 102 Glover St, Cremorne, ph 9908 3611.

Ryda Home Entertainment

Palatial airconditioned premises and great deals on Akai, Grundig, Panasonic, Sony, and Toshiba televisions and VCRs.

■ 676 Pacific Highway, Chatswood, ph 9411 1133.

Rentlo

One of the few rental firms that can give you access to all the biggest names in the electronics business, such as Philips, Panasonic, Sharp, Sony, Sanyo and Samsung. Rentlo deals in conventional and teletext sets, large-screen and projection TVs, and home-theatre sound systems as well as complete home entertainment systems. Free delivery and installation, plus free repairs.

■ 101 Silverwater Rd, Silverwater, ph 9648 3355. Also at Dee Why, ph 9972 2980.

Radio Rentals

This long-established firm has a lowest-rate guarantee. Although it specialises in televisions, video recorders and stereo systems, it's a one-stop shop where you can just as easily rent a computer, a fax machine, colour printer, washing machine or home and office furniture.

■ Shop 12a, MLC Centre, King St, City, ph 13 1181. Also nine suburban stores.

Valtel

Need to hire a video camera to capture that special occasion on tape? Camcorders are a speciality at Valtel. This company is also expert at short-term hire for conferences, weddings and special events.

■ 13 Lawndale Ave, North Rocks, ph 9873 3377.

Other good hire organisations are **Cumberland Electronics** (215 Parramatta Rd, Auburn, ph 9737 8499) and **Redihire** (ph 13 1501).

Greg Borrowman

Television, video & stereo repairs

Twenty years ago, you would have had the name of your local TV repair store permanently stuck to the door of your fridge. These days, hi-fi and TV equipment is so reliable that few Sydneysiders have any experience in how to locate a good electronics technician. Any search is made more complicated by the increasing complexity of modern electronics which has meant that many repair stores now specialise in certain types of components and sometimes only particular brands. When booking your equipment in for repair, save yourself time and money by providing a complete written explanation of the fault, the time it occurred and any unusual circumstances, such as a thunderstorm, or the connection of a new household appliance.

Dr Hi-Fi

Specialist repairer of domestic and professional audio/hi-fi equipment (not video or TV).

■ 74 Carrington Rd, Waverley, ph 9369 2008.

Associated Technicians

Expert CD/MiniDisc repairer as well as general hi-fi. Will repair VCRs, but not TVs.

■ 17 Tramore Place, Killarney Heights, ph 9975 1410.

Allison Audio

Specialises in car audio, particularly car CD players, also general hi-fi components and TV/video equipment.

■ 46 Wattle Rd, Brookvale, ph 9905 5613.

Crystal TV

TV repairs a speciality but will fix VCRs and accepts general hi-fi repairs.

■ 9 Crystal St, Petersham, ph 9569 1790.

Vienna Hi-Fi Electronics
Repairs mainly European-made TVs, but also works on all other brands.
- 220 Waldron Rd, Chester Hill, ph 9645 1384.

Cohen TV
All TV and video repairs.
- Shop 3, 3 Gondola Rd, Narrabeen, ph 9913 9963.

Greg Borrowman

Tennis

see also sporting goods

In comparing golf to tennis, an American golf writer once observed the difference between the two was that if you've played one tennis court you've played them all, while each golf course had its own story to tell. That may be true up to a point, but there remain courts in Sydney, either for playing or watching, that can only heighten the enjoyment of the game. Sydney will never be the same after the Olympics, and that is also true for one of its most beloved sporting venues – White City – under threat of subdivision now that tournament tennis is moving to a 16-court complex seating 10,000 on centre court at Homebush Bay. The same could be said for Sydney suburbia, where hundreds of antbed courts adjoining even modest family homes have vanished under the relentless pressure of subdivision. But tennis is still an affordable pleasure for most, with public and private courts across Sydney available for $10–15 an hour.

White City
A permanent place in the city's history and memories, particularly for the crowd of 25,578 who turned up to watch the first day of the Davis Cup final between Australia and the United States in December 1954. The Garden Enclosure, the second 'stadium' court which seats about 1,500, is without doubt *the* best place in Australia to watch tournament play.
- 30 Alma St, Paddington, ph 9360 4113.

Rushcutters Bay Tennis Centre
Five loam-surfaced courts alongside one of Sydney's most picturesque cricket grounds. An early-morning match will get you a serenade from a few thousand lorikeets in the Queensland black bean trees on one side, and a view past the boats moored at the Cruising Yacht Club of Australia and down the harbour to the sunrise.
- Waratah Ave, Rushcutters Bay, ph 9357 1675.

Primrose Park Tennis
A different surface and a different water view – of the Long Bay arm of Middle Harbour. These four synthetic grass courts are nestled in a valley just above the water. Located on the less unit-infested side of Cremorne, you can contemplate the local real estate between points, and ponder what might have been if you'd turned pro at 17.
- Young St, Cremorne, ph 9908 2366.

Bayview Tennis Court
This one is a personal favourite, again for the surrounds, rather than the court surface, which is fairly careworn bitumen. It is a single court, just beyond the summit of one of the hills overlooking the entrance to Pittwater. Surrounded by gum trees, you can be deafened by cicadas or heckled by kookaburras; just the thing when you're facing break point with that dodgy second serve.
- Kara Cres, Bayview, ph 9997 6992.

Marrickville Tennis Club
Possibly the cheapest grass court tennis in Sydney. The surface isn't exactly day one at Wimbledon, but it's in better shape than your backyard. The court closest to Livingston Rd has a pronounced slope away from the deuce

court, allowing a right-handed server to enjoy briefly the fantasy of the massive swinging serve otherwise the exclusive property of left-handers.
- Livingston Rd, Marrickville, ph 9569 1348.

Strung Out

Phil Colin has been stringing racquets for the pros – a notoriously finicky breed – at the NSW Open since 1985, and did likewise for the Australian Indoor before its demise in 1994. More recently, Frenchman Guy Forget would not let anyone else touch his racquets during the 1997 Davis Cup tie against Australia.
- 137 Bayswater Rd, Rushcutters Bay, ph 9360 9905.

Cockatoo Tennis and Golf

This has more to do with fashion than equipment. Joan Harris's clothing line has already proved itself popular with the kids at White City each January, proof that there is a market for something distinctively Australian apart from serve and volley tennis.
- 145 Edgecliff Rd, Woollahra, ph 9387 5745.

Love On Deuce

It's the little things that matter. The headquarters of the Northern Suburbs Tennis Association is one of the more innovative centres on the North Shore, with corporate days, tiny tots' training and breakfast competitions. This is a *real* breakfast comp – the clubhouse/pro shop has its own espresso machine.
- Talus St, Naremburn, ph 9901 3144.

The Tennis Ranch

An aggressive advertiser of its substantial range of everything and anything related to the game. Arguably the most comprehensive in Sydney.
- 128 Victoria Rd, Gladesville, ph 9816 3666.

Wally Masur

Without doubt the best qualified of any of the Sydney coaches, if you regard 13 years on the pro tour and a recent stint looking after the now-retired Wimbledon champ Michael Stich as a suitable background. You would, however, need to be extremely good or extremely wealthy to get his attention. Other coaching queries should be directed to Ray Parker at the NSW Tennis Coaches Association (ph 9548 3880).

Gerard Wright

Further information
- Tennis NSW, ph 9331 4144

Thai restaurants

Thai food has taken the world by typhoon over the last two years, but rarely does it reach the heights it manages to achieve in Sydney. If you're looking for the real thing and don't mind the good honest prickle of a little chilli on the tip of your tongue, then follow your nose to the following.

Darley St Thai

This may well be the best Thai restaurant outside of Thailand. David Thompson is a dedicated flavour raider, taking from ancient Thai cookbooks to reproduce dishes you'd be hard pressed finding in their home country. Nothing is toned down for Western tastes so come ready for anything.
- 28-30 Bayswater Rd, Kings Cross, ph 9358 6530.

Prasit on Crown

Prasit Prateeprasen has had more Thai restaurants than most of us had pad thais, but this is without a doubt his finest effort to date. Try not to be too distracted by the garish purple colour scheme (it's a royal Thai purple) and just focus on his wonderful masaman lamb curry, and tom yum scampi.

- 413 Crown St, Surry Hills, ph 9319 0748.

Phat Boys

It's as white and as glossy as the inside of a plastic lunchbox. But in spite of the cooler than cool space, you can always be sure of a warm welcome and some good hot Thai food. Just follow the chilli rating on the menu and let owner Nick Townsend steer you towards a suitably compatible wine.

- 118 Crown St, East Sydney, ph 9332 3284.

Sailors Thai

If Darley St is the designer label of Sydney's Thai restaurants, then it's younger sibling, Sailors Thai, is the ready-to-wear. Located in the old Sailor's Home in the historic Rocks district, it's a classy, distinctive space full of good, gutsy, pull-no punches Thai food.

- 106 George St, The Rocks, ph 9251 2466.

Terry Durack

Theatre

see also pre-theatre dining, late-night dining, buskers

While for some the Star City casino and the Olympics are mixed blessings, they've provided a windfall for the performing arts in Sydney. The 2,000-seat **Star City Lyric Theatre**, the city's newest venue, opened in early 1998. And the four annual Olympic Arts Festivals will culminate in 2000 with **Harbour of Life**.

Sydney's two biggest cultural events run back-to-back over the summer. In January, there's the **Sydney Festival**, and in February, it's the **Gay and Lesbian Mardi Gras**, which celebrates its 21st birthday in 1999 – without doubt the city's most colourful arty party.

The **Sydney Theatre Company** and Belvoir St Theatre, both city-based, offer subscription seasons which mix the best of contemporary plays from here and overseas with revivals of the classics. The North Shore is well looked after with seasons at the **Ensemble Theatre** and **Marian Street Theatre**. The venerable and eclectic **New Theatre** serves Newtown.

For the adventurous, there's plenty of theatre beyond the mainstream. At Sydney's smaller theatres, the curious can be inexpensively entertained or, at least, provoked by the next generation of actors, writers and directors. Venues of note include the **Lookout Theatre**, **Performance Space**, **Pilgrim Theatre** and **Belvoir St Downstairs**.

The Griffin Theatre Company

Griffin's single-minded commitment to developing and presenting the work of Australian playwrights must put it in the running as Sydney's best theatre company. Then there's its canny artistic director, Ros Horin, and its wonderfully intimate theatre space, The Stables. An unbeatable combination.

- 10 Nimrod St, Kings Cross, ph 9361 3817.

Neil Armfield

Arguably the best director in Australia, let alone Sydney, Neil Armfield's work can be seen at the Belvoir St Theatre, where he leads the city's finest ensemble of actors.

- 25 Belvoir St, Surry Hills, ph 9699 3444.

Rent

One for fans of the musical: *Rent*, the rock version of *La Bohème*, won both a Tony and a Pulitzer on Broadway and will surely be one the year's must-sees. Opening at the Theatre Royal in November 1998.

- Theatre Royal, MLC Centre, King St, City, ph 9250 1777.

Theatre

The Performing Arts Bookshop
Sydney's best theatre bookshop is number one in a field of one but entirely deserving of a mention for its extensive range of play scripts. It also has a good-size section on the theory and craft of acting and knowledgeable and helpful staff.
- 7th Floor, 280 Pitt St, ph 9267 2257.

Theatre suppers
The best of after-theatre suppers is at The Wharf, which shares Pier 4 with the STC. Good food, great views and a 'theatrical' owner, Dov Sokodi. Chat to your favourite actors at the bar.
- The Wharf, Pier 4, Hickson Rd, ph 9250 1761.

Colin Rose

Further information
- See Sydney Morning Herald Metro and CitySearch for listings

Tiles & pavers

see also **floors, tradespeople**

In Sydney there are a handful of tile and paving specialists that shine out among the rest.

Bisanna Tiles
Even the most hardened style junkies go weak at the knees over Anna Murray's extraordinary range of stones (some semi-precious), terracottas, limestones, marbles, mosaics and frosted glasses all in impeccable shades and textures. She has elevated colour almost to high art.
- 423 Crown St, Surry Hills, ph 9310 2500.

Country Floors
Provincial border tiles perfect for splashbacks and kitchen walls, plus good range of tiles for flooring and benchtops.
- 28 Moncur St, Woollahra, ph 9326 2444.

Domus
First to bring fab Italian fossilised limestone to Sydney. Honed, non-reflective finish or rougher stuff in grey, green, beige and charcoal with more than eight different varieties to choose from. Textures and colours are endless. Pricey, but headache-free.
- 499 Crown St, Surry Hills, ph 9698 1755.

Fred Pazotti
The acknowledged king of terracotta in Sydney. Take your pick from the wide range of sunbaked terracottas in various shades of earth. Also good selection of limestone and marble.
- 64 Moncur St, Woollahra, ph 9327 1850.

Haddonstone
A favourite of well-heeled Sydney. The massive showroom sells a full range of reconstituted stone paving. It is impossible to tell this man-made material from its sandstone twin.
- 104 Bourke St, Woolloomooloo, ph 9358 6688.

Jolly Rogers
Cast-concrete pavers that can be custom made in an infinite range of colours. Also produces reconstituted sandstone paving.
- 1 Myoora Rd, Terrey Hills, ph 9450 1646.

Taps Design
Loads of pre-sealed stones in delightfully colour-free hues plus a disciplined palette of mosaics in half penny and hexagonal shapes. Also Italian glazed ceramics in all the new-look brights.
- 115 Flinders St, Darlinghurst, ph 9332 4800.

Tuscan Pavers

Heinz Schweers makes all manner of classic reconstituted sandstone pavers in two popular hues: dirty yellow and dusky orange. It looks like sandstone but is tougher. All pavers are hand finished and delivered with sharp 90 degree edges.

- 110 Old South Head Rd, Bondi Junction, ph 9387 6228.

Melissa Walker Smith

Toys & hobbies

The question is, how seriously do you take your fun? Toys are an important part of a child's development. In play, they learn cognitive and social skills not always explored while simply swinging on the monkey bars. Hobbies are generally the playtime we carry to adulthood – a chance to get enthralled with something that isn't work or a social obligation. Maybe it's worth taking a trip down memory lane to one of the following centres – it could even save on therapy sessions.

World 4 Kids

More toys than you'd ever realised existed. This toy conglomerate has six stores throughout Sydney. Take children of all ages to this shop and watch them enjoy the supermarket wonderland.

- Bankstown Shopping Centre, ph 9790 2733; Westpoint Shopping Centre, Blacktown, ph 9622 2000; Chatswood Chase, ph 9411 7411; Westfield Shopping Centre, Hornsby, ph 9482 7566; MacArthur Square, Campbelltown, ph (046) 28 7886; Riley St, Penrith, ph (047) 21 3399.

Hobbyco

Hobbyco is conveniently located in the city centre. As well as supplies for more predictable pastimes, it is the largest supplier of materials for making doll's house furniture. If you don't have a hobby when you arrive at the shop, you might end up with one by the time you leave.

- S402 Gallery Level, Mid City Centre, 197 Pitt St, City, ph 9221 0666.

Teach 'em Toys

This shop specialises in educational toys that are still lots of fun. Stocks an impressive range of wooden toys and distributes POD Toys which share the premises.

- 55 Flinders St, Darlinghurst, ph 9332 3134.

Yennora Hobbies

Stockist of radio-controlled models, model railways, Scalextric and AFX Slot Cars, this shop bills itself as the complete hobby specialist. It also sells new and second-hand goods on consignment.

- 76 Railway St, Yennora, ph 9632 5002.

Campbelltown Doll and Toy Hospital

This repair centre is for Humpty Dumpty and his friends when all the king's horses and men couldn't help out.

- 7 Griffiths Place, Eagle Vale, ph (02) 4626 1720.

Train Trader

Train Trader is a specialist in Marklin and Hornby. This is a model train enthusiast's Central Station, where you can do more than simply trainspot. Kids of all ages come here to buy, trade and talk gear ratios.

- 15 Waterloo St, Narrabeen, ph 9913 1362.

Woodpecker Model Railways

Specialist in the British brands Hornby and Bachmann, the shop also has an impressive range of diecast buses and trucks to go with

Toys & hobbies

your trainscape. Woodpecker does repairs and has an impressive range of second-hand trains for serious collectors.
- 10 Joyce St, Pendle Hill, ph 9636 3855.

Penrith Toy and Hobby Centre

More a hobby specialist than a toy supplier these days, this centre concentrates on radio-controlled cars, planes and boats by makers Tamiya and Kyosho, painting-by-numbers kits and doll's house ceramics, and has one of the most comprehensive adult jigsaw collections in Sydney.
- 417 High St, Penrith, ph 4721 8314.

Einsteinz Toy Box

A generation ago, children had a few toys and big imaginations. Today, parents are paranoid the genius within will be stifled without the right toys. Before lashing out and buying everything, get some advice from the experts at this new shop. Free workshops and discussion groups are run by early childhood teachers for parents, mothers groups, early childhood centres and playgroups.
- 330 Norton Street, Leichhardt, ph 9569 8788.

Kate Ryan

Tradespeople

see also building contractors, carpenters & cabinetmakers, electricians, painters, plumbers

Finding a reliable and professional tradesperson in Sydney can be daunting, but don't be overly concerned. According to the Department of Fair Trading the number of complaints they deal with in a year is a fraction of the number of jobs undertaken. For the past two years the Sydney Morning Herald's weekly home section, Domain, has received thousands of letters from readers recommending tradespeople for the Quote Unquote column. The majority of the nominations for are builders, carpenters, electricians, painters and plumbers (see separate listings) but we have also selected a range of specialist tradespeople who have received multiple nominations and listed them below.

To find a good tradesperson you can also call the Master Builders Association (MBA) on 9281 3511, the Housing Industry Association on 9633 4488 or ask at big suppliers.

For the best results, the MBA recommends that you:
- Ensure the builder is licensed – by calling the New South Wales Department of Fair Trading on 9895 0111 – and is a member of an industry body such as the MBA.
- Ask the builder for references and contact recent clients to check performance. Did they do a good job? Was the work completed on time? Did the builder explain things? Were they satisfied with the quote and final cost?
- Check with your solicitor before signing the contract, if you have any concerns.
- Never pay a deposit of more than 10 per cent for work less than $20,000 or five per cent for work more than $20,000.

Troy's Repairs

Robert and Troy Morris provide good old-fashioned service and reliability on any general repairs and maintenance of a non-structural kind. Trade licence 38361C.
- ph 9371 7858, 0416 221 468 or 0416 221 469.

Mark Hinton

Plasterer: Internal lining specialists, renovations, extensions and restoration work. Trade licence 46987C.
- ph 9570 6162 or 0414 395 222.

Robert Everett

Specialises in re-roofing and slate work. Federation houses, Eastern Suburbs, North Shore and Inner West. Trade licence R97951.
- ph 9868 4175 or 0411 601 616.

Morrissey Paved Ways

Daniel Morrissey does paving, landscaping and retainer walls. Bobcat and tipper for complete service. Trade licence 58531C.
- ph 9589 0425 or 0411 171 764.

John Senti

Specialising in paving, retainer walls, stonework and all other aspects of landscaping. Trade licence 86730C.
- ph 9988 4289.

Bede Saville

Stonemason specialising in building and repairs of stonework. Trade licence R89340.
- ph 9521 2905 or 0419 984 869.

Penny Harrison

Trains

Some of Sydney's rail commuters are truly spoiled, gliding through stretches of the most spectacular scenery in the State. Take a trip and check out what you are missing out on.

West

Do the commuters route to Katoomba in the heart of the Blue Mountains. CityRail travels there hourly from Central Station. For $11.20 (offpeak return) you can sit in airconditioned comfort and and head off into the blue yonder.

North

Catch any train to the Central Coast for a leisurely and spectacular view of the bushland and waterways of the Hawkesbury. Stop off at the village of Brooklyn and hire a boat for a closer view of river life. Hawkesbury River Boat Hire (ph 9985 7252) is just one of many spots to hire boats.

South

Trains on the southern line to Bomaderry pass through the Royal National Park and along the spectacular Illawarra escarpment north of Wollongong, where rainforested mountains and coal mining villages hug the ocean. Have lunch at the terrific Due Mezzi in pretty Bulli.

3801 Limited Steam Rail Tours

Travel on a 1932 steam train on the 'Cockatoo Run' between the coast and the Southern Highlands or north to the Hunter Valley and Newcastle.
- Ph 9699 2737.

Toy and Railway Museum

Travel to the Blue Mountains to see this beautifully maintained collection of trackside and station memorabilia. There's also the largest collection of model trains in Australia on display. Open every day from 10- 5, $6 for adults, $2 for children.
- 36 Olympian Pde, Leura, ph (02) 4784 1169.

Scenic Railway, Katoomba

Built in the 1880s by coalminers, it's more an inclinator than a railway with its 45 degree slant making it one of the steepest in the world. The open cars drop 200 metres to the bottom of Jamison Valley.
- Cliff Dr and Violet St, Katoomba, ph (02) 4782 2699.

Monorail

Links the city centre with Darling Harbour in a continuous 3.6 km loop. The six-car train travels the circuit in around 12 minutes winding high above the city streets. More a joyride for tourists, but also popular with commuters and shoppers who can park more cheaply at Pyrmont.
- Inquiries: ph 9552 2288.

Cerentha Harris

Further information
- **Countrylink**, for State Rail country timetables and bookings, ph 13 22 32

Translators

see also languages

Sydney's multilingual and culturally diverse citizens guarantee no shortage of skilled translators and interpreters.

National Accreditation Authority for Translators and Interpreters

NAATI can refer you to accredited translators working in the more than 50 languages. Buy its directory for $35 or check out entries on the group's website.
- Level 2, 60 Clarence St, City,
  ph 9299 4144;
  http://people.enternet.com.au/~naati/

Associated Translators and Linguists

ATL provides translating and interpreting services in more than 100 languages. Clients include insurance companies, courts and the Immigration Review Tribunal.
- Level 5, 72 Pitt St, City, ph 9231 3288.

Language Professionals International

The business has operated for 10 years translating everything from business cards to legal documents, brochures to film scripts.
- 32 York St, City, ph 9299 1500.

Language Services

A division of the NSW Ethnic Affairs Commission, this service provides translation and interpreting services in more than 90 languages.
- 164 Liverpool Rd, Ashfield,
  ph 1300 651 500.

SBS

The multicultural broadcaster can translate, and produce voice-overs and subtitles in more than 60 languages.
- 14 Herbert St, Artarmon, ph 9430 3819.

Peter Jordan

Travel agents & tour operators

see also guided tours

On a bright, clear day, when the harbour and the sky challenge each other to produce the more dazzling blue, you might wonder why anyone would ever want to leave Sydney. But if you must go, where will it be? Putting on the ritz in Paris, a shutter safari in Africa, shopping in Bangkok or marvelling at the wonders of the Hermitage in St Petersburg?

Do you take your travel with a drop of fine wine or some gourmet food? Perhaps you prefer to come back lighter, rather than heavier, so perhaps it should be a little hiking, cycling, trekking. Or maybe you'd like to just veg out on a cruise or a coach tour.

Whatever. Wherever. Whether your taste is champagne or strictly soft drink, here's a selection of the city's top travel agents to get you wherever you want to go. Bon Voyage!

Alumni Travel

Music in Europe? The architecture of South America? The native cultures of North Africa? Alumni thinks travel should broaden the mind, not just the waist.
- 100 Clarence St, City, ph 9290 3856.

Bench International

Been in Africa since Rhodes was a boy.
- 36 Clarence St, City, ph 9290 2877.

CiT World Travel Group

Well-priced packages for Italy in particular and Europe in general.
- 263 Clarence St, City, ph 9267 1255.

Eastern Europe Travel Bureau

The name says it all.
- Level 5, 75 King St, City, ph 9262 1144.

Flight Centre
No matter where you're going – Lagos to Lyon, Lima to Launceston – air travel at rock bottom prices.
- Ph 131 600 for your nearest office.

Helen Wong's Tours
The most experienced when it comes to China.
- 456 Kent St, City, ph 9267 7833.

Mary Rossi
To do it in the height of style – anywhere.
- Suite 3, 65 Berry St, North Sydney, ph 9957 4511.

Pacific International Travel Centre
If it's an island and in our region, PITC is the way to go.
- Level 1, 91 York St, City, ph 9244 1811.

Russia and Beyond
Knows the former Soviet Union so well it can even get you home stays.
- 100 Clarence St, City, ph 9299 5799.

STA
You're young? So are they.
- 855 George St, City, and branches, ph 1300 360 960.

UK Flight Shop
The cheapest way to Britain (and back).
- 7 Macquarie Place, City, ph 9247 4833.

Venture Holidays
Keenly priced holidays just about anywhere in Asia. Pick up the brochure at any travel agent.
- 5 Elizabeth St, City, ph 9236 5222.

Wiltrans Australia
For anything afloat.
- 189 Kent St, City, ph 9255 0899.

TTW Marketing
Also a cruise specialist.
- 5 Elizabeth St, City, ph 9236 5255.

World Expeditions
If you must holiday in hiking boots or kayaks (here or overseas), an affordable adventure specialist.
- Level 3, 441 Kent St, City, ph 9264 3366.

Peregrine
Also an adventure specialist.
- Level 5, 38 York St, City, ph 9290 2770.

Greg Lenthen

Triathlon

see also cycling, swimming, lifesaving, running

Triathletes claim to have the best bodies of all sports people. Swimming develops good shoulder, chest and arm muscles, cycling tones the legs and buttocks and running keeps the fat off the hips and thighs. After just a few years of intense lobbying, triathlon has emerged from being a fringe event borne from the 1970s fun-run boom to become a major international sport that will debut at Sydney 2000. The kudos of being part of the biggest sporting show on earth has made triathlon hugely popular. At the elite end, Australia leads the world in both the individual and team events. Sydney's Emma Carney and Chris McCormack are undisputed leaders, both holding the world champion and world number one titles.

About 500 triathletes compete on the elite tour, but there's triathlons for everyone, from juniors and novices to veterans. There is also a wealth of clubs, circuits, camps, event calendars, awards, magazines, school and junior development programs and speciality stores. The best way to get into the sport is through a club, of which there are 18 in the Sydney metropolitan area. But remember, even the shortest

Triathlon

events – a 300m swim, 11km cycle and 3km run – require some degree of fitness.

The Olympic triathlon course, starting with the swim in the harbour from the Opera House with run and cycle legs through the Botanic Gardens to Mrs Macquarie's Chair, will be one of the Olympics' most spectacular events.

Triathlon NSW
For a $45 sign-on fee with Triathlon NSW you get racing and training insurance, the State association magazine, event calendar and a card that lets you race around the country.
■ ph 9518 7766.

Cronulla
The city's best credentialled club. It has won the State title three times in the past four years and boasts some of the sport's biggest stars. Weekly run, bike group sessions, plus individual groups training.
■ ph 9552 4427

Balmoral
Saturday-morning cycling sessions in Centennial Park, track sessions, organised group runs, wind-trainer cycle sessions, social functions and trips. World top 10 triathlete Greg Bennett is a member.
■ ph 9977 6142

Sydney International Aquatic Club
Wind-trainer cycle, swim, run sessions weekly. Friday night dinners. Functions and club championship trip.
■ ph 9752 3666.

Saucony B.R.A.T. (Bondi Running and Triathlon)
$25 membership buys monthly newsletter, group training and entry into about six club races a month. Large social club of 330 members.
■ ph 9665 5079.

Albion Cycles
The major expense of triathlon is the bike. A $500 model will get you started but if you get hooked into this highly-addictive social sport, expect to pay a $1,000 for a racing bike and up to $7,500 for a hi-tech carbon-fibre model. Talk to Frank Conceicao, the Australian triathlon team bike mechanic. He also runs squads and training.
■ 285 Bronte Rd, Waverley, ph 9387 1144.

Louise Evans

Tutors & coaching

see also musical tuition

Increased competition at all levels of education in Sydney seems to be driving up demand for coaching and tutorial services. Despite repeated assurances from education officials that students cannot be coached to improve their performance in selective school and opportunity class entrance tests, parents are not convinced and are sending their children off for extra tuition in growing numbers. Students as young as eight years are attending coaching and tutorial centres in an attempt to gain an educational edge. Centres also offer help to students needing help to keep up in class and, of course, offer HSC coaching.

But parents should beware. According to the Department of Consumer Affairs there is no registration or accreditation process for tutorial centres, so it is important to check the qualifications of the tutors. Some of the centres make extravagant claims about their students' success in gaining entry to selective schools and winning scholarships but there is often very little evidence of just how much the coaching college actually contributed to the success.

Look for a centre that is aware of changes to HSC courses and is up to date on the best way to prepare for exams. Rates vary from $14 a session upwards, depending on the year level and whether students are working in groups or privately.

HSC UniLink
The University of NSW runs tutorials courses for maths, physics and chemistry. Sessions run one night a week for each subject and there are two sessions on a Saturday morning. Students work through the HSC syllabus and the courses run from February to September. There are also revision programs held in the school holidays at various locations. All tutors are qualified Year 12 teachers and the centre carries the imprimatur of one of the State's leading universities.
- ph 9385 6305.

North Shore Development and Coaching Centre
One of the largest coaching centres in Australia with 18 branches in Sydney, from Bankstown to Wahroonga, and four in Melbourne. It offers coaching for selective school and opportunity class exams as well as the HSC and scholarship tests. Subjects on offer include economics, business studies, maths, chemistry and physics.
- Head office: 66-70 Archer St, Chatswood, ph 9415 1860.

The Swot Shop
Opened five years ago, the shop started as an education centre for gifted students. The programs are aimed at extending students rather than accelerating them through school work and there are lots of games. The centre also offers courses for talented maths students and while it runs a selective high school entrance course, it will tell you quite honestly its course is no guarantee of success.
- 2 Packard Ave, Castle Hill, ph 9634 2000.

Stephanie Raethel

Upholstery

see also soft furnishings & fabrics
Starting from scratch? A well-designed and sprung sofa (or chair, stool, bedhead) doesn't come cheap, so you must invest in just the right piece – a design that will stand the test of time. Make sure your flop zone is comfortable for the long haul, and stick to Sydney's best craftspeople.

Aaron Upholstery
Steve Shaw is a trade secret among leading designers and decorators. Shaw can build modern and traditional sofas, armchairs and stools (with hardwood frames) that fit a brief of fashion, function and form. Check out the Kingsway and Selwood sofa designs. He can also rejuvenate old upholstered pieces with new covers.
- 1611 Botany Rd, Botany, ph 9666 5696.

Eric Ahlfors
If you dream of sumptuous upholstered walls, you won't go wrong with French-born Ahlfors, a specialist in wall upholstery, cladding your rooms in fabric. Pricey, but definitely worth it.
- ph 9371 5353.

Elio Upholstery
A big favourite with young Sydneysiders wanting to feather their nests on a budget. Elio can build upholstered furniture with hardwood frames or simply recover any existing pieces with new fabric. You can't get a cheaper upholstered bedhead in town.
- 65 Goodhope Ave, Paddington, ph 9360 6170.

Carlos Malta
Upholsterer for high-end Sydney furniture retailers and antique dealers and a trade secret. His know-how will instantly update any pre-loved piece or he can custom-build you something to order.
- 676 Parramatta Rd, Croydon, ph 9799 2820.

Upholstery

Stephen McDonald
If you have a sofa or chair with good bones and want some new loose covers, this Englishman is Sydney's slip-cover king. The Terrigal-based McDonald travels to Sydney weekly to tailor loose covers for the devoted clientele he has built up over the past eight years. He works the old-fashioned way, cutting the fabric into panels on site, then piecing them in place on the chair or sofa and pinning the lot together. He returns a few weeks later to fit the finished cover. Very affordable.
- ph 4385 2290.

Bill O'Hehir
The concept of the well-made sofa and chair takes on new meaning in the hands of O'Hehir who has been building pieces for A-list Sydney for more than three generations. Crafted with expertise and time-consuming perfection, his upholstery is the best – built to last a lifetime. He will also happily re-upholster existing pieces.
- ph 9389 1972.

John E Puddick Furnishings
Puddick is renowned for his reliable and good workmanship. He can build whatever you want or re-upholster a world-weary piece of furniture.
- 304 Bronte Rd, Waverley, ph 9389 3038.

Cameron McFarlane
From re-upholstery of antiques and classic styles to custom building of contemporary furniture, always using the best quality materials and traditional upholstery skills. Received multi recommendations in the *Sydney Morning Herald* Tradespeople of the Year Awards.
- 5b North St, Balmain, ph 9810 3785.

Melissa Walker Smith

Vegetarian restaurants

Blame k.d. lang or Lisa Simpson if you like, but something strange is happening in the world of vegetarians. No longer are they prepared to be fobbed off with a slice of hunza pie and wholemeal muffin that tastes like soggy knitting yarn. They even want to be able to taste something when they eat out. What a concept!

Bodhi
By day, you can order from a variety of dim sum dumplings that look (and sometimes even taste) like the real thing, but don't worry, what looks suspiciously like pork, is really tofu and those seafood rolls aren't. At night, there is a good range of claypots, beancurd dishes and rice combinations, with no MSG, prepared stocks or tinned ingredients used.
- 187 Hay St, Haymarket, ph 9281 9918

Cicada
Cicada is not a vegetarian restaurant, it's a big-night-out restaurant. But even vegetarians deserve a big night out occasionally, which is why chef Peter Doyle has instituted a special vegetable menu with sublime, beautifully honed dishes such as his spinach and eggplant curry with fried polenta.
- 29 Challis Ave, Potts Point, ph 9358 1255

Iku wholefoods
Iku has a bright liveliness about it that attracts even non-vegetarians. The delights of a creamy tofu and blueberry cheesecake appeals to all denominations, as do the frittatas, the miso soup and the roast vegetable and legume casserole.
- 25a Glebe Pt Rd, Glebe, ph 9692 8720; Shop 2, The Grove, Grosvenor Lane, Neutral Bay, ph 9953 1964.

Malabar
Not strictly a vegetarian restaurant, but Malabar specialises in the cooking of South India, which has a large vegetarian population. Therefore there is plenty on the menu to tempt, including a popular vegetarian thali – a selection of delicious little tidbits served with

a mighty Malabar dosa (rice and lentil pancake).
- 332 Pacific Highway, Crows Nest, ph 9906 7343.

Terry Durack

Video stores

You can find a well-stocked Blockbuster Video, Video Ezy, Top Video or Civic Video in almost any suburb in Sydney but if you're after a more specialised range or a bit of character, your best bet is an independent.

Videodrama
Destined to be known forever as the shop where Muriel worked and picked up a date in *Muriel's Wedding*, this Oxford St institution specialises in art house, foreign, gay and lesbian and cult films. Open until midnight on Friday and Saturday nights.
- 90 Oxford St, Darlinghurst, ph 9331 3158.

Dr What
With more than 25,000 tapes, this is the place to find that classic you've been hunting down since the 1970s. Be quick or your copy of the latest art house sensation will end up in the hands of a socialite or cinephile.
- 562 Oxford St, Bondi Junction, ph 9387 1100.

Lounge Lizards Video
Finding a children's film that really is suitable for kids can be hard. This shop has a great range though, along with a full range of classics and foreign films.
- 9 Plumer Rd, Rose Bay, ph 9362 3864.

Rebecca Wallwork

Further information
- Australian Video Retailers Association, ph 9235 3866

Vietnamese Sydney

The best of Vietnamese Sydney is dirt cheap but not so easy to discover. That's because of the sheer quantity. There are more than 50,000 Australians of Vietnamese origin living in metropolitan Sydney and most of them seem to own a shop or work in one. In New York and Europe, Vietnamese food is very much in fashion. So beat the rush and try one of Sydney's value-for-money Vietnamese restaurants before they become trendy. You will be rewarded by a meal that is as subtle and as beautifully balanced as it is exotic.

Cabramatta
Better known as Vietnamatta, this is good old western Sydney suburbia except for a concrete oasis of shops and restaurants straddling the local train station. Crowds ebb and flow up and down the main John Street strip: an unrelenting mass of young and old, fast and slow, colourful and the plain bewitched, caught up in the sounds, the smells and the energy that is Cabramatta. It's a crazy labyrinth with dozens of restaurants, bread stalls, Hong Kong fashion houses, Chinese medicine stores, hairdressers, hi-fi and video outlets, $2 shops, greengrocers, butchers, cafes and the ubiquitous restaurants.

BKK Shopping Centre
While you could spend a whole day trawling through every smelly nook and charming cranny of Cabramatta, if time is not on your side and you have to do some shopping, try here. Under BKK's square roof are shops selling weird cuts of meat, BBQ roast duck, fresh Vietnamese herbs, spices and vegetables, some of the cheapest seafood in Sydney, videos, beauty products, cheap plastic knick-knacks and underwear by the kilo.
- 53 Park Rd, Cabramatta, ph 9726 8088.

Dong Ba

Specialises in a dish that comes from the ancient capital, Hue, in central Vietnam. The eponymously named dish, *bun bo hue* (spicy beef noodles from Hue), is a princely delight that will leave you sweaty but happy. Main dishes start from $5.
- Shop 5–6, 40 Park Rd, Cabramatta, ph 9755 0727.

Thanh Binh

This is Cabramatta's most versatile and accommodating Vietnamese restaurant. The English menu explains every dish perfectly, but if you still don't know what to order, try the chicken *pho*, sugar cane prawns, deep fried quail and *bun bo hue*.
- 52a John St, Cabramatta, ph 9727 9729.

Bankstown

Compared with Cabramatta, Bankstown, in Sydney's south west, is a sleepy hollow. It's a much gentler, quieter and prettier place. Bankstown is the home of various Vietnamese community groups and newspapers. If Cabramatta is the stomach, Bankstown is the head. On any day, you can stroll through The Mall, off Chapel Road, and watch huddles of old and young men playing Vietnamese chess under the eucalypts.

The Vietnamese Community in Australia

This staunchly anti-Communist group is located in an oddly Soviet-style building. You can pop in and talk to one of the many volunteers there about the local community.
- 300 Chapel Rd, Bankstown, ph 9796 8035.

Thuy Nga

Not far from where the chess players congregate is this music shop, which has the biggest and best selection of Vietnamese music imported from the USA and the homeland.
- 323–325 Chapel Rd, Bankstown, ph 9796 7227.

An

To call Vietnamese *pho* a noodle soup is like calling the noble French cassoulet a stew. At An, you will find the pho by which all others must be judged. The beef special *pho* is a veritable kitchen sink of goodies, while the prices look like typing errors.
- 29–31 Greenfield Pde, Bankstown, ph 9796 7826.

Pasteur

Known for its *pho* beef (beef and rice noodle soup), but as the old waiter's saying goes 'everything is special'. Try the red rice, barbecued spare ribs, crisp skin chicken and *bun bo hue* – thick rice vermicelli in a spicy soup laced with pork, beef and blood jelly.
- 209 Chapel Rd South, Bankstown, ph 9790 2900.

Marrickville

This was the first suburb the Vietnamese anchored when they started arriving n the mid–70s. It's to the Vietnamese what Leichhardt is to the Italians. Illawarra Road was a more bustling place 10 years ago. It's still the main drag today but many in the community have decamped to the outer west or elsewhere, taking their businesses with them.

Minh

This friendly neighbourhood restaurant has a huge range of authentic Vietnamese dishes including the curiously named campfire beef and sizzling hot plate dishes including crocodile, kangaroo and venison. By day, a lunchtime *pho* is the go.
- 508–510 Marrickville Rd, Dulwich Hill, ph 9560 0465.

Chinese New Year

The most important festival in the Vietnamese calendar, normally at the end of January or the first week of February, depending on the wax and wane of the moon. For three days, the shopping streets of Cabramatta are festooned with bright red and yellow decorations. The shops are normally closed during the first day and re-opened thereafter to welcome the New Year with firecrackers and dragon dancers.

Le Phat Dang

The month of May is Buddha's birthday, and celebrations are held at many temples scattered around the Fairfield municipality. The biggest of them is Phuoc Hue on Victoria Street, Wetherill Park.

Lantern Festival

This popular festival, dedicated to children, falls in September. It is the Vietnamese equivalent to America's Halloween night, where kids walk around the unlit village streets carrying paper lanterns dangling at the end of bamboo sticks.

Minh Bui and Terry Durack

Vintage & recycled fashion

Opportunity, recycled or vintage clothing shops can be the source of fantastic one-off accessories or garments. Sydney has many a great 'Vinnies' (ph 9560 8666 for your nearest store) or Lifeline (ph 9635 0700), but when it comes to that extra special bargain designer label, funky pair of recycled shoes, or wild retro pair of sunglasses, these stores have the second-hand business down pat.

Blue Spinach

The list of clothing and accessories labels in this store reads like the schedule for Milan, Paris and New York fashion weeks, with the likes of Issey Miyake, Dolce & Gabbana, Giorgio and Emporio Armani, Gianni Versace, Gucci, Jil Sander, Yohji Yamamoto, Vivienne Westwood, Donna Karan, Prada, and Calvin Klein among the many, all individually selected by owners Mark Thompson and Jane Wigzell.
- 348 Liverpool St, Darlinghurst,
  ph 9331 3904.

Di Nuovo

Specialising in second-hand avant-garde labels, including Zambesi, Martin Margiela, Comme des Garçons, Yohji Yamamoto, Issey Miyake, Helmut Lang, and Jean Paul Gaultier. Di Nuovo has adjoining stores for women and men.
- 92-94 William St, Paddington,
  ph 9361 4221.

Mister Stinky

For thoroughly individual, one-off pieces, visit Sydney's cult op-shop. Alongside of standard op-shop '60s and '70s retro clothing, Mister Stinky also makes its own pieces from recycled fabrics, such as great psychedelic print body shirts, Hawaiian shirts, flares, and funky dresses.
- 482 Cleveland St, Surry Hills,
  ph 9310 7005.

King St, Newtown

Sydney's cutting-edge street fashion arena has a constantly changing variety of great recycled and vintage clothing stores. Wander down King St, starting at **Value Village** (131 King St, ph 9517 1789) and **The Look** (230 King St, ph 9550 2455), right down to the end, to **Chiconomy** (399 King St, ph 9557 4072) and **Trade Roots** (475 King St, ph 9550 4778).

Pelle Recycled Designer Footwear

Large range of recycled designer footwear and leather accessories, including coveted international labels Gucci, Prada, Dolce & Gabbana, Sergio Rossi, Patrick Cox, Manolo Blahnik, Michel Perry and Chanel. With styles from the '60s through to the '90s, expect at least one-third off original prices.
- 90 William St, Paddington,
  ph 9331 8100.

Revivre

For the well-heeled shopper after bargain-priced, classic styles from international designer labels, Revivre has a selection of Giorgio Armani, Prada, Anna Sui, Gianni Versace, Gucci, Valentino, Byblos, Fendi,

Moschino, Chanel (the only time you will find a 'bargain' Chanel, as they never have sales). The store also carries new end-of-season Italian stock from Iceberg and Bazar by Christian Lacroix, at nearly half price.
- Shop 4, 49 Bay St, Double Bay, ph 9362 0597.

Route 66
Recycled American clothing, such as retro and classic style jeans, including a range of new Lee and Levis jeans, Hawaiian shirts, men's 'garage' shirts, and a range of Western shirts, pants and cowboy boots.
- 255 Crown St, Darlinghurst, ph 9331 6686.

The Vintage Clothing Shop
Great for retro that is not the standard '60s/'70s psychedelia. They have '40s, '50s, '60s stock, including great period overcoats, jackets, and embroidered and beaded cardigans. The extensive range of accessories covers gloves, ties, shoes, costume jewellery, and handbags, with fantastic silk, woollen, and faux fur scarves and wraps.
- 147 Castlereagh St, City, ph 9267 7135.

Zoo Emporium
Inner-city street urchins and party-goers shop here for anything funky from any period over the last 40 years. Known for its range of retro clubbing shoes.
- 332 Crown St, Darlinghurst, ph 9380 5990.

Felicity Ward

Volleyball

see also beaches, sporting goods
The beach used to be just for swimming and sun-baking – now it's the setting for Sydney's coolest summer sport, beach volleyball. With swim togs, wrap-around sunglasses and a dollop of SPF15, you're set for hours of spiking, digging and serving in the soft sand of Sydney's famous beaches. And when summer has faded into autumn, it's time to head indoors for more of the same. Bondi will be the location for the Olympic beach volleyball competition.

Manly
Beach volleyball mecca, not only in Sydney but all of Australia. The country's most dynamic elite players, like Olympic bronze medallist Kerri Pottharst and world top 10 player Julien Prosser, are based on the northern beaches and train daily at Manly. There are also five courts permanently open to the public.
- Manly Beach, North Steyne. Contact the Northern Beaches Volleyball Association.

Northern Beaches Volleyball Association
Organises beach competitions every weekend, plus mid-week twilight and social leagues for the public. NBVA also runs regular volleyball coaching clinics (ph 9973 1234). The NSW Volleyball Association (see below) can also help with indoor clubs to join.
- Ph 9223 4200.

Redsand
The 'in' beach gear for Sydney volleyballers. Available at Grace Bros stores. Other popular brands are Mossimo, Sideout and Primitive Prints, plus Bolle and Oakley for sunnies.

Sydney Entertainment Centre
The indoor volleyball Olympic venue in 2000. Sydney is hosting international Test series against countries such as China, Italy, the USA and Korea during 1998, plus rounds of the Australasian Volleyball Tour, played from May–August, which the public can attend. For details, call the Australian Volleyball Federation (see below).

Heather Quinlan

Further information
- NSW Volleyball Association, ph 9223 4200

Volunteering

see also charities, activism

It's tricky defining the best of volunteering because this depends on the nature of your convictions. Volunteering is a two-fold reward – helping other people or the environment or both means you'll probably feel better about yourself. Listed below are groups that perform a wide range of non-profit work, from pollution control to well digging in Somalia. Big issues with lots of uncertainties – one thing is sure, if you have appropriate skills or just plain old enthusiasm, you can help.

Volunteer Centre of NSW

This group provides a referral and placement service for volunteers, and accredited training for co-ordinators and managers of volunteers. The centre also has a phone-in service that allows volunteers to ask questions about various issues.
- 2/105 Pitt St, City, ph 9231 4000.

Community Aid Abroad

CAA relies on regular donations, fundraising activities and merchandising and has built a sound reputation in rural Australia, Africa, Asia and Central America. Volunteers can work in the office, at a CAA shop, or join a local group and attend regular meetings regarding annual fundraising events, such as Walk Against Want.
- Level 2, 16-22 Wentworth Ave, Surry Hills, ph 9264 1399.

Bobby Goldsmith Foundation

BGF provides financial help for people disadvantaged as result of AIDS-related illnesses. Their main goal is to maintain the quality of life of its clients by paying bills and lending appliances. BGF volunteers help by visiting the ill and insuring their needs are met. Volunteers also collect money on Shop Yourself Stupid Day and before the Mardi Gras Parade. All volunteers gain entry to a reserved viewing area opposite the BGF stand, to watch the parade.
- 2/9 Commonwealth St, City, ph 9283 8666.

St Vincent de Paul Society

Australia's largest charity group has limitless opportunity for those wanting to help people such as abused women, homeless men and under-privileged children. Call head office and it will direct you to the centre nearest to you.
- Head Office: West St, Lewisham, ph 9560 8666.

Clean Up Australia

Clean Up Australia was founded in 1986 after Ian Kiernan, while on a solo around-the-world yacht race, noticed badly polluted oceans and decided to do something about it. Clean Up Australia Day in 1997, when Australians were forced to look at their own backyard, had the co-operation of more than half a million volunteers. The day is held annually in March.
- 117 Harris St, Pyrmont, ph 9552 6177.

Chris Dobney

Wallpaper

Sydney homes are facing radical change. Wallpaper mania is upon us, with fashionable home decorators storming around the city for the latest looks. Here's where they are heading.

Arkitex

You can't beat these dull metal papers by New York based company Donghia which are delightfully colour free.
- 44-46 McLachlan Ave, Rushcutters Bay, ph 9331 4544.

Wallpaper

Boyac Decorative Furnishings
If you want to go over the top, check out the big, bold designs in ecclesiastical purple and gold by Watts of Westminster.
- 19c Boundary St, Rushcutters Bay, ph 9360 4515.

Decortex Wallcoverings
Lots of tactile stuff here with a full range of Italian paper-backed raffia, jacquard, silk and thread plus an assortment of plain or patterned vinyl papers.
- 5-15 Dunning Ave, Rosebery, ph 9663 0521.

Karman Grech
Create your own groovy patterns and get artist Grech, who has been handprinting wallpaper for more than 35 years, to silk-screen it from $40 for 10 metres. He also specialises in restoration work and can recreate original designs by hand from a small scrap.
- ph 9597 5430.

Order Imports
Legendary company Zuber et Cie produces designs that cover the full spectrum from Empire to convincing vistas.
- 11a Boundary St, Rushcutters Bay, ph 9360 3565.

St James Furnishings
Lots of decorative grandeur here with big names that include Brunschwig & Fils, Coles & Son, Mauny, Fardis, G.P & J. Baker and Bradbury & Bradbury.
- 15-19 Boundary St, Rushcutters Bay, ph 9332 1900.

Wallpaper to Go
Here you'll find bargain neo-baroque paper with lots of fab flock designs in gold, silver and burgundy.
- 54 Joseph St, Lidcombe, ph 9646 2666.

Wardlaw
Those dedicated to the art of understatement will delight in the range of elegant papers here. Lots of traditional favourites such as Osborne & Little, Nina Campbell, Designers Guild, Schumacher, Warner and Liberty.
- 100 Harris St, Pyrmont, ph 9660 6266.

Melissa Walker Smith

Water polo

Water polo – strangely – is not like Kerry Packer's favourite game minus the horses. It's actually an action-packed combination of soccer, basketball and ice hockey skills played while swimming up and down a pool. It's exciting to watch, aerobically-demanding to play and, happily, in Sydney you can do both – easily.

Flippa Ball
This is the modified game of water polo suitable for children under 10. Most water polo is taught in schools, or at coaching clinics for 12- to 13-year-olds. Keen adults, though, can learn the fundamentals of the game through any of the 25 Sydney clubs. Contact NSW Water Polo (see below) for details.

Sydney International Aquatic Centre
The place to see water polo at its best. Sydney-based Australian players such as Mark Oberman, Grant Waterman, Liz Weekes and Bronwyn Maher train here regularly. The SIAC is also the Olympic venue in 2000 and the site for the 1999 World Cup tp be held in July.
- Sydney Olympic Park, Homebush, ph 9752 3666.

National League
The men's National League is played from October to February/March at venues such as the Warringah Aquatic Centre and Sutherland pool. There are four strong Sydney teams, plus international sides from Canada, Brazil, etc.

The leading east coast women's teams, from NSW, Queensland and Victoria, compete in the Sydney premiership, which runs concurrently with the men's National League.

Heather Quinlan

Further information
■ NSW Water Polo Inc., ph 9552 1574

Waterskiing

see also powerboating

As social as a backyard barbecue, waterskiing is a declaration that summer has arrived. Family and friends queue at the door with picnic hampers and coolers, flash wetsuits, bright buoyancy vests, ropes, waterskis and wakeboards. And somehow they all find a place aboard. A good ski-boat is a social creature, but for the motor, usually a big one, which bursts into life with a throaty roar. When it does, the search begins for that perfectly smooth bend of water, free from jellyfish, and with a white-sand beach from which to ski and spread out in the shade for lunch.

You'll find beautiful bends for waterskiing on the upper Hawkesbury River and adjoining Cowan Creek in north-western Sydney. You can waterski anywhere there aren't speed restriction signs in Botany Bay, Port Hacking and Sydney Harbour, though water traffic will confine you to skiing in the early morning. These days, keen skiers are strutting their stuff on a whole new breed of waterski, often made from carbon-fibre, with adjustable fins and channels, and wider tips and ends. Where speed once ruled the waves, slalom skiing has taken off. And that's where you'll find the young at heart – performing a new bag of tricks on the latest craze, wakeboards.

Hawkesbury River
Head for the fresh and brackish water reaches of the Hawkesbury River between Sackville and Wisemans Ferry, where calm, quiet bends beckon to be carved, slashed and crashed. Downstream, Cowan Creek in Kur-ing-gai National Park has deep, clear water – some say sharks – stunning scenery and as much protection from wind as you will find anywhere in Sydney. The Bridge to Bridge Water Ski Race is held on the Hawkesbury River from Brooklyn to Windsor each November.

Lewis Ski Boats
Designed and built locally, Lewis is the household name in ski-boats in Australia and exports to the United States. Inboard, stern-drive and outboard models, as well as three new up-market craft – described as the BMWs of ski-boats – recently released.
■ 152 Adderley St, Auburn, ph 9748 1983.

The Waterski Factory
In business for 35 years and well stocked with the latest wide-bodied parabolic skis, twin-tip wakeboards, ski tubes, wetsuits, vests, ropes, gloves, everything you need to get going. Big on the locally made Ron Marks brand of slalom skis and wakeboards.
■ 199 Parramatta Rd, Homebush Bay, ph 9763 1333.

The Ski Shack
Run by Geoff Hardaker, winner of the Hawkesbury's Bridge to Bridge race seven times and triple Men's Open Champion. All the latest American skis, wakeboards and tubes for sale and weekend hire.
■ 915 Old Northern Rd, Dural, ph 9651 4056.

Jack Ellison Water Ski Resort
There is caravan accommodation on the shores of the Hawkesbury River and a ski school from September to May each year. Lessons and week-long camps are run by Jack and Deon Ellison, champion and demonstration skiers. They teach

barefooting, ski-boarding, slalom, trick skiing, jumping, show skiing, freestyling, kneeboarding, air chairing – and lots of beginners.

- 505 Pitt Town Bottoms Rd, Pitt Town, ph 02 4572 3733 or 018 44 2340.

David Lockwood

Further information

- NSW Water Ski Association, ph 9552 4311

Weddings

see also catering, event management, function venues, party supplies

Weddings: a girl's dream, and sometimes her worst organisational nightmare, all rolled into one. Sydney has a range of fantastic venues, registry services, cakes and, of course, so many possibilities for that inimitable dress.

Alex Perry

In business for seven years, this made-to-measure designer has recently launched a reasonably priced, ready-to-wear line, for basic separates and gowns, for evening and bridal. Famous for dressing Kimberley Davies for the big day, Perry is known for his glamorous, full-skirted evening dresses, rather than traditional wedding gowns.

- 2nd level, 16-18 Cross St, Double Bay, ph 9326 2126.

Geoffrey Parker

A little left of traditional, Parker's fashion-driven, made-to-measure wedding designs cover everything from trouser suits, to sheath dresses, or your big construction numbers. Very special fabric treatments and expert, unique cutting and construction.

- Ph 9356 4548.

Jonathan Ward

For glamour and elegance visit Double Bay's society couturier. With a client list including the likes of bride Antonia Kidman and matron of honour, sister Nicole, Ward creates simple, flattering gowns in an array of top quality fabrics from all over the world.

- 66 Cross St, Double Bay, ph 9363 5689.

Mariana Hardwick

Five times FIA award winner, Hardwick's eclectic, romantic gowns are individual and special enough to make her one of the few successful off-the-rack designers in her industry. Look to the especially unique beaded and embellished veils.

- Shop 60-61, Lemongrove, Victoria Ave, Chatswood, ph 9415 1415.

Other dress designers

For more traditional wedding styles with modern fabrications, visit the following made-to-measure designers: **Rhonda Hemmingway** (Rose Bay, ph 9371 6716); **Velani** (124 Great North Rd, Five Dock, ph 9712 5020); **Diane Lewis** (536 Parramatta Rd, Petersham, ph 9550 9005); **Bizzaro Haute Couture** (271 Homer St, Earlwood, ph 9558 7145).

Fabric Fantasy

Stockists of Sydney's most unique and beautiful top-quality fabrics, all imported from Italy, this fabric haven's extensive bridal section includes beaded and embroidered panels, silks, tafettas, and French and Italian laces, all wrapped up with very helpful advice.

- 110 Commonwealth St, Surry Hills, ph 9221 5536.

Wendy Louise Designs

Fifteen years of experience with antique and contemporary materials have culminated in Louise's perfectly crafted accessories, such as sweet headpieces scattered with tiny strawberries and ivy leaves, or more traditional matching brushed gold rose earrings, tiaras

and necklaces. Men's accessories and gift ideas also available.
- Shop 36, The Ritz Carlton Promenade, 33 Cross St, Double Bay, ph 9362 0196.

Panache
Wedding shoe specialists Panache will construct a pair of shoes for you from scratch in your chosen fabric. But an enormous collection of colours, shapes and materials for the whole bridal party should satisfy most needs.
- Shop 56, Gallery Level, Lemongrove, Victoria Ave, Chatswood, ph 9411 3934.

Sweet Art
For wedding cakes, try Sweet Art's fabulous designs that have moved on from the traditional fruit-packed, white-clad cake. Mud cake is their most popular, followed by carrot, banana and orange.
- 96 Oxford St, Paddington, ph 9361 6617.

Peter's of Kensington
This is the perfect place for shopping for wedding presents. Packed with top-quality classics in the china, crystal, bed linen, towels and cookware departments, it is preferable to visit during the week to avoid weekend queues that stretch onto the street.
- 57 Anzac Pde, Kensington, ph 9662 7373.

Vaucluse House Tearooms
A great spot for the quintessential Sydney outdoor wedding ceremony experience, on the beautiful lawns over looking the house.
- Wentworth Ave, Vaucluse, ph 9388 8188.

The Wharf Restaurant
This glass-encased space has sparkling night views of the harbour and simple, fresh, modern Australian cuisine. Bookings are taken well in advance as wedding receptions are held only on Sundays.
- Pier 4, Hickson Rd, Walsh Bay, ph 9250 1761.

Felicity Ward

Weekends away

see also drives
When Sydneysiders need a weekend break to recharge their batteries, they don't have to travel far. Within a two- to four-hour drive of the city are a swag of destinations where visitors can indulge in a multitude of activities or simply sit back, relax and be pampered. The accommodation is just as varied. Budget travellers should check out the camping opportunities or try backpackers' hostels or caravan parks. Motels and self-catering cottages or apartments are good mid-price options. If money is no object, there are luxury resorts, guest houses and secluded hideaways that match the world's finest. It's best to book in advance, particularly during school holidays and for long weekends.

Blue Mountains and beyond
Breathtaking scenery and crisp mountain air have lured generations of Sydneysiders west to the most accessible section – by both road and rail – of the Great Dividing Range. With hundreds of kilometres of walking tracks along the sandstone escarpments and through the forested valleys, it's a bushwalker's paradise. A great half-day trek is the one through the lush Grand Canyon. Or sit back and enjoy the views from the Zig Zag Railway, the Scenic Railway or the Scenic Skyway. Other less strenuous activities include exploring the galleries, antique shops and eateries of Leura and neighbouring heritage towns, strolling through the manicured formal gardens of Mount Wilson's grandest mansions and visiting the cold climate botanic garden at Mount Tomah. The gardens are particularly impressive in late October and early November, when the rhododendrons bloom, and in autumn. During winter, get a taste of a northern hemisphere Christmas at a traditional Yulefest celebration. Further afield, explore the underground world at the Jenolan Caves, where nine of some 300

caves are open to the public; the historic townships of Yerranderie, Hartley, Hill End and Gulgong — the last famous for its excellent Pioneer Museum; or taste the wines at Mudgee.

Southern Highlands and beyond

The rolling green hills, olde worlde villages and towns and four distinct seasons that characterise the Southern Highlands give them an English country feel. Antique shops and craft galleries abound in Berrima, Moss Vale, Mittagong and Bowral, which is also home to the Bradman Museum and a colourful tulip festival each spring. Don't miss *Babe* country near Robertson, Kangaroo Valley or spectacular Fitzroy Falls, one of the many scenic splendours of rugged Morton National Park. The region is also the gateway to Canberra, which boasts Parliament House, the National Gallery, the War Memorial and Museum and a host of seasonal attractions.

South Coast

Beach-lovers will find some of the best and most unspoilt beaches in Australia as they follow the coast road south from Sydney. Catch a wave at Seven Mile Beach or take a walk along dazzling Hyams Beach in Jervis Bay, which claims to have the whitest sand in the world. Look out for dolphins, whales and fur seals basking in the sheltered waters of Jervis Bay, which are also a paradise for divers and snorkellers. Further south at Pebbly Beach, share the beach — and perhaps even the surf — with the resident eastern grey kangaroos. If you tire of beaches, the coastal hinterland has much to offer. The quaint town of Berry is brimming with antique stores, galleries and cafes, while Morton and a number of smaller national parks offer good bushwalking and spectacular scenery.

Central Coast and beyond

Great beaches and waterways, unspoilt bush and a laid-back lifestyle are the major attractions of this region, a comfortable 90-minutes from the city by road or rail. Explore the waters of Broken Bay by boat and seek out one of the many good fishing spots, find a secluded beach or catch a wave at one of a string of surf beaches. There are national parks aplenty and if you tire of natural attractions, get a taste of pioneer life at Old Sydney Town or browse round the boutiques of Terrigal. Lake Macquarie is a mecca for watersports, fishing and swimming and it's a similar story further north at Port Stephens and Myall Lakes, where eagle-eyed visitors may spot koalas and kangaroos as well as dolphins, pelicans and a host of birds.

Hunter Valley and beyond

If you're looking for indulgence, the Hunter Valley is your place. First-class accommodation and eateries have blossomed in the past few years to match the region's liquid assets — the high-quality wines for which it is famous. Visit some of the dozens of wineries that offer tastings and cellar-door sales and picnic among the vines or eat at one of the many excellent restaurants. Want to work off those extra calories? Nearby World Heritage-listed Barrington Tops National Park has walking trails through the rainforest to idyllic swimming holes and waterfalls or, for the less energetic, superb forest drives.

Activity and adventure breaks

Looking for action? Then consider one of the multitude of adventure and activity breaks that offer everything from abseiling to whitewater canoeing. The Blue Mountains offer abseiling, canyoning, caving, rock climbing, horseriding and overnight bushwalking while further west at places like Hill End you can fossick for gold. On the coastal strip try scuba diving at Jervis Bay and Port Stephens; canoeing, sailing and windsurfing on Myall Lakes or one of the other sheltered waterways that dot the coastline, and deep sea fishing or whale watching off Wollongong. Inland, there is whitewater canoeing in Barrington Tops or four-wheel driving or fly fishing in numerous locations. For the ultimate high, try hang gliding at Stanwell

Tops, skydiving at Camden or hot air ballooning at Camden or in the Hunter Valley. The only limits are your imagination.

Long weekends

If you're planning a three- or four-day weekend and don't mind driving for five or six hours, consider heading further north or south along the coast for even quieter beaches and bush backdrops, north-west to the magnificent Warrumbungle National Park, west to Dubbo for its world-famous zoo or south-west to the Snowy Mountains, a year-round destination.

Jenny Stanton

Further information
- Tourism NSW, ph 9931 1111: www.tourism.nsw.gov.au
- Sydney Morning Herald's Saturday Travel section
- NRMA Holiday Guides ($10 each, free to members)

Weightlifting

see also bodybuilding, sporting goods

Weightlifting is often confused with weight training and body building in local gyms. If you're not sure of the difference, remember this: weightlifting is the sport where you win if you lift more than your rivals. Body building is when you eat egg whites for the rest of you life and aspire to look like the Incredible Hulk. It may surprise many to learn that the experts do not recommend going to your local gym to learn or improve your weightlifting. This is primarily because suitably-trained coaches are few and far between in Sydney. Close contact with a trainer boasting Australian Weightlifting Federation coaching credentials is advised instead. Sydney is home to Johnny Nguyen, the Vietnamese-born Commonwealth and Oceania Champion ranked no. 1 in the Commonwealth in the 56kg class. His closest rival is Mehmet Yagci, also Sydney-based. Dividing his time between his native Bulgaria and his adopted Sydney is Kiril Kounev, ranked no. 1 in the Commonwealth since 1990 in the 85kg class. He is considered an outside chance for medal in 2000.

Burwood Police Citizens Youth Club

National and NSW coach Luke Borreggine is based at this major training centre for weightlifters of all levels in Sydney. The club provides all equipment and training and welcomes beginners.
- 17 Deane St, Burwood, ph 9744 0136.

Darling Harbour Convention Centre

Scene for the weightlifting competition at Sydney 2000, where women will compete for the first time.
- ph 9282 5000.

NSW Weightlifting Association

The best place to call for anyone looking to get involved in serious competition. Produces the only monthly magazine updating the comings and goings in NSW weightlifting.
- State Sports Centre, Australia Ave, Homebush, ph 9763 0101.

York Fitness

Supplier of weightlifting equipment for the serious lifter such as barbells, plates and weight benches.
- Lot 12 Airds Rd, Minto, ph 9603 8444.

Berrico Weightlifting Equipment

Supplier of gear the professionals use.
- ph 9763 7936.

Peter Vincent

Further information
- Australian Weightlifting Federation, national controlling body for the sport, ph (03) 9813 1399

Weight loss

see also **fitness clubs, personal trainers, aerobics**

It's generally accepted nowadays that diets are the enemy of anyone who is serious about trying to lose weight. The secret to long-term successful weight loss is changing habits permanently and finding what works for you.

Weight Watchers

The longest established and largest weight loss organisation, there are 308 Weight Watchers groups, meeting in almost every corner of Sydney. There are no up-front fees, you pay as you go. Meetings are conducted by WW success stories and they emphasise you can eat what you like and still lose weight.
■ ph 9928 1300.

Gut Busters

Established by Aussie blokes for Aussie blokes, and now also running courses for women, its six-week lifestyle course focuses on changing habits, eating differently (not less) and 'trading' extra indulgences for extra exercise.
■ 98 Arthur St, North Sydney,
  ph 9956 6877.

The Diet Factory

The dietitian's answer to meals on wheels, the Diet Factory prepares and delivers your choice from a weekly menu. Your three meals a day consist of a mixture of fresh and frozen food. Starting at $83 a person a week, they are nutritionally balanced and calorie controlled.
■ 1 Sutherland St, Granville,
  ph 9682 7322.

Nutritionist – Jane Barnes

The word dietitian is a no-no nowadays, says Barnes, who has been practising in Sydney for more than a decade. All diets are bound to fail eventually, she says, emphasising that how much fat you can keep off is more important than how much weight you can take off. Weight 'cycling' (drastic weight loss followed by rapid gain) is more damaging than leaving the weight on permanently, she says.
■ 75 Paraween St, Cremorne,
  ph 9909 1598.

Christopher Dobney

Wildlife

see also **national parks, zoos**

An extraordinary diversity of wildlife can still be seen in Sydney, although overdevelopment is diminishing it rapidly. Remember, you are dealing with wild animals. They will only survive if you treat them with the utmost respect. Observe them from a distance and never frighten or threaten them.

North Head

The jewel in Sydney's wildlife crown. It is the only place in the entire harbour area where you can still see bandicoots, while the city's only penguins nest and fish nearby. Bandicoots are best seen in the evening on St Patricks Estate and Little Manly point.

Royal Botanic Gardens

Inner-city birds abound. Blue wrens (now vanished from much of the city), tawny frogmouths and boobook owls grace the more dense vegetation, while a diversity of waterfowl use the lakes.
■ Between Mrs Macquarie's Rd and
  Macquarie St, City, ph 9231 8125.

Darling Harbour

The stone wall on the western side of Darling Harbour is a favourite place to enjoy Chinese takeaway. Normally wary bream have come to know that occasional spills of rice fall into the water there. Let our harbour's smartest fish enchant you. Better than seeing them at Costi's.

Taronga Zoo
While not strictly wild, a diversity of species that were once common around the harbour can now only be seen here, including echidnas, platypus, swamp wallabies and grey kangaroos. Wild native birds abound, while skinks such as blue-tongue lizards can be glimpsed in the adjacent National Park at Bradley's Head.
■ Bradleys Head Rd, Mosman, ph 9969 2777.

Maroubra Beach
Around September each year, Sydney is visited by southern right whales. Hunted to near extinction last century, they return to calve in the city's bays and beaches. Maroubra is often visited but magnificent sightings have also been had in Long Bay and off Manly.

Gordon bat colony
Each year, up to 60,000 grey-headed flying foxes roost in a bush gully in the northern suburb of Gordon. The sight of their nightly exit, which can be had from a number of vantage points in the area, is breathtaking. Flying foxes can be seen feeding in inner-city parks each evening. City restaurants with outdoors eating areas offer particularly good locations from which to observe these extraordinary creatures.

Tim Flannery

Wine

see also bars, liquor stores
Sydney is relatively well served for fine wine, with a handful of top retailers, educators and sommeliers who can lead you to the best of Australian and imported wines.

Ultimo Wine Centre
Sydney's most extraordinary wine shop, with an obsession for imported wines, and its own separate accessory shop a couple of doors down the street. The combined wisdom of Jon Osbeiston, Kevin Facey, David Burkitt and Philippe Morin is formidable and the regular newsletter is as good a read as most wine magazines. Regular forays into Europe keep the shelves filled with an astonishing range of direct imports.
■ Shop 99, 460-480 Jones St, Ultimo, ph 9211 2380.

More top retailers
Five Ways Cellars Paddington, Best Cellars East Sydney, Vintage Cellars Double Bay, Camperdown Cellars, Roseville Cellars, Wahroonga Cellars, Grapefellas of Epping, The Wine Gallery Pyrmont, Sixty Darling Street Balmain, Kemeny's of Bondi.

Winebanc
This is the wine bar Sydney has always deserved, but had to wait ages for. Romantically lit, vaulted like a Burgundian grower's cave, and with an encyclopedic wine list of 500 featuring a tempting by-the-glass list of 23, this is the wine buff's ultimate subterranean hangout. Sit at the bar or at low tables and mix and match your wines with delicious snacky food.
■ Basement, 53 Martin Place (entrance in Elizabeth St), City, ph 9233 5399.

Forty-One
The exception to the usual cynicism about restaurants with views. The vista is stunning, 41 floors above Sydney and its harbour, with food to match and an outstanding wine list. The by-the-glass list is also exemplary and not as pricey as you might expect in such an elite eatery. You can have a mature Grange by the glass, and any wine you like from the Krug stable: vintage, non-vintage, rosé, blanc de blancs or a mature vintage.
■ Level 41, Chifley Tower, 2 Chifley Square, City, ph 9211 2500.

Wine

Franck Crouvezier

Franck Crouvezier is what every great restaurant should have: a top-notch sommelier (specialist wine waiter). At bel mondo, in The Rocks, he not only combines with an unusually wine-knowledgeable chef (Stefano Manfredi) to select an outstanding wine list, he is also on hand to recommend the ideal wine to suit your palate and the dish you're ordering. Italian wines are a specialty, notably the reds of Tuscany and Piedmont.

■ bel mondo, Level 3, 12-24 Argyle St, The Rocks, ph 9241 3700.

More great lists

As well as bel mondo, Forty-One and Winebanc, the following restaurants have excellent wine lists: Armstrong's, Banc, Bathers Pavilion, Bilson's, Bistro Moncur, Bistro Deux, Bistro Pavé, Catalina, Centennial Hotel, Cicada, Claudine's, Darling Mills, Grand Pacific Blue Room, Kables, La Grillade, l'Avventura, Merrony's, Moran's, Pavilion on the Park, Pier, Rockpool, San Francisco Grill, Stuyvesants House, Vetro, Watermark.

Peter Bourne

Sydney's liveliest wine courses are conducted by this long-time retailer/wholesaler/wine writer/ promoter. Chatty, unstuffy approach and 30 to 40 of the best wines, hand-picked by Peter. Small, intimate classes at introductory ($195) and advanced ($275) levels on four consecutive Tuesday nights, throughout the year.

■ ph 9365 0033.

The Wine Society

Sydney's busiest schedule of wine tutoring, ranging from beginners through advanced to specialist courses, tutored tastings, wine dinners and guided tours (Australia and overseas). The society, a non-profit direct-marketing wine club, is NSW's biggest wine retailer. Courses cost $145 for members, $160 for non-members.

■ ph 132 046.

New South Wales Wine Exhibition

Taste wines from the State's tried and true regions (Hunter Valley, Mudgee, Riverina, etc.) and exciting new ones (Orange, Canberra, Hilltops, Cowra, Port Macquarie and more). At the Hotel InterContinental in September 1998.

■ Hotel InterContinental, 117 Macquarie St, City, ph 9230 0200.

Huon Hooke

Women's shoes & accessories

see also international designer fashion

If you're as mad about shoes as Imelda Marcos, Sydney shoe stores are for you. They cater for all tastes – the chicest of international labels (at a price) to mass market knock-offs. These are the specialists but don't forget the David Jones for shoes and accessories in the Elizabeth St store.

Donna May Bolinger

Bespoke shoemaker Donna May Bolinger specialises in handmade shoes, made to measure on her Sydney premises, as well as her own designer label shoes which are made in Italy. She moonlights as one of the designers for Italy's sought-after Sergio Rossi shoes.

■ 379 South Dowling St, Darlinghurst, ph 9360 7898.

Belinda Gunn

Charming and original handbags are designed and created by Belinda Gunn in her own shop/studio, a recent addition to the happening William St terrace row in Paddington. Belinda Gunn's eclectic array includes calfskin wallets, hand-embroidered silk evening bags, funky snakeskin handbags, to patchwork velvet totes.

■ 88 William St, Paddington, ph 9380 5085.

Women's shoes & accessories

Evelyn Miles
The chicest must-have shoe labels from around the world like Sergio Rossi, Manolo Blahnik, Michel Perry, Jimmy Choo, Patrick Cox and Richard Tyler. Utterly covetable and utterly expensive.
- Ritz Carlton Promenade, 33 Cross St, Double Bay, ph 9327 5732; MLC Centre, Cnr King & Castlereagh Sts, City, ph 9233 1569.

Gary Castles
The absolute latest in shoe trends imported primarily from Italy. Clever interpretations of the hottest designer styles at more affordable prices.
- Strand Arcade, City, ph 9232 6544; Piccadilly, 210 Pitt St, City, ph 9267 4713. Also at Paddington, ph 9361 4560; Double Bay, ph 9327 5077.

Gucci
The hot shoes and bags from the label that influences style directions around the world.
- 136-140 George St, The Rocks, ph 9252 1663; Shop 7/23, MLC Centre, City, ph 9232 7565.

Hunt Leather
Established in 1975, Hunt Leather is a leading Australian retailer of high quality luggage, business cases, handbags, wallets and leather accessories. Their label imports include French staple Longchamp (which they have stocked for over 20 years), along with Italian labels Il Bisonte, Enny, and MH Way and top-of-the-range luggage by Tumi. Recently opened a boutique in Sky Gardens devoted exclusively to Longchamp.
- Castlereagh level, MLC Centre, City, ph 9233 8702.

Midas
Bringing affordable shoe imports to Australia with all the latest trends.
- Imperial Arcade, City, ph 9233 3612;

The Glasshouse, 135 King St, City, ph 9221 5620. Also at Bondi Junction, ph 9387 1241; North Sydney, ph 9929 6508.

Prada
The cult label for aficionados of Italy's Miuccia Prada hits Sydney at last, with Prada's sought-after bags and shoes for women and men.
- 44 Martin Place, City, ph 9231 3929.

Oroton
Australian designer leathergoods with the international-feel handbags, wallets and briefcases made in Italy and Spain to Australian concepts.
- Centrepoint, City, ph 9232 2242. Also at Queen Victoria Building, ph 9261 1984; International Airport Terminal, ph 9669 2656; North Sydney, ph 9956 5112; Parramatta, ph 9687 0393.

Raymond Castles
Ritzy luxury shoe imports for the ladies who lunch and the cocktail set, including Italian favourites Bruno Magli, Di Sandro and Casadei plus the glitzy Stuart Weitzman, American designed but made in Italy. An evening shoe mecca.
- Gallery Level, Centrepoint, City, ph 9232 2147. Also at Double Bay, ph 9327 3864; Mosman, ph 9960 2518; Parramatta, ph 9663 5112.

Zomp
Younger label shoe imports, particularly from Italy, at affordable prices.
- George St level, Mid City Centre, Pitt Street Mall, ph 9221 4027. Also at Double Bay, ph 9362 3422; Mosman, ph 9960 2504; Paddington, ph 9361 3800.

Jane de Teliga

Womenswear

see also international designer fashion, women's shoes & accessories

Sydney's buzzing with the hottest Australian labels. No more cultural cringe on the frock front, with local heroes stocked side by side with the best from overseas. With many of the world's prestigious stores snapping our labels up, we can now get them earlier and cheaper right here. Don't forget the huge selection of both international and designer labels at David Jones and Grace Bros department stores.

Akira Isogawa

Akira Isogawa's layered blend of East and West has made him a rising star on the Australian fashion scene and a find for savvy overseas boutiques like Browns, London.
- 12a Queen St, Woollahra, ph 9361 5221.

Amanda Garrett Designs

Evening wear, in limited editions, now discovered by Bloomingdales for their Los Angeles and New York couture departments.
- 14a Queen St, Woollahra, ph 9360 2732.

Bare

The stretchy, sexy designs of Sydney designer Becky Davies have been snapped up by supermodels such as Claudia Schiffer and Linda Evangelista.
- 200 Oxford St, Paddington, ph 9331 2607; 45a Bay St, Double Bay, ph 9363 3232.

Belinda

One of Sydney's chicest stores, due to Belinda Seper's impeccable eye for upcoming and hot labels from Europe and Australia. Look for international names like Ann Demeulemeester, Stephen Slowik, Lawrence Steele, and Australia's Collette Dinnigan as well as charming accessories from around the world.
- 8 Transvaal Ave, Double Bay, ph 9238 6288.

Black Vanity

Affordable interpretations of the season's latest looks from day to evening, often with an ethnic flavour.
- 400 Oxford St, Paddington, ph 9360 5130. Also at the Strand Arcade, City, ph 9233 6241; Surry Hills, ph 9331 4801.

Bracewell

Hip mix of their own label and imports like New Zealander Karen Walker, Costume National shoes and Joseph, London.
- 264 Oxford St, Paddington, ph 9331 5844; 139 Elizabeth St, City, ph 9264 7271.

Carla Zampatti

Thirty-three years in the business, Zampatti keeps up with the fashion trends and gives them a classy and classic finish.
- 143 Elizabeth St, City, ph 9264 3257. Also at Double Bay, ph 9326 2248; Mosman, ph 9960 2585; Chatswood Chase, ph 9411 1212.

Claudia's Collection

Boutique with an eclectic mix of designer labels including Sydney's Leonie designs.
- The Argyle Department Store, Argyle St, The Rocks, ph 9252 4060.

Collette Dinnigan

The original terrace house boutique of Australia's best known international designer who shows at the Paris pret a porter and sells her romantic creations in the world's most prestigious department stores.
- 39 William St, Paddington, ph 9360 6691.

Womenswear

Country Road
Defining easy and contemporary Australian style, Country Road has stores throughout Australia, the US and Asia.
- Shop T12, Level 1, Chatswood Chase, Victoria Ave, Chatswood, ph 9419 5570. Also at many other locations including the Queen Victoria Building, City, Mosman, Parramatta, Castle Hill.

Directions
Mix of Australian labels for the Eastern Suburbs gal – lunching, running the kids to school or dressing up. Names include Ashley Fogel, Jane Lamerton, Phoebe Rose Hats, Simona Sport, Sara Sturgeon, Trent Nathan, Trent Resort.
- 401 New South Head Rd, Double Bay, ph 9328 1991.

Done Art and Design
Judy Done creates weekendwear and swimwear using imagery from her artist husband Ken Done's vivid designs.
- 123-125 George St, The Rocks, ph 9251 6099. Also at Queen Victoria Building, City, 9283 1167; Sydney International Airport, ph 9667 0996.

Entity
North Shore haven for Australasian designer labels – Collette Dinnigan, Sally Smith, Akira Isogawa, Zambesi, Workshop, Jenny Bannister, Allanah Hill, Deborah Hill, Matthew Eager, Victoria Loftes, Helen English, and Ellin Ambe.
- Westfield Shoppingtown, Victoria Ave, Chatswood, ph 9412 4410; Greenwood Plaza, North Sydney, ph 9957 2552.

Five Way Fusion
For 24 years Paul Jellard's clothing store has bought top international designer labels to Sydney, first for men and for the past four years for women. Names include Issey Miyake, Dolce & Gabbana, Comme des Garcons, Anna Molinari and Missoni.
- 205 Glenmore Rd, Paddington, ph 9360 2572; Queen Victoria Building, City, ph 9264 9268.

Leona Edmiston
Perfect chic for the modern working girl from Leona Edmiston, now solo after her split with fellow designer Peter Morrissey.
- Shop 68, Level 1, Strand Arcade, City, ph 9231 2266. Also in Chatswood, ph 9410 2255.

Lisa Ho
Designer fashion looks by Sydney's Lisa Ho run from drifty evening wear to hip leather.
- 2a-6a Queen St, Woollahra, ph 9360 2345; Chatswood Chase, Victoria Ave, Chatswood, ph 9411 8442.

Naked
An Inner West boutique for labels like Ashley Fogel, Mela Purdie, Penny Black, Sara Sturgeon, Mulberry, Susan Nurmsalu, Charlie Brown, Matthew Eager and George Spyrou.
- 313 Darling St, Balmain, ph 9818 3778.

Matthew Eager
This Sydney designer's forte is contemporary evening wear which is also popular with bridal parties.
- Strand Arcade, City, ph 9221 7575.

Nicola Finetti
Italian-born, Sydney-based designer whose ethereal layered looks have been taken up enthusiastically by the fashion magazines.
- 92 Queen St, Woollahra, ph 9362 1685. Also at Mosman, ph 9960 2806.

Pierucci
Well-priced, Italian-inspired women and menswear from Western Australia.
- Chifley Plaza, 2 Chifley Square, City, ph 9231 5232. Also at Paddington, ph 9380 6336; Bondi Junction, ph 9386 1103.

Reads
Packed to the gunnels with Australian labels from weekend separates to career suiting –

Womenswear

labels like Easton Pearson, Saba, Trent Nathan, Simona Sport, Helen Kaminski, and accessories galore.
- 130 Queen St, Woollahra, ph 9328 1036.

Riada
A smart boutique specialising in beautiful Italian labels like Romeo Gigli, Alberta Ferretti and Philosophy by Alberta Ferretti, Alberto Biani, Antonio Fusco and French labels Jean Paul Gaultier and Victoire, as well as shoes by JP Tods and Robert Clergerie.
- 118 Queen St, Woollahra, ph 9363 0654. Also at Mosman, ph 9969 4269.

Robby Ingham stores
With four stores side by side, Robby Ingham carries imports with a little bit of difference – English label Paul Smith, knitwear label Tehen, Comme des Garçons and G. Gigli.
- 422-428 Oxford St, Paddington, ph 9332 2124.

Saba Melbourne
Over 30 years old and still hip, happening, and hot on contemporary trends. Just opened in New York.
- 39 Bay St, Double Bay, ph 9362 0281. Also at Skygarden, City, ph 9231 2183; Mosman, ph 9960 7045.

Sally Smith
Upcoming Sydney label for the fashionable young things around town.
- 263 Crown St, Darlinghurst, ph 9380 6726.

Scanlan & Theodore
Melbourne's talented Fiona Scanlan's contemporary clothing for the urban and hip.
- 443 Oxford St, Paddington, ph 9361 6722; Greenwood Plaza, North Sydney, ph 9955 2383.

Simona
One of the classic labels. Has been in the business for more than 30 years with new young label Simona Speed and popular Simona Sport.
- 478 Oxford St, Paddington, ph 9332 1447. Also at Mosman, ph 9969 6943; Chatswood, ph 9411 6366.

Sonya Hopkins
Now you can find the delectable knitwear of this Sydney designer in her own little boutique.
- 6 Glenmore Rd, Paddington, ph 9380 8030.

Sportsgirl
One of the best fashion chains around with labels for all ages from the young and trendy Elle B, sophisticated David Lawrence and the more mature Sportscraft.
- Skygarden, 77 Castlereagh St, City, ph 9223 8255. Also at many other locations, including Chatswood, ph 9419 7883; North Sydney, ph 9955 4585; Miranda, ph 9524 1397; Parramatta, ph 9687 0343.

Tea Rose
Refined romantic dresses, fine handcrafted knits in beautiful fabrics and limited editions.
- Shop 3, 24 Bay St, Double Bay, ph 9362 0976.

Third Millennium
Contemporary lingerie dressing with a retro mood for the groovy set.
- Strand Arcade, City, ph 9221 4089.

Tour
Young and strappy evening wear by Suska and Andrew Dunshea that is hugely popular for school formals.
- Strand Arcade, City, ph 9233 3180; Westfield Shoppingtown, Victoria Ave, Chatswood, ph 9415 3440.

Von Troska

The latest trends made wearable for 30-somethings.
- 294 Oxford St, Paddington, ph 9360 7522. Also at VTX Paddington, ph 9331 2212; Strand Arcade, City, ph 9223 3925; Double Bay, ph 9327 7799; Mosman, ph 9968 1514.

Vreelands

Delve through tightly packed stock for good Australian labels like Easton Pearson from Queensland.
- 696 Military Rd, Mosman, ph 9960 3893.

Wayne Cooper/Brave

Hip and trendy modernism from London-born Sydney designer Wayne Cooper with two labels – the young and sexy Brave and more upmarket Wayne Cooper.
- Strand Arcade, City, ph 9221 5292, 9235 1114. Also at Paddington, ph 9332 2940.

Witchery

A Melbourne-based fashion chain that has had a mega style revamp both in product and stores. Good for the season's must-have basics.
- Central Plaza, 436 George St, City, ph 9231 1233. Also at many locations from Bankstown to Parramatta, ph 1800 640 249.

Zambesi

New Zealand label whose contemporary deconstructed looks have a strong following.
- 160 Castlereagh St, City, ph 9267 7277.

Zimmermann

Hip young styles by Sydney's Nicky Zimmermann. The big hit is her modern swimwear now selling in London's Harvey Nichols, CK Tang's, Singapore, Barneys, New York and Japan.
- 24 Oxford St, Woollahra, ph 9360 5769.

Jane de Teliga

Woodworking

For some, there's nothing like the smell of sawdust and beeswax, and the touch of the grain, to really evoke passion for a piece of furniture. Perhaps it's because of the individuality of craftsmanship, or maybe it's because you know it'll stand the test of time. Whatever the reason, woodwork is in a league of its own, combining functionality and art with contemporary design and craft traditions.

Timber and Working with Wood Show

This annual show, held in mid-year at the Homebush Bay Exhibition Centre, is for anyone who enjoys working with wood. More than 200 exhibitors on hand to discuss the latest products, techniques, woodcrafts, carvings, furniture, sculptures, rare timbers and the latest tools. For information, contact:
- Riddell Exhibitions, ph 9565 1099.

Nicholas Dattner & Co.

Boasting the 'most beautiful tables in the world', Nicholas Dattner & Co. specialise in Australian native-hardwood timber tables, chairs and sideboards. Tables are its passion, and it designs and produces original pieces. They range from the humble kitchen table to the corporate boardroom piece, with everything in between.
- 41 Bridge Rd, Glebe, ph 9518 8777.

The Wood Works Book & Tool Co.

This is not your average hardware store. This gem of a shop sells a broad range of high-quality speciality woodworking hand-tools and woodworking books. They have a large selection of tools from the US, Japan, Germany and the UK, including speciality carving chisels, saws, fine sharpening stones, turning tools and planes.
- 8 Railway Rd, Meadowbank, ph 9807 7244.

Nicola Shenton

World music

see also rock music, blues music, folk music, country music, jazz

Sydney prides itself on its multiculturalism and enthusiastically supports world music acts – Mali's Salif Keita and Benin's Angelique Kidjo, and groups such as South Africa's Ladysmith Black Mambazo and the US's Sweet Honey in The Rock can fill major venues. The city's commitment to local musicians and performers is less passionate. There are many groups working within their own cultures – Greek, Italian, Portuguese, Spanish – but there are some notable bona fide world music acts. Keep an eye out for Sirocco, a local band which rarely plays Sydney.

Blindman's Holiday
An a cappella female group which tends to perform in churches and quality acoustic spaces.

Mara
Any musical configuration with Mara Kiek is worth checking out.

Colin Offord
As much a performance artist as a world musician, a tantalising mixture of Celtic and Pacific Rim.

Harbourside Brasserie
The city's preferred world music venue with semi-regular local performers. It is used by most overseas acts with a strong dance component to their music. Occasionally world music acts appear at **The Basement** (ph 9251 2797) and **The Three Weeds** (ph 9810 2244).
- Pier One, City, ph 9252 3000.

HMV Shop
Boasts the city's most comprehensive world music section and is an endless source of information. Both Gordon Mignot and Dave Robson are a great source of knowledge and advice.
- Shop 1, Midcity Centre, Pitt St Mall, City, ph 9221 2311.

Folkways Music
An extensive world music section and can order hard-to-get titles.
- 282 Oxford St, Paddington, ph 9361 3980.

Bruce Elder

Further information
- See Sydney Morning Herald Metro and CitySearch for listings

Wrestling

see also sprting goods

Wrestling, one of the few ancient Olympic Games sports to survive into the modern era, is well represented in Sydney. There are a range of clubs spread across the Emerald City, although most are stronger in the junior grades than in the seniors. Victoria, although we hate to say it, has Australia's elite seniors. In Sydney, the Sutherland, Hornsby and Eastern Suburbs clubs are fertile ground for young champions, while St George has our best senior wrestlers. All these clubs welcome women and learners. St George's Masgood Sadeghpour is probably our best senior, while Hornsby's Gabriel Szerda and the Cash brothers, Brett and Graham, each hold Australian and Oceanic junior Greco-Roman and Freestyle titles. Two of Sydney's best young seniors, Igor Praporschikov and Russell Mirny, of the Eastern Suburbs club, represented Australia at the ill-fated 15th Maccabiah Games in Israel in 1997. Igor, in particular, was one of the heroes of the accident, saving several fellow competitors from drowning. Sadly, neither has wrestled since the tragic bridge collapse, but officials hope both will be able to continue their promising careers. In 2000, Olympic competition will be held at Darling Harbour's Exhibition Halls in the second week of the Games.

State Sports Centre
This is where Sydney's elite wrestlers train on Tuesdays and Thursdays, with top coach John Kinsella.
- Australia Ave, Homebush Bay, ph 9763 0111.

St George PCYC
This Police Citizens and Youth Club is home of the State's best seniors. Also provides training and tuition for all ages and skill levels.
- Ador Ave, Rockdale, ph 9567 0408.

Eastern Suburbs Wrestling Club
Sydney's main eastern club, with strong links to the Jewish community.
- Underwood St, Paddington, ph 9386 1502, 019 463 782.

Hornsby PCYC
North Shore club encouraging beginners and women.
- 94 George St, Hornsby, ph 9477 2310.

Sutherland PCYC
Large club specialising in training for 8- to 16-year-olds.
- Waratah Park, Forest Rd, Sutherland, ph 9521 5690.

Don Brown
Don, who is also Australia's highest-ranked referee, orders Tiger and Adidas wrestling boots, earguards and costumes from the US, which are hard to find in Australia.
- PO Box 276, Warilla, NSW, 2528, ph 042 970 986.

Peter Vincent

Further information
- NSW Wrestling Association, ph 4392 6479 (Les Neal, president)

Yoga

see also tai chi, alternative medicine
Hatha yoga originated as an Indian philosophy some 2,000 years ago and today its postures and breathing techniques are widely practised in either its basic form or derivative styles, such as Iyengar and Ashtanga.

Kings Cross Yoga Centre
Caroline Coggins is the principal teacher and chairs the introductory teachers' assessment committee for the Iyengar yoga movement in Australia. This style focuses on correct alignment, through the use of props, for an uninhibited flow of breath through the cells. The centre has remedial, pranayama (breathing) and intensive morning classes, retreats, workshops, and discussion groups.
- 157 Brougham St, Woolloomooloo, ph 9357 7103.

Sydney Yoga Centre
Its teaching moves away from the strictness of the Iyengar system with a slower approach to attaining alignment and strength, by being receptive to the levels of stress, anxiety and exhaustion of students. An eclectic meditation class on Sundays addresses modern problems.
- 69 Archer St, Chatswood, ph 9369 5324; Clifton Reserve, Surry Hills, ph 9369 5324.

Yoga Synergy
As the name suggests, teachers combine traditional yoga with medical science, working on posture, but maintaining the flow of classes by limiting the use of props. Teaching focuses on

Yoga

improving structure, line, flexibility and strength and relaxation and meditation are incorporated into the classes.
- 196 Australia St, Newtown, ph 9389 7399; 115 Bronte Rd, Bondi Junction, ph 9389 7399.

Yoga Moves

The Ashtanga style is a vigorous, almost aerobic, continuous series of movements where each posture is held for five 'fire' breaths. The advanced Ashtanga-Mysore style emphasises Ujjayi breathing which generates heat or energy with sound, and is said to help detoxify the body.
- Verona Centre, 17 Oxford St, Paddington, ph 9360 7602.

Yoga in Daily Life

Each centre teaches hatha yoga classes combining breathing, general stretches for tension prone areas, a cycle of energised postures, relaxation and meditation.
- Head office: 102 Booth St, Annandale, ph 9518 7788. Also at Gymea, Dee Why, Chatswood, Parramatta, St Ives.

Trisha Treanor

Yum cha

see also Chinese restaurants, Chinese Sydney

The Cantonese answer to tapas and antipasto, this happy, steamy, messy lunch of delicate little dim sum is one of the world's great bargains. Don't worry if you don't know what things are called, just point at the trolleys as they roll by and look hungry. Yum cha is cheap, noisy, crowded, filling, invariably varied and a great deal of fun.

Chequers

Tucked away in a modern shopping centre cum cinema centre, Chequers is very Kowloon in style with its marble-clad entrance, fish tanks and glittering chandeliers. The variety of yum cha served is huge, with the har gau and sharks fin dumplings recommended.
- Shop 220-221, Mandarin Centre, 65 Albert Ave, Chatswood, ph 9904 8388.

The Dragon

Basically a Chiu Chow seafood specialist, The Dragon still manages to dish out an authentic Cantonese yum cha of infinite variety. Anything steamed is invariably good, but do try the scallop dumplings, shark fin dumplings and *cheung faan* steamed rice roll filled with prawn.
- 445 Victoria Ave, Chatswood, ph 9415 2785.

Imperial Peking

Miles from the steamers and woks of Chinatown, you can still enjoy a buzzy daily yum cha amid rosewood furniture and hanging lanterns. The Imperial Peking goes beyond *siu mai* to stuffed eggplant and coconut rice cake wrapped in lotus leaf.
- 979 King Georges Rd, Blakehurst, ph 9546 6122.

Kam Fook

This 800-seater is madly noisy, tenement-crowded and completely and utterly Chinese in concept, with a seemingly haywire but utterly logical numbering system for those who wait. The *har gau* (prawn dumpling) is close to perfect, *siu mai* are gems and *cheung faan* rice rolls have just the right amount of wobbliness.
- Level 3, Market City, 9-13 Hay St, Haymarket, ph 9211 8988.

Marigold Citymark

Welcome to two floors of yum cha fun, where 700 people converge most weekends for, among other things, wonderful *siu mai* dumplings, perfect, crisp *woo gok* (yam dumplings) and the tenderest *pai gwat* steamed spare ribs.
- Levels 4 & 5, 683 George St, Haymarket, ph 9281 3388.

Terry Durack

Zoos

see also wildlife

The idea of exotic animals locked up for safe viewing by the public may be a bit un-PC these days, but zoos have moved beyond the idea of wildlife behind bars.

Taronga Zoo

The animals here must have some of the best harbour views in Sydney. An easy ferry ride from Circular Quay, Taronga is a Sydney institution which has moved with the times with a world-class collection of exotic and native animals and a renowned breeding program.
- Bradleys Head Rd, Mosman,
  ph 0055 20218 (inquiries), 9969 2777 (administration).

Featherdale Wildlife Park

It is 50 minutes from the city to a park full of koalas. Also home to Tasmanian devils, rare wallabies, emus, dingoes and wombats.
- 217-219 Kildare Rd, Doonside,
  ph 9622 1644.

Koala Park Sanctuary

You've seen them on TV and longed to give them a pat. Well indulge yourself at the Castle Hill Koala Park. It was the first privately owned park in the country when it opened in 1930. You can see the koalas being fed at 10.20am and at 2 and 3pm.
- Castle Hill Rd, West Pennant Hills,
  ph 9484 3141.

Australian Wildlife Park

Part of the Australia's Wonderland, the largest theme park in the country, this zoo contains only Australian native animals. Check out the fairy penguins and the five-metre crocodile. There's also a huge woolshed where you can watch sheep being sheared.
- Eastern Creek, ph 9830 9187.

Sydney Aquarium

Take a break from the furry critters. The best thing here are the glass tunnels under the tanks full of marine life. Like a Chinatown restaurant really but you can't eat any of it. Come nose to snout with a huge big shark. The kids will love the interactive displays.
- Per 26, Darling Harbour, ph 9262 2300.

Cerentha Harris

BEST OF SYDNEY LOCALITY GUIDE

CITY NORTH

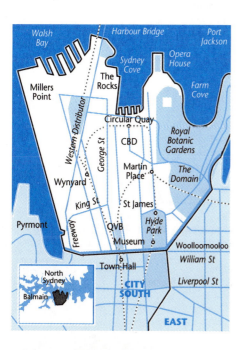

 ## ARTS AND ENTERTAINMENT

The Basement, Circular Quay, ... p.80, 191
Art Gallery Of NSW, ... p.55, 57, 234
Birdland Records, ... p.192
Class Act at Sublime, ... p.160
Dendy Cinemas, ... p.142
Discount Art and Drafting Materials, ... p.59
Eckersley's, ... p.59
Fletchers Fotographic, ... p.235
HMV Music Store, ... p.81, 111, 314
Harbourside Brasserie, ... p.314
Hyde Park Barracks, ... p.56
Julian Ashton Art School, ... p.58
NSW State Library, ... p.234
Performing Arts Bookshop, ... p.123, 225
Red Eye, ... p.246
Rent, ... p.286
Soup Plus, ... p.191
State Library of NSW-Conservation Access, ... p.56
State Theatre, ... p.246
Strand Arcade, ... p.254, 259
Sublime, ... p.221
The Basement, ... p.80, 191
The Performing Arts Bookshop, ... p.286
Time Warp Records, ... p.246
Wynyard Hotel, ... p.191
Australian Music Centre, The Rocks, ... p.110
National Aboriginal and Islander Skills
    Development Association, The Rocks, .. p.42
Sounds Australian, The Rocks, ... p.192
Ausdance, Walsh Bay, ... p.123
Bangarra Dance Theatre, Walsh Bay, ... p.42, 123

 ## FASHION AND LIFESTYLE

Andrew McDonald, ... p.258
Angus & Coote, ... p.136
Aveda Environmental Lifestyle Store, ... p.77
Baubridge & Kay, ... p.208
Bow Blue, ... p.103
Budget Eyewear, ... p.160
Bulgari, ... p.192
Carla Zampatti, ... p.311
Cartier, ... p.192
Celine, ... p.184
Chanel, ... p.184
Chifley Shoe Worx, ... p.258
Cobra Athleisure, ... p.272
Country Road, ... p.209, 311
Crabtree and Evelyn, ... p.77
David Jones, .. p.65, 71, 77, 112, 128, 163, 203, 237
DKNY, ... p.184
Dioptics, ... p.273
Dotti, ... p.272
Downtown Duty Free, ... p.135
Emporio Armani, ... p.184, 209
Fairfax & Roberts, ... p.193
Fila, ... p.272
Gary Castles, ... p.309
General Pants, ... p.272
Gianni Versace, ... p.184
Giorgio Armani, ... p.184, 209
Gowings, ... p.129
Grace Bros, ... p.128
Gucci Boutique, ... p.309
Guess, ... p.184
Hairline Institute, ... p.169
Hardy Bros, ... p.193
Hermes, ... p.185
House of Cerrone, ... p.192
Hunt Leather, ... p.115, 204, 309
IM Bodywear, ... p.203

321

Locality Guide

Ian McMaugh, ... p.210
Jayem Underfashion, ... p.203
Joh Bailey Hairdressers, ... p.168
John Pardoe, ... p.209
Jurlique, ... p.77
Kenzo, ... p.185
Leona Edmiston, ... p.312
Loewe, ... p.185
Louis Vuitton, ... p.185, 205
Lush, ... p.77
Makers Mark, ... p.193
Marcs, ... p.131, 210
Matthew Eager, ... p.312
Max Mara, ... p.185
Midas, ... p.309
Moray Hats, ... p.171
NSW School of Therapeutic
   Massage, ... p.207
Oroton, ... p.204, 310
OshKosh B'gosh, ... p.103
Paradise Perfumery, ... p.78
Paris Miki Optical Vision Express, ... p.161
Paspaley Pearls, ... p.193
Percy Marks, ... p.193
Perri Jewellers, ... p.193
Pierucci, ... p.312
Plot, ... p.210
Polo Ralph Lauren, ... p.185, 210
Prada, ... p.185, 310
RM Williams, ... p.210
Raymond Castles, ... p.310
Red Earth, ... p.78
Rox Gems and Jewellery, ... p.193
Salvatore Ferragamo, ... p.185
Shades, ... p.273
Sportsgirl, ... p.313
Stefano Designer Jeweller, ... p.193
Strand Arcade, ... p.254, 259
Strand Hatters, ... p.171
Sunglass Hut, ... p.273
Surf Dive 'n Ski, ... p.278
The Academy of Hair Transplantation, ... p.169
The Original Michel's Shoe Repairs, ... p.258
The Vintage Clothing Shop, ... p.298
The Watch Gallery, ... p.193
Third Millennium, ... p.313
Tiffany & Co, ... p.193
Tour, ... p.313
Trumps, ... p.79
Vince Maloney, ... p.211
Wayne Cooper, ... p.313
Wink Hair, ... p.168
Witchery, ... p.313
Zomp, ... p.310
Showface, Millers Point, ... p.78
Claudia's Collection, The Rocks, ... p.311
Done Art and Design, The Rocks, ... p.311
Gap, The Rocks, ... p.184
Gucci, The Rocks, ... p.309
The Argyle Department Store, The Rocks, ... p.128
The Rocks Market, The Rocks, ... p.206

FOOD AND DRINK

Concourse, Opera House, ... p.239
Harbour Restaurant, Opera House, ... p.257
Bilson's, Circular Quay, ... p.143, 151
Merrony's, Circular Quay, ... p.151, 199, 240
Banc, ... p.91
Bennelong, Opera House p.72, 143
David Jones, ... p.65, 71, 77, 112, 128, 203, 237
Edna's Table, ... p.42
Forty One, ... p.143, 308
Kable's, ... p.269
Kamogawa, ... p.190
Kingsley's Australian Steakhouse, ... p.270
L'Espresso Stop, ... p.111
Matsukase, ... p.190
San Francisco Grill, ... p.91
Slip Inn, ... p.72
The Krug Room, ... p.72
The Olive Italian Food Bar, ... p.254
The Sidewalk Cafe Coffee Lounge, ... p.254
Torres Cellars & Delicatessen, ... p.126
Vanderwee Chocolates, ... p.108
Winebanc, ... p.71, 308
Pavilion on the Park, The Domain, ... p.226
Anti Bar, The Rocks, ... p.73
Horizons Bar, ANA Hotel, The Rocks, ... p.71
Lord Nelson Brewery Hotel, The
   Rocks, ... p.79, 241
MCA Fish Cafe, The Rocks, ... p.257
Number Seven, The Rocks, ... p.211
Rockpool Catering, The Rocks, ... p.99
Rockpool, The Rocks, ... p.144, 212
Sailors Thai, The Rocks, ... p.285
Shiki, The Rocks, ... p.190
Sydney Cove Providore, The Rocks, ... p.163
Unkai, The Rocks, ... p.190
bel mondo, The Rocks, ... p.143, 187
The Wharf Restaurant, Walsh Bay, ... p.303

HOME SHOPPING AND SERVICES

Alan Landis, ... p.51
Bottom of the Harbour Nautical Antiques, p.113
Camera House, ... p.135
Corso de Fiori, ... p.189
Country Road Homewear, ... p.154
Department of Fair Trading, ... p.214

Locality Guide

Dinosaur Designs, ... p.192, 280
Downtown Duty Free, ... p.135
Dymocks, ... p.83, 116
Gateway 2000, ... p.114
Grace Bros, ... p.51, 128
Hunt Leather, ... p.115, 204, 309
Loot, ... p.155
Luggage Land, ... p.115
Paxton's Camera and Video, ... p.136
R.G. Madden, ... p.177
Roses Only, ... p.149
Strand Arcade, ... p.254, 259
Dinosaur Designs, The Rocks, ... p.192, 280
The Rocks Market, The Rocks, ... p.206

SPORT AND LEISURE

Australian Rugby League (ARL), ... p.248
Bloch for Dancers, ... p.47
Clarence St Cyclery, ... p.122
Compleat Angler, ... p.146
InSki, ... p.262
International Wing Chun Academy, ... p.206
Mick Simmons Sports Store, ... p.85, 268
Rebel Sports, ... p.74, 268
Andrew (Boy) Charlton Pool, The Domain, .. p.276

RECREATION AND HOBBIES

Abbey's Bookshop, ... p.82
Australian Institute of Modern
   Languages, ... p.198
Australian Institute of Music, ... p.217
Billiards & Snooker Association of NSW, ... p.237
Club CBD, ... p.109
Dymocks, ... p.83, 116
Galaxy Bookshop, ... p.83
Hobbyco, ... p.287
Kingsleys Steakhouse and Cigar Lounge, .. p.109
Museum of Contemporary Art, ... p.57, 153
Paddy Pallin, ... p.91
Pierpont's Lounge Bar, ... p.108
Sound Devices, ... p.217
Sydney Conservatorium of Music, ... p.217
Sydney Observatory, The Rocks, ... p.60
The Rocks Market, The Rocks, ... p.206

TOURISM

Alumni Travel, ... p.291
Bench International, ... p.291

CIT World Travel Group, ... p.291
Eastern Europe Travel Bureau, ... p.291
Hunt Leather, ... p.115, 204, 309
Hyde Park/Archibald Fountain War
   Memorial, ... p.56
Hyde Park Barracks, ... p.56
International Travellers Advisory
   Service, ... p.66
Justice and Police Museum, Circular
   Quay, ... p.215
Kyle Management Resources, ... p.67
Louis Vuitton, ... p.185, 205
Luggageland, ... p.115
Museum of Contemporary Art, Circular
   Quay, ... p.57, 153
Museum of Sydney, ... p.216
Oroton, ... p.204, 310
Pacific International Travel Centre, ... p.291
Peregrine, ... p.291
QVB, ... p.55
RM Williams, ... p.210
Recruitment Solutions, ... p.67
Rox, ... p.193
Russia and Beyond, ... p.291
Strand Arcade, ... p.254, 259
Strand Hatters, ... p.171
Strandbags, ... p.205
Student Uni Travel, ... p.66
TTW Marketing, ... p.291
The Regent, ... p.43
The Ritz Carlton, City, ... p.43
Travellers' Contact Point, ... p.66
UK Flight Shop, ... p.291
Venture Holidays, ... p.291
Wiltrans Australia, ... p.291
YHA Travel Centre, ... p.66
Art Gallery of NSW, The
   Domain, ... p.55, 57, 106, 234
The Observatory, The Rocks, ... p.43
The Park Hyatt, The Rocks, ... p.43
The Russell, The Rocks, ... p.44
The Stafford, The Rocks, ... p.44
The Wharf, Walsh Bay, ... p.303

GENERAL

Associated Translators and Linguists, ... p.290
Career Edge, ... p.245
Language Professionals International, ... p.290
National Accreditation Authority for
   Translators and Interpreters, ... p.290
United Way, ... p.100
Volunteer Centre of NSW, ... p.299

Locality Guide

CITY SOUTH

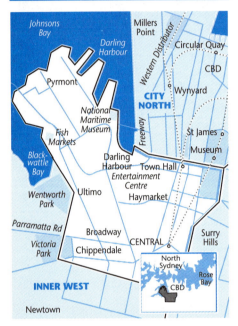

FASHION AND LIFESTYLE

Julia's Perfumery, ... p.77
The Illustrated Man, ... p.281
Gavala, Darling Harbour, ... p.42
DB 2, Haymarket, ... p.106
Solomoda, Haymarket, ... p.106
UTS Chinese Medical School, Ultimo, ... p.49

FOOD AND DRINK

BBQ King, ... p.198, 239
Capitan Torres Restaurant, ... p.267
Casa Asturiana Restaurant, ... p.239, 267
Costi's at David Jones, ... p.146
Don Quixote Restaurant, ... p.267
Golden Century, ... p.104, 198, 257
Helen's Cake Shop, ... p.105
Hellenic Club Restaurant, ... p.164
Miro Restaurant, ... p.267
Serendipity Ice Cream, ... p.181
The Spanish Club, ... p.267
Wockpool, Darling Harbour, ... p.226
Yoshii, Darling Harbour, ... p.191
BBQ King, Haymarket, ... p.198, 239
Bodhi, Haymarket, ... p.294
Cyril's Delicatessen, Haymarket, ... p.126
Golden Century, Haymarket, ... p.104, 198, 257
Haymarket Seafoods, Haymarket, ... p.146
Kam Fook, Haymarket, ... p.104, 317
Marigold Citymark, Haymarket, ... p.104, 317
Thai Kee Meats, Haymarket, ... p.207
Thai Kee Supermarket, Haymarket, ... p.105, 274
B. & J. Lizard, Pyrmont, ... p.152
Blackwattle Deli, Pyrmont, ... p.90
Simon Johnson Purveyor of Quality
   Foods, Pyrmont, ... p.101, 112, 116, 126
Sydney Seafood School, Pyrmont, ... p.117
Waterside Fruit Connection, Pyrmont, ... p.153
Chinese Grocery Shop, Ultimo, ... p.105
Ultimo Wine Centre, Ultimo, ... p.308

ARTS AND ENTERTAINMENT

Boomalli Aboriginal Artists' Co-operative,
   Chippendale, ... p.42
Anthem Records, ... p.246
Chinatown Cinema, ... p.106
Cinestore, ... p.142
Dalia Stanley, ... p.63
Dendy Cinemas, ... p.142
Greek Art and Book Shop, ... p.165
Michael's Music Room, ... p.225
Odeon Music, ... p.165
The Metro, ... p.246
Utopia Records, ... p.246
Gavala, Darling Harbour, ... p.42
IMAX Theatre, Darling Harbour, ... p.142
Showroom, Darling Harbour, ... p.93
Sydney Entertainment Centre, Haymarket,
   p.246, 209
Jokers, Pyrmont, ... p.114
Showroom Star City, Pyrmont, ... p.93

HOME SHOPPING AND SERVICES

Alexander Tzannes Associates,
   Chippendale, ... p.53
Resource Office Pty Ltd, Chippendale, ... p.224
Dalia Stanley, ... p.63
Studio Wilkhahn, ... p.156, 224
WEA, ... p.116
Books Buy & Sell, Haymarket, ... p.116

Locality Guide

Thai Kee Supermarket, Haymarket, ... p.105, 274
Nomadic Rug Traders, Pyrmont, ...p.113, 249
Secom Security, Pyrmont, ... p.258
Wardlaw, Pyrmont, ... p.266, 300
Nomadic Rug Traders, Ultimo, ... p.113, 249
Terrace House Factory Building
    Materials, Ultimo, ... p.89, 244
Total Office Solutions, Ultimo, ... p.224

SPORT AND LEISURE

Smith's Sports Store, ... p.259
The Adventure Shop, ... p.46
Chinese Youth League, Haymarket, ... p.107
Jin Wu Koon – Kung Fu and Kick
    Boxing Academy, Haymarket, ... p.107
Sydney City Karate, Ultimo, ... p.206

RECREATION AND HOBBIES

Drum City, Chippendale, ... p.216
Greek Art and Book Shop, ... p.165
InSearch Language, University of
    Technology Sydney, ... p.198
Sol Levy Tobacconist, ... p.109
Sutherland's Hotel, ... p.237
Triple–8 Hotel, ... p.195
World News Centre, Darling Harbour, ... p.221
Po Hong, Haymarket, ... p.106
Havana Tobacconist, Pyrmont, ... p.109
Star City, Pyrmont, ... p.157

TOURISM

World Wide Workers, Chippendale, ... p.67
Greyhound Pioneer Australia, ... p.67
Helen Wong's Tours, ... p.291
STA, ... p.291
World Expeditions, ... p.291
YHA, ... p.66
Sydney Aquarium, Darling Harbour, ... p.318
Aaron's, Haymarket, ... p.44
Australian National Maritime Museum,
    Darling Harbour, ... p.215
Simon Johnson Purveyor of Quality
    Foods, Pyrmont, ... p.116, 126
Powerhouse Museum, Ultimo, ... p.118, 216
Tinkers Well Fountain, Ultimo, ... p.151

GENERAL

China Ginseng and Herbs Co, ... p.106
Kinko's, ... p.240
Sydney City Mission, ... p.100
APHEDA, Haymarket, ... p.100
John Wong, Haymarket, ... p.106
Clean Up Australia, Pyrmont, ... p.300
Amnesty International, Ultimo, ... p.45

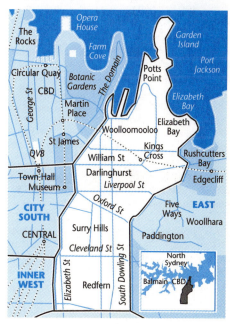

INNER EAST

ARTS AND ENTERTAINMENT

Wemyss, ... p.63
DCM, Darlinghurst, ... p.222
The Dugout Bar, Darlinghurst p.109
Gitte Weise Gallery, Darlinghurst, ... p.58

325

Locality Guide

National Art School, Darlinghurst, ... p.58
David Stein Fine Art Conservation, East Sydney, ... p.57
Griffin Theater Company, Kings Cross, .. p.285
The Griffin Theatre Company, Kings Cross, ... p.285
The Underground Cafe, Kings Cross, ... p.222
The Milk Bar, Potts Point, ... p.222
On the Other Side at X Site, Potts Point, ... p.160
Performance Space, Redfern, ... p.123
Neil Armfield, Surry Hills, ... p.286
Opera Australia, Surry Hills, ... p.225
PRIDE (Sydney Gay & Lesbian Community Centre Ltd), Surry Hills, ... p.159
Ray Hughes Gallery, Surry Hills, ... p.58, 250
ReZerection, Surry Hills, ... p.191

FASHION AND LIFESTYLE

Ahead In Wigs, Darlinghurst, ... p.169
Ciao Bella, Darlinghurst, ... p.78
Donna May Bolinger, Darlinghurst, ... p.309
Harry's Tattoo World, Darlinghurst, ... p.281
Hellerwork at Zen, Darlinghurst, ... p.49
Morrissey, Darlinghurst, ... p.210
Route 66, Darlinghurst, ... p.298
Sally Smith, Darlinghurst, ... p.312
The Piercing Urge, Darlinghurst, ... p.281
Toni and Guy, Darlinghurst, ... p.168
YPV, Darlinghurst, ... p.273
Zen and the Art of Body Maintenance, Darlinghurst, ... p.79
Zoo Emporium, Darlinghurst, ... p.298
Blue Spinach, East Sydney, ... p.297
Hotel Capital Relaxation Centre, Kings Cross, ... p.207
Kings Cross Rotary Market, Kings Cross, ... p.205
Spa Chakra Potts Point, Potts Point, ... p.79
The Costume Design Centre, Redfern, ... p.118
Beauty on Crown, Surry Hills, ... p.78
Blondes, Brunettes, Redheads, Surry Hills, ... p.168
Fabric Fantasy, Surry Hills, ... p.303
Helmet, Surry Hills, ... p.168
Liu Lily, Surry Hills, ... p.48
Mister Stinky, Surry Hills, ... p.298
TSB, Surry Hills, ... p.168
The Costume Shop, Surry Hills, ... p.118
Wheels & Doll Baby, Surry Hills, ... p.273
Kings Cross Yoga Centre, Woolloomooloo, ... p.316

FOOD AND DRINK

Tonic, City p.86
Bar Coluzzi, Darlinghurst, ... p.94
Burgerman, Darlinghurst, ... p.138
East Village, Darlinghurst, ... p.72
Fu Manchu, Darlinghurst, ... p.139
Infinity Sour Dough Bakery, Darlinghurst, ... p.68
Loreto's Larder, Darlinghurst, ... p.255
Midnight Shift, Darlinghurst, ... p.160
Oh! Calcutta!, Darlinghurst, ... p.182
Riberries Taste Australia, Darlinghurst, ... p.42
Ristorante Riva, Darlinghurst, ... p.188
Stonewall, Darlinghurst, ... p.160
The Arch, Darlinghurst, ... p.189
Uno Uno Pizzeria, Darlinghurst, ... p.236
bills, Darlinghurst, ... p.86, 94
Beppi's, East Sydney, ... p.187
Eleni's, East Sydney, ... p.164
Phat Boys, East Sydney, ... p.285
Ristorante Mario, East Sydney, ... p.91
The eDGE, East Sydney, ... p.235
Isaribi, Elizabeth Bay, ... p.190
Sebel Townhouse, Elizabeth Bay, ... p.72
Bayswater Brasserie, Kings Cross, ... p.72
Darley St Thai, Kings Cross, ... p.285
Penthouse Bar, Gazebo Hotel, Kings Cross, ... p.72
The Fireplace, Kings Cross, ... p.199
The International, Kings Cross, ... p.211
Cafe Hernandez, Potts Point, ... p.112, 198
Cicada, Potts Point, ... p.143, 295
Mezzaluna, Potts Point, ... p.187, 226
Morans, Potts Point, ...p.94, 211
On the Other Side at X Site, Potts Point, ... p.160
Paramount, Potts Point, ... p.211
Athenaikon Continental Cake Shop, Surry Hills, ... p.164
bills, Surry Hills, ...p.86, 94
Fuel, Surry Hills, ... p.86
La Vina, Surry Hills, ... p.267
MG Garage, Surry Hills, ...p.71, 143
Pazzo, Surry Hills, ... p.187
Prasit on Crown, Surry Hills, ... p.285
The Restoration Centre, Surry Hills, ... p.244
The Mode Group, Woolloomooloo, ... p.99

HOME SHOPPING AND SERVICES

Wemyss, ... p.63
Form, Darlinghurst, ... p.154, 249
Gelosa, Darlinghurst, ... p.195
Home, Darlinghurst, ... p.176, 254

Ken Neale, Darlinghurst, ...p.113, 155
Lightwise, Darlinghurst, ... p.202
Pad, Darlinghurst, ... p.155
Space, Darlinghurst, ... p.155
Taps Design, Darlinghurst, ...p.75, 287
Thurlstane, Darlinghurst, ... p.254
Clifford Powell, East Sydney, ... p.214
Dedece, East Sydney, ...p.154, 202
QCC Grande Cuisine, East Sydney, ... p.254
Sampford and Staff, East Sydney,.......p.52, 75
Stylecraft, East Sydney, ... p.156
de de ce, East Sydney, ... p.227
Make, Elizabeth Bay, ... p.155
Brook Street Trading, Kings
 Cross, ...p.176, 202
Carroll's Hardware, Kings Cross, ... p.170
Kings Cross Rotary Market, Kings Cross,...... p.205
Grandiflora, Potts Point, ... p.148
Hordern House, Potts Point, ... p.112
Anibou, Redfern, ...p.154, 249
Tangent Central, Redfern, ... p.202
Allen Jack + Cottier, Surry Hills, ... p.54
Bisanna Tiles, Surry Hills, ... p.286
Chee Soon & Fitzgerald, Surry Hills,...p.113, 154
Cloth, Surry Hills, ... p.266
Delta, Surry Hills, ... p.127
Domus, Surry Hills, ... p.286
Engelen Moore, Surry Hills, ... p.54
Grose Bradley, Surry Hills, ... p.54
No Chintz, Surry Hills, ... p.265
Norman and Quaine, Surry Hills, ... p.155
Planet Furniture, Surry Hills, ... p.155
Ray Hughes Gallery, Surry Hills, ...p.58, 250
Spence & Lyda, Surry Hills, ...p.155, 202
Sydney Antique Centre, Surry Hills, ... p.51
Sydney Building Information Centre,
 Surry Hills, ... p.89
Sydney Kitchen Centre, Surry Hills, ... p.196
Darryl Gordon, Woolloomooloo,......p.154, 183
Echo Echo, Woolloomooloo, ... p.154
Haddonstone, Woolloomooloo, ... p.286
Sedia, Woolloomooloo, ... p.155
West Eight, Woolloomooloo,...........p.156, 202

SPORT AND LEISURE

City Gym Health & Fitness Centre,
 East Sydney, ...p.47, 81, 147
Nat Craig's City Boxercise, East Sydney,.. p.85
Storm Hughes, East Sydney, ... p.231
Bayswater Fitness, Kings Cross, ... p.81
NSW Bodybuilding Supplies, Surry Hills,.. p.82

RECREATION AND HOBBIES

Animal Antics, Darlinghurst, ... p.232
Green Park Hotel, Darlinghurst, ... p.237
Midnight Shift, Darlinghurst, ... p.160
Stonewall, Darlinghurst, ... p.160
Taylor Square Newsagency,
 Darlinghurst, ... p.221
Teach 'em Toys, Darlinghurst, ... p.287
The Temple, Darlinghurst, ... p.222
Videodrama, Darlinghurst, ... p.295
Kings Cross Rotary Market, Kings Cross,.. p.205
Nick's Tobacconist, Kings Cross, ... p.109
Locomotive Workshops, Redfern, ... p.153
Billy Hyde's Drumcraft, Surry Hills, ... p.216
Central Newsagency, Surry Hills, ... p.221
PRIDE (Sydney Gay & Lesbian
 Community Centre Ltd), Surry Hills,.. p.159
Tai Chi Hung Ging Academy, Surry
 Hills, ... p.281

TOURISM

Australian Museum, City p.214
L'otel, Darlinghurst, ... p.44
Sydney Jewish Museum, Darlinghurst, ... p.216
Elizabeth Bay House, Elizabeth Bay, ... p.175
Sebel of Sydney, Elizabeth Bay, ... p.43
Backpackers World, Kings Cross, ... p.67
El Alamein Fountain, Kings Cross, ... p.151
Kings Cross Rent-A-Car, Kings Cross, ... p.97
Oz Experience, Kings Cross, ... p.67
Pegasus Rental Cars, Kings Cross, ... p.67
Travellers Auto Barn, Kings Cross, ... p.67
Simpsons of Potts Point, Potts Point, ... p.44
Sydney Mounted Police Stables,
 Redfern, ... p.180

GENERAL

AIDS Council of NSW, ... p.159
Bobby Goldsmith Foundation
 (BGF), ... p.159, 299
People Living With HIV/AIDS,
 Darlinghurst, ... p.45
Australian Chinese Community
 Association of NSW, Surry Hills, ... p.107
Community Aid Abroad, Surry
 Hills, ... p.100, 299
Planet Ark Environmental Foundation,
 Surry Hills, ... p.45

Locality Guide

EAST

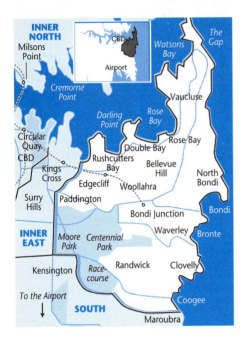

 ## FASHION AND LIFESTYLE

Bondi Beach Markets, Bondi Beach, ... p.205
Highest Aspirations, Bondi Junction, ... p.220
Masterspecs, Bondi Junction, ... p.161
Run For Your Life, Nike, Bondi
  Junction, ... p.272
Bikini Island, Bondi, ... p.277
Cool for Cats, Bondi, ... p.278
Hang Out Bondi Laundry, Bondi, ... p.135
Siren Song, Bondi, ... p.221
Adrienne and The Misses Bonney,
  Double Bay, ... p.66, 203
Alex Perry, Double Bay, ... p.302
Andrea Connolly Hairdressing Double
  Bay, Double Bay, ... p.168
Belinda, Double Bay, ... p.310
Directions, Double Bay, ... p.311
Evelyn Miles, Double Bay, ... p.309
Homegrown, Double Bay, ... p.103
Jan Logan, Double Bay, ... p.193
Jane Lambert, Double Bay, ... p.171
Jonathan Ward, Double Bay, ... p.303
Neil Grigg Millinery, Double Bay, ... p.171
Revivre, Double Bay, ... p.298
Saba Melbourne, Double Bay, ... p.312
Smyth and Fitzgerald, Double Bay, ..p.79, 168
Sylvia Deitch Beauty Therapy, Double
  Bay, ... p.78
Tea Rose, Double Bay, ... p.313
The Ali Hamylton Makeover Shop,
  Double Bay, ... p.78
Wendy Louise Designs, Double Bay, ... p.303
White Ivy, Double Bay, ... p.202
The Baby's Ark, North Randwick, ... p.65
Amazing Costume Hire Company,
  Paddington, ... p.118
Antony Whitaker, Paddington, ... p.169
Aquila, Paddington, ... p.208
Aveda, Paddington, ... p.78, 207
Bare, Paddington, ... p.310
Belinda Gunn, Paddington, ... p.309
Bisonte, Paddington, ... p.209
Black Vanity, Paddington, ... p.31
Bracewell, Paddington, ... p.311
Brave, Paddington, ... p.209
Calibre, Paddington, ... p.209
Collette Dinnigan, Paddington, ... p.203, 311
D-PO, Paddington, ... p.272
Declic, Paddington, ... p.208
Di Nuovo, Paddington, ... p.297
Dinosaur Designs, Paddington, ... p.192, 280
Face It, Paddington, ... p.273
Five Way Fusion, Paddington, ... p.209, 311

 ## ARTS AND ENTERTAINMENT

Double Bay Comedy Club, Double
  Bay, ... p.114
Academy Twin, Paddington, ... p.141
Albury Hotel, Paddington, ... p.160
Australian Centre for Photography,
  Paddington, ... p.235
Byron MAPP Gallery, Paddington, ... p.235
Campus Art Store, Paddington, ... p.58
Chauvel Cinema, Paddington, ... p.141
European Cameras, Paddington, ... p.235
Folkways Music, Paddington, ...p.81, 192, 315
Josef Lebovic Gallery, Paddington, ... p.235
Roslyn Oxley9, Paddington, ... p.58
STILLS Gallery, Paddington, ... p.234
The Verona, Paddington, ... p.141
Unicorn Hotel, Paddington, ... p.114
Randwick Ritz, Randwick, ... p.142
Michael Commerford Gallery,
  Rushcutters Bay, ... p.57
Woollahra Hotel, Woollahra, ... p.191

328

Locality Guide

Fragile Maternity Wear and Kids,
  Paddington, ... p.103
George Skoufis Optometrist,
  Paddington, ... p.273
Hot Tuna, Paddington, ... p.278
K Optica, Paddington, ... p.273
Lorna Jane, Paddington, ... p.278
Mambo, Paddington, ... p.131, 278
Napoleon, Paddington, ... p.77
OPSM, Paddington, ... p.161
Paddington Bazaar, Paddington, ... p.206
Rif Raf, Paddington, ... p.272
Robby Ingham stores, Paddington, p.210, 312
Saba, Paddington, ... p.312
Scanlan & Theodore, Paddington, ... p.312
Simona, Paddington, ... p.313
Sonya Hopkins, Paddington, ... p.313
South West Trader, Paddington, ... p.210
Sweet Art, Paddington, ... p.303
Swellstore, Paddington, ... p.273
Venustus, Paddington, ... p.79
Von Troska, Paddington, ... p.313
Yoga Moves, Paddington, ... p.316
Isabella Klompe, Queens Park, ... p.171
Decorating Recycled, Rose Bay, ... p.266
Akira Isogawa, Woollahra, ... p.310
Anne Schofield, Woollahra, ... p.51, 192
Axel Mano, Woollahra, ... p.171
Lisa Ho, Woollahra, ... p.312
Nicola Finetti, Woollahra, ... p.312
Reads, Woollahra, ... p.312
Riada, Woollahra, ... p.254, 312
The House of Maxwell Mouse,
  Woollahra, ... p.103
Zimmermann, Woollahra, ... p.278, 313

FOOD AND DRINK

David Jones, Bondi
  Junction, ...p.65, 71, 77, 112, 128, 203, 237
Costi's at David Jones, Bondi Junction, .. p.146
David Jones Food Hall, Bondi
  Junction, ... p.163
Macro Wholefoods, Bondi Junction, ... p.173
Belinda Franks' Catering, Bondi, ... p.99
Bondi Icebergs, Bondi p.276
Bondi Diggers, Bondi, ... p.276
Burgerman, Bondi, ... p.138
Gusto, Bondi, ... p.163
Kemeny's Food and Liquor, Bondi, ... p.203
Paris Patisserie Francaise, Bondi, ... p.69
Ravesi's, Bondi, ... p.44, 211
Sean's Panaroma, Bondi, ... p.86, 212
The Health Emporium, Bondi, ... p.173
Bronte Chippa, Bronte, ... p.138
Sejuiced, Bronte, ... p.86
Direction of Cure, Clovelly, ... p.94
King Wally's Pies, Coogee, ... p.138
Elise Pascoe Cooking, Darling Point, ... p.117
Bon Bon Chocolates, Double Bay, ... p.108
Double Bay Steakhouse, Double Bay, ... p.137
Game Birds, Double Bay, ... p.237
Penny's Quality Meats, Double Bay, ... p.207
The Blue Monkey, Double Bay, ... p.112
Top Fruit, Double Bay, ... p.152
DeliFarm, Edgecliff, ... p.237
Flavour of India, Edgecliff, ... p.182
Juste Nous Catering, Edgecliff, ... p.99
Albury Hotel, Paddington, ... p.160
Bonaventura, Paddington, ... p.126, 189
Buon Ricordo, Paddington, ... p.187
Grand Pacific Blue Room, Paddington, ... p.72
Gusto, Paddington, ... p.163
La Gerbe d'Or, Paddington, ... p.69
La Mensa, Paddington, ... p.240
Lucio's, Paddington, ... p.187
Nice Cream, Paddington, ... p.180
Simmone Logue, Paddington, ... p.163
Sweet William Chocolates,
  Paddington, ... p.108
la mensa, Paddington, ... p.240
Eastern Suburbs Brewmaker, Randwick, ... p.79
T.J. Wright's Gourmet Meats,
  Randwick, ... p.208
Catalina Rose Bay, Rose Bay, ... p.226
Parisi's of Rose Bay, Rose Bay, ... p.152
Pier, Rose Bay, ... p.257
Vaucluse House Tearooms, Vaucluse, ... p.303
Watsons Bay Hotel, Watsons Bay, ... p.241
Bistro Moncur, Woollahra, ... p.151, 269
Centennial, Woollahra, ... p.72
Claudes, Woollahra, ... p.143, 151
jones the grocer,
  Woollahra, ... p.101, 112, 126
Pasta Rosa, Woollahra, ... p.163
Penelope Sach, Woollahra, ... p.112

HOME SHOPPING AND SERVICES

Bondi Beach Markets, Bondi Beach, ... p.205
Amazing Paint Discounts, Bondi
  Junction, ... p.228
Anglo Master Chimney Sweeps, Bondi
  Junction, ... p.174
Porter's Original Paints, Bondi
  Junction, ... p.228
Sound & Vision, Bondi Junction, ... p.282
Tuscan Pavers, Bondi Junction, ... p.287
Barry's Garage Sale, Bondi, ... p.194
Funkis, Bondi, ... p.154

329

Locality Guide

Kalinka, Bondi, ... p.227
Basic Essentials, Double Bay, ... p.118
Bay Street Nursery, Double Bay, ... p.197
Grafton Galleries, Double Bay, ... p.50
Hamilton Beach, Double Bay, ... p.98
Mondo, Double Bay, ... p.177
Nicholas Pounder Bookseller, Double
  Bay, ... p.84, 113
Papaya Studio, Double Bay, ... p.177
Pavillion Christofle, Double Bay, ... p.280
Robyn Cosgrove Rugs, Double Bay, ... p.250
Harvey Norman Computer Superstores,
  Moore Park, ... p.115
IKEA, Moore Park, ... p.80, 154, 202, 280
Antiques Avignon, Paddington, ... p.50
Astro Design, Paddington, ... p.250
Bibelot, Paddington, ... p.176
Dinosaur Designs, Paddington, ... p.192, 280
ECC Lighting, Paddington, ... p.202
Elio Upholstery, Paddington, ... p.294
Empire, Paddington, ... p.176
Josef Lebovic, Paddington, ... p.112
Paddington Bazaar, Paddington, ... p.206.
Raymond & Victoria Tregaskis Oriental
  Decorative Arts, Paddington, ... p.51
The Butler's Pantry, Paddington, ... p.280
The Country Trader, Paddington, ... p.50
Tracey Deep Floral Sculptures,
  Paddington, ... p.148
Randwick Restoration Store,
  Randwick, ... p.174
Order Imports, Rushcutter Bay, ... p.266, 300
Arkitex, Rushcutters Bay, ... p.266, 300
Ascraft Fabrics, Rushcutters Bay, ... p.266
Boyac Decorative Furnishings,
  Rushcutters Bay, ... p.266, 300
Order Imports, Rushcutters Bay, ... p.266, 300
St James Furnishings, Rushcutters
  Bay, ... p.266, 300
Brian Barrow, Waverley, ... p.156
Commercial and Domestic Flooring,
  Waverley, ... p.98
Dr Hi-Fi, Waverley, ... p.282
John E Puddick Furnishings, Waverley, ... p.294
Andrew Simpson, Woollahra, ... p.112
Anne Schofield, Woollahra, ... p.51, 192
Art of Food and Wine, Woollahra, ... p.113
Bay Tree, Woollahra, ... p.117
Candana, Woollahra, ... p.75
Caspian Gallery, Woollahra, ... p.113
Castone, Woollahra, ... p.176
Christie's, Woollahra, ... p.62
Copeland & de Soos, Woollahra, ... p.113
Country Floors, Woollahra, ... p.286
Fred Pazotti, Woollahra, ... p.286
Hamish Clark, Woollahra, ... p.50
Howell & Howell Antiques, Woollahra, ... p.50

I & B Perryman, Woollahra, ... p.113
Inne, Woollahra, ... p.155
Janet Niven, Woollahra, ... p.51
Ken Latona, Woollahra, ... p.54
Lynette Cunnington Oriental Art,
  Woollahra, ... p.50
Ma Maison en Provence, Woollahra, ... p.280
Martyn Cook, Woollahra, ... p.50
Mobili, Woollahra, ... p.155
Orson and Blake, Woollahra, ... p.177
Phillips, Woollahra, ... p.63
Pigott's Store, Woollahra, ... p.177
Sotheby's, Woollahra, ... p.62
Susan Avery Floral Decorator,
  Woollahra, ... p.148
The Art of Wine and Food,
  Woollahra, ... p.280
Tibet Gallery, Woollahra, ... p.249
Tim McCormick Rare Books,
  Woollahra, ... p.113
Tyrone Dearing, Woollahra, ... p.113
Woollahra Antique Centre,
  Woollahra, ... p.51

SPORT AND LEISURE

Easts Leagues Club, Bondi Junction, ... p.64
Healthland International, Bondi
  Junction, ... p.47
STM, Bondi Junction, ... p.262
Bondi Icebergs, Bondi, ... p.276
Randwick Rugby Club, Coogee, ... p.248
Temple of the Body & Soul, Edgecliff, .. p.147
Eastern Suburbs Wrestling Club,
  Paddington, ... p.315
Sydney Swans Football Club,
  Paddington, ... p.64
White City, Paddington, ... p.283
Centennial Park Cycles, Randwick, ... p.122
Royal Randwick Racecourse,
  Randwick, ... p.178
Eastsail, Rushcutters Bay, ... p.239, 252
Rushcutters Bay Tennis Centre,
  Rushcutters Bay, ... p.283
Strung Out, Rushcutters Bay, ... p.284
Parsley Bay, Vaucluse, ... p.276
Albion Cycles, Waverley, ... p.292
Cockatoo Tennis and Golf, Woollahra, ... p.284

RECREATION AND HOBBIES

Bondi Beach Markets, Bondi Beach, ... p.205
Dr What, Bondi Junction, ... p.295

Locality Guide

Hutchings, Bondi Junction, ... p.216
National English Academy, Bondi Junction, ... p.198
Pets Pantry, Bondi Junction, ... p.234
Beach Road Hotel, Bondi, ... p.237
Hotel Bondi, Bondi, ... p.194
Centennial Park, Centennial Park, ... p.121, 179, 233, 250
Kite Site, Coogee, ... p.196
Double Bay Bridge Centre, Double Bay, ... p.86
Lesley McKay's, Double Bay, ... p.83
Nicholas Pounder Bookseller, Double Bay, ... p.84, 113
Ariel Booksellers, Paddington, ... p.82
Berkelouw Books, Paddington, ... p.83
Louella Kerr Lorraine Reed Old Fine & Rare Books, Paddington, ... p.84
Paddington Bazaar, Paddington, ... p.206
Lounge Lizards Video, Rose Bay, ... p.295
Sydney Harbour Sea Planes, Rose Bay, ... p.149
Eastsail, Rushcutters Bay, ... p.239, 252
Riviera Sales Sydney, Rushcutters Bay, ... p.238
Lesley McKay's, Woollahra, ... p.83

TOURISM

Ravesi's, Bondi Beach, ... p.44, 211
Discount Car and Truck Hire, Bondi Junction, ... p.97
Marathon Steps, Darling Point, Darling Point, ... p.55
The Ritz Carlton, Double Bay, Double Bay, ... p.43
Hot Tuna, Paddington, ... p.278
Mambo, Paddington, ... p.131, 278
South Head Cemetery, Vaucluse, ... p.125
Wentworth Memorial Church, Vaucluse, ... p.55
Waverley Cemetery, Waverley, ... p.125

GENERAL

Fleet Taxi Training Centre, Paddington, ... p.134
Eastern Suburbs Driving School, Randwick, ... p.134

INNER NORTH

ARTS AND ENTERTAINMENT

L&P Photographics Supplies, Artarmon, ... p.235
International Conservation Services, Chatswood, ... p.56
Cremorne Orpheum, Cremorne, ... p.141
Windsor Lab, Crows Nest, ... p.235
Eckersley's, North Sydney, ... p.59
Royal Art Society, North Sydney, ... p.58
Walker Cinema, North Sydney, ... p.142
Eckersley's, St Leonards, ... p.59

FASHION AND LIFESTYLE

Chatswood Chase, Chatswood, ... p.260
Country Road, Chatswood, ... p.209, 311

331

Locality Guide

Efbee Hair, Body & Beauty,
    Chatswood, ... p.78, 168
Entity, Chatswood, ... p.311
Esprit Kids, Chatswood, ... p.103
Jurlique, Chatswood, ... p.77
Mariana Hardwick, Chatswood, ... p.303
Max & Co., Chatswood, ... p.185
Musson, Chatswood, ... p.193
Panache, Chatswood, ... p.303
Sydney Yoga Centre, Chatswood, ... p.316
Jane Barnes-Nutritionist, Cremorne, ... p.306
The Little Shop for Horrors, Crows
    Nest, ... p.118
ABC TV Marketing, Gore Hill, ... p.118
Bonza Brats, Mosman, ... p.102
Gumboots, Mosman, ... p.103
Higher Octave, Mosman, ... p.220
Riada, Mosman, ... p.254, 312
Vreelands, Mosman, ... p.313
Destiny, Neutral Bay, ... p.220
Blue and White Dry Cleaning, North Sydney, ... p.135
Gut Busters, North Sydney, ... p.306
North Sydney Market, North Sydney, ... p.206
Polo Ralph Lauren, North Sydney, ... p.185, 210
Tarasin Jewellers, North Sydney, ... p.193
Nature Care College, St Leonards, ... p.49

FOOD AND DRINK

Watermark, Balmoral Beach, ... p.226
Chequers, Chatswood, ... p.104, 316
Claudines, Chatswood, ... p.143
The Dragon, Chatswood, ... p.317
Top Score Fruit Market, Chatswood, ... p.153
Annabel's Natural Food Store, Crows Nest, .. p.173
Azuma, Crows Nest, ... p.190, 257
Blue Elephant, Crows Nest, ... p.59
Bravo Trattoria, Crows Nest, ... p.181
Central Court Restaurant, Crows Nest, ... p.59
Five Star Gourmet, Crows Nest, ... p.126, 274
Malabar, Crows Nest, ... p.182, 295
Sakana-ya, Crows Nest, ... p.190
Sea Treasure, Crows Nest, ... p.104, 257
Accoutrement, Mosman, ... p.117
Arena's L'antipasto Deli, Mosman, ... p.126
Arena's Quality Fruit and Vegetables,
    Mosman, ... p.152
Cliff Penny's Butchery, Mosman, ... p.208
The Cheese Shop, Mosman, ... p.101
Iku wholefoods, Neutral Bay, ... p.295
Otello Chocolate & Patisserie, Neutral Bay, .. p.108
Shimbashi Soba, Neutral Bay, ... p.190
Woolworths Neutral Bay, Neutral Bay, ... p.274
Armstrong's, North Sydney, ... p.269
Bistro Pave, North Sydney, ... p.91, 151
Rengaya, North Sydney, ... p.270
To's Malaysian Gourmet, North Sydney, ... p.60
Joe and Sam Antico's Northbridge
    Fruitworld, Northbridge, ... p.152
Tokyo Mart, Northbridge, ... p.191, 274
Fink's Fabulous Food, Waverton, ... p.69

HOME SHOPPING AND SERVICES

Amtico Studio, Artarmon, ... p.98
Cotswold Garden Furniture, Artarmon, .. p.227
Murobond Coatings, Artarmon, ... p.228
Restoration Scene, Artarmon, ... p.156
Roof Rack City, Artarmon, ... p.214, 262
Alpha Appliances Repair Company,
    Cammeray, ... p.52
Capell of Chatswood, Chatswood, ... p.195
Chatswood Chase, Chatswood, ... p.260
Designer Homeware, Chatswood, ... p.52
Dulux Trade Centres, Chatswood, ... p.228
Ryda Home Entertainment, Chatswood, ...p.282
DME, Cremorne, ... p.282
Five Star Gourmet, Crows Nest, ... p.126, 274
Kitchen Kapers, Crows Nest, ... p.117
Len Wallis Audio, Lane Cove, ... p.270
Litsa Flowers, McMahons Point, ... p.149
Alex Popov Architects, Milsons Point, ... p.54
Harry Seidler & Associates, Milsons Point, ... p.53
Accoutrement, Mosman, ... p.117
Australian Squatters Chair Company,
    Mosman, ... p.227
Glenn Murcutt, Mosman, ... p.53
Tempo Interiors, Mosman, ... p.266
White & White, Mosman, ... p.177
Woolworths Neutral Bay, Neutral Bay, ... p.274
Laptop Land, North Sydney, ... p.115
North Sydney Market, North Sydney, ... p.206
Telstra Big Pond, North Sydney, ... p.115
The Bath House, Northbridge, ... p.75
Tokyo Mart, Northbridge, ... p.191, 274
North Shore Locksmiths, St Leonards, ... p.204
De Gabrielle Kitchens, Willoughby, ... p.195
Metropolitan Framing, Willoughby, ... p.57
Michele Shennen's Garden Centres,
    Willoughby, ... p.223
No Chintz, Willoughby, ... p.265
Porter's Original Paints, Willoughby, ... p.228
Sydney Kitchen Centre, Willoughby, ... p.196

SPORT AND LEISURE

Balmoral Boat Shed, Balmoral Beach, ... p.145
Abbey Archery, Chatswood, ... p.53

Locality Guide

NORTH

Charltons Horseland, Chatswood, ... p.180
Chatswood Cycles, Chatswood, ... p.122
Janet Norton, Chatswood, ... p.230
MacCallum Pool, Cremorne Point, ... p.276
Primrose Park Tennis, Cremorne, ... p.283
Alpine World, Crows Nest, ... p.262
Ausail Sailing School, Mosman, ... p.253
Balmoral Snowboards, Mosman, ... p.262
Sydney Yachting Centre, Mosman, ... p.253
Love On Deuce, Naremburn, ... p.284
Mountain High Travel, Naremburn, ... p.262
Pumphouse, Neutral Bay, ... p.147
Bodyline Fitness Centre, North Sydney, ...p.47, 82
North Sydney Olympic Pool, North Sydney, .. p.276

RECREATION AND HOBBIES

Partytime Hire, Chatswood, ... p.230
Canine Coiffure, Cremorne, ... p.233
Cremorne Pet Centre, Cremorne, ... p.232
Constant Reader Bookshop, Crows Nest, ... p.83
Theme and Variations Piano Services,
   Greenwich, ... p.217
James Gordon Workshop, Lavender Bay, ... p.137
Athol Hall Function Centre, Mosman, ... p.153
Sirius Cove, Mosman, ... p.233
Taronga Zoo, Mosman, ... p.307, 317
Trumps Bridge Centre, Mosman, ... p.79
Four Legged Friends, Neutral Bay, ... p.232
North Sydney Market, North Sydney, ... p.206
Ensemble Musical Instruments, Northbridge, .. p.216
The Bridge Shop, Willoughby, ... p.87
Tytaff Grooming, Willoughby, ... p.233

TOURISM

Taronga Zoo, Mosman, ... p.307, 317
Mary Rossi, North Sydney, ... p.291

GENERAL

SBS, Artarmon, ... p.264, 290
North Shore Development and Coaching
   Centre, Chatswood, ... p.293
Norman Driving School, Lane Cove, ... p.134
Chinese Christian Church, Milsons Point, ... p.107
The Centre for Worklife Counselling,
   Mosman, ... p.244

ARTS AND ENTERTAINMENT

Sorlies, Frenchs Forest, ... p.93
Manly Art Gallery and Museum, Manly, .. p.215
The Old Manly Boatshed, Manly, ... p.114
Roseville, Roseville, ... p.142
The Stockade, Terry Hills, ... p.144
Rose Seidler house, Wahroonga, ... p.55

FASHION AND LIFESTYLE

Yoga in Daily Life, Dee Why, ... p.316
Merringtons, North Ryde, ... p.161

FOOD AND DRINK

La Banette, Avalon, ... p.68
Seafood at the Beach, Dee Why, ... p.138
Crown of the Hill Cellars, Forestville, ... p.203

Locality Guide

Northern Lights, Hornsby, ... p.137
Peking Inn, Lindfield, ... p.104
Cliff Pennys Butchery, Mona Vale, ... p.208
Newport Arms Hotel, Newport, ... p.241
Otello Chocolate & Patisserie, West Pymble, ... p.108

HOME SHOPPING AND SERVICES

Home Hardware, Asquith, ... p.171
Coastal Care Horticultural Services, Avalon, ... p.197
Freedom Furniture, Balgowlah, ... p.227
Allison Audio, Brookvale, ... p.283
Brookvale Bazaar, Brookvale, ... p.194
Edwards Engineering, Brookvale, ... p.139
Balmain Floorsanding, Carlingford, ... p.148
Affordable Office Furniture, Castle Hill, .. p.224
Unique Autosports, Castle Hill, ... p.214
Elders Stockmans, Dural, ... p.224
Rainbow Ridge Nursery, Dural, ... p.223
Swane Bros, Dural, ... p.222
BBC Hardwarehouse, Epping, ... p.139
Accoutrement, Gordon, ... p.117
IKEA, Gordon, ... p.80, 154, 202, 280
3D Paint Stores, Hornsby, ... p.228
Storage Australia, Hornsby, ... p.272
Associated Technicians, Killarney Heights, ... p.283
De Gabrielle Kitchens, Kings Park, ... p.195
Grosvenor Antique Centre, Lindfield, ... p.224
QuikTrak Networks, Lindfield, ... p.258
The Wood Works Book & Tool Co.,
   Meadowbank, ... p.314
Just Blinds, Mt Kuring-gai, ... p.80
Cohen TV, Narrabeen, ... p.283
Stutchbury & Pape, Newport, ... p.54
North Manly Garden Centre, North Manly, ... p.223
Valtel, North Rocks, ... p.282
The Brick Pit, North Ryde, ... p.89
Nouvelle Designer Kitchens, Pennant Hills, .. p.196
Glass Bricks and Skylights, Putney, ... p.263
Specialised Security Systems, Ryde, ... p.258
Camellia Grove, St Ives, ... p.223
Imperial Gardens, Terrey Hills, ... p.197
Jolly Rogers, Terrey Hills, ... p.287
Decorator Flooring & Interiors, Thornleigh, .. p.147
Parkers Nursery, Turramurra, ... p.223
Rast Bros, Turramurra, ... p.222
Joanne Green Landscape Design,
   Warriewood, ... p.197

SPORT AND LEISURE

Bayview Tennis Court, Bayview, ... p.284
The Ski Shack, Dural, ... p.302

Epping YMCA, Epping, ... p.167
Warringah Aquatic Centre, French's Forest, ... p.276
Hornsby PCYC, Hornsby, ... p.315
Equitrek, Ingleside, ... p.179
Boules To You, Manly, ... p.85
Manly Blades, Manly, ... p.261
Manly Skate Park, Manly, ... p.262
Sydney Harbour Parasailing, Manly, ... p.46
The Quiksilver Boardriders Club, Manly, p.278
The Sailing Scene, Mona Vale, ... p.253
Narrabeen Bait, Narrabeen, ... p.146
Bashford International, Newport, ... p.253
Hugh Treharne Sailing, Newport, ... p.252
Vicsail Pittwater, Newport, ... p.253
Macquarie Ice Rink, North Ryde, ... p.261
Kellyville Riding Club, Rouse Hill, ... p.180
Riverview Squash Centre, Ryde, ... p.269
Seaforth Badminton Club, Seaforth, ... p.68
Campo's, St Ives, ... p.248
Northside Riding Club, St Ives, ... p.180
NSW Gun Club, Terrey Hills, ... p.259
Thornleigh Squash Centre, Thornleigh, .. p.269

RECREATION AND HOBBIES

Clipper Cruiser Holidays, Akuna Bay, ... p.239
The Papershoppe, Baulkham Hills, ... p.221
Time & Tide Hotel, Dee Why, ... p.195
Contented Cat Inn, Glenorie, ... p.231
Syd Howard Fireworks International,
   Glenorie, ... p.144
World 4 Kids, Hornsby, ... p.287
Halvorsen Boats, Ku-ring-gai Chase
   National Park, ... p.239
Humphreys Newsagency, Manly, ... p.221
Manly, Manly, ... p.76, 299
Tai Chi College of Australia, Manly, ... p.280
Curzon Hall, Marsfield, ... p.153
Train Trader, Narrabeen, ... p.288
Monika's Mouse, Moggy & Mutt
   Minding, Turramurra, ... p.232
Turramurra Music Centre, Turramurra, ... p.217

TOURISM

Featherdale Wildlife Park, Doonside, ... p.317
East's Lane Cove River Van Village, North
   Ryde, ... p.95
Rose Seidler house, Wahroonga, ... p.55
Koala Park Sanctuary, West Pennant Hills, ... p.317

Locality Guide

GENERAL

Stay Upright School, Annangrove, ... p.134
The Swot Shop, Castle Hill, ... p.293

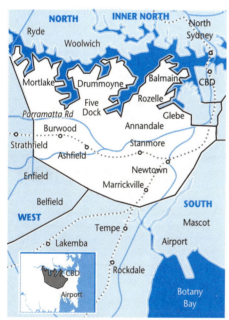

ARTS AND ENTERTAINMENT

Annandale Galleries, Annandale, ... p.57
Jacksons Rare Guitars, Annandale, ... p.81
Lawsons, Annandale, ... p.63
The Loaded Dog, Annandale, ... p.150
Unity Hall Hotel, Balmain, ... p.191
Rose of Australia, Erskineville, ... p.80
Sydney Gay and Lesbian Mardi Gras Ltd,
  Erskineville, ... p.159

Point Light, Glebe, ... p.235
The Comedy Hotel, Glebe, ... p.114
Tranby Aboriginal Co-operative College,
  Glebe, ... p.42
Valhalla, Glebe, ... p.142
Marrickville RSL, Marrickville, ... p.93
Dendy Cinemas, Newtown, ... p.142
The Comedy Store, Petersham, ... p.114
Photographer's Showcase, Stanmore, ... p.235
Macleay Museum, University of
  Sydney, ... p.215
Nicholson Museum, University of
  Sydney, ... p.165, 216

FASHION AND LIFESTYLE

Herbal Solutions Annandale, Annandale, .. p.49
Yoga in Daily Life, Annandale, ... p.316
Mysteries in Balmain, Balmain, ... p.221
Naked, Balmain, ... p.312
Flash Trash, Camperdown, ... p.254
Birkenhead Point Shopping Centre,
  Drummoyne, ... p.253
Essential Energies, Glebe, ... p.220
Glebe Markets, Glebe, ... p.205
Baby's Stuff, Leichhardt, ... p.65
Leichhardt Sunday Market, Leichhardt, .. p.205
Celtic Dragon Tattoo Art Studio,
  Newtown, ... p.281
Essential Energies, Newtown, ... p.220
Polymorph Body Piercing Studio, Newtown, .. p.281
Yoga Synergy, Newtown, ... p.316
Diane Lewis, Petersham, ... p.302

FOOD AND DRINK

Beer Importers & Distributors, Alexandria, ... p.79
Annandale Hotel, Annandale, ... p.241
Iseli Swiss Butcher, Ashfield, ... p.208
Music Front, Ashfield, ... p.268
Emile's, Balmain, ... p.152
Much Ado About Cooking, Balmain, ... p.117
Ralph's Delicatessen, Balmain, ... p.189
Riverview Hotel, Balmain, ... p.241
Simmone Logue Fine Food, Balmain, ... p.163
Victoire, Balmain, ... p.68, 101
Essential Ingredient, Camperdown, ... p.71
Rio's Brazilian Cabaret, Camperdown, ... p.267
The Essential Ingredient, Camperdown, ... p.90
The Truffle Group, Camperdown, ... p.99
Lennons, Drummoyne, ... p.270
Sixty Darling Street, East Balmain, ... p.204
Gabriel's on Swanson, Erskineville, ... p.181

335

Locality Guide

Blue Bells, Five Dock, ... p.138
Culinary Edge, Five Dock, ... p.99
Architectural Heritage, Glebe, ...p.174, 244
Boathouse on Blackwattle Bay, Glebe, ... p.257
Helios Demeter Bakery, Glebe, ... p.69
Iku wholefoods, Glebe, ... p.295
Russell's Natural Food Markets,
  Glebe, ... p.173
The Boathouse on Blackwattle Bay,
  Glebe, ... p.211
The Mixing Pot, Glebe, ... p.187
A&P Sulfaro, Haberfield, ... p.93
Haberfield Bakery, Haberfield, ... p.68
La Disfida, Haberfield, ... p.236
Napoli in Bocca, Haberfield, ... p.236
A.C. Continental Butchery,
  Leichhardt, ... p.71, 188, 208
Balmain Stripping Factory, Leichhardt, ... p.243
Bar Italia, Leichhardt, ... p.94, 181, 189
Elio, Leichhardt, ... p.187
Chippendale Restorations,
  Lilyfield, ... p.174, 244
Franklins Big Fresh, Marrickville,
  Marrickville, ... p.274
Paesanella Cheese Manufacturers Pty
  Ltd, Marrickville, ... p.189
Picuba Food Wholesalers, Marrickville, ... p.165
Victoria Yeeros, Marrickville, ... p.139
Delicacies on King, Newtown, ... p.126
Macro Wholefoods, Newtown, ... p.173
Steki Taverna, Newtown, ... p.164
Perama Greek Restaurant, Petersham, ... p.164
Belle Fleur Fine Chocolates, Rozelle, ... p.108
Rozelle Fishbowl, Rozelle, ... p.257
Tetsuya's, Rozelle, ... p.144

HOME SHOPPING AND SERVICES

B 'n' S Locksmiths, Alexandria, ... p.204
Gavan Hardy, Alexandria, ... p.63
Major & Tom, Alexandria, ... p.156
Booth & Taylor Hardware,
  Annandale, ... p.170
Fabric with Finish, Annandale, ... p.265
Lawsons, Annandale, ... p.63
Recycling Works, Annandale, ... p.194
Cameron McFarlane, Balmain, ... p.294
Juliet Justice Floral Design, Balmain, ... p.148
Cheminee Philippe, Camperdown, ... p.173
John Williams, Camperdown, ... p.63
Silent Gliss, Camperdown, ... p.80
Carlos Malta, Croydon, ... p.294
Sydney Appliance Centre, Croydon, ... p.52
Audio Excellence, Drummoyne, ... p.270

Birkenhead Point Shopping Centre,
  Drummoyne, ... p.253
Paul Pribia Art Restoration, Dulwich
  Hill, ... p.56
Amalgamated Textiles, Enmore, ... p.249
Sky Solutions, Five Dock, ... p.263
123 Removals and Storage Australia,
  Gladesville, ... p.243
Australian Wrought Iron, Gladesville, ... p.139
Storage Australia, Gladesville, ... p.272
Architectural Heritage, Glebe, ... p.174, 244
Glebe Markets, Glebe, ... p.205
Nicholas Dattner & Co., Glebe, ... p.314
3D Paint Stores, Leichhardt, ... p.228
Audio Connection, Leichhardt, ... p.270
Designer Rugs, Leichhardt, ... p.249
Leichhardt Sunday Market, Leichhardt, .. p.205
Barlow, Lilyfield, ... p.227
Chippendale Restorations, Lilyfield, ...p.174, 244
Franklins Big Fresh, Marrickville, ... p.274
Reverse Garbage, Marrickville, ... p.194, 230
John Sommerlad, Newtown, ... p.113
Zebra Discounts, Newtown, ... p.271
Crystal TV, Petersham, ... p.283
Carrier APAC, Rozelle, ... p.48
Velux Skylights, St Peters, ... p.263
Natural Floorcovering Centre,
  Stanmore, ... p.98

SPORT AND LEISURE

Sydney Flames, Alexandria, ... p.74
Burwood Police Citizens Youth Club,
  Burwood, ... p.306
Hockey NSW, Concord, ... p.176
Five Dock Leisure Centre, Five Dock, ... p.68
Stay-Fit Equipment, Five Dock, ... p.82
The Tennis Ranch, Gladesville, ... p.284
Wentworth Park, Glebe, ... p.165
Marrickville Tennis Club, Marrickville, ... p.284
Newtown Police Citizens Youth Club,
  Newtown, ... p.85
Ultimate Fitness, Newtown, ... p.147
Ultimate Gym, Newtown, ... p.81
Majestic Rollerink, Petersham, ... p.261

RECREATION AND HOBBIES

Europress Distributors Pty Ltd,
  Alexandria, ... p.189
Fivestar Karaoke, Annandale, ... p.194
Jackson's Rare Guitars, Annandale, ... p.217
Planet Entertainment, Annandale, ... p.230

Locality Guide

WEST

The Bass Player, Annandale, ... p.216
The Pet Health Food Shop,
  Annandale, ... p.233
Art on King: Discounted Art & Craft
  Supplies, Ashfield, ... p.59
Action 8 Ball Tables, Balmain, ... p.237
Balmain Art School, Balmain, ... p.58
Steve Giordano, Camperdown, ... p.217
Australian Academy of Tai Chi,
  Croydon, ... p.280
Chapman Marine, Drummoyne, ... p.238
Blackbooks, Glebe, ... p.42
Glebe Markets, Glebe, ... p.205
Gleebooks, Glebe, ... p.83
Harold Park, Glebe, ... p.179
The Well-Connected Cafe, Glebe, ... p.116
Astam Books, Leichhardt, ... p.123
Einstelnz Toy Box, Leichhardt, ... p.288
Leichhardt Sunday Market,
  Leichhardt, ... p.205
Messy Mutts, Leichhardt, ... p.233
Mini Grand Prix, Marrickville, ... p.161
Reverse Garbage, Marrickville, ... p.194, 230
Elite Pool Table & Amusement
  Machines, Petersham, ... p.237
Libreria Italiana, Petersham, ... p.189
Tai Chi Qi Gong Centre & Yoga
  Centre, Petersham, ... p.281

TOURISM

Frontline Camper Conversions,
  Croydon, ... p.95
Sydney Gay and Lesbian Mardi Gras
  Ltd, Erskineville, ... p.159
Tranby Aboriginal Co-operative College,
  Glebe, ... p.42
YHA, Glebe, ... p.66
European Hire Cars, Rozelle, ... p.97

GENERAL

Language Services, Ashfield, ... p.290
The Exodus Foundation, Ashfield, ... p.100
The Smith Family, Camperdown, ... p.100
Royce Driver Training School, Five
  Dock, ... p.134
The Wilderness Society, Glebe, ... p.45
St Vincent de Paul Society,
  Lewisham, ... p.300

ARTS AND ENTERTAINMENT

The Vietnamese Community in
  Australia, Bankstown, ... p.296
Thuy Nga, Bankstown, ... p.296
Campbelltown Catholic Club,
  Campbelltown, ... p.119
Eckersley's, Parramatta, ... p.59
Fletchers Fotographic, Parramatta, ... p.235
Yesterday & Today Records,
  Parramatta, ... p.119
St Marys Sound Centre, St Marys, ... p.119

FASHION AND LIFESTYLE

Elandra's Baby Kingdom,
  Bankstown, ... p.65
The Diet Factory, Granville, ... p.306
Cobra Athleisure, Parramatta, ... p.272

337

Locality Guide

 ## FOOD AND DRINK

An, Bankstown, ... p.296
El Bahsa, Bankstown, ... p.200
Golden Nights, Bankstown, ... p.199
Pasteur, Bankstown, ... p.297
BKK Shopping Centre, Cabramatta, ... p.296
Dong Ba, Cabramatta, ... p.296
Thanh Binh, Cabramatta, ... p.296
La Torre Cake Shop, Fairfield, ... p.268
Martinez Bros, Fairfield, ... p.126
Martinez Continental Deli, Fairfield, ... p.268
Sydney Markets, Flemington, ... p.152
Abhi's, North Strathfield, ... p.181
Temasek, Parramatta, ... p.60

 ## HOME SHOPPING AND SERVICES

Autopro, Auburn, ... p.214
Dick Smith Electronics, Bankstown, ... p.115
Steel Fitter Security, Bankstown, ... p.139
Gasweld Discount Tool Centre,
  Blacktown, ... p.88
Hudson Timber & Hardware,
  Bonnyrigg, ... p.89
Khai Hi-Fi, Cabramatta, ... p.270
Tim's Garden Centres,
  Campbelltown, ... p.223
Materials in the Raw, Casula, ... p.224
Vienna Hi-Fi Electronics, Chester Hill, ... p.283
Daikin Australia, Chipping Norton, ... p.48
Ronnies Demolition, Chipping
  Norton, ... p.127
Sydney Flooring Pty Ltd, Chipping
  Norton, ... p.147
Dumaster Paint Discounts, Enfield, ... p.228
Parra Power Tools, Granville, ... p.88
Mr Antenna, Harris Park, ... p.49
By Dezign, Homebush, ... p.196
De Gabrielle Kitchens, Homebush, ... p.195
Homebush Home Improvement Centre,
  Homebush, ... p.195
In Kitchens, Homebush, ... p.196
Wreckair Hire, Homebush, ... p.88
Bassett Demolition, Lidcombe, ... p.127
Grace Removals, Lidcombe, ... p.243, 271
Wallpaper to Go, Lidcombe, ... p.300
Independent Locksmiths,
  Parramatta, ... p.204
Freedom Kitchens, Prospect, ... p.195
IKEA, Prospect, ... p.80, 154, 202, 280
Email, Silverwater, ... p.48

Gray Eisdell Timms Auctioneers &
  Valuers, Smithfield, ... p.89
NRMA Automotive Service Centre,
  Villawood, ... p.214
Annandale Timber, Wetherill Park, ... p.89
Law's Auctions, Wetherill Park, ... p.89
VIP Car Care, Yagoona, ... p.214

 ## SPORT AND LEISURE

Lewis Ski Boats, Auburn, ... p.302
Revolution Racegear, Auburn, ... p.213
Club Marconi, Bosley Park, ... p.264
Camden Lakeside, Catherine Field, ... p.162
Eastern Creek Raceway, Eastern
  Creek, ... p.212
Olympic Softball Stadium, Eastern
  Creek, ... p.265
Benson Archery, Granville, ... p.53
Parramatta City Raceway,
  Granville, ... p.212
Greenacre YMCA, Greenacre, ... p.279
Race and Rally, Greenacre, ... p.213
5Motorcycling NSW, Harris Park, ... p.213
NSW Weightlifting Association,
  Homebush Bay, ... p.306
Olympic Hockey Centre, Homebush
  Bay, ... p.175
Ross Pavilion, Homebush Bay, ... p.67
State Sports Centre, Homebush
  Bay, ... p.74, 167, 315
Sydney International Aquatic Centre,
  Homebush Bay, ... p.132, 276, 279, 301
The Waterski Factory, Homebush
  Bay, ... p.302
Just Hockey, Homebush, ... p.176
State Sports Centre,
  Homebush, ... p.74, 167, 315
Horsley Park Gun Shop, Horsley
  Park, ... p.259
Anne Clarke Netball Centre,
  Lidcombe, ... p.140
Cumberland College, Lidcombe, ... p.279
EG Whitlam Centre, Liverpool, ... p.74
Metapower Martial Arts Supplies,
  Liverpool, ... p.206
York Fitness, Minto, ... p.306
Liverpool City Archers, Moorebank, ... p.53
Oran Park Raceway, Narellan, ... p.212
Confederation of Australian Motor
  Sport, Parramatta, ... p.213
Fernwood Female Fitness,
  Parramatta, ... p.82
Peter Wynn's Score, Parramatta, ... p.248, 268

Locality Guide

International Regatta Centre, Penrith, ... p.247
Sydney International Regatta Centre, Penrith, ... p.96

RECREATION AND HOBBIES

World 4 Kids, Blacktown, ... p.287
Campbelltown Pet and Aquarium Centre, Campbelltown, ... p.232
World 4 Kids, Campbelltown, ... p.287
CRG Racing Centre, Chipping Norton, ... p.162
Campbelltown Doll and Toy Hospital, Eagle Vale, ... p.288
Eastern Creek International Karting Raceway, Eastern Creek, ... p.161
Australian International Conservatorium of Music, Harris Park, ... p.218
Adelar Pet Motel Boarding Kennels, Leppington, ... p.231
FastLane Go-Karting, Minto, ... p.161
Woodpecker Model Railways, Pendle Hill, ... p.288
Penrith Toy and Hobby Centre, Penrith, ... p.288
World 4 Kids, Penrith, ... p.287
Rosehill Gardens, Rosehill, ... p.178
Rossmore Dog Pool, Rossmore, ... p.233
Warwick Farm, Warwick Farm, ... p.178
NSW Animal Welfare League (AWL), West Hoxton, ... p.232
RSPCA, Yagoona, ... p.232
Yennora Hobbies, Yennora, ... p.287

TOURISM

All Districts Limousines, Homebush, ... p.97
Boots Great Outdoors, Lidcombe, ... p.95
Rookwood Cemetery, Lidcombe, ... p.125
St John's Cemetery, Parramatta, ... p.125
Boots Great Outdoors, Prospect, ... p.95
NSW Caravan, Camping and 4WD Supershow, Rosehill, ... p.95
Fulchers Caravans, Wentworthville, ... p.95

GENERAL

Go Yui Temple, Bonnyrigg, ... p.106

SOUTH

ARTS AND ENTERTAINMENT

Dharawal Education Centre, La Perouse, .. p.41
La Perouse Community Development Corporation, La Perouse, ... p.41

FASHION AND LIFESTYLE

Yoga in Daily Life, Gymea, ... p.316
Baby Things, Kensington, ... p.65
Moore Park Supa Centa, Kensington, ... p.260
Roselands, Roselands, ... p.261
Clothing Clearance Warehouse, Sydenham, ... p.65

FOOD AND DRINK

Imperial Peking, Blakehurst, ... p.104, 317
Mohr Food, Botany, ... p.146
Rimal, Brighton-Le-Sands, ... p.200
Sam Won Garden, Campsie, ... p.59
Adora Handmade Chocolates, Earlwood, . p.108

339

Locality Guide

Golden Kingdom, Kensington, ... p.104
Ratu Sari, Kingsford, ... p.60
La Perouse Community Development
   Corporation, La Perouse, ... p.41
El-Manara, Lakemba, ... p.139
The Arabic Bookshop, Lakemba, ... p.200
Venice Nuts, Lakemba, ... p.200
Caffe Italia, Mascot, ... p.94
Patchett's Pies, Mascot, ... p.138
Summerland, Punchbowl, ... p.199
Star Light, Riverwood, ... p.199
Paul's Famous Hamburgers, Sylvania, ... p.138

HOME SHOPPING AND SERVICES

Jetmaster, Arncliffe, ... p.174
American Auto Parts, Beverly Hills, ... p.214
Tool Tech Australia, Bexley, ... p.88
Aaron Upholstery, Botany, ... p.294
Designer Iron Craft, Botany, ... p.139
Paul Kenny, Botany, ... p.112
Freedom Kitchens, Caringbah, ... p.195
Fence Magic (Southside) Pty Ltd, Engadine, ... p.139
Freedom Kitchens, Kensington, ... p.195
Moore Park Supa Centa, Kensington, ... p.260
Peter's of Kensington, Kensington p.117, 254, 303
Verosol, Kingsgrove, ... p.80
Antenna Shack, Maroubra Junction, ... p.49
China Bear, Mascot, ... p.243
Hardwarehouse, Mascot, Mascot, ... p.170
Second Hand Building Centre, Rockdale, ...p.89
Decortex Wallcoverings, Rosebery, ... p.300
Louis Poulsen Lightmakers, Rosebery, ... p.202
Roselands, Roselands, ... p.261
Town and Country Vehicle Accessories,
   Roselands, ... p.214
Co-Ordinated Landscapes, Sutherland, ... p.197
Planet Floorcoverings, Sydenham, ... p.147
Attic Access Company, Taren Point, ... p.263
Sydney Chimney Sweep Company, Tempe, ... p.174
Tempe 4x4 Spares, Tempe, ... p.214
Porter's Original Paints, Waterloo, ... p.228
Premier Carpets, Waterloo, ... p.98
Stitches Soft Furnishings, Waterloo, ... p.265
Sydney Plantation Shutters, Waterloo, ... p.80

SPORT AND LEISURE

Sutherland National Park, Audley, ... p.250
Canterbury-Bankstown Leagues Club,
   Belmore, ... p.269
NSW Touch Association, Beverly Hills, ... p.248
Macs Bait, Blakehurst, ... p.146
NSW Golf Course, Henry Head, ... p.162
Bates Bikes, Hurstville, ... p.122
Kenso Discount Sports, Kensington, ... p.251
Kurnell Boarding Stables and Riding
   School, Kurnell, ... p.179
Manhattan Super Bowl, Mascot, ... p.84
HotBodz, Miranda, ... p.47
The Strike Zone, Panania, ... p.265
Danz Design, Penshurst, ... p.279
Soccer City, Rockdale, ... p.264
St George PCYC, Rockdale, ... p.315
Combined Sports Traders, Roselands, ... p.279
Southside Runners, Sutherland, ... p.250
Sutherland Leisure Centre, Sutherland, .. p.276
Sutherland PCYC, Sutherland, ... p.315
Peter Cosgrove, Sylvania, ... p.230

RECREATION AND HOBBIES

Sydney Pet Grooming Centre, Bexley, ... p.233
Hunts Marine, Blakehurst, ... p.238
Botany Dog Beach, Botany, ... p.233
Canterbury Park, Canterbury, ... p.178
Bloomin' Books, Caringbah, ... p.83
E.G. Waterhouse National Camellia
   Garden, Caringbah, ... p.158
Hanrob Pet Care Centre, Heathcote, ... p.231
Accent Entertainment, Hurstville, ... p.194
Discount Art and Drafting Materials, Hurstville, ... p.59
Joseph Banks Native Plants Reserve, Kareela, ... p.158
Kingsgrove Megatrack, Kingsgrove, ... p.161
Andrew Short Marine, Taren Point, ... p.238

TOURISM

Cronulla National Park Ferry Cruises,
   Cronulla, ... p.140
Caravan Accessories, Kogarah, ... p.95
Dharawal Education Centre, La Perouse, .. p.41
La Perouse Community Development
   Corporation, La Perouse, ... p.41
Backpacker Campervans, Mascot, ... p.67
Boomerang Car Mart, Mascot, ... p.67
Eastern Suburbs Memorial Park and
   Crematorium, Matraville, ... p.125

GENERAL

Jim Murcott's Advanced Driving Centre,
   Jannali, ... p.134
ABC, Kogarah, ... p.134
Centatime, Rosebery, ... p.240

BEST OF SYDNEY CALENDAR OF EVENTS

JANUARY

ARTS & ENTERTAINMENT

2–26 January: Sydney Festival, Sydney, ph 8248 6500. www.sydneyfestival.org.au

3–9 January: Flickerfest, The 8th International Short Film Festival, ph 9211 7133

6 January–11 March: Opera Australia Summer Season, ph 9319 1088

18 January: Symphony under the Stars, The Domain, ph 8248 6500 www.sydneyfestival.org.au

26 January: Survival Concert (Aboriginal music), ph 9331 3777. www.niaaa.com.au

26 January: Australia Day Celebrations, Australia Day Council, ph 9247 2130

26–28 January: Blue Mountains Folk Festival, Blue Mountains, ph 02 4782 7734. www.bluemts.com.au

30 January: Opera in the Park, The Domain, Sydney, ph 9318 1099. www.opera_australia.org.au

SPORT

26 January: Cricket Test Match. Australia v England. Sydney Cricket Ground, ph 9360 6601. www.acb.com.au

13 January: One-Day Cricket. Australia v Sri Lanka. Sydney Cricket Ground, ph 9360 6601.

10–16 January: Adidas International Tennis Tournament, White City, Sydney, ph 9331 4144. www.tennisnsw.com.au

15–16 January: 1999 FINA World Cup Swimming, International Aquatic Centre, Homebush, ph 9752 3666. www.siac.nsw.gov.au

17 January: One Day Cricket. Australia v England. Sydney Cricket Ground, ph 9360 6601. www.acb.com.au

23 January: Manly Surf Carnival, Manly, ph 9984 7188. www.lifesavingnsw.org.au

26 January: 1999 Australia Day 10k International Wheelchair Road Race, Circular Quay, ph 9809 5260. www.nswwsa.org.au

28–31 January: Summer International Wheelchair Tennis Open, ph 9809 5260

GENERAL

30 January: Australian Stock Exchange Share Day, Sydney, ph 1300 300 279

FEBRUARY

ARTS & ENTERTAINMENT

3–27 February: 1999 Sydney Gay and Lesbian Mardi Gras Festival, Sydney, ph 9557 4332. www.mardigras.com.au

4–26 February: Sydney Symphony Orchestra Summer "Pops" Season, ph 9334 4644

6 February–28 March: The Tower Twilight at Taronga Summer Concerts, ph 1800 675 875

17–21 February: Kiama Jazz Festival, Kiama, ph 02 4232 3322. www.tourism.nsw.gov.au

21 February: Tropfest (short film festival), ph 9368 0434

22–28 February: Artexpress: Outstanding artworks from Higher School Certificate visual arts students. State Library of NSW, ph 9561 8446. www.det.nsw.edu.au

26–28 February: Blue Mountains Folk Festival, Blue Mountains, ph 02 4782 7734. www.bluemts.com.au

27 February: 1999 Sydney Gay and Lesbian Mardi Gras Parade, Sydney, ph 9557 4332. www.mardigras.com.au

SPORT

3 February: One day cricket series. England v Sri Lanka. Sydney Cricket Ground, ph 9360 6601. www.acb.com.au

4–7 February: Greg Norman Holden International, Lakes Golf Club, Sydney, ph 9262 1122

Calendar of Events

5 February: One day cricket series. England v Australia. Sydney Cricket Ground, ph 9360 6601. www.acb.com.au

5–7 February: Bungendore Country Muster, Bungendore, ph 02 6238 1373

10 February: One day cricket series. First final. Sydney Cricket Ground, ph 9360 6601. www.acb.com.au

14 February: Harbour Challenge (Sydney City Mission charity paddle race from Putney to Darling Harbour), ph 9286 0100

21 February: The Botany Bay Gift Foot Race, Botany Ph 9366 3507, 9315 8509

GENERAL

10–12 February: Vietnamese New Year Celebrations, ph 9790 3934

16 February: First day of the Chinese New Year (year of the rabbit)

20–21 February: Chinese New Year Celebrations, Darling Harbour, ph 9286 0100

MARCH

ARTS & ENTERTAINMENT

6 March–18 April: Archibald, Wynne and Sulman Prizes, Art Gallery of NSW, ph 9225 1700

6–21 March: Botanica: an Exhibition of Botanical Art and Etched Glass by eminent Australian botanical artists, Royal Botanic Gardens, Sydney, ph 9231 8182. www.rbgsyd.gov.au

17–20 March: Illawarra Folk Festival, Jamberoo, ph 02 4233 1073. http://wollongong.starway.net.au/~gsmurray/jamberoo/

20–22 March: Central Coast Jazz Festival, ph 02 4385 2708

29 March–1 April: Festival of Fools, Sydney City, ph 9265 9007. www.sydneycity.nsw.gov.au

March-April: The Australian Ballet season, ph 1800 335 646. www.austballet.telstra.com.au

SPORT

1 March: Opening of Olympic Stadium, Sydney Olympic Park, ph 9297 2000

7–13 March: Paralympic Week, ph 9297 2000

6 March–17 April: Sydney Autumn Racing Carnival:

6–27 March: Sydney Turf Club Golden Slipper Festival, Rosehill Gardens Racecourse, Sydney, ph 9930 4000

14 March: Macquarie Fun Run/Walk for MS (Multiple Sclerosis), ph 9413 4166

21 March: Walk Against Want, ph 1800 034 034

26 March–11 April: International Womensport Festival, Sydney, ph 9268 2199

GENERAL

5–7 March: The Chilli Festival, Erina, Central Coast, ph 02 4367 7322. www.fragrantgarden.com.au

7 March: Clean Up Australia Day, ph 9552 6177

8 March: International Women's Day

12–14 March: Castle Hill and District Agricultural Show, ph 9634 2632

14 March: Kings Cross Bed Race, Kings Cross, ph (02) 9358 1144

15 March–2 April: Bandaged Bear Appeal (Bandaged Bear Day 23 March), ph 9845 3481

17–21 March: Commonwealth Bank Home Show, Darling Harbour, ph 9565 1099

20–21 March: Sydney Bridal Expo, Darling Harbour, ph 9362 0278

21 March: International Day for the Elimination of Racial Discrimination

21–28 March: Seniors' Week, Sydney and Regional New South Wales, ph 9367 6839. www.add.nsw.gov.au

26 March–10 April: Sydney Royal Easter Show, Homebush Bay, ph 9704 1111

Calendar of Events

APRIL

ARTS & ENTERTAINMENT

1–18 April: Archibald, Wynne and Sulman Prizes, Art Gallery of NSW, ph 9225 1700

2–5 April: Darling Harbour Circus & Street Theatre Festival, ph 9286 0100

2–26 April: Darling Harbour Autumn Holiday Program, ph 9286 0100

10–11 April: NSW, Australian & International Dragon Boat Championships, Darling Harbour, ph 9585 2000, 9525 2422

25 April–2 May: Australian Dance Week, ph 9241 4022.

SPORT

3–17 April: AJC Autumn Carnival, Royal Randwick Racecourse, Sydney, ph 9663 8400.

24 April–2 May: RTA Big Ride for Multiple Sclerosis, ph 9413 4166

April-May: Autumn Greyhound Racing, Wentworth Park, Sydney, ph 9649 7166

April 10–11: Cycling (Mountain Bike), UCI World Cup. Olympic Test Event, ph 9297 2000.

GENERAL

1–10 April: Sydney Royal Easter Show, Homebush Bay, ph 9704 1111

7 April: World Health Day

10–18 April: Caravan, Camping & 4WD Supershow, Rosehill Gardens, ph 9633 9377

17–25 April: Heritage Festival, Sydney and Regional NSW, ph 9258 0123. www.tenden.aust.com/nationaltrust/

21 April: Secretaries' Day, ph 9633 4888

25 April: Anzac Day

MAY

ARTS & ENTERTAINMENT

17–23 May: Sydney Writers' Festival, ph 9566 4158

1–30 May: Songs of the Wind, arts and music festival, Blue Mountains, ph 02 4784 2552. www.bluemts.com.au/-songs

SPORT

2 May: ITU Triathlon World Cup, Sydney, ph (02) 9596 2340

4 May: 500 Days to the Sydney 2000 Olympic Games

23 May: The Sydney Morning Herald Half Marathon, ph 9282 3844

May: Sussan Women's Classic (Fun Run) ph 03 9819 6888.

May-June: The National Rugby League State of Origin Series, ph 9339 8500, www.nrl.com.au.

GENERAL

1–8 May: Lifeline Awareness Week, ph 9635 0700

1–9 May: National Science Week, ph 6205 0281, www.abc.net.au/science

2 May: Buddha's Birthday, ph 9286 0100

10–15 May: Mercedes Australian Fashion Week, Sydney, ph 9332 2100, www.afw.com.au

14–16 May: Sydney Pet and Animal Expo, Homebush, Sydney, ph 9876 4600

26 May: National Sorry Day

27 May–3 June: Reconciliation Week, ph 1800 060 266

30 May: Air League Ceremonial Parade (Scout Parade) ph 9286 0100

30 May: Salvation Army Red Shield Day, ph 9266 9820

31 May: World No Tobacco Day, ph 9334 1900

Calendar of Events

JUNE

ARTS & ENTERTAINMENT

2–7 June: The Australian Folk Festival, Kiama, ph 02 4236 0701
4–18 June: Sydney Film Festival, ph 9660 3844
12–14 June: Darling Harbour Jazz Festival, ph 9286 0100
12 June–6 November: Opera Australia Winter Season, ph 9319 1088
June: Winter Magic Festival, Katoomba, ph 02 4739 6266
June-August: Yulefest Blue Mountains Festival, ph 02 4739 6266
June: Sydney Cabaret Convention, ph 9265 9089
June: Central Coast Country Music Festival, Warnevale Country Music Park, ph 02 4332 2547
June-September: McDonald's City of Sydney Performing Arts Challenge, ph 9261 8366

SPORT

June: Fisher & Paykel Plate, Netball, ph 9633 2533
6 June: 500 Days to the Sydney 2000 Paralympic Games
23 June: Olympic Day. 9297 2000
June: The National Rugby League State of Origin Series, ph 9339 8500, www.nrl.com.au.

FOOD & DRINK

5–6 June: Manly Food and Wine Festival, ph 9977 1088
12 June: Feastability - A Feast for the Senses. Newtown, ph 9335 2249
19–27 June: Feast of Sydney: The Food and Wine Festival, ph 132 077. www.tourism.nsw.gov.au
20 June: Darling Harbour Waiters' Race, Longest Buffet, ph 9286 0100
21 June: International Hotels Restaurant Week, ph 9281 6922

GENERAL

5 June: World Environment Day
14–19 June: Home Computer Show, ph 03 9646 6822
24–27 June: The Australian Women's Weekly Needlework, Art and Craft Fair, Sydney, ph 9977 0888
26–27 June: Australia's Premier Bear Affair Teddy Bear Show, Sydney Town Hall ph 02 4868 1338
18–20 June: Filex 99 (Fitness & Health) Sydney Convention Centre, Darling Harbour, ph 9908 4944
18–25 June: NSW Tourism Week, ph 9931 1111
25 June: Red Nose Day (Sudden Infant Death Syndrome), ph 9681 4500

JULY

ARTS & ENTERTAINMENT

5–12 July: International Music Festival, Opera House, Sydney Town Hall, Martin Place, Darling Harbour etc 9929 5447
5–18 July: Darling Harbour Winter Music Program, ph 9286 0100
17–21 July: Sing Australia Festival, Sydney Town Hall, ph 9268 2199
17–21 July: The International Choral Festival, Sydney. Ph (02) 9268 2199
27 July–1 August: World Championship of Marching Show Bands, Sydney, ph 9268 2199
July: The Shakespeare Festival Australia, Bowral, ph 02 4872 2799

SPORT

July 2–4: Weightlifting, International Invitation. Olympic Test event ph 9297 2000

Calendar of Events

GENERAL

4–11 July: NAIDOC (National Aboriginal & Torres Strait Islander) Week. Contact your local council or aboriginal organisation
22–27 July: Sydney International Boat Show, ph 9438 2077
30 July–1 August: Timber and Working with Wood Show, venue TBA, ph 9565 1099, ph 9712 5623
July: Terrigal Beach Food and Wine Festival, ph 02 4385 4074

AUGUST

SPORT

August 5–8: Volleyball, International tournament, Olympic Test Event 9297 2000
August 8: Sun-Herald City to Surf, Sydney City to Bondi Beach, ph 9282 2747
August 19–22: Wrestling, Youth World Championship. Olympic Test Event ph 9297 2000
22–29 August: Pan Pacific Swimming, International Aquatic Centre, Homebush, ph 9752 3666. www.siac.nsw.gov.au
28 August–18 September: Sydney Turf Club Spring Carnival, Rosehill Racecourse, ph 9930 4000

GENERAL

3 August: Internet World 99, ph 9310 5544
4–6 August: The Australian Women's Weekly Our House Expo, Darling Harbour, ph 9977 0888. www.exevents.com.au
6 August: Jeans for Genes Day (Children's medical research Institute) ph 9687 2800
August: Courier & Kemeny's Festival of Food and Wine. Royal Randwick Racecourse, ph 9353 0092
August: Japan Festival, Usually Opera House and Lower Town Hall, ph 9954 4824
August: Festival of Health & Harmony, ph 9413 3322

SEPTEMBER

ARTS & ENTERTAINMENT

11 September–4 October: Carnivale (Statewide multi-cultural arts festival), ph 1800 064 534
15 September–4 October: Olympic Arts Festival: Reaching the World, Powerhouse Museum, ph 9217 0111
26 September–11 October: Darling Harbour Spring Holiday Program. ph 9286 0100

SPORT

September 1–5: Badminton, Australian Championships. Olympic Test Event, ph 9297 2000.
1–18 September: Sydney Turf Club Spring Carnival, Rosehill Racecourse, ph 9930 4000 Olympic Test Event, ph 92972000
September 10–12: Gymnastics (rhythmic), Australian Invitation, Olympic Test Event, ph 92972000
September 15–28: Tennis, World Youth Cup, Olympic Test Event, ph 9297 2000
September 16–26: Sailing, Sydney Harbour Regatta, Olympic Test Event, ph 9297 2000
September 20–26: Archery, International Invitation, Olympic Test Event, ph 9297 000
September 22–24: Rowing, Australasian Championships, Olympic Test Event, ph 9297 2000
September 22–26: Handball, International Invitation, Olympic Test Event, ph 9297 2000
September 22–26: Hockey, International Invitation, Olympic Test Event, ph 9297 2000
September 23–26: Equestrian, Sydney

Calendar of Events

International 3-day event, Olympic Test Event, ph 9297 2000

September 26–28: Canoe/Kayak (Sprint), Sydney International Regatta, Olympic Test Event, ph 9297 2000

September 23 -October 3: Water Polo, FINA Men's World Cup, Olympic Test Event, ph 9297 2000

25 September–4 October: AJC Spring Racing Carnival, Royal Randwick Racecourse, ph 9663 8400

29 September–3 October: Bathurst 1000 Touring Car Motor Race, Mt Panorama, Bathurst, ph 9672 1000

September 30 - October 3: Canoe/Kayak (Slalom), World Cup Final, Olympic Test Event, ph 92972000

September: RTA Cycle Sydney: North Sydney to Parramatta Park, ph 9283 5200

September: Rugby union finals. Ph 9956 3444. www.rugby.com.au

September: The National Rugby League Final series, ph 9339 8500. www.nrl.com.au

GENERAL

9–12 September: Australian Springtime Flora Festival, Mount Penang, Kariong, Central Coast, ph 02 4385 4430

12 September: Festival of the Winds (kites), Bondi, ph 9130 3325

24–26 September: South Pacific Ballroom Dancing Championship, NSW State Sports Centre, Homebush, ph 9144 3800

25 September–10 October: Tulip Time Festival, Bowral, ph 02 4871 2888

September: Penrith City Festival, ph (02) 4721 4015

September: Sydney Deaf Festival, ph 9286 0100

September: Spring in Sydney, Sydney City Council, ph 9265 9007

September: Blessing of the Fleet, Darling Harbour, ph 9286 0100

September: Freedom from Hunger Appeal, ph 9264 1399

September-November: Blue Mountains Spring Gardens, ph 02 4739 6266

OCTOBER

ARTS & ENTERTAINMENT

1–4 October: Manly Jazz Festival, ph 9977 1088

October: Pacific Circle Music Convention, ph 9211 1466

October: Central Coast Country Superstar Show, Warnervale Country Music Park, ph 02 4332 2547

4 October–5 October: Darling Harbour Fiesta (Latin Festival, food, craft and music), ph 9286 0100

SPORT

1–4 October: AJC Spring Racing Carnival, Royal Randwick Racecourse, ph 9663 8400

1–3 October: Bathurst 1000 Touring Car Motor Race, Mt Panorama, Bathurst, ph 9672 1000

13–17 October: Tennis: Telstra Smart Champions - Sydney Entertainment Centre, ph 9566 1662. www.auschampions.com.au

23–31 October: Commonwealth Bank Cycle Classic: Sydney to Canberra, ph 9542 5699

October-November: Greater West Games, Western Sydney, ph 9890 1804

October 5–10: Beach Volleyball, FIVB World Tour. 9297 2000. Olympic Test Event, ph 92972000

October 16–17: Modern Pentathlon, World Cup Final 9297 2000. Olympic Test Event, ph 9297 2000

FOOD & DRINK

24 October: Belgenny Farm Food & Winefest, Camden, ph 02 4655 9651

October: Taste of the Nation. Kings Cross, ph 9264 1399

October: City of Sydney Food & Wine Fair, Hyde Park, ph 9265 9007 www.sydneycity.nsw.gov.au

October: Sydney Morning Herald Good Food Month, ph 9282 2822

Calendar of Events

GENERAL

1–10 October: Tulip Time Festival, Bowral, ph 02 4871 2888

16–17 October: Doll & Teddy Bear Collector Show, Sydney Town Hall ph 02 4868 1338

29–31 October: Getaway Holiday Expo, Sydney, ph 9977 0888

October: Sydney International Motor Show, ph 9286 0100

NOVEMBER

ARTS & ENTERTAINMENT

1 November: Kings Cross Carnival, ph 9326 9995

7 November: Symphony on the Sand, Freshwater Beach, Harbord, ph 9942 2658

26–27 November: Schools Spectacular, Sydney Entertainment Centre, ph 9816 4150

November-December: The Australian Ballet summer seasons, ph 1800 335 646. www.austballet.telstra.com.au

SPORT

November 4–14: Baseball, Intercontinental Cup. 9297 2000. Olympic Test Event, ph 9297 2000

November 27-December 3: Judo, International Invitation, Olympic Test Event, ph 92972000

7 November: Sydney to the Gong Bicycle Ride, ph 9413 4166

November: Australian PGA Golf Championships, NSW Golf Course, La Perouse, ph 9439 8111

November: Greater West Games, Western Sydney, ph 9890 1804

GENERAL

23–11 November: Remembrance Day

28 November: Australian Craft Show, Sydney Showground & Exhibition Centre, Homebush, ph 9876 3905

25 November: Christmas Parade and Christmas Tree lighting Ceremony, Martin Place Amphitheatre, Sydney, ph 9265 9007. www.sydneycity.nsw.gov.au

November: Wooden Boat Festival, Darling Harbour, ph 9552 7777

November: Matsuri Fiesta, Darling Harbour, ph 9386 9494

November: Sydney Mind Body & Spirit Festival, ph 9286 0100

November: Backpackers Expo, Sydney Town Hall, ph 9955 6963

November: Fishers Ghost Festival, Campbelltown, ph 02 4645 8922

DECEMBER

ARTS & ENTERTAINMENT

4–5 December: Tuggerah Lakes Mardi Gras Festival, The Entrance, ph 02 4385 3788

10 December: Darling Harbour Christmas Pageant, Darling Harbour, ph 9267

18 December: Carols in the Domain, Ph 03 9596 8199, www.activetv.com.au

26–31 December: Sydney Harbour Jazz Festival, ph 9931 1111

31 December: Year 2000 Celebrations, Sydney Observatory, ph 9217 0111

31 December: New Year's Eve in Sydney, ph 9265 9007
www.sydneycity.nsw.gov.au

December: Carols on the Harbour, ph 9286 0100

SPORT

December 3–5: Fencing, World Cup/Challenge Australia Olympic Test Event, ph 9297 2000

December 4–5: Taekwondo, International Invitation, Olympic Test Event, ph 9297 2000

December 6–12: Athletics, Australian

Schools Championships, Olympic Test Event, ph 92972000

December 6–10: Cycling (track), Oceania Championships, Olympic Test Event, ph 9297 2000

December 7–11: Boxing, International Invitation, Olympic Test Event, ph 9297 2000

December 12 and 14: Cycling (road races), Oceania Championships, Olympic Test Event, ph 92972000

16–19 December: Sydney International Regatta, Sydney Harbour, ph 9922 4333

26 December: 1999 Sydney to Hobart Yacht Race, Sydney Harbour to Hobart, Tasmania

December: North Cronulla Surf Carnival, Cronulla, ph 9984 7188.
www.lifesavingnsw.org.au

GENERAL:

December: World AIDS Day

BEST OF SYDNEY
VISITORS' GUIDE

Visitors' Guide

Airlines

All international airlines servicing Australia have offices in Sydney. Qantas (ph 13 1313) and Ansett (ph 13 1300) are the two major domestic airlines. All domestic flights in Australia are non-smoking.

Airport

Sydney's Kingsford Smith Airport is 15–30 minutes south of the central business district by car, taxi or bus. A shuttle service runs between the international and two domestic terminals. Car hire agencies can be found in all terminals.

Business hours

Banks Most Banks are open 9.30am–4pm Monday-Thursday; 9.30am–5pm Friday.
General office hours are 9am–5pm, Monday-Friday.
Post offices are open 9am–5pm Monday-Friday.
Shops: generally 9am–5.30pm Monday to Friday, with late-night shopping on Thursday till 9pm. Saturdays: generally 9am–4pm, with larger stores open similar hours on Sunday.
Restaurants: many close on Mondays

Customs & quarantine

Each adult has a duty-free quote of one litre of alcohol, 250 cigarettes and dutiable goods up to a value of $400. Strict quarantine restrictions apply to any animal or vegetable matter brought into the country. Penalties for importation of illegal drugs or endangered species products are severe.

Climate

Sydney has a warm and temperate climate with sunshine most days of the year. Seasons are the reverse of the Northern Hemisphere.
Average temperatures:
Spring: September to November 17°C (63°F)
Summer: December to February 22°C (72°F)
Autumn: March to May 18°C (64°F)
Winter: June to August 13°C (55°F)

Driving

A bona-fide tourist may drive in Australia on a valid overseas driver's licence for the same class of vehicle. Licences must be carried when driving, in addition to a valid passport. An International Driver's Permit is not sufficient by itself and must be accompanied by a valid driver's licence.

Driving is on the left side of the road. Speed limits vary from 50kmh in built-up areas to 110kmh on some freeways. Seat belts for all vehicle occupants are compulsory and there are heavy penalties for drink driving (in excess of a blood alcohol reading of .05.)

Many international motoring organisations have reciprocal arrangements with the NRMA, which offers a 24-hour breakdown service. Phone 13 1111.

Petrol comes in leaded and unleaded grades and is sold by the litre. Petrol costs between $A0.66–$A0.80 per litre. Prices are often higher in country areas. Petrol stations are plentiful; trading hours vary. Most accept international credit cards.

Electricity

220–240 volts, 50 Hz. Adaptors widely available for foreign appliances.

Embassies & consulates

Most embassies are in Canberra, but many countries maintain Sydney consular offices. Look in the Yellow Pages for details.

Emergency

For serious emergency calls to ambulance, fire or police, dial 000.
Dental: ph 9692 0333
Chemist prescriptions: ph 9235 0333
Poisons: ph 13 1126
Rape: ph 9819 6565
Legal: ph 9219 5000
Interpreting: ph 9221 5866

Health

You will encounter few health hazards in Sydney. Standards of hygiene are high, particularly in food preparation. Doctors and dentists are highly trained and hospitals are well equipped. Overseas visitors are strongly recommended to take out health insurance before departure to cover the duration of their stay. Visitors who are covered by Australia's national health insurance scheme, Medicare, are those who are residents of one of the seven countries with which Australia has reciprocal health-care agreements – the United Kingdom, New Zealand, Italy, Malta, Finland, Netherlands and Sweden. The agreements provide health care for immediately necessary medical treatment only.

Information

The Sydney Morning Herald is Australia's leading quality broadsheet, publishing Monday to Saturday (except Christmas Day), with daily news, business, sports and arts sections. Saturday's paper has nine sections, including News Review, Spectrum (features, books, arts) Real Estate, Motoring, Employment, Travel, Icon (home computing) and the Good Weekend (colour magazine). It also publishes a range of specialised sections during the week:

The Guide (Monday): Television and radio programs, news and home entertainment features.
Good Living (Tuesday): Restaurants, food, wine, fashion and beauty
I.T: Information technology for business
Money (Wednesday): Personal finance
Domain (Thursday): Home and Garden, Property
Metro (Friday): Going out guide. Film, Theatre, Art, music, leisure listings
Drive (Friday): Motoring
The Form (Friday): Horse racing, greyhounds.

Detailed information on current city events, attractions, performances, restaurants, etc. is available online on Sydney Morning Herald CitySearch (www.sydney.citysearch.com.au).

The Sun-Herald is the best Sunday newspaper while *The Australian Financial Review* is a national daily business newspaper.

Liquor laws

General licensing hours for public bars are Monday to Saturday 10am to 10pm. Sunday hours vary. Restaurants, clubs and hotel lounges have more flexible hours. You must be 18 years or older to buy or consume alcohol in public. Packaged alcoholic beverages are sold at hotels, liquor stores and other licensed premises. Many restaurants allow patrons to BYO (Bring Your Own) wine for which they may charge a small corkage fee.

Medications

Visitors are permitted to bring reasonable quantities of prescribed (non-narcotic) medications. All should be clearly labelled and identifiable. For large quantities it is advisable to bring a doctor's certificate to produce for Customs if necessary, and to an Australian doctor if required. Local pharmacies, called chemists, can fill most prescriptions (which must be written by an Australian-registered doctor).

Money

Australian currency is decimal with the dollar as the basic unit (100 cents equals one dollar). Notes come in $100, $50, $20, $10, $5 denominations. Coins come in 5c, 10c, 20c, 50c, $1, $2 denominations.

Travellers cheques can be cashed and currency exchanged at Sydney International Airport as well as at banks and large hotels. Banks will accept most travellers cheques in every currency. Most widely accepted are American Express, Thomas Cook, Visa, Barclays, Bank of America and Mastercard. ATM (Automatic Teller Machine) cards can be used as long as they have been converted for international access. Travellers should contact their bank at home for information on availability and service charges.

Public holidays (1999)

January 1: New Year's Day
January 26: Australia Day

April 2: Good Friday
April 5: Easter Monday
April 25: Anzac Day
June 14: Queen's Birthday
August 2: Bank Holiday
October 4: Labour Day
December 25: Christmas Day
December 27: Boxing Day Holiday

Public transport

For bus, ferry and Cityrail train timetables, phone State Transit Authority on 13 1500. The main bus stops in the City are Circular Quay (to the East and South), Railway Square (West) and Wynyard (north). The City Circle is an underground service for the Central Business District. Town Hall and Central Stations serve all suburban train lines, with country and interstate services leaving from Central. All ferries depart from Circular Quay. The privately run Monorail and Light Rail (9660 5288) link the Darling Harbour/Pyrmont area to the City.

Religion

Christianity is the predominant faith but all major religions are represented. Your hotel desk can advise you on places of worship.

Sun protection

Enjoy outdoor activities such as sightseeing, bushwalking, boating and camping without the risk of harmful exposure to the sun by using simple skin protection. Wear a shady hat, a shirt with a collar and sleeves, and SPH 15+ broad-spectrum, water-resistant sun screen. Try to avoid the sun during the middle of the day, between 10am and 2pm (11am and 3pm in daylight saving time) when the ultraviolet rays are at their strongest.

Surf safety

Popular beaches are patrolled by volunteer Surf Life Saving Association members. Always remember to swim between the flags and observe the 10 safety hints. Most beaches are patrolled from October to April.

Taxis

Meter operated taxicabs service all major cities and towns. You will find taxi ranks at transport terminals, major hotels or shopping centres or you can hail them in the street. The Yellow Pages of the telephone directory list taxi companies which will send a radio-controlled cab to pick you up (for a small charge). There is a minimum 'flagfall' charge, then a charge for the distance travelled. Small additional charges are made for luggage and telephone bookings, otherwise the account shows on the meter. Taxi drivers do not expect to be tipped, but happily accept gratuities.

Telephones

Public telephones take coins and phonecards (available from post offices and newsagents) and some take credit cards. Local calls cost 30 or 40 cents for unlimited time. Long distance (STD) and international calls are timed.

Tipping

Tipping is not the general custom in Australia and service charges are not added to accounts by hotels and restaurants. Porters at airports, taxi drivers and hairdressers do not expect to be tipped although you may do so if you wish. At railway terminals porters have set charges, but not at hotels. In better class restaurants it is usual to tip food and drink waiters up to 10 per cent of the bill for good service. At any time tipping is your choice.

Television & radio

There are five TV channels, three commercial and the government funded ABC and SBS (multicultural), along with about 20 radio AM and FM radio stations.

Time

Summer daylight saving time: Greenwich Mean Time plus 11 hours
Winter time: GMT plus 9 hours

Tourist information

Sydney Visitors Centre, 106 George St, The Rocks, ph 9255 1788
NSW Visitor Information Helpline, ph 13 2077
Tourist Information Service, inquiries 9669 5111

Vaccinations

Vaccinations are not required if you are travelling direct unless you have come from or visited a yellow fever infected country or zone within six days prior to arrival. You do not need any other health certificate to enter Australia.

Visas

All visitors except New Zealanders require a visa Tourist visas are free for stays of up to three months. A $30 fees for longer stays of up to six months within a 12-month period. All visa applications should be made to an Australian diplomatic mission. Working holiday visas are available for 18- 26-year-olds from the UK, Ireland, Canada, Holland and Japan. For information on student visas, write to IDP Education Australia, 210 Clarence St, Sydney 2000: ph 61 2 9373 2700, fax 61 2 9373 2724.

Weights & measures

Australia uses the metric system of weights and measures. Speed and distance are measured in kilometres; goods in kilograms and litres; temperature in Celsius (Centigrade).

■ *The visitors' guide has been compiled with the assistance of Tourism NSW (www.tourism.nsw.gov.au).*